BIG
DEAL

BRUCE WASSERSTEIN

BIG DEAL

2000 and Beyond

WARNER BOOKS

A Time Warner Company

Warner Books, Inc., 1271 Avenue of the Americas, New York, NY 10020

Visit our Web site at www.twbookmark.com

Ⓦ A Time Warner Company

Printed in the United States of America

First Warner Books Printing: January 2000

10 9 8 7 6 5 4 3 2 1

Library of Congress Cataloging-in-Publication Data

Wasserstein, Bruce.
     Big deal : 2000 and beyond / Bruce Wasserstein.—Rev. ed.
         p.   cm.
     Includes bibliographical references and index.
     ISBN 0-446-52642-8
     1. Consolidation and merger of corporations — United States   2. Conglomerate corporations — United States.   3. Corporate reorganizations — United States. 4. Corporations — United States.   I. Title.

HD2746.55.U5 W37 2000
338.8'3'0973 21—dc21

                                                                99-044624

To my wife, Claude,
my love and inspiration

Acknowledgments

This is the culmination of many people's helpful insights and assistance. In particular, I wanted to thank my research directors, my colleagues at Wasserstein Perella, my clients and the law firms who have shared so much of their wisdom.

Lucie Longworth, Lisa Desmond, and Crissy Kerr have worked tirelessly to support the effort, and Mort Janklow, my agent, my partners, Jeffrey Rosen, Robert Pruzan, and Mike Biondi, and Larry Kirshbaum, my publisher, were always generous with their time. Most of all, the tolerance and love of my children, Pam, Ben, Scoop, Jack, and Dash, the inspiration of my parents and sisters, and the support of my wife, Claude, were essential to writing the book. I will forever miss the love and assistance of my deceased sister, Sandra W. Meyer.

Bruce Wasserstein
East Hampton
September 1999

Contents

Introduction

This is the millennium edition of *Big Deal*, prompted by the fact that many of the largest deals in history were announced this past year. This book is less about particular financial transactions and more about understanding the process our economy uses to adapt to change. The swirl of mystery and controversy surrounding the deal business continues to spiral. Recent big deals—MCI World-Com–Sprint; Viacom-CBS; Chrysler-Daimler; BP-Amoco-ARCO; Travelers-Salomon-Citicorp; AT&T's deal frenzy; AOL-Netscape; SBC-UBS; Dean Witter–Morgan Stanley; NYNEX–Bell Atlantic; Wal-Mart–Asda—suggest a seismic shift in the structure of the world economy. We are at the dawn of a post-industrial age, a world of microchips, services, and outsourcing, and as part of it, the tide of globalization will continue to rise.

The movement and restructuring of assets—mergers, acquisitions, and divestitures—are currents in this evolutionary whirlpool. Front-page news and trends are inexorably reflected in a deal.

Indeed, growth by merger has been a part of American economic history since the coming of the Industrial Revolution. Over the years, the rationale, style, and intensity of successive merger waves have varied, and a rich assortment of knaves and fools, heroes and winners, have played cameo roles. Millions of people and thousands of companies have felt the reverberations.

Change of this sort has been inherent in business since the Age of Discovery. But the image of the merger process is clouded by technical jargon and the premise that somehow the structure of

Dow Jones Industrial Average

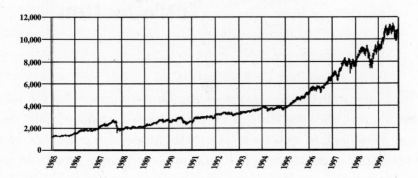

business is static, gray, unchanging, and unfathomable. The key barrier to comprehension is that changes in the structure of the economy have not come smoothly. Cycles of recession, depression, and growth have battered our experience. By 1932, the stock market declined over 70 percent from its 1929 highs. Yet from the Crash of 1987 to 1999, the market appreciated by over 500 percent.

Further, the wisdom of the moment often is misleading. The last decade has seen a breathtaking bull market, as stock market valuations of companies have soared. As a result, the 1980s turned out in hindsight to have been a time of relative bargain shopping. Curiously, little is said today of the fact that the carping at the end of the 1980s about prices paid in deals being too high turned out in hindsight to have been wrong. Today, the scope of the bull market is hard to comprehend as it unfolds, obscuring the fact that companies are being bought at all-time highs in the sensible 1990s.

Nor are hustlers anything new. In 1720, shares in the glamorous English conglomerate the South Seas Company were hot: Its interests in whaling, exploration, and the slave trade were a window on the future. The bubble eventually burst, and the company passed into history.

The process of change can also bring pain and destruction, a reflection of the cruel face of capitalism. That is why it is easy to attack mergers and acquisitions on an anecdotal basis. Such criticism
calls to mind what Samuel Johnson once said about London: "When
a man is tired of London, he is tired of life; for there is in London all
that life can afford."

Similarly the mergers business reflects the hubbub of our society
with all its bustling and pretense. It is at the edge of change and
fashion, and yet a minefield for the unwary. Mistakes are common.
Still, good, bad, or indifferent, mergers and acquisitions are an essential vehicle for corporate change, and the pace of change is increasing.

This edition is an attempt to put the deal business in context of our
changing times. Part One surveys the broad sweep of merger history,
from the nineteenth century to the 1990s. Part Two focuses more
closely on the strategy and tactics behind some active industries in
the 1980s and 1990s and the deals that transformed them. Part Three
describes the implementation of the modern transaction.

The emphasis here is on the structural forces, tactics, and personalities that shape the deal process. My hope is that the spirit
emerges in these clashes of corporate will, the uncertainty, fear and
emotion, the failure and the triumph.

Of course, this book reflects many prejudices and experiences.
Some twenty years ago, I wrote a book on corporate finance law from
a young lawyer's point of view. I have since worked on well over 1,000
deals, including many of the larger transactions. With the inflation
of asset values during this period and the dramatic rise in the Dow
Jones Average, most deals have worked well, but there certainly have
been disappointments.

My perspective today is influenced by a particular combination of
five experiences in this field. While at Harvard law and business
schools, I worked for Ralph Nader examining government merger

policy. Mergers were the natural intersection of my interest in law, business, economics, and public policy. After Harvard, I studied economics and British merger policy at Cambridge University and wrote an article for the *Yale Law Journal* on the subject.

When I went to work as a young lawyer at New York's Cravath, Swaine & Moore, I was sent off to specialize in mergers partly because of the article. At the time, mergers were less exciting to many of my colleagues than the booming public offering practice.

After five years of lawyering, one of my clients, First Boston, convinced me to become an investment banker. I stayed there for over ten years, eventually as Co-Head of Investment Banking. Then for the past twelve years at Wasserstein Perella & Co., I have continued to advise clients on deals as well as investing in businesses directly as a principal.

Because the scope of this book is so broad, it cannot purport to be exhaustive. The intent is rather to provide a sensitivity and a context for an appreciation of the traits of an important part of our economic history and an inevitable phenomenon.

Part One | # Past as Prelude

"Go where you will on the surface of things, men have been there before us."

—Henry David Thoreau,
*A Week on the Concord and
Merrimack Rivers*

The Digital World Cometh

*"Empires of the future are
the empires of the mind."*

—Sir Winston Churchill,
Speech at Harvard,
September 6, 1943

The dawn of the new millennium has been accompanied by a frenetic quest for the business model of the future. Companies are scrambling to respond to and anticipate a new industrial revolution in which business is globalized, new technologies emerge, the Internet becomes a vital medium for commerce, and regulatory barriers begin to break down—in short the coming of the digital age.

WorldCom: Challenging AT&T

In the whirlwind of this digital age, the pace of change has accelerated. The dramatic $129 billion merger of MCI WorldCom with Sprint to challenge AT&T for leadership in global telecommunications underscores the intensity of the restructuring. The Telecommunications Reform Act of 1996, new digital technologies such as fiber optic cables, the Internet, and wireless telephony, and soaring share prices have unleashed a frenzy of record-breaking deal activity in the industry.

MCI WorldCom Chief Executive Bernie Ebbers will now be able to provide fully integrated voice and data services, over wireless or land lines. The combined company merges the second- and third-largest long-distance carriers in the U.S. to control a third of the nation's $90 billion business, provides a majority of the country's Internet backbone, and owns one of the fastest-growing nationwide wireless PCS service providers, Sprint PCS, which has focused on wireless Internet communication.

Viacom-CBS: Media Giant of the Digital Age

Supersalesman Mel Karmazin had just emerged from a boardroom coup, becoming the new CEO of CBS to a roaring ovation from the stock market. Throughout his career the tenacious Karmazin was able to anticipate the implications of the changes in the regulatory environment, such as the allowance of multiple radio station ownership. With the recent modifications in the limits on TV station ownership and the explosive impact of technology such as the Internet, he saw a pressing need for greater mass and distribution muscle.

The street-savvy Karmazin made his pitch to Sumner Redstone, the seventy-six-year-old controlling shareholder of Viacom, the home of Paramount, Nickelodeon, and MTV. Redstone brushed Karmazin away. Redstone had just completed focusing Viacom on its core media and entertainment assets and cleaning up its balance sheet: Paramount studios had a series of box office hits; Blockbuster, Viacom's video rental chain, had a successful initial public offering; and non-core assets such as Simon & Schuster's educational division had been divested; Viacom's debt burden had been pared down substantially.

Mel kept coming. Finally, he convinced Redstone that the digital future of the media industry required the participants to pool their assets, culminating in the announcement on September 7, 1999, of the seminal $41 billion Viacom-CBS merger.

DaimlerChrysler: An Automotive Leader

As Juergen Schrempp chainsmoked through a pack of cigarettes, Robert Eaton listened with great interest. The two executives were sitting at the President Wilson, a hotel by Lake Geneva, hashing out the plans for the merger between their companies: Daimler-Benz and Chrysler. Finally Schrempp seduced Eaton into the largest industrial deal ever.

Each company was attempting to solve its own dilemma. Daimler saw a future with stagnant sales: Its existing markets were becoming saturated and its vehicles were too expensive for most emerging markets. It lacked either minivan or broad SUV products.

Chrysler too was finding its home market, the U.S., increasingly saturated, but found options abroad limited, since it did not have the same presence overseas that GM and Ford enjoyed. Furthermore, because it was the smallest of the three U.S. carmakers, it had fewer vehicles over which to spread its costs, making it increasingly less able to invest in advanced technology. Globalism and changes in technology had driven the necessity to larger scale.

BP-Amoco and Exxon-Mobil: The Titan Recombined

In 1911, with the mere stroke of a pen, the government broke up John D. Rockefeller's empire: Standard Oil. The company, which before the proceedings controlled 85 percent of the country's oil production, emerged as seven separate pieces: Standard Oil of New Jersey (Exxon), Standard Oil of New York (Mobil), Standard Oil of California (Chevron), Standard Oil of Ohio (BP's American subsidiary), Standard Oil of Indiana (Amoco), Continental Oil (Conoco), and Atlantic (ARCO).

But in 1998, as if by magnetic force, the pieces of Standard Oil began to recombine in a whirlwind of activity. The search for global economies of scale was again the spark that ignited the fire. In an environment in which oil exploration costs were rising steeply but oil prices were at half the level of the previous year—down from $20 to $11 a barrel—oil combinations looked especially attractive. Indeed, it was an industry in distress. The dreams of lower exploration costs, lower administrative costs, and greater stability could be realized through mergers.

Sir John Browne, chief executive of British Petroleum, moved first, announcing a merger with Amoco in August 1998 to form Britain's largest company.

Exxon and Mobil quickly followed with an announcement of their $86.4 billion combination. When the deal closes, Exxon Mobil will be one of the world's largest companies in terms of revenue, surpassing Royal Dutch/Shell in both output and sales, and will produce more oil than the entire country of Kuwait.

But Browne was not to be outdone. When an ailing ARCO, badly bruised from the crash in oil prices, shopped itself around to suitors, Browne sprang to action. In April 1999, BP Amoco announced its purchase of ARCO for $33.7 billion. The deal vaulted BP Amoco to the top of the pack, the largest non-OPEC producer of oil in terms of output.

Citigroup: The Global Financial Institution for the New Millennium

Catching digital fever, Travelers and Citicorp merged, hoping to be poised to be the leading financial institution for the new millennium. It is a global powerhouse, whose stated goal is to provide insurance, mutual funds, and consumer, commercial, and investment banking services to 100 million customers in 100 countries. It manages over $700 billion—nearly one third the federal budget. Its immense asset base will be a source of enormous competitive advantage and will help Citigroup weather market downturns. Its brand, "Citi," is recognized worldwide.

The deal was most stunning, however, because its success was predicated upon the tearing down of a law that has regulated the banking sector for half a century: the Bank Holding Company Act, which prohibits banks from engaging in insurance underwriting. If the act is not repealed or revised, Citigroup will have five years to divest itself of its noncomplying insurance operations, which comprise approximately 20 percent of Citigroup's revenues and whose combination with Citicorp's banking assets was one of the strategic imperatives of the deal. But it is increasingly likely that the law will be altered so as to make such transactions legal.

AT&T: Telephony for the Twenty-first Century

AT&T, once a sleepy monopoly phone company, has attempted to reinvent itself for the twenty-first century. Though in the last few decades the telco frequently stumbled, it seems as though AT&T might have traction. Over the course of the past year, AT&T has acquired a premier group of assets to create a global leader in telephony, Internet, cable, and data services.

The prelude to this shift was long and painful for AT&T. Facing competition from newcomers MCI and Sprint in the 1970s, AT&T realized that its core long distance service was rapidly becoming a commodity business and therefore sought to expand into what it saw as a growth area: computers. But its partnership with Olivetti and takeover of NCR proved disastrous. AT&T retrenched, unwinding the Olivetti deal and spinning off NCR.

For a time, AT&T's future again looked uncertain. CEO Robert Allen promised a radical overhaul of the company, but none of the benefits of a restructuring ever materialized. Soon Allen was out and Michael Armstrong came in. Under Armstrong's leadership, AT&T has set itself on a new course, transforming through acquisitions.

In June 1998, AT&T announced the $70 billion acquisition of TCI. It is this combination that is to transform AT&T. TCI's cable assets will be combined with AT&T's phone assets to allow the phone company to provide an integrated package of services—local and long distance telephone service, Internet access, and cable—over TCI's cable network. AT&T will be back at the cutting edge of technology.

Despite the scale of this move, AT&T pressed ahead with its acquisition spree. To make itself into a truly global player, in June 1998 AT&T announced the merger of its global operations with the international business of British Telecom. In April 1999, AT&T's $63 billion bid for cable operator MediaOne was accepted, moving the company closer to its goal of becoming a digital communications leader.

However, other telecom giants such as MCI WorldCom–Sprint and SBC-Ameritech have merged to challenge Ma Bell's leadership.

These deals, like others in the past, are part of a pattern of adapting to industrial change. Of course, the patterns are crude and imperfect. There is no clear road map.

However, there do seem to be elemental forces, Five Pistons, which drive the merger process. They are regulatory and political reform, technological change, fluctuations in financial markets, the role of leadership, and the drive for scale.

Regulatory and Political Change   Many of the most active M&A sectors over the past few years—media and telecommunications, financial services, utilities, health care—have been stimulated by deregulation or other political turmoil.

Before deregulation, a number of industries owed their very existence to regulatory boundaries. In the financial services sector, for example, specific rules carved up the world into commercial banking, investment banking, insurance, mutual funds, credit unions, and so forth. These rules defined everything from the role of the local bank to that of the largest financial institution. Competition across the metaphysical regulatory boundaries was forbidden. However, lately these barriers have been relaxed, and in some cases completely removed. An Oklahoma land rush of deals has ensued, as companies struggle to make sense of this new competitive landscape.

Likewise, Congress literally rewrote the rules for the media and telecommunications businesses in the Telecommunications Reform

Act of 1996. In the past, the various telecommunications players had defined realms. Local and long distance companies were not allowed to compete against each other; cable television companies generally had monopoly status. By contrast, the 1996 legislation eventually will allow local and long distance phone companies to compete in each other's markets. Cable companies also will be permitted to offer local service. Television and radio broadcasting companies may now own more stations. Though the regulations to implement this vision are currently tied up in litigation, the churning of the economic structure of the industry has already begun.

Technological Change   Technology creates new markets, introduces new competitors, has spurred globalization, and is intertwined with regulatory change. Changes in technology make old regulatory boundaries obsolete and sometimes silly. For example, the media and telecommunications business is an industry shaken by technological change and by regulatory reform. Technology has created industries like wireless telephony and satellite television, and promises a convergence of voice, video, and data transmission that will dissolve the boundaries between market participants. The emergence of thousands of new businesses in the last decade based on new technologies assures a heated merger pace in the future.

Financial Change   Financial fluctuations have a similar catalytic effect. A booming stock market encourages stock deals. A low market with low interest rates can spur cash deals after a period of high inflation in which the cost of hard assets has increased more rapidly than stock prices. In this environment, it may be cheaper to buy hard assets indirectly by purchasing companies on the stock market. Falling interest rates and available capital lubricate the process.

This was the story of the early 1980s. After a decade of relatively steep inflation, the replacement cost of assets had appreciated considerably. Yet, the stock market remained flat into the early part of the decade. As a result, a company's breakup value often exceeded its stock market value. The gap provided a powerful incentive for takeover entrepreneurs and financial buyers. On the other hand, tight money chokes the deal flow.

In the late 1990s, the opposite situation prevailed: the combination of financial fluctuations and technological change has created frothy stock market valuations in the technology and communications sectors, providing these companies with strong acquisition currencies. Sometimes, like the 1960s, companies with vibrant valuations can beat competing cash offers with stock, but the danger is that on some occasions the froth collapses like a soufflé.

Leadership   Of course, corporate combinations do not occur in a mechanistic fashion. A human element is involved—the man on horseback who leads a company to seminal change. Jack Welch at GE, Mike Armstrong at AT&T, Louis Gerstner at IBM, Philip Purcell at Dean Witter, make a difference, just as J.P. Morgan or Harold Geneen made the difference. As in political history, there have been arguments made about economic determinism, but people have an impact.

Size   Scale matters, and bigger seems to mean better to most managers. Maybe it's critical mass, or technology and globalization, or integration, or sheer vanity and ego, but there is a natural imperative toward scale. However, just as some companies keep getting bigger, others shed their skin and became smaller. The imperative toward focus and simplicity is as strong as that for size. The two competing elements create a vortex of change. Generally, today size has momentum within an industry, and diversified large companies tend to divest. However, even focused companies shed subsized or underperforming units, and some conglomerates such as GE keep getting bigger.

Technology, deregulation, and globalization fuel one another to shape this global digital age with a profound impact on our lives. Yet, we are only on the brink.

Mel, Barry, and Sumner Go Digital | 2

"A billion here, a billion there, and pretty soon you're talking about real money."

—Former U.S. Senator Everett Dirksen

Barry Diller, Sumner Redstone, and Mel Karmazin are extraordinary entrepreneurs who have repeatedly been catalysts for media industry change. Almost single-handedly, Diller transformed the ABC network and built up Fox as the fourth television network. Karmazin helped define the radio broadcasting industry as it is today by rolling up radio stations across the country. Redstone foresaw years ago a world of specialized programming, and spent the past decade and a half developing the country's leading cable television assets such as MTV and Nickelodeon that have defined the youth culture. The three men's paths have crossed as they have gone about creating their vision of the future, a series of events that culminated in the merger of CBS and Viacom.

Redstone and Diller clashed in the first of the digital age deals: the battle between Viacom and QVC for control of Paramount. It was a battle responding to changing regulations and the need for scale, driven by the tenacity of the two media moguls. Redstone not only won, but the price he paid was, in hindsight, low. The Viacom-Paramount deal fueled Viacom to be a potent media conglomerate—

a vertically integrated player combining powerful distribution and content assets—which enabled it to consummate the CBS deal.

Sumner Redstone, Mel Karmazin, and Barry Diller all are transitional men, one foot in old media and one in the digital age. They have spent their careers assembling media assets through acquisitions, mergers, and organic growth. They will spend the next decade building upon these old media assets and adapting them to bridge over to the evolving world of the Internet and positioning themselves for the broadband revolution.

Diller left QVC not long after losing Paramount to Redstone. His relatively short stint at QVC had left him considerably richer, but without a platform for his talents; so he went about creating his own company by combining a collection of humdrum media assets, sprucing them up, and attempting to move into the digital age.

Diller started his new empire from scratch. In 1995, he obtained control of a comparatively modest, unremarkable asset: twelve Silver King UHF-TV stations. These paled in comparison to companies Diller had run in the past, but he had a grand vision: Silver King would form the basis for a new broadcast network.

From this humble base, and backed by a $320 million equity infusion from John Malone's TCI, Diller embarked on an ever-larger string of acquisitions. First was Savoy Pictures Entertainment in November 1995 for $210 million in stock. Then came Silver King's purchase of the Home Shopping Network for $1.3 billion in a stock swap. The deal combined Silver King and Savoy's TV stations with HSN's retail TV network. Before, his twelve UHF stations' only source of revenue was the $45 million annual fees for carrying HSN's broadcasting. But by shifting the broadcasting of HSN solely to cable, Diller freed up the TV stations to launch his new network.

Diller bought content next. In October 1997, he struck a deal to buy Seagram's Universal Studios television assets—including cable channels USA Network and the Sci-Fi Channel, with 72 million subscribers and lucrative syndicated shows like *Xena: Warrior*

Princess and *Law & Order*. HSN paid Seagram $1.2 billion cash and granted a 45 percent stake in the new company, renamed USA Networks. Diller's collection of broadcasting and content assets finally had the potential to take on the established networks, command comparable advertising premiums, and also collect cable subscriber fees. Aiming to control another network, Diller held discussions in June 1998 with General Electric, owner of the NBC network, to merge NBC with USA Networks. However, that deal was vetoed by Edgar Bronfman Jr., CEO of Seagram, who did not want to have his stake in USA Networks diluted.

Barry Diller had a media empire again, but he was restless—he saw the world moving ahead while his company was stuck in old media assets. The imperative was clear: Participate in the Internet revolution or be left behind. USA Networks acquired a controlling stake in Ticketmaster and merged Ticketmaster's online efforts with CitySearch, a Pasadena-based producer of Internet guides to entertainment, businesses, and services, and then spun off the combined venture in a highly successful initial public offering.

The deal, however, that Diller hoped would transform USA Networks for the digital age was announced in early 1999: a three-way merger involving the Internet assets of USA Networks, Lycos, and Ticketmaster Online–CitySearch. The deal would unite the cable home shopping company with the Internet portal and allow Diller to push his commerce content over the web as well. USA Networks would own 61.5 percent of USA-Lycos, with 30 percent to be held by Lycos and 8.5 percent by Ticketmaster. USA Networks would contribute to the new venture its Home Shopping Network, Ticketmaster, and Internet Shopping Network–First Auction assets, which together represent about 50 percent of its cash earnings. Cable operations would remain with USA Networks.

While Lycos was, as is true of most Internet companies, a business with no earnings, the deal was to bring it "real assets" and positive "EBITDA" (earnings before interest, taxes, depreciation, and amortization—a measure of the company's cash earnings), allowing the market to value the company on a traditional cash earnings basis rather than as a multiple of revenues, as Internet companies tend to trade.

Despite its strategic promise, the market and investors gave the deal a thumbs-down. They thought Diller hadn't valued Lycos highly enough. USA-Lycos company, with positive earnings, would be measured against comparable companies in the industry; but companies that actually have earnings and that, like USA-Lycos, are not composed primarily of Internet assets, enjoy nowhere near Lycos' valuation because of the fear of old media dilution on their equity. Ultimately, the prospect of high growth for Lycos holders was more alluring. The Lycos deal was called off.

Diller had attempted to transition to the digital age but was essentially unwilling to pay a new age price for the digital future. Some might think Internet values frothy, but not Lycos' shareholders. Despite his strategic adaptability, the new age market saw him as too stuck in the old media mindset, not a product of the Internet generation, although he would contend he was ahead of an immature market.

Redstone and Karmazin may be ahead one step, but Diller has shown he can bob and weave. Barry will be back. Meanwhile, the entire industry will be completely restructured.

Mel Karmazin has built a career on exploiting changing FCC regulations. He built Infinity Broadcasting to be one of the most successful collections of broadcasting assets by aggressively acquiring top radio stations in major cities whenever regulations permitted— first in the 1981 and 1984 relaxation of multiple radio station ownership, then again in 1996. At the time of the 1996 change of regulations, Karmazin aimed bigger and approached CBS to buy all of its radio stations. CBS was not a seller. Karmazin reconsidered and sold his company to CBS. Subsequently, in a boardroom coup,

Karmazin, who also had become one of the biggest equity holders at CBS, took over the reins of CBS as the new CEO.

Karmazin inherited a broadcast network with a limited demographic profile—and not only were CBS' viewers older than advertisers' preferences, but broadcast networks in general were losing viewers in droves to alternative specialized entertainment sources such as cable television and the Internet. Mel successfully shook up the status quo and revitalized CBS' staid image. He saw a new opportunity with the recently relaxed regulation on TV station ownership and the scrapping of the "fin/syn" rule, which had prevented network and studio mergers in the past.

In the Viacom-CBS deal, Redstone will remain the CEO of the new Viacom and retain voting control. In a highly unusual provision, baked in to the merger agreement was Karmazin's role—he would be the COO and president for the next four years and only a fourteen-person majority of the eighteen member board of directors could remove him.

The merger of Viacom and CBS is Redstone and Karmazin's response to rapid regulatory and technological changes. The combination of a focused Viacom and CBS under Mel Karmazin brings together Viacom's premier cable assets such as MTV, VH1, and Nickelodeon, Paramount motion picture studio, Simon & Schuster consumer book publisher, Blockbuster Video, a movie theater chain, theme parks and television stations, with CBS' broadcast television network, Infinity radio and outdoor media assets, television stations, and prime syndication assets such as King World Productions, television's largest program syndicator.

But Redstone and Karmazin are not only combining old media content and distribution under one umbrella. Combined, they have the power to dominate in new media as well. Viacom has developed its Internet program through promoting MTV and other strong brands online. CBS, on the other hand, has been investing in Internet startups by swapping Internet equity for valuable advertising time on its radio and television stations. Viacom's Internet program will benefit from ad exposure through CBS' radio stations and television network. Likewise, CBS' myriad Internet investments will benefit from Viacom's depth of experience in developing strong brands and specialized programs, especially important in a broadband world. A platform has been established for the digital age.

Barry Diller

Barry Diller is regarded as unique in Hollywood, a cut above the rest. He retains a genuine creative capability in addition to outstanding business management and leadership skills.

Diller was born and raised in California. Lured by the world of show business, he dropped out of UCLA at age nineteen and convinced neighbor Danny Thomas to secure him an interview at the William Morris Agency. Eventually, Diller landed a job in the famed William Morris mail room. He rose from there to become an agent and then, at age twenty-four, an executive at ABC.

Diller spent ten years at the television network, cementing his reputation as a creative force. In those years, he launched ABC's popular and successful *Movie of the Week* format and the first successful miniseries.

In 1974, Diller left ABC to become the head of Paramount and, with a highly successful team that included Michael Eisner, Frank Mancuso, and Jeffrey Katzenberg, drove the studio to renewed success. The studio produced such hits as *Saturday Night Fever* and *Raiders of the Lost Ark*. However, when Martin Davis succeeded Charles Bluhdorn in 1983, Davis and Diller clashed.

Diller then moved to Twentieth Century Fox, which was undergoing its own period of instability under owner Marvin Davis (who is unrelated to Martin Davis), and created "the comeback studio of the year." Diller, along with the next Fox owner, Rupert Murdoch, built Fox Television into a successful fourth network with popular series such as *The Simpsons.*

In February 1992, Diller stunned the entertainment industry by abruptly resigning his post at Fox. His explanation for leaving the studio was simple: "It's not mine," he said. He landed at QVC with the express desire to own a major entertainment property and started eyeing Paramount.

Watching Diller, both during the Paramount battle and since, he dazzles with his ability to take on different roles for different crowds. When appropriate, he can be as emotional as any director. The fire blazes from his eyes. Other times, he is as businesslike and efficient as a button-down IBM executive. Diller has learned all the parts and is in total control. His attempt to transition to new media, however, is a reminder that the transition to the digital age is difficult to accomplish, even for the smartest and most nimble.

The Battle for Paramount

The Viacom-CBS deal and Diller's quest for a digital empire both flowed from the battle for Paramount. The price was steep, but the value was there.

In addition, the Paramount epic foreshadows many of the themes of this book: the impact of changing technology, the dominant roles of personalities, the changing strategies of major corporations, the importance of the courts, and issues of pricing and takeover tactics.

While the contest for Paramount raged on, it dominated the financial news. Newspapers, television, radio, online information services—all were filled with the latest word on the bidding. In fact, the back-and-forth received so much attention for so long that at least one reporter openly professed to be "sick of writing about Paramount."

However, many Americans were captivated with the struggle. One reason for this interest was the nature of Paramount's business. Paramount was, as then-Viacom president Frank Biondi described it, one of the great American "dream machines."

Diller Decides

A host of lawyers and investment bankers trooped into the dark granite Manhattan office tower on the corner of Sixth Avenue and 52nd Street in January 1994. Known to New Yorkers as "Black Rock," the building houses the main executive offices of CBS Television. However, the lawyers and bankers were in the building to visit the new offices of Wachtell, Lipton, Rosen & Katz, a powerhouse takeover law firm, which in a typically shrewd move had leased space at the bottom of the real estate cycle from the downsizing CBS network.

QVC chairman Barry Diller arrived last in the thirty-third-floor Wachtell, Lipton conference room. The epic battle for control of Paramount Communications, pitting home shopping channel QVC against Sumner Redstone's Viacom, had dragged out over months. Now it came down to this one moment. As the clock ticked toward the impending February 1 deadline for final bids, Barry Diller and his partners had to decide whether to raise QVC's $10 billion bid for Paramount.

When Diller arrived in the conference room, he found a small crowd that included Marty Lipton, one of Wachtell, Lipton's founding partners, and high-profile media banker Herb Allen of Allen & Co. A bevy of advisers including a team from Wasserstein Perella & Co. represented Diller's partners in the bid.

The meeting opened with a description of the situation. Viacom had just raised its bid from $104 to $107 a share for 50.1 percent of Paramount's stock. Media mogul Sumner Redstone was a tenacious and skilled adversary. Earlier, hoping to craft a "Diller killer," Viacom had added a contingent value right (CVR) to the complicated pack-

age of securities it was offering in exchange for the remaining 49.9
percent of Paramount's stock. The rest of the Redstone package was
easy to beat. Consequently, the CVR was the main topic of Diller's
conversation with his advisers.

The CVR provided that Paramount shareholders would receive
additional Viacom securities if Viacom's stock failed to reach a specific price target within three years. Although there were substantial
loopholes in Viacom's CVR, a consensus quickly developed among
Diller's advisers that, due to the CVR and the downside protection
the CVR provided, the arbitrageurs, or professional speculators, who
held a majority of Paramount's stock would favor Viacom over QVC.
QVC would lose the bidding war unless it offered a similar security.

The debate raged. Was gaining Paramount worth taking the additional risk inherent in a CVR? If QVC added such a right to its bid,
QVC's existing shareholders might be forced to pay a steep price:
Should QVC's stock not hit the price target, new QVC shares would
have to be issued to the former Paramount stockholders, diluting the
interest of the other QVC shareholders. Was the price for Paramount so high that the winner of the bidding would really be the
loser?

Diller closed the debate and asked his friends to make their personal recommendations to him in private. Lipton, Allen, and all the
others realized that a "win" was within grasp and that Diller's destiny
was to run Paramount. They all strongly endorsed the raise. Diller
said he needed time to think the issue over and would be back
shortly. While Diller's advisers waited, he walked the halls.

Paramount was the transitional deal, the last of the contested
brawls of the 1980s, the first of the digital strategic transactions of
the millennium. Only a true believer in the full valuation of content
would pay the price; the cynic would back down.

Finally, Diller returned and in a soft voice told the exhausted en-
tourage his decision—he would not let the emotional momentum of

the contest push him; QVC would not raise. He would rather lose than overpay. The battle for Paramount was over.

Paramount Communications—the company being fought for—had not always been a sexy sought-after media company that could command a steep price in the market. Not long before, the company called Paramount Communications had been Gulf + Western, a plodding corporate conglomerate. Of course, the Paramount movie studio—one division of Gulf + Western—had a long and compelling history. Founded in 1916 by Adolph Zukor, Paramount Pictures was a Hollywood powerhouse in the 1930s and 1940s, boasting a stable of stars that included the Marx Brothers, Gary Cooper, W.C. Fields, Claudette Colbert, Bob Hope, and Bing Crosby.

In those early days, Paramount not only made movies, it also owned a captive chain of theaters. To the politicians of the late 1940s, this arrangement smacked of a dangerous monopoly. Eventually in something called the "Paramount Decrees," the government forced Paramount and other movie studios to sell off their captive theater chains.

By the 1950s, however, Paramount was wounded and dying. Then along came the highly controversial Charles Bluhdorn—dubbed the "Mad Austrian" by *Life* magazine—and his company, Gulf + Western. Even before it bought Paramount in 1966, Gulf + Western was a corporate menagerie, having evolved from a car bumper business into one of America's largest conglomerates. Bluhdorn's company made building products, owned racetracks, marketed consumer products and cigars, ran a publishing company, held land in the Dominican Republic, mined titanium, peddled panty hose, and so on. The various operations were known as "Charlie's cats and dogs."

In the end, Gulf + Western's performance was lackluster. The sudden death of Bluhdorn in 1983 and rise of Martin Davis to the position of CEO only underscored what had been clear for several years—Gulf + Western needed to slim down and refocus.

On taking the helm, Davis, a tough former publicist with an instinct for survival, quickly assessed the situation. In a radical departure for a company once known as "Engulf & Devour," he launched Gulf + Western on a campaign to sell off more than 100 unrelated businesses. By 1989, this effort was largely complete. In that year, the company sold its large finance division to Ford Motor Company for $2.6 billion, rechristened itself Paramount Communications, and made an unsuccessful $12 billion hostile bid for Time Inc.

Having failed to win Time, Davis and Paramount sat in the early 1990s on a large hoard of cash and looked for another strategic partner. Potential acquisitions reportedly included Geffen Records, Thorn EMI, and even MCA. Rumors also periodically circulated of an impending Paramount-Viacom merger. In talks with Viacom's Sumner Redstone, as well as with other potential partners, Davis reportedly insisted that he control the surviving entity as CEO. But Redstone found this demand unacceptable, as did other potential partners. A match failed to materialize, and the pressure began to mount.

A New Kind of Rumor

In the summer of 1993, Martin Davis heard a new rumor. Word on the street had QVC's Barry Diller preparing a bid for Paramount. Davis and Diller knew each other well, as both had worked together under Bluhdorn in the old Gulf + Western days. But a clash of wills after Davis took over had led Diller to leave Paramount.

Given the antipathy between Diller and Davis, Davis viewed the prospect of a QVC bid with alarm. Soon he received confirmation of his worst fears: Early in 1993, Davis heard from John Malone, the leader of both Tele-Communications Inc. (TCI), a cable company, and Liberty Media, an affiliated owner of cable television channels and QVC's largest shareholder, who told Davis that QVC intended to purchase Paramount. At the time, Malone was regarded by his enemies as the Darth Vader of the cable industry, an all-powerful, brilliant overlord with his fingers grasping for every media opportunity.

According to court papers filed in later litigation, Malone recalls Davis responding that the Liberty Media boss should keep Diller "on a leash."

In July, Davis had a tense lunch with Diller at Paramount headquarters. According to Davis, Diller denied the rumors of QVC's interest in Paramount, but only in a "vacant" fashion. Diller, who claims he was noncommittal when asked about his intentions, describes the meeting differently. In a later deposition, he testified that the lunch was cut short when Davis became incensed, yelling "I know you're coming after me."

Meanwhile, Redstone and Davis had been in serious discussions since June 1993. The negotiations were at times difficult. Everything was hotly debated, including the total price, the amount of cash to be paid for Paramount, as well as a whole slew of governance issues, including who would be CEO and the name of the surviving entity.

However, the approaching shadow of Diller apparently motivated the Paramount side to come to terms. A little over a month after Davis' lunch with Diller, Davis took a proposed merger with Viacom to the Paramount board. The deal called for Viacom to pay Paramount shareholders $9.10 a share in cash plus Viacom stock then valued at $60 and valued Paramount at roughly $8.2 billion.

To facilitate the merger, Paramount agreed to amend its existing "poison pill," a takeover defense device. Moreover, as approved by the Paramount board, the deal also contained two lockup provisions designed to keep other bidders from busting apart the Viacom-Paramount marriage: First, Paramount granted Viacom an option to acquire 20 percent of its stock, and second, Paramount agreed to pay Viacom a $100 million fee if it backed out of the deal. Finally, for Davis, the deal had another important feature—he would be CEO of the proposed Paramount Viacom International, though Redstone would control the company.

Stroke, Counterstroke

On Sunday, September 12, 1993, the Viacom and Paramount boards approved a merger agreement. The transaction would bring the two companies together into a combined entity with a market capitalization of roughly $18 billion. Two days later, papers were filled with the news, heavily sprinkled with words like "mega," "mogul," and "giant."

"We think we've created the number one software company in the world," Sumner Redstone told reporters at a press conference in Viacom's cafeteria. "Only a nuclear attack" would break the deal. When asked, he dismissed the notion that Davis had agreed to the deal only to stave off Diller. "Martin has never had any fear of those people," he said. "We're not concerned about them."

Redstone's confidence in the Viacom-Paramount deal stemmed largely from his assessment of developments in the media business. While distributors of programming, in particular cable providers, currently had a powerful position as access providers, content, according to Redstone's vision, would soon reign supreme. New technologies promised to allow phone companies to transmit video over phone lines. Cable providers would have to share their distribution monopoly with telephone companies and satellite dishes. In a 500-channel world, content manufacturers like Viacom and Paramount would have a sought-after product.

From this perspective, the Viacom-Paramount combination made compelling strategic sense. Viacom brought cable channels MTV, Nickelodeon, VH-1, and Showtime to the table. Paramount produced movies and television shows, owned a successful publishing house, and had a library of over 850 films. The distribution boom—digital cable, movies on demand, global satellite television, and hot international movie and videocassette markets—dramatically increased the leverage and value of content.

However, as soon as the deal was announced, it became clear that the market doubted Redstone's confident assertions that no other bidder would emerge. Arbitrageurs—the speculative investors who buy up the stock of merger targets in the hope a deal will go through at a higher price—elbowed to buy up Paramount stock. The price was bid up from the mid-50s to the high 60s.

There was good reason for the arbs to hope. On a breakup basis, most observers valued Paramount's treasure chest of media assets at between $9 and $10 billion. A buyer could easily outbid Redstone and make up the difference with asset sales. Paramount's theme parks, Madison Square Garden, which owned the Knicks and Rangers sports teams, and seven TV stations were likely candidates for easy sale.

Eight days later, with the stroke of a pen, Barry Diller indicated his intention to break up the deal. In a letter that began "Dear Martin," Diller proposed a merger of Paramount and QVC "on terms far more attractive to Paramount stockholders than the transaction proposed with Viacom." In the merger, Diller continued, each share of Paramount stock would be converted into $30 cash and .893 share of QVC stock. The package was valued at $80 a share, or $9.5 billion in the aggregate, based on QVC's market price at the time. When compared to Viacom's offer, by this time valued at around $63 a share, Diller's bid was superior. In essence, Diller thought the Viacom deal was vulnerable because Viacom had lowballed its bid.

According to Diller, QVC would finance the generous offer, which included $3.5 billion in cash, with the help of several equity investors. At the time of his letter, cable operators Liberty Media and Comcast already had agreed to invest $500 million each in QVC. Another $1 billion would come from Paramount itself. When asked about the final $1.5 billion, Diller responded with a question: "Is there anybody in the world who doesn't think we can borrow $1 billion, $1.5 billion? I'm not paying for any bank commitments . . . until we know more." True to form, Diller soon had another $1 billion of equity commitments, $500 million each from Cox Enterprises, a cable and newspaper company, and Advance Publications, the New-house family's publishing company.

Like Redstone, Diller had a sweeping strategic vision to back his offer. A combination of QVC—with support from cable providers Liberty and Comcast—and Paramount would create a vertically integrated media company. In addition, Diller brought a strong creative history, running both Paramount and other studios, and a demonstrated ability to turn a flagging media company around.

Diller's bid naturally threw the Viacom-Paramount deal into great turmoil. Paramount shareholders were not likely to tender shares to Viacom in light of QVC's steep premium over the existing Viacom offer. Still, Paramount management stuck to its position that a combination with Viacom represented the "best fit for growth" of its businesses. The Paramount board slowly considered the QVC offer but continually put off discussions with Diller. First, Paramount required QVC to provide information on its financing. Then, when that condition was satisfied, Paramount delayed signing the confidentiality agreement needed before QVC could safely share further information with Paramount.

Finally Diller tired of the foot-dragging. He launched a public tender offer for Paramount stock, contingent on the removal of both Paramount's poison pill and the costly termination fees provided for in the Viacom deal.

Viacom responded by renegotiating its deal with Paramount, raising the total consideration to $80 per share in cash for 51 percent of Paramount's stock plus a package of securities for the remaining 49 percent. The total package was worth roughly $9.4 billion. Even with the raise, however, the lockup provisions were left in place.

On November 16, the Paramount board met and rejected QVC's offer as unduly conditional. Even though the most recent QVC bid remained appreciably more valuable than Viacom's best offer to date, the board urged shareholders to favor the Viacom merger. In support of this stance, a company spokesman pointed out that QVC's tender offer was contingent on the removal of Viacom's lockup provisions, which had escalated in value and were now worth more than $600 million.

Sumner Redstone

Sumner Redstone—ranked as one of the 400 wealthiest Americans by *Forbes* magazine—has built an estimated $9 billion fortune on the strength of shrewd judgment and a tough competitive spirit. He was born on May 27, 1923, in a Boston, Massachusetts, tenement. An entrepreneurial spark was bred into Redstone from the start—he watched his father transform a single drive-in movie theater into a small but profitable chain.

Though the seeds of a business career were planted early, Redstone didn't return to the family business until the mid-1950s, after graduating from Harvard College and Harvard Law School and spending a number of years as a Washington lawyer. Then in 1954, Redstone joined his father and brother in the family's chain of twelve drive-ins, known then as Redstone Management.

Redstone soon spotted the trends that would reshape the movie business. People were moving out of the cities into booming suburbs, and land was becoming increasingly scarce and more valuable. Redstone put these two trends together and realized that drive-in theaters were not the future. Rather, there was value in clustering more screens at single indoor locations. So the multiplex was born—a concept and a term that Redstone is credited with creating.

In time, Redstone expanded the family chain from fifty-nine to 129 theaters. He carefully picked sites and bought the underlying land, giving his company a hedge on the volatile movie business.

By his fifties, Redstone was a wealthy movie exhibitor with a reputation for an unyielding negotiating style.

However, the course of Redstone's life changed dramatically in
1979. Caught in an early morning hotel fire, he barely survived.
This near-death experience seems to have sharpened Redstone's
drive. He continued to expand the family business, now known as
National Amusements, but became increasingly concerned at the
lack of further growth potential. Good theater locations near
major highways were scarce. Looking for growth, Redstone began
investing in the content side of the movie business, just as the
1980s deal frenzy took off.

In 1986, Redstone made a toehold investment in Viacom, a
cable television and movie company then the subject of takeover
rumors. Soon, sparked by what he viewed as a lowball management bid to buy the company, Redstone launched his own
takeover, ultimately winning Viacom after a heated round of bidding. The original management offer had been $2.7 billion; Red-
stone agreed to pay $3.4 billion.

Some observers scoffed at Redstone's initial foray into the
big-deal business. He was portrayed in the media as a novice
dealmaker who got caught up in the zeal to win and seemed to
have overpaid. Yet, very soon after the deal closed, Redstone
looked like a genius. Viacom's MTV and Nickelodeon channels
continued to captivate young audiences around the world, while
the value of Viacom's cable system doubled very quickly in a rising market. This growth allowed the company to service its debt,
and the value of Redstone's stake multiplied, providing the capital to launch his Paramount bid.

On a personal level, Redstone exudes congeniality and charm.
He almost gurgles with enthusiasm about his business in every
technical aspect. Yet the sunshine fades rapidly when Redstone is
crossed. In such circumstances, he displays the bulldog tenacity
of a former litigator.

The Battle Shifts

Both sides in the Paramount fight soon ran to court. Not surprisingly, Redstone, a litigator by training, was first out of the gate. Two days after Diller announced his bid, Viacom filed suit in New York federal court challenging QVC's offer on antitrust grounds. In a press release, Viacom claimed that the lawsuit, which was broadly focused on the allegedly anticompetitive practices of John Malone's Liberty Media and Tele-Communications Inc., had been in the works even before the QVC bid. In light of its Paramount bid, however, QVC was added to the complaint.

Redstone had repeatedly used litigation in his career as an integral part of business strategy. He shrewdly judged that Diller's glass jaw was his Malone connection. As CEO of TCI and chairman of Liberty, Malone controlled the largest cable operator in the country as well as a number of cable channels. Critics charged Malone made a practice of using to unfair advantage his status as a gatekeeper to millions of cable subscribers.

Liberty Media's partial ownership of QVC gave Redstone an opening, and he pounced. According to Viacom's complaint, Diller was nothing more than a front man for Malone. Diller's offer was just another manifestation of Malone's "conspiracy to monopolize" the cable television business. Malone was painted in stark terms, as a buccaneer, a "bullyboy" monopolist, who used his company's dominance in the cable market to exact tolls from content providers like Viacom.

By November 12, the Malone connection cracked. Facing mounting scrutiny and political pressure, QVC had dropped Malone's Liberty Media from its group of financial backers. A week later, John Malone announced a settlement with the Federal Trade Commission that required Liberty Media Corporation to sell its interest in QVC within eighteen months if QVC bought Paramount.

But the resourceful Diller bounced back. He scrambled and replaced Liberty Media's planned $500 million investment with a much larger $1.5 billion commitment from regional telephone company BellSouth Corporation, our client. BellSouth had been lying in wait, hoping for a crack in one side or the other so that it could acquire a relatively low-cost window on expertise for video content. Meanwhile, NYNEX, the New York regional Bell phone company, took a position backing the Viacom bid.

Notwithstanding Viacom's initial success, the central litigation took place in Delaware courts as Diller mounted a counterattack masterminded by Herb Wachtell, the senior litigator at Wachtell, Lipton. Delaware prides itself on, and profits from, its position as the leading legal home for corporations, and because of this role, takeover litigation most often involves the Delaware courts. In this arena, the fiery Wachtell was a star, smooth, articulate and yet passionate. He proceeded to cut Paramount's board to ribbons.

From a technical legal standpoint, the case *Paramount v. QVC* revolved around whether the Paramount board had treated its shareholders fairly: By agreeing to merge with Viacom, did the Paramount directors effectively put their company up for sale? Wachtell maintained that the company was on the auction block, and the process the directors followed was unfair. The Paramount-Viacom deal was not a strategic marriage, according to Wachtell. Rather, Paramount had sold itself to Viacom. Under that circumstance, according to an earlier case involving industrialist Ronald Perelman's hostile bid for the Revlon Corporation, the Paramount board had a responsibility to open the sale to all bidders and conduct a fair auction.

Ironically, Paramount and its lawyers were in the awkward position of relying on the case they had lost three years earlier in Paramount's effort to split apart the Time-Warner merger. The *Time* case, won in part by Herb Wachtell, stands for the proposition that a board of directors is not required to cancel a planned "strategic" merger when faced with a higher cash bid.

After hearing arguments, the Delaware court sided with QVC. In his November 24 opinion, Vice Chancellor Jack Jacobs lambasted the lockup provisions in the Viacom-Paramount merger agreement as "draconian" and enjoined Paramount from modifying its poison pill to favor the Viacom deal or honoring the lockup option. Instead, an auction would have to be held consistent with the *Revlon* case.

Fifteen days later, after a hearing broadcast live on Court TV, the Delaware Supreme Court affirmed the opinion. The court sided with Diller—the proposed Viacom-Paramount merger was a sale of control that triggered the *Revlon* duties. The Paramount board should have focused single-mindedly on securing the highest price for Paramount shareholders. This conclusion rested in part on the fact that Redstone would control 70 percent of Viacom's voting stock after a Viacom-Paramount merger, and in part on the court's distaste for the Paramount board's and advisers' procedures.

To the court, the board was too swift to act and too generous to Viacom, and therefore the court proceeded to rap the board and its advisers on the knuckles. Moreover, the Paramount board could not hide behind the "no-shop" provision in its agreement with Viacom, which prohibited Paramount from seeking other offers, for the board had originally given "insufficient attention to the potential consequences of the defensive measures demanded by Viacom" and the measures were therefore unenforceable.

Barry Diller now had a level playing field.

The Auction

Reacting to the Delaware Supreme Court, the Paramount board met into the evening of December 13, 1993. The deliberations were in one sense a formality—in light of the court's decision, Paramount would be auctioned to the highest bidder. Still, a long, heated debate ensued. Certain directors felt a committee of independent, non-management directors should be appointed to oversee the bidding procedures, especially in light of the court's concerns. However, Davis argued that the entire board could administer a fair auction.

Ultimately, Davis carried the day and the entire board approved a set of auction procedures.

Under the procedures, each bidder was required to submit a closed "final" bid by 4:00 P.M. on December 20, 1993. Paramount agreed to drop its poison pill defense with respect to the bidders so that shareholders would be free to select either offer. In addition, the bidders were required to hold their offers open for at least ten days after gaining enough stock to complete the acquisition. This stipulation would allow stockholders who had tendered to the losing bidder to switch sides, thereby eliminating the incentive to tender early. Without this rule, only those shareholders who tendered to the winner prior to its deadline would receive a share of the cash consideration offered.

When the auction opened, QVC had a decided edge over Viacom. QVC's latest offer for Paramount was a $9.8 billion package of cash and securities. Viacom, with the help of a $600 million investment from Blockbuster Entertainment and a $1.2 billion investment from NYNEX, had cobbled together a $9.6 billion counteroffer. However, even this offer threatened to overwhelm Viacom's resources. The combined Viacom-Paramount entity would barely have enough cash flow to cover its massive debt unless both companies performed far better than they had over the past few years.

On December 20, the parties submitted their bids. However, reflecting Viacom's cash crunch, its bid remained unchanged from its last offer. QVC, on the other hand, raised the cash portion of its new bid to $92 per share for 50.1 percent of Paramount. At the same time, the stock portion of the bid was reduced, so that the shift did not raise the total value of the offer. A day later, in a blow to CEO Martin Davis, the Paramount board adhered to the Delaware Supreme Court's admonition and endorsed the higher QVC bid. Putting the best face on these developments, Davis emphasized that Viacom could still raise its bid.

Davis' wish came true during the first week in January. Sumner

Redstone announced an $8.4 billion merger with cash-rich Block-buster Entertainment. By paying stock for the acquisition, Redstone acquired new fuel for his battle with Diller and, with this new part-ner, dramatically raised the cash portion of his bid to $105 a share. However, like Diller, Redstone adjusted the stock portion of his bid, so that the total value of Viacom's offer was around $9.4 billion, still well short of QVC's $9.8 billion bid. Redstone, it seemed, was count-ing on the greater cash pool to entice the arbitrageurs, who now held most of Paramount's stock.

In an angry response to Viacom's new bid, QVC charged that its rival had violated the bidding procedures by entering a new bid with the same value as the old bid. Earlier, QVC had charged Redstone with attempting to manipulate the price for Viacom stock higher to keep the Paramount purchase price down.

The New York Times sparked these claims when it reported in De-cember that Redstone's National Amusements Inc., Viacom's parent company, had been buying Viacom stock in July and August and that WMS Industries, a company 25 percent owned by Redstone, made similar purchases around the time of QVC's original bid. The WMS Industries purchases amounted to about 20 percent of the volume in Viacom Class B shares, at the time a large component of Viacom's acquisition currency. For his part, Redstone insisted that he was ig-norant of the purchases by WMS Industries. Meanwhile, both com-panies had secret talks as to a compromise settlement with no success.

At a January 11 media conference in Los Angeles, Diller told re-porters, "The bids are in. The public, the shareholders, should de-cide. As for me, I'm finished."

The bidding had reached the presumed upper limit of Para-mount's breakup value. To some degree, Redstone's fierce competi-tive reputation was an asset to him. No matter the obstacle, Redstone seemed determined to overcome it. Redstone was betting that efficiencies and the opening of new windows for the use of creative content would leave room for adequate returns on Viacom's $10 billion investment. Diller disagreed.

Implicit in Diller's thinking was a relatively high value for Paramount's movie studio and a relatively low value for both Paramount's publishing businesses and Madison Square Garden and its sports teams. The studio business was pegged at between $3.5 and $4.0 billion, roughly 15 times cash flow from operations. The publishing business was valued at between $2.5 and $3.0 billion, or roughly 10.5 times cash flow from operations. The Garden, the sports teams, and the theater chains together were valued at between $800 million and $1.0 billion. This was about 15 times operating cash flow. Adding all Paramount's assets up, Diller couldn't get to a number higher than he had already bid. Redstone was in a different position because he already had a large asset base in Viacom. Diller also had to bring along his partners in a complex and difficult situation.

Diller, however, was not just concerned about the Paramount purchase price and persuading his partners; he also was thinking ahead to life after the deal. Additional money would need to be invested in Paramount to realize his vision. If QVC paid much more than $10 billion for Paramount, Diller would be hard-pressed for capital. Improvements would be difficult. Diller refused to parachute into what he saw as an untenable situation.

On February 15, Viacom announced it had enough shares to complete the deal. The evening before, with the "cruel, abusive, and sometimes ridiculous battle for Paramount" (as Redstone described it) winding down toward a midnight resolution, Redstone, Viacom CEO Frank Biondi, and two other Viacom executives dined at Manhattan's "21" Club. At around 8:30 P.M., a call came in from Viacom's proxy solicitor. Viacom already had the 50.1 percent it needed to complete the deal. A few weeks later, Redstone described his reaction: "I picked up a champagne glass and said, 'Here's to us. We won.' It was not said in arrogance. The frustration, the stress, the meanness that had taken place all disappeared."

Diller, on the other hand, was philosophical about losing the biggest takeover fight of the year. He told the *Los Angeles Times,* "One of the things I learned long ago about auctions . . . you have to remember it's not ego or talent. It's simply raising your hand for the next bid. You don't always get to win."

In the aftermath, Sumner Redstone felt like the winner, Barry Diller expected to be a winner, and the rest of the world was waiting to see.

Diller's official statement about the Paramount contest—"They won. We lost. Next."—turned out to be prophetic. Diller soon bounced back.

Meanwhile, Redstone profited more directly from the coming of the digital age. Despite Diller's concern about overpaying for Paramount, in the end, its assets were worth more than previously thought. The cash received from the divestitures of Madison Square Garden ($1.0 billion), its sports teams, the educational publishing business of Simon & Schuster ($4.6 billion), and half the USA and Sci-Fi cable networks brought in a collective $7.5 billion. The assets that remain from the deal, excluding the studio business—Paramount's TV stations, Simon & Schuster's consumer publishing, a movie theater chain, and a music publishing company—are valued at more than $4 billion by analysts. Therefore, Paramount's nonstudio assets alone are today worth more than $11.5 billion, several billion dollars in excess of the $9.8 billion paid for Paramount. Effectively, Redstone got the studio for free, proving his critics wrong.

Despite serious setbacks with Blockbuster, the vehicle whose copious free cash flow enabled Redstone to enter the nearly $10 billion bid, Redstone seems to have turned things around. The new CEO, John Antioco, has refocused Blockbuster on its core video rental strategy and has instituted an innovative revenue-sharing plan with

studios: To make it affordable for Blockbuster to offer plentiful supply of the most popular tapes, Blockbuster will pay studios a substantial cut of revenues in exchange for huge discounts on video
rental tapes. The program appears to be successful, and Blockbuster
had a successful August 1999 IPO. This enabled Sumner to take advantage of the CBS opportunity.

History's Shadow | 3

"The best prophet of the future is the past."

—Lord Byron, *Journal*

The Five Pistons—regulatory and political change, technological developments, fluctuations in financial markets, leadership styles, and the drive for scale—run throughout the CBS and Paramount stories. These merger dynamics pervade the 1980s and 1990s megadeals and have been part of the long history of M&A and the adaptation of industry and financial markets to change.

The Fight for the Erie

In 1868, Cornelius Vanderbilt had been in a battle to gain control of the Erie Railroad for more than two years, but had been stymied at every turn. The Erie Three—Daniel Drew, Jay Gould, and Jim Fisk—had skillfully defended their positions as incumbent managers. In the process, Vanderbilt had lost about $5.5 million, a phenomenal sum in those days. Vanderbilt faced a quandary: Raise or fold?

Daniel Drew—titular head of the Erie—received Vanderbilt's cryptic answer late in the summer of 1868. "Drew," wrote Vanderbilt, "I'm sick of the whole damned business. Come and see me."

The seventy-one-year-old former cattle driver made his first fortune in the rough-and-tumble cattle business, bringing herds to market. Along the way, Drew reputedly fed salt to the cows, keeping them thirsty during the trip, then let them drink their fill just before reaching the scales at market. The scheme, called "watering stock," later became a metaphor for the issuance of corporate securities with an inflated value, a strategy used by Drew in his later incarnation as a stock market player. Still, by the time he received Vanderbilt's note, even the pugnacious Drew had wearied of the constant back-and-forth battle over the Erie.

The struggle for the Erie had begun in 1866 when Vanderbilt, a seasoned master of corporate growth through timely acquisitions, was a ripe seventy-two years old. By that time, the gruff old man had parlayed a small shipping company into a massive transportation empire with the New York Central Railroad as the linchpin. An amalgamation of the New York & Harlem, the Hudson River, and the old New York Central railroads, the reconstituted New York Central had lines running from New York City to Buffalo. Vanderbilt also owned an interest in the Lake Shore line, which gave him connections as far west as Toledo, Ohio. But Vanderbilt saw the need for a further link with the bustling hub of Chicago. The Michigan Southern line possessed such a link, and Vanderbilt wanted it. There was a problem, though: Another suitor, Drew's Erie Railroad, was after the Michigan Southern.

For a shrewd corporate acquirer like Vanderbilt, the answer was clear—he would pursue Erie itself. Vanderbilt thought himself well positioned. His agents were given orders to buy up Erie shares in the market; but as they did so, Erie's stock price rose dramatically. Still, the Commodore kept buying, paying a hefty premium in the process.

Unbeknownst to Vanderbilt, many of the Erie shares he was buying in the market were coming directly from the Erie Three. Their main strategy was both simple and probably illegal (notwithstanding its validation after the fact by corrupt public officials). Fundamentally, it was very similar to the poison pill defense adopted by Para-

mount and others in the 1980s. As Vanderbilt feverishly tried to corner the market in Erie shares, management kept the printing press
whirling, issuing more and more new shares.

Not fazed by the Erie Three's tenacity, Vanderbilt again com-
manded his brokers to buy, but to no avail. Each time they waded
into the market, the printing press spun out a new batch of certificates, and Vanderbilt's ownership interest was diluted. Finally, Vanderbilt understood that he would not wrest control of the Erie in the
market. Vanderbilt then resorted to a common raider's tool—he went
to court. These were the days of Boss Tweed and Tammany Hall,
when corrupt politicians controlled the New York political infrastructure. Not surprisingly, Vanderbilt was able to find a friendly
judge who complied with Vanderbilt's request and issued a warrant
for the Erie gang's arrest.

Fortunately for the Erie Three, sources at the courthouse warned
them of the impending arrest. Gould and Fisk hurriedly stuffed $6
million from the Erie treasury into several suitcases and fled with
Drew across the river to New Jersey, where they settled in at Jersey
City's Taylor Hotel. Then, as now, the press loved the dramatic. They
dubbed the hotel "Fort Taylor" after the Erie incumbents installed a
stout antitakeover defense—fifteen policemen and three small can-
nons mounted on the waterfront.

Finally, after some time, Vanderbilt tired of "kicking a skunk," as
he is reputed to have characterized the battle. He sent the note to
Drew, offering to meet and come to terms. Drew responded favorably, and the two men met at Vanderbilt's house. The Commodore
was not, however, in the mood to give up quietly. He demanded in
excess of $4.5 million as partial repayment for his losses from the
fight. This was an early case of a spurned raider seeking a payment
to go away—what became known as "greenmail" in the 1980s.

Vanderbilt was not without a negotiating position. If one believes
Jim Fisk's description, Vanderbilt threatened to continue his legal assault: "He said . . . he would keep his bloodhounds [the lawyers] on

our track; that he would be damned if he didn't keep them after us if we didn't take the stock off his hands." Though Vanderbilt's price was steep, Drew and his compatriots accepted.

PROFILE

Cornelius Vanderbilt

Cornelius Vanderbilt's ability to spot and capitalize on new technologies was the essence of his success.

Vanderbilt was born in 1794 and as a boy cared little for schooling. When pressed to attend, he would instead volunteer to work on his father's farm or ferry passengers or freight to New York City in the family boat. Noting her son's passion for his father's ferry business, Mrs. Vanderbilt agreed to lend him $100 to buy his own small ferry boat.

Vanderbilt began his ferry service at an opportune time. He was able to repay his parents within the first year, and gave them an additional $1,000. When during the War of 1812 British ships blockaded the harbor, vessels like Vanderbilt's provided the only means to transport goods up and down the seaboard.

By the end of the war, Vanderbilt had a small fleet of sailing ships at his command. When new steamboat technology threatened to make his wind-powered vessels obsolete, Vanderbilt jumped on the technology and slashed prices to keep out competition.

At the time the Civil War broke out, Vanderbilt was in his late sixties and, again, saw the rise of a new technology—railroads. He realized that the United States must "span its imperial distances . . . or else crumble apart from the deadweight of its size."

Once more, Vanderbilt adapted to change. He divested his shipping company for $3 million and bought railroads. By the time Commodore Vanderbilt died in 1877, he had left a railroad empire and an estate valued at more than $100 million.

The Consolidation of the Railroads

Railroading was the high-tech industry of the nineteenth century, promising to open the great American expanses to commerce and development. After the founding of the Baltimore and Ohio Railroad in 1828, the craze for railroads spread. Entrepreneurs recognized the railroad's potential and began to build a massive coast-to-coast network. While most of the early roads were built between cities along the Eastern seaboard and carried primarily passengers, by 1849 freight revenue began to exceed passenger revenue. By the 1880s, iron and steel tracks crisscrossed the country.

This massive expansion was funded partly with federal land grants but also absorbed a considerable amount of private and public capital. Almost $300 million was invested in the railroads in the 1840s, and $840 million more was invested in the 1850s, mostly by foreign investors. By 1890, the railroads suffered from both overcapacity and overleverage.

With the onset of the Panic of 1893 and a sagging in the economy from 1893 to 1897, a mess ensued in the railroad industry. At that time, approximately 60 percent of the companies trading on the New York Stock Exchange were railroads and many had become unable to pay their creditors. The Interstate Commerce Commission counted 192 insolvent railroad corporations, which represented roughly 25 percent of the country's combined railroad capitalization. Thousands of workers were thrown out of work. Those companies that survived barely limped along. The industry was in chaos.

Investment banker J.P. Morgan stepped into the breach. Over the next several years, working to advance the interests of his many European clients who had loaned money to the railroads, he played a key role in merging and restructuring their operations.

Morgan was a man of few words. Though notorious for a sharp tongue and booming baritone, his physical appearance was perhaps his most recognized feature. A permanent skin disorder, rhino-phyma, left his face, and particularly his nose, swollen, gnarled, and scarred. Business acquaintances struggled to keep from staring. A reputed mistress said: "I have never met anyone so attractive. One forgets his nose entirely after a few minutes."

In the late nineteenth century, Morgan was one of the gatekeepers to the supply of capital for U.S. companies. Both J.P. Morgan & Company and Morgan's personal dominance grew by mediating between the concentrated European supply of wealth and the American burgeoning need for capital. With developed European contacts, especially among wealthy Britons, Morgan earned his commissions floating American bonds in Europe.

PROFILE

J.P. Morgan

John Pierpont Morgan was the catalyst for the expansion of the American economy near the turn of the century. His famous bank Drexel, Morgan, later J.P. Morgan & Co., after the death of his partner, Anthony Drexel, provided capital to the leading firms of the day. On several occasions, it also played a key role in bailing out the government and stabilizing the capital markets.

By 1912, J.P. Morgan was in control of a syndicate consisting of the major financial houses in the country which, together, were acting as a central bank. Just as the railroad trust, the steel trust, and the sugar trust had been created, Morgan had created the banking trust.

Recent J.P. Morgan biographer Jean Strouse describes Morgan's role in shaping the American economy: "In the 1850s, when America needed much more capital than it could generate on its own, the Morgans and their associates had funneled money from Europe to build railroads and float government bonds. By the turn of the century, Pierpont Morgan was organizing giant industrial corporations, largely with American money, and the vital center of world finance had shifted from London to New York."

The House of Morgan was regarded by investors as a stamp of quality. Businesses Morgan underwrote were steady performers that provided unwavering profits and long-term growth. But when necessary, Morgan would take control over companies to which he supplied capital to stabilize them. It took this personal commitment and involvement with American industry to assure investors that their money was secure with Morgan. By being one of the first to undertake this role, Morgan ensured his success.

Central to his Morganization of failing railroads and his key role in the formation of U.S. Steel was Morgan's philosophy about competition. Morgan believed in the need and efficacy of administered markets, but had no faith in the government's ability to do the administering. Morgan viewed himself as something of a financial doctor.

In fact, Morgan and his bankers acted as financial doctors not only to industry but to the federal government as well. By 1893, the federal treasury was in the midst of a crisis, with its gold reserve fallen below $60 million. At that time, the only way to replenish the gold supply was to sell bonds to the public and use the proceeds to buy gold in the market. But if bonds could not be sold, the treasury would be insolvent and would have to default on its obligations, potentially inducing the collapse of the financial markets. As the gatekeeper to these markets, Morgan saw his role clearly: He would have to help stabilize the government by underwriting the bond issue.

By February 1895, the situation had become dire, with only $9 million of gold left in the treasury and $12 million in drafts against the gold. The government was technically insolvent. On February 12, 1895, J.P. Morgan & Co. offered the government bonds for sale at 112¼, almost 8 points more than the syndicate had paid for the bonds. The entire subscription sold out in less than twenty minutes. Crisis had been averted.

In subsequent months, public outrage mounted at the large fees made by Morgan and the other underwriters in the gold bond financing. But the financiers felt they had taken on substantial risk, for which they deserved to be compensated.

In another dramatic story, Morgan saved the markets from widespread panic in May 1897. When he and his syndicate were buying up shares of the Northern Pacific railroad, the stock shot up from about $127 to $149 in a day. Speculators believed that this kind of a rise could not be supported and began to short-sell the stock at $140. But in fact, the short sellers cornered themselves in, having pledged to sell 100,000 more shares than had ever been issued. So while the Morgan group had stopped buying at $146, the stock continued to rise all the way to $1,000 in anticipation that the short sellers would need to buy to cover their shorts. At that point, J.P. Morgan stepped in to avert a crisis and stabilize the markets, offering some of his shares in Northern Pacific at $150.

J.P. Morgan was not a candidate for sainthood. His actions were often driven by his quest for personal short-term profit. In 1863, for example, he created an artificial gold shortage, so that he could then sell at a large profit. Morgan's livelihood was dependent on stable financial markets and a strong U.S. government. He did what was necessary to ensure their order and his own future potential for profit. Morgan understood that with the power of gatekeeper of the markets also came responsibility.

Railroads, with their immense fixed costs, were the primary beneficiaries of this European money supply: By 1893, Morgan's clients held a large volume of American railroad bonds. Understandably, then, when the railroads began to default on their obligations, Morgan became quite concerned.

To Morgan, the railroads' grief seemed self-inflicted. There were simply too many competing lines, resulting in harrowing competition and razor-thin profit margins. Railroad companies in this hyper-competitive market had become vulnerable to every economic downdraft. Morgan and his father had both devoted their lives to developing a mature capital market, the maintenance of which depended on preserving the trust of European investors. The idea that sniping competition between the railroads could destroy this trust incensed Morgan.

Rather than sit by and watch this happen, Morgan set about re-structuring the roads in a process that came to be known as "Morganization."

In the usual Morgan restructuring, the stockholders placed their shares in a voting trust to be controlled by Morgan until the railroad's debts were paid. Then, fixed costs were slashed and Morgan's people carefully projected the railroad's future cash flow. Bondholders received new replacement debt that provided payments in line with the railroad's projected cash flow. New stock was also issued to the stockholders and bondholders which, while of only speculative value at the time of issue, would be quite valuable if the railroad survived. Because Morgan was overseeing many different railroads at once, he was able to reduce the warfare that had so debilitated the industry: He minimized the overlap between railroads by shutting down some lines and, when possible, merging companies.

Though Morgan asserted that he was doing a public service by saving the railroads, critics had a different opinion about his activities. He was, they argued, too powerful. By dominating the railroads, he reduced competition and forced higher prices upon consumers. Morgan also made himself and his firm incredibly wealthy in the process. Despite the protestations of detractors, however, Morgan's reorganization practices were successful and by 1900 the survivors were returning to economic health. Railroad bonds, which had been anathema to investors during the lean years, became a glamour investment once more.

The process of Morganization formed the basis of today's bankruptcy and distressed securities practices.

Steel and Oil

Many other industries developed along trajectories similar to that of railroading. Steel and oil are prominent examples. The steel industry was born from the centuries-old iron business. In 1860, over 250 firms produced almost 1 million tons of iron. However, iron is a product of limited strength and is costly to produce. Steel, an alloy of pure iron and a controlled amount of carbon, by contrast, is a stronger product.

In 1856, Henry Bessemer and William Kelly each independently discovered a cheap and effective method for purging iron of its impurities. A series of subsequent discoveries improved the process, and a new industry was born. Large mills were built throughout the 1850s and again in the 1870s and 1880s. Output increased accordingly.

Andrew Carnegie was perhaps the best-known steel man. Having originally founded a company to make iron railroad bridges, Carnegie built an enterprise that in 1899 produced 75 percent of all U.S. steel exports and more than 50 percent of the plate steel made in America. He accomplished this feat through a two-tiered strategy. First, he drove his subordinates relentlessly to pursue technological innovations and cost savings. Second, he retained a considerable portion of earnings in his company and bought his competitors at bargain prices when times were hard.

In the oil business, John D. Rockefeller followed a similar path in building what would become Standard Oil, beginning with a 1862 investment in a small Cleveland refinery. By 1870, the company had been reorganized as Standard Oil (a name intended to reflect the standardized quality of its product) and boasted the world's largest refining capacity. At that time, just as during the railroad boom, enthusiasm about the prospects for new oil companies had caused significant overcapacity in the oil industry. According to one source, the total oil refining capacity in 1870 was three times as great as the volume of crude oil actually being pumped. The fierce competition that ensued meant that few companies turned a profit. Much like Carnegie, Rockefeller detested the unremitting competition in the oil industry. Rockefeller's motto was "pay a profit to nobody." Vertical integration was his goal, and acquisitions his weapon of choice.

By the spring of 1872, about 80 percent of all Cleveland refineries had sold out to Rockefeller. Standard Oil's capacity increased to 12,000 barrels a day, or about one third of all U.S. production. Rockefeller then repeated his Cleveland pattern in other cities—Pittsburgh, New York, Philadelphia, and Baltimore. As his empire spread, transportation and distribution efficiency became critical, leading Rockefeller to buy into pipeline projects and pipeline companies. Rockefeller's strategy worked well, and by 1880, Standard Oil controlled at least 90 percent of the nation's oil business. Standard Oil was everywhere.

Rockefeller used the immense scale of his business to drive competitors out of the market. He formed strategic alliances with railroads which provided Standard Oil, but no other refiners, substantial rebates on shipping costs. In this way, Rockefeller raised the costs of his rivals, forcing them either to sell to him or be forced to shut down.

Rockefeller rationalized the ownership structure of Standard Oil in 1882 with the formation of the Standard Oil Trust. In exchange for their shares, each stockholder received trust certificates. The Trust was governed by a board, which was controlled by Rockefeller. The arrangement was ordered broken apart by an Ohio court on the ground that it violated the state's monopoly statute; but Rockefeller simply remade the Trust into a holding company in New Jersey—a state whose laws permitted such trusts—that survived until 1911.

John D. Rockefeller

The enigmatic John D. Rockefeller was born in Moravia, New York, to parents of modest means. His early years in poverty were pivotal in defining his quest to become wealthy and successful, ruthless and virtuous. Rockefeller's father instilled in John the need to keep meticulous accounts. But while John's traveling salesman father was a hedonistic, scandal-ridden figure, it was his mother who brought up the children and enforced discipline, as well as a strong sense of religion. Rockefeller soon came to believe that "God wanted his flock to earn money and then donate money in a never-ending process." As a youth, Rockefeller was also deeply interested in music, even briefly considering becoming a professional musician and practicing the piano for up to six hours a day.

In 1855 Rockefeller began the search for his first job in Cleveland. He spoke in his later years of his job: "As I began my life as a bookkeeper, I learned to have great respect for figures and facts, no matter how small they were." He threw himself zealously into his work, knowing if he didn't he would have to rely on his flighty father. Rockefeller, according to biographer Ron Chernow in *Titan,* embodied the Protestant work ethic in its purest form.

In 1862, Rockefeller formed a partnership to refine oil into kerosene, not realizing that oil would soon be his most important product. Creating a business model that he would follow for years to come, Rockefeller located near railroad tracks. By age twenty-five, he bought out his business partners for $72,500 and founded a second Cleveland refinery. Critics, even at this early stage, criticized Rockefeller for setting oil prices at the market-place "at whim." He proceeded to buy up competitors and lever-age his power into advantageous deals with railroads.

Even in the early years, Rockefeller understood the impor-tance of having a war chest for acquisitions. He noted that he had won many bidding contests simply because he had more avail-able cash than the next bidder. Not surprisingly, Rockefeller was detested by competitors and reviled by consumer advocates, most notably Ida Tarbell, who wrote the muckraking classic his-tory of Standard Oil, which told a tale of raw power and regula-tory corruption.

Living in Cleveland with his wife, Cettie, and his four children, Rockefeller tried to remain untouched by the excesses of the Gilded Age. Indeed, Chernow notes that what set Rockefeller apart from the other capitalists of his day is that he wanted to be "rich *and* virtuous and claim divine sanction for his actions." In-deed, Rockefeller was a great philanthropist, endowing the Uni-versity of Chicago and Rockefeller Institute of Medical Research, but he also knew charity was good for his public relations image.

Up until the very end of the Standard Oil empire, Rockefeller proved particularly shrewd. When questioned in 1907 in a court investigation of Standard Oil's operations, the titan feigned igno-rance and senility. Many wondered how this seemingly bumbling, charitable, kind old man could have been responsible for the col-lusion and price fixing of which he was accused. Standard Oil was broken up nonetheless, although the pieces became even more valuable than the whole.

Economic Rhythms

The evolution of the railroad, steel, and oil industries, from the rapid pre–Civil War expansion to the turn-of-the-century consolidation, followed a pattern common to most American industries. Initially, as a promising new technology was commercialized, certain producers experienced rapid growth, and investors thronged to support the industry. This growth eventually resulted in overcapacity and an ensuing period of retrenchment. While some market participants thrived in this difficult environment, others collapsed under the weight of new competition. The strong bought the weak. Companies combined in the race to gain new efficiencies, to curtail competition, or just to survive. These same themes would also play a significant role in the strategic mergers of the 1980s and 1990s.

This evolutionary process sparked a great leap toward industrialization between the end of the Civil War and the turn of the twentieth century. With the close of the war, more than a million men returned from service and threw themselves into the workforce. This influx, combined with the pent-up demand for industrial expansion, sparked an economic boom. Heavy industry in particular grew at a breakneck speed. Great railroad and shipping empires were pieced together, the steel mills of Pennsylvania took shape, and the immense meat-packing yards of Chicago blossomed. The boom period lasted for almost ten years.

Then, in September of 1873, financier Jay Cooke's once powerful Philadelphia bank failed, creating shock waves that toppled related business firms and eventually pushed the country into the Panic of 1873. It was the most serious depression yet experienced by Americans. More banks teetered, calling in loans in an effort to stave off failure, and thus forcing many debtor firms into bankruptcy.

America came out of depression in the late 1870s, only to sink back again in 1893. By the turn of the century, though, the country was well on the road to industrialization and was becoming a nation of large enterprises. Around this time, a merger wave took off, with the peak period of activity between 1898 and 1902.

Statutory revisions in New Jersey and elsewhere helped spark the wave by creating the legal framework for the modern holding company. Prior to 1888, corporations were required to be operating entities and could not own companies operating in another state. The 1888 New Jersey Holding Company Act put the business trust on statutory footing by explicitly permitting New Jersey corporations to buy and sell the securities of any corporation, New Jersey or otherwise. Whether cause or effect, this new legal structure provided a mechanism for consolidation.

By some measures, this turn-of-the-century wave was the most consequential boom in history. During the period, companies with roughly 40 percent of the nation's manufacturing capital participated in some type of combination. The boom ended with the stock market crash of 1904 and the Bank Panic of 1907.

More than three quarters of the mergers during the first wave were horizontal combinations—transactions involving companies in the same industry. By 1907, consolidating industries, including oil, sugar, tobacco, chemicals, and canning, were often left with only one or two concerns controlling an overwhelming majority of the market. Over 3,000 companies had disappeared.

While many of these transactions were financially defensible, they often caused social turmoil. Many of the leading individuals and corporations of the day attracted the ire of social critics, who found the financial workings of the age needless and harmful. The cruel side effects of industrialization and monopoly power were attacked and sometimes curbed, but the deals went on.

The Great American Steel Deal

Andrew Carnegie's high-tech, consolidation-based strategy ultimately generated the landmark deal of the first merger wave—the formation of U.S. Steel. The transaction netted Carnegie more than $225 million, over $4 billion in 1999 dollars.

In 1900, the steel business was entering a new age. A series of mergers had already consolidated the production of raw steel into the hands of Carnegie Steel, the Morgan-controlled Federal Steel

Company, and the Moore brothers' National Steel Company. While the market for steel had been booming for a number of years, demand had recently softened and steel processing firms, which turned the raw product into finished goods, were beginning to feel the pinch. The Morgan and Moore camps, each of which controlled a number of processors, had recently announced their intention to stop purchasing steel from Carnegie. Carnegie had countered with an ambitious plan to build a series of fabricating facilities, an area he had previously left to other companies. Difficult competitive times lay ahead for everyone involved.

On a cold December evening in 1900, eighty guests gathered at Manhattan's elegant University Club. Chiefly industrialists and investment bankers, the men came to honor Charles Schwab, the president of the largest and most prosperous steel company in the country: Carnegie Steel. J.P. Morgan, the leading banker of the day, sat to Schwab's right. Others in attendance included Andrew Carnegie, railroad magnate E.H. Harriman, Standard Oil president H.H. Rogers, and investment bankers August Belmont and Jacob Schiff.

After dinner, the honoree—a smooth, energetic orator—rose to deliver a short speech. Being a steel man, he talked about steel. The industry faced tough times ahead, he told the group. Every last production efficiency had been wrung out of Carnegie Steel's operations. Foreign competition loomed on the horizon. The economic future was uncertain.

But all was not gloom, Schwab told the audience. He suggested an alternative. If several firms banded together, substantial distribution savings could be achieved. Overlapping sales forces could be eliminated. Shipping costs could be slashed. New low prices would result, and the market for steel would expand accordingly.

By December of 1900, Schwab's boss, Carnegie, was sixty-five years old and growing impatient to begin a stage of more active philanthropy. Schwab's speech may have been a thinly disguised sales pitch.

Morgan was clearly intrigued by Schwab's vision and arranged a follow-up meeting. Four weeks later, a deal creating the nation's largest steel company was inked.

The formation of U.S. Steel, which combined Carnegie Steel and nine other companies, was valued at $1.4 billion. Carnegie's business was purchased for $480 million, $130 million more than the federal government's budget in 1901. J.P. Morgan brokered it all.

Trust Busters Win a Round

The first merger wave left many industries highly consolidated. However, shifting regulatory winds soon reversed some of the earlier combinations.

At the start of the twentieth century, Standard Oil and U.S. Steel dominated their respective industries. The American Cottonseed Oil Trust, the National Linseed Oil Trust, and the National Lead Trust each controlled a large portion of the market for their particular commodities. At its peak, the American Sugar Refining Company controlled nearly the entire refining business. The Pullman Palace Car Company held 85 percent of the market for railroad passenger cars. The International Harvester Company held 85 percent of the market for farm machinery. The American Tobacco Company was formed in 1890 through the merger of the five leading cigarette manufacturers and at its peak produced 80 percent of the nation's tobacco.

Business leaders justified the trusts, and later holding companies, as a necessary means to increase efficiency and gain economies of scale. In addition, they sought the elimination of unrestrained competition, which many saw as the cause of the successive depressions of 1873 and 1893. Critics, on the other hand, condemned the combinations, arguing that the concentration of market power in the hands of one or two producers left consumers vulnerable to price gouging.

Politicians like President Theodore Roosevelt fueled the fear by playing on the populist sentiment against the great concentrations of wealth and power represented by the leading industrial combinations.

Despite the potential backlash against these trusts, however, more failed than succeeded. Some industries found the trust structure favorable; others—especially those that were particularly labor-intensive or exhibited few economies of scale—did not.

Reacting to this popular dissatisfaction, Congress passed the Sherman Antitrust Act of 1890. However, the law at first proved largely ineffectual: In its first application in 1895, the Supreme Court ruled in favor of the American Sugar Refining Company, holding that it was not a monopoly in restraint of trade.

President William Taft, Roosevelt's successor, however, was more effective in breaking apart several trusts. His administration vigorously prosecuted U.S. Steel, American Sugar Refining, General Electric, and International Harvester. In 1911, Taft's Justice Department won a huge victory in the Supreme Court, forcing the breakup of Standard Oil into seven pieces.

While the former parts of the monopoly thrived for many years, they remained a shadow of their former selves, never again to dominate the industry. Yet these newly independent companies were themselves quite large, indicating the enormous size of Standard Oil before the breakup. The largest of them was Standard Oil of New Jersey—which later became Exxon—and ended up with close to half the aggregate net value. The second largest piece, Standard Oil of New York, later renamed Mobil, had 9 percent of the total net value. Standard Oil (California) became Chevron, Standard Oil of Ohio became the American subsidiary of British Petroleum, Standard Oil of Indiana became Amoco, which also merged with British Petroleum, Continental Oil became Conoco, and Atlantic became part of ARCO, the most recent addition to BP.

By the 1980s, however, the situation worsened considerably in the oil industry. Prices fell to new lows, and the market hammered oil companies' share prices. Oil could be purchased more cheaply on Wall Street by buying companies outright than it could in the oil markets. A wave of consolidation ensued. Yet regulation opposed recombination of the old Standard Oil empire at that time. The threat of antitrust scrutiny constituted a formidable defense to many of the hostile oil deals of the 1980s.

But by the late 1990s, the political tide turned in recognition of the fact that America's oil companies had ceased to be global leaders. Exxon had been overtaken by Royal Dutch/Shell and state-owned enterprises. Another consolidation wave ensued—this time between the former pieces of Standard Oil. The opening shot was the merger of British Petroleum with Amoco. The company that resulted—BP Amoco—subsequently announced its intent to acquire ARCO as well. And in a deal that would form one of the largest companies in the world measured by sales, Exxon announced a merger with Mobil. Only two of the seven pieces of Standard will remain independent: Standard Oil (California)—Chevron; and Continental Oil—Conoco.

Before the Fall: The Roaring Twenties

In the early years of the twentieth century, the business cycle continued its dramatic rise and fall, but the secular trend with regard to capacity and wealth was decidedly upward. The nation's real wealth, placed at $88.5 billion in 1900, more than doubled by the end of World War I (which had spurred a considerable expansion in productive capacity). The country experienced a brief postwar depression in the early 1920s but soon boomed again, with industrial output nearly doubling over the remainder of the decade.

Industries established in earlier periods, such as oil, steel, and electricity, continued to expand. At the same time, several new industries were born. Automobiles, airplanes, movies, and radio all became commercial realities in the 1910s and 1920s. The number of radio stations increased from thirty in 1922 to 500 in 1924. The number of registered cars went from 8.1 million in 1920 to 23.1 million in 1929. Meanwhile, on Wall Street, the stock market boomed. Volume climbed from 143 million shares in 1918 to 460 million in 1925, to 920 million in 1928, and to 1,125 million in 1929. The Dow Jones Industrial Average nearly quadrupled, from 100 in late 1924 to over 380 five years later.

The rising market and strong industrial growth combined to fuel a second merger movement, which ended with the Great Crash of 1929. Over 4,600 mergers were announced during the most active years, between 1926 and 1930. By the end of the 1920s, the nation's top 200 companies controlled an estimated half of the nation's corporate wealth.

Baby Blue Chips Grow by Merger

The volcanic activity of the second merger boom spawned many of the great creations of American industry. Dozens of today's major, established companies—such as GM, Ford, International Harvester (now Navistar), and Merrill Lynch—were formed during this period. These were the start-ups of the age, often pieced together with the help of funding from the overcharged stock market. General Motors' history illuminates the dynamic nature of the period.

General Motors founder William Durant got his start selling wagons and carriages. When the car company of his neighbor, David Buick, ran into difficulties in 1904, Durant took over. He reorganized the business and by 1908 was producing more than 8,000 cars. In that same year, after an aborted attempt at merging Buick with Reo, Ford, and Maxwell-Briscoe in what would have been a combination of the four leading automakers, Durant instead formed General Motors as a New Jersey holding company with Buick as its main subsidiary. He then used $8.75 million in GM stock and the cash dividends from Buick to go on a massive buying binge. He had two aims. First, he would broaden General Motors' product lines. Second, he would arrange a guaranteed supply of parts.

Durant quickly fulfilled both goals. First, he purchased the W.F. Stewart Body Company, the supplier of Buick's bodies, and 49 percent of Weston-Mott, the supplier of Buick's axles. Durant also established a joint venture to make AC spark plugs with Albert Champion, a promising young Frenchman. Then, in November of 1908, GM acquired a second line of cars with its approximately $3 million stock purchase of the Olds Motor Works. However, the intervening deals all paled in comparison to Durant's coup—GM's acquisition of the Cadillac Motor Car Company for $4.75 million—paid for primarily with cash. After a long courtship, Durant had finally succeeded in putting together two of the five largest carmakers.

Despite this accomplishment, GM suffered from considerable acquisition-related indigestion. In 1910, Durant was ousted as president of GM in favor of a team selected by the company's creditors. The bankers controlled GM through 1915, when enough of the company's debts were paid down to warrant a return to stockholder control. Durant, still a major owner of GM stock, had in the interim co-founded the Chevrolet Motor Company. Though Chevrolet was becoming successful in its own right, Durant badly wanted to regain control of GM and therefore launched a raid on the company he once ran.

Durant began by feverishly buying GM shares in the market. The price, which was around $80 at the start of the year, rose to a high of $558 by December 1915. While he could not realistically hope to gain control of GM by purchasing its stock in the market, Durant had a plan. He lobbied his friends for their proxies and, claiming at a GM meeting that he held 50 percent of proxies, forced GM's bankers to pay a massive $50 per share dividend on GM. This enormous cash inflow, combined with the proceeds from a public offering of

Chevrolet stock, allowed Durant to accumulate 44 percent of the outstanding GM stock.

However, Durant sought an absolute majority. Ever the tactician, he devised a clever scheme to accomplish this goal. After a meeting with other Chevrolet shareholders on Christmas Eve in 1915, he launched an exchange offer for GM in which Chevrolet would exchange five shares of its stock for each GM share tendered. The offer, which represented a premium on GM's current stock price, would remain open for just a month. To make the offer more attractive, Durant and a syndicate of backers began buying Chevrolet stock in an effort to force its price higher. When the price responded, Durant cut his offer to GM shareholders from five to one to four to one.

For the bankers who controlled GM, the situation was dire. The smaller Chevrolet, which Durant had unsuccessfully offered to sell to GM, now threatened to gobble the larger GM. The bankers, who still had visions of controlling GM, fought Durant's effort, but were unsuccessful. By May of 1916, Chevrolet—and indirectly, Durant—owned 54.5 percent of GM.

With control assured, Durant brought in the DuPont Company as a financial partner and shareholder—a tactic that would become more widely used in 1980s to guard against unwelcome attacks. By the end of 1919, DuPont controlled approximately 28 percent of GM and represented a friendly, stable shareholder base. Durant then launched a second acquisition tear, using GM to acquire Chevrolet in 1918 and reversing the corporate hierarchy so that GM again sat at the top. The following year, GM purchased 60 percent of the Fisher Body company, a major supplier. Numerous other acquisitions were added to the fold, including what later became the Frigidaire Division.

Then, in 1920, history repeated itself for Durant. Personal reverses in the stock market forced him to sell the large majority of his interest in GM to DuPont, and he was again pushed out of his management position. Though this was not the most ceremonious way for Durant to exit, his acquisition strategy had positioned GM for the future. As Alfred Sloan—who served as CEO of GM for twenty-three years starting in 1923—later wrote, "General Motors had then the makings of a great enterprise." Ultimately, however, Durant proved to be a creative high-wire artist who operated without a net. He simply lacked the discipline to transform the hodgepodge of companies he brought together into a large industrial enterprise. That role fell to Sloan.

Between 1923 and the Great Depression, Sloan made a few additions to the GM enterprise through acquisition. The remaining 40 percent of the Fisher Body Corporation was purchased in 1926 in a stock deal designed to assure supply and harvest economies of scale. Primarily, Sloan spent these years installing a set of financial and operational controls at GM. He created committees and a command-and-control structure. Inventories were closely managed. Cash flow was tracked. By successfully employing what were highly innovative practices at the time, Sloan had created the American management structure that would be replicated by other industrial companies.

GM's management structure and the strength of its fundamental business allowed it to ride out the Great Depression relatively unscathed. Sales dropped off dramatically, yet the company still earned $248 million between 1929 and 1933. Even more astonishing, GM paid out more than $343 million in dividends over the same period.

The command-and-control structure also had a wider impact. In the words of legendary management guru Peter Drucker, this structure was "a foundation for America's economic leadership in the forty years following World War II."

Frenzy, Then Collapse

During the 1920s, Wall Street achieved new highs, both in financial terms and in social standing. This was the Jazz Age, the time of Gatsby, and the booming stock market. Between the end of 1924 and the end of 1925, the Dow Jones Industrial Average jumped from 120 to 159. The market jumped another 22 percent in 1927. Then, the real boom began—with the market up 48 percent in 1928.

Individual stocks performed even more amazing feats. Radio Corporation of America—at the time a speculative flier—jumped from $85 to $420 in 1928. DuPont almost doubled. Montgomery Ward went from $117 to $440.

However, the upward progression was not smooth. RCA would jump 20 points one day, open up another 20 the next, then crash back 30 by the market close. The volatility was widely attributed to the manipulations of the big-money players. Trying to piggyback on these anonymous market insiders, investors fixated on the tape, the strip of paper churning out current prices. The hope was to spot a big move in the early stages and jump on for the ride.

There was certainly an element of truth to the belief that insiders had an advantage over Middle America when it came to stock trading. Corporate reporting was relatively unregulated, making accurate data on companies often hard to come by, and insider trading had not yet been made illegal. As a result, board members, corporate insiders, and bankers often had access to information before it became disseminated in the market.

The presumption of inside information was a powerful force, with the thirst for such information strong. The classic example is the market reaction to comments made by J.P. Morgan partner Thomas Cochran. Cochran, on his way to Europe, granted an interview aboard ship where he reportedly said that General Motors, in which he, J.P. Morgan, and its ally DuPont owned large stakes, was due for a 100 point increase. The Dow Jones ticker flashed a quote from this interview while Cochran was at sea. Traders presumed Cochran knew what he was talking about and bought the stock in bulk. It soared 25 points in two days.

While Cochran's comments appear to have been offhand, touting stocks was not an uncommon practice in the 1920s. Stock pools and syndicates, later outlawed, were commonplace, even fashionable. A group of investors would pool capital and appoint a manager. The manager would buy heavily into a company, trade back and forth, and attempt to create the impression of strong market activity. Some pools planted rumors in the press and often public relations men were hired to flog the stock. When investors piled in, driving up the price, the pool would sell out at a large profit. Without the support of the pool, the price often fell back dramatically.

Though now viewed as unethical, in the 1920s pool membership was not restricted to shady market operators. Rather, prominent bankers, partners of J.P. Morgan, the president of large banks, and corporate heads all participated.

In October 1929, the market came to a screeching halt. While the broader market had been depressed for a period of months, on Black Thursday, October 24, pessimism spread to the stocks of companies in the Dow Jones Industrial Average. Within a matter of weeks, stocks listed on the New York Stock Exchange lost almost 40 percent of their value. The market would continue to slide downward for years thereafter.

Following the Great Crash of 1929, America's bankers were the object of scornful Senate hearings. Ferdinand Pecora, a fiery assistant district attorney from New York, was deputized by the Senate Banking Committee to lead the charge. Over a period of months, this public servant, on a salary of $12.75 a day, went toe-to-toe with America's most powerful bankers and most able corporate lawyers. He dragged John Pierpont Morgan Jr. (known as Jack), the son of the first J.P. Morgan, before his tribunal and battered the sixty-six-year-old banker with tough questions and sardonic asides. A senator with pro-Morgan leanings decried the spectacle. "We are having a circus," he said, "and the only things lacking now are peanuts and colored lemonade."

The remark spawned one of the humorous oddities of history. A Ringling Brothers press agent, hearing of circuses and lemonade, thought to bring Lya Graf, a thirty-two-year-old midget, to Capitol

Hill for the next day's hearings. During an intermission, an enterprising photographer put Ms. Graf together with Jack Morgan, and a classic photo was born. The image of Graf, perched on Morgan's lap like a doll, went out to newspapers around the world. Here was the proof—the Pecora hearings had become an out-and-out circus.

Still, in the end, Pecora caught his prey. Other Morgan partners followed Jack. Each was forced to answer publicly for the speculative excesses of the previous decade. Eventually, it came out that, during the feverish 1920s, the House of Morgan made a practice of selling stock to those on its "preferred list"—prominent politicians, bankers, corporate executives, and friends of the Morgan partners—at a bargain. The press and public reacted with disbelief. Despite protestations from the Morgan partners, this practice looked and smelled like influence peddling. As a result of these and other revelations uncovered by the Pecora hearings, the banking sector became one of the scapegoats for the 1929 stock market collapse.

Whether the banking industry deserves the brunt of the blame for the Crash is to this day hotly contested. However, banks certainly played a prominent role in fueling the speculative binge in both their traditional capacity as lenders and also in their emerging role as marketers of corporate securities.

Banks began to enter the securities underwriting and brokerage business in the 1920s as a logical extension to their traditional lending operations. Due to the stock market run-up, which sparked considerable investor demand for new securities, companies were increasingly finding the capital markets to be a cheaper source of funds than traditional bank loans. With a portion of the fees they had formerly enjoyed now shifted to the capital markets, many of the nation's largest banks set up securities affiliates to participate in the booming brokerage business.

For example, the National City Bank, the largest American bank and the predecessor of Citibank, was an enthusiastic purveyor of securities through its National City Company. City had 1,900 fast-

talking brokers spread around the country who concentrated on selling to Middle America, often taking on a carnival barker's tone. In
addition to stocks, they hawked foreign bonds, mostly from Latin
American countries. Only later would it be revealed that many of
these bonds were repackaged bank loans that had gone sour.

PROFILE

Charles Mitchell

Charles Mitchell, president of National City, shattered the image
of bankers as gray-haired conservative types. He was a bear of a
man, a glad-handing salesman who traveled the country in a specially outfitted luxury railroad car. Mitchell thought of National
City as a manufacturer. Stocks and bonds were its product, and
they had to be pushed out the door.

Mitchell did all he could to whip his sales force into a frenzy.
He organized rallies and contests, awarded points for each share
sold, and paid prizes to top performers. The National City sales
force was built in Mitchell's image, filled with talkative salesmen
who could charm average citizens into buying Peruvian bonds or
shares in Anaconda Copper. When the Crash came, many of the
shares pushed by National City proved worthless—the Peruvian
bonds hyped only a few years before became a popular metaphor
for foolishly speculative investments.

At his height, Mitchell was both famous and rich. National City
paid him over a million dollars in bonus for 1928, and again in the
first half of 1929. However, like his customers, Mitchell would not
emerge from the Crash unscathed.

Mitchell's problems stemmed largely from the planned merger
of National City and the Corn Exchange Bank. Under the terms of
the deal, Corn Exchange stockholders could take either cash or
stock. The exchange ratio was designed such that, before the

Crash, holders would undoubtedly opt for stock. After the Crash, however, with the stock value of National City far below pre-Crash levels, shareholders opted for the cash alternative. National City would therefore have to come up with $200 million to complete the deal. Seeking to avoid this unpleasant prospect, Mitchell first tried to support National City's stock by borrowing $12 million from J.P. Morgan to buy shares in the market. His efforts, however, were unsuccessful and the deal fell apart. In the process, Mitchell had mortgaged himself to the hilt.

Mitchell's larger problems came in 1933, when he was arrested on charges of tax evasion. Toward the end of 1929, he had "sold" a block of National City shares to his wife in order to generate a tax loss that would offset his large income. The shares were later "repurchased" from his wife. Mitchell resorted to this wash-sale tactic—which was then fairly common—rather than sell the shares in the market because the shares were tied up as collateral on the J.P. Morgan loan. Though he was ultimately acquitted on the criminal charges, a large civil tax liability was entered against him. Mitchell retired from National City a broken man.

National City was perhaps the most unabashed when it came to selling securities, but it was not alone. The Chase National Bank, the nation's second-largest bank, opened brokerage offices coast to coast. Together with securities dealers, the banks encouraged average Americans to invest in stocks, oftentimes on margin. At the time, the margin rules allowed customers to purchase a dollar of stock for as little as 10 cents. The remaining 90 cents would be borrowed from the bank.

This leverage, responsible for stellar returns in an up market, left investors extremely vulnerable to a downturn. When the crash came, many investors were ruined. The inability of investors to pay their loans in turn contributed to the hundreds of bank closings during the Depression years.

Part of the problem, which can be seen clearly after the fact, was that banks' motivations were conflicting. On the one hand, they were charged with safeguarding customer deposits. On the other hand, as the underwriters of securities offerings, they wanted to sell securities and therefore encouraged customers to make what were sometimes risky investments, often loaning out these deposits on margin. With banks borrowing funds from the Federal Reserve at 5 percent and loaning them out at 10 percent, the whole process was quite lucrative in the face of a steady market.

Pyramids and the Power of Leverage

The 1920s spawned a unique capitalization structure known as the pyramid holding company, which allowed a small group of investors to control large companies with relatively little invested capital.

The basic structure involved the creation of a holding company with layered subsidiaries. Stock and debt of the second-, third-, and fourth-tier subsidiaries was offered to the public, but always in such a way that the ultimate parent company retained control.

PROFILE

The Van Sweringen Brothers

For a time, the Van Sweringen brothers were two of the most prominent financiers in America. Making their start in real estate, they soon discovered the enormous profit potential of leverage. In time, however, they also discovered its downside.

Otis and Mantis Van Sweringen were born in Wooster, Ohio, in 1879 and 1881, respectively. When their father died in 1893, they left school to enter the workforce. By 1900, the brothers decided to branch out on their own in the real estate business, buying an acre of land with their life savings and reselling it at a profit.

Inspired by their early success, Otis and Mantis took more options, sold more land, then borrowed enough capital to purchase 4,000 acres. The brothers also extended the scope of their vision: They sought a railroad line that would run from their development to the center of Cleveland, a goal realized in 1916 with the acquisition of the Nickel Plate Railroad for $8.5 million. The deal was financed with borrowed cash and bank notes.

Subsequent to their purchase, the Van Sweringens founded a holding company, Nickel Plate Securities, to hold their railroad, property, and debts.

Pleased with the now-thriving Nickel Plate line, the Van Sweringens continued buying up properties. Borrowing against the Nickel Plate, the brothers bought the Lake Erie & Western from the New York Central, as well as the Toledo, St. Louis & Western line, and consolidated all three lines in 1923. By late 1925, Otis and Mantis' holdings included control of 9,200 miles of railroad and assets of about $1.5 billion.

However, this empire was short-lived. In October 1929, the stock market crash caused a sharp fall in prices of the Van Sweringens' securities. Because the majority of their holdings were pledged to banks as securities for loans, the pyramids quickly came tumbling down. The end came in September 1935, when the Van Swerigen holdings went up for sale. The brothers were wiped out.

The pyramid structure was the foundation of many acquisition programs carried out in the 1920s, especially among public utilities. Power company executives like Sidney Mitchell of the Electric Bond and Share Company and Samuel Insull of Middle West Utilities pieced together dozens of small power companies through the use of highly leveraged holding company structures.

Insull's empire, for example, had as many as six layers of sub-holding companies. At the apex of the pyramid was Insull Utility Investments, Inc. The Corporation Securities Company of Chicago occupied the next tier, though it owned part of Insull Utility in a circular relationship. Beneath this were Insull's four operating systems—Middle West Utilities (holding 111 subsidiaries), People's Gas, Light & Coke (eight subsidiaries), Commonwealth Edison Company (six subsidiaries), and the Public Service Company of Northern Illinois.

When the Great Depression hit, the effects among the utility holding companies were somewhat mixed but overall were negative. Mitchell's company, one of the stronger utilities, continued to pay dividends on its common stock through the mid-1930s. Insull's companies, on the other hand, collapsed into bankruptcy, with investors losing between $500 million and $2 billion. After a period of flight, Insull was eventually tried and acquitted on charges of mail fraud.

The stock market collapse of 1929 brought with it a good deal of recrimination. One chief target of criticism was the overuse of debt to fuel the recent acquisition boom. Like the railroads after the Panic of 1893, these highly leveraged companies were unable to service their debt and collapsed as a result. Both the use of debt to fund acquisitions and the ensuing difficulty of servicing debt during downturns have been recurring trends in American economic life.

Depression, War, the 1950s

From the perspective of business and industry, the 1930s were a lost decade. The stock market crash of 1929 ushered in a long, three-year economic slide. While the economy bottomed out in 1933, it didn't really bounce back until 1939 and the onset of World War II in Europe. Merger activity was scant during the Depression, but picked up slightly in the war years.

The 1950s witnessed one of the first proxy fights, a spectacle that would set the stage for the hostile takeovers to come. Robert Young, through the Allegheny Corporation that he controlled, also had an interest in the Chesapeake & Ohio Railroad, which he sought to combine with the New York Central Railroad to create a more powerful Eastern player. He launched a hostile takeover of the New York Central in 1948, but his attempt was defeated by an Interstate Commerce Commission ruling against him.

Undeterred, in 1954 Young was poised to make another run at the New York Central. He resigned as director of the C&O and caused Allegheny to divest itself of its interest in the New York Central. With this potential regulatory hurdle removed, Young launched a proxy fight. He positioned himself as the friend of a small shareholder, "Aunt Jane." He promised to improve service and also to raise the railroad's dividend. Young ultimately won the proxy fight and became chairman of the New York Central.

By and large, the late 1940s and 1950s were mainly a period of organic industrial growth, as the United States underwent the transition to a peacetime economy. This growth, like the broad expansion following the Civil War, set the stage for yet another major merger wave, one that would come to pass in the "Go-Go Years" of the 1960s.

The Rise and Fall | 4
of the Conglomerate

"A man lives not only his personal life, as an
individual, but also, consciously or unconsciously,
the life of his epoch and his contemporaries."

—Thomas Mann, *The Magic Mountain*

The 1960s witnessed the full emergence of the American postwar industrial economy. These were the Go-Go Years of the stock market, with the increased power of professional institutional money managers and their emphasis on the leading, "Nifty Fifty" stocks.

The decade began with the optimism of Kennedy's Camelot and the extolling of professional management. The "Whiz Kids" and numbers men were in style in Washington and Wall Street, and Robert McNamara and Harold Geneen were revered as the best and the brightest.

By the end of the decade, the nation was deeply divided, and disillusionment eroded the government's monopoly on truth. The Vietnam War was a fiasco, and the numbers boys were discredited.

The Third Merger Wave

The 1960s spawned a third merger wave. By the end of 1968, the 200 largest industrial corporations controlled more than 60 percent of the total assets held by all manufacturing firms—a share equal to that held by the 1,000 largest firms in 1941. In 1968 alone, twenty-six of the nation's 500 largest corporations, were swallowed in mergers or acquisitions, sometimes by much smaller acquirers. However, since many of the acquisitions were diversifying moves, concentration in specific markets did not increase materially.

Much of the deal activity of the mid-1960s now looks strange: the pairing of RCA, a defense, technology, and broadcasting company, with Banquet frozen foods; Jimmy Ling's golfball, goofball, and meatball combination of sporting goods, pharmaceuticals, and meat packing; Textron's crazy quilt of companies making zippers, chain saws, fountain pens, rocket engines, and helicopters. In fact, much of the activity of the 1980s and 1990s involved undoing the deals made in the 1960s.

Unlike in previous merger waves, diversification, not concentration, was the goal, with targets operating in industries unrelated to those of the acquirers. Four factors drove this trend. First, federal regulators heightened antitrust scrutiny of horizontal and vertical mergers. Therefore, executives who wished to grow by acquisition were forced to look outside their core competencies for consolidation partners.

Second, the intellectual community in the early 1960s believed that the "best and the brightest" could manage anything and management skills were easily transferable between companies in unrelated industries. In light of the 1960s regulatory environment, it was this theory, in part, that encouraged the formation of conglomerates. As the conglomerates spread into seemingly incongruous industries, investment analysts and other stock watchers began to hear from executives about "critical mass" and "free-form management." Jargon aside, the basic theory was that each unit of a larger enterprise could draw as necessary on a central management pool, generating operating efficiencies.

Third, in the heated stock market of the 1960s, there was a need for growth in earnings per share and a higher stock price. The institutional market was inexperienced and naive and viewed these conglomerates' transactions—which, at least on paper, were accretive to earnings per share—favorably. Numbers seemed so scientific; common sense and strategy were out of fashion.

Fourth, the men running these companies believed in the manifest destiny of corporate growth. Bigger was better.

As a result of these four factors, the 1960s were the decade of large diversified conglomerates like ITT, Litton Industries, Teledyne, and Textron. The heads of these companies—Harold Geneen, Royal Little, Henry Singleton, and Charles "Tex" Thornton—and their peers molded their own legacy.

Ling: The King and His Realm

Of all the conglomerators, Jimmy Ling's career is among the most colorful. A high school dropout and Navy veteran, Ling's management career began in 1947 with the creation of an electrical contracting business in Dallas. Ling raised an initial $2,000 and founded the Ling Electric Company.

The early days were anything but glamorous. Ling hustled for wiring jobs in homes and small office buildings. However, frenetic energy, salesmanship, and a chugging Dallas economy combined to make Ling a success. After a period of steady earnings growth, Ling embarked on the acquisition campaign that would make him famous.

Ling Electric's first acquisitions were very small, consisting of a series of small electronic and defense contractors. Over time, however, the cumulative effect of these small deals made Ling Electric much larger. Then, in 1958, Ling found an investment bank willing to underwrite an offering of convertible bonds. With this burst of fresh capital, Ling began to hunt for bigger companies.

Results came quickly. A stock-for-stock merger of Temco Electronics into Ling Electric, followed by a stock-for-convertible-debt hostile takeover of Chance-Vought Aircraft, transformed Ling Electric into Ling-Temco-Vought, which became LTV. The combined entity earned 158th place on the Fortune 500.

For several years after the Chance-Vought acquisition, Ling busied himself shifting LTV's capital structure. First, he reduced the company's debt load by swapping debt for equity at opportune times. Then in 1965, in a restructuring dubbed Project Redeployment, Ling put into place a capital structure resembling the pyramid holding structures of the 1920s. He first separated LTV's operations into three separate subsidiaries. Then, he effected a stock swap with LTV shareholders, whereby they would receive a portion of the stock held by LTV in each of its subsidiaries in exchange for their LTV stock and some cash. Now publicly traded, the subsidiaries' stock was bid up by the market, which in turn increased the value of LTV stock.

Thus repositioned and recapitalized, Ling reenergized his acquisition campaign with the hostile takeover of Wilson & Company, a company operating in meat packing, sporting goods, and pharmaceuticals. The deal was structured as "two tiers" of just over $81 million in cash for 53 percent of the company and $115 million face value of preferred stock for the remainder. The transaction underlined Ling's willingness to make acquisitions ranging far afield from his core business.

The Wilson acquisition was well received in the market. Enthused with the momentum, Ling next acquired GreatAmerica, a diversified company that owned an insurance operation, Braniff Airlines, a bank, the National Car Rental Company, and real estate. Finally, Ling acquired a majority stake in the Jones & Laughlin Steel Company for $425 million in what was, at the time, the largest ever cash tender offer. By 1969, LTV had moved up to fourteenth place on the Fortune 500 list.

But Ling's last acquisition would bring his downfall. The Justice Department challenged the deal on antitrust grounds, leaving Ling unable to recapitalize and restructure the company as he had before. In the general downturn that affected all conglomerates, LTV's stock price eventually fell from $170 to $16. LTV shareholders lost a lot of money, and Ling lost his job.

James Joseph Ling

The bulk of Jimmy Ling's personal history is inextricably woven together with the history of his company—LTV. In the company's heyday, Ling received glowing press and business publications referred to him as "Jimmy Ling, the Merger King." He spun one complicated restructuring plan after another, making his prowess as a financier legendary.

A self-starter, Ling got his introduction to high finance hawking shares in his company at the 1955 Texas state fair. In short order, he became a master of the "Chinese paper" financings of the 1960s. LTV was built on a foundation of complicated deals— paper swaps, triangular mergers, debt restructurings, and so on. Each deal brought some new variation of complex securities.

Ultimately, Ling became the magician of the deal business. Attention to the fundamentals, however, was only of secondary concern. Rather, he seemed consumed by an insatiable desire to fashion a larger and larger enterprise.

As LTV's financial health worsened, so too did Ling's. He had over the years pledged most of his assets, including his stock in LTV, as security for personal loans. Nervous bankers tightened the screws when LTV's stock price tanked in the early 1970s, and Ling's personal finances were thrown into a shambles.

Eventually, Ling made several comeback attempts. The first— Omega-Alpha—was a small-fry conglomerate which Ling hoped to convert into a major company. The second—Xenerex—was an oil services company. Ling's convoluted financial structures, which captivated the market in the 1960s, did not play well in the 1970s and 1980s. Both efforts failed. His companies collapsed into bankruptcy, and Ling receded into retirement.

ITT Diversifies

Another continuing tale of the 1960s was ITT—International Telephone & Telegraph—created in 1920 through a combination of telegraph, telephone, and communications equipment manufacturers. The company, with operations around the world, was largely international in focus until 1959, when Harold Geneen became president.

Geneen left the presidency of Raytheon to join ITT. His résumé included time at several other old-line industrial companies, including Jones & Laughlin Steel and American Can. In the process of hopscotching his way up the corporate ladder, he had developed a reputation for strong and disciplined management: Raytheon's stock, trading at $64, dropped 6½ points the day his departure was announced. Yet, in retrospect, Geneen's previous experiences only prefaced the dramatic transformation he would work at ITT.

The forty-nine-year-old Geneen brought a time-tested management style to ITT. More importantly, however, he arrived with a pre-existing strategic vision: growth through diversification. Geneen favored this approach for a variety of reasons, but primarily because he saw it as less risky than building a business from scratch. At each of his previous jobs, he had unsuccessfully pushed diversification as a corporate goal. Now, ITT would be the laboratory for this vision.

If Geneen had any doubts about the virtues of his plans, they were quickly eliminated when in 1960 ITT's operations in Cuba were privatized by the new Castro regime. This experience highlighted the vulnerability of ITT's core business and spurred Geneen to reshape ITT. Geneen sought both diversification and a greater mix of income from the U.S.

After nine years of voracious merger activity, with more than 100 deals consummated, Geneen had achieved his goal. Included in the ITT fold were operations like Sheraton Corp., Avis Rent-a-Car, Bobbs-Merrill publishers, and Levitt & Sons. Despite a failed bid for the American Broadcasting Company and a few other setbacks, Harold Geneen compiled an impressive record during his first decade in office: In the span of years between 1959 and 1970, ITT grew from a company with $766 million in sales to a company with $6.4 billion in sales and had become one of the twenty largest industrial companies in America.

Harold Geneen

Unlike many other conglomerators, Harold Geneen was known as much for the way he ran companies as for the pace of his acquisition program. Tales of Geneen hustling to his plane, staff in tow, with multiple briefcases full of financial statements and memoranda for his review defined his popular image. He was legendary for his fourteen-hour days, incredible memory, and inquisitorial management style.

Geneen believed that information was the key to good management. "Facts" was his favorite word. After one 1965 meeting, he wrote a memo blasting those present for playing fast and loose with the term. In Geneen's mind, facts were incontrovertible, an expression of "final and reliable reality." "Apparent facts" or "reported facts" were not facts at all. However, once "true" facts were uncovered, management decisions became easy.

Geneen designed the entire ITT management structure around his passion for uncovering facts. Monthly General Management Meetings (GMMs) were at the heart of the process. In advance of the meetings, line and staff managers would prepare monthly reports—the documents that filled the numerous suitcases shepherded around by Geneen's personal staff. He would review several reports each evening, on weekends, even on vacations.

However, this was all just preparation for the GMMs. The

meetings took place in a specially designed, Orwellian conference room atop the ITT Americas Building in New York City. The giant windowless room had an oval table that could seat ninety-two, with sophisticated microphones and screens to project slides of the data being discussed. Geneen would sit at the midpoint of the table. Company executives would fill the other ninety-one chairs, with their own staff in even more chairs behind them.

Ostensibly, the GMM provided a forum for management interaction and centralization. A manager in one division might raise a problem that a manager from a different division had dealt with in the past. Really, though, the managers who presented their monthly reports at the meetings had an audience of one—Harold Geneen.

The questions, sometimes picayune but always discerning, would start shortly after a manager launched into a presentation. Woe to the manager who was not on top of his or her data. Geneen would ask four, five, ten, or more follow-up questions on the same point. For example:

> If you presented Geneen with what might seem an elementally simple fact—say, the value of physical assets in your unit—his first question might be, How do you know? If you told him, Our controller told me, his next questions would be, How does he know? Did you ask? Or have you uncritically accepted his statement and passed it along as fact without bothering to determine whether it is a fact, an opinion, or a guess? [Robert J. Schoenberg, *Geneen,* p. 193.]

Some participants found Geneen's confrontational style demeaning. Others found his attention to small details a waste of time, especially with more than 100 people often in attendance at the GMMs. Yet, for Geneen, his questions, and the lessons they taught, were a critical part of knitting together the diverse units under the ITT umbrella. He wanted all his managers to be tough detectives capable of uncovering problems before they mushroomed.

In the early years, the Geneen system seemed to work almost infallibly. ITT sailed along. Then, in 1969, problems began to surface. Geneen agreed to acquire the Grinnell Corporation, the leading maker of fire protection sprinkler systems, and the Hartford Fire Insurance Company. Richard McLaren, the government's antitrust chief, opposed both acquisitions. The attack had little grounding in existing antitrust law: McLaren seemed more concerned with ITT's burgeoning size than any actual anticompetitive effects. Both a federal district court and an appeals court ruled in ITT's favor.

Nevertheless, on the eve of the government's Supreme Court appeal, Geneen settled the case, agreeing to divest Avis, Levitt, and certain other businesses in exchange for the right to retain Hartford. For a time, Geneen put the turmoil surrounding Hartford behind him. But, in 1972, Washington political correspondent Jack Anderson uncovered a memo from Dita Beard, a lobbyist for ITT, which linked the Nixon administration's willingness to settle the antitrust case against ITT with a $400,000 contribution from ITT to the city of San Diego to support its bid to host the 1972 Republican convention. Anderson alleged a political bribe.

Though ITT had violated no laws, the company's image suffered as a result of the Dita Beard affair. The fallout, however, paled in comparison to the problems for ITT—and Geneen—when Anderson made his next revelation. About a month after he published the Beard memo, Anderson ran a series on a link between ITT and the CIA, again supported with memos from ITT lobbyists. ITT, the CIA, and other American business interests had apparently been working together in an effort to forestall socialist Salvador Allende Gossens' election to the Chilean presidency.

Several high-ranking ITT executives were indicted for perjury as a result of the Chilean affair. The charges against these executives ultimately were dropped on national security grounds, and Geneen escaped prosecution. Critics alleged a cover-up. Even without being directly implicated, Geneen's reputation was severely damaged, and

ITT became associated in the public mind with questionable practices.

The damage was only exacerbated when the IRS challenged the tax-free status of the Hartford merger. ITT successfully appealed the case, but for a time, former Hartford shareholders faced a potential $100 million tax liability.

While Geneen and ITT weathered the political problems of the early 1970s, the company's acquisition program cooled. The next decade would be spent repairing the damage.

The Earnings-per-Share Game

Although it may seem hard to fathom from the perspective of the 1990s, conglomerates such as LTV and ITT were actually thought of as high-growth companies during the third merger wave. Therefore, the market rewarded such companies with P/E ratios—a measure of the growth potential of a company—of over 40 at their peak, well in excess of the market average. Of course, to keep these high P/E ratios, the companies had to keep growing—and growing. When in 1968, Litton announced its first earnings decline in fourteen years, conglomerate share prices collapsed. The game was over.

Conglomerates often maintained earnings growth by acquiring firms which had lower price/earnings multiples, paying a premium in the process. These deals typically were funded with common stock. Under the right circumstances, this strategy provided an easy mechanism both to create instant growth in earnings per share and to boost an acquirer's stock market price.

As an example, take the case of a diversified growth firm trading at 20 times earnings and contemplating the acquisition of a target with equal earnings but trading in the market at 8 times earnings. Factoring in the control premium the acquirer would need to pay, let us assume that the acquirer could purchase the company for 10 times earnings. In such a combination, earnings would double for the new firm, assuming that no write-down of the purchase price were required. But the total number of shares outstanding would not double because of the difference in price/earnings ratios. If both the acquirer and target firms had 1 million shares outstanding, the acquirer would only have to issue an additional half a million shares to purchase the target because the market value of one acquirer share would equal the market value of two target shares. As a result, the earnings per share would rise by 33 percent, as the following table illustrates.

GROWTH IN EPS BY ACQUISITION

	Acquirer	Target	Merged Firm
P/E	20X	10X	20X
Earnings	$1 million	$1 million	$2 million
Shares outstanding	1 million	1 million	1.5 million
EPS	$1.00	$1.00	$1.33
Market valuation per share	$20.00	$10.00	$26.67

This effect could become even more pronounced if securities other than common stock were offered. For example, companies such as LTV specialized in devising hybrid securities to be issued in connection with mergers. Debt convertible into common stock was a frequent choice because tax laws permitted a company to deduct the interest on convertible debt issued in an acquisition. By contrast, dividends on stock were not deductible. This rule was later tightened in reaction to the perceived abuse of convertible debt.

Conglomerates also boosted EPS by targeting stodgy, old-line companies with buried earnings potential. For example, such companies might have had conservative depreciation or capitalization policies that could be altered to enhance accounting earnings. The possibility that such companies might have understated their assets, which the conglomerate could then revalue to create an accounting gain, was another potential source of one-time earnings growth. These transactions typically did not add economic value, however.

Through these mechanisms, deals could bring favorable earnings-per-share growth results, even though the individual businesses held by the conglomerate may not, in fact, have been growing. This situation caused a snowballing effect on conglomerates' price/earnings ratios: For a time, conglomerates' track records of strong EPS growth led markets to reward them with higher P/E ratios, allowing them to perpetuate their acquisition sprees and again be rewarded with higher P/E ratios. But this market imperfection was a short-run phenomenon which, like other bubbles, would soon correct itself.

This earnings game had obvious weaknesses. First, in order for the game to work, it had to continue in perpetuity. When the string of earnings increases stumbled, the market responded by punishing conglomerates' share prices, causing their price/earnings multiples to plummet, and making new acquisitions with stock substantially more expensive. Those companies that chose instead to issue so-called Chinese paper, the innovative hybrid securities issued to target company stockholders, began to feel the heavy burden imposed by their dividend or yield features.

Second, a key presupposition was that the stock market would treat the growth in EPS from acquisitions as if it were from internal growth—that is to say, that it would not penalize the acquirer's P/E—its measure of growth potential—when it acquired low-growth companies. While this was true in the short term, the market eventually caught on to the conglomerates' game, and gradually the P/Es of the conglomerates began to shift downward.

Third, the use of the leverage of hybrid securities became less efficacious. Again, analysts began pinpointing the effect undue leverage was having on earnings and began discounting the results for the additional risk imposed by the leverage. Meanwhile, the government began to limit the tax deductibility of interest on certain debentures issued in merger transactions, and, as will be discussed, accounting authorities began to reform the treatment of acquisitions to reflect costs more realistically.

Fourth, in the mad rush to make deals, some were necessarily rotten. Companies began to sag under the weight of interest costs and low internal growth from ill-thought-out acquisitions.

This focus on earnings growth, which set the stage for the conglomerate boom, was driven in part by the return of institutional investors, who sought EPS growth in companies, as a key governing force. Professional money managers had not played a major role in the market since the highly popular and eventually disastrous investment trusts of the 1920s. However, between 1949 and 1960, the amount of money managed by institutional investors went from $9.5 billion of NYSE-listed investments to about $70 billion. The 1960 total constituted roughly 20 percent of all NYSE-listed securities.

The money management business was highly competitive in the 1960s and, as is also the case today, performance was key. Fortunately for money managers, the 1960s were also a time of almost uninterrupted growth in stock prices. Significant returns were not difficult to achieve in this environment, and the reputation of money managers in general soared. A popular book titled *The Money Game*, written under the pseudonym "Adam Smith," christened the term "gunslingers"—money managers who jumped quickly on hot stocks. These gunslingers followed the market closely, traded regularly, and were generally considered to have a significant edge over individual investors.

Money managers lived and died on their quarterly performance and needed short-term gains to maintain momentum. Consequently, they became frequent supporters of corporate takeovers and were quick to accept hostile cash offers that included a premium to the previous market price. Investment bankers therefore often focused on a company's ownership structure as a key in advising on takeover strategy.

RCA: A Case of Mission Creep

The hot-blooded markets of the 1960s caused even the most established American companies to rethink corporate strategy. RCA—the Radio Corporation of America—was one company that fully embraced the new trend toward diversification.

RCA was founded in 1919 at the encouragement of Franklin Roosevelt and with the assistance of General Electric. Then assistant secretary of the Navy, Roosevelt wanted an American firm in the radio business for security reasons. In 1922, RCA began selling its first crystal radio sets, and four years later, RCA, GE, and Westinghouse established the National Broadcasting Company. RCA was also a pioneer in the record industry and was the first company to commercialize television sets.

Reversing course in the 1930s, government authorities forced GE to end its partial ownership of RCA. Free of GE's influence, RCA developed into a major competitor with operations in electronics, communications, and aerospace technology. However, RCA lost its way in the 1960s and 1970s, purchasing Hertz Car Rental, Gibson Greeting Cards, and CIT Financial. Other new businesses included frozen food and carpeting.

The acquisition program added debt to the balance sheet and increased RCA's annual interest burden. By the early 1980s, the company had almost $3 billion in debt and dramatically rising interest costs. CIT and Hertz, both capital-intensive businesses, were largely the culprits and therefore odd partners for an already cash-hungry electronics and technology firm.

While these new businesses consumed capital, RCA largely ignored its core markets, giving Japanese competitors the room to move in. While RCA had once been an industry leader, with an edge in radios, tape recorders, record players, and TV sets, by the early 1980s, RCA made little other than TV sets and was losing out even in that market. The company's famed Princeton, New Jersey, research center had focused for too long on a failed attempt to get into computers, leaving RCA with dated TV technology. Meanwhile, the company's main new product—the videodisc—flopped.

NBC also struggled for want of attention. The network's ratings fell off badly, and NBC became an also-ran in the three-way ratings wars.

Nor did the newcomers to the corporate fold make up for failings in the old core businesses. CIT proved a fiasco. RCA had wildly overpaid, ponying up an 80 percent premium to snare the lackluster unit. RCA's management compounded the problem by agreeing to leave enough cash in the CIT business to maintain a favorable credit rating.

Hertz had its own problems. The company made an aggressive effort to move into commercial truck rental, but the program floundered, and RCA was forced to write off the investment. At the same time, sudden oil price increases forced Hertz to shift its fleet over to compact and subcompact cars. Management was stuck with an overstock of costly gas guzzlers.

Some of RCA's problems can be attributed to financial fluctuations, chiefly steep jumps in interest rates and the price of oil. However, RCA's diversification program, compounded by management turmoil, certainly was also responsible.

The Collapse of Penn Central

The final blow to the 1960s merger boom came from the collapse of the Penn Central railroad. The diversifying acquisitions and horizontal merger that spurred its collapse put the final pin into the 1960s bubble.

The 1968 horizontal combination of the New York Central and Pennsylvania railroads sought to transform two unprofitable operations into a single successful unit. With the increasing orientation toward the automobile and the airplane, rail passenger traffic declined precipitously, and the great trunk lines of the Middle Atlantic had, by the late 1950s, become moribund and weak. Both the Pennsylvania and the New York Central had lines linking New York City with the Midwest and competed head-to-head for business.

As far back as the late 1950s, management of the Pennsylvania and the New York Central had explored a merger as the potential answer to mounting competitive difficulties. In 1961, the situation had become so dire that they came to terms. The merger, however, did not close until 1968 due to antitrust and integration concerns. One of the conditions of the merger was that the merged entity divest itself of its interest in the Norfolk & Western line. Deprived of this revenue stream, the railroad began a major diversification program. Investments in a diverse group of companies were to replace revenues lost from the sale of the Norfolk & Western. Nevertheless, the combined entity—dubbed the Penn Central—first and foremost was a railroad, with lines stretching from New York City west to Chicago and 1967 combined revenues of nearly $2 billion.

Just two years later, however, Penn Central was insolvent with a loss of $500 million—one of the largest bankruptcies in American history. Among other factors, the failure was attributed to mismatched management styles, excess debt, and ill-advised spending on diversification—money that could have been used to pay down debt. However, the fundamental factor in the decline appears to have been the failure to plan for the operational integration of the two roads—plain bad management.

Hints of trouble at Penn Central began leaking out in the spring of 1968 and into 1969. The stock price fell from the post-merger high of $86 to under $30. Meanwhile, because the railroad operations were burning through cash, David Bevan, the company's chief financial officer, and other executives were struggling to finance the company. Assets were sold off and cash squeezed out of subsidiaries. While the Nixon administration's efforts to control inflation had caused a run-up in interest rates, the Penn Central could not afford to wait out the market.

Bevan raised as much capital as he could from banks, but they had become wary. In March 1968, Bevan turned to investment bank Goldman Sachs because of his personal relationship with Gustave Levy, the firm's managing partner. Over the next several months, Goldman raised $200 million for the Penn Central in the short-term commercial paper market. However, this was a risky source of funding for the railroad's long-term capital needs because the paper, with a maximum nine-month term, would have to be rolled over on a regular basis. If the railroad were unable to do so, it would face a huge, immediate liquidity crisis. However, Bevan could not afford to be conservative. He did the best he could, backstopping half of the commercial paper with standby bank loans.

These precautions proved inadequate. The Penn Central turned in an awful performance for the first quarter of 1970. Institutional investors dumped its commercial paper, which the railroad was forced to repurchase. Bevan attempted to secure additional bank loans, even help from the government. Neither was forthcoming. On June 21, 1970, the railroad collapsed into bankruptcy.

The Pennsylvania and New York Central lines were eventually reorganized with government help as part of Conrail, and would later be the centerpiece of a 1996 takeover battle.

The Air Goes Out of the Conglomerates

Of course, like all bubbles, the conglomerate era was destined to end. Starting in 1968, the conglomerates were battered with a string of bad news. Litton Industries announced an earnings decrease for the first time in fourteen years. Trust-buster McLaren was busily making war on the conglomerates, both in the press and in the courts. Ling was hamstrung over the Jones & Laughlin purchase, and Geneen struggled with the Hartford deal.

In part reflecting this bad news, a major bear market swept the Street in 1968, taking the Dow from 1,000 down to 631 in May 1971. With their stock prices deflated, the conglomerates could no longer play the P/E game that had fueled all their previous earnings increases. Then, Penn Central collapsed, striking the final nail into the coffin.

The flaws in the conglomerate financial model had been exposed. The model didn't account for the possibility of fluctuations in the financial markets. Ling, Geneen, Tex Thornton, and their compatriots needed a strong and increasing stock market to keep their companies' inflated stock prices aloft. Without valuable stock as a currency, the acquisition spree came to a crashing halt; and without acquisitions, the conglomerates went from high-fliers to humdrum plodders. The conglomerate movement was dead.

Indeed, most diversified companies suffered through the next decade along with the nation. Watergate, war in the Middle East, and two major Oil Shocks diverted attention from the economy. The conglomerates struggled with anemic earnings and share prices and were ultimately dismantled.

The Early Evolution of Hostile Takeovers

During the 1970s, the deal business was in something of a recession, recovering from the collapse of the conglomerate merger wave. Yet, here and there, inklings of the future were apparent. For example, it was during this era that the hostile takeover in its modern form first moved from the corporate fringes to become an established practice.

In the 1960s, the hostile takeover was beginning to enter the corporate landscape. Though not successfully used against major American companies, medium-sized companies like Wilson were the subject of rough-and-tumble unregulated hostile bids. Federal securities laws only stipulated that an offer be left open for at least seven days. Therefore a potential acquirer could make an exploding cash tender for just enough shares to control its target, leaving it little time to respond to such a "Saturday Night Special" offer, and putting shareholders under intense pressure to come to a quick decision.

By the late 1960s, blue-chip corporate America was given an inkling of the hostile battles to come. At the close of the decade, in 1969, three major companies were targeted: Olympian Pan American World Airways by upstart Resorts International, Chemical Bank by Leasco Data Processing, and B.F. Goodrich by Northwest Industries.

Each attempt failed, but corporate executives got an early taste of the no-holds-barred tactics necessary to fight off an unwanted suitor. B.F. Goodrich, for example, fired out negative ads against Northwest and successfully lobbied the state and federal governments to block the deal on antitrust grounds. In addition, Goodrich completed two defensive mergers and altered its accounting method to pump up reported earnings. In the end, the company remained independent. But not all early hostiles were so easily thwarted.

In 1974, the International Nickel Company of Canada, a large, established corporation with a long history, met with Frederick Port, the president of ESB, and offered to buy the company. More importantly, Inco made clear that it would go ahead with a public tender offer whether or not ESB agreed to the proposition.

Inco's offer for ESB was spurred by its desire to diversify so as to be less exposed to fluctuations in nickel prices. In the early 1970s, the company began to look for new lines of business that would be less cyclical and more likely to experience growth. After the Oil Shock of 1973, Inco management settled on energy as an attractive sector, and eventually narrowed its focus to the subcategory of "packaged energy." After a failed attempt was made to acquire a British car battery maker, ESB (formerly the Electric Storage Battery Company)—the world's largest battery maker and Philadelphia's eleventh-largest company—seemed a good second choice.

When Port turned down Inco's offer, Inco was encouraged to proceed with a hostile bid by its banker, Morgan Stanley, which saw an opportunity to carve out a leadership position in aggressive offers. On the day of the meeting between the parties, ESB's stock closed at $19.50 a share. After the market close, however, Inco announced a $28 per share cash tender offer, and the fight for control began.

With the large differential between ESB's stock price and Inco's offer, ESB soon concluded that public relations and other defensive measures would not be sufficient to keep ESB independent. Very quickly, the company began to look for a "white knight" (i.e., a friendly acquirer) to take Inco's place. United Aircraft—later renamed United Technologies—was approached and by Sunday, July 21, had agreed to terms. Sometime after 6:00 P.M. the following day, United announced a $34 per share counteroffer for ESB shares, which ESB management endorsed as fair. Thinking he had fended off Inco, Port was jubilant. But his happiness was short-lived.

Two days later, Inco upped its offer to $36 a share, which United matched. Inco raised again, first by $2 a share, then by $3 a share. When the price reached $41 per share, however, United dropped out and a few weeks later the tender offer closed. Inco received 90 percent of the shares. In the space of less than a month, Inco had fought and won the first takeover contest initiated by a major strategic buyer. The purchase price came to roughly $227 million.

In hindsight, the ESB acquisition turned out to be a belly flop for Inco and vastly overpriced. Inco suffered a replay of Jimmy Ling's Pyrrhic Jones & Laughlin acquisition when antitrust authorities attacked the ESB deal as anticompetitive due to Inco's perceived dominance of the nickel market (then a raw material for batteries). The process dragged out for over three years during which Inco exercised little direct control over ESB. The same CEO who had tried to fight off Inco was left in place.

But even more significant than the antitrust battle was the fact that Inco simply was unable to manage a consumer goods business. Duracell and others thrashed ESB's Ray-O-Vac line at the checkout counter.

ESB also failed to invest in new battery technologies due both to lack of foresight and to lack of available capital for investment. First, the company was slow to develop its alkaline battery alternative. But Duracell was not so shy, and its copper-topped alternative became the prototype. Similarly, in the market for automotive batteries, ESB stuck with its low-maintenance battery rather than getting on the no-maintenance bandwagon. Competitors again came to market with better alternatives, and consumers shifted away from ESB's products. But even if management at Inco had wanted to explore these technologies more aggressively, Inco's capital woes prevented the necessary investment. A downturn in the nickel market during the 1970s caused the company's earnings to plummet and made excess capital scarce.

Nine years later, Inco gave up. ESB had been thoroughly trounced by Duracell and Eveready in the race to develop the long-life dry-cell batteries used today. Sears, Delco, and others owned the automotive battery category. Having already poured another $300 million into the ESB business, Inco saw little room for a turnaround and decided to divest ESB. The parts were sold off piecemeal and by the end Inco had lost more than $200 million on the failed diversification attempt.

The Deal Decade: 5
Early Years

"For now I stand as one upon a rock,
Environed with a wilderness of sea,
Who marks the waxing tide grow wave by wave,
Expecting ever when some envious surge
Will in his brinish bowels swallow him."

—William Shakespeare, *Titus Andronicus*

The cauldron of American economic activity in the 1980s resulted in the cresting of America's fourth merger wave. Death throes of mature industries, the spawning of new engines of economic growth, and innovations in financial markets all swirled to create the surge and a frenzy of excess. The bubble collapsed with a legacy of deflated expectations and acrimony. Yet, by the end of the decade, America had structurally revamped its corporate economy and was poised for an unprecedented boom.

The decade began as a period of retrenchment for many of America's large companies: Between 1979 and 1988, the Fortune 500 shed more than 3 million jobs. While some of these cuts were associated with a merger, buyout, or other transaction, the majority were not. The job loss at big companies reflected a trend that had begun in the 1960s and 1970s: American industry faced increasing foreign competition where none had existed before. At the same time, several key industries, such as steel and automobiles, faced relatively saturated markets.

In contrast to the situation faced by large companies, small and midsized companies as a group were experiencing phenomenal growth and new growth industries were emerging, creating new opportunities. Cable television, wireless communications, consumer electronics, computers, and overnight courier services, to name just a few examples, all grew into major industries. Notwithstanding the layoffs and restructurings among major corporations, America gained millions of jobs in the 1980s.

This juxtaposition of growth in new industries and the maturation of others created powerful incentives for mergers and acquisitions: Entire industries were in need of building or restructuring. During this period—from 1981 to 1989—over 22,000 deals were announced.

TEN LARGEST DEALS OF THE 1980s

Rank	Acquirer	Target	Approximate Price Paid (Millions)	Year Announced
1.	Kohlberg Kravis Roberts & Co.	RJR Nabisco Inc.	$24,561.6	1988
2.	Beecham Group PLC (U.K.)	SmithKline Beckman Corp.	$16,082.4	1989
3.	Chevron Corp.	Gulf Corp.	$13,205.5	1984
4.	Philip Morris Companies, Inc.	Kraft Inc.	$13,099.8	1988
5.	Bristol-Myers Co.	Squibb Corp.	$12,001.8	1989
6.	Time Inc.	Warner Communications Inc.	$11,650.3	1989
7.	Texaco Inc.	Getty Oil Co.	$10,128.9	1984
8.	DuPont Co.	Conoco Inc.	$8,039.8	1981
9.	British Petroleum Co. (U.K.)	Standard Oil Co. (remaining 45%)	$7,762.2	1987
10.	U.S. Steel Corp.	Marathon Oil Corp.	$6,618.5	1981

Source: MergerStat

The 1980s were distinguished by three distinct trends: first, strategic purchases by corporate buyers; second, going-private transactions funded by financial buyers; and third, the move by foreign multinationals into the U.S. merger market.

Strategic deals—mergers or acquisitions involving major corporate acquirers—predominated during the first half of the 1980s but became less important toward the end of the decade. These deals sought to satisfy a strategic imperative, such as building critical mass or diversifying into a new industry. Part Two of this book is about the strategy and deal implementation of these strategic mergers in the 1980s and 1990s.

Financial buyers—entities and individuals in the business of buying and selling companies—also emerged as major players in the early part of the 1980s. Kohlberg Kravis Roberts & Co. (KKR), one of the first financial buyers, became particularly visible starting in 1984, when it took part in three of that year's top thirty announced transactions. In the late 1980s, the financial buyers rose to even greater prominence. KKR became a household name in 1988 with its $24 billion purchase of RJR Nabisco. Buyout shop Hicks, Haas—later Hicks, Muse, Tate and Furst—put itself on the map with its LBO of Dr. Pepper and Seven-Up. In fact, three of the top ten deals in that year involved financial buyers.

International acquisitions formed another significant part of the late 1980s merger dynamic. Reflecting the pace of the larger merger market, many early cross-border deals involved targets in the oil business. Nevertheless, foreign multinationals had a spotty U.S. presence in the early part of the decade, failing to successfully consummate many transactions. For example, Seagram of Canada bid for Conoco in 1981, only to have its target snatched away by DuPont. Similarly, Rupert Murdoch's Australia-based News Corporation made a run at Warner Communications but was rebuffed.

By the second half of the decade, though, foreign acquirers had become a force in the market, entering into cross-border deals in a wide range of industries—from pharmaceuticals to consumer goods, from retailing to insurance, from publishing to movie studios.

Backlash

Hostile takeovers were another visible sign of the 1980s takeover boom, although relatively few in number. Even the peak year of 1988 saw only forty-six contested tender offers. Yet, these contested deals often involved very large companies such as Time Inc., Sterling Drug, and RJR Nabisco and, as a result, received a good deal of press and captured the public imagination. Terms like "corporate raider," "greenmail," "white knight," and "arbitrageur" or "arb" entered the common lexicon.

As the profile of hostile deals increased, so too did the political heat directed toward the individuals involved. The Business Roundtable, a lobbying group for the Fortune 500's corporate management, along with labor unions, decried what they saw as the negative impact of hostile deals.

This campaign against takeovers had a pronounced effect. During the 1980s, Congress considered hundreds of bills designed to curb the merger market. While no general antitakeover laws were enacted on the federal level, various changes in the tax code were used to reduce the incentive to merge. The Securities and Exchange Commission meanwhile appointed an Advisory Committee on Tender Offers on which I served along with Bob Rubin, Marty Lipton, and Joe Flom, among others. The committee's report, released in 1983, adopted a hodgepodge practical approach that failed to please either side in the debate but was meant to achieve a fairer process. Fifty specific recommendations were made, but few were enacted.

While the federal government did not enact general legislation on takeovers, antitakeover laws were passed at the state level. Delaware passed such a law in 1988. Not coincidentally, the law was made retroactive to December 1987, when corporate raider Carl Icahn began buying stock in Texaco Corporation and commenced a hostile takeover attempt. The law generally bars an unwanted bidder who buys more than 15 percent of a company's stock from merging with or selling the assets of the company for three years after obtaining a 15 percent stake. There are three exceptions to this rule, however: If the acquirer buys 85 percent or more of the target's stock, if two thirds of the stockholders approve the acquisition, or if the board of directors and stockholders waive application of the statute. Several other states have adopted similar laws.

The Role of the Courts

Litigation played a key role in almost every boisterous takeover battle of the 1980s. Like any other fight, these corporate struggles needed a referee—a role filled by the courts—with raiders and defenders fighting hard to tip the rules in their favor. Takeover litigation generally fell into two broad categories: antitrust litigation and fiduciary obligation litigation.

The large majority of the legal battles took place in the paneled courtrooms of Delaware. Because many major American companies are incorporated in that state, its judges often hear corporate cases and consequently have developed a reputation and expertise in the area.

From the perspective of those in the deal business, the Delaware courts have another key advantage: Delaware has a well-oiled system in place that allows a complex takeover case—often involving billions of dollars—to be heard and resolved in an extremely short time. Other state and federal courts now have similar procedural systems, but Delaware remains the key forum. The result is a rapid-fire brand of legal sparring. Lawyers on either side work around the clock to build documentary evidence. Hearings are short, jury trials are nonexistent.

The six weeks or less needed to resolve a Delaware case must be contrasted with the months or years which pass before a general civil dispute is resolved in the courts.

In the heyday of takeover litigation, a single situation would sometimes generate multiple suits in various jurisdictions. The target would challenge the bidder in federal court on antitrust and other grounds. The acquirer would challenge the target's board of directors in state court on fiduciary obligation grounds. Forum shopping was common, with targets tending to favor hometown courts and acquirers looking more often to the specialized Delaware courts.

Though the legal mudslinging at times got quite ferocious in heated takeover battles, litigation rarely proved an effective defense to a well-funded takeover offer. Over time, the federal courts wearied of antitrust challenges to takeovers, which seemed to have more to do with delay than actual competitive effects. The U.S. Supreme Court consequently raised a number of roadblocks to such antitrust challenges. Fiduciary obligation litigation, on the other hand, could be used as an offensive weapon to force the hand of a target company's board. Here, too, the courts developed a number of impediments to legal challenges.

Milken, Drexel, and the Emergence of Junk Bonds

A distinctive element of the 1980s was the development of a liquid market for debt obligations below investment grade—a market created largely by Michael Milken.

Fresh out of the Wharton School, Milken joined the firm Drexel Harriman Ripley in 1970 as its director of research for low-grade bonds. While the firm had a distinguished name, its business was not particularly strong. But despite Drexel's shaky standing, Milken's new job matched his interests. While in school, he had become fascinated with the idea of investing in what would eventually come to be known as junk bonds.

In 1970, a thin but established market for low-grade debt existed. The securities fell into two main categories: "fallen angels" and original issuances. The fallen angels, greater in number, were bonds that had lost their original investment grade rating due to the issuers' poor performance. Original issuances below investment grade, on the other hand, were rare instances. The issuers typically were small companies, or sometimes acquisitive conglomerates like LTV.

Milken first became interested in low-grade bonds while helping out his father, an accountant, with work for a client. He later chose to pursue the topic while in school, where he happened upon a particularly interesting 1967 study by Professor W. Braddock Hickman. Hickman's analysis showed that lower-rated bonds actually outperformed higher-rated bonds over certain periods of the economic cycle. The study had received little attention when published, but Milken found it inspirational.

In his early years at Drexel, Milken traveled the country, speaking to money managers and wealthy individuals. He tried to interest them in investing in the higher-yielding junk bonds and assured them Drexel would make a market in the securities: If they ever wanted to sell, he would buy. Slowly, he developed a following. Initially, Milken focused on the existing issues of conglomerates and the fallen angels, and as it turned out, these securities performed quite well through the volatile economic times of the middle 1970s.

Milken prospered as his audience grew. In 1974, he was permitted to organize a separate junk bond unit within Drexel which at first was comprised of salesmen, traders, and research analysts and had a $2 million capital base. Milken was also given the freedom to distribute a third of his unit's profits to whomever he liked. Until the late 1970s, the group was primarily a sales and trading operation.

The success of Milken's junk bond sales and trading unit effected a financial turnaround at Drexel. But when Milken made the shift into junk bond original issuance, he transformed Drexel into a household name.

Drexel was not the first firm to issue junk bonds. Goldman Sachs and Lehman Brothers underwrote a series of junk securities for LTV, Zapata, and Pan American World Airways in early 1977. However, Milken's strong network of loyal customers gave him a strong advantage over other firms. Drexel managed seven issues worth $124 million in 1977.

The added business was extremely profitable for Drexel. By the middle 1980s, Drexel dominated the approximately $50 billion new issuance market for junk bonds, enjoying a 60 percent market share. Entrepreneurs were the primary customers for Drexel's corporate finance services: Milken financed MCI, Ted Turner, Craig McCaw, Ron Perelman, and many other creative but cash-poor managers. Cable television, cellular operators, and casinos were big Drexel-backed issuers of junk bonds.

Drexel profited from the expanded market for junk securities in a number of different ways. First, the firm charged the borrower an underwriting fee to issue junk—generally about 3 percent of the total issuance.

On top of these investment banking fees, Drexel made a considerable profit trading junk bonds. Its position as a dominant market maker in junk securities allowed Drexel to set fairly broad spreads between the price at which its traders would buy and sell securities.

In 1984, Milken decided to expand Drexel's burgeoning empire even further. He sought to parlay his junk bond financing empire into an M&A operation as well, hoping that companies and LBO shops would come to him for "one-stop shopping" when doing leveraged buyouts and corporate takeovers: Milken would provide both M&A advice and the deal financing. Milken hoped that his alliances with financial buyers would eventually propel the firm into the center of some of the decade's largest deals.

PROFILE

Michael Milken: The Glory Years

In 1978, against the wishes of his nominal superiors at Drexel, Milken moved the bulk of his operation—traders, salesmen, research analysts, and investment bankers—from New York to Beverly Hills. A native of California, Milken wanted to return home to be with his father, who had recently been diagnosed with cancer, and with his children. In addition to his personal reasons, Milken felt that being in California would provide a competitive advantage precisely because it was far from New York: He would be able to operate away from the watchful eyes of competitors.

Milken did not slow down once he left New York. Rather, he took advantage of the time difference between the two coasts. He would arrive in Drexel's high-tech office at 4:00 A.M., where he could then work two hours before the markets opened in New York, and still be out of the office in time to see his children.

With Milken's staff matching his dedication, Drexel's Wilshire Boulevard offices became the center of the junk bond world. Chief executives would gladly agree to 5:00 A.M. meetings just for the opportunity to pitch Milken on their companies. Invitations to the annual High-Yield Bond Conference, later dubbed the "Predators Ball," were sought after as a prized ticket.

The eagerness with which potential issuers approached Drexel and Milken was a reflection of the junk bond market's dynamic and the strength of Milken's network. There was no shortage of companies and individuals who wanted to sell junk bonds. It was buyers who were the scarce commodity, and Milken was the gatekeeper to capital.

Amidst all the glory and glitter was also hustle and sleaze. Anyone could sense the exuberance, but only the naive could miss the recklessness. Milken himself sounded like a reasonable man, even soft-spoken, always playing with ideas. Some disciples were among the brightest on Wall Street. But the tone of the organization was out of control and some of the staff inappropriate for a major firm. The tragedy of Drexel was that the excess and illegality weren't necessary to its success.

The Financial Buyers Come to the Fore

The withering of the 1960s conglomerates, the fashionability of divestitures, and the availability of financing spawned a boom for financial buyers in the 1980s.

Financial buyers were beneficiaries of a new market orthodoxy which favored slimmed-down, "pure-play"—or single-business—companies. Time and again, the financial buyers teamed with managers to purchase a moribund division from a conglomerate. If all went as planned, the leveraged acquisition would be followed by a period of debt reduction during which operations would be streamlined and costs slashed. Within a couple of years, the cleaned-up company would be sold for a substantial gain.

The financial buyers filled a vacuum in the relatively inefficient market for corporate control. Many major public companies focused on return on assets (ROA) as the appropriate measure of whether an acquisition would pay off, where assets were defined as both the debt and equity component of the total purchase price. So, for example, if a company with a 20 percent ROA threshold paid $100 for an acquisition, it would need to be comfortable that the target would return $20 in the first year from some combination of earnings and appreciation of asset value.

Financial buyers took a different view, focusing more narrowly on return on equity. They might fund the same $100 acquisition with $20 of equity and $80 of debt. But because debt holders' return is fixed—if the interest rate on debt were 10 percent, for example, they would be entitled to $8—the $20 equity investment would yield a much higher return on equity. If the target returned the same $20 in the first year, the stockholders would receive the remaining $12, for a 60 percent return on invested equity.

Through this mechanism, a financial buyer could pay a substantial premium over current public market value by financing a deal primarily with debt and still earn a sizable return. Success came from both performance improvement and simple financial arbitrage. That the period was inflationary and stock market prices were cheap made this formula even more successful.

Jerome Kohlberg Jr. was one of the early practitioners of the leveraged acquisition. He began arranging small leveraged deals in the mid-1960s as a partner at Bear Stearns & Co. While leveraged transactions were not a specialty of the firm, so-called bootstrap acquisitions, featuring the use of a company's own borrowing capacity to finance its purchase price, intrigued him.

In 1965, Kohlberg arranged a $9.5 million buyout of Stern Metals, a dental supply company owned by its seventy-one-year-old founder. Stern wanted to sell the business, but couldn't bear to see it swallowed by a larger company. Finally, Kohlberg and his associates came up with another alternative—a bootstrap acquisition financed with considerable debt and a sliver of equity from Bear Stearns and members of the Stern family.

The Stern Metals transaction proved extremely profitable, and Kohlberg's success led to more deals. In the early 1970s, Kohlberg added two new associates—cousins Henry Kravis and George Roberts—to help with the effort. By then, Kohlberg and others had developed a profile for a company best suited to a successful LBO. First, a stable cash flow stream which could support leverage and ultimately pay down acquisition debt was key. Cyclical or speculative growth companies were therefore eliminated as possibilities. Rather, the typical LBO company was like Stern Metals—in a mature industry, steady, almost boring. As a corollary, a suitable LBO target— whether currently public or private—was undervalued, with the ability to service debt its measure of value. A company with $1 million of operating cash flow (before interest payments and taxes), for example, might be able to support $5 million in borrowings. If payments on a portion of the debt could be delayed for several years (through instruments such as PIKs—pay in kind securities—for example), even more debt capital might be raised. A financial buyer then would add a sliver of equity—generally 10 to 20 percent of the purchase price.

A motivated seller was another important piece in the LBO puzzle. There were two primary paradigms. In the first category were privately held companies, like Stern Metals, where the owners wanted to cash out of their investments.

In the second category were large companies which, pressed to maximize shareholder value, were eager to sell off underperforming subsidiaries. From the perspective of managers in the subsidiaries, an LBO was an attractive alternative because it would allow them to run an independent company.

The Leveraged Acquisition Model

Mastery of the leveraged acquisition model was the cornerstone of the financial buyers' initial success. Stripping away the technical and legal jargon, the leveraged acquisition process is quite simple— the acquisition of a company is financed largely with borrowed money. The company's own cash flow or assets serve as the main security for the loan.

A legendary early LBO involved Gibson Greeting Cards. In 1981, Wesray, an investment partnership owned by former Treasury Security William E. Simon and investment manager Ray Chambers, purchased Gibson Greetings from a stumbling RCA. Debt financing provided $79 million of the $80 million purchase price. Gibson's existing managers, who stayed on to run the company, owned 20 percent of the common equity.

A year later, Bill Simon looked like a genius. The country was coming out of recession, operating profits were up dramatically, and the bulls began to charge on Wall Street. On May 19, 1983, Wesray took Gibson Greeting Inc. public, selling about 30 percent of the company for just over $96 million. The IPO valued the whole company at $330 million. Wesray had earned a $250 million pretax paper profit on its $1 million equity investment.

Some observers wrote off Wesray's success as a fluke, a case of a pair of sophisticated investors who outwitted an unusually dense conglomerate. Others attributed Wesray's phenomenal profit to opportune timing. A strong economy, a booming stock market—a confluence of unpredictable events—allowed the partners to cash out quickly.

However, other early LBOs proved equally remarkable, and the vitality of this transaction structure soon became widely recognized. Over time, three different variations of the LBO structure developed—each during a different stage of the 1970s and 1980s. The long bull market of the last decade has been kind to LBOs in general. Nevertheless, each of the three variants has its own unique risks and pressure points which could become exposed in a less exuberant market.

The Classic LBO   The classic LBO capital structure was designed so that an acquirer could buy the greatest amount of assets with the least amount of equity investment. By borrowing against the assets and cash flows of an acquisition target, an LBO buyer can put up one dollar of equity and buy five or six dollars of business.

The effect of this leverage is striking. Simply shifting the capital structure allows a buyer to more than double the company's return on equity. So, while the classic LBO structure reigned during the late 1970s and early 1980s, financial buyers didn't need to perform any miracles to earn excellent returns on equity.

Of course, if a financial buyer did manage to improve the acquired business, the added appreciation in value would be compounded due to the effects of leverage. Financial buyers recognized this phenomenon and developed an approach to maximize the likelihood of positive results. As a rule of thumb, existing corporate management was encouraged to participate in most early LBOs, with top management allowed to purchase a significant portion of the common equity, often at a discount.

Management participation was part carrot, part stick. The carrot came in the form of promised riches if the company met its financial plan and were sold: The managers, as part-owners, would share in the gains from the sale. The stick came from the fact that managers had a significant portion of their net worth tied up in the typical LBO. Failure had a steep price, and this prospect tended to concentrate the mind.

In fact, structuring the classic LBO is not quite as simple as choosing the desired portions of debt and equity. Rather, the capital structure is typically sliced into various pieces, spanning a spectrum between common equity and "pure" debt so as to appeal to as wide a base of potential investors as possible. The ability to appeal to a large potential investor base facilitates the speedy placement of securities issued in the LBO at terms favorable to the issuer. For example, a bank might want a more secure, lower-paying instrument, but an insurance company may have more appetite for risk if it means getting a higher yield. Junk bond investors would take on even more risk to get a better payoff.

At the top of the LBO capital structure is the senior debt provided by banks or other traditional lenders, defined by the fact that it stands first in line to be paid in case of bankruptcy. Senior debt also can be "secured" by a claim on specific assets of the debtor, similar to a mortgage on a house. These two features—seniority and security—make senior secured debt a low-risk, low-yield instrument.

In the classic LBO, the space between the common equity and the senior debt is filled with successive layers of increasingly senior capital sources—for example, preferred stock, subordinated debt, or senior unsecured debt. Because these other instruments occupy an intermediate space, they are referred to as mezzanine financing.

Like senior debt, the mezzanine financing offers a fixed return. This return generally declines as an instrument becomes more senior. Lenders also frequently demand an equity "kicker"—an option to buy equity at a favorable price—as an inducement to provide financing.

The proportions of different debt securities issued as part of an LBO must be designed with the target company's cash flows in mind. Lenders who provide each layer or tranche of debt generally require at least a threshold cash flow to support each dollar of debt. Cash flows, rather than accounting earnings, are key because the purchased company's cash flow is the sole means to service the debt issued in the LBO. In this particular structure, the new debt generally is scheduled to be paid off within seven years.

Projecting cash flows, however, is more art than science. Furthermore, the financial buyers in the classic LBO who prepared projections faced conflicting incentives that simultaneously favored aggressive and conservative projections. On one hand, the growing competition in the market for target companies caused their prices to be bid up to increasingly higher levels in auctions and thus necessitated aggressive cash flow projections to justify these high prices. But on the other hand, cutting the cash flow margin too closely could cause problems later on: The business might be unable to service its debt burden, which could force it into bankruptcy. This situation explains why early financial buyers selected businesses with stable cash flows as LBO candidates.

A firm grasp of tax law was also essential to a successful execution of the classic LBO model. Tax rules made the levered structure even more palatable because, unlike dividends on stock, interest on debt generally is tax-deductible. Therefore, increasing a company's leverage decreases its tax bill, generating additional cash which can be used to pay down additional debt.

However, nothing in the federal tax law is simple. Reacting to the outcry over hostile takeovers and leveraged acquisitions, politicians and regulators built a thicket of interlocking rules regarding the deductibility of corporate interest expense. As a result, financial buyers spent considerable time devising creative structures to maximize tax benefits.

The Breakup LBO The vitality of the classic LBO structure depended both on leverage and the ability to pay existing target company shareholders an acquisition premium. As prices for target companies were bid up, however, the model became less tenable. By the mid-1980s, when financial buyers looked at potential targets, projected cash flows often weren't sufficient to pay interest on the desired level of debt. Something had to give.

Over time, a second-stage LBO model developed, dependent upon breakup values. However, the company was not expected to service its debt solely from operating cash flow. Divestitures of businesses were planned from the outset, with the proceeds to be used to pay down the debt, typically by half within seven years. Though relying on asset sales for success exposed this structure to additional risk, the tactic generally worked well in the hot merger market of the mid-1980s.

The new importance of asset sales required increased attention to underlying asset values. Diversified conglomerates—which often traded at a discount to underlying values—became favorite targets.

In 1987, however, the attraction of the breakup LBO was severely limited by tax law changes. Specifically, a 1987 change in the applicable tax rules eliminated the popular "mirrors" liquidation technique which had allowed an acquirer to split up a target company on purchase. The basic technique required four steps. First, the acquirer would set up a parent company to hold "mirror" subsidiaries, each of which would be funded with cash in an amount equal to the fair market value of the assets to be put into them. Second, the newly created parent company would purchase the target company in a tax-free stock deal. Third, the parent would liquidate the target into its various mirror subsidiaries, placing unwanted assets into a separate subsidiary. Finally, the mirror subsidiary containing the unwanted company could be sold to a third party with no tax gain or loss, since the parent's tax basis in the mirror subsidiary—the amount of cash with which it originally funded the subsidiary—would be equal to the fair market value of the assets sold.

Unwanted assets could in this way be sold off with little or no resulting corporate tax liability. The death of mirrors was also the death of many breakup LBOs because the tax impact on value was so large.

The Strategic LBO   At the beginning of the 1990s, LBO practitioners found themselves in need of a new LBO structure. The first-stage LBOs had eliminated the "low-hanging fruit"—mismanaged companies with inefficient balance sheets to which leverage could be applied and generate returns. And tax law changes had destroyed the benefits to the second-stage breakup LBO. Finally, the market became more hesitant than it was in the 1980s to lend at high debt to equity ratios. Therefore, a third-stage LBO model was developed in which returns are not generated through capital structure change but rather by growing the business and increasing earnings. The exit strategy contemplated, as before, is an IPO or a sale to a strategic buyer. This approach has two variants.

In the first variant, a private company or a division of a public company is bought. The operations and finances of the company are then improved. More glamorous management might be installed. Then, when the time is right, the company is taken public in an IPO.

The second strategy is to buy up and integrate several small business units which would not have received favorable public market valuations as stand-alone entities. As an integrated, well-managed whole, however, the new "rolled-up" company would make an attractive IPO candidate or purchase by a strategic buyer. In either case, the strategic LBO is a departure from the leverage-driven models of the 1980s. Rather, in the strategic LBO, financial buyers provide the managerial expertise and capital necessary to "dress up" companies in a way that will appeal to strategic buyers or investors in the public markets. Operational savviness, as opposed to mere financial engineering, is key.

Managing the LBO   The variety of LBO pursued determines not only capital structure and investment focus but management style as well. Very different approaches are necessary in a classic LBO versus a strategic LBO. In the former case, management focuses on operational efficiency only to the extent necessary to ensure successful debt paydown and sale of the company. However, in a strategic LBO, the financial buyer takes a more hands-on role, building up infrastructure rather than cutting it. Furthermore, the financial buyer must identify synergies between rolled-up companies and capitalize upon them. The ultimate stock market value and investment return might be maximized by investing cash to build future earning potential in a strategic LBO.

Catalysts

The basic LBO structure may not have been an innovation of the 1980s, but the dollar volume of deals during the decade was unprecedented. About $2 billion of LBO transactions were completed in 1980. In 1988, 239 deals were executed for a total purchase price of $81.2 billion.

A number of factors—financial, regulatory, market, and technological—explain the dramatic growth in LBO volume. On the financial front, the availability of credit and easier lending terms formed a critical spark. Capital flowed into New York's money center banks from oil-producing nations which had benefited from the successive Oil Shocks of the 1970s. Eager to recycle these petrodollars into income-producing loans, however, these banks were finding many of their traditional lending markets being closed off.

Faced with this dilemma, financing LBOs—which were known in the banking community as highly leveraged transactions, or HLTs—was extremely attractive to the banks, giving them the po-

tential to earn high interest rates and up-front fees. Risks for an individual bank were reduced through syndication—passing to another bank a portion of a loan in return for a cut of the fees. Credit
standards loosened further when Japanese banks made a major push
into the U.S. lending market with vast pools of capital to invest.

Junk bonds provided a new source of liquidity for financial buyers. Where Drexel had once concentrated on financing entrepreneurs and operating businesses, in the mid-1980s Milken decided to
open the junk bond market to financial buyers and began to underwrite takeover entrepreneurs and LBO firms.

Meanwhile, regulatory changes increased the flow of equity capital into the buyout business. In the early 1980s, many states began
to allow their public employee pension funds to make a broader
range of investments. As a result, many chose to shift a portion of
their holdings away from the conservative stocks and bonds they
were previously required to hold and toward LBO investment pools.

Capital may have been the spark for the LBO boom, but market
factors provided the kindling. The stock market began the 1980s at a
level seen in the early 1960s. Diversified large companies faced a particularly unforgiving environment and were pressured by the market
to divest subsidiaries. Financial buyers stepped into the void created
by this market imbalance.

The Financial Players

KKR—The Early Years   In 1976, Kohlberg, Kravis, and Roberts
left Bear Stearns to pursue leveraged buyouts full-time. Kohlberg,
then in his fifties, radiated a sense of solidity and prudence and was
the elder statesmen of the group. His wire-rim glasses gave him a
stern countenance, offset by bursts of droll humor. Cousins Kravis
and Roberts were in their early thirties and hungry.

There was little fanfare when KKR opened its doors. Not sure
how long it would take to find a first deal, Kohlberg, Kravis, and
Roberts husbanded their $120,000 start-up capital where they could.

Kohlberg and Kravis leased space in a shabby Manhattan office suite, using the metal furniture left behind by the previous tenant. Roberts, who had worked out of Bear Stearns' San Francisco office, found similar space.

By the time they started KKR, Kohlberg, Kravis, and Roberts had honed their approach. The CEO in transition was their ideal target audience. When a takeover loomed, ornery investors threatened, or estate tax issues pressed, KKR had a viable option. The firm would join with existing management in a leveraged buyout, after which the CEO and his team would have considerable autonomy to run things as they saw fit—as long as they hit their financial plan. Top management, KKR, and its investors would share in any gains.

As it turned out, Kohlberg, Kravis, and Roberts opened KKR at an opportune time. The stock market was in a swoon, and mature companies in particular received relatively low valuations. Executives who once had rushed to go public began to question the merits of their decisions.

In the fall of 1976, KKR financed a $26 million management buyout of a small conglomerate. They closed three more deals the next year. Then, in 1978, KKR broke into the big time, financing the acquisition of its first Fortune 500 company: Houdaille Industries.

Houdaille manufactured steel, machine tools, pumps, and car bumpers. Spurred by rumors of an impending takeover, Kohlberg approached CEO Gerald Saltarelli.

Saltarelli's aversion to debt could be seen on Houdaille's balance sheet, which in 1978 contained $40 million in cash and $22 million in debt. The conservative Saltarelli needed convincing, but, urged on by his subordinates, ultimately signed off on a leveraged buyout. KKR's investment group bid $40 a share for the company's stock, which was then trading at around $25. The total purchase price— about $350 million—was more than three times larger than any KKR had previously paid. Financed with 85 percent debt, the deal closed in April 1979.

Over the next few years, Houdaille faced rough times and KKR's projections proved in retrospect too rosy. Faced with strong foreign competition in its core business, Houdaille was forced to shed operations and redeploy capital. Despite these problems, however, KKR and its investors still earned a healthy 22 percent return on common equity over a seven-and-a-half-year period.

LBOs in the Early 1980s   News of the Houdaille purchase put the LBO on the map. But a few other players were already in the LBO business before KKR. Gibbons Green van Amerongen was formed in 1969 to do leveraged acquisitions. Forstmann Little was formed in 1978 by the two Forstmann brothers—Ted and Nick—and Brian Little and pioneered the practice of raising pools of equity and subordinated debt capital from pension funds. Clayton & Dubilier, which had started as a firm specializing in turnaround situations, switched to LBOs in the same year. Its CEO, Martin Dubilier, had been exposed to bootstrap acquisitions as chairman of Stern Metals.

After the Houdaille deal, Wall Street was abuzz. Copies of the public documents for the deal were passed around like trading cards, and people began to see the profit potential in leveraged acquisitions. Within the space of a few years, many of the major investment banks, including Morgan Stanley, First Boston, and Merrill Lynch, jumped into the business.

Still, KKR benefited from its position as an early entrant, and the Houdaille deal opened a lot of doors. Executives began to return calls, the business press took notice, and deals came more easily. As a result, the firm dominated the business: In dollar terms, KKR accounted for 40 percent of all leveraged buyouts in 1981.

KKR Moves into Billion-Dollar Territory   Things accelerated dramatically for KKR when the country came out of recession in 1983. Over the next two years, the firm acquired seven companies, spending in excess of $2.8 billion. Awareness of KKR, previously more or less limited to readers of the business press and investment professionals, began to spread. Then, in 1986, the $6.2 billion Beatrice transaction thrust KKR fully into the limelight.

Beatrice was a hodgepodge collection of food and consumer products businesses staggering under the eccentric and autocratic leadership of CEO James L. Dutt. Despite his ultimate removal by the board and the ensuing appointment of an interim chief executive, the company's situation remained unstable.

KKR had studied Beatrice for years. But it was not until Dutt's departure that KKR could act with any hope of success. Aided by Donald P. Kelly, a flamboyant but savvy executive of Esmark (a minor Chicago-based conglomerate bought by Beatrice), KKR sent a "bear hug" letter—an unsolicited offer at a significant premium—to the Beatrice board offering to buy the company for $5.6 billion.

While refused by the board as inadequate, the offer nevertheless put the company into play and very soon shareholders irate at Beatrice's record began to pressure the board of directors. A group of Beatrice executives tried to arrange an alternative LBO, but they lacked credibility. KKR upped its bid and ultimately persuaded the board to accept.

The capital structure proposed by KKR's deal called for $4 billion of bank loans, $2.5 billion of junk bond financing, and $407 million of equity. While these sums seemed phenomenal at the time, Beatrice was operationally strong and had easily salable assets, including such major brands as Tropicana orange juice, Playtex, Hunt-Wesson grocery products, Orville Redenbacher popcorn, among dozens of others.

The energetic Kelly promised to dedicate himself to restructuring the company's operations. He would slash frivolous expenses, such as the millions spent on auto racing by Dutt, and would sell $1.5 billion of Beatrice's noncore business and grow the remainder.

The banks' and bondholders' faith in KKR paid off. Kelly trimmed more than 15 percent out of a bloated $975 million marketing budget, in part by eliminating spending in markets where the company didn't even sell the products being advertised! He reduced corporate overhead and initially sold off more than $3 billion in assets—Wesray bought Avis for $275 million, Coke bought the Los Angeles bottling business for more than $1 billion, and a group of managers bought Playtex in a leveraged buyout. With the cash from these transactions, debt was reduced to manageable levels.

Soon, it became apparent that a frothy stock market and frenzied takeover environment would allow KKR to sell the remaining 75 percent of Beatrice for a healthy gain. First, the nonfood businesses—with Kelly at the head—were sold to the public in a $420 million stock offering. After the intervening Crash of 1987, Seagram bought Tropicana for $1.2 billion. ConAgra then bought the remaining businesses in 1990 for $1.3 billion in cash and stock, plus the assumption of over $1 billion in debt.

In the final tally, after paying down Beatrice's debt, KKR and its co-investors retained net proceeds of approximately $2.2 billion. Over the four years of the investment, KKR had earned an annual return of roughly 50 percent on the $420 million equity invested. Beatrice was a triumph.

PROFILE

Henry Kravis

Today, Henry Kravis is probably the most visible embodiment of the LBO movement. The son of a wealthy Oklahoma oilman, he started working at Bear Stearns with Kohlberg after graduating from Columbia Business School.

Kravis had the advantages of an analytical mind honed by Kohlberg's training and a natural gift for persuasion. He understood early on that the LBO business had four equally important elements: raising money, investing it well, running the company, and selling well. Much of his early days in the business involved wooing investors and persuading companies to sell.

The firm's annual investor conference was an important forum to bond with investors, and Kravis exerted great efforts to assure that the presentations were unusually thorough. Although West Coast cousin George Roberts never quite got the glare of attention, he was equally important in spotting deals and in persuading the large state pensions of the wisdom of investing in this new "alternative investment" category.

When Kravis and Roberts parted with Kohlberg, the business continued to expand. Kravis received unrelenting attention, both professionally and socially. Inevitably, his success created resentment, and criticism therefore mounted when the deal business stumbled in the early 1990s. Walter Industries, a Tampa-based conglomerate acquired by KKR, in 1987, sought bankruptcy protection two years later. Seaman Furniture also experienced operating difficulties unforeseen by KKR. Through it all, Kravis managed to retain his stamina and his calm. His large investors gave him complete support, mainly because they remembered past gains, and because he and Roberts excelled at communicating with them.

Today KKR is more successful than ever. The cumulative years of business experience and social contacts give Kravis a clear edge in the business and his tight organization has mellowed and gained patina. Based in wood-paneled suites with a stunning view of Central Park, the operation is highly professional.

Kravis' success has brought wealth and power. With an estimated net worth around $1 billion, Kravis has become a major philanthropist, contributing tens of millions of dollars to museums, universities, and other causes. The shock of his success has worn off, and KKR is accepted as the senior partner of the LBO business.

Tapping the Money Source   Few if any other buyout shops at that time pursued acquisitions on the scale of Beatrice. However, all buyout shops had a considerable thirst for capital—senior and subordinated debt, as well as equity.

For equity capital, KKR initially relied on a group of passive investors—primarily wealthy individuals who agreed to pay a portion of KKR's expenses in exchange for the opportunity to invest alongside KKR's partners. KKR typically would form a separate investment vehicle for each deal. Kohlberg, Kravis, and Roberts would put in 1 or 2 percent of the equity and the passive investors would supply the remainder.

As KKR's deal flow began to multiply, however, its thirst for equity outgrew the capacity of a handful of wealthy individuals. In 1978, Kohlberg, Kravis, and Roberts raised their first "blind pool" of $30 million. The money, supplied mainly by insurance companies and banks, could be invested in deals as KKR saw fit. This arrangement gave the firm the flexibility to act quickly. Another $316 million blind pool was raised in 1982, a $1 billion pool in 1984, and a $5.6 billion pool in 1987.

As the pools got bigger, KKR was forced to expand its fundraising efforts. Adopting a practice that Forstmann Little had pioneered in the late 1970s, KKR began to look to pension funds as a major capital source. State pension funds proved the most receptive, and the list of KKR limited partners eventually came to include the state employee pension funds of Washington, Oregon, Michigan, Massachusetts, among others.

LBO firms make money in a number of different ways under the blind pool arrangement. First, they often charge investors a management fee, usually about 1.5 percent of committed capital until the funds are invested, and a lesser percentage thereafter.

Second, LBO firms usually charge a transaction fee for arranging a deal, whether purchase or sale. These fees range as high as 1 percent of the purchase price, but generally are lower in large transactions. KKR's 1996 sale of Duracell to Gillette, where KKR was paid $20 million on a $7 billion deal, is a recent example.

Third, firms retain any director's or monitoring fees paid to its professionals, who often sit on the boards of acquired companies. A typical director's fee might be in the range of $25,000 to $50,000 per year.

Fourth, firms earn a 20 percent share of the profits realized by the pool if they perform above some threshold percentage, usually around 8 percent. This arrangement gives the firms a huge performance incentive.

Though the blind pools eventually became quite large, they only provided one tranche in the leveraged acquisition capital structure. LBO firms also needed to raise the two remaining tranches—the senior debt and the mezzanine financing. For senior debt, financial buyers generally went to banks. Mezzanine financing, on the other hand, traditionally came from insurance companies. However, as the junk bond market developed, KKR and other financial buyers increasingly turned to Michael Milken and Drexel Burnham Lambert for junior debt.

During the early 1980s, there was a cachet to investing with KKR or one of its competitors. Proximity to the glamorous world of big-dollar deals was part of the attraction. But glamour alone was not enough to keep investors coming back. Hundreds of millions of dollars were at stake, and the investors directing these sums were sophisticated and demanded substance.

The first few generations of buyout funds delivered. Investors in KKR's early funds, for example, earned annual returns in the range of 30 to 50 percent even after deducting KKR's fees. Other funds showed similar results. Of course, the frothy market environment played a key role in these returns: A leveraged investment in the S&P 500 also would have showed a handsome return. However, that would not have been a feasible alternative for most investors.

As news of past successes spread, more and more money flowed into the buyout funds. This level of demand for investments had created over 200 buyout firms by 1988 controlling an estimated $30 or $40 billion in equity capital. With the power of leverage, this gave the funds the ability to spend over $200 billion on acquisitions.

Hicks, Muse, Tate & Furst

Founded by six-foot-three Texan Tom Hicks, Hicks, Muse, Tate & Furst has been highly active in the buyout market. The firm, under Hicks' direction, pioneered the "buy and build" strategy of using a core acquisition as a platform to acquire related businesses. The firm is perhaps best known for its investments in radio broad-casting companies, an understandable specialty, given Tom Hicks' background. Hicks' father, originally an advertising salesman for TV and radio stations in Dallas, built up a business of several Dallas-area radio stations. When Tom was in high school, he worked at his father's station after school, learning the radio business from the ground up.

Tom Hicks studied finance at the University of Texas, after which he pursued his developing interest in venture capital, help-ing to set up a venture capital division at Continental Illinois in Chicago. He later went on to USC Business School, with the ulti-mate goal of entering the venture capital market in California.

However, the elder Hicks hoped that Tom and his other three sons would come back to Texas to work at his radio stations. While Tom's heart was really in the deals business, he did return to Texas, where he had big plans for his father's company. At that time, regu-latory restrictions prohibited a radio operator from owning more than seven stations and from owning more than one AM and one FM station in a single market. Therefore, Hicks encouraged his father to sell his stations and upgrade to larger markets. The elder Hicks, however, was attached to his business and did not want to sell.

Hicks left Dallas and took a venture capital job at J.P. Morgan in New York but soon moved back to Dallas to become head of the venture capital group of First National Bank. He then left his job in 1977 to do what would be the first in his long string of successful LBOs. Partnering with Louis Marx Jr., Hicks purchased a small aluminum window and door manufacturing company for $4 million. The two investors quadrupled their money in seven years.

When their father was ready to retire in 1980, Tom and brother Steve purchased three of their father's small stations in a $3 million LBO and added an additional station in Denton, Texas, for $3.3 million. Steve ran the stations while Tom went back to the deal business. In 1986, Hicks executed a highly successful $416 million LBO of Dr. Pepper and Seven-Up (Forstmann Little had already sold Canada Dry, nine bottling plants, and other assets) with partner Robert B. Haas and set up a single management company to run both operations. He sold the two companies two years later for almost $700 million.

But Hicks would soon find his way back into the radio business. In 1987, the Hicks brothers together bought another station—WSIX in Nashville—which they modernized, converted to a country music station, and sold for a handsome profit. Steve envisioned a radio empire. But regulations still prevented ownership of more than one AM and one FM station in a single market. Drawing upon his experience in the Dr. Pepper and Seven-Up deal, Tom Hicks devised a method to circumvent these regulations—Local Marketing Agreements (LMAs). These LMAs were designed to allow one company to manage another without actually owning it: The managed company would pay the management company a predetermined fee in exchange for its services. Under this arrangement, the Hicks brothers converted weaker radio stations, which through competition drove down advertising revenue in the entire market, to a different music genre. The stronger station was then able to increase advertising rates. What had been the weaker station—now a different format—had a new target audience and too could gain more advertising revenue.

Tom Hicks formed Hicks, Muse in 1989 when he and Haas split up due in part to differences of opinion about how to fund deals. Hicks wanted to raise an investment pool, while Haas wanted to fund deals on a deal-by-deal basis. Hicks soon after teamed up with John R. Muse, a Prudential Securities banker, Charles W. Tate, a Morgan Stanley managing director of venture capital, and Jack D. Furst, a former partner at Hicks & Haas, as well as three others.

With the 1991 recession and Gulf War, radio stations that had taken on too much debt ran into difficulties. As a result, the FCC began to loosen rules for ownership and Hicks, Muse started buying. Subsequent regulatory changes have also been key in allowing the buyout shop to build its radio empire: The Telecommunications Reform Act of 1996 allowed operators to acquire up to eight stations in the same market representing up to 35 percent of total market advertising revenue and erased limits on the number of markets a single operator could enter.

It was the promise of these and future regulatory changes that spurred Hicks, Muse to build up its best-known investments—Dallas-based Chancellor Media and Austin-based Capstar Broadcasting—from scratch. In 1998, these two portfolio companies combined in a $4.1 billion transaction in which Chancellor Media acquired Capstar Broadcasting, forming the largest radio concern in the United States. The Chancellor stations are active in the top twenty radio markets, including New York, Chicago, and Los Angeles; Capstar is active in small and midsized markets. While perhaps not as glamorous as investments in cable or the Internet, these investments in radio have been very good to Hicks, Muse. The firm has been able to earn an operating profit of 45 percent of revenue in this technologically mature, seventy-five-year-old industry, while growing revenues at more than 10 percent per year.

In February 1997, Hicks, Muse accomplished its goal of leveraging its radio assets into control of TV assets with the acquisition of Sunrise Television—a Florida-based broadcaster. LIN Television was added in March 1998; while initially LIN was to be folded into Chancellor Media, in March 1999 that plan was scrapped. In June 1999, Chancellor reached an agreement to sell its outdoor billboard operations to Lamar Advertising for $1.6 billion.

Meanwhile, by 1999, Chancellor's performance had stalled. Its stock suffered amid the market's perception of strategic difficulties at the company. Hicks himself took over the CEO mantle, renamed the company AMFM Inc., and expanded its Internet presence. By the end of 1999, Hicks, Muse decided to sell AMFM rather than operate it. In October, Clear Channel agreed to acquire AMFM for $23.5 billion. Hicks, Muse had made a handsome profit from a radio station roll-up strategy.

While Hicks, Muse is most heavily invested and perhaps best known for its media empire, it has also successfully invested in a wide variety of other industries, including energy, food and consumer products, industrials, insurance, real estate, and retail. Recent deals have included a $1.2 billion purchase of American Home Products' food division, maker of Chef Boyardee pasta, PAM cooking spray, and Jiffy Pop popcorn; Triton Energy; Regal Cinemas (with KKR); and Glass's Group. Hicks, Muse has extended its buy-and-build strategy to nonmedia investments as well. It has enlarged its $208 million investment in consumer products brands into a $1 billion portfolio, for example.

Hicks, Muse has had no trouble finding new capital for its lucrative investments. Over the past two and a half years, the buyout fund received a total $7.5 billion in new investor capital, of which $4 billion was just raised in its recently formed fourth fund.

Tom Hicks, an avid sports fan along with his brother Steven, also owns the Dallas Stars, a hockey team, and the Texas Rangers, a baseball team.

The Takeover Entrepreneurs

The new financing techniques of the 1980s also spawned a second category of financial players—the takeover entrepreneurs. These men used the liquidity of the 1980s to build empires or amass fortunes. Many were self-made, others inherited their initial table stakes. In general, the takeover entrepreneurs were more likely than LBO shops to entertain hostile takeovers as a strategic alternative. Some put up a large percentage of the equity in their deals and therefore captured the lion's share of any profits.

The takeover entrepreneurs—T. Boone Pickens, Sir James Goldsmith, Nelson Peltz, Oscar Wyatt, Saul Steinberg, Ronald Perelman, Carl Icahn—all initially relied on the junk bond prowess of Drexel to finance their efforts. Some profited immensely by putting companies in play so as to have their shares bought out at a substantial profit. Others actually took control of major industrial empires.

Ronald Perelman   From an early age, Ronald Owen Perelman wanted to be an industrialist. He learned the mergers and acquisitions game on the job while working for his father, who owned a number of medium-sized companies. Together, the two men built the family holdings with a string of acquisitions.

Perelman struck out on his own in 1978 at the age of thirty-five, moving to New York to scout for deals. His first deal came together within a matter of months: Perelman bought 40 percent of a small jewelry company for $1.9 million, borrowing the entire amount on his personal credit and assets. He rapidly set about liquidating nonproductive stores. Then, he threw himself into marketing the company's products. A year later, Perelman had repaid the original acquisition loan, netted a $15 million profit, and still controlled a large stake in the remaining business.

In 1980, Perelman acquired MacAndrews & Forbes, a supplier of licorice extract and chocolate. The deal was originally financed by a syndicate of banks, but Perelman soon convinced Bear Stearns and Drexel Burnham to float $35 million in junk bonds as part of a refinancing. Perelman paid considerable attention to the company's operations, taking sales trips to meet executives at cigarette companies—major consumers of licorice extract—and also broadened his company's supply base of licorice beyond the politically unstable Iran and Afghanistan.

Perelman next added Technicolor to his budding empire. He sold off its unproductive one-hour developing labs and refocused the company on its entertainment business, bulking it up with $150 million in add-on acquisitions of other film and video processing companies. Less than five years later, Perelman sold Technicolor for $780 million (plus the roughly $300 million in operating profits he earned while owning the company).

In 1984, Perelman took MacAndrews & Forbes private in a Milken-financed deal, thereby gaining new freedom to continue his acquisition program. Consolidated Cigar was added in 1984, and grocery chain Pantry Pride in 1985. The grocery company had been poorly run but had a valuable tax loss carry-forward. Perelman liquidated its operating business but retained the shell company so as to use its loss carry-forwards to shelter other business income from taxation.

By 1984, Perelman had created a diversified, highly leveraged business empire with businesses in jewelry, cigars, licorice, and film processing. But Perelman wanted more.

In 1985, Perelman used Drexel to underwrite a $761 million junk bond offering to finance future, as-yet unidentified acquisitions. Perelman needed this blind pool of capital to step up to the big leagues.

With money in hand, Perelman could pursue a much larger acquisition: Revlon. The cosmetics company—which had diversified into health products, pharmaceuticals, and eye care—was in an operational slump, and its stock market valuation suffered accordingly. Yet, in Perelman's judgment, the Revlon brand name remained powerful. He could buy the company, divest the noncore assets for a substantial premium over their original purchase price, and rejuvenate the cosmetics operation.

Perelman met with Revlon CEO Michel Bergerac, hoping to negotiate a friendly deal. The negotiations never got off the ground, though, as Bergerac made little effort to conceal his disdain for Perelman and his team. Perelman responded on August 20, 1985, with a $1.8 billion public offer for the company.

A drawn-out takeover contest ensued. LBO shop Forstmann Little tried to lock up the company in a white knight bid, but the Delaware court ruled in the landmark *Revlon* decision that once a company was for sale, the board had to deal fairly with the higher bidder. With superior tactics and an intense hunger to win, Perelman outbid Forstmann Little and won his prize. Key factors in his success were pre-selling part of the Revlon assets and understanding the operational changes he would need to make at Revlon.

Within a few months of taking over, Perelman had sold various health and pharmaceutical operations, raising over $1 billion. He also moved to shore up Revlon's cosmetics core with two acquisitions: Max Factor and Almay, purchased from Playtex Products. Then, he added a group of top-line cosmetic brands.

With the necessary pieces in place, Perelman set about to improve them, increasing research and development, modernizing factories, and refocusing advertising. While MacAndrews & Forbes initially had difficulty digesting Revlon, after a number of years Perelman turned around the cosmetics giant and then engineered a marketing triumph in 1994 with Revlon's Colorstay long-lasting cosmetic line.

More recently, however, Revlon has run into trouble. Perelman's 83 percent stake in Revlon plunged $2 billion in value in 1998 following an announcement that third-quarter profit would be 70 percent below analyst expectations. The stock dropped 44 percent. Difficulty with lower inventory levels at retailers and competition from new brands were two culprits. The company's operations continued to deteriorate through 1999. Perelman put Revlon on the auction block, but after six months no bidder was willing to pay his asking price.

PROFILE

Ronald Perelman

Ronald Perelman, once a small businessman in Philadelphia, is, despite recent setbacks, today one of the richest men in America. Part of the explanation is his intense drive and operational skill.

We watched Perelman closely in the Revlon deal when representing two buyers of assets he intended to pre-sell. His personal energy level is frenetic and exhausts those around him. However, it is his intensity about operational details which sets him apart from other leveraged buyers. He thinks and breathes industrial strategy and operations, peppering his conversations with statistics and questions.

Perelman's team is like a brotherhood, sharing breakfast and lunch. Key meetings are held at their art-filled headquarters in a town house in Manhattan's East Sixties. Calling on one officer is like calling on all as each wanders in and out of the meetings.

As was the case with KKR, Perelman employed the leveraged acquisition model in his acquisitions. This, together with a deft understanding of how to turn around an ailing business, gave him the ability to magnify a relatively small equity stake across increasingly larger deals. Recently, however, Perelman's investments have become more and more volatile, rising and dropping by billions.

After the Revlon purchase, Perelman's collection of companies kept him increasingly occupied. Still, he continued to pursue major deals, making runs (although unsuccessful) at Gillette and investment bank Salomon Brothers. Then, at the end of 1988, he snared a particularly favorable acquisition: MacAndrews & Forbes put up about $160 million in equity to buy a group of failed savings and loans. In return, as part of a larger program, the government granted the company a number of lucrative—and later controversial—incentives.

Today, Perelman's empire includes First Nationwide Bank and Panavision, among others. Consolidated Cigar was sold to Seita SA for $730 million.

Of course, things go wrong, even for the most able managers. The value of Perelman's stake in Sunbeam, obtained when he sold also-troubled Coleman to the company in March 1998, was down almost 90 percent between March 1998 and December 1998, to the tune of $660 million of Perelman's personal fortune. Ironically, Perelman had sold his stake in Coleman to rid himself of its troubles. The camping equipment maker, under Perelman's control, expanded too far downmarket with backpacks, coolers, lanterns, and tents sold through mass-market retailers. The company was also hurt by troubles in Asia. Its 1996 purchase of Camping Gaz was also a disaster, adding $400 million in debt but virtually no earnings.

Perelman's Marvel Entertainment Group—purchased in 1989 for an estimated $83 million—also collapsed into bankruptcy. In 1988, before Perelman purchased the company, Marvel earned a lackluster $2.3 million, mainly from publishing its comic books. Perelman, however, had a larger vision for the company, envisioning Marvel's valuable library of characters licensed for everything from toys to movies.

Initially, Perelman's strategy was highly successful. A booming market for comic books, new TV shows, and licensing deals pumped revenues up to $415 million by 1993. Flush with success, Marvel bought out two trading card companies—Fleer and Skybox. Perelman then took Marvel public in 1991 and over the next few years his stake grew to more than $2 billion. Perelman sold bonds secured by his stock interest and used part of the money to fund other parts of his empire.

Starting in 1994, though, two of the markets for Marvel's products—comic books and trading cards—took dramatic turns for the worse. Demand for comic books—which had before been driven by speculative collecting activity—fell off a cliff and a number of competitors crowded into the trading card business. The quality of Marvel's art also went downhill. Then, the 1994 baseball strike stopped interest in trading cards cold. By early 1997, Marvel was in deep trouble. Perelman attempted a restructuring, but Carl Icahn and other investors who had bought up the distressed Marvel bonds didn't like the terms. They took control of the company in bankruptcy proceedings.

Measured from the market peak, the collapse of Marvel cost Perelman over $2 billion. Nonetheless, the deal proved lucrative for Perelman. He recouped his initial investment in Marvel through the stock and bond offerings. Separately, he realized a huge gain on the sale of New World Entertainment Group—a company on the rocks when Perelman took over—to Rupert Murdoch for $2.7 billion.

Carl Icahn   As the merger boom of the 1980s matured, more and more dealmakers became corporate managers. Nelson Peltz bought National Can, Sir James Goldsmith bought Crown Zellerbach, Oscar Wyatt's Coastal Corporation bought American National Resources. But not all dealmakers found the role an attractive one. Carl Icahn's stint as the owner-manager of TWA is a cautionary tale.

After college, Icahn gravitated toward the excitement of Wall Street and became a successful options trader. Then, in 1979, he made the shift from his small brokerage operation into a new business: He was going to invest in and take over undervalued companies.

Tappan, a company that made stoves, was Icahn's first target. He took a position in the company's stock and launched a proxy contest. When a white knight swooped in to acquire the company, within a few months Icahn had netted $2.7 million on his stock.

Over the course of the coming decade, Icahn would go after increasingly larger companies such as Marshall Field and American Can, efforts initially fueled with the help of a group of limited partners who each chipped in $100,000 or $200,000. Buying on 50 percent margin, Icahn leveraged the money into large stakes in his target companies.

Once Icahn had a stock position, he would approach management, present a plan to improve the company, and ask for a board seat. The request was generally denied. Icahn would then threaten a proxy fight or an outright takeover, exciting interest in the company among other acquirers.

Known for acting on instinct rather than exhaustive due diligence, Icahn has had a mixed record with his takeovers. In 1980, for example, Icahn and his investors took a large position in Hammermill, a paper company. He met with CEO Albert Duval soon after the group's ownership stake was filed and asked for two board seats, telling Duval he wanted to see Hammermill sold to the highest bidder.

Duval and the Hammermill board rejected Icahn and initiated a number of defensive maneuvers. Icahn countered with a proxy fight. The parties exchanged lawsuits. After an acrimonious battle, Icahn lost the proxy vote. Ultimately, though, Duval wanted Icahn to go away and eventually agreed that Hammermill would pay part of his expenses. In return, Hammermill received an option to purchase Icahn's shares, which was exercised shortly thereafter. Icahn's investors made a profit on the Hammermill stake when the option was exercised.

In 1984 Icahn transitioned from hostile raider to leveraged industrialist. In June of that year, surprising many observers, he followed through on his $405 million offer to buy ACF Industries. While Icahn had been after the rail car and automotive products manufacturer for months, he eventually agreed to a standstill agreement designed to give management time to arrange financing for an LBO. When management came back with a rich offer, market observers expected Icahn to accept the offer and take his profits. Instead, Icahn topped the management bid, not once but twice. Icahn was no longer content to put companies in play: He wanted to run them.

ACF was to Icahn what Houdaille had been to KKR: The deal brought a measure of respect that had previously eluded him. More important, Drexel Burnham began returning his calls. By the end of 1984, Milken's troops had refinanced ACF and provided Icahn with his own $150 million "blind war chest." A few months later, he played a cameo role in the Phillips Petroleum takeover fight initiated by T. Boone Pickens.

Then, in early 1986, Icahn completed what he hoped would become his signature deal, the acquisition of TWA. The preceding takeover fight, which had dragged out over many months of 1985, had been particularly bruising, featuring the usual litigation and public relations attacks on Icahn. In addition, TWA management unsuccessfully attempted to lobby Congress to block an Icahn bid and searched for a white knight.

Frank Lorenzo of Texas Air turned out to be the most promising prospect from management's perspective. Lorenzo was, however, deeply flawed in the eyes of TWA's unions because he had recently taken Continental Airlines through voluntary bankruptcy to force concessions from its employees. Therefore, TWA's unions were viscerally opposed to a Lorenzo bid. Their willingness to negotiate concessions with Icahn ultimately swung the contest in his favor.

The TWA Icahn took over had a proud tradition but was a poor financial performer. Howard Hughes, who owned the airline after World War II, had set it back considerably with a foot-dragging transition to jet aircraft. In the 1960s, management had diversified, buying Canteen Corp. and Hilton International Hotels. The airline, deemed a cyclical dog, was spun off in 1983.

Despite a promising start, Icahn's days as an airline CEO turned out to be a disaster. A few months after the takeover, a terrorist hijacked one of TWA's planes. At about the same time, TWA's flight attendants, the one group which had not agreed to a contract in advance of the takeover, walked out in a bitter strike. Icahn, after moving to replace the attendants with nonunion employees, broke the union, but was tarred in the press with the same brush previously applied to Lorenzo.

In 1988, Icahn took TWA private, first issuing junk bonds through Drexel Burnham and then buying out the public shareholders with this cash plus debt securities. Icahn cashed out his original investment in the process.

After the restructuring, matters went steeply downhill. Critics argued Icahn failed to invest in the airline's planes or employees. Service was dismal. Finally, the recession of the early 1990s crippled TWA. Notwithstanding these problems, though, Icahn continued to press potential merger partners or acquirers for top dollar. However, no savior emerged. In total, the airline had a few profitable years.

TWA eventually went through bankruptcy. Icahn suffered a few harrowing months during which it looked like he might be on the hook for the airline's underfunded pensions. But when that matter was resolved, Icahn gladly gave up his position as a failed industrialist and returned to the life of a takeover entrepreneur.

Today, Icahn remains active in the financial markets, most recently focusing on investments in distressed bonds and real estate. One such investment, a large position in the bonds of Marvel Entertainment, put him at odds with Ron Perelman over a reorganization plan for the troubled company. Icahn, however, was the winner in bankruptcy court and became chairman of Marvel until July 1997. The company emerged from bankruptcy in October 1998 and merged with Toy Biz. Icahn was also involved with other firms in bankruptcy, including Pam Am, casinos Arizona Charlies and Stratosphere Corp., and Philip Secur and National Energy Group. Icahn has also maintained a large position in RJR Nabisco and agitated on several occasions in favor of splitting the company's food and tobacco operations apart. In December 1998, Icahn had again accumulated 5 percent of RJR Nabisco stock, a stake he raised to 8 percent in February 1999. As before, he called for RJR Nabisco to split its tobacco business from its food business.

In March 1999 RJR did announce its intent to split off its U.S. cigarette business and the sale of its international tobacco business to Japan Tobacco for $7.8 billion. It will continue to hold 80.6 percent of Nabisco. Yet Icahn professed not to be happy with RJR Nabisco's plan, preferring that the food business, rather than the U.S. cigarette business, be spun off. In a bid to control the company, Icahn nominated his own nine-member board in March 1999 but by May had backed down.

In retrospect, the activities of financial entrepreneurs and financial buyers have come to define the pace, the rhythm, and the scope of the 1980s merger boom. The irony is that many of these financial entrepreneurs and financial buyers were able to expand their horizons vastly because of financing by Drexel. Yet, after Drexel's fall, most of these players survived and prospered. Other institutions had stepped in to take Drexel's place.

M&A Goes Global

Large cross-border deals were another significant part of the 1980s merger dynamic. Though relatively uncommon as late as the early 1980s, a rush of deals in the latter part of the decade broke the boundaries of geography.

TEN LARGEST CROSS-BORDER DEALS OF THE 1980s

Rank	Acquirer	Target	Approximate Price Paid (Billions)	Year Announced
1.	Beecham Group PLC (U.K.)	SmithKline Beckman Corp.	$16.1	1989
2.	British Petroleum Co. (U.K.)	Standard Oil Co. (remaining 45%)	$7.8	1987
3.	Campeau Corp. (Canada)	Federated Department Stores, Inc.	$6.5	1988
4.	Grand Metropolitan PLC (U.K.)	Pillsbury Company	$5.6	1988
5.	Royal Dutch/Shell Group (Netherlands)	Shell Oil Co. (remaining 30.5%)	$5.5	1984
6.	BAT Industries PLC (U.K.)	Farmers Group Inc.	$5.2	1988
7.	Société Nationale Elf Aquitaine (France)	Texasgulf Inc.	$4.3	1981
8.	Amoco Corp.	Dome Petroleum Ltd. (Canada)	$4.2	1987
9.	Exxon Corp.	Texaco Canada Inc. (Canada)	$4.1	1989
10.	Private Group—Led by Alfred Checchi/KLM Royal Dutch Airlines	NWA Inc. (Northwest Airlines)	$3.5	1989

Source: MergerStat

Like the domestic merger market, the international merger market went through cycles reflecting worldwide macroeconomic conditions, currency fluctuations, politics at home, and home-country regulatory attitudes. In the 1980s, the number of foreign firms acquiring U.S. firms was larger than the number of U.S. firms acquiring foreign firms. During the decade, there were an average of 218 transactions per year involving a foreign bidder and a U.S. target with an average yearly value of $23.4 billion; by contrast, there were an average of 147 transactions per year involving a U.S. acquirer and a foreign target with an average yearly value of $8.5 billion. These foreign firms used M&A to gain access to the lucrative U.S. market. Many of these transactions came—seemingly illogically—at a time when foreign currencies were at an all-time low against the dollar. A prominent example was Nestlé's $3 billion acquisition of Carnation.

As the chart indicates, the largest cross-border deals of the 1980s were in oil and pharmaceuticals. Indeed, the stable U.S. economy and weak dollar in 1988 made U.S. companies attractive targets for foreign acquirers. However, there was also prominent cross-border M&A activity in consumer products. The takeover of Pillsbury by consumer products conglomerate Grand Metropolitan is a notable example. In addition to its food business, Pillsbury also owned Burger King, Bennigan's, and Steak & Ale restaurants. GrandMet won its victory when the Delaware Court of Chancery barred Pillsbury from, as announced, spinning off Burger King, and invalidated its poison pill defense. In the deal, Grand Met gained control of brands including Green Giant frozen vegetables, Häagen-Dazs ice cream, and Pillsbury cake mixes, which it added to its own line of Alpo dog food, Smirnoff Vodka, and J&B Scotch whisky. In 1997, Grand Metropolitan merged with Guinness to form Diageo.

Also in 1988, British tobacco, paper, and retailing conglomerate BAT Industries (later merged with Rothmans in 1999) announced its $5.2 billion takeover of California-based insurer Farmers Group. Nineteen eighty-eight was also a hot year for contested European deals. Twenty-seven were announced in France alone. By contrast, in 1984 only one hostile bid was launched in France. Bernard Arnault was one of Europe's most aggressive raiders of the 1980s. Allied with Guinness, Arnault obtained control of LVMH Moët Hennessy Louis Vuitton.

Nineteen eighty-eight also witnessed the merger of Sweden's Asea with Switzerland's Brown Boveri and France's Cie. Financière de Suez's takeover of Société Générale de Belgique—then Belgium's biggest company.

In Britain, Europe's biggest M&A market, $46 billion worth of companies were sold in 1987. British companies spent $3.4 billion in 1998 for acquisitions in Europe, with Spain in second place. In 1988,

Drexel Burnham set up Europe's first junk bond fund, reportedly with $380 million.

The increasing maturity of the global capital markets in the 1980s also helped spur cross-border activity. Companies came to look for financing wherever they could get it—not necessarily just in their home countries. Eurobonds—bonds issued by European companies denominated in U.S. dollars—also became popular for capital raising. Global swaps helped companies hedge currency risk.

Companies from different countries were active at different times. Due to a common language, British and Canadian companies were consistently active in the United States. Japanese companies on the other hand enjoyed a window of opportunity in the second half of the decade when both the Japanese home market and the Japanese currency were strong. Rich with cash, a number of Japanese companies made large U.S. acquisitions in the last several years of the decade. Then the cycle turned, and the Japanese pulled back.

In the 1980s, U.S. companies also began to look internationally for acquisition candidates. From autos to financial services, from entertainment to pharmaceuticals, industries became increasingly global. While at one time foreign companies were reluctant to sell businesses, often due to pride and a long-term view, the experience of U.S. businesses in the 1980s caused European companies to regard divestitures as valuable tools in corporate strategy and enterprise value creation. In the 1980s, the acquisition market therefore globalized: Companies up for sale were shopped simultaneously to European, American, and Japanese acquirers.

The globalization trend gathered momentum throughout the decade, surging to create a whirlwind of cross-border activity in the 1990s.

Troubled | 6
Years

"Each organic being is striving to increase in a geometrical ratio . . . each at some period of its life, during some season of the year, during each generation or at intervals, has to struggle for life and to suffer great destruction. . . . The vigorous, the healthy and the happy survive and multiply."

—Charles Darwin, *On the Origin of Species*

The leveraged acquisition business was rocked by change in the second half of the 1980s. By 1986, the business had matured, and the field had become crowded. Longtime market participants had immense pools of capital at their fingertips and faced pressure to invest the money.

RJR Nabisco

The new realities in the buyout market were highlighted in 1988 when a bidding war erupted over giant RJR Nabisco. RJR chief executive F. Ross Johnson's management buyout bid triggered what history would come to view as a legendary takeover battle. The ensuing auction was the Roller Derby of deals, a chaotic process replete with underhanded tactics. Outside board members never fully got control of the situation; management continued to make access to information difficult and relied on leaks from the boardroom to target their own bid.

The press had a field day lampooning everyone involved and fictionalized some events to protect favored sources. Two *Wall Street Journal* reporters even became best-selling authors based on their well-written parody, *Barbarians at the Gate*, although their credibility was injured when one of the reporters subsequently attacked a key source as a congenital liar. Nevertheless, the HBO movie based on the book was hilarious and made everyone involved look like a fool.

Johnson set the bidding war in motion on October 13, 1988. An able manager with a taste for the perks of office—jets, golf tournaments, and club memberships—Johnson proposed a management buyout of RJR Nabisco in which he, a small group of top managers, and investment banks Lehman Brothers and Salomon Brothers offered to buy the company for $75 a share. The stock—which had closed at about $56 the day before the announcement—recently was trading in the 40s. Meanwhile, stock analysts put the breakup value of the company at about $100 per share.

Many members of the board felt blindsided by Johnson's offer. Rather than endorse the offer or give management exclusive rights to negotiate, the board appointed a committee of nonmanagement directors to consider his proposal and made the details of the offer public. This action effectively put the huge company into play.

When news of the bid came out, Henry Kravis was surprised. KKR had approached Johnson a few months earlier to discuss the possibility of a buyout, but had been turned away. Now, with Johnson advancing what Kravis considered to be a lowball bid, KKR threw itself into the game: Within a few days KKR responded with a higher offer, $90 a share for 87 percent of the company.

A number of other bidders had also expressed interest in a deal. Forstmann Little pulled together a bidding syndicate, but ultimately dropped out. And First Boston cobbled together a proposal, but it wasn't regarded as a serious offer.

The board now faced a difficult decision. Should it accept one of the buyout offers or attempt a restructuring? Although a lawsuit would inevitably result no matter what the board decided, the special committee members needed a defensible alternative.

After working through the bids, the board committee opted for the old auctioneer's ploy: It asked for another round of bids. Curiously, again the bids were leaked. In the middle of the bidding process, our Tokyo office called to tell us that the "secret" bids were being described in minute detail on the Asian feed of the Dow Jones News Service!

In second-round bidding, both Johnson and KKR—the two strongest bidders—offered complicated packages of cash and securities to which the board's investment bankers ascribed approximately equal value. At a climactic meeting in the Manhattan offices of law firm Skadden, Arps, the board finally picked KKR's offer as the winner primarily because, economic values being equal, the outside board members didn't want to be perceived as backing a controversial management.

From first bid to closing, the RJR transaction took less than three months. Nearly $20 billion in debt capital was raised, $15 billion from a large syndicate of banks and $5 billion in junk bonds. The $25 billion price paid for the company represented almost a 100 percent premium over RJR's recent market valuation. Although the dollars involved were huge, the valuation was not excessive based on the facts known at the time.

At several times in the course of the deal, opportunities presented themselves for a compromise joint bid between the major bidders, which would likely have been less costly. However, the underwriters for the rival bidders were too busy fighting for their own turf to make it happen.

History has not been kind to the RJR deal. The public visibility was simply too much, and the deal's doings became too easy to equate with the excesses of an overheated market. However, the most immediate financial threat to the deal came from a security Drexel had recommended to finance the purchase: the increasing rate note. The instrument—at the time considered an aggressive Drexel marketing innovation—was designed to reset periodically so it would always trade at face value. By assuring selling shareholders that the paper they were to receive would always be worth face value, Drexel managed to dispel the unsavory image associated with the packages of securities often included in buyout offers.

However, RJR's $6 million issuance in increasing rate notes boomeranged in 1990. Confidence in the tobacco company's ability to service its debt plummeted on January 26 when Moody's downgraded the company, and the bond's price plunged accordingly. Due to this price decrease, the coupon on the note would have to be reset at sky-high levels for it to trade at face value.

Often increasing rate notes have a cap—a limit on the top interest rate—but RJR's advisers and Drexel had not included that term. To prevent RJR from defaulting on its interest payments, KKR negotiated a recapitalization in which it agreed to put $1.7 billion of additional equity capital into RJR and refinance the outstanding junk bonds.

Disaster was averted in the reset crisis, but competitor Philip Morris was relentless in attacking RJR on the pricing side, and the tobacco liability threat didn't die. Perhaps the only heroes of the RJR deal were Kravis and Roberts, who remained calm throughout and, when adversity hit, handled the situation with dexterity and dignity.

Eventually, KKR's investment was liquidated in an exchange for Borden stock at a low rate of profit. Ironically, after KKR sold, RJR stock rose as its prospects improved. More recently, though, RJR stock has been in something of a slump, not materially increasing in value over the past few years. Recent agitation by shareholder Carl Icahn, which resulted in a sale of the international tobacco business and the spin-off of the U.S. tobacco business, might improve investor perceptions.

Teddy Forstmann and the Anti–Junk Bond Crusade

Teddy Forstmann and his partners at Forstmann Little were troubled by the junk bond–fueled buyout wars sweeping the market, and the RJR circus just reinforced their view. In his stance as outspoken critic of junk bonds in the press and on the editorial pages, Forstmann earned a reputation on Wall Street as something of a Cassandra.

Forstmann had three principal complaints about junk-financed deals. First, he argued many companies were being overleveraged. The inflexible principal repayment schedule typically structured into LBOs combined with regular interest payments left the debt-laden companies with little margin for error.

Second, Forstmann argued the easy credit provided in the junk bond market—"funny money," as he termed it—allowed financial buyers to bid unreasonable amounts for target companies. Due to these frothy valuations, Forstmann Little, which on average had bought two companies a year in the early 1980s, was forced to curtail its efforts in the late 1980s and sit on a good part of its $2.7 billion fund. When the firm did make an offer, it was often outbid by Drexel-financed acquirers: Perelman snatched Revlon away and Kravis took RJR Nabisco. To Forstmann, his competitors were using "wampum" with high risks of default.

Finally, Forstmann complained that junk bonds were an expensive capital source. Drexel and its competitors took an up-front percentage of any money it raised in junk bond underwritings and typically demanded equity in the issuer. Once the capital was raised, junk bond investors charged relatively steep interest rates that ate into potential LBO returns.

Rather than rely on junk bonds for subordinated debt financing, Forstmann turned to the same pension funds that had provided the lion's share of LBO equity. Starting in the late 1970s, Forstmann Little raised mezzanine debt funds as companions to its equity funds. These mezzanine debt funds promised investors a fixed return on the loans plus a portion of the equity upside. The combination proved to be extremely lucrative: In the mid-1980s, the mezzanine funds were averaging total returns of approximately 25 percent a year.

The fund arrangement allowed Forstmann to commit debt capital extremely quickly and cheaply: The current cash interest liability on the debt generally was 2 to 4 percentage points lower than on comparable junk bonds. The principal repayment schedule associated with the captive financing was similarly favorable. Moreover, the Forstmann-controlled funds provided greater flexibility than junk bonds would have, as they were a ready source of capital.

PROFILE

Theodore Forstmann

During the 1980s, Ted Forstmann and his partners matched the success of KKR, though on a smaller scale. Forstmann Little broke into the big time in 1984 with the purchase of Dr. Pepper. At the time observers tagged the $650 million purchase as too high and the deal earned the distinction as the 1984 LBO "most likely to fail." But within two years, Forstmann Little confounded the critics. The firm netted more than eight times its original investment, having sold Canada Dry, nine bottling plants, and other assets to pay down debt.

The Dr. Pepper buyout and similar investments earned Forstmann Little's investors very high returns—60 percent annual returns on invested equity and 20 percent on debt in 1986. Of course, competitors point out that it is more sensible to take a blended return.

The son of a wealthy industrialist who went bust, Forstmann graduated from Yale University and Columbia Law School. By his own admission, his performance in school was mediocre. He practiced as a lawyer for a few years, then worked at a number of Wall Street jobs. At the age of thirty-five, he was trying to broker deals on his own, but was quickly running out of money.

Summing up his own background, Forstmann told a reporter, "I never went to business school. I was basically never in an investment banking firm worthy of mention. I've always been a guy who had ideas."

The LBO caught his fancy in the late 1970s when his younger brother Nick was working at KKR. As a favor, Ted arranged a meeting between Kravis and Derald Ruttenberg, a president of an industrial company whom Ted had met in his early days as a dealmaker. Forstmann had heard of bootstrap acquisitions before, but had never done one. Ruttenberg liked the buyout idea, but wondered why he and Ted couldn't carry it out on their own. Forstmann jumped at the chance, and with initial funding from Ruttenberg and his friends, Forstmann, his brother Nick, and Brian Little set up their firm.

In those early days, Forstmann Little thrived by concentrating its efforts on executing the classic LBO deal, where "reasonable prices [were] paid for mature companies with steady cash flows and with dominant positions in industries that were less volatile than the economy." Brian Little, who had a reputation as one of the nicest guys on Wall Street, charmed clients while Ted ran the shop.

Eventually, Ted became more dominant and driven. Sleek and silver-haired, he takes control of Forstmann Little investments himself when necessary. For example, when corporate jet maker Gulfstream was sputtering with indifferent sales, Forstmann took over as chairman and started selling the planes himself.

The Insider Trading Scandal

In May 1985, a Merrill Lynch compliance officer opened an anonymous letter from Caracas, Venezuela, which alleged that two of Merrill Lynch's brokers in Caracas were trading on inside information. As it turns out, the letter set off a chain of events that resulted in the arrest of Drexel investment bankers Dennis Levine and Martin Siegel and guilty pleas by Ivan Boesky and Michael Milken.

Levine was the first to fall. An affable fellow, he was regarded as a mediocre professional who lacked the analytical skill to be an effective deal strategist. Levine began his career at Citibank, but dreamed to be on the inside of large deals. After several attempts, he finally landed a spot at Smith Barney where his jocular nature was rewarded with a spot in the firm's M&A department.

Despite Levine's aggressive self-promotion, his superiors at Smith Barney ultimately were unimpressed with his abilities, passing him over for promotion a few years after he joined the firm. Incensed, Levine moved to Lehman Brothers. His flashy cars and habit of paying cash for expensive meals raised some eyebrows at the firm, but Levine prospered in a boom environment from his penchant for knowing deal stories. He joined Drexel in 1984 as part of the firm's push into M&A.

The source of many of Levine's tips turned out to be a ring of insiders—lawyers and investment bankers—he had cultivated to provide information on unfolding transactions. Levine also developed a relationship with arbitrageur Ivan Boesky in which Levine agreed to provide tips to Boesky in exchange for a share of Boesky's trading profits.

This web began to unwind in 1986 when Merrill Lynch, and later the SEC, followed the anonymous letter of 1985 to an account under the name Mr. Diamond at a bank in the Bahamas. It was revealed that Levine had opened the account in 1980 to conduct insider trading. Impatient for wealth and prestige, Levine had found what he saw as an easier road. However, the success of his trades became his downfall. The bank executive that Levine used to make his trades began mirroring Levine's trades on his own behalf and eventually the circle of people involved widened to the two brokers in Merrill Lynch's Caracas office.

In the spring, federal officials finally were able to crack the bank secrecy laws that hid Mr. Diamond's true identity, and on May 12, 1986, Levine was arrested on charges of insider trading. Less than a month after the arrest, Levine pled guilty to four felonies and agreed to forfeit his $11.6 million in trading profits. Despite his downfall, Levine failed to see anything wrong with his trading, likening his behavior to that of a worker in a deli who "takes home pastrami every night for free. It's the same with information on Wall Street."

PROFILE

Rudolph Giuliani

At the time of the insider trading scandal, Rudolph Giuliani was the U.S. attorney responsible for federal prosecutions in New York City. He had already earned a reputation as a bulldog prosecutor, primarily for his pursuit of the New York Mafia, and had demonstrated a thirst for publicity. When the SEC unearthed the Levine case, Giuliani and his staff turned their attention to insider trading.

Once incited, Giuliani's staff members pursued the new brand of criminals with zeal using broad racketeering statutes—written to break the Mob—against defendants. In addition, Giuliani made headlines by supporting longer prison sentences for those convicted of insider trading and a stricter definition of the insider trading law in order to eliminate any potential ambiguities.

Critics complained that Giuliani was engaging in a reign of terror designed to boost his own image and political career, pointing to the constant press conferences and leaks to the news media regarding ongoing investigations. Giuliani's staff appeared to have adopted a strategy of using media pressure to force suspects to plea-bargain.

Even worse to civil libertarians, Giuliani seemed to delight in treating white-collar criminals with particularly draconian measures, despite his mixed conviction record. In 1987, he arrested three arbitrageurs in a particularly dramatic fashion: Tim Tabor, formerly of Kidder, Peabody, Richard Wigton, head of arbitrage at Kidder, and Robert Freeman, head of arbitrage at Goldman Sachs. Tabor was arrested in the evening so that he would have to spend a night in jail, and Wigton and Freeman were dragged off their trading floors, handcuffed and led away while forewarned television crews looked on. But two years later, Giuliani was forced to drop charges against the first two men. Freeman pled guilty to a single charge and was sentenced to four months' jail time.

In 1993, Giuliani was elected mayor of New York City, where he has achieved considerable popularity and successfully reduced crime. In November 1997, he won a sweeping victory for a second term and is now eyeing running for the Senate.

Feeling the heat, Levine decided to cooperate with government prosecutors. He implicated the members of his information-gathering ring, all relatively minor figures in the takeover business. Then, in a surprise revelation, Levine also pointed a finger at Ivan Boesky—a prominent arbitrageur who had made millions trading on takeover rumors. Giuliani and his allies at the SEC salivated at the prospect of bringing Boesky down.

Unfortunately, Levine could not provide ironclad proof that Boesky had been trading on inside information. He did, however, reveal the tips he had provided to Boesky, providing a road map for authorities. They subpoenaed Boesky for records of all his trades.

As it turned out, Boesky was extremely vulnerable to the threats of prosecution. Not only had he traded on information from Levine, but he also had relationships with investment bankers like Michael Milken and Martin Siegel, the latter formerly at Kidder, Peabody before he joined Drexel. Boesky and his lawyers had discounted the government's ability to build a case around Levine, who had previously lied under oath and had admitted to orchestrating his insider trading ring. But Boesky feared one of his other sources might make a deal with the government. He raced to cut his own deal before it was too late.

On November 14, the SEC made the stunning announcement that Boesky had agreed to become a government witness: He would pay $100 million in fines and plead guilty to a single felony count. Giuliani and Gary Lynch, the head of enforcement at the SEC, thought the government had struck a tough bargain. However, shortly after the announcement, *The Wall Street Journal* reported that Boesky had made more than $200 million on tips from Levine alone.

Criticism mounted when it later came out that Boesky had been allowed to sell some of his firm's stock positions in advance of the announcement, driving down the price of many takeover stocks. To some, this seemed like government-sanctioned insider trading. Furthermore, allowing Boesky to plead guilty to just one count rather than Levine's four counts seemed out of proportion to their relative wrongdoing. Boesky's three-year sentence—of which he served a bit more than half—seemed light in view of his wide-ranging involvement.

Ivan Boesky

Ivan Boesky was born on March 6, 1937, the son of a Russian immigrant milkman turned pub owner, and grew up in an upper-middle-class neighborhood in Detroit, Michigan. A hyperactive youth with a short attention span, Boesky attended a number of different high schools and colleges, although he never actually graduated from college. He did, however, eventually earn a degree from the Detroit College of Law, which did not require an undergraduate degree for admission. Boesky married Seema Silberstein, the daughter of a wealthy real estate developer, at about the same time he graduated from law school.

Intrigued by Wall Street, Boesky used his law degree to secure a position as a securities analyst, but soon found the job unappealing. Boesky's dissatisfaction led him to discover arbitrage, a business more in tune with his energetic nature and that satisfied his lust for quick results. After several false starts, brokerage firm Edward & Hanley hired Boesky to do professional arbitrage work.

At Edward & Hanley, Boesky was an overnight sensation. Like other arbitrageurs, Boesky typically bought on margin, which allowed him to take larger positions. Edward & Hanley had modest capital but Boesky nonetheless invested as much as $2 million in single situations. His tactics, however, grew too daring, and eventually contributed to the ruin of the firm. When Edward & Hanley went out of business, Boesky opened his own arbitrage boutique—Ivan F. Boesky & Co.—whose founding fortuitously coincided with the beginning of the takeover boom.

The new Boesky firm opened for business in late 1975, backed by $700,000 of his in-laws' money. Again, Boesky demonstrated a talent for the business. In the 1980s, Boesky made large sums by placing heavy bets on pending takeovers: He reportedly made

$50 million on Getty stock when it was taken over by Texaco and $65 million on Chevron's purchase of Gulf.

Not all of Boesky's bets were winners, however. He lost considerable sums on the busted Cities Service and Phillips Petroleum takeovers in the middle 1980s—transactions which reportedly triggered his increased interest in obtaining inside information.

Information is the lifeblood of arbitrage. Before placing a large bet on a particular merger or acquisition, Boesky needed to believe that the transaction would proceed and therefore cultivated the image of an expert information gatherer. In the heat of a contest, he would have people posted at courthouses, legislative hearings, and companies' headquarters. Only later did it become apparent that his success had come at least partly by building a network of informants, eager to receive cash payoffs for their tips.

With the help of Siegel and others, Boesky won far more often than he lost. By 1985, he was on *Forbes*' list of America's 400 wealthiest individuals. As Boesky became more successful, he was thrilled at the attention. He set himself up as the icon of arbitrage, preaching the glories of greed as a mantra. While the exposure helped Boesky raise money, his practices invited severe criticism from fellow risk arbitrageurs who were horrified by his tactics.

In retrospect, Boesky's punishment was light. He was released from prison in April 1990.

Of course, the merit of the Boesky plea agreement also depended on Boesky's value as a witness. Once allied with the government, Boesky in turn implicated others, including both Siegel and Milken.

In February of 1987, Martin Siegel pled guilty to two felonies in what was perhaps the most troubling story to come out of the insider-trading scandal. Siegel was a golden boy, a capable professional with movie-star looks and a captivating personality. He had risen to prominence at Kidder, Peabody & Co. by building a reputation in takeover defense and promoted himself as the "Secretary of Defense." He moved in 1986 to Drexel Burnham Lambert, where he was guaranteed a $3.5 million salary and a $2 million bonus.

Siegel's downfall stemmed from an earlier arrangement with Boesky. In 1982, Kidder, Peabody was having a rocky time financially and seemed in danger of being pushed to the fringes of the M&A business. At the same time, Siegel felt pressure to maintain an expensive lifestyle. While Siegel had already developed a professional relationship with Boesky, in 1982, Boesky proposed a different kind of relationship: Siegel would pass tips on pending takeovers to Boesky, and Boesky would pay Siegel a "consulting" fee.

Siegel's first tip came some time later that year and Boesky made $120,000 trading on the information. From then on, Siegel exchanged tips with Boesky in return for a share of Boesky's trading profits. Boesky made good on the deal by having messengers deliver suitcases full of $100 bills to Siegel in the lobby of Manhattan's Plaza Hotel. Siegel received between $700,000 and $800,000 in cash. Finally, in 1984, the pressure of dealing with Boesky got to Siegel. He stopped taking Boesky's calls. However, the damage had already been done.

Following Boesky's lead, Siegel plea-bargained his way out of serious jail time. Ultimately, he agreed to pay a $9 million penalty and keep only his two residences and pension contributions, and was sentenced to a light two months in prison—even though the information he provided the government was of dubious value. The main result of Siegel's cooperation was the unsuccessful arrest of arbitrageurs Freeman, Wigton, and Tabor.

Unlike Giuliani's other targets, Tabor, Wigton, and Freeman refused to roll over. They asserted their innocence and prepared to fight the charges against them. Nine days before the trial was to begin, the government was forced to admit it was not ready. Then, in a highly unusual move, the charges against the three were dropped. Wigton and Tabor were not reindicted. But unwilling to admit complete defeat, the government pursued Freeman.

After fighting for two and a half years, Freeman pled guilty to a single charge of mail fraud and was sentenced to four months in prison. The charge stemmed from the following situation: Before his arrest, Freeman had been head of arbitrage at Goldman, where he had taken a large position in Beatrice during KKR's takeover of the company. At some point, rumors began to circulate that the deal was about to collapse, potentially creating a big loss for Goldman Sachs. As was customary, Freeman called around the Street looking for confirmation. A fellow arb named Bernard "Bunny" Lasker told Freeman the deal was indeed in trouble and therefore Freeman called Siegel, who had been talking to Freeman on and off for some time and who was working for KKR on the deal. Freeman asked if the rumor relayed by Lasker was true. Siegel responded, "Your bunny has a good nose." Freeman promptly dumped his position. Of course, Siegel's information soon proved to be false. KKR's Beatrice deal went through and Freeman would have earned a big profit if he had held on.

The most significant personal fallout from the 1985 letter to Merrill Lynch was the 1989 indictment of Michael Milken on ninety-eight counts of mail fraud, securities fraud, tax evasion, and racketeering. Milken eventually pled guilty to just six counts, none of which involved insider trading or stock manipulation.

Several of the counts related to stock parking arrangements with Boesky—arrangements designed to put companies in play or support the prices of Drexel clients' stock. In one case, Milken encouraged Boesky to buy stock in the Fischbach Corporation to create the appearance that Boesky was after Fischbach, thereby freeing a Drexel client from an agreement not to pursue Fischbach. As an inducement, Milken agreed to guarantee any losses Boesky might incur while he held the Fischbach stock.

Other charges against Milken related to an arrangement to charge one client slightly more for certain stock trades rather than taking a commission and to an arrangement to help a client evade taxes by creating current losses to be offset by guaranteed future gains.

Milken and his staff clearly broke a number of rules. However, while stock parking arrangements involved regulatory violations, they had never before been the subject of criminal convictions. In past cases, the defendants had been permitted to plead guilty to lesser civil charges.

In an effort to make a statement against perceived Wall Street excesses and to pressure Milken to finger others, federal judge Kimba Wood sentenced Milken to a stiff ten years in prison, although the sentence was later reduced in 1992. Milken ended up serving twenty-four months in prison and forfeiting over $1 billion to settle various criminal and civil charges.

Drexel Implodes

Allegations against Drexel as an institution began to surface soon after the Boesky plea bargain. For a time, the firm's management considered fighting the charges, but in December 1988, Giuliani threatened to indict the firm on federal racketeering charges.

Drexel management was in a tight spot. If they fought the charges, legal proceedings might drag on for months, or even years, and in the interim, the firm's clients likely would flee the firm. Fearing the associated uncertainty, the firm decided to settle and came to terms with the government.

Drexel agreed to plead guilty to six counts and to pay a $650 million fine, the largest ever for a securities violation. Three outside directors, appointed by the SEC, would be added to Drexel's board in an effort to address the fundamental problems with the culture of

Drexel. The firm also agreed to place Milken on a leave of absence and withhold $200 million of his earnings for 1988. The settlement was a calculated gamble: Drexel management traded the short-term pain of the penalty and the loss of the firm's star for a chance at survival. As it turned out, the gamble failed to pay off.

Drexel survived 1989 and actually had a number of successes, among which was the raising of $5 billion in a junk bond offering for KKR's purchase of RJR Nabisco. That single deal—a strong statement of the firm's continuing distribution capabilities—brought Drexel a fee of $250 million.

Yet, without Milken at the helm, Drexel began to unwind. The first hint of real trouble came in June 1989 when Drexel was unable to re-fund $40 million of commercial paper for Integrated Resources. These short-term securities were used by Integrated to finance its working capital needs and were expected to be rolled over when due, replaced with new paper. The failure to raise a mere $40 million for Integrated forced the company into default on $1 billion of junk bonds. Market observers wondered whether the failure would have happened with Milken still on the job. In the past, he had managed to find creative solutions to similar problems.

Drexel's lackluster defense of Integrated Resources becomes more understandable, however, when seen in the context of the time. Drexel was reeling, with its credit rating lowered to the point where it could not re-fund its own outstanding commercial paper. Still, to have any hope of survival, Drexel felt it had to defend its junk bond franchise and therefore, as the $200 billion junk bond market tanked, in part due to Milken's departure, continued to act as a buyer of last resort. The firm's inventory of troubled securities grew to over $1 billion.

By the start of 1990, it was becoming clear that Drexel had been forced into a classic mistake—funding its long-term cash needs (primarily to carry its junk bond inventory) with short-term borrowings.

Drexel was facing a major liquidity crisis and was on the brink of bankruptcy.

Fred Joseph, CEO of the firm, spent the fall and winter months looking for someone willing to put up the money needed to save Drexel. There was precedent for such a rescue: E.F. Hutton had a near-death experience in 1987 and was resuscitated by the coordinated efforts of the government and other financial institutions.

But when Joseph called around to other investment banks, none was willing to buy equity in Drexel—not even to gain the firm's once vaunted junk bond operation. The potential for liability was just too great. Furthermore, there was little goodwill toward Drexel on the Street, as the other big investment banks had been bullied by Drexel over the years. Now they turned their backs on the former upstart.

As Drexel struggled, its client base evaporated. Employees began to sense trouble and circulated résumés. The firm lost a number of stars. Rumors flew around the Street about the impending failure of the once-proud firm.

Because he had kept the heads of the Federal Reserve, SEC, and Treasury Department informed about Drexel's problems, Joseph looked to the government to lead a rescue effort. However, Federal Reserve Chairman Alan Greenspan and Treasury Secretary Nicholas Brady declined to act.

Greenspan and Brady apparently decided the financial markets could withstand the failure of Drexel. There would be no government bailout. In fact, on the evening of February 12, the Fed and the Treasury told Joseph that Drexel would either have to file for bankruptcy or go into liquidation.

The next day, February 13, 1990, Drexel announced its bankruptcy.

Tough Times

Drexel was not alone in facing difficulties in 1989 and 1990. The second half of 1989 ushered in a rocky period for the financial markets in general. The RJR Nabisco deal was a high-water mark for the 1980s buyout boom and in the remaining months of 1989, a series of negative events rocked the financial world. Tough times followed, a dramatic shakeout period during which many financial buyers struggled for economic survival.

Milken's 1989 indictment and resignation from Drexel were major blows to the junk bond market on which so many financial buyers relied for liquidity. A further blow came in October 1989 when a management buyout of United Airlines fell apart.

UAL, the airline's parent company, had announced a $6.75 billion employee-led buyout in September 1989 in which United pilots had agreed to team up with management and British Airways to buy the airline. The deal was to be funded with cash from British Airways and management and wage concessions from the pilots. In addition, $7.2 billion would be borrowed to fund both the deal and operating cash flow needs.

Reflecting the turmoil in the junk bond market, UAL intended to raise the money entirely from a syndicate of banks led by Citicorp and Chase Manhattan. These two leads banks promised $3 billion and agreed to raise the remaining $4.2 billion from other banks.

However, only a few weeks after the deal was first announced, Citicorp and Chase gave the market a jolt: The two banks could not raise the additional $4.2 billion. The major Japanese banks, to which they had looked for most of the money, had blanched at the deal's financial and fee structure. The buyout collapsed in disarray. Both the stock and junk bond market reacted sharply downward.

The problems in the credit markets were exacerbated by a nascent economic recession: Companies struggled at the operational level, and a number of junk-financed LBOs had slipped into default. KKR was in the market attempting to refinance $624 million of debt issued by its Hillsborough Holding Company. The Southland Corporation, owner of the 7-Eleven chain, was on the ropes after a 1987 buyout. Gibbons Green van Amerongen was unable to refinance a

$450 million bridge loan related to its purchase of Ohio Mattress, popularly known on the Street as the "burning bed" bridge. As the economy slumped further into 1990, bad news kept coming. KKR's re-funding crisis at RJR Nabisco opened the year.

For a time, the credit markets were almost nonexistent. Banks were extremely hesitant when it came to making any new loans. The market for new junk bond issuances dried up almost completely. Even the secondary market for junk bonds almost disappeared.

The financial buyers were particularly vulnerable to the credit crunch that ensued, as capital was the oxygen that gave life to the leveraged acquisition structure. When tough times came, the financial buyers were forced to retrench. KKR was consumed for a time with reshuffling the capital structure at RJR Nabisco. Forstmann Little had its problems with Gulfstream. These tight credit markets together with the fact that the market for corporate control was relatively quiet made it extremely difficult to sell portfolio companies at a favorable price.

Retailing was another extremely troubled industry of the late 1980s. Robert Campeau's Federated and Allied Stores chains collapsed into bankruptcy in 1990. Carter Hawley Hale followed suit the next February. Macy's, which had been taken private by CEO Edward Finkelstein in a 1986 LBO, lingered on life support for several years. Finally, in 1992, the chain also entered Chapter 11. Bankruptcy did not spell the end for most of the troubled retailers, though. They possessed valuable brand names which, despite tough competition from discounters, remained strong. After difficult years of restructuring and debt reduction, the retail industry has come back.

The problem for Finkelstein, Campeau, and other retailers was not that they overpaid. Indeed, in hindsight, these late 1980s deals were good asset values. Rather, the buyers didn't finance well, taking on too much debt, often of the wrong maturity. Campeau funded his Federated acquisition with a $1 billion short-term bridge loan from

First Boston. First Boston, Campeau's financial adviser, correctly advised Campeau to refinance his bridge or sell assets, but Campeau balked because he thought he could get better terms later. He also became enamored of several assets, such as Bloomingdale's, and refused to divest them as part of a previously planned delevering of the company. As a result, Federated had a classic mismatched book. The short-term Federated and Allied Stores debt was financing long-term obligations.

A highly leveraged capital structure of this sort is particularly precarious in retailing, a cyclical business financed by flighty trade debt. When the economy stalled in 1989 and 1990, retail sales fell off. Then, as is common in retailing, suppliers began to get jittery and called in their trade credits—a crucial source of funding for inventory—accelerating the downward spiral.

The Legacy

The abrupt pricking of the 1980s bubble led to an explosion of common wisdom about the mergers process: Merger deals were overpriced, junk bonds dead, and the stock market too frothy. All these insights would be proven wrong in the remarkable 1990s.

The Merits of Mergers: 7
The Good, the Bad,
and the Ugly

"[Should] . . . large corporations . . . be treated like
artichokes and simply torn apart without any
regard for employees, communities, or customers,
solely in order to pay off speculative debt?"

—Felix G. Rohatyn,
investment banker and diplomat

During the 1980s, the debate about the merits of mergers raged not only in New York and Washington, but also in towns like Bartlesville, Oklahoma. For Bartlesville in particular, the issue hit home on February 22, 1985.

Rain lashed the city's streets that day, and the unpleasant weather matched the mood among Bartlesville's 38,000 residents. In the coffee shops and at the meat counters, everyone focused on the same thing. For nearly three months, the town had been hunkered down in what many saw as a life-or-death fight. Now, in an auditorium filled with lawyers, shareholders, and bankers—out-of-town folk— Bartlesville's fate would be decided.

"Corporate raiders" had targeted Phillips Petroleum, the economic anchor of this small company town forty miles north of Tulsa. In Bartlesville, Phillips was a whole lot more than a faceless corporation—it was the heart of the town—employing about 7,700 of the town's residents, a fifth of the community. Countless other small business owners depended on the Phillips money that flowed into their cash registers each year.

Everything came down to this shareholder vote: Phillips shareholders were being asked to approve a management plan designed to turn back the raiders. If Phillips lost the vote and was taken over, many Bartlesville residents feared the entire town would be shuttered. Bartlesville would become a run-down, post-industrial shell.

The last few months had been a stressful roller-coaster ride. First came T. Boone Pickens, the flamboyant independent oilman who had been shaking up Big Oil for the past several years—making a hefty profit for his Mesa Petroleum in the process. Late in 1984, Pickens, his company, and a group of investors had bought up a large chunk of Phillips stock in order to put an end to what he saw as management's wasting of shareholders' money.

Management disagreed with Pickens' assessment, but was over a barrel. If Phillips didn't get rid of Boone, another more powerful company might bid. Therefore, Phillips bought Pickens' stock for $53 a share and paid his $25 million of expenses. At the same time, the company pledged to buy back 38 percent of its stock and carry out a recapitalization designed to give shareholders the same $53 a share in value.

Boone had, once again, greenmailed a company to buy out his stock position for cash. The deal was announced just before Christmas, and Bartlesville breathed a sigh of relief.

The widely held view, however, was that the securities offered by Phillips to the rest of its shareholders were worth less than $45 per share. Not surprisingly, other shareholders were not pleased, especially speculators who were betting on a takeover of Phillips at a higher price. Carl Icahn—one of the leading speculators—took up the assault on Phillips, announcing he would lobby shareholders to reject the Phillips recapitalization. He instead suggested a $55 a share leveraged buyout, placing Bartlesville back on the ropes again. Still, as a local car dealer told a reporter, "We're tired, but we're not ready to quit."

The fight over Phillips, first between Pickens and management, then between Icahn and management, involved a debate from two very different angles. On the offense, Pickens and Icahn cast their actions as a campaign for shareholder rights. Shareholders, they argued, owned Phillips, and management ought to do whatever was necessary to maximize shareholder value. Instead, by their reckoning, management had been depleting Phillips' holdings of natural resources while living a perk-filled life—with private planes and fishing lodges—all at the considerable expense of shareholders. The insurgents purported to speak for all shareholders, including retirees and pensioners—the "little people" who indirectly owned a majority of Phillips through institutional money managers. For their sake, Phillips was in need of restructuring, with or without the blessing of incumbent management.

Ranged against this image, management had the people of Bartlesville. The fight for Phillips was about jobs and community, about preserving the American middle class from grasping, money-hungry financiers. Sure, the company's stock price was down a bit. But management was working hard to correct the situation. They just needed a couple years, time to take the long-term view. Of course, that would be impossible without freedom from Pickens and Icahn, "speculators" out to make a fast buck.

This latter vision certainly carried the day in and around Bartlesville. "I doubt that I could be elected mayor of Bartlesville," Pickens joked to a television reporter. And Icahn was no more loved. In fact, a few days before the stockholder meeting on that rainy February day, people had gathered for a pep rally of sorts. They stood around a bonfire and burned proxy solicitations from Icahn. "Burn, Icahn, burn," they chanted in unison.

But the shareholders, not the town, had the final vote. By the time of the vote, Phillips stock was held mostly by institutions and arbitrageurs—an unsentimental lot who wanted to keep the company in play. Therefore, a majority voted against the recapitalization.

The company scurried in desperation to placate Icahn and his fellow-traveling institutional friends and finally came up with a sweeter but riskier recapitalization plan. The new package of securities offered was valued by the Street in the $53 to $56 range. Icahn withdrew his tender offer, but only after Phillips also agreed to pay him $25 million for expenses.

Bartlesville again celebrated. The barbarians had been turned back at the inner wall, but at a steep cost to the Phillips balance sheet. Ultimately, the town would not emerge unscathed. To service its debt, Phillips planned to cut its workforce by 10 percent and sell off assets.

PROFILE

T. Boone Pickens

The life of Boone Pickens is full of irony. Oil was in his blood from the start. Born and raised in the small town of Holdenville, he grew up in the oil patch of the Oklahoma panhandle where his father was a land man, an itinerant broker who put together deals between farmers and oil companies.

Coming out of college with a geology degree, Pickens got his start in the oil business at Phillips Petroleum, the same company he would later bring to its knees. But he chafed in the world of Big Oil, and within four years he had set out on his own as an independent oilman. He founded Mesa Petroleum in 1964 where he built his initial $2,500 investment into a company with $400 million in sales. By the early 1980s, he was a rich man, yet by the standards of the oil business, Pickens was a fairly small player. That was soon to change.

Pickens began to realize that oil companies were undervalued relative to the worth of their proven reserves. Furthermore, his experience working for Phillips had left Pickens with a distaste for the bureaucratic tendencies of Big Oil. He felt the companies were dramatically undermanaged. Executives were more concerned with perks than performance.

Pickens may not have been the first to recognize the value of prospecting for oil on Wall Street, but he was certainly one of the most enthusiastic promoters of the practice. Though he never actually was able to buy a major oil company, his early hostile tenders were nonetheless successful. Following the Phillips model, Mesa profited in each case when a third-party suitor appeared.

In the process, Mesa became the "terror of the oil patch." Pickens soon became caught up in his campaign and the publicity it brought, founding a group called the United Shareholders Association to lobby against entrenched management and for better governance provisions.

Then, in the ultimate irony, Pickens himself became a target of shareholder dissent. Mesa had recorded miserable performance starting in the late 1980s, largely because Pickens made a bad bet on natural gas prices. He fought to keep control, but, in 1996, was forced out of Mesa by a group of dissidents.

The Merger Movement

The press understandably loved the battle for Phillips. Its contrasting images formed a compelling drama: Boone Pickens, a direct descendant of Daniel Boone, fighting for the "little guy"; the twenty-four-hour prayer vigils in Bartlesville; the children with heart-shaped Phillips balloons standing in the rain outside the shareholder meeting; the local women who brought "I love Phillips" cookies to a meeting in New York City. The pictures and stories crystallized opposing views about the wave of mergers and acquisitions sweeping over the oil business, and America in general.

By now, the shibboleths have become familiar. Are mergers good because they restructure inefficient companies and allow good companies to continue to grow? Or do they strip-mine America communities for the benefit of Wall Street profiteers? Do mergers benefit or harm shareholders? The intensity of this debate flares whenever the periodic merger cycle booms. In fact, the discussion is usually clouded more by rhetoric than elucidated by penetrating thought.

A key problem with the quality of the debate is that each party is usually a self-interested advocate, proselytizing a point of view. In the 1980s labor unions and target corporations joined in an unholy alliance, together using public relations and lobbying firms to machine-gun the deal process. To stir up the political fires, pressure was focused on constituents who feared job loss. On the other hand, to espouse their views and defend the deal process, the investment banks led by Morgan Stanley hired consultants like McKinsey, whose studies reflected the views of the banks that hired them. The politicians were more than pleased. They received donations from all and did very little.

Truth also is obscured by the fact that both critics and supporters of deals "data-mine" the M&A bank to find support for their own conclusions. Critics lambaste the deal process with anecdotes such as: Ling went under, Macy's went bankrupt, RJR didn't work for KKR, etc. On the other hand, proponents of deals note that KKR turned Duracell around and the merger between Chase and Chemical banks slashed costs, increased efficiency, and built shareholder value.

However, with all their limitations, it is useful to summarize the arguments for and against mergers, first those from proponents:

- Mergers and acquisitions provide specific economic benefits;
- Mergers and acquisitions maximize overall shareholder wealth;
- An active market for corporate control motivates incumbent management to act in the interest of shareholders;

- Economic activity as a whole is benefited by the active acquisition and divestiture marketplace, which allows young companies to be bought and mature companies to adapt to changing circumstances; and

- The ability to cash out of investments through mergers and acquisitions encourages business start-up and venture capital activities.

Economic Benefits for Target Company

Managers involved in a merger or acquisition, as well as takeover proponents, generally project economic benefits to justify such transactions. Particular benefits include enhanced operating and financial efficiency, or the need for critical mass and sheer size.

Operating Efficiencies   The combination of two companies into one presents the opportunity to achieve economics of scale, a common source of merger-related economic benefits. Such savings typically result from the elimination of redundant overhead or capacity, allowing the combined firm to service customers more efficiently.

Enhanced operating efficiency is so important that it has often been cited as the primary driver of bank mergers. Chemical Bank's 1991 acquisition of Manufacturers Hanover suggests why. At the time the deal was announced, the two banks projected $650 million in annual cost savings from reducing duplicative overhead. Indeed, when the dust settled these cost savings materialized: The new Chemical had shed branches, cut back-office staff, and reduced overlapping marketing expenses. In fact, the annual cost savings actually totaled more than $750 million. Its success integrating Manufacturers Hanover led it to undertake a similar combination, the recent merger with Chase, which resulted in similar benefits. Driven by these cost-cutting combinations, Chemical's (now Chase's) stock price has zoomed.

Obviously, however, not all attempts to reduce total costs through merger succeed. Meshing two organizations into one can be incredibly complex. There may often be economics of scale besides the benefits of sheer size. But the reverse can happen as well—diseconomies of scale—as was seen in the conglomerate era. Furthermore, many observers note that these "efficiencies" come at the expense of employees, who often find themselves out of a job after mergers.

Financial Efficiencies   Increase in an organization's size can be a source of financial efficiencies. Many academics argue that such efficiencies in theory should not exist, but anecdotal evidence suggests otherwise. In the early 1990s, for example, small and medium-sized firms found it incredibly difficult to raise capital. The first problem was the expense: Banks demand a premium from smaller firms to compensate them for making what they view as a riskier loan. Furthermore, in times of really tight money, lenders will take care of the needs of larger firms first both to minimize exposure to risk and to maintain vital business contacts. Third, the public market, which lately has been accessible to small companies, periodically dries up, as it did in the early 1970s. Indeed, the cyclical lack of money for financing results in a larger firm having more "staying power" in the face of adversity than a smaller concern. Unfortunately, even a well-managed small firm may find itself insolvent in a cash crunch.

Academics have argued that institutional investors should be able to attain the diversification benefits of investing in larger firms by buying securities of many different smaller firms. But the world does not seem to work that way when money is short. Institutions are inclined to purchase securities in large blocks, but such a large investment in smaller firms could be illiquid in a cold public market. Quite often in such a situation, the only way for a small firm to attain financing or liquidity is to sell out to another corporation.

The Merger Market and Management Incentives

The possibility of being taken over can also act as a curb on management that otherwise would not exist. In the 1930s, Adolph A. Berle and Gardiner C. Means charged that in the modern corporation ownership and control were becoming separate: The shareholders bore the financial risk but the professional managers controlled the company. With each individual investor typically owning a diversified portfolio and investing only a small portion of his net worth in a single corporation, he has little incentive to monitor management carefully. In addition, even if an investor has the motivation and the time to follow a particular company, he has little power to effect change. Rather, a dissident investor must lobby a large group of fellow shareholders in order to build a sufficient base of support to challenge management. Such an endeavor is usually very costly, especially relative to the size of the dissident investor's holdings.

From the perspective of hostile takeover proponents, the situation recognized by Berle and Means has two practical implications. First, ineffective managers have little incentive to perform and face few repercussions as a result of poor results, barring extreme crisis. Second, absent self-imposed restraint, managers have little reason to curb expensive perks. The saga of Ross Johnson is the critics' favorite. F. Ross Johnson was the flamboyant CEO of RJR Nabisco at the time it was purchased in 1989 by KKR. At shareholder expense, RJR Nabisco maintained an "air force" of corporate jets, twenty-four country club memberships, and numerous sports stars on retainer as expensive "consultants."

The presence of a strong M&A market may address these two concerns: The mere possibility that an outsider might bid for corporate control forces management to be less complacent about poor results and limit perks. Moreover, takeovers provide a vehicle to oust particularly bad management.

Shareholder Wealth Effects of Mergers

The case for mergers may also be made based on a simple dollars-and-cents analysis: Mergers put money in shareholders' pockets. Shareholders in target companies on average gain a considerable premium from selling their shares in a takeover, roughly 33 percent over the years, but varying considerably in particular years depending on the pace of the takeover market. This additional shareholder wealth could have favorable macroeconomic effects if redeployed in the marketplace through investment or spending.

On the other hand, it is possible that over time shareholders could have reaped such returns without selling out. Furthermore, if the transaction does not improve the value of the acquiring company sufficiently to justify the premium, the payment to target shareholders amounts to nothing more than a transfer of wealth from acquirer shareholders to target shareholders. If the merger results in job cuts, the acquisition premium similarly can be viewed as a wealth transfer from employees to target shareholders (at least until they find new jobs), a transfer that may not be acceptable to some.

Mergers and Economic Flexibility

Mergers also may encourage efficient allocation of economic resources. Economic circumstances change over time, creating new opportunities and making old approaches obsolete. The ability to react to these changes through mergers and acquisitions may help to keep the American economic system from becoming sclerotic. The pace and scope of change should not be underestimated: In the 1980s, for example, more than one third of all companies in the Fortune 500 were merged with other companies or taken private.

Mergers and the Capital Markets

Finally, mergers—along with stock offerings—provide an incentive to invest in new businesses, creating a mechanism to cash out of an investment. If these capital markets options were over-restricted, potential investors would likely be discouraged from starting new businesses or putting venture capital into start-ups.

Against the Tide

Mergers have long been the target of populist rancor. The outraged reaction to J.P. Morgan's turn-of-the-century U.S. Steel amalgamation was a foreshadowing of the future. One critic, Yale president and economist Arthur Hadley, argued that the continuing concentration of corporate power, if unchecked, would lead to the appearance of "an emperor in Washington within twenty-five years." *The Wall Street Journal* expressed "uneasiness" about the risky capital structure Morgan and his team had devised. "Would U.S. Steel ever be able to pay a dividend?" the newspaper wondered.

Then there were the phenomenal fees. Wall Street interests earned $57.5 million (somewhere north of $1 billion in today's dollars) for underwriting the issuance of various U.S. Steel securities. How could the mere reshuffling of corporate ownership earn so much money for so few? Unethical or dishonest practices were suspected.

Today's critics raise very similar issues. They put forward the following basic arguments:

- Mergers and acquisitions have often induced the overleveraging of corporate America, with disastrous consequences;

- Mergers and acquisitions can have destructive effects on communities;

- The premiums paid to target shareholders in corporate takeovers derive from inappropriate wealth redistribution;

- Management self-interest drives most strategic corporate acquisitions; and

- By and large, mergers destroy rather than create value and have serious social costs.

Naturally, proponents of corporate takeovers have attempted to counter these arguments.

The Overleveraging of America

According to takeover opponents, as the 1980s came to a close, America was drowning in a rising tide of speculative debt. Raiders like Carl Icahn and Boone Pickens, with the help of funds raised in the junk bond market by Michael Milken and Drexel Burnham Lambert, were making assaults on some of the largest bastions of the Fortune 500. Meanwhile, Henry Kravis and his partners at KKR were taking public companies private in highly leveraged transactions.

When the 1980s merger wave picked up steam, so did the criticism of leverage. In a newspaper editorial, investment banker Nicholas Brady, who later became secretary of the Treasury under George Bush, warned of dire consequences. Under the heading "Equity Is Lost in Junk-Bondage," Brady predicted that "speculative, highly leveraged financing techniques involving junk takeover bonds, if unchecked, will leave misery in their wake."

Corporate executives, many of whom experienced firsthand the power of leverage when threatened with takeovers, also complained, carrying out their campaign under the auspices of the Business Roundtable. Andrew Sigler, spokesman for this big business lobbying group and CEO of Champion International, called leveraged acquisitions "one of the most destructive phenomena of the twentieth century." Fred Hartley, CEO of Unocal (one of the Boone Pickens' targets), concurred: "What this all comes down to is simply withdrawing the warm blood of equity and replacing it with the cold water of debt."

The debt-based criticism of takeovers has taken hold in the public consciousness. For example, in the 1980s, Marty Lipton, the dean of takeover defense lawyers, was able to play to the grandstands with his invectives against "bust-up, junk bond deals" as management buyout specialist Ted Forstmann pilloried Henry Kravis for his leveraged acquisitions. *Fortune* magazine reached the following verdict on the "deal decade" of the 1980s:

> Too often the debt driven deals imposed suffocating interest charges and repayment schedules on once solid businesses. Scores of companies, unable to withstand this year's [1991] brief and mild recession, have defaulted in record numbers on their junk bond payments or have fled behind the shield of Chapter 11. Junk holders have watched a lot of their paper crumple in value. . . . Turning corporations into Flying Wallendas is not what the U.S. economy needs.

A few years later, a *Business Week* cover story compared the "debt-laden" leveraged buyouts of the 1980s to the "thoroughly discredited" conglomerate mergers of the 1960s. Yet a more recent 1999 *Business Week* article is decidedly pro-merger, asserting that mergers help companies achieve global scale, cut costs, and deal with overcapacity. Mergers are a market mechanism to reduce supply. Even though megamergers entail megalayoffs, the economy is creating more jobs than mergers are destroying. Yet another 1999 article expresses the worry that large companies can exert undue pressure on the government, which may not be in the interest of citizens.

Rhetoric aside, critics argue that high levels of takeover-induced indebtedness have several unattractive side effects: an increased likelihood of bankruptcy, cost cutting that displaces workers and disrupts communities, and a management focus on the short term that leads to reduced competitiveness.

Bankruptcy Effects　Former SEC chairman John Shad, before joining Drexel Burnham, stated the first criticism in a widely publicized 1984 speech: "The more leveraged takeovers and buyouts today, the more bankruptcies tomorrow." Mired in his fight with Pickens, Fred Hartley of Unocal used more apocalyptic imagery. "This speculative binge," he warned, "this chain letter, must eventually collapse, leaving wreckage of ruined companies, lost jobs, reduced U.S. oil production, failed banks and savings and loans, and government bailouts, not to mention unemployment and empty buildings." Takeovers, according to Hartley and others, allow fast-buck financiers to play high-risk games with America's big companies.

This vision proved accurate during the early 1990s. Several major companies—Federated, Macy's, Revco, TWA, among others—that had been involved in highly leveraged transactions sank into bankruptcy. Moreover, in 1991, *Fortune* magazine reviewed the status of the forty-one companies that had been featured on its "Deals of the Year" lists between 1985 and 1990. While nineteen companies had managed to pay down their debt, twenty-two were treading water or had added even more debt. One of the twenty-two had defaulted on outstanding bonds, three were in bankruptcy, two had been restructured out of court, and one was liquidated.

Yet an active merger market can also be a powerful source of economic rejuvenation. As Icahn put it during a 1985 congressional hearing, "Did any raider take over the railroads? And yet these companies had to be closed down. . . . Thousands and thousands of people, indeed a whole section of this country, has been closed down . . . not because raiders came in but because raiders did not come in." More often than not the target companies of the 1980s were troubled long before any takeover. The fact that some attempts were unsuccessful should be unsurprising.

Some academics point out that the frequency of failure, not the fact that some firms failed, should be the yardstick for measuring the

success or failure of takeovers. A few sensational failures are insufficient to discredit the entire merger movement.

The Short-Term View   Another major charge is that the need to
pay down debt incurred in mergers and takeovers has a stultifying effect that leads to reduced investment in research, development, and
capital improvements.

The American news media repeated this shibboleth throughout
the 1980s, with a *Forbes* story calling the practice "mortgaging the future." "When companies start worrying about sharks," the story
began, "practically the last thing they care about is tomorrow. As a
result, one of the first items to go in corporate restructurings is the
R&D budget."

People in the antitakeover camp label such behavior "managing
for the short term," which they identify as a major cause of America's
perceived lack of competitiveness in the 1980s. For example, Andrew
Sigler made the point for the Business Roundtable: "This kind of
game-playing imposes short-term attitudes and strategies on companies which are just the opposite of what is needed if this country is
to remain competitive."

Empirical research on capital spending and post-deal R&D is
generally inconclusive. The market price of companies that announce "strategic investments" with a projected long-term payoff appears to be slightly positive, suggesting that the market actually
rewards managing for the long term. Obviously, whole industries
such as biotech and the Internet have been spawned by the market's
belief in the value of long-term development expenditures, even if
such expenditures lead to no profit or negative profitability in the
near term.

Some studies have found measurable cuts in strategic spending
following takeovers, but the aggregate numbers were low and the definition of development is ambiguous. In fact, companies involved in
takeovers and buyouts in the 1980s tended to be in industries with

little emphasis on R&D anyway. According to an SEC study, 77 percent of the companies involved in going-private transactions during the 1980s reported no R&D spending in the prior year. Nevertheless, it is important to keep in mind that the existence of the merger market increases R&D at start-ups: Mergers are the mechanisms by which investors cash out of the venture capital process.

These arguments that debt can increase the probability of bankruptcy and encourage short-term cost slashing are less valid today than in the 1980s because most deals in the 1990s have been stock-for-stock strategic mergers. These stock-for-stock mergers involve no additional financial leverage and therefore do not involve increased bankruptcy risk or an incentive to slash costs indiscriminately. In fact, stock-for-stock mergers *increase* incentives to invest in the future, because the stock that target shareholders receive is valued by the market based on its perceived future growth prospects.

When debt is used, however, the burden of regular interest payments can force discipline upon corporate managers, compelling them to cut unnecessary costs and streamline operations. This focus on improving operations has created some of the most efficient companies in the world. For example, Safeway Stores, once an ailing industry laggard, has become a leader in the supermarket industry following a KKR takeover. Today it enjoys some of the highest operating margins and, consequently, one of the highest market valuations of any retailer.

Community Impact   Critics also point out that merging companies often results in closed plants and job cuts in an effort to reduce duplicative positions. In fact, the market rewards companies handsomely for job-reduction announcements. While such cutbacks may benefit the few investors who hold company stock, on a broader level, some find the associated social cost unacceptable. Stated in sensational fashion, mergers result in "the strip-mining of communities."

These are the concerns that animated Bartlesville, Oklahoma, during the 1984–85 fight for Phillips Petroleum. It did not matter how often Boone Pickens professed in his drawl, "I'm from Hold-enville, a little town just south of Oklahoma." Nor did it matter that he claimed to have no plans to move the company from Bartlesville. Residents remembered well what had happened at Cities Service, another Oklahoma company Pickens had targeted. The company had avoided selling out to Pickens only by agreeing to be acquired by Occidental Petroleum. In the aftermath, Cities Service's 22,500 employees had been reduced to 4,000.

Like Bartlesville, organized labor was strident in its opposition for takeovers due to its fear of job losses. Lane Kirkland of the AFL-CIO lambasted "corporate raids" as "an outrage and a bloody scandal." By his estimate, mergers cost 90,000 union members their jobs during the 1980s. Such cutbacks, merger opponents argued, often had painful collateral effects beyond the few hundred, or few thousand, jobs lost. Entire communities suffered.

The dislocations from plant closings and layoffs stuck a chord and generated political rumblings. In the 1988 presidential election, plant closings and layoffs became a political issue. Legislation was passed to require sixty days' notice for certain closings.

Beyond the personal suffering that these layoffs have caused, mergers can also result in economic turmoil for the country as a whole. Consumers who are unemployed don't have as much money to spend and therefore don't inject as much money into the economy. While this result is mitigated by the transfer of wealth from the unemployed to the target shareholders and the investment bankers and lawyers—who will in turn pump their economic gains back into the economy—it is still unclear whether such gains will "trickle down" to benefit the workers who have lost their jobs. Furthermore, merger-related job loss could result in a greater tax burden on the rest of the population due to the unemployment benefits that taxpayers must shoulder.

It is, however, true that over time unemployed workers can be re-trained and redeployed more efficiently in the economy. In theory, mergers can be a catalyst for change, as expressed in Carl Icahn's congressional testimony. Or, as Michael Jacobs puts it in his book *Short-Term America*:

> For a nation to be competitive, it is vital that labor—like capital—is deployed efficiently. Some layoffs may be appropriate if they involve nonproductive workers, or workers in nonproductive business units. In this sense, LBOs may expedite the painful but necessary process of restructuring noncompetitive or declining businesses by laying off unnecessary workers.

But retraining and redeployment has proved to be more myth than reality—at least in the short term—with most government re-training programs woefully expensive and ineffective. This is more true than ever in our increasingly high-tech world, where jobs are most easily available for the new "technocrat" class.

Some argue that the connection between mergers and unem-ployment has been exaggerated. A 1989 government study found that less than 5 percent of major layoffs were related to a change in cor-porate control. Another study found that employment actually in-creased slightly at a group of companies involved in LBOs between 1980 and 1986.

But many will counter that in the strategically motivated megadeals of the 1990s, the rationale is almost entirely synergy and cost cutting. That means layoffs. Combining companies have seen their market values shoot up by announcing just how many people they would slice from the corporate payroll. For example, it was es-timated that the combined Travelers and Citibank would lay off 8,000 workers, 5 percent of the combined workforce, shortly follow-ing the merger; and the combined Exxon and Mobil would reduce head count by 15,000. Curiously, therefore, the labor reallocation argument for mergers may be most true in boom times.

Wealth Redistribution

Critics also doubt whether takeovers in fact create wealth. Rather, critics claim, the premiums paid to target company stockholders represent a wealth transfer, not wealth creation, and have little if any social utility. In particular, critics have identified bondholders and the government (in the form of the federal treasury) as possible sources for the premiums paid to existing target shareholders. An additional possible wealth transfer—from stockholders to management—has also been singled out for concern.

Bondholders   Bondholders, and to a lesser extent preferred stockholders, complain that the premiums paid to common stockholders come at their expense if the debt owed to them is not paid off. The leveraged buyout of RJR Nabisco is perhaps the most cited example. Prior to the announcement of the deal, RJR Nabisco had outstanding A-rated investment grade bonds that were held largely by insurance companies and other institutional investors. This all changed when the deal was announced. The bonds were downgraded to BB, below investment grade, and thus became fallen angels in the lingo of the market. As a result, they lost as much as 15 percent of their value.

Naturally, RJR Nabisco's bondholders were furious at the sudden turn of events. Metropolitan Life Insurance Company—holding a paper loss of $40 million on RJR Nabisco bonds—ultimately filed suit, arguing the company implicitly promised not to act in a way so as to dramatically alter its credit rating. Metropolitan Life, however, lost the case. Some creditors began to demand provisions giving them the right to a refund of their principal upon a takeover-related downgrading, but the concept has not had widespread support. This concern is becoming increasingly less important with the stock-for-stock strategic mergers of the 1990s.

The Tax Man   The tax man is another potential victim of a negative wealth transfer, a point harped on by antitakeover politicians and critics at the height of the 1980s merger wave. Mergers, they argued, took money out of the federal and state treasuries and used it to pay premiums to stockholders and profits to dealmakers and their financial backers.

In one scenario, leveraged buyouts take advantage of the tax deductibility of interest payments. By increasing a company's debt load, a takeover can reduce the company's tax liability, sometimes to zero. But this analysis is incomplete. The target company in a cash acquisition is not the only relevant taxpayer: Individual shareholders who sell their stock and lenders receiving interest all provide offsetting tax revenue. However, in a second scenario, the tax revenue is not offset. Tax-free, pooling-of-interests transactions allow premiums to be paid to target shareholders so long as the target shareholders receive stock in the acquirer. Target shareholders pay no tax until they actually sell their stock.

The loss of tax revenue has broader social implications—including reduction in government spending programs—that affect many citizens. It can be further argued that taxes on individuals have been increased to offset the loss in corporate taxes, requiring Americans to shoulder the burden of corporations' M&A activity. On the other hand, some might argue that trickle-down effects from greater target shareholder and dealmaker wealth have offset the loss in tax revenue. The data are inconclusive on this point.

Target Stockholders to Management   In management-led takeovers or marriages, another kind of wealth transfer has been singled out as troubling—from existing shareholders to management (and any financial allies). The perceived conflict of interest inherent in management's dual role as a custodian for shareholders and as a self-interested acquirer had real vitality in the mid-1980s.

A series of mishaps have made the courts leery of management self-dealing. The colorful Ross Johnson of RJR was accused of attempting a lowball steal of the company for his LBO investor group. In the auction of Macmillan, the management leaked details of one offer to a group with which it was affiliated. But these obvious conflict problems have been addressed by case law on conflicts and the use of special committees of independent directors.

Management Self-Interest

Even in cases where managers do not have as obvious a direct economic stake in their company as a result of a management buyout, opponents argue management self-interest, not potential gains to the acquiring firm, drive most mergers. Critics argue managers do deals simply because managing a larger business provides greater prestige, as well as access to more perks, a higher salary, or a higher share price—increasing the value of their stock options.

A related hypothesis is that pride or ego causes managers to launch overpriced transactions and pay steep (and unwarranted) premiums for target companies.

Value Destruction

In perhaps the most direct attack on mergers and acquisitions, a constituency contends that takeovers simply do not make economic sense for the corporate buyer. More often than not, according to this view, mergers destroy rather than add value from the acquirer's perspective. Harvard Business School Professor Michael Porter advanced this thesis in a famous 1987 *Harvard Business Review* article. He studied the diversification strategies of thirty-three major American companies, involving acquisitions, joint ventures, and start-ups. As Porter put it, the data "paint a sobering picture." On average,

Porter's subjects divested over half their acquisitions in new industries and over 60 percent of their acquisitions in entirely new fields.

In a 1995 article entitled "The Case Against Mergers," Phillip
Zweig of *Business Week* reported the results of a similar study. *Business Week* measured the post-deal stock market performance of 150
deals from the 1990s against the S&P 500. Relative to this benchmark, half the deals reduced shareholder value, and another third
added only marginal value.

The *Los Angeles Times* reported in 1999 that of the 182 mergers
completed in 1998 valued at $1 billion or more, 40 percent saw their
closing deal value decrease from the announced value, 18 percent
saw their deal value increase, and the remainder noticed virtually no
change in value.

A recent *Fortune* article blasted most recent mergers on the basis
of EVA®—economic value added, a popular method for measuring
return on investment. The article estimated the market's growth expectations for various acquirers based on their cost of capital and
contrasted those rates with the growth rates required to break even
on their acquisitions. The authors of the article were skeptical that
mergers could generate the additional growth compelled by the premiums paid.

By way of contrast, many studies show acquiring companies
breaking even on mergers in terms of stock price.

But all of these studies are in some way misleading. First, the
benefits of most deals are long-term, not immediate, and the markets
might not reflect these benefits immediately in stock prices. Second,
while some deals have led to declines in acquirer stock prices, it is
unclear what would have happened to acquirers that didn't undertake the transactions. Might their stock prices have dropped even
further? The market provides no control group against which to test
hypotheses. The group of companies that is often supposed to act as
a control group—such as the S&P 500, for example—is distorted because it includes the takeover candidates themselves in its sampling.

Third, the size of the deal relative to the company purchasing is key. Equity deals require some time for shares to be redistributed. Larger deals take more time. Fourth, acquirer stock prices at the time of or shortly before the deal announcements may *already* have included an assumption of deal-related growth. Therefore, stock price movement around the time of the deal announcement could be unrelated to the deal itself.

More fundamentally, the problem with many academic studies is that they make questionable assumptions to squeeze untidy data points into a pristine statistical model. For example, the assumption that the sale of an acquired company makes the original purchase a bad deal is misguided. Many acquirers exist to buy and sell companies—and make money in the process—including the diversified conglomerates, financial buyers, and the companies they control.

After the Transaction: The Integration

What happens after the transaction will likely depend on the success with which the acquirer and the target integrate their operations. It is from this integration process that the vaunted synergies arise—the reductions in unnecessary head count and the sharing of "best practices"—and therefore the creation of shareholder wealth. It is difficult to generalize about whether mergers and acquisitions build shareholder value because whether or not the acquirer and target successfully integrate depends so much on management vision, foresight, and cooperation.

The challenges acquirers face are as varied as the nature of the business that are acquired. Sometimes, the initial transition is smooth and the follow-through clear. However, surprises do crop up, as the Union Pacific Railroad discovered in its $3.9 billion acquisition of the Southern Pacific Rail Corporation.

In 1997, trouble integrating the two railroads' computer systems and other operational snafus slowed traffic on Union Pacific's tracks to a crawl. Rail cars destined for Kentucky ended up in Mexico. The company, the nation's largest railroad, could not locate other cars for weeks on end, a situation which ultimately required the government to step in and force open part of Union Pacific's system to competitors. The company meanwhile struggled to clear up the difficulties.

Different types of acquirers also have different goals for their purchased companies. Financial buyers focus on financial performance and the broad strategic sweep of the business, with day-to-day management left to operating executives. Strategic acquirers, however, tend to take a more hands-on approach. These acquirers may have premised their purchase price on the realization of synergies. Post-closing integration therefore is crucial to success.

BACK FROM THE BRINK

Ted Forstmann Flies Gulfstream

When a buyout hits bumps, financial buyers necessarily must take a more active role. Forstmann Little's investment in Gulfstream illustrates the advantage of stamina and vision.

Forstmann Little bought Gulfstream, a maker of corporate jets, in 1990 in an $850 million management buyout led by Gulfstream CEO Allen Paulson. Forstmann Little and management invested $100 million of equity, while Gulfstream took on $750 million of debt, much of it provided by Forstmann Little's mezzanine debt fund.

The early years of the buyout were rocky. Almost immediately after the deal closed, the economy slumped, and the bottom fell out of the corporate jet market. Gulfstream hit a wall in 1993 with a $275 million loss. Ted Forstmann lost confidence in Paulson, and Gulfstream touched the brink of bankruptcy, coming within a few weeks of defaulting on its bank loans.

Yet Forstmann did not turn away from Gulfstream. He instead took over the company chairmanship and plunged headfirst into

Gulfstream's daily operations. The first order of business was to stanch the bleeding: Forstmann hired new financial and operations people who restructured operations and cut costs. At the same time, he converted the $450 million in subordinated debt held by his fund into preferred stock that would not require current cash payments.

Forstmann also renewed his commitment to Gulfstream's ongoing project to develop a new long-distance business jet. Forstmann had conceived of the plan to build a Gulfstream V model, but now saw the project as the key to the company's survival. Competitors were working on similar prototypes and the first to market would gain valuable market share.

Today, Gulfstream has soared back to profitability. The $800 million G-V program has turned out a leading-edge plane which Forstmann's tenacity and foresight allowed the company to bring to market at the end of 1996—well ahead of a comparable product from competitor Bombardier. Sales are up, helped along by personal calls from Forstmann and other high-profile members of the Gulfstream board he assembled.

The strong results allowed Forstmann Little to raise $1 billion in a 1996 Gulfstream IPO and, ultimately, to sell the company to General Dynamics for $4.6 billion in 1999.

Post-Closing Implementation

Businesses are complex and unique. There is no by-the-numbers approach that will ensure successful post-deal implementation. Attention to four basic rules, however, can go a long way toward avoiding major problems.

At the outset, it is important to have a good strategic concept of the deal, grounded in industry fundamentals. Post-deal management is made much easier if a clear vision is defined as part of the acquisition process. Furthermore, the vision should be fleshed out to the level of specific operating directives. Once the deal closes, a further review of the business from the inside can then be followed up with rapid implementation.

The second rule feeds off the first: Studies show that intense post-deal implementation is more successful than a slower process. Major strategic and operational changes should be made in the first six months after the deal closes because in that period the acquirer has the traction to make changes. Managers and employees can be focused on new initiatives. After about six months, the newness wears thin, and change becomes far more difficult.

Given the importance of fast and decisive action, acquirers that provide strong leadership are the most successful. Top management can come from within the target or from the outside, but in either case, the presence of a focused and able executive team with the firm backing of the acquirer is necessary to implement the strategy. Because the first few months are so critical, having executives in place at the outset is absolutely critical.

Finally, if the strategic and operational framework is indeed defined before the acquisition, operating executives should be involved early in the process. These are the individuals who know the industry and may be the same people charged with implementing the strategy. Therefore, it makes sense that they be involved in defining the future path.

Of course, these are just rules of thumb. Volumes have been written on the topic of acquisition management and scores of management consultants are in the business of providing assistance. The point is that the follow-up on a deal can be as determinative of success as the deal itself.

But management that is too strong can also pose problems for the newly integrated company. A case in point is the acquisition of Morgan Grenfell, a British merchant banking firm, by Deutsche Bank in 1989. The deal was regarded universally as a failure because

Deutsche was not sensitive to Morgan Grenfell's decentralized management structure. Instead, Deutsche pulled management authority back to Frankfurt from London and the departure of many of the Morgan Grenfell rainmakers followed. Some analysts wonder if the same fate will befall DaimlerChrysler. Due to pay disparities between Chrysler and Daimler-Benz, it is possible that an American manager working in Germany might end up reporting to a German manager who earns half his salary. If former Chrysler executives' pay were cut, managers could depart to other U.S. automakers; yet is it likely that DaimlerChrysler will increase the pay for German executives across the board?

The lesson to be learned is that acquirers must be sensitive to the acquired firm's culture and must integrate it successfully with its own—easier said than done and often called impossible by industry analysts. Yet for all the talk about "clashing cultures," many deals have proved to be home runs. The merger of Dean Witter and Morgan Stanley is a prime example. Many questioned how a white-shoe investment bank—whose employees were known for their high pay packages—and a retail brokerage could combine. Yet today the bank is one of the strongest financial institutions on Wall Street, weathering the shocks of the markets well.

Technical integration also presents a challenge for merging companies. The marriage of Wells Fargo and First Interstate was a disaster because the two banks did not successfully integrate their computer systems. Depositors were unable to access their deposits and a customer service fiasco ensued, giving a bad name to the new institution and to mergers in general. Thousands of customers left, and Wells Fargo's stock took a beating in the market. Information technology is not easy to integrate, a fact the market easily forgets in its awe over multibillion cost saving figures.

Lack of management cooperation can also cause deals to go awry. The 1998 megamerger of Travelers with Citigroup had the best of initial publicity. Yet disagreements at the top soon led to the ousting of

Jamie Dimon, president of Travelers and co-CEO of Salomon Smith Barney. As of late, management disagreements have killed deals before they have even gotten off the ground. The proposed merger between American Home Products and Monsanto, for example, died because neither CEO was willing to cede control.

Part of the fault lies with the market, which focuses on the deal but rarely the post-deal integration. Companies also often underestimate the difficulty of melding two different cultures, two different information systems, or two different egos into one coherent institution.

Although these stories, like many of the arguments made against mergers, are sensationalized, post-merger planning is going to become increasingly important in the digital age.

Thoughts on the Debate

Many, if not most, companies bought eventually do get resold, a fairly startling thought and perhaps the most searing indictment of the critics of mergers. My favorite example is Entenmann's Bakery, which my partner Bill Lambert has worked on four times. Lambert, whose career has centered on creating acquisition ideas for clients, figured that the New York City–centered regional specialty bakery, known for its chocolate donuts, could use the help of a major corporation to push for national expansion. Furthermore, the owners were aging and might be willing to sell. Bill first represented Warner-Lambert, then a food and drug company, in buying Entenmann's.

Then Warner-Lambert decided to focus on drugs, and Bill sold Entenmann's to General Foods. Bill later represented Philip Morris when they bought General Foods, including Entenmann's. Philip Morris eventually decided to exit the baked goods business, and Bill worked on selling Entenmann's to its proud, new buyer, CPC International spin-off Bestfoods.

Each time Entenmann's was sold, the company increased in

value and quality. This churning of assets was not necessarily "bad," but rather reflective of the changing strategic needs of its acquirer and the adaptability of the American corporation.

The criticisms of mergers were much more stinging in the late 1980s than the mid-1990s. When the stock market is high and defaults low, much of the attack withers. Even the anecdotal evidence shrivels into the dustbin of history. Of course, there is also some learning from experience. Managers are increasingly motivated by their own stock price and are, therefore, unlikely to make an imprudent deal merely for the sake of empire. Leverage in deals has subsided, with the markets unwilling to let debt-to-equity ratios climb as high as in the 1980s, and some have learned the lesson of the mismatched book—borrowing all short-term against the acquisition of long-term assets.

Of course, there is no guarantee for companies that attempt to move with the times, but there is a virtual certainty that those who rely on the past will fail. One of the envies of foreign companies and, especially, government-owned companies is the speed at which American businesses can change. There is both a silliness in the pace of change and a glory, a crudeness and a marvelous flexibility. It is quintessentially part of the American economic experiment.

Part Two | # The Strategic Challenge

"Everything in strategy is very simple, but that does not mean that everything is very easy."

—Carl von Clausewitz, *On War*

The Strategic | 8
Dilemma

After a dramatic decline in the late 1980s, M&A activity has exploded in recent years. Each of the last five years has seen a record dollar volume of announced deals. In the aggregate, between the start of 1993 and mid-1999, more than $7 trillion of corporate assets changed hands. As a result, the 1990s will be remembered as the fifth merger wave of the twentieth century.

However, M&A trends in the 1990s have been different from those in previous decades. Going-private transactions have decreased from 27 percent of all M&A transactions in 1988 to less than 3 percent in 1998, and major hostile takeover attempts have declined from forty-six in 1988 to twenty-seven in 1998.

Strategic buyers have been driving M&A activity in the 1990s. Corporate managers view acquisitions and mergers as critical tools to position their companies for success in the face of their industry's competitive dynamics. The resulting strategic combinations have been both horizontal, as in the banking and health care industries, and vertical, as in the media business, but rarely diversifying.

Globalization has been another trend in 1990s deals. Many of the decade's most prominent combinations have been cross-border transactions: BP's acquisition of Amoco and ARCO, Daimler's merger with Chrysler, Deutsche Bank's purchase of Bankers Trust, Vodafone's merger with AirTouch, Deutsche Telekom's failed deal with Telecom Italia, and LMVH's attempted bid for Gucci. This pattern will continue to accelerate.

TEN LARGEST DEALS OF THE 1990s

Rank	Acquirer	Target	Approximate Deal Value (Billions)	Year Announced
1.*	MCI WorldCom Inc.	Sprint Corp.**	$129	1999
2.*	Exxon Corp.	Mobile Corp.	$86	1998
3.	Travelers Group	Citicorp	$73	1998
4.*	SBC Communications Inc.	Ameritech Corp.	$72	1998
5.*	Bell Atlantic Corp.	GTE Corp.	$71	1998
6.	AT&T Corp.	Tele-Communications Inc.**	$70	1999
7.	Vodafone Group PLC	AirTouch Communications	$66	1999
8.*	AT&T Corp.	MediaOne Group	$63	1999
9.	NationsBank Corp.	BankAmerica Corp.	$62	1998
10.	British Petroleum Co. PLC	Amoco Corp.	$55	1998

Source: Securities Data Corporation, as of October 6, 1999. Starred deals are pending. Deal Value includes debt assumed by acquirer.
**Includes valuation of tracking share units.

Finally, deals in the 1990s have been some of the largest combinations ever. The ten largest mergers and acquisitions in history were announced in 1998 and 1999 alone. Furthermore, the 1990s saw the recombination of five pieces of Standard Oil into BP Amoco ARCO and Exxon-Mobil as well as the combinations of five of the Baby Bells: SBC-Ameritech (pending), Bell Atlantic–NYNEX, and a contested match between upstarts Qwest and Global Crossing for Baby Bell US West.

The merger wave of the 1990s parallels the boom at the turn of the century. In both periods, business was rocked by fundamental shifts in the business environment. The late nineteenth century was the brink of the industrial age, the managers groped for the appropriate strategic platform, the model of a successful industrial company. Now, companies are scrambling in a search for a post-industrial model appropriate to the digital age.

In this new environment, strategic thinking is the driver. Managers struggle with fundamental issues, such as how to compete in a world where the South Koreans can bend metal cheaper. After several lean years of downsizing and cost cutting, companies are now seeking to increase revenues and earnings in the face of low U.S. population growth. "What kind of company do we want to be?" is the essential question.

The specifics driving each deal are different, but there is a common pattern to the process. Existing business strategies and structures ossify over time. These structures may survive for some period with the protection of systemic inertia, but eventually external catalysts give a sharp jolt to the system. Outmoded practices become apparent and limiting to success. Mergers and acquisitions, a kind of rough-hewn evolutionary mechanism, then are undertaken as companies react to the new business realities. The companies with the greatest foresight may recognize these industry changes sooner than the rest and become the consolidation leaders in their industry. Initial transactions often spark a consolidation wave among their competitors who don't want to be disadvantaged.

With a booming stock market, many financial buyers have concluded that the mechanical application of financial leverage will not guarantee satisfactory returns on their money. By adopting the strategic LBO model, financial buyers have expanded the range of potential acquisition targets. Stable, no-growth enterprises are no longer the primary target; indeed, very few of these pieces of "low-hanging fruit" still exist after the financial buyers' acquisition sprees of the 1980s and 1990s. Instead, there is a new interest in finding promising companies with the potential for revenue growth.

For example, Forstmann Little in 1990 acquired General Instrument, a maker of cable set-top boxes and other electronics, because Ted Forstmann saw the company as a growth play. He believed technological advances—primarily the shift to digital systems—would greatly expand the market for General Instrument's products. However, the company would need to make a major investment in new technology to serve this market. Compared to the 1980s deals, in which capital expenditures were trimmed substantially after the takeover, the General Instrument deal was a break from the LBO norm.

The Strategic Dilemma

Regulatory change, technological change, fluctuations in financial markets, scale, and the role of leadership propel the dynamics of corporate transformation. What is a company's strategic dilemma and how should it be addressed? How should resources be deployed? Success depends on managing in the face of these uncertainties. This is the core of the merger business: the development of a sound and executable corporate strategy at a justifiable price.

Most companies face significant dilemmas in the evolution of their objectives. Buggy whips, sewing machines, slide rules, typewriters, adding machines—at different times, the manufacture of each of these products represented a strong, attractive business. Yet technological volatility changed the competitive landscape practically overnight. The products slipped into obsolescence and manufacturers were forced to react.

We live in a world of risks, contradictions, and limited resources. Making the tough strategic choices with consistent tactical follow-up is the province of good management. Ambling along, oblivious of the need for change, is a prescription for trouble; inconsistency between strategy and tactics brings a fiasco.

The problems that constrain a company's growth can be described with a Rosen's Cube, named after our senior international partner, Jeffrey Rosen, who innovated work on the link between strategy and mergers. The three-dimensional Rosen's Cube shows a company inside the box anxious to burst out and achieve growth, but constrained by external limitations and its resources. Breaking through the box of constraints is the obsession of top management. To do so requires taking a calculated but disciplined risk on one or more of the six barriers.

In 1998, Daimler-Benz faced a strategic dilemma: Mercedes cars were reaching the limit of their market potential. Traditional markets were mature and quickly becoming saturated, and the company's cars were too expensive for customers in developing countries. Furthermore, the automaker had no minivan and was only just beginning to sell an SUV. Remaining a niche player could cause Mercedes to lose its competitive edge in new technology, such as airbags or ABS. While at one time Mercedes was the only carmaker offering such technology, mass-market automobile makers were beginning to catch up. Suppliers, who before had granted Daimler exclusive use of new technologies, were becoming increasingly reluctant to do so for more than a short time, desiring a faster return on their investment. Other attempts at diversification away from autos had been ill-fated and had to be dismantled.

But Daimler's problem was a circular one. Daimler had difficulty growing its revenues because its cars were too expensive for yet-untapped markets; but its cars were so expensive, at least in part, because its small production base did not afford it the economies of scale enjoyed by larger carmakers such as Honda or GM. (Of course, the other reason for the high price of Mercedes cars was to maintain a prestige brand image.) To survive into the twenty-first century, Daimler needed to broaden its product base to appeal to a wider demographic in such a way that it would not dilute the brand image of Mercedes cars. Yet to do so would require enormous capital investment in new production lines and dealer networks—money that would have to be recouped through high automobile sticker prices, which would in turn narrow Daimler's potential customer base. Daimler did try to branch into the smaller-car market with its A-Class, but the car quite literally proved a flop when it rolled over in a "moose test." Unless this circular dilemma could be resolved, Mercedes would have few prospects to grow its profits and would have difficulty investing in new technology—unless it raised the prices on its existing cars even further.

In other words, Daimler faced the following Rosen's Cube:

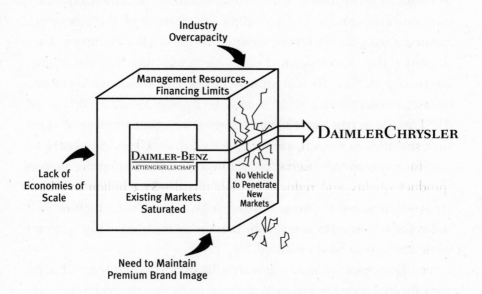

Chrysler too faced its own strategic dilemma. In fact, Chrysler's history was particularly volatile. Things first came to a head in 1981, when the U.S. Treasury had to bail out the insolvent carmaker. Subsequently, during his tenure in the 1980s, Lee Iacocca turned the automaker around, concentrating on minivans, pickups, and sport utility vehicles. But then things began to head south. Iacocca diversified into aerospace, buying Gulfstream in the mid-1980s, only to sell the company a few years later when profits had deteriorated. In 1994, build quality began to decline after four years of improvement, and *Consumer Reports* blasted Chrysler for the poor reliability of its most popular models, such as its Jeep Grand Cherokee and its Dodge Intrepid. But even more problematic, earnings dropped because customers had begun to buy less expensive models.

As the smallest U.S. carmaker, with insignificant operations overseas, Iacocca tried to forge alliances with foreign automakers like Volkswagen and Fiat to gain bulk—but to no avail.

In 1990, when Robert Eaton succeeded Iacocca as CEO of Chrysler, the automaker was again near collapse. Eaton effected a second transformation of the company, and by 1994 Chrysler had turned a $3.7 billion profit. Yet still, as the smallest U.S. carmaker, Chrysler had fewer production units over which to spread ever-increasing R&D costs and capital expenditure, making it a relatively less-efficient operator.

Then came the dilemma of shareholder agitation. In April 1995, investor Kirk Kerkorian, 13.6 percent owner of Chrysler, launched a bid for the company. Kerkorian wanted Chrysler to improve its poor product quality and reduce its cash hoard—$7.3 billion in March 1995—that should have gone to stockholders. Not insignificantly, Chrysler was also trading at about a third of the average market multiple at the time of the bid. Kerkorian embarked upon a plan to take over the company from the inside and to oust Chrysler's "ultraconservative financial management."

In the end, Kerkorian's agitation led Chrysler to agree to buy back $3 billion of its stock over a two-year period. Kerkorian also gained a board seat and implemented corporate governance policy changes allowing fully financed buyers to make an offer for more than 15 percent of Chrysler's stock without triggering its poison pill. In return, Kerkorian's stake in Chrysler was limited to 13.6 percent.

Chrysler's basic strategic dilemmas remained: It had virtually no presence in Europe, lacked penetration in the luxury car market, was overly dependent on two products—minivans and Jeeps—and was run by an aging management team. If those two types of automobiles were to go out of fashion, Chrysler would again flop. In fact, by the second quarter of 1997, that is what seemed to be happening. Sales of its most popular vehicles—Jeeps, Dodge Rams, and Jeep Grand Cherokees—were slipping. Furthermore, the company's U.S. market share slipped to 14.6 percent from 16.5 percent a year before.

By 1997, the industry had become plagued by overcapacity. Chrysler's goal of 20 percent sales growth per year now seemed overly aggressive given the saturated U.S. market. Furthermore, Daimler's market share was being eroded by mass-market brands which had launched higher-end models, such as Toyota's Lexus line and Honda's Acura line. Daimler chairman Juergen Schrempp placed a call to Chrysler chairman Robert Eaton.

While the deal provided a solution to both Daimler's and Chrysler's strategic dilemmas, it also marked the end of Chrysler as an institution. Despite protestations from Chrysler's publicity department, the deal was really a takeover of Chrysler by Daimler. The deal was pitched to the public, however, as a marriage of equals, a combination to create a truly cross-border company. Dual headquarters in Auburn Hills, Michigan, and Stuttgart, Germany, were symbolic. A new global share that would trade freely and with a minimum of transaction costs on both the Frankfurt and New York stock exchanges was also designed so as to make the company an attractive investment to both Germans and Americans.

It has become increasingly clear that DaimlerChrysler is really a German company. The global share was excluded from the S&P 500 index because DaimlerChrysler's ownership is 58 percent German. This exclusion exacerbated the disparity in ownership because U.S. S&P 500 index funds were forced to sell the stock. Management power also flowed to Stuttgart. Many Chrysler managers left on their own, and some were paid off to leave. The deal is a sign of the times: In an increasingly global economy, it is possible that the pride of a country may land in the hands of a foreign acquirer.

Daimler was able to assume the upper hand because at the time of the deal, Chrysler was valued at approximately 8 times earnings, while Daimler was valued at more than 18 times. Daimler had the much bigger market capitalization and was playing the 1960s P/E game—buying on the cheap with its high-flying stock.

The consummation of the $41 billion deal on November 12, 1998, marked the creation of the third-largest automaker in the world in terms of revenue and the biggest acquisition of an American company by a foreign buyer at the time.

PROFILE

Juergen Schrempp

Juergen Schrempp has earned the reputation as one of Germany's most aggressive managers. Becoming chairman of Daimler-Benz in 1994, Schrempp began to address the issues plaguing the company. He restructured Daimler's nonauto business and stripped Mercedes of its traditional independence by eliminating its separate board of directors and removing its chairman, Helmut Werner. When he took over, Daimler posted a $3.45 billion operating loss. The next year, Schrempp helped the company turn a profit.

In many ways, Schrempp seems more like a tough American CEO than a traditional German company chairman. Having cut head office staff by 75 percent, he has been quoted as saying: "You have to sweep the stairs from the top down." Schrempp set an aggressive goal of 12 percent return on capital for each division and whittled the company down to twenty-three units from thirty-five.

Schrempp has enjoyed a lifelong career at Daimler, starting out as a mechanic at a Mercedes-Benz dealership in southern

Germany. Subsequently, he left his job to pursue an engineering degree at a technical college, and after graduation returned to work at Daimler's head office in Stuttgart. From there, he held a number of jobs within the company, including as a local board member for engineering in Daimler's South African subsidiary, the manager of the Euclid heavy trucks subsidiary in Cleveland, head of the Deutsche Aerospace division—securing him a board seat—and finally, chairman.

Schrempp is a colorful character. A chain smoker, Schrempp also consumes vast amounts of mineral water each day—"for his health." He is a jazz trumpeter who taught himself to play without reading music and is an avid mountain climber. Friends and business associates remark at his seemingly boundless energy.

Schrempp has been praised for his focus on the bottom line and building shareholder value. At Aerospace, he trimmed 40,000 workers. Mercedes-Benz also eliminated 40,000 jobs between 1991 and 1995. Unlike many top CEOs, he is remarkably willing to admit mistakes. After buying Fokker, the Netherlands-based regional aircraft manufacturer, in 1993, Schrempp sold the company in 1996, unable to improve its performance. He has proved willing to pull the plug on projects that have the support of other executives and pushes his employees to achieve. Observers have admired his decisive action. Indeed, Schrempp is a self-styled German Jack Welch of GE.

While detractors wonder whether Schrempp will be able to integrate Daimler with Chrysler, industry observers seem to trust in his visionary leadership and cunning. Meanwhile, Schrempp thinks he outnegotiated the Americans.

The corporate cultures of Daimler and Chrysler were very different, making integration a potentially daunting task. Daimler was run as a conglomerate with twenty-three separate businesses, whereas

Chrysler was run as a highly centralized operation. Daimler has been known as a conservative and slow-moving corporation, whereas Chrysler prides itself on making decisions quickly and bringing new vehicles to maket in short order.

The former Daimler operations will benefit from Chrysler's immense dealer network, its experience selling cars in the United States, and distribution network; former Chrysler operations will gain logistical aid in Europe from Daimler, which will use its existing relationships to help Chrysler gain dealerships on the Continent. Daimler's fuel cell and diesel technologies will also be shared with Chrysler.

Both the Daimler and Chrysler operations will also benefit from the economies of scale they did not previously enjoy as smaller-volume producers. Purchasing synergies will likely account for $500 million in savings in 1999, rising to $1.5 billion in 2001. Despite the logistical difficulties of merging a German company with a U.S. concern, Daimler was able to break through its Rosen's Cube.

Strategic Models

Of course, there is no magic answer that will point a company in the right strategic direction. Giving advice on corporate strategy is an increasingly crowded cottage industry teeming with gurus of the moment. Old models regularly lose favor, and new ones gain faddish popularity. Fundamentally, though, all the models merely formalize the attempt to arrive at common sense.

Four of the more popular theories are:

- The McKinsey Formulation
- The Boston Consulting Group Model
- Michael Porter's Five Forces
- Hamel and Prahalad's Core Competencies

Each of these models has been ascendant in a different era and, at least in part, results from a different definition of strategy. Peter

Drucker, for example, defines strategy as the theory of the business, while Michael Porter describes it as "the creation of a unique and valuable position." Different definitions of strategy have led to different objectives and thus different theories. McKinsey's concepts were innovations in the Kennedy years. The Boston Consulting Group Model came to prominence during the conglomerate boom of the late 1960s. Michael Porter introduced his Five Forces in a seminal 1980 book. Hamel and Prahalad popularized their strategic concepts in the early 1990s. In each case, I don't purport to do them justice as they would express their concepts, just to summarize their gut impact on CEO thinking.

The McKinsey Formulation Company after company has brought in teams from McKinsey and learned the golden rule of corporate strategy: He who rules makes the gold. The leading companies in the leading industries will make more money and are, therefore, more attractive acquisitions. Of course, adding to market share is also encouraged because greater power yields higher profitability.

The obvious problem with this analysis is that it doesn't encourage investment in emerging industries and does not address the price one should pay for a company or the feasibility of merging with the best companies. McKinsey's lack of practicality spawned the corporate guru industry and created a vacuum for investment bankers to assert a wider expertise as "practical" strategists.

The Boston Consulting Group Model The Boston Consulting Group Model attacks the nondynamic nature of the McKinsey Formulation. It is really an amalgamation of three different but inextricably related ideas: the experience curve, the product life cycle, and portfolio balance. The experience curve theory maintains that as the total historical volume of output produced by a company increases, unit costs decline geometrically. Hence, the company with the most historical output should have the lowest unit cost. If the relationship holds, companies presumably should target early market entry and price products to maximize volume.

The product life cycle is a model for industry evolution. According to this view, each product or business line goes through four stages: development, growth, maturity, and decline. The first two phases are marked by strong sales growth and low barriers to entry. In the later phases, entry becomes more costly and difficult as market participants move down the experience curve and volume growth slows. Once the business enters decline, unprofitable or marginally profitable firms are squeezed by falling prices and volume, sparking consolidation. Thus, high market share leads to higher production volumes, lower production costs, and higher profits.

The model dictates that a successful company should hold a portfolio of products with different growth rates and different market shares—the portfolio balance theory. Both high-quality and low-growth operations are necessary because their cash flow characteristics are synergistic: Low-growth operations that produce high cash flow can be used to fund the investment needed to build market share for companies that produce little cash but have the potential for a high level of future growth. High market share will translate into higher margins and the ability to generate cash. But the cash generated by slow-growing cash cows should not be reinvested into those businesses because to do so would depress returns and would produce little or no profit or cash benefit.

The Boston Consulting Group Model classifies companies this way:

- Cash Cows: Mature, slow-growth companies that generate cash in excess of their cost of operations
- Dogs: Companies with low market share and slow growth and thus no cash generation abilities; they are best liquidated

- Problem Children: Require more cash than they generate; cash must be supplied, or they will turn into dogs
- Stars: High-market-share, high-growth companies; nearly always report profits but may require cash investment; when reinvestment needs diminish, will become cash cows

Therefore, conceptually, portfolio balance theory is related to movements along the product life cycle. These theories were the intellectual foundation for conglomerate activity and rationalize the corporate churning of an asset portfolio. Of course, this approach was widely discredited in popular opinion when conglomerates crashed.

Michael Porter's Five Forces   In his strategic model, Michael Porter blasts his predecessors for being too diffuse and not focusing on a company's specific competitive environment. For Porter, the environment is defined by Five Forces: rivalry among competitors, substitute products, potential entry, bargaining power of suppliers, and bargaining power of buyers. The stronger each factor is in a particular industry, the more intense competition will be. Because the mix and relative strength of these forces vary by industry, strategy has to be tailored to the circumstances.

Porter places particular emphasis on three of the forces: 1) the threat posed to existing market participants by industry competitors, 2) potential entrants, and 3) product substitutes, all of which can erode a company's strategic position dramatically. Strong rivalry, usually the most powerful of the Five Forces, is caused by factors such as a plethora of firms of equal size and capability, slow market growth, low cost for customers to switch brands, high industry exit costs, and high payoffs to successful strategic moves, among others. Second, high barriers to entry lessen competitive forces and make industry players more profitable. But the irony of potential entry is that those industries that are most attractive to enter are those that cannot be entered because of high barriers to entry. Third, close product substitutes put a ceiling on how much firms in a particular industry can charge for a good.

Powerful bargaining positions enjoyed by suppliers to a company and buyers from a company can also place pressure on a firm's competitive outlook. For example, customers may be able to dictate pricing in a saturated industry, whereas the reverse may be true in an industry dominated by a few major players.

Porter agrees that there are two basic types of competitive advantages a firm can possess: low cost or product differentiation. Which advantage a given firm possesses will determine which of three strategies a company chooses to achieve "above-average" performance: cost leadership, differentiation, or focus. But companies must choose one of these three generic strategies because being all things to all people is a recipe for disaster.

Hamel and Prahalad's Core Competencies   Gary Hamel and C.K. Prahalad have popularized the concept that corporate strategy should attempt to exploit a company's core competencies to achieve its goals. In their view, strategy should be about stretching to shift industry structure, or to develop an entirely new industry.

However, any expansion activity should be grounded in a firm understanding of a company's limited core competencies or bundles of skills, a constraint that has favored the more focused strategic deals of the 1990s and the divestiture of the excess baggage of 1960s diversification.

A company's core competency should not, however, be defined too narrowly. If a buggy whip company defines its competence as making really good whips, it will be out of business when the buggy disappears. Perhaps the business is better defined as the manufacture of small hand tools. Or maybe the focus should instead be on the company's branding power. The problem is that a good slide rule maker is not necessarily a competitive personal computer manufacturer. Core competencies must be defined taking into account the expertise and strengths of the company. Mere strategy alone—empty words—cannot effect a transformation. Nevertheless, the theory espouses constant organizational self-renewal through learning. General Electric has been highly successful in adopting a variant of this approach.

Practical Reality

Each of these approaches has obvious elements of insight and can help a company both conceptualize its strategic dilemma and determine a solution. In the 1980s and 1990s, many of these solutions came in the form of mergers and acquisitions activity. Depending on the market environment and the specific industry dynamics, each theory has its place.

The practical reality, however, is that the phenomenal bull market of the past decade has acted as a wide safety net for strategic acquirers. Whether or not these strategies helped companies achieve success—or whether companies implemented them at all—is unclear, as assets across a wide spectrum of industries generally have appreciated: Tenacity and a rising stock market cure many ills. The risk for the future may be the impact of buying at a cyclical peak. Indeed, most CEOs do not take as formal an approach to strategic planning as their academic counterparts.

Many companies in the oil, financial services, media and telecommunications, and health care industries faced strategic dilemmas in the 1980s and 1990s punctuated by changes in technology and in the regulation of global markets. Firms have relied on mergers and acquisitions to break through their Rosen's Cubes. As a result, leading companies have undergone frenzied reshuffling of assets in a short time span and have repeatedly redefined themselves to adapt to their rapidly changing environments and to find the next growth concept. This section describes the strategic context of this journey for many of the key industries driving our economy.

The Energy Wars: 9
Globalization Reigns

*"We're eyeball to eyeball,
and I think the other fellow just blinked."*

—Secretary of State Dean Rusk
on the Cuban Missile Crisis

On a hot day in August 1998, two companies that had been sep-arated for eighty-seven years announced their plan to recom-bine.

The former Standard Oil of Ohio and Indiana—British Petro-leum and Amoco—were to form one of the world's largest companies ranked by both net income and petrochemical sales and would sell 12 percent of the gasoline used in the United States.

The deal was the brainchild of Sir John Browne, chief executive of British Petroleum. After engineering a turnaround of the once-ailing company, Browne made BP a global leader. His remarkable coup, a takeover of Amoco, would add size, scope, and allow for massive cost reductions. What resulted was Britain's largest public company and the largest ever foreign takeover of a U.S. company— surpassing DaimlerChrysler in transaction value.

The combination made compelling strategic sense. Browne pounced on Amoco when crumbling crude prices and the increasing risks of global exploration had cracked the resolve of Amoco's management. They wanted out, and Browne, who had prepared for the cyclical downturn, was ready to jump on the historic opportunity.

The strengths and weaknesses of the two companies complement each other perfectly. BP currently has twice Amoco's crude oil production capability, while Amoco has twice BP's natural gas production. Amoco is the world's third-largest polypropylene producer but is not a producer of polyethylene; conversely, BP produces polyethylene but not polypropylene.

Sir John has been quick to reduce costs at the former Amoco in order to bring the company up to industry-standard profitability-per-employee levels. At least $2 billion in cost cuts have already been specifically identified and virtually none of the former Amoco top management remains. As the joke in London states, one pronounces BP Amoco with a silent Amoco.

Browne recognized the strategic advantage to being the first mover and had the vision to create a leading oil company for the twenty-first century. As in the 1980s, macro factors in the oil industry were a significant force driving merger activity in 1998. The oil business was once again in dire straits, with prices at about half the levels they were the year before, down from $20 per barrel to $11 per barrel. The drop in oil prices could be explained by two factors: a warmer winter than usual and economic recession in Asia that lowered demand. OPEC, which for years had acted to prop up oil prices by lowering production, was becoming increasingly reluctant to do so. Now controlling only 40 percent of the oil market, OPEC realized that its efforts to increase oil prices could easily be undermined by major non-OPEC producers like Russia: non-OPEC producers could fill the void left by OPEC's production cutbacks and increase production, thereby stealing market share from OPEC, and causing no increase in oil price.

Furthermore, the oil industry's continuing push to explore in further and further away places—offshore, in rain forests, and in the Arctic—had driven up exploration costs and risks considerably. It seemed as if only the largest companies would be able to afford exploration in the future. For example, Mobil was unable to match Royal Dutch/Shell's offer to build a pipeline in Turkmenistan for $1 billion or more.

In the face of lowered oil prices and higher exploration costs, U.S. oil companies—higher-cost producers than their OPEC counterparts—were further encouraged to reduce costs. The weaker companies—Amoco, Mobil, and ARCO—were also encouraged to seek healthier partners. Amoco and ARCO ended up with BP. Mobil is to partner with Exxon. The possibility that OPEC producers might reverse their historical strategy and begin to compete for market share by flooding the market with oil made the situation even more dire.

With the weaker companies feeling the pressure, the strategic-minded larger companies had the advantage. Oil company valuations were no longer low enough that companies could buy oil on the cheap on Wall Street; but mergers represented an opportunity to cut costs and make Big Oil more competitive. Becoming bigger would also allow companies to spread exploration risk over a great number of projects—akin to diversifying a stock portfolio. Even giant companies like Exxon and Mobile were finding increasing size imperative—especially when competing with state-owned titans such as Saudi Aramco, Mexico's Pemex, and Petróleos de Venezuela (which owns Citgo).

The market too realized the benefits of scale, rewarding larger companies such as Royal Dutch/Shell with higher price/earnings multiples (approximately 21 times) than smaller companies, such as BP (approximately 17 times before the merger announcement). Thus while strategic combinations would undoubtedly provide a means to cut costs, they could also provide the opportunity to gain higher valuation multiples.

Because the key driver of these deals was cost reduction, job cuts are expected to be big. One analyst has predicted that up to 15,000 could be fired in the wake of the Exxon-Mobil combination, which is expected to generate $2.8 billion in cost savings: $1.1 billion from production rationalization, $750 million from organizational efficiencies, $300 million from adoption of best practices, and $300 million from a more selective exploration program.

Sir John Browne

Sir John Browne, chief executive of BP Amoco, is a very impressive man. In 1989, when put in charge of restructuring BP's ailing oil and gas business, Browne effected a radical transformation of the company. At that time, acquisitions had swelled BP's debt to about 50 percent of capitalization; capital spending climbed steeply; and weak oil prices hurt earnings. Browne slashed costs. He reinvented the entire management structure of the company, restructuring BP into small business units, linked to enable groups across the world from each other to share ideas and technology advances.

Within a few years, BP became one of the strongest players in the oil industry. Browne's 1998 move to take over Amoco was a visionary step. His subsequent bold play to buy ARCO shortly thereafter vaulted BP past Royal Dutch/Shell to be the world's largest nonstate oil producer.

In an industry known for the machismo of its chief executives, Browne is something of an anomaly. He is a refined, wiry intellectual, and yet a coiled bundle of intense energy. Despite his friendly demeanor, Browne is an intensely private person, uncomfortable with speaking about himself. A known sympathizer with the Green environmental movement, Browne has a passion for opera, as well as pre-Columbian art. But Browne never takes his eye off the bottom line.

John Browne was born in Hamburg after the Second World War, the son of a British soldier and a Romanian linguist. He graduated with a first in physics at Cambridge and top in his class at Stanford Business School. Browne's first job, as a petroleum engineer at BP, was also the first step in his lifelong career at BP, capped with his 1995 appointment as the youngest chief executive in the company's history. Browne is a workaholic who puts in a seventy-five- to eighty-hour workweek.

The BP-Amoco combination changed the competitive dynamic in the oil industry. Once BP moved, others could not stand still. Exxon, the largest U.S. oil company, had long insisted that it was not interested in a partner. But John Browne had changed everything.

Exxon-Mobil Forced into action by the announced BP-Amoco merger and by its lagging position relative to industry leader Royal Dutch/Shell, Exxon announced a merger with Mobil in December 1998. CEO and chairman of Exxon Lee Raymond, who will head the new company, expressed that size per se was not what motivated the combination: "I have no interest in being the largest company in the Fortune 500. Revenues mean nothing to me. What counts is profit." Nevertheless, the deal would combine the number one and number two U.S. oil companies.

Again, while this deal too was nominally a merger of equals, it is clear that Exxon will be taking over Mobil: Exxon shareholders will own approximately 70 percent of the combined company. Mobil, financially a much weaker company than Exxon, had been in talks with other companies, including BP, Amoco, and Conoco. Like Amoco, the crunch of the oil cycle made the management a seller.

The deal would combine another two of the several pieces of John D. Rockefeller's Standard Oil empire: Standard Oil of New Jersey and Standard Oil of New York. Despite the size of the combined company—larger than Royal Dutch/Shell—Exxon Mobil would still not be nearly big enough to control world prices, with less than 12 percent of U.S. refining capacity and about 7 percent of worldwide refining capacity. This figure contrasts sharply with the 85 percent U.S. market share enjoyed by Standard Oil before it was broken up in 1911. It is also a lower concentration level than in other industries, such as automobiles, where GM and Ford together hold about 50 percent of the U.S. market.

Browne Strikes Again   But Exxon's reign as the world's largest nonstate oil company was a short one. John Browne had a vision to create the world's largest, most efficient public oil producer. In April 1999, when the opportunity arose, he seized it.

On April 1, 1999, BP Amoco announced its acquisition of Atlantic Richfield (ARCO) for $33.7 billion. Low oil prices had bruised ARCO badly, especially after the company narrowed its focus by divesting its coal mining and petrochemical operations in 1997 and 1998. Indeed, the decision to bid for ARCO must have been a difficult one for Browne. The timing was far from perfect, as Browne was in the midst of integrating Amoco: The acquisition of ARCO would throw a monkey wrench in the whole process and divert management focus. Yet ARCO was shopping itself, and if Browne didn't bite, someone else would, most likely Chevron. Browne swallowed hard and jumped.

To help fund the deal, the combined group would likely sell $3 billion in assets. It is also expected that 2,000 jobs will be eliminated. This deal, like that with Amoco, makes BP an even more powerful global player. It will be the largest non-OPEC producer in terms of output, the third-largest group in terms of sales, and will benefit from ARCO's reserves in Southeast Asia and its retail operations on the West Coast. The Alaskan position of ARCO is an ideal fit with both BP and Amoco.

These recent friendly deals stand in stark contrast to the contested takeover battles of the 1980s. What was a ferocious battle scene a decade ago has mellowed into an orderly mating ritual today. Indeed, a unique set of factors paved the way for the dramatic 1980s Oil Wars.

On the Brink of the Oil Wars   The seeds of the 1980s Oil Wars were planted the decade before when a worldwide shift away from politically secure U.S. oil that led to two major Oil Shocks—dramatic increases in the price of oil. By the early 1980s, the oil market was plagued by overcapacity, which had dramatic consequences for Big Oil.

For a time, Big Oil profited from the higher oil prices during the 1973 Oil Shock. The aggregate net income for these largest of oil companies had grown at an anemic pace in the five years prior to 1972. But on the cusp of the Shock, net income had risen to $11.7 billion in 1973, almost double the $6.9 billion earned in 1972, and then to $16.4 billion in 1974. Big Oil was looking for places to invest these phenomenal cash flows.

Motivated by their large pools of cash and industry-wide predictions of continuing oil shortages, in 1973 Big Oil undertook a helter-skelter race to discover new oil reserves—a project that would continue into the 1980s. Billions of dollars were invested in exploration, and prices for everything related to the hunt for oil shot up dramatically. The oil cities of Houston, Dallas, and Denver experienced boom times. The thrill of wildcatting and the independent oil business was popularized in the hit television series *Dallas*.

One of the primary assumptions justifying the push for new capacity was that demand for oil products would continue to increase. The so-called Iron Law—an observed relationship that demand for oil and energy grows at the same rate as the overall economy—lay at the heart of this prediction.

But this Iron Law soon proved false. During the late 1970s and early 1980s, the major economies embraced conservation and efficiency as a new mantra and, as a result, demand for oil shrank while the economy grew. Between 1973 and 1985, the United States became 25 percent more energy-efficient and 32 percent more oil-efficient. But oil-producing capacity had continued to grow, and the industry was producing 13 million barrels of unneeded oil each day.

Observers soon came to believe that the oil industry was dying a slow death. Sooner or later, the world's supply of oil and gas would be depleted and new energy sources—solar, hydro, nuclear—would replace oil and gas. Diversification became the industry byword. Exxon spent roughly $500 million on a start-up office electronics business amid talk of taking on IBM. The company also spent $1.2 billion to acquire Reliance Electric Co. and invested heavily in the copper industry. Mobil Oil shelled out $1 billion for retailer Montgomery Ward. Standard Oil acquired copper producer Kennecott for $1.8 billion. But as was true in the 1960s diversification, these deals would later haunt the buyers.

The early 1980s—the brink of the Oil Wars—saw a growing buyer's market for petroleum and petroleum products, with a deep recession in 1981 and 1982 contributing to the erosion in demand for oil. At the same time, three major, non–Middle Eastern oil sources came on-line—in Alaska, Mexico, and the North Sea. The Alaskan oil fields—completed in 1977—by themselves had an enormous impact, shipping over 1 million barrels per day in 1978, and transporting more than 2 million barrels per day by the early 1980s. At that time, Alaskan fields accounted for 25 percent of U.S. crude oil production.

The combination of the recession and new capacity put downward pressure on oil prices, hitting many of the Big Oil companies hard. Big Oil had poured billions of dollars into exploration and production, all premised on an oil price north of $30 a barrel. Exxon, for example, had spent a billion dollars in the early 1980s to develop shale oil technology, but was forced to back out of the project in 1982: Such expenditures no longer made sense in a world of $10 a barrel oil.

The huge administrative staffs built up during the 1970s also began to look increasingly out of proportion as the price of oil continued its downward progression. Not only was this infrastructure incredibly costly to maintain, it created a built-in bias for further inefficient exploration and production.

As prices bottomed out near $10 a barrel, continuing exploration became hard to justify. A series of major exploration disappointments highlighted the issue, including the failure of a $2 billion Alaskan wildcat project called Mukluk, known in the industry as the most expensive dry hole in history. The Mukluk disaster led Big Oil to believe that it would be cheaper to buy existing oil reserves than to develop new ones. In 1982, for example, major oil companies spent an average of $14.22 a barrel to develop new domestic oil reserves, while oil reserves could be purchased in the market for approximately $4 a barrel.

Measured against this benchmark, Wall Street valued most major oil companies at a steep discount to the underlying value of their proven oil and gas reserves, a situation that allowed an acquirer to pay a premium for an oil company's stock without paying an above-market price for its oil. This market imperfection sparked numerous takeover attempts by Big Oil companies who wanted to acquire new oil reserves. In this "bargain hunting" environment, the transactions were often highly contested.

Early Landmark: Belridge

The tide of the oil megadeals began in 1979, when a little-known California producer named Belridge Oil was put on the auction block. The company, founded in 1911 by three land speculators, owned the rights to a large oil patch north of Los Angeles containing approximately 380 million barrels of proven reserves of heavy crude. Relatively undesirable, this gooey, viscous oil adhered to underground rock formations and was costly to extract. The company was

55 percent owned by descendants of the company's three founders and 34 percent owned by Mobil and Texaco together.

Belridge was put on the market under pressure. In July 1979, the two majors attempted to buy out the other shareholders, negotiating with each shareholder individually so as to gain the company on the cheap. However, the members of the founding families, mostly in their sixties and seventies, would not be pushed around, and instead decided to run an auction. When the result was announced, Shell Oil had snatched Belridge away from Mobil and Texaco on the strength of a $3.6 billion offer.

The deal was stunning on several counts. Shell reportedly had topped the next highest bidder by $500 million, making the transaction the largest corporate acquisition to date. The deal also required the largest debt financing to date. Furthermore, the purchase price valued Belridge's reserves of low-quality oil at roughly $8.75 a barrel, considerably higher than the going rate in the market of $5 or $6 a barrel. Most observers thought Shell was crazy to spend so much on Belridge.

Shell CEO John Bookout had shocked the industry. But Bookout was betting that Shell's then-unique steam injection technology—pumping steam into oil reserves to make oil flow more freely—would enable it to capitalize on Belridge's reserves. While his competitors stumbled, Bookout was able to apply the steam injection technology, causing output from the California wells to more than triple. While so-called proven oil reserves were estimated at approximately 380 billion barrels, Shell had in fact found nearly 660 billion barrels, making the price paid per barrel more like $3.50! Bookout had bought himself a bargain and earned the reputation as one of the smartest men in the industry.

The Conoco Brawl

Belridge set off a bruising competitive atmosphere. Shortly thereafter, Conoco—the nation's ninth-largest oil company—became a target, and once again the oil industry was thrust into the public spotlight. The battle would drag out over three months and involve four separate bidders. The tactical maneuvering was at a level of complexity that set precedents for years to come. With Conoco, the Oil Wars exploded, and the 1980s merger boom began.

The jousting commenced on May 6, 1981, when Canada's Dome Petroleum tendered $65 per share for up to 20 percent of Conoco's stock. The stock had opened at just under $50 on the morning of the announcement.

Dome, a much smaller company than Conoco, explicitly stated it was not out to gain control of Conoco. Rather, Dome wanted to swap the Conoco stock it would purchase for Conoco's majority interest in its Canadian subsidiary, Hudson Bay Oil and Gas. Dome suggested a stock swap and not an outright cash purchase because the swap structure would be tax-free to Conoco.

The Dome tender should not have come as a surprise to Conoco. Ralph Bailey, Conoco's chairman, had committed a classic error: He had not firmly rejected an earlier informal offer from his counterpart at Dome and therefore had encouraged Dome to strike. Bailey simply felt no sense of urgency about the Dome offer, believing that his company was worth more than $65 a share and that his shareholders would concur. They didn't. Nearly 53 percent of the company's shareholders tendered to Dome.

Meanwhile, Seagram chairman Edgar Bronfman Sr. had been on the prowl for an acquisition for almost a year. His liquor company recently had sold its own oil and gas properties for $2.3 billion and was looking for a way to invest the sale proceeds. Conoco looked like an intriguing possibility.

Bailey and Bronfman met to discuss a deal, but Bailey once again did not make his position clear. He was eager to use Seagram as an offset to Dome, but feared Seagram's long-term intentions. Without telling Bronfman, Bailey rushed from Conoco's Stamford, Connecticut, headquarters to a waiting corporate jet bound for Oklahoma

City, the headquarters of Cities Service. Bailey approached Charles Waidelich, the CEO of Cities Service, to propose a merger.

The next day, Bailey returned to Conoco's headquarters. While he hadn't made a definitive agreement with Cities, he felt that his bargaining position was strong. Meanwhile, Conoco's board protected its flanks by approving an agreement with Dome whereby the Canadian oil company would swap its Conoco stock plus $245 million in cash for Hudson Bay, approximately double the amount promised in its initial tender offer.

With Dome in hand, Bailey tried to pursue the Cities merger while keeping Seagram at bay. Feeling abused, Edgar Bronfman commenced a hostile tender offer for 41 percent of Conoco's stock at $73 a share—just as Bailey and Waidelich were preparing the press release to announce the merger of their two companies. The Seagram offer ripped the foundations out from under that deal and put Conoco irretrievably into play.

Bailey reacted angrily to his new predicament and rushed to find a white knight. Blue-chip DuPont had been pondering the future of energy prices and had calculated that buying oil interests would be a sound hedge against the volatile costs for its vast chemical operations. Conoco seemed an ideal vehicle, and we were brought in to advise DuPont. A deal was put together at a breakneck pace over the July 4th weekend and announced the following week.

DuPont's bid was structured carefully, taking into account the opening left by Seagram's failure to tender for all of Conoco's stock. DuPont wanted at least 51 percent of Conoco's stock, but didn't want to pay cash for fear of adversely affecting its debt ratings. The resulting offer took the form of a two-tier package: DuPont offered for 50 percent of the company on the front end—80 percent in cash and 20 percent in stock—and the remaining 50 percent for stock in a back-end merger. Effectively, DuPont would pay $87.50 per share for 40 percent of the company and 1.6 DuPont shares for each remaining Conoco share.

A bidding war ensued. Seagram was not willing to give up easily, but couldn't compete with DuPont's offer. Yet as it turned out, all the maneuvering between DuPont and Seagram was just a prelude: On July 16, 1981, giant Mobil Corporation, a jilted Belridge suitor, weighed in with its own offer.

Finally, three months after the initial Dome offer, top executives from DuPont gathered at the Hotel du Pont in downtown Wilmington, Delaware. When the clock struck midnight on August 5, the team lifted champagne glasses in a toast. Then DuPont began sending out payments to make good on its tender offer for shares in the Conoco Corporation.

The festivities that evening were not without cause, for DuPont had just completed the largest takeover in history; but such records are made to be broken. The real surprise, however, was that shareholders had tendered to DuPont in the face of Mobil Corporation's $120 per share offer, a more than 20 percent improvement on DuPont's price. DuPont had raised sufficient concern about how antitrust authorities might treat a Mobil-Conoco deal that shareholders opted for the lower, but certain, payout from DuPont.

In fact, from the moment Mobil bid, DuPont publicly stated that price alone should not decide the winner. Mobil's offer, argued DuPont, had to be discounted for the risk that a merger between Mobil and Conoco would be blocked by the government on antitrust grounds. Therefore, when Mobil ultimately raised its bid to $120 per share (compared to DuPont's $98), DuPont consciously decided against a raise, relying instead on the antitrust argument to carry the day.

Though the antitrust law is incredibly complex and typically involves sophisticated economic analysis, the DuPont antitrust strategy was simple—keep yelling "two and nine"—a catchphrase intended to emphasize that a Mobil and Conoco merger would combine the nation's number two and number nine oil companies. Such a combination, DuPont and Conoco argued, *had* to have antitrust implications.

This tactic was targeted specifically toward the audience that really mattered: the institutional investors and arbitrageurs who held large blocks of Conoco stock. The intent was to play on these investors' fear that antitrust issues eventually would kill the Mobil deal—a disastrous outcome for any investor who tendered to Mobil. To feed this fear, Conoco promptly sued Mobil on antitrust grounds.

The government played an important role in determining the winning bidder because antitrust laws afforded it the power to delay any of the bids for Conoco. In particular, the Hart-Scott-Rodino Antitrust Improvements Act required each bidder to file a notice with both the Justice Department and the Federal Trade Commission, after which the government would review the filings for antitrust implications.

In the Conoco contest, the Justice Department antitrust review process was scheduled to end on a different date for each player. If both DuPont and Mobil received approval in the first round, DuPont would have to wait until August 7 to purchase shares, a week later than Mobil. Even worse for DuPont, if it were to be faced with an information request from the government, DuPont could not effect its tender for Conoco until at least August 27. But if Mobil received an information request but DuPont did not, Mobil would be delayed until after August 10. Conoco would likely be sold to the first party to navigate the antitrust gauntlet.

With so much riding on the review process, DuPont's antitrust lawyers worked hard to satisfy the Justice Department. In fact, they did everything short of bringing the government lawyers coffee, and, as a result, DuPont sailed through the process three days early. The response—no further information request—played right into DuPont's bidding strategy.

On July 31, however, Mobil was faced with an information request. Mobil's in-house counsel George Birrell, who received the call from the government, described the result this way: "With that phone call, it was over for us." Investors tendered to DuPont, and the battle ended. The Justice Department and the antitrust laws decided the outcome of the multibillion-dollar fight for Conoco.

Meanwhile, Seagram had purchased 32 percent of Conoco's stock through its tender offer, but did not gain control, and ultimately tendered its Conoco stake in return for a 20 percent stake in DuPont. Years later, Seagram sold this stock back to DuPont and used the sale proceeds to purchase the movie studio MCA.

PRORATION POOLS

Among the confusing exotica of the public merger process is the proration pool. If a company offers $100 cash per share in a tender offer for 50 percent of a company and $80 per share in stock for the remainder in a back-end merger, the average price paid by the acquirer is $90. If 100 percent of target shareholders tender, then all shareholders will receive an average of $90 per share— $100 for the first 50 percent of their shares and $80 for the other 50 percent.

But the math becomes more complicated when fewer than 100 percent of shareholders tender. For example, if only 90 percent of shareholders tender, the 10 percent of shareholders not tendering automatically receive $80 in stock on the back end. But in order for a total of 50 percent of shares outstanding to be exchanged for cash according to the terms of the offer, the 90 percent of shareholders who do tender are entitled to exchange more than 50 percent of their shares for cash. Under this scenario, the 90 percent tendering can exchange 55.56 percent of their shares for cash (because 55.56 percent x 90 percent equals 50 percent), and 44.44 percent of their shares for stock in the back end. The

average price received by the tendering shareholders is therefore
$91.11—55.56 percent x $100 plus 44.44 percent x $80.

Because of the importance of the eligibility dates (which determine the pool of shareholders eligible for proration), a tender
offer for less than 100 percent of shares has been called a coercive device: If a shareholder misses the pool eligibility date, he
receives the less valuable back-end offer. To prevent the coercive
effect of hostile partial offers, poison pills (which are discussed in
more detail in Part Three) were developed. However, partial offers
remain commonplace in friendly deals and are a flexible tactical
tool.

Always a Bridesmaid . . .

Mobil's defeats in Belridge and Conoco did not kill the large
company's thirst for acquisitions, however. Heavily dependent on
Saudi oil, Mobil desperately wanted to expand its U.S. reserves,
leading the company to spend $4.3 billion on domestic exploration
and production between 1976 and 1980. But despite its aggressive exploration activity, Mobil's U.S. reserves fell 6 percent over the period. Mobil chairman Rawleigh Warner and president William
Tavoulareas sought to reverse the decline.

It didn't take long for the two men—who worked without the
meaningful help of outside advisers—to find another target. In October 1981, about a month after Conoco slipped away, Mobil announced a $5 billion, two-tier bid for Marathon Oil.

Ohio-based Marathon, the nation's sixteenth-largest oil company,
was a particularly inviting target due to its rich U.S. reserves—especially its 49.5 percent interest in the massive Yates oil field in West
Texas. Many oil analysts placed Marathon's breakup value well above
Mobil's bid, which nonetheless represented an approximate 27 percent premium over the trading price of Marathon stock.

We were brought in by Marathon's management to defend against the offer, building upon our Conoco experience. The Marathon board was eager to find a corporate white knight, ideally an industrial company that would protect the employees, the legacy of the company, and the community—Findlay, Ohio—as well as offer a higher price. Mobil was one of the richest and toughest companies in the nation, but Marathon had learned from Conoco how to make Mobil stumble: raise enough antitrust issues so that shareholders would discount Mobil's bid and instead vote in favor of a white knight.

The list of companies capable of absorbing Marathon was not long, and within a matter of weeks, U.S. Steel expressed interest. Negotiations progressed quickly and a U.S. Steel team flew into Ohio for meetings at Marathon's headquarters. Not careful about secrecy, the U.S. Steel team came aboard one of the company's jets, with the corporate logo emblazoned on the fuselage. Arbitrageurs and the local press had people stationed at the airport who saw the U.S. Steel plane and rumors of a deal began to circulate in the market.

Later, the Marathon team flew to Pittsburgh for the final negotiations at U.S. Steel's corporate headquarters. As our plane (without markings) touched down, it was quickly whisked directly into a separate hangar. The scene was out of a James Bond movie. Ground crew members dressed in neon orange suits stood all around the hangar along with security guards. We were ushered to the roof, where a helicopter was waiting to take the Marathon team to the U.S. Steel building. The helicopter landed on the top of the Pittsburgh skyscraper, we climbed down one flight of stairs, and were in the U.S. Steel executive offices.

The next day, the deal terms were announced. U.S. Steel offered $125 a share in cash for half the outstanding Marathon shares and securities worth about $86 for the remainder. U.S. Steel also agreed to a provision to preserve employment in Marathon's hometown by keeping Marathon intact as a separate subsidiary headquartered in Findlay, Ohio—what has become known universally as a "Findlay, Ohio" provision.

When the U.S. Steel offer was announced, Mobil raised its bid. But in the meantime, Marathon had won a valuable temporary injunction against Mobil on antitrust grounds. Mobil scrambled to respond and soon negotiated a deal to sell the operations that would not comply with antitrust law. But this proved too little, too late.

Mobil's bid was about $200 million higher than U.S. Steel's, but again Mobil was thwarted by the threat of antitrust scrutiny. One can imagine Mobil's frustration. Unwilling to wait for the ambiguities regarding Mobil's offer to be resolved, shareholders overwhelmingly tendered their shares to U.S. Steel.

T. Boone Pickens

T. Boone Pickens was one of the most colorful figures in the 1980s Oil Wars. Through his company, Mesa Petroleum, Pickens launched numerous takeover battles for other companies, hoping to buy oil on the cheap on Wall Street. But on the Friday before Memorial Day, 1982, the tables were turned. Cities Service, the nation's nineteenth-largest oil company, announced a public tender offer to purchase all of Mesa's stock for $17 per share. At that price, Cities Services would pay a scant 25 cents above Mesa's latest closing price. Pickens' company, which itself had been contemplating a bid for Cities, was being Pac-Manned. Pickens canceled his plans for the long weekend.

Takeover professionals had been discussing the possibility of a so-called Pac-Man defense for some time. The idea was relatively simple. When faced with a hostile bidder, a takeover target could tender for the shares in the hostile bidder. In this way, the hunted could swallow the hunter, eliminating the threat.

We represented Cities with Lehman Brothers, and all the bankers were having a great time. Our team and the Lehman bankers—Henry Breck, a former CIA agent with a sense of humor, and Jack Lentz, who had played a year of professional football—all had an instinct for the jugular and saw an unusual opportunity. We felt there was a good chance for the "pool shot"—to break up Pickens' assault before it could be mobilized.

Though on paper it was hard to believe, at the time of the Cities bid, little Mesa Petroleum posed a very real threat to the larger company. After all, in addition to being the nineteenth-largest oil company, Cities was also the thirty-eighth-largest industrial company in America with $8.5 billion of revenues in 1981. By way of comparison, Mesa had roughly $400 million of revenues, one third the assets of Cities, and only 900 employees compared to 20,000.

However, Pickens possessed other assets. The press loved this twangy Oklahoman. Pickens wrapped himself in the classic frontier spirit and projected a David-versus-Goliath mentality. He was a master of spinning zippy quotes. For example, when asked by a *Wall Street Journal* reporter if his attack on Cities was a bluff, Pickens responded, "Well, we didn't come to town on a load of watermelons." This down-home homily threw the reporter, who asked for clarification. Pickens laughed. "I may not be from Wall Street," he said, "but I know what I'm doing."

Indeed, in Cities, Pickens had picked a vulnerable target. The company's main problem was its poor operating performance. In each of the last ten years, it had depleted reserves more quickly than it discovered new oil, and over the previous five years, its reserves had fallen by about 20 percent. Meanwhile, to no avail, the company had been pouring more and more money into exploration.

Reflecting this track record, Cities' stock price lingered in the mid-30s, implying a market value of less than half the appraised value of its proven oil and gas reserves. The board was known to be upset with the company's performance, and sensitive to shareholder complaints. Consequently, Mesa could acquire oil in the ground at a below-market price even if it paid a large premium to Cities' share-holders.

Pickens had recognized this situation in 1979, when he began purchasing Cities stock for Mesa's account. By late May 1982, Mesa had acquired slightly more than 5 percent of Cities' outstanding stock. Pickens also had four partners waiting in the wings with another $1 billion to invest. Preparations were under way for a June 4 hostile tender offer. But word leaked to Cities, and it launched its surprise bid to the bankers' delight. As a backup, though, the board also deputized us to explore the interest of other bidders in Cities. If the price were high enough, the board would seriously consider selling, even if Boone were no threat.

While the Pac-Man defense was a well-known possibility, Cities had taken the idea one step further. Rather than passively waiting for the bid from Mesa, Cities attacked first. As a result, Cities gained an important tactical advantage. Federal law required that a tender offer remain open for at least twenty days. So, because Cities beat Mesa out of the blocks, the Cities offer would expire first. This time difference would allow Cities to buy Mesa before the opposite happened.

Pickens was in danger of being boxed in. It had taken months to find financial backers willing to throw in with Mesa. Now, in the face of the Cities bid, the lead investor backed out, taking $500 million with it. Pickens had to scramble to keep his other partners from following suit, or he might lose control of Mesa itself.

But Pickens was not about to give up. If Mesa walked away, it stood to lose $60 million. So, instead, Pickens shot back a classic bear hug letter—an offer made directly to Cities' CEO and announced to the world. Mesa was prepared to pay $50 a share for Cities stock, part in cash and part in securities. This was not a tender offer; the Cities board would have to give its approval for the deal to go forward. The likelihood of that happening was slim. However, that wasn't the point. Pickens just wanted to build pressure on Cities' incumbent managers and board of directors. The tactic was a failure.

Pickens and his advisers scrambled for a stronger counterattack. They kept coming back to the same stumbling block—where to get the cash for an all-out tender? Eventually, with the clock ticking on Cities' offer for Mesa, Pickens settled on an unusual partial tender offer. On June 7, Mesa announced the terms: It would pay $45 per share for an additional 15 percent of Cities stock, which would give Mesa more than 20 percent in total.

Given the steep premium over the market price for Cities stock, more than 15 percent of the shareholders might very well tender their shares to Mesa. If that happened, Pickens would have a powerful lever to raise additional cash. Moreover, Mesa would argue that the tender offer was a referendum on incumbent management's performance. Even if the Mesa bid were to be turned away, another predator might attempt to capitalize on the palpable shareholder discontent, and Boone would make a profit.

Meanwhile, Cities faced a dilemma. The strike against Boone looked like a winner: Boone would be knocked out before he could punch. But an insistent Gulf Oil wanted to make an offer as well. So Gulf was told Cities didn't need a white knight rescue bid with the Boone situation under control; on the other hand, if Gulf bid a preemptive price, the board would listen. Basically, the board was a seller and was using Boone as a stalking horse.

On June 17, Gulf Oil took the bait and offered $63 per Cities share in a friendly deal. This was a slam-dunk bid at a price well above what Pickens could ever afford. We urged Gulf to continue the bid for Mesa and buy it too, but Gulf settled. Boone gave up the fight, and sold Mesa's shares in Cities back to the company for $55 a share, less than the other shareholders were to receive, but still a $30 million profit.

Though matters with Pickens was settled, the Cities story was not over. Less than two months after agreeing to its deal with Cities, Gulf backed out. The company cited irreconcilable antitrust problems. Observers on Wall Street found the explanation implausible. Gulf, they argued, could have settled its differences with the government by selling certain assets. According to this view, Gulf had just gotten cold feet over the price it was paying. The antitrust issue was a convenient way to save face, and Gulf was sued for its insincerity. After years of legal sparring, a Tulsa jury finally hit Gulf—now part of Chevron—for $742 million in damages. In March 1999, the Oklahoma State Supreme Court upheld the judgment.

With Cities left at the altar, Dr. Armand Hammer's Occidental Petroleum stepped in and tried to scoop up the company at a bargain price. Although the board was eager to sell, the directors all agreed that Hammer, as the culminating gesture of a long and controversial career, was even more eager to buy, and therefore taunted Hammer by threatening to sell Cities' assets on a piece-by-piece basis. Hammer eventually overruled his staff and bought the wounded Cities Service for $53 a share, about $1 billion less than Gulf, but still higher than Boone's offer. The shareholders were also entitled to a slice of any proceeds received from the Gulf lawsuit. Cities' board members were thrilled. Cities was finally sold.

1984—The Year of the Megadeal

In 1984, the merger storm hit the majors with full force.

Superior Oil   First, a bitter feud between siblings Howard Keck and Wilametta Day Keck—son and daughter of the company's founder—led to the sale of Superior Oil, the country's largest independent.

Wilametta hated her brother—director and retired CEO of Superior—and chose to use Superior as a tool for revenge. Angry at her brother's control of the company, Wilametta launched a proxy fight to facilitate a change in control. Ultimately, with the help of Boone Pickens—who, spotting potential for profit, had bought into Superior—and others, Wilametta won the fight: Mobil eventually swooped in to buy the company for $5.7 billion. After years of searching, Mobil finally had a willing partner.

A Closer Look

Valuing a public oil company is more art than science. The starting point for a valuation is the SEC-mandated analysis—known as
the "standardized measure of discounted future net cash
flows"—found in oil companies' annual reports.

It is insufficient, however, to rely exclusively on these reports
because they make three key oversimplifications: 1) they fail to
include any reserves in excess of proven reserves; 2) they provide
only a one-time snapshot based on constant (as of fiscal year-
end) price and cost assumptions; and 3) they employ a discount
rate of 10 percent rather than the company's true cost of capital.
Consequently, the reported figures must be supplemented with
data from other sources.

Oil companies routinely use independent engineering firms
such as de Golyer & McNaughton and Ryder Scott to prepare internal reports that detail not only proven, but also probable and
possible reserves. While these reports can supplement those
found in SEC documents, the reader must keep in mind that reports prepared by different independent engineering firms are not
necessarily comparable: A given firm may tend either to overstate
or understate reserves. Furthermore, engineers must base their
assessment on assumptions including the recovery techniques
available to the company in question (some of which may extend
the lives of reserves) and recovery results from similar or adjacent
properties. Assessments of raw undeveloped acreage are even
more difficult to make, and therefore can vary wildly. Indeed, the
Belridge auction proved that an engineer's report was the beginning—not the end—of inquiry.

Even if the reserve quantities were easily determinable, however, the quality of reserves—the level of impurities as well as the

specific gravity of the oil—is not always known. Oil quality is important in valuation of reserves because poorer oil quality requires more costly refining techniques.

Similar concerns exist in valuing natural gas. For example, natural gas values are enhanced if the gas is rich in liquids (such as propane, ethane, or butane) that can be stripped out and sold. Conversely, gas's value is reduced by the presence of impurities like hydrogen sulfide and other sulfur compounds, which necessitate expensive processing.

To value oil and gas reserves, one must discount the cash flows expected to be generated by the reserves. The math is as follows: The quantity of oil available for sale at each period in time is multiplied by the likely sales proceeds, net of costs, and is discounted at the company's cost of capital. The key assumption lies in the sales proceeds figures, which are based on one's view of the future price of oil, known as a "price deck."

In recent years, more sophistication has been applied to the volatility factor in the price deck. Even if a deal makes sense on an expected value basis, the bounce of the oil cycle may be too much risk for many buyers. The advantage of John Browne's BP is that it is geared to operate profitably at the downside of the cycle.

In practice, potential buyers alter the price deck and/or cost of capital when looking at large strategic deals to reflect their opinion about the quality of the target's reserves. Confidence in one's engineers, the level of familiarity with the particular field, and recovery technology have a lot to do with the valuation.

Of course, the most precise valuations arise when the method is applied to proven reserves; the valuation of probable and possible reserves usually involves "haircutting" the estimated reserves and is far more subjective.

Getty Oil Getty Oil was the next big oil company to be acquired. While Boone Pickens and Mesa Petroleum played a cameo role in the transaction, billionaire Gordon Getty, son of Getty Oil's founder, J. Paul Getty, was at the center of the process.

Gordon's passion was opera, and he passed many hours composing music in a soundproof studio in the basement of his twenty-five-room San Francisco mansion. But despite an apparent lack of interest in the details of day-to-day business management, Gordon retained considerable power over his father's company. His position as trustee of the Sarah C. Getty Trust, which held 40 percent of Getty Oil's shares, made his opinion very important to the company's future.

Over time, Gordon began to insert himself more forcefully into company affairs, having become increasingly disenchanted with the performance of CEO Sidney Petersen and with the company's strategic dilemma: As was true for most of the majors, Getty was depleting its reserves faster than it was finding new oil, and its stock was trading at a fraction of the value of the company's proven reserves.

Gordon Getty found this situation intolerable. He met with Boone Pickens and others, looking for ideas about what should be done. Sidney Petersen meanwhile attempted an unsuccessful boardroom coup, seeking to reduce the influence of Gordon Getty, whom Petersen regarded as not capable of managing the company. Instead, however, Petersen merely increased the animosity on both sides. With boardroom hostilities in the open, Pennzoil announced a $1.6 billion tender offer for 20 percent of the outstanding Getty Oil stock at $100 a share.

Pennzoil's partial tender represented an attempt by chairman J. Hugh Liedtke to become the swing voter who would align with Gordon Getty to decide Getty Oil's fate. Before the offer, the Getty Trust owned 40 percent of the company and the J. Paul Getty Museum another 12 percent. The museum, advised by takeover lawyer Martin

Lipton of Wachtell, Lipton, Rosen & Katz, had previously acted as a swing voter: However, at the end of 1983, the museum was unwilling to partner with Gordon. Liedtke jumped into the opening provided by this unrest.

The Pennzoil bid put both Gordon and the museum in a tough spot. If they allowed Pennzoil to proceed, its above-market tender offer might be oversubscribed—sending a clear signal of upheaval to the marketplace—and potentially causing Gordon to lose control of Getty Oil in the process. But, after much public rumination about the future of Getty Oil, Gordon made an agreement with Liedtke in which the trust and Pennzoil together would pay $100 per share for the 60 percent of Getty Oil not owned by the trust; but the agreement would survive only if approved by the Getty board at the meeting that same day. The insiders and independent members of the board, however, resisted and recessed the meeting to convince Gordon to auction the company to the highest bidder.

In the interim, investment bankers from Goldman Sachs representing Petersen and the company had been canvassing for a white knight. One of these calls excited the interest of Texaco, which engaged a team to follow up, including us. Then the Getty board reconvened, and after nudging a few extra dollars out of Liedtke, approved the Pennzoil agreement "in principle," with a "definitive merger agreement" to be negotiated later. An announcement was made to that effect.

With the cooperation of Lipton and Petersen, Texaco made a $10.8 billion bid the very next day. The deal made sense for Texaco. Total reserves had declined by 1.4 billion barrels in the previous five years, leaving Texaco with just 1 billion barrels in the ground by 1983, while the company's exploration cost had soared to roughly $21 a barrel. If these trends could not be reversed, Texaco would soon be out of business. Therefore, the deal looked like a home run for Texaco. Even with the premium paid for Getty, Texaco was buying several billion barrels of oil for less than $5 a barrel.

The deal's value for Texaco, however, was reduced by the subsequent Pennzoil litigation, which alleged that Texaco had induced a breach of contract. None of the New York or Delaware lawyers working on the deal thought there was any issue. However, due to a procedural blunder in which Texaco's lawyers failed to file an answer to Pennzoil's complaint, Pennzoil was able to remove the case from Delaware and instead drag New York–based Texaco into a Texas court, where the hometown jury ruled in Pennzoil's favor. (Under Delaware rule 41, a plaintiff may dismiss a lawsuit without prejudice and refile it elsewhere if the defendant has not yet answered the complaint.) The jury awarded Pennzoil $10.5 billion in damages. Texaco eventually settled the case for $3 billion, but only after years of legal wrangling.

The Fight for Gulf   Ironically, by the summer of 1983, Mesa Petroleum was in trouble—even by Pickens' admission. Like other oil companies, it had overextended itself in a massive exploration program in the Gulf of Mexico.

In search of a quick fix, Pickens put his staff on the lookout for another Cities Service, and eventually settled on Gulf Oil. The company—one of the Seven Sisters, as the world's seven largest oil companies were known—had $20 billion of assets, $30 billion in annual revenue, and roughly 40,000 employees. However, Gulf was vulnerable because it traded at a huge discount to its estimated breakup value and had a history of poor management.

Mesa planned to make a major investment in Gulf and then agitate for strategies to increase Gulf's stock price. Specifically, Pickens planned to advance a favorite proposal that he had employed at Mesa: to spin off at least half of Gulf's oil and gas reserves into a royalty trust from which shareholders could receive cash flows undiluted by corporate taxes. By investing heavily in Gulf, Mesa would profit on any increase in shareholder value resulting from its efforts.

To put his plan in motion, Pickens had Mesa Petroleum invest $350 million in Gulf stock. Mesa bought its 4.9 percent stake—just

below the 5 percent threshold for a mandatory public filing—
through numbered bank accounts spread around the country to conceal its identity as the purchaser. By staying below the 5 percent
threshold, Mesa was able to maintain secrecy long enough to raise
the additional funds necessary to invest in Gulf stock. While creative
at the time, the tactic wouldn't work today because of the Hart-Scott
antitrust notification process required on purchases above $15 mil-
lion.

In late September, Pickens set about the business of raising an
additional $200 million of capital. He canvassed a small group of
wealthy individuals, and by October 4, had formed the Gulf Investors Group, a partnership with $550 million of equity (including
the $350 million already invested by Mesa). This war chest provided
Mesa $1.1 billion of purchasing power, including margin loans. Pick-
ens had learned a lesson from the Cities Service Pac-Man defense:
The Gulf Investors Group agreement provided that voting control of
the Gulf stock acquired would shift to one of the investors if Mesa
were to undergo a change in control.

Shortly after the meeting, Mesa returned to the markets and
began buying more shares. Ten business days after acquiring 5 percent of Gulf stock, the Gulf Investors Group made a mandatory public filing with the Securities Exchange Commission of its then 9
percent ownership. But rather than indicating an intention to take
over Gulf, the group characterized its holding of Gulf stock as "for
investment purposes."

Though the statement was arguably accurate—Pickens intended
to advocate management changes without actually assuming control—Gulf management was naturally skeptical and indeed had reason to worry. Gulf undeniably had problems, stemming from a
scandal in the 1970s over illegal political contributions in the United
States and questionable foreign payments. The ensuing purge of senior managers had left Gulf indecisive during the tumultuous times
following the first Oil Shock, and in 1975 the company's oil rights in

Kuwait—responsible for a large proportion of earnings—were nationalized. At the same time, the company was rapidly depleting its U.S. reserves.

When the identity of Gulf's new large shareholder became known, management acted immediately to defend against Pickens, announcing a special shareholder meeting in December 1983, to change Gulf's state of incorporation from Pennsylvania to Delaware. Delaware did not require cumulative voting, and incorporation in that state therefore minimized the possibility that Mesa would be able to elect a strong minority of the board.

Pickens turned the ensuing proxy contest into a referendum on Gulf's management—a contest that management won, but only barely. ARCO, which had been waiting on the sidelines anticipating Gulf's vulnerability, jumped at the opportunity. We were brought in to work with their team, and the time to strike had come. ARCO offered $70 a share to buy out Gulf, causing the beleaguered board to collapse and announce an auction of the company. A race broke out among three main bidders: ARCO, Chevron, and KKR.

The auction represented another watershed in takeovers—the arrival of a financial buyer in the oil business: KKR, with a few dozen employees, was bidding against two of America's largest and richest companies in a multibillion-dollar auction. Pickens was content to ride out his gain on the Gulf stock his group held.

On March 5, the Gulf board held a dramatic "one-shot" auction at the company's Pittsburgh headquarters. Each of the three bidders was given one opportunity to present its case and its highest offer. ARCO took a dive. It went first with a slightly sweetened $72 bid, knowing it was a loser. Having had the opportunity to conduct extensive due diligence, ARCO had enough concerns not to raise its bid materially. KKR followed with a mix of cash and stock valued, according to the buyout firm, at $87.50 a share. Chevron, third and last, offered $80 a share, all cash.

After hearing the presentations, the board debated the three offers. Very quickly, the directors narrowed the choice to one between Chevron's all-cash offer and KKR's ostensibly higher-valued package of cash and securities (although the investment bankers advising the board could not put a precise value on the KKR securities). It initially appeared that KKR's was the winning proposal.

However, some directors became concerned about the perception of impropriety that might result from management remaining in place in the KKR buyout. Therefore, after seven hours of debate, the board settled on Chevron's $13.2 billion offer. Mesa took home roughly $300 million after taxes.

Phillips Petroleum Under Seige   About six months after the Gulf transaction was approved by shareholders, three very interested observers were hunting in Spain. The trio—Fred Hartley, the CEO of Unocal, William Douce, the CEO of Phillips, and John McKinley, the CEO of Texaco—had been invited on the trip by the head of a construction company that worked with all three oil giants. But while they stalked around the Spanish countryside, Douce and Hartley must have felt something like the red-legged partridge they were hunting: Both of their companies' stock was under accumulation. Rumors swirled in the marketplace that Pickens was responsible.

On December 2, while Douce, Hartley, and McKinley were having dinner, the call came. Someone interrupted the dinner to say Douce was wanted on the phone. It was urgent.

Douce took the call. He learned from his company's treasurer that Mesa Petroleum had just filed notice of its 6 percent ownership of Phillips. The day the filing became public, Pickens also announced his intent to tender for an additional 14.9 percent at $60 a share, providing a hefty premium over the company's current trading price of approximately $40 a share. With such a large difference between the tender and the market price, there likely would be a stampede to offer shares to Pickens.

Douce was on his way back to Bartlesville, Oklahoma, within

hours, and we were called in with Morgan Stanley to fend off Mesa. Over the next four months, Douce would fight off first Pickens and then Carl Icahn.

Phillips had the quintessential hometown defense: The management and community campaigned hard to keep the company intact. In the end, Phillips remained independent, but only after putting in place a complicated recapitalization plan that gave shareholders a package worth between $53 and $56 a share. The transaction put more than $4.5 billion of new debt on the Phillips balance sheet, but was ultimately successful.

PROFILE

Fred Hartley

Canadian-born Fred Hartley earned his reputation as the toughest CEO in Big Oil long before Pickens came on the scene. The consummate Organization Man, Hartley joined Union Oil in 1939 after earning his degree in chemical engineering. He worked his way up the ranks, spending his entire career at the company.

Over time, Hartley also became known for an irascible nature, sharp tongue, and fiery temper. He was fond of calling his financial advisers "bums" and, proud of his tough reputation, named his fifty-one-foot boat *My Way*.

Hartley became president and CEO of the Union Oil Company of California in 1964 and within months presided over the then-largest oil takeover in United States history: Unocal's acquisition of Pure Oil. The merger's success led Hartley to pursue an aggressive acquisition policy, expanding Unocal into overseas exploration, chemicals, and geothermal energy. In the process, Hartley transformed Unocal from a regional player to the nation's twelfth-largest oil company. Despite all his acquisitions, Hartley never stopped plowing profits back into the company.

Even before the Oil Wars of the 1980s, Hartley was a regular in the press. After an oil spill coated the California coast in the late 1960s, he told a Senate committee, "I am always amazed at the publicity for the loss of a few birds." He also received considerable attention as an outspoken critic of early environmentalists.

In the early 1980s, Unocal suffered along with other members of Big Oil. Yet Hartley remained wedded to exploration and his expensive pet project—a massive oil shale mining effort in the Sierra Nevada mountains. To Hartley, remaining in charge of Unocal was not just best for the company—it was best for the country. Exploration and R&D were a matter of patriotism and national security: American companies needed to search for more oil to "secure oil supplies for the United States and low energy costs for the free world."

Hartley held to his belief even as exploration costs outpaced the market value of oil. This commitment, and its financial repercussions, eventually would lead Pickens to go after Unocal.

Unocal's Line in the Sand

Though Fred Hartley was spared in Spain, soon he too came under attack. On St. Valentine's Day, 1985, he received the news. Pickens had filed another 13D with the SEC and Unocal was the target: Pickens already held 7.9 percent of the company's stock. Hartley came out with guns blazing and a bruising war ensued. Unocal would emerge bloodied, but Pickens would be beaten.

Unocal first turned to the courts. Pickens had already negotiated a $1.1 billion credit facility—a standing agreement with a number of banks to provide loans—and Security Pacific National Bank in Los Angeles, Unocal's traditional lead bank, was one of the banks in the syndicate. Although the bank was only a small player, to the tune of a $54 million commitment, on March 12, Unocal filed a lawsuit against Security Pacific, claiming that the bank, with long-standing access to confidential Unocal information, had violated its contractual and fiduciary obligations.

To maximize the political impact of the suit, Unocal's public relations firm sent a copy of the lawsuit, along with a letter from Hartley calling for an investigation of banks involved in takeovers, to chairman of the Federal Reserve Paul Volcker, to every member of Congress, and to every director at Pickens' banks.

Hartley decried raiders and the "merger mania" they had fashioned. People like Pickens left "ruined lives, corporate cadavers, and poorer prospects for reserve replacement and future economic development for the nation" in their wake. The banks were also to blame. "Under the guise of 'protecting the small shareholders,' corporate raiders and their bankers and brokers are engaging in stock and bond and credit schemes reminiscent of those of the 1920s— but on a multibillion-dollar scale." At times, Hartley became even more animated, calling Pickens a financial barbarian and a "communist," and asserting that takeovers were "cannibalizing" the oil industry. Hartley hired squads of PR men and lobbyists to follow up.

Hartley's antimerger shibboleths had some sticking power. A lot of antitakeover rhetoric was generated by his machine, much of which is invoked even today.

Pickens struggled as the Unocal lawsuit took effect. Security Pacific and two other banks pulled out of the Mesa credit syndicate. While the banks were eventually replaced, this turn of events caused Pickens to worry that his vital loan capacity could be destroyed. Therefore, on March 21, Mesa struck back, filing a complaint against Unocal in a California state court that alleged Unocal had engaged in "unlawful efforts to interfere with the banking relationships" of Mesa.

To underline its commitment to the Unocal investment, Mesa then bought a huge block of stock, $322 million worth, raising its ownership to over 13 percent. Pickens also began to consider a hostile tender offer, and met with investment bankers from Drexel to explore the possibility of raising capital through a junk bond offering. Drexel was enthusiastic.

After a meeting on Good Friday with a group of New York bankers, lawyers, and other advisers, Pickens made the decision to tender for enough shares to give Mesa control of Unocal. With the help of Drexel's $3 billion in junk bond commitments, Mesa was able to offer $54 a share in cash for enough stock to give it over 50 percent of Unocal, and a package of securities for each additional Unocal share.

Unocal responded quickly. Its board rejected the Mesa offer as "grossly inadequate" despite the premium it would pay shareholders over the recent trading range of Unocal stock. Then Unocal announced a complicated self-tender offer in which Unocal would repurchase 49 percent of its stock for a package of securities valued at $72 a share. The self-tender had two key features: First, it would only became active if Pickens succeeded in buying his 51 percent interest; second, Pickens was excluded from the offer. Therefore, if Mesa went forward with its takeover attempt, it would end up the only shareholder in an insolvent company.

Pickens denounced the Unocal offer as "just another poison pill in a new bottle." The offer, he argued, was illusory. If Mesa withdrew its planned purchase, Unocal would not be obligated to give shareholders anything and its shareholders would be back where they started, owning a stock projected to trade in the mid-30s.

Reacting to Pickens, Hartley revised the Unocal tender offer, providing that Unocal would unconditionally repurchase 29 percent of its shares. In addition, Unocal would consider placing 45 percent of its oil and gas reserves in a limited partnership, with the ownership interests in the partnership to be distributed to shareholders, much like in a royalty trust.

Yet the terms of the revised Unocal tender still excluded Mesa: If the Unocal plan were carried out, Mesa's Unocal stock would suffer a dramatic loss in value. Pickens attacked the selective exclusion as a dangerous departure from the legal principle that all shareholders must be treated equally. Many experts agreed.

In line with expectations, Delaware judge Vice Chancellor Carolyn Berger held that Unocal would have to include Mesa in the tender offer if it wished to go forward. Unocal appealed Vice Chancellor Berger's ruling to the Delaware Supreme Court within hours. Each side filed a 100-page brief and the case was argued within three days. The court handed down its decision on Friday, May 17—and it was a shocker. The opinion stated that Unocal's selective tender offer was "reasonable in relation to the threat that the board rationally and reasonably believed was posed by Mesa's inadequate and coercive two-tier tender offer." The decision was final and could not be appealed. Pickens could, therefore, be excluded.

Knowing he had been beaten, Pickens reached out to Unocal within hours, seeking a settlement. Hartley, savoring victory, was initially not in the mood to negotiate but soon realized that, as Unocal's largest shareholder, Pickens could make a lot of trouble. Over the weekend, the two sides struggled through tough negotiations.

A deal was announced on Monday morning. Pickens' shares would be included in the $72 Unocal tender—though at a lower percentage than other shareholders. Pickens agreed to a twenty-five-year standstill under which he would not buy more Unocal stock and also promised to retain his current shareholding for at least a year. The press roundly described the settlement as Pickens' first major defeat, although Mesa would actually make close to $100 million in the transaction.

THE *UNOCAL* CASE

The issue in the *Unocal* case was whether the business judgment rule applied to the Unocal directors' decision to institute a discriminatory self-tender. The basic notion of the rule is that the Delaware courts will generally defer to the business judgment of a board of directors as long as there is no self-dealing or lack of care.

According to the *Unocal* court, a board may enact takeover defenses which thwart a bid, but the board will then be subject to an enhanced duty of care. Under this enhanced review, a court will look at the board's decision process as well as its ultimate decision and determine whether both are reasonable in relation to the threat involved. In the case of Mesa's takeover attempt, the court held that the Unocal board had acted reasonably.

The SEC eventually disallowed selective tenders. However, in a broader sense, *Unocal* created a key standard of takeover law, a rule which instantly became a focus of future takeover litigation: Were the board actions proportional to the threat? A variant of the Unocal discrimination technique is incorporated in the more sophisticated defense device, the poison pill.

Self-Restructuring

While Unocal marked the final major hostile fight in the 1980s Oil Wars, the underlying economic currents continued to favor change, and a number of major oil companies undertook self-restructurings during the late 1980s and early 1990s. ARCO chairman Robert O. Anderson, with a view of the Unocal building from his fifty-first-floor office, made his move even as the fight for Unocal was under way.

ARCO's plan—"a sort of self-acquisition"—was announced on April 29, the day for which Unocal had originally scheduled its annual meeting. In the restructuring, money would be borrowed and used to repurchase $4 billion of ARCO stock. In addition, the company's exploration budget would be slashed and write-offs taken on its mining division, a previous diversification that would be divested. Most dramatically, ARCO would shed its downstream gasoline business east of the Mississippi.

As one analyst put it, ARCO was "doing exactly what Wall Street's been telling it to do for three years." The stock price responded: It had been lingering in the mid-40s, but two weeks after the announcement, it had risen above 60. With this new higher trading price and extra debt on the balance sheet, ARCO effectively immunized itself from the Pickenses of the world. In 1997 and 1998, ARCO slimmed down and refocused, shedding coal mining and petrochemical operations; but the management no longer had Anderson's resolve. They were grooming the company for sale.

During the late 1980s to early 1990s, many of the other majors also felt compelled to act. Royal Dutch/Shell spent $5.7 billion to acquire the 31 percent of Shell Oil U.S.A. it did not already own. British Petroleum bought the 47 percent of Standard Oil of Ohio it did not already own for $7.6 billion. And Exxon spent $16 billion on a stock repurchase program between 1983 and mid-1990. At the same time, the company pursued smaller asset acquisitions and slashed its overhead.

The 1985 collapse in oil prices put added pressure on Big Oil: Profits plummeted and shareholders began to revolt. At the urging of shareholders, oil companies began to unwind their diversifications. Exxon wrote off Office Systems. Mobil faced agitation in favor of selling Montgomery Ward and eventually did so in a 1988 management-led LBO. Montgomery Ward limped along for almost ten years, and ultimately filed for bankruptcy in 1997. (We advised the company in its restructuring.)

Marred by the overhanging Pennzoil judgment, Texaco declared bankruptcy in 1987. Carl Icahn, sensing an opportunity, began accumulating Texaco shares in the market at a steep discount to prior trading levels and its intrinsic asset value and, with this large stake in place, pushed the company to settle the Pennzoil case. He also bought 24 million shares from wealthy but financially troubled Australian investor Robert Holmes à Court. Icahn believed, correctly, that the amount of the judgment imposed on Texaco would not be nearly as great as the market feared.

The company finally settled under compulsion from the bankruptcy court and due to significant agitation from Icahn himself. As Icahn had predicted, Texaco's stock jumped. However, Icahn kept hounding the company to sell assets and use the proceeds to pay shareholders a large dividend. While the proxy fight Icahn subsequently waged was unsuccessful, company management finally agreed to pay a special dividend, and Icahn sold his shares for a reported $500 million profit, at that time the second-largest block trade on the New York State Exchange.

Oil Services Companies   The 1990s opened with consolidation among oil services companies. The sector—populated with drilling equipment and service firms, and production companies—has over the past fifteen years gone through a feast-or-famine cycle closely tied to oil price gyrations. Given this dynamic, the early 1980s were a boom time: As oil prices rose, exploration and the demand for oil services increased. Companies invested heavily in oil rigs and other production capacity, which then was leased out to producers. However, the 1985 crash in prices ushered in a long lean period. Excess capacity drove prices and margins down and many weaker competitors were forced to exit the market.

The tough times were a hothouse for deal activity. In one high-profile combination, Baker International and Hughes Tool merged in a $1.2 billion stock swap, creating the industry's third-largest company. The merger brought together Hughes' drill bits and Baker's drilling equipment, and allowed for the parties to ride out the downturn by slashing costs. In another deal, Falcon Drilling Co., an onshore drilling concern, combined with Reading & Bates Corp., an offshore drilling company, to extend the breadth of their product offerings.

Downstream Combinations   In recent years, oil companies have focused on cleaning up their downstream refining and marketing operations, plagued by razor-thin margins. For example, in 1997, Texaco and Royal Dutch/Shell agreed to merge their U.S. refining and marketing businesses into a joint venture, and Mobil entered into a downstream joint venture with BP in Europe. A similar deal between Phillips and Conoco was in the works but fell apart. Cost reduction was the main driving force behind these deals.

Big Oil—Together Again   In the oil industry, the kick-off deal in the late 1990s consolidation boom was Union Pacific Resources' unsuccessful $4 billion hostile bid for Pennzoil. The bruising fight—with the opposing sides trading barbs in the press and in court—was reminiscent of the 1980s Oil Wars. However, Pennzoil's effective defense also highlighted how much defensive techniques had evolved since the 1980s.

Union Pacific Resources (UPR) first approached Pennzoil in April 1997 with a friendly $80 a share offer. Pennzoil had underperformed the market over the prior five years, but management had a turnaround plan in place which appeared to be taking hold. Confident that this plan would deliver greater value to shareholders than UPR's $84 per share bid, Pennzoil management rejected attempts to negotiate a deal.

UPR went public on June 23, 1997, with a two-tier, $84 a share hostile bid representing a 56 percent premium to Pennzoil's thirty-day average trading price. At the same time, UPR management kept pressuring the Pennzoil board to turn friendly.

Pennzoil shareholders embraced the UPR acquisition, with more than 60 percent tendering into the front end of UPR's offer. Yet

Pennzoil's board remained steadfast in its defense. The board rejected UPR's offer as inadequate and ordered a full defense. Pennzoil decided to "just say no."

Two key innovations of the 1980s gave the Pennzoil board its strong defensive position. First, the company had a poison pill in place which effectively precluded a hostile deal unless the Pennzoil board chose to pull the pill. Second, Pennzoil had a reinforced board that could not be removed immediately by the consent of shareholders. Because the terms of directors were staggered, UPR would need at least two annual meetings to capture the board and force the removal of the pill.

Protected by this strong defensive perimeter, Pennzoil began punching holes in the UPR bid. Pennzoil first attacked the value of the stock UPR was offering in the back-end merger, leading UPR to shift to an all-cash offer. The Pennzoil board also continued to insist that its strategic plan would provide superior returns to shareholders. Eventually, UPR concluded it would not be able to capture Pennzoil without a long and costly battle and therefore withdrew its offer. Though UPR's bid was unsuccessful, Pennzoil would soon find a friendly consolidation partner.

In April 1998, Quaker State announced its merger with the motor oil, refined products, and fast lube operations of Pennzoil Company. The merger created the biggest chain in the fast lube business, with 2,688 facilities, versus the 535 locations owned by its nearest competitor, Valvoline Instant Oil Change. The merged entity— Pennzoil–Quaker State—will be a "total car care" company.

As part of the transaction, Pennzoil's oil exploration and production operations were spun off to shareholders as a separate, publicly traded company called PennzEnergy. The restructuring created two pure-play companies, and allowed the market to value PennzEnergy's and Pennzoil–Quaker State's operations fully. In May 1999, PennzEnergy and Oklahoma City–based Devon Energy merged in a $2.4 billion deal.

Other small integrated players—Unocal and Ashland Oil—have also demerged their upstream and downstream operations in a trend that is likely to continue as other small to midsized players find their margins increasingly squeezed. These demerged operations will, as in Pennzoil–Quaker State, be positioned to merge with other pure-play companies.

Meanwhile, the smaller independents have been getting together in a search for competitive bulk. Our client Diamond Shamrock's 1996 merger-of-equals with Ultramar is a good example: By combining, the companies strengthened their retailing presence. Furthermore, with strong operations in California and Texas, the new company is positioned to take advantage of the growing Southwestern market.

Following the Pennzoil deal, a flurry of oil mergers was announced. Like the Big Oil deals of the 1980s, these combinations broke new records for size. First, BP and Amoco announced their $55.0 billion merger. In December 1998, Exxon agreed to buy Mobil for $86.4 billion. Then BP struck again, agreeing to buy ARCO in April 1999. Texaco and Chevron held merger discussions in May, but talks broke down over control issues and price.

Despite unfavorable short-term economic conditions in oil, the healthier players remained well positioned to ride out the storm. Even during this time of turmoil, Conoco, a subsidiary of DuPont, commenced an IPO to break loose from its corporate parent.

Both Mobil and Texaco had also been in merger discussions with Conoco, then a division of DuPont in the late 1990s. But ultimately Conoco decided to go at the oil business alone—at least for now. In early May 1998, Conoco CEO Archie W. Dunham sent a cryptic e-mail to top management. It said: "The leopard is out." The so-called Project Leopard was the code name for DuPont's plan to take Conoco public.

The market was trading DuPont at a multiple lower than that of the weighted sum of its individual businesses—specialty chemicals, life sciences, and oil: The IPO would unlock hidden value embedded in DuPont's stock. Furthermore, the environment that had originally prompted DuPont to buy Conoco no longer existed: DuPont no longer needed to insulate itself from rising oil prices, as oil prices had fallen drastically. The sale proceeds would allow DuPont to build up its drug and biotechnology businesses.

In October 1998, DuPont launched an IPO to sell 30 percent of Conoco to the public, which, at $4.4 billion, was the biggest IPO in U.S. history. The market assumes that eventually Conoco itself may become a takeover target.

In Europe, Total and Petrofina announced their $11.8 billion combination to create TotalFina, the third-largest oil company in Europe, just hours after Exxon and Mobil's announcement. Total chairman Thierry Desmarest remarked that the announced merger was a response to the growing industry consolidation: "There are a number of mergers now. It would be a danger to stay out of this process." Furthermore, economies of scale are becoming necessary to facilitate investment required by the European Union's auto oil regulations, effective 2005. The Total-Petrofina merger was a prelude to the inevitable consolidation of Europe's oil companies.

Recent deals have reflected the European market's emerging acceptance of hostile transactions, and true to Thierry Desmarest's observation, the sentiment among European oil companies has become "Eat or be eaten." Elf Aquitaine, TotalFina's French rival, made a run at Saga Petroleum, Norway's third-largest oil company, but eventually lost to local bidder Norsk Hydro (in no small part due to Norwegian regulators' lack of impartiality). Elf itself became a victim of a hostile bid when the newly created TotalFina, in its aggressive drive for scale, launched a $43 billion takeover bid for the company. Not to be outdone, Elf invoked, in a move reminiscent of the bitterly fought oil deals of the 1980s, the classic Pac-Man defense strategy against TotalFina and launched a $51.5 billion counterbid for the hostile bidder. Ultimately, failing to win investor support, Elf chairman Philippe Jaffre was forced to capitulate to TotalFina, but not before extracting a further meaningful premium to the original bid for a total enterprise value of $55 billion. A TotalFina–Elf Aquitaine combination promises to be a significant milestone in the consolidation of Europe's oil companies in not only the tone of European dealmaking but also the future landscape of the global oil industry. The combined company would be Europe's third-largest oil group, after Royal Dutch Shell and BP Amoco. National or regional oil champions are emerging to take on the global supermajors.

Natural Gas

Big Oil has not been the only energy sector rocked by change. The natural gas business, a close cousin to the oil business, has experienced similar volatility. The resulting hostile takeover fights in natural gas matched the billion-dollar oil mergers of the day in the blaze of their intensity.

Two factors made the natural gas business a particularly fruitful field for takeover activity. First, in the late 1970s and early 1980s, many companies had agreed to "take or pay" contracts—contracts obligating companies to buy a fixed amount of product at a set price each year, whether they needed the product or not—as a way to ensure supply in a tight market. When the market price of gas plummeted, these contracts hammered profits. Many of the companies eventually renegotiated and paid pennies on the dollar, but for a time they looked particularly vulnerable.

The impact of price volatility was magnified by deregulation in the early 1980s. Previously, the natural gas business had been a sleepy industry that earned stable returns due to government regulation. Suddenly, deregulation allowed producers to charge whatever the market would bear. In 1985, regulators went a step further, allowing utilities and industrial customers freedom to shop around for gas. Third parties other than pipeline companies also were permitted to enter the gas sector, and a host of independent natural gas marketing companies sprang up. As a result, pipeline companies, which previously had lived in a world of muted pricing and marketing pressures, were thrown into a competitive marketplace. Companies had varying degrees of success dealing with the new environment. Some floundered around for a few years until they found their stroke. Others took advantage of the uncertainty to build strong competitive positions. A spate of deals resulted, and the industry consolidated.

Coastal Corp.'s Man on Horseback   Coastal Corp.'s Oscar Wyatt saw his pipeline competitors' troubles as an opportunity. He hoped to jump-start Coastal's expansion effort by acquiring a company with existing capacity instead of spending the years required to build new pipelines.

Wyatt launched his first major takeover attempt in 1983, a $550 million hostile bid for Texas Gas Resources. However, Texas Gas eluded him when white knight CSX Corp. stepped forward. The next year, Wyatt offered $1.3 billion for Houston Natural Gas, which we represented. This bid also was beaten back by incumbent management, which bought out Coastal's stake after threatening a Cities Service–type Pac-Man bid for Coastal.

While these two attempts failed, the strategic imperative for a major acquisition remained, and Wyatt's appetite was further whetted. He took two steps to improve his chances for the next battle. First, Wyatt restructured the charter of Coastal so that it was immune to takeover itself, a "Deathstar" not subject to the Pac-Man defense. In a creative proxy, Wyatt asked his shareholders to approve the Deathstar vehicle so that he could attack other companies without being vulnerable. They overwhelmingly supported him. Second, he raised a $600 million blind pool of capital through a Drexel Burnham Lambert junk bond offering. Investors only knew the money would be used for acquisitions, not the identity of the targets.

Wyatt launched his next fight early in 1985. While rumors of an impending bid had been swirling in the market for weeks, the target's identity was not revealed until the first week in March, when Coastal launched a $2.27 billion hostile tender offer for American Natural Resources. Initially, management at the Detroit pipeline and natural gas production company resisted. But Wyatt was desperate to win and ANR finally agreed to be acquired by Coastal after Wyatt bumped his offer to $2.5 billion.

After two failed attempts, Wyatt had a major victory. The price looked steep at the time, yet Wyatt's vision was vindicated. From an operational perspective, the addition of ANR's Midwest pipeline gave Coastal a strong position in that market. From a financial perspective, ANR's growing cash flow proved more than sufficient to service the debt incurred in the transaction. In fact, Coastal was able to pay down approximately $1 billion of debt by 1989, and the additional cash flow provided by ANR gave Wyatt the ability to pursue further expansion.

By 1989, Coastal had digested ANR but still lacked a major connection to the Northeast. Wyatt was ready for another acquisition. He quickly settled on a target—Texas Eastern Corp.—a company that possessed such a link. The company also owned valuable North Sea oil reserves and a portfolio of Houston real estate which could be sold off to fund an acquisition.

Ultimately, Panhandle Eastern Corp. snatched Texas Eastern from Wyatt, topping Wyatt's $2.5 billion offer with a $3.2 billion bid. While it was a beleaguered company, Panhandle was willing to gamble that the combination of its Midwestern pipes and Texas Eastern's Northeastern pipes would create a powerful nationwide distributor: Panhandle had more miles of pipe, but Texas Eastern had three times the revenue. Even though Panhandle's debt would increase more than fourfold, the company faced a buy-or-be-bought situation and decided the potential reward was worth the risk.

After losing the Texas Eastern fight, Wyatt decided that natural gas properties had become overpriced in the market. He therefore turned to investing money in building new pipes and expanding Coastal's network internally.

Oscar Wyatt

Born in Beaumont, Texas, during the 1920s, Wyatt kicked around the shipyards and oil fields in the summertime. He served as bomber pilot in World War II, after which he earned an engineering degree and started a small oil business that would grow into $9 billion-a-year Coastal Petroleum. Along the way, Wyatt earned a reputation as a tough customer.

During the early 1970s, Wyatt became a pariah in his home state. His companies had supply contracts with hundreds of Texas towns. But when the Oil Shock jacked up the price of natural gas, Wyatt's companies didn't have enough reserves to fill the contracts. Caught between producers and customers, he shut off gas supplies to San Antonio and Austin in the middle of winter and fought customer lawsuits for years.

Name calling didn't seem to bother him. "My job isn't to win a popularity contest," he would say. "My job is to win a profitability contest." In the early 1980s, Wyatt's maxim led him to become involved in hostile takeover attempts. In fact, Wyatt did have an advantage over other bidders: He was willing to be much more aggressive in the valuation of disputed supply contracts, figuring rightly that he could settle disputes on a more favorable basis than existing management.

The Consolidation Widens   Oscar Wyatt was not the only player targeting natural gas companies in the middle 1980s. Other strategic purchasers, as well as financial buyers, saw the consolidation potential in the industry. Rocked by price fluctuations and facing an uncertain deregulated future, many natural gas companies had traded down in the market, making the nation's roughly twenty pipeline companies—some with relatively stable cash flows—appealing targets.

One big consolidation move came in May 1985 at the instigation of investor Irwin Jacobs. Smelling vulnerability, Jacobs built a stake in InterNorth, an energy transmission and production company with access to low-priced reserves and little debt. Sam Segnar, chairman of InterNorth, preferred to act rather than react, and therefore he contacted his counterpart at Houston Natural Gas to suggest a merger. Two weeks later, the pair announced a $2.3 billion deal in which InterNorth would acquire Houston Natural Gas, with HNG's CEO Kenneth Lay to take over the top spot as of January 1, 1987. Board representation would be split relatively evenly.

The combination of HNG and InterNorth made compelling strategic sense. Together, the two companies possessed a 37,000-mile pipeline system spanning coast to coast, giving the new company—renamed Enron in 1986—access to almost every major market and a wide range of supply sources. Enron therefore had the ability to provide customers and suppliers with efficient, effective service.

Once in the CEO job, Lay set about consolidating Enron's operations. He sold off noncore businesses to pay down debt, pared Enron's workforce, and reorganized operations. Very shortly, the strategic vision that brought NHG and InterNorth together was vindicated. Enron was on the way to becoming a model for the competitive new superpipeline companies that have come to dominate the business.

The final plank in pipeline deregulation came in 1992, when federal authorities opened the sale, distribution, and storage of natural gas to all entrants. Margins in gas production narrowed further as commodity pricing took over, providing a final shove to the natural gas companies. Most accelerated their drive into the still-profitable marketing and distribution side of the business and another wave of consolidation swept the industry.

The experience of Panhandle Eastern, the company which saved Texas Eastern from the clutches of Oscar Wyatt, is indicative. For Panhandle, the early 1990s were a rocky period as the price of natural gas went into free fall and margins collapsed. The company's problems were exacerbated by the debt burden from the Texas Eastern deal, which had jacked up Panhandle's debt load to over $2.8 billion. While the associated interest expense looked manageable in 1989, it became burdensome when competition ate into profit margins. Meanwhile, a number of land mines buried in Texas Eastern's operations—primarily environmental problems—surfaced shortly after the deal closed. Panhandle was forced to slash its dividend by 60 percent and its stock lost over 60 percent of its value in the immediate aftermath. The company's CEO left under pressure.

Over the next few years, Dennis Hendrix, the former chief executive of Texas Eastern who returned to be the CEO, concentrated on reshaping Panhandle. He settled several disputes with customers, negotiated his way out of uneconomical take-or-pay contracts, and wrote off impaired assets.

Then he shifted Panhandle's focus: Production was downplayed and distribution became key. Rather than spend money to find new gas, Panhandle would make money moving other people's gas through a new Northeast distribution system that it would build. A second major acquisition also played a crucial role in Panhandle's overhaul. In 1994, the company purchased Associated Natural Gas, a marketing outfit, for $591 million in stock and $239 million of Associated's debt.

The desire to gain further exposure to marketing and distribution capabilities was not unique to Panhandle. Enron Corp., Coastal, and other natural gas players also were busily buying up marketing capacity during the early 1990s.

Deals in the 1990s

As in the oil industry, companies have increasingly begun to use joint ventures to address their strategic dilemmas. Midsized firms frequently lack the relationships and deep pockets to undertake the most attractive exploration opportunities or to fund a diversified project portfolio; joint ventures provide a way. Furthermore, joint ventures provide many of the same risk-sharing and cost-reduction benefits of outright mergers but are easier to execute and, because they are more limited in scope, are easier to dissolve, if necessary.

Examples include a joint venture between both Canada's Ranger Oil and the U.S. independent Chesapeake Energy and between Amoco Canada and Northstar Energy to develop a natural gas prospect in British Columbia, and a venture announced on February 3, 1999, by Chevron and ARCO, to combine their natural gas and oil assets in West Texas and southeastern New Mexico to reduce costs.

Other natural gas companies have engaged in more traditional M&A activity. For example, Sonat acquired Zilkha Energy—with its valuable Gulf of Mexico reserves. Subsequently, Sonat was acquired by El Paso Energy for $6 billion. Duke Energy, primarily a power company, has also been an active participant in the 1990s natural gas industry consolidation. In 1997, Duke acquired gas pipeline company Pan-Energy Corp., the old Panhandle Eastern, for $7.7 billion in an effort to control the commodity that powers its generators. And in November 1998, Duke agreed to purchase the natural gas processing business of Union Pacific Resource for $1.35 billion, shortly following the sale of two gas pipelines to CMS Energy for $2.2 billion. The two deals allowed Duke to exchange a business whose rates were regulated for a business whose rates it could set freely. The UPR deal makes Duke the nation's largest producer of natural gas liquids.

Indeed, Duke's latest acquisition was timely. Depressed oil prices have depressed the market price for natural gas liquids and the trading prices of natural gas liquid companies. Duke was able to get in at the bottom of the economic cycle and buy assets on the cheap.

Electric Utilities

Deregulation is just beginning to take shape in the utilities business. The breakdown of regulation—the mechanism used to induce companies to build up a national utility infrastructure by guaranteeing a return on investment in exchange for government pricing control—has brought with it a flurry of M&A activity.

Historically, utilities were guaranteed a stable return on investment in the form of cost-plus pricing: Regulators allowed the companies to charge whatever rate was necessary to earn a "reasonable" return on capital invested. Utilities were permitted to increase their rates each time they invested more capital to build a new power plant or purchase a new transformer. Theoretically, regulators policed the companies to avoid unnecessary spending.

The monopoly system may have been effective and appropriate in the power industry's developmental era, but its rigidity caused the industry to become inefficient as it matured. Under cost-plus pricing, when a company made an unsound expenditure decision, government regulators nonetheless usually added the expenditure to the company's rate base. In effect, bad decisions by utility company executives and investors, as well as lax regulatory oversight, were paid for by utility customers.

Nuclear power facilities are the classic example of ill-advised projects that have led to increased rates. When oil prices skyrocketed in the 1970s, utilities began planning construction of nuclear reactors. In many cases, by the time building began, oil prices had already settled back to more reasonable levels. Yet these nuclear facilities were built anyway at great cost—often more than originally projected. Given these "stranded costs"—costs that are so high that open markets will not allow companies to recover them—utility rates skyrocketed.

The impact of this system is apparent today in the dramatic variations in rates charged by different utilities. Northern California's Pacific Gas & Electric, for example, charges its customers about 10 cents per kilowatt-hour for electricity. Oregon's Portland General Corporation, on the other hand, runs the meter at an average of 5½ cents per kilowatt-hour. On the eastern tip of New York's Long Island, customers dole out roughly 16 cents per kilowatt-hour.

Today, the technology and infrastructure is now in place to transfer power generated in Wisconsin to customers in California. States like California and New York have begun to relax monopoly protection, and other states promise to follow. A low-cost producer will be able to enter the market of a high-cost producer, forcing the high-cost producer to adapt or go out of business. We are on the edge of a revolution in the structure of the utility business. Many companies have chosen M&A to adapt to these new realities.

As the industry suffers through the painful intermediate period between regulation and deregulation, there will no doubt be confusion. The market for energy itself remains highly imperfect. Summer heat waves in 1998 drove electricity prices up to exorbitant levels, causing energy trading companies to default on delivery contracts. Chicago-based Commonwealth Edison Co. was forced to pay $5,000 per megawatt-hour to buy energy on the spot market—more than 100 times the regular price. It was the Oscar Wyatt fiasco all over again. Vestiges of regulations can also have a chilling effect on M&A activity. For example, Baltimore Gas & Electric's 1998 plan to purchase Potomac Edison fell apart when Maryland regulators decided that 70 percent of cost savings generated—as opposed to the 50 percent common in most states—should be given back to consumers.

Industry Trends   Five overlapping trends can be discerned amid the growing flood of utilities deals: 1) divestiture of power generation assets to focus on distribution and service; 2) merging "horizontally" to gain scale; 3) industry globalization; 4) mergers between different types of energy companies; and 5) diversification into new business lines.

First, like Panhandle in the natural gas industry, many companies in the electric utilities business have strategically chosen to focus on distribution rather than generation. A string of generation asset sell-offs has resulted. Niagara Mohawk sold its stake in the Nine Mile Point Nuclear plant located in Scriba, New York. And in December 1998, the company sold two coal-fired electric generating stations as well as seventy-two hydroelectric power plants. These moves are part of NiMo's Power Choice restructuring agreement in which the utility will focus on the service and delivery business.

Similarly, Consolidated Edison, the New York utility, has been in the process of auctioning its power plants. As has been true for several utilities, this move was required by regulators who sought to create a more competitive market and reduce stranded costs. Expected proceeds are over $2 billion. Similarly, Montana Power has recently sold nearly all its electric generating facilities to PP&L Global of Fairfax, Virginia, choosing instead to focus on distribution and telecommunications services.

PP&L, on the other hand, has chosen the opposite route: to consolidate its position in the power generation business. The utility agreed to acquire the generation facilities of Bangor Hydro-Electric Company to gain a stronger foothold in the New England market. Likewise, Entergy is buying up nuclear plants in an effort to develop nationwide nuclear power generation capability. Its $80 million bid to acquire Boston Edison's Pilgrim nuclear station marked the first time a U.S. nuclear power plant was sold in a competitive bidding process.

Second, utilities have also been engaging in horizontal M&A activity to benefit from economics of scale. In December 1997, the American Electric Power Company and Central and South West Corporation announced their plans to merge. At the time, the combined company would have been the nation's largest electric utility in terms of generation, customers, and kilowatt-hours sold. In September 1999, Unicom and PECO Energy announced a $32 billion merger of equals making the combination the largest electric utility deal to date and the number-one utility in terms of customers. These two deals have redefined the scale in the industry and have created two emerging giants who will be future consolidators.

Third, facing the prospect of growing competition, utility companies have been looking abroad for high-growth markets. One manifestation of this trend has been the race to invest in projects in the emerging markets of South America and China. Another has been a rush by U.S. utilities into the U.K. market. For example, in 1996, we represented Virginia-based Dominion Resources in a $2.2 billion acquisition of the U.K.'s East Midlands Electricity. Other major U.K. acquisitions include Entergy Corporation's $2.1 billion deal for London Electricity, CalEnergy's $1.3 billion hostile buyout of Northern Electric, and Texas Utilities' $10.9 billion purchase of The Energy Group, completed in June 1998.

Great Britain represents a particularly attractive market for U.S. companies because deregulation has proceeded more quickly there. All generating companies currently sell their power into a clearinghouse that sets prices at half-hour intervals based on market demand. The U.K. companies have already begun offering telecommunications and other services, and are a laboratory for what might happen in the U.S. market. Moreover, U.K. companies have outpaced their U.S. counterparts in terms of growth. To date, American companies have taken over eight of the U.K.'s twelve regional electrical utilities.

Similarly, deregulation is taking hold in Australia, where Texas Utilities just completed a $1 billion purchase of the Westar natural gas distribution and Kinetik Energy retailing facilities from the state government of Victoria in 1999. Victoria is the first Australian state to auction its electric power and gas assets in a privatization effort, a move that could spark similar auctions in other states, providing more growth markets for U.S. companies.

Emerging markets are beginning to become targets for U.S. energy companies. Teco Energy, a Tampa utility, announced it was acquiring a $25 million joint venture stake in Energía Global International's investments in El Salvador, Panama, Costa Rica, and Guatemala. Reliant Energy and Enron have also been investors in Central America, and Duke Energy made a failed $3 billion bid for 60 percent control of the Chilean electric company Empresa Nacional de Electricidad.

The soon-to-be-deregulated U.S. market will likely prove attractive for foreign energy companies, however. Scottish Power announced its intent to acquire PacifiCorp in 1998, making it the first foreign company to buy a big U.S. utility. This combination comes after the failure of Scottish Power's earlier attempts to merge with Florida Light and Power and Cinergy.

Fourth, integration of natural gas companies and utilities has been another strategic response to coming deregulation. Some deals have come at the instigation of the gas companies—Enron's $3.2 billion purchase of the Portland General Corporation, for example. More commonly, though, utilities have reached out to buy the experience and marketing savvy of the natural gas concerns. For example, Houston Industries spent $2.4 billion for NorAm Energy. Similarly, Duke Power of North Carolina nabbed Panenergy—the renamed Panhandle Eastern—for $7.7 billion. On February 22, 1999, electrical utility Dominion Resources entered into a $6.3 billion merger agreement with Consolidated Natural Gas, a company that produces, distributes, and transports natural gas primarily in Ohio, Pennsylvania, New York, Virginia, and West Virginia. Ironically, Dominion had sold Consolidated its Virginia Natural Gas subsidiary in 1990 so that it could focus on its core electricity business. But the changing economics of the business as well as deregulation have made reentry into natural gas attractive for Dominion.

Its friendly merger offer spurned by Consolidated in February, Columbia Energy Group—another natural gas company— launched a $6.9 billion hostile bid for the company in April 1999. The offer, a combination of cash and stock, offered Consolidated shareholders a 21 percent premium over Dominion Resources' bid, as the price of Dominion's stock had slipped between February and April. Nevertheless, Dominion had a higher market value than Columbia and the ability to outbid Columbia. In the end, Dominion won with a sweetened $6.3 billion deal and Columbia became the target of a $5.7 billion hostile bid from NiSource, the former Nipsco Industries.

LEADING THE WAY

Kenneth Lay and Enron

Enron CEO Kenneth Lay stitched HNG and InterNorth together into the leading gas pipeline and marketing company. The purchase of Portland General signaled the next phase in Enron's growth. The goal was to bring skill developed in the deregulated gas market to the deregulating electricity market.

Lay saw that the fragmented gas industry was bound to consolidate under the force of deregulation and understood that marketing would become the key to future success. Enron capitalized on these visions of the future by pioneering the practice of trading natural gas. Very quickly, Enron's trading operation became a de facto market maker for natural gas contracts and developed into the nation's leading wholesaler of natural gas.

Part of the Enron success has been transforming a staid utility company into an entrepreneurial, driving competitor. Lay has accomplished the shift by bringing in new people—trained in business disciplines like marketing and finance—to recharge the Enron culture.

As deregulation proceeds in the electricity market, Lay hopes to repeat his earlier success. The acquisition of Portland General gave Enron a captive supply source. Meanwhile, Enron's traders have begun to swap electricity and already are a leading provider, behind the Bonneville Power Administration and the Tennessee Valley Authority.

Of course, a great deal of competition exists in the electricity business as hundreds of companies scramble to get a piece of this $320 billion market. California opened its market in January 1998 and several other states have followed thereafter. Lay has a staff of several hundred working on retailing strategies and a nationwide advertising program. Enron is leading the way toward a future integrated energy market.

The frenzied pace of these utilities-gas deals mark utilities' search for marketing expertise. The natural gas companies have already undergone deregulation and know how to compete in a free market.

Fifth, the utilities hope eventually to provide bundled services—gas, electricity, etc.—to customers on a nationwide basis once deregulation has run full course. One company, Topeka-based Western Resources, has even decided a natural extension of its business is in the home security industry.

This diversification strategy appears promising, given the extremely valuable customer recognition, access, and information possessed by utilities. The hope is that the envelope from the power company, which arrives at homes each month, ultimately can be used as an entrée to provide all manner of other services. Another company, Conectiv—formerly known as Delmarva Power and Light Co.—has begun to offer local phone service to compete against incumbent carrier Bell Atlantic. Meanwhile, Montana Power—through its subsidiary Touch America—is laying fiber-optic cable in an attempt to enter the telecommunications market. The company expects telecommunications to account for half of its total earnings within five years. Western Resources is also bulking up its security services business with a merger with Protection One and Centennial Security Holdings.

Further competitive pressure on the utilities industry could come from the piston of new technology: The "microturbine" promises to revolutionize the power generation and distribution market. Benjamin Rosen, who founded Compaq, described the new technology this way: "The little turbine engine has the same relationship to larger power plants that the PC had to the mainframe. It puts the source of power at the site." Generation may, in the future, come from these smaller devices—about the size of a refrigerator—rather than from central generation facilities. Currently microturbines are expensive and have relatively small output: One microturbine can only power a small restaurant.

The way we seek and pay for the energy that powers our lives will continue to be a topic of intense activity over the next decade.

Metamorphosis: 10
Conglomerates Transformed

> *"As Gregor Samsa awoke from unsettling dreams one morning, he found himself transformed in his bed into a monstrous vermin. . . . 'What has happened to me?' he thought. It was no dream."*
>
> —Franz Kafka, "The Metamorphosis"

The Oil Wars had sparked a corporate treasure hunt. As the oil industry restructured through the early 1980s, Wall Street buzzed with talk of "breakup value." Assuming that undervalued assets were not unique to the oil business, investors began to prowl for other companies whose parts were worth more than the whole. Conglomerates provided such an opportunity.

After faltering at the end of the 1960s, many large, diversified companies limped through the 1970s. In the 1980s these conglomerates became a punching bag for critics: Corporate diversification was widely held to be a failed experiment and conglomerates were punished in the marketplace.

As a result, ITT, Gulf + Western, Tenneco, City Investing, Westinghouse, Wickes, Teledyne, RCA, IC Industries, Allied, Litton, Rockwell, and Textron were all torn apart. In fact, much of the deal activity in the 1980s and 1990s was based on the undoing of the deals of the 1960s. But at the same time as this trend toward unbundling conglomerates was unfolding, some companies—Seagram, Cendant, Tyco, Berkshire Hathaway, and GE—attempted to laugh in the face of the trend toward pure-play businesses.

Brave New World: 1960s Conglomerates Restructure

The early 1980s presented a caustic business environment. Interest rates topped out above 20 percent, and the Dow Jones Industrial Average fell to the low 700s, where it had been in 1963 and again in 1970. Stockholders in the conglomerates put together in the 1960s suffered particularly. LTV's stock closed as high as $136 in 1968 and below $12 in 1980. ITT's stock traded as high as $63 in 1968 and as low as $25 in 1980. Investors were irate.

A number of key factors shaped the pace and scope of this trend:

Financial   The debt and interest expense burden created by the conglomerates' buying sprees of the 1960s and early 1970s had dragged down earnings per share and turned off investors. In many cases, rising interest rates in the 1980s exacerbated the problem, incentivizing managers to convert unproductive assets into cash.

ITT, for example, carried nearly $5 billion of debt in 1980. While the resulting interest expense was manageable while interest rates were relatively low, when the prime rate hit 20 percent, ITT began to feel the squeeze. In 1981, the company was forced to pay out almost $800 million in interest, a tremendous drag on its reported earnings. Rand Araskog, Harold Geneen's successor, made debt reduction a major goal; divestitures were the only way to accomplish this task.

Increased Sophistication   The early conglomerates were built on a premise of ever-increasing earnings, the interchangeability of financial management skills among various industries, and an adoring analytical and money management community. All of these ideas were anachronistic by the early 1980s.

Analysts came to recognize that centralized administration could, in general, not effectively manage a diverse group of companies. There were, in fact, benefits to specialization and focus. These conglomerates which had reveled in their image of having the best of "modern" management were in the 1980s perceived to be the most antiquated. Stern Stewart's newly developed EVA® analysis indicated that conglomerates were destroying shareholder wealth by not focusing on the costs of capital employed—not just debt but also equity and working capital—in relation to the return generated by the capital. Indeed, one reason the LBO buyers of conglomerate divestitures did so well is that the companies were so poorly managed. Furthermore, investors already held widely diversified portfolios: They did not need conglomerates to add a second layer of diversification—especially if diversification came at the expense of the high takeover prices.

Shifting Market Orthodoxy   Due to these financial and management factors, market forces coalesced to favor the pure-play company. Because the market had penalized the share prices of conglomerates, research analysts soon noticed that the conglomerates' market values were lower than the sum of the fair market value of their subsidiaries. The realization that selling off these companies could build shareholder value sparked a divestiture wave in the early 1980s.

The success of the Gibson Greeting Cards buyout sparked a sequence of similar deals in which leveraged entrepreneurs snatched assets away for a fraction of their true value. Yet the conglomerates were unable or unwilling to unlock the same values on their own. The buyers took the risk and seemed more sophisticated than the lumbering companies of the 1980s. That the market rewarded conglomerates for divesting subsidiaries and that financial buyers earned sizable returns on their purchases led eventually to the slimming down of the conglomerates.

A Passing of the Guard   To understand the story of the conglomerates, one must understand the personalities that shaped them. Many of the companies—Textron, LTV, Gulf + Western—were built up by founding entrepreneurs. Other companies that blossomed in the 1960s featured strong-willed, almost autocratic leaders like ITT's Harold Geneen.

Starting in the late 1970s, the leaders of the conglomerate era began to pass into retirement, some more gracefully than others. These men, who had spent their professional careers building up major diversified companies and had—in the environment of the 1960s—earned a reputation for genius, quite understandably resisted the notion that their companies needed to adjust with the times. The idea that the companies they had built up should be broken apart was anathema.

The successors who took over top management positions were not as closely tied to the Go-Go Years and were not as emotionally invested in retaining the pieces as a combined whole. The change in management philosophy was sometimes traumatic.

Turmoil at ITT

ITT is the classic example. The company suffered through a difficult period in the early 1970s, with its stock, which had traded as high as $67 per share in 1971, hitting $12 in 1974. Earnings also suffered: ITT's string of fifty-eight straight quarterly earnings increases came to an end in 1974 when yearly earnings came in 13 percent below 1973. The downward trend continued into 1975.

The economic problems at ITT were magnified by political controversies—the company's involvement in Chile, alleged improprieties surrounding the San Diego Republican Party convention, the Hartford Insurance antitrust and tax cases. The bad news at times threatened to bury Harold Geneen.

Despite the tumult, however, Geneen survived. A somewhat reluctant board granted him a two-year contract extension in August

1974, ignoring ITT's mandatory retirement age of sixty-five. When his contract expired at the end of 1977, Geneen relinquished CEO title to Lyman Hamilton, but remained chairman.

Notwithstanding the formal transfer of day-to-day authority, Geneen was not ready to release the reins of power and, within months, began openly sniping at Hamilton. The main source of friction was the new CEO's decision to redirect ITT's strategic focus: Geneen favored the long-standing emphasis on revenue growth, the foundation of ITT's 1960s buying frenzy, while Hamilton was more concerned with the bottom line and return on equity. Hamilton's strategy dictated that underperforming businesses be divested.

Things came to a head in June 1979. Hamilton had been at the helm for eighteen months and was ready to make a bold move—the sale of ITT's European consumer goods business. Geneen was irate when he heard the news. He leapt into action while Hamilton was away on a three-week business trip in Asia, furiously lobbying his fellow board members. Two weeks later, Hamilton was out as CEO and Rand Araskog, Geneen's new pick as successor, was in.

Araskog inherited an incredibly complex, troubled company. During the Geneen years, ITT had bought or merged with more than 250 companies. Revenues had climbed from $765 million to over $22 billion. But the 1970s found earnings and revenues down, and the stock price continued to languish. The debt burden left over from Geneen's acquisition program was at least partly to blame.

Araskog was determined to reverse the downward slide. His intermediate-term goal was to reduce the company's debt load—at that point approximately 50 percent of total capital—and, like Hamilton, he saw a divestiture program as the way to do it. However, unlike Hamilton, Araskog first cleared a major impediment out of the way: Geneen. Araskog gave ITT's board members an ultimatum. The board caved, and Geneen was forced to resign his chairmanship.

Free to act, Araskog went on a selling spree. Between 1979 and 1983, ITT sold approximately $200 million of assets each year. However, the stock price failed to respond, remaining significantly below its 1970 trading levels. A number of predators began to circle, including Jay Pritzker, the Chicago real estate developer and investor, and financier Irwin Jacobs. Further pressure was put on ITT by insurgent shareholders, who kept pounding away at Araskog. In November 1984, the company received requests to put the liquidation of the company to a shareholder vote. ITT ultimately prevented such a vote, but the request spurred Araskog and the ITT board to adopt an even more aggressive divestiture program. On January 16, 1985, the company announced a plan to sell additional companies.

Araskog followed through with the plan. By 1986, the tally of divested businesses reached ninety-five, with proceeds received totaling $4 billion. Debt as a share of total capital slipped below 30 percent in 1988. Finally, in a particularly dramatic move, ITT abandoned its roots as an international telephone company, selling its telephone subsidiary to a French company in 1992 for $3.6 billion. Its international telephone directories company was ITT's only remaining link to the phone business. The divestiture left ITT with operations in forest products, financial services, manufacturing, and leisure.

Then, Araskog stunned his shareholders and the market by announcing ITT's new strategy: The company's new core focus would be its leisure and gaming business. The forest products company, Rayonier, was spun off to shareholders. The company next paid $3 billion to acquire casino operator Caesars World and partial ownership of Madison Square Garden (which held the New York Knicks and Rangers)—purchases intended to complement ITT's Sheraton Hotels division.

The culmination of his gaming and leisure strategy came in 1995, when Araskog embraced the new market orthodoxy: Bowing to persistent market pressure, Araskog announced plans to split up ITT.

By December 1995, three distinct companies carried the ITT name. ITT Industries operated a manufacturing and defense business, ITT Hartford Group operated a financial services business, and ITT Corporation operated the hotel, gaming, and sports properties, with Araskog as CEO.

The Strategic Merits of the Spin-off

The spin-off has become a common feature in the business landscape. The roster of recent spin-off participants includes not only ITT, but also General Motors, AT&T, Viacom, Sprint, Pepsi, and U S West. Although each company's situation is unique, all of these companies embraced the spin-off in an attempt to benefit from Wall Street's preference for focused, pure-play companies.

Given the prevailing market view, Araskog's decision to spin off ITT's manufacturing and financial services operations made sense: The three resulting pure-play companies would no longer be tagged with ITT's conglomerate discount. Furthermore, a spin-off transaction, if properly structured, would be tax-free to the company and its shareholders. By contrast, an outright sale of ITT's industrial and financial services businesses would likely have triggered a significant tax liability: The company would have been taxed on any gain realized on the sale, and shareholders would have been taxed individually on any special dividends paid out from the sale proceeds.

Finally, a spin-off would afford ITT shareholders the upside benefit from future improvements in the spun-off businesses. And indeed, it seemed likely that such benefits would materialize. A body of empirical evidence suggests that both spun-off companies and their former parents tend to outperform the market in the years following the spin-off. Some explain this phenomenon by positing that spin-offs unlock the entrepreneurial potential of employees. One may further argue that close market scrutiny forces the spun-off company to manage its costs and grow its earnings, something it might not have had to do as part of a larger business. Smaller subsidiaries often succumb to the "rich uncle syndrome": The parent company protects the subsidiary in lean times and may not force the subsidiary to live up to its potential.

Although ITT's stock ran up on the announcement of its three-way split, Araskog soon came under intense pressure. Many investors believed he had "gone Vegas" during his recent acquisition spree and that the disparate parts of the new enterprise made little sense together. Further criticism mounted when Araskog launched an expensive plan to build several Planet Hollywood hotel and casino complexes. As a result, the market once again pummeled ITT's stock, taking away much of the market value added from the spin-off.

With its market value again depressed, ITT Corporation became a target of Hilton in what would be one of the most contentious takeover fights of the 1990s. Araskog soon tried to split ITT into yet another three pieces, but a Nevada judge prevented him from doing so, as this restructuring was seen as part of a larger plan solely intended to entrench management. ITT was ultimately purchased by Starwood Hotels and Resorts Worldwide. Soon after, however, Starwood was forced to give up its unique paired-share REIT status, which had given it special tax privileges, and its share price crashed.

Unlocking the Hidden Value

Throughout the 1980s, conglomerate leaders battled to close the gap between the stock market and breakup values of their companies. Making operational changes was a key part of this process: Costs were trimmed, marketing refocused, and divisions reorganized.

Despite valiant attempts, however, internal operational adjustments rarely proved sufficient to close the value gap. As a result, many conglomerates also carried out financial and structural changes. Standard strategic options developed over time. A company might follow ITT's approach and sell or spin off assets not vital to its core business. Alternatively, the company might issue tracking stock in a subsidiary. The common thread was that these strategies were designed to appeal to the new market orthodoxy.

The Alchemy of Divestiture

Charlie Bluhdorn's Gulf + Western followed a similar trajectory to that of ITT. Bluhdorn built one of America's largest conglomerates, involved in businesses ranging from race tracks and cigars to mining titanium and publishing. Eventually, like most conglomerates, Gulf + Western's performance became lackluster. Under Martin Davis, the new CEO in 1983, the company shed 100 unrelated businesses and refocused the company into a relatively debt-free media company. Rechristened Paramount Communications, the company remained focused on the media business subsequent to slimming down. In 1989, Davis made an attempt to bust up the Time-Warner merger and purchase Time Inc. When that effort failed, Martin Davis continued on the prowl until settling upon Viacom in 1993, triggering his slugfest with Barry Diller.

Westinghouse: The Strategic Transformation

The many changes undergone by Westinghouse—from focused industrial company to conglomerate, back to a focused media company—dramatically illustrate the fluidity of corporate existence.

Westinghouse Electric Corporation began life as a single-line company. Founded in 1886 by engineer George Westinghouse, the company's product was its alternating current electricity distribution system. Over time, however, Westinghouse grew into a diversified conglomerate, and by 1981 it owned a 7-Up bottler, a financial services company, radio stations, and cable television systems. The company manufactured kitchen ranges, fighter jets, nuclear power plants, office furniture, and light bulbs.

Like many other conglomerates, Westinghouse started the 1980s in too many businesses and with too much debt. Corporate raiders circled and investors criticized the company's poor performance. In response, a string of chief executives slashed costs and pruned operations. More than seventy businesses were sold between 1985 and 1990, netting $3.5 billion.

However, Westinghouse remained a laggard. The company's managers desperately sought a vehicle for growth and bet on financial services, hoping to match the success of rival General Electric. On paper, Westinghouse Credit Corporation boomed, generating as much as 16 percent of the parent company's profits in peak years.

As the nation went into the recession of 1991, however, it became clear Westinghouse was no General Electric: The Credit Corporation's loan portfolio was in shambles, with its real estate loans and junk bonds underwater to the tune of at least $5 billion. The finance subsidiary had taken on too much risk in search of fast revenue and profit growth, and in the recession, the downside to that risk reared its ugly head. Westinghouse was forced to take two charges against profits in 1991, the first for $975 million and the second for $1.7 billion. Another $2.7 billion charge was taken in 1992.

Westinghouse's problems were not limited to its finance subsidiary. For even after the asset sales of the 1980s, the company remained a diversified conglomerate, with roughly seventy-five business lines arranged in seven groups, and a correspondingly messy balance sheet. The company was weighed down with more than $7 billion of debt—$9 billion, or roughly 80 percent of capital, if the debt of nonconsolidated subsidiaries were to be included.

Finally, a 1993 boardroom revolt forced the incumbent CEO to resign. Michael H. Jordan, a PepsiCo executive, was hired in his place and made an early commitment to reshape Westinghouse.

Westinghouse was not without bright spots, however. Both the Group W broadcasting operation and the Thermo King refrigerated-transport unit were performing well. But while Jordan wanted to fix rather than jettison lagging businesses, he realized that Westinghouse's mammoth debt compelled him to sell assets if he wanted to save the company. In his first two years as CEO, Jordan sold five major businesses: office furniture, defense electronics, electric distribution, electrical supply stores, and real estate development, raising more than $5 billion in the process. Jordan was able to prune away a significant amount of debt.

The resulting slimmed-down balance sheet gave Jordan freedom to execute the next step in his strategy: to strengthen Westinghouse's high-margin, high-growth broadcasting operations. His first move, the $5.4 billion acquisition of CBS, came in August 1995. The next year, Westinghouse spent another $4.9 billion to acquire Infinity Broadcasting, led by the ebullient Mel Karmazin, which owned a major syndicate of radio stations, and then followed up with the purchase of the Gaylord country music cable channels.

These acquisitions left Westinghouse something of an ungainly Siamese twin, a single company with one foot in the glamorous media business and another in the staid industrial world. In a market that valued pure-play companies highly, the media division was being tarnished by its association with the industrial business.

Jordan had to decide what strategic direction the new Westinghouse would take. The company could rely on operational improvements to drive its stock price higher. But choosing this status quo option would not address the "conglomerate discount" plaguing Westinghouse's stock. To eliminate the conglomerate discount issue, Jordan could effect more asset sales, a spin-off, or a tracking stock issue.

Initially, Westinghouse selected a spin-off in which the company would be divided into two separate public companies. The first, Westinghouse Electric Corporation, would harbor the industrial and power generation businesses. The second would hold the television and radio broadcasting businesses, with the CBS franchise as the linchpin.

However, the Street was skeptical that a spin-off would work. Many of Westinghouse's industrial businesses—power generation and nuclear power, for example—had not been strong performers. In addition, perceived litigation and environment risk weighed down operations like nuclear power. Thermo King, the company's success-ful refrigeration equipment business, was the only real sizzle on the industrial side. But when that business was sold to Ingersoll-Rand for $2.6 billion in September 1997, the market consensus was that a spin-off of the remaining industrial business would trade poorly.

Perhaps because of this market skepticism, Westinghouse instead opted to sell off the major remaining pieces of its industrial empire, while continuing to build its media business. Engineering firm Morrison Knudsen teamed up with BNFL to buy the Westinghouse Electric Company in July 1998 for $1.2 billion. In August 1998, Westinghouse sold its conventional power generation business to Siemens for $1.5 billion. The proceeds from the Thermo King sale were used to pay down debt and to fund the acquisition of ninety-eight additional radio stations from American Radio.

In the end, Westinghouse became an entirely new company, completely divested of its industrial operations. What was once just one of its portfolio companies—CBS—has come to embody Westinghouse's new strategic vision. In fact, though, Westinghouse had come full circle. A pioneer in the early days of radio, Westinghouse, whose KDKA station produced the first U.S. commercial radio broadcast in 1920, has returned to its roots over seventy years later. To reflect this monumental shift, Westinghouse changed its name to CBS. Shortly after the christening of the new company, Chairman and CEO Michael Jordan became the target of a boardroom coup, and Mel Karmazin took over. Jordan represented the company's conglomerate past, and Karmazin its media future. Since Mel came to CBS, he has driven its stock price steadily upward. It was the end of one era and the beginning of another as CBS agreed in September 1999 to merge with Viacom to form a new media giant.

Building a Conglomerate in the 1990s

While ITT, Gulf + Western, and Westinghouse were restructuring, some companies clung to their conglomerate structures. Other companies that once were pure-play companies, such as Seagram, began to diversify themselves.

Seagram

Seagram is a company that has bucked the trend toward the pure-play business, recently making the transition from liquor producer to conglomerate. Seagram was founded by current chairman Edgar Bronfman Jr.'s grandfather Samuel Bronfman, the son of Russian Jewish immigrants. Samuel, along with his three brothers, started out running hotels on the Canadian frontier and eventually built up one of the world's largest liquor businesses.

Edgar Jr., however, was at first not interested in the family business, forgoing college to become a film producer in Hollywood. While in his twenties, Bronfman produced the Jack Nicholson movie *The Border*. He then came to Universal Studios—the company he would later buy—in 1978, a then-stodgy place best known for TV movies. After the birth of his first child, Edgar Jr.'s father asked him if he would like to join Seagram, with the intent to someday run it. Bronfman said yes.

In the heat of the 1980s Oil Wars, Seagram had made a hostile bid for Conoco in an attempt to diversify. While DuPont eventually acquired the oil company, Seagram did accumulate a large stake in Conoco, which it eventually exchanged for DuPont stock. It was this stock that enabled Bronfman to launch Seagram into the entertainment business.

In April 1995, Seagram shed its 24.2 percent stake in DuPont and used the cash proceeds to buy 80 percent of MCA—which Bronfman renamed Universal—from ailing Matsushita. Through this transaction, Seagram gained the Universal Studios and Universal Music businesses.

This diversification, however, soon led to disarray in management. Bronfman, dissatisfied with old MCA management, replaced the diehard managers with executives whom observers have called inexperienced. Acquired record labels were discontinued or combined, irritating bands that had long-standing relationships with record executives. In fall 1997, Seagram sold a majority interest in its television and cable assets to Barry Diller—retaining a minority interest—in what many thought was an odd move: What was an entertainment company doing without these valuable assets? But Bronfman realized that he would have to invest a huge amount of capital into the cable operation if he wanted to compete with Time Warner or Viacom. Therefore, Bronfman brought in Diller as a partner, who presumably would be able to do more with the assets. Bronfman also wanted the money for an even bigger investment to come.

Movie flops further compounded Seagram's problems. *Blues Brothers 2000, Dante's Peak, Mercury Rising,* and *Primary Colors* performed poorly at the box office. Had the company best known for its Chivas Regal and Seagram V.O. brands made a mistake with this foray into the world of entertainment? The DuPont stock that Seagram sold had outperformed Seagram's own stock, which had in turn grossly underperformed the S&P 500. Furthermore, the company underperformed the S&P indexes for both beverage and entertainment companies. The market was applying a conglomerate discount to Seagram's operations rather than recognizing it with Disney-like media valuations.

Nevertheless, on December 10, 1998, Bronfman pushed Seagram even further toward media conglomerate in a $10.4 billion merger with Polygram. Entertainment now would account for two thirds of Seagram's total revenues. To fund the purchase, Seagram arranged to sell its Tropicana drinks business to PepsiCo. Polygram—75 percent international—would complement Universal's 75 percent domestic operation, and combined with Universal would give Seagram the largest music business in the world. In 1999, Seagram announced that it was launching an Internet music venture with Germany's Bertelsmann.

Today, in addition to its Universal-Polygram and beverages businesses, Seagram holds interests in a diverse group of media and entertainment companies: a 46 percent interest in the USA television and networks group, a 26 percent interest in Loews Cineplex, a 50 percent interest in Interscope Records, a 50 percent interest in sit-com production company Brillstein-Grey Entertainment, Wet 'n Wild Water Parks, an entertainment park in China, and May Islands of Adventure in Orlando, among others. As well as its number one worldwide position in the music business, which Bronfman hopes to leverage into a leading online retail position in its joint venture with Bertelsmann, Bronfman views Seagram's number two place in the recreation segment (Disney is number one) as key. Bronfman believes that consumers will spend their ever-increasing disposable income on recreation—especially at his theme parks.

Cendant

Cendant is another conglomerate built up in the 1990s, the product of the 1997 merger of conglomerates HFS and CUC. HFS, before the merger, was a highly successful conglomerate formed by CEO Henry Silverman, starting with the 1990 purchase of the companies that owned the franchise rights to Ramada and Howard Johnson hotels. Silverman added Days Inn's franchise system in 1992, and in 1996 car rental company Avis, which he proceeded to split into two pieces: One consisted of Avis's rental sites and vehicle fleet, while the other was a franchising company that owned the rights to license the Avis name. Silverman took 75 percent of the operating business public, while retaining the franchise business. Critics noted that Avis was ailing and were skeptical that Silverman could turn it around; but he proved them all wrong. Century 21 and Coldwell Banker franchising were also folded into HFS. Indeed, Silverman had a unique vision for HFS—if it could be franchised, it fit with the company.

CUC International ran shopping clubs, such as Shoppers Advantage and Travelers Advantage. In essence, CUC was a middleman, forging deals with consumer products manufacturers, travel companies, and hotel and car rental companies. It then pitched the products by phone, mail, and online to customers. CUC charged a membership fee and took a small cut of all purchases.

At first, the merger of HFS and CUC looked like a home run. Cendant was a company that could do no wrong and was on a wild acquisition streak. After the merger, Cendant had acquired Providian Auto & Home Insurance Co. and had agreed to buy American Bankers Insurance Group. But in April 1998, the truth came out: Widespread accounting fraud was discovered on CUC's books. CUC's former CFO and controller had directed practices to inflate CUC's income from discount shopping, travel, and other services to fee-paying members by $500 million. The adjustments were made to bring CUC's income in line with analyst expectations. Cendant's once high-flying shares lost 41 percent of their value almost immediately. By October 1998, Cendant had lost three quarters of its value. The stock had recovered some of its value by late 1999 but was still half off its high.

The scandal surrounding Cendant led it to call off its proposed $219 million Providian deal and its $3.1 billion deal to buy American Bankers in October 1998. The sharp decline in Cendant's stock value, which it had previously used as acquisition currency 1960s-style, made the deals unworkable. The company would either have had to issue much more stock to pay for the purchases, or to pay for part of them in cash. In a most unusual turn of events, Cendant paid American Bankers a $400 million breakup fee because of its inability to comply with its acquisition contract.

While its accounting problems did not stop Cendant from buying RAC Motoring Services from the U.K.'s RAC Holdings Ltd., the company was forced to use bank financing rather than its stock to finance the $732 million purchase. Cendant is seen as the story of the 1990s conglomerate that almost succeeded and then pancaked—the LTV of the 1990s.

Tyco: The Focused Conglomerate

Tyco is quite a different story. This company is the poster child industrial conglomerate of the 1990s. Tyco is the world's largest manufacturer and installer of fire protection systems, the largest provider of electronic security systems, and the largest manufacturer of flow control valves. Other operations include medical equipment—a sector in which Tyco is an aggressive industry consolidator—undersea communications systems and services, plastics, adhesives, and electrical and electronic components. Recently, the company made headlines when acting as white knight in the AlliedSignal-AMP takeover battle, paying $11.3 billion for AMP, the electrical connector company.

The pace of Tyco's acquisition streak is astounding. Since the beginning of CEO Dennis Kozlowski's tenure in 1992, the company has made about 100 acquisitions. In the six years between 1992 and late 1999, Tyco's market capitalization has also climbed from about $1.8 billion to $80 billion. Earnings have increased over fifteenfold. Despite the current market preference for the pure-play company, investors have clearly bought into Kozlowski's management philosophy.

The key to Tyco's success is Kozlowski's discipline. Despite this fast-paced acquisition activity, Tyco remains a relatively focused conglomerate, choosing to be a leader in several industry sectors. The majority of acquisitions have been add-ons to build scale in these sectors: disposable supplies (primarily medical), fire protection/security systems, flow control products, and electronic components/fiber optics. Kozlowski speaks about his acquisitions as follows: "I've never once ventured out of the businesses we were already in." The company is also fanatical about cost control, with a corporate staff of only fifty, thirty of whom are responsible for SEC and IRS filings.

Tyco's disposable products line consists primarily of medical products, an industry which the company has gradually been rolling up. In November 1998, Tyco acquired Graphic Controls Corp. for $460 million. Previous acquisitions included the $3.2 billion purchase of U.S. Surgical, a minimally invasive surgical products company, the $1.8 billion purchase of Sherwood-Davis & Geck, and the 1994 purchase of Kendall International. These deals have given Tyco the largest market share in disposable medical products.

Similarly, Tyco built up its fire protection business starting with the 1976 purchase of ITT's Grinnell Fire Protection Systems; a string of subsequent acquisitions made Tyco the market leader. The company's 1997 purchase of security systems operator ADT positioned Tyco strongly in the security systems sector as well.

Flow control has been something of a laggard compared to other businesses, however. Acquisitions to move into servicing and maintaining flow control equipment will make the business segment less vulnerable to cyclical fluctuations.

Finally, Tyco is growing quickly in electronic components and fiber-optic cable. Contracts with independent phone carriers, like Global Crossing, to lay undersea fiber-optic cable are fueling this expansion. As in other business lines, acquisitions have also been an essential part of Tyco's business strategy: For example, in 1997, Tyco purchased the submarine systems division of AT&T in a move to expand further.

The strong stock market performance of Tyco, especially in the face of Wall Street's preference for pure-play companies, has validated the company's business model. As long as Tyco remains able to slash costs and integrate targets into its own operations, the company can continue to be a high-flier.

Berkshire Hathaway: The Conglomerate with the Cult Following

Warren Buffett's Berkshire Hathaway is legendary. Its stock is by far the highest priced on the New York Stock Exchange, trading for approximately $62,000 per share as of September 1999. This high price reflects Buffett's aversion to stock splits, which might threaten the integrity of his target shareholder base of wealthy well-informed, long-term investors and induce uninformed speculative trading activity in Berkshire Hathaway stock. Nevertheless, approximately half of the company's 250,000 shareholders came on board in 1998.

Not a conglomerate in the traditional sense, Berkshire Hathaway is a bit of a hybrid of a mutual fund, a diversified conglomerate, and an insurance company, maintaining substantial investments in companies such as Coca-Cola, American Express, and Gillette. At one time in 1998, Berkshire Hathaway had even accumulated 20 percent of the world's silver!

In addition to its investment activities, Berkshire Hathaway also operates companies in a wide range of industries, including insurance, pilot training, furniture, jewelry, shoes, private jet time-sharing, and candy. Some of the more well-known businesses wholly owned by Berkshire Hathaway include Dairy Queen, Dexter Shoes, See's Candy Shops, Flight Safety, and Executive Jet. But unlike many conglomerates, the company makes no effort to create synergies between its various portfolio companies.

Despite its diversified appearance, however, Berkshire Hathaway actually derives approximately 79 percent of both its total revenue and operating income from its insurance operations. By themselves, Berkshire Hathaway's insurance operations, which include the recently purchased General Re as well as GEICO and National Indemnity, are the fourth largest in the United States based on premiums and would rank 100th in the Fortune 500 based on 1997 pro forma revenues and sixty-seventh based on 1997 earnings. So really, Berkshire Hathaway can be viewed as an insurance company that holds diversifying, risk-hedging investments in other industries.

The capital controlled by Berkshire Hathaway is immense. In August 1998, rumors swirled on Wall Street that the company would buy out failing hedge fund Long Term Capital Management. In fact, Berkshire Hathaway is one of few companies that would have had the financial capacity to hold on to LTCM's investments for the extended period necessary for them to become profitable.

The story of Berkshire Hathaway is inextricably tied to Warren Buffett's investing philosophy. This "Sage of Omaha" has developed a following due to his highly successful strategy identifying and investing in undervalued but fundamentally strong companies.

But Buffett is now modest about the prospects for Berkshire Hathaway. He wrote in the 1998 annual report: "Our rate of progress in both investments and operations is certain to fall in the future. At our present size, any performance superiority we achieve will be minor." The company is so large, and its investments so diverse, that it will be difficult for its stock price performance to exceed meaningfully the broader market. But investors still know that somehow Buffett seems to come out ahead.

PROFILE

Warren Buffett

The investment record of Warren Buffett—the "Sage of Omaha"—is a testament to the value of fundamental analysis. Stock in his investment company, Berkshire Hathaway, has appreciated a phenomenal 27 percent a year over a period of thirty years, far outstripping the performance of broad market averages. Berkshire Hathaway is now one of America's twenty largest companies.

Buffett owes this success not to skill as an operating manager but to investing skill, much of which he credits to his years under the tutelage of Benjamin Graham, the co-author with David Dodd of the seminal 1934 tome *Security Analysis*. Published in the midst of the Depression, Graham and Dodd's book faced an extremely skeptical audience, as few investors were interested in putting money into stocks. Yet, over time, the work became recognized as the foundation text of fundamental analysis.

Buffett's exposure to Graham began in college, when he read Graham's *The Intelligent Investor*. Buffett was taken with Graham's analytical approach and enrolled in Columbia Business School in 1950, where he quickly distinguished himself and came to be Graham's star pupil. He learned how to analyze a company's financial statements, how to sniff out fraud, and how to measure a company's "intrinsic value."

The secret, according to Graham, was to remain objective. His portfolio had been badly scarred by the Crash of 1929 and the ensuing market slide. Having survived that experience, Graham emphasized the importance of a long-term view. Historical performance over a number of years, investigated through financial ratio analysis, was the arbiter of value; current trading prices were not.

In 1956, Buffett returned to Omaha and began his career as an independent money manager, raising money from friends and family and on the strength of recommendations from Graham. Following Graham's precepts, Buffett would buy up major stakes in companies that were trading below their intrinsic value. Buffett proved incredibly adept at managing money, and racked up a decade and a half of superior returns. Then, in 1971, he liquidated his investment partnerships and in return received $25 million and a controlling interest in Berkshire Hathaway. He then turned to running the company on a full-time basis.

When Buffett acquired control of Berkshire Hathaway, it was a failing New England textile company. However, he looked past the warts and saw the business's potential to generate cash. He installed professional management, then used the Berkshire cash flow to fund investments in other businesses. In this fashion, Buffett built up a major portfolio of diversified businesses.

Buffett has had stunning successes. He tripled his investment in General Foods when it was bought out by Philip Morris in 1985. He helped fund Capital Cities' successful purchase of ABC. Major stakes in Coca-Cola, Gillette, and *The Washington Post* have paid off handsomely. Of course, Buffett has had his share of troubling setbacks. An investment in USAir fared poorly, and an investment in Salomon Brothers earned only a modest return when Travelers acquired the company in 1997. On balance, though, Buffett's returns have been staggering.

The essence of Buffett's approach—a refined Graham and Dodd analysis—is deceptively simple. His concern for fundamental financial analysis remains. However, numbers must be understood in a context. Buffett invests only if he sees a strong business behind the financials.

This analysis takes place on two levels. From a strategic perspective, Buffett looks for companies with a "great franchise." In the 1970s these were newspaper and broadcasting companies which not only met the threshold condition of being cheap in the market but also enjoyed strong market positions with little competition. In the 1980s and 1990s, Buffett shifted to consumer products companies with strong brands and market share. Coca-Cola and Gillette are examples.

In addition to a strong strategic position, Buffett looks for able managers he likes and admires. When he finds a company that meets all these criteria, he buys stock and holds.

Picking good companies is not the only key to Buffett's success. He brings considerable insight and an impeccable reputation. Managers and board members are flattered to have him as an investor. Even people sitting across the table from Buffett in a negotiation get a charge from dealing with him. This aura—and an understated, but tenacious style—work in Buffett's favor.

Buffett also knows when to sacrifice a pawn. When we negotiated the sale of ABC to Capital Cities, Buffett realized that the television network was a prize and was willing to be flexible on the issuance of warrants to clinch the deal, even though he philosophically disliked issuing warrants.

GE: Against the Pure-Play Trend

Laughing in the face of the conventional wisdom against conglomerates, Jack Welch, chairman of General Electric, has led the company to tremendous success.

In fact, GE is widely hailed as one of America's best companies of the 1990s and Jack Welch as one of America's top corporate leaders. These accolades have been reflected in the performance of the company's stock, whose price increased from a split-adjusted $15 range in 1990 to about $115 in mid-1999. The company is something of an anomaly—a successful conglomerate of the 1990s.

GE's strong record raises an obvious question: What sets GE apart from other, less successful diversified companies? Jack Welch is the easy answer, and perhaps the most insightful.

During the Welch years three overlapping strategic initiatives become apparent: a drive to reduce operating costs through restructuring, to expand revenues through major acquisitions, and to shift the company onto a post-industrial footing.

When Welch was passed the leadership baton in April 1981, the world saw GE as a company with a long and proud history, a history against which Welch's performance would be measured. Thomas Edison had founded the company—then known as the Edison Electric Light Company—in 1878, with his patents for the electric light bulb and other inventions the crown jewels of the enterprise.

For all his technical genius, Edison had made a blunder: He favored a direct current distribution system over the alternating current system advanced by George Westinghouse and others. Edison ultimately lost this "war of the currents" and his company suffered because of his refusal to adopt the new technology. Finally, in 1892, Edison Electric was merged with another company that held alternating current patents, forming General Electric.

Until World War II, GE, like Westinghouse, focused primarily on its core business of supplying electrical and electronic equipment. On the industrial side, GE made equipment for the generation and distribution of electricity. For consumers, GE produced fans, irons, toasters, refrigerators, washing machines, air conditioners—appliances that required an electrical power source.

The electricity and electrical goods business began to mature after the war and, in keeping with the times, GE diversified far afield during the 1960s. Computers, commercial jet engines, nuclear energy, plastics, financial services, medical systems, chemicals, and defense contracting became areas of business. And the laundry list of businesses grew from one year to the next. After the first Oil Shock, a major natural resources company was added.

For all its diversity, GE weathered the 1970s better than most conglomerates. GE earned $1.5 billion in 1980 on revenues of just under $25 billion, had over 400,000 employees and a strong balance sheet. The company was the world's number one manufacturer of electrical equipment and had strong positions in nuclear power, commercial aviation, and consumer goods.

An Early Commitment to Restructuring   In 1981, Welch's main concern was to improve the bottom line by cutting costs. As the process began, Welch developed a yardstick against which each of GE's 350 businesses would be measured: A business would be retained only if it was or could become number one or number two in its market. Welch and his team took a hard look at every business in this light. "Fix, close, or sell" was the general rule.

When Welch came on board, GE was engaged in 350 businesses organized into forty-three business units, from nuclear reactors to time-sharing services to Australian cooking coal. How was Wall Street to analyze such a company? Jack Welch provided the answer. He took out a pad of paper and drew three circles. The first was GE's core businesses: lighting, major appliances, motors, transportation, turbines, and contractor equipment. The second contained GE's high-technology businesses: industrial electronics, medical systems, materials, aerospace, and aircraft engines. And the third contained GE's service businesses: GE Credit Corporation, information, construction and engineering, and nuclear services. These were the areas that Welch wanted to pursue; any businesses falling outside these circles were to be discarded. As it turns out, 20 percent of GE's businesses—valued at $9 billion—fell outside these three circles.

A new generation of management was in control and nothing was sacred. Utah International, the natural resources business acquired in the 1970s, was sold in 1983 for $2.4 billion. Just seven years before, GE management had identified the company as an engine of future growth.

In 1984, Welch made the even more wrenching decision to sell GE's housewares business to Black & Decker for $300 million even though housewares were part of GE's long history. The waffle irons, fans, and toasters turned out by this division had made GE into a household name. Yet Welch saw a different reality. These products had largely become commodities, and GE could never hope to outsell competitors in Asia and Europe that churned out irons and blow dryers far more cheaply. Similarly, while the consumer electronics business was then ranked fourth in the world market, Welch realized that it would be nearly impossible to turn it into a number one or two player. Therefore, it was sold to Thomson S.A.

Welch saw that GE's strengths were in areas requiring tremendous amounts of capital and technological resources, not commodity businesses. GE, unlike many upstart companies, has the resources to develop new jet engines, medical imaging equipment, etc.

Therefore, Welch was not indiscriminate in the businesses he sold. Some units which were not number one or number two were worth saving. The turbines business, for example, was retained even though it was in a slump. Power generation had been the cornerstone business at GE for a century, and was historically quite profitable. Fundamentally, the business was cyclical and would bounce back.

Welch's early commitment to restructuring served GE well, and by 1985 much had been accomplished. More than $5.6 billion worth of businesses had been divested. Payroll was reduced by 130,000 employees through layoffs and divestitures. And the results could be seen on GE's income statement. Between 1981 and 1984, revenues were flat, but earnings rose almost 15 percent per year.

Twice since the early 1980s, Welch has renewed cost-cutting efforts at GE. The first initiative, introduced in 1989, became known as Work-Outs and involved an attempt to empower employees. Town meetings were held at factories and offices. An open dialog was encouraged. The goal was to push decision making down the chain of command. The second effort, a push for greater quality, was introduced in 1996 and is ongoing.

GE Revisits the Go-Go Years   Welch's first few years as CEO were spent focusing on cost cutting. Then, confident with the state of GE's existing businesses, Welch began to look for ways to expand revenues. Internal growth was part of the story, and Welch invested billions in capital expenditures. However, acquisitions were also a major focus. Though GE had been acquiring companies in the market fairly consistently, the major marker of GE's new acquisitive phase came in 1985. On December 12, Welch stepped to a podium and announced that GE had agreed to purchase RCA, the owner of the NBC television network, for $6.28 billion in cash.

For RCA, the friendly deal with GE represented the culmination of its own restructuring effort. Thornton Bradshaw, a former oil executive, had taken over as chairman of RCA in the same year Welch became chairman of GE and saw as his mission stabilizing the faltering company. He promptly divested businesses: Hertz, CIT, Gibson Greetings, Banquet Foods, Random House were all sold to outsiders who did much better with them than RCA had. Welch bought the remaining company, including the jewel of its defense business, at a bargain price.

The RCA purchase, and GE's acquisition program in general, helped to fuel dramatic growth at GE. Between 1985 and 1995, revenues increased from $28.3 billion to $70.0 billion. However, this road to growth was not without bumps.

The integration of NBC proved especially challenging. GE executive Robert Wright, whom Jack Welch charged with day-to-day management of the network, made his first order of business to reduce expenses. But this was a task that proved politically difficult. NBC employees had grown up in a creative culture where the three broadcast networks had an assured future and therefore initially balked at budget cuts. By 1988, NBC News was losing $126 million per year.

Late-night television host David Letterman was the most vocal critic, openly razzing the folks from GE. But in time, GE silenced the critics, both internal and external. Wright ultimately built a creative team that led the network to new ratings dominance in the 1980s and expanded NBC into a global media company with interests in cable networks and online entertainment.

NBC has also proved a useful vehicle to take advantage of the growth opportunities afforded by the Internet, having partnered with Microsoft to create online news programming MSNBC and purchased 19 percent of CNET's Snap! Internet portal (with an option to acquire a total 60 percent ownership) as well as 4.99 percent of CNET itself. These moves mark a further step on the part of Jack Welch to integrate into the digital age.

Recently, Barry Diller attempted to buy NBC from GE, but 45 percent owner of Diller's USA Networks Edgar Bronfman Jr. vetoed the deal, which would dilute his ownership stake. CBS's Mel Karmazin had also been eyeing the network. Despite the fact that network viewership is on the downswing, NBC remains a hot asset and will be restructured.

The outcome of GE's 1986 entry into the securities business, with its $600 million purchase of Kidder, Peabody, was also a cautionary experience. Problems emerged almost from the moment GE took control of the struggling investment bank. First, Kidder's former M&A superstar Marty Siegel was implicated in the insider trading scandal of the late 1980s. Then, the stock market crash of 1987 drained profits and morale. GE's industrially trained Kidder management team became the butt of Wall Street jokes. And finally, in the early 1990s, a government bond trader at Kidder named Joseph Jett allegedly engaged in a string of fictitious trades that were designed to inflate the profits of his unit.

The Jett scandal, together with the collapse of the mortgage-backed securities market, brought Kidder to its knees. GE—which invested a total of $1.4 billion in Kidder over the years—sold part of the operation to PaineWebber and liquidated the remainder. As a result, GE reported $1.2 billion in losses and charges related to Kidder in 1994, although GE later covered much of these losses with gains on the PaineWebber stock it received.

However, notwithstanding the problems with Kidder, Welch remained committed to growth through acquisition, particularly in the financial services area. Over the course of three years in the early 1990s, GE spent more than $6 billion acquiring insurance companies, which were folded into the highly profitable GE Capital subsidiary.

A Post-Industrial GE   Third on the list of strategic initiatives at GE was a drive to create a post-industrial company. From the time he took over as CEO, Jack Welch recognized the need for this transition. The world manufacturing economy was maturing and margins in GE's old-line industrial businesses were being squeezed: Growth percolated along at 1 or 2 percent a year and cost cutting can only go so far. Given the situation, GE needed to evolve into new markets and find new ways to make money.

GE's transition to a post-industrial company meant to Jack Welch an increasing emphasis on services as a revenue source. This emphasis can be seen in Welch's commitment to GE Capital and NBC. By 1997, services generated about 60 percent of GE's income, as compared to 16 percent in 1980. Welch wants to increase this figure to 80 percent. GE Capital is rapidly adding new businesses globally through acquisitions such as Eagle Star Reinsurance of the U.K., Lake Co. Limited, a Japanese consumer finance company, and its information technology services division.

Welch also recently launched a new push to leverage existing industrial expertise and equipment to gain additional service revenues. Assignments might range from the servicing of equipment to general operations and business consulting.

Welch acknowledges that a number of his businesses, including GE Capital, could stand well on their own, if spun off. But he sees no advantage in such a maneuver. While in conglomerates of years past management was allowed to become bloated and unfocused, Welch is a disciplined manager, determined to make each business the best in its class.

When Welch retires in late 2000, after he turns sixty-five, he will have left an impressive legacy; but it is unclear that GE's supremacy will outlast Jack.

The Conglomerators' Legacy

With the right management and strategy, a diversified company can thrive. Assets must be shuffled to match the existing economic circumstances, and leadership must be willing to work hard at renewing mature businesses. However, history teaches that reaching beyond core competencies is very difficult and can lead to market mistrust. Few managers can be Jack Welch or Dennis Kozlowski.

Financial Services in the Digital Age

"Future shock . . . the shattering stress and disorientation that we induce in individuals by subjecting them to too much change in too short a time."

—Alvin Toffler, *Future Shock*

The gales of change have transformed the financial services industry. A complex interaction between technology, globalization, and regulatory change has shaped this new economic order, causing a frantic search for size, scope, and purpose. Mergers and acquisitions activity has skyrocketed.

Technology has directly impacted the way financial institutions conduct business. Retail customers are demanding that banks adopt technological innovations that make their lives easier: ATMs, online transactions, Internet trading. Not to offer these services puts a bank at a severe competitive disadvantage. Possessing sophisticated back-office technology is also essential to providing good service. But investments in technology have proved exceedingly expensive, and banks which combine gain substantial savings. Expenditures in a merged entity can be spread over a larger base of customers, improving the bottom line. The technological innovations of the digital age have also had a more indirect impact: They have led to the rise of asset management and the retail investor.

The Charles Schwab story is a startling indication of the rapidity of change.

Schwab keeps reinventing itself as the world rotates. Once just a discount brokerage outfit, the company remade itself into a mutual fund seller, riding the mutual fund boom. Today, it is also the largest Internet stock trading service. While rivals like Merrill Lynch stood still, Schwab seized the opportunities provided by the digital era, and as a result, investors have rewarded its stock with a severalfold rise between early 1998 and mid-1999. With over $30 billion market capitalization, Schwab today is larger than financial institutions like Merrill Lynch and Goldman Sachs.

Technological change and the wealth it brought also played a large role in the globalization of the financial services industry. Geographic boundaries are beginning to fall. Europe is becoming unified. Investors in Europe and Asia are now eager to invest in the United States. And American investors are equally eager to put their money into Europe, Asia, and emerging markets. But to capture this international investment business requires a global presence.

One of the most significant manifestations of the globalization of finance is the euro. The euro—a single currency for Europe—will dramatically alter the state of the European capital markets, imposing price transparency throughout Europe, allowing a European company to shop around for capital at any bank in the EU with no currency risk, and creating a more competitive market for capital.

The dawn of this newly integrated European financial sector has been one of the primary sparks of an unprecedented wave of European M&A activity: Only the strongest institutions will survive the brutally competitive environment to come. Europe's financial institutions have realized that they cannot stand still.

The onset of technological change and globalization has also induced agitation for even more regulatory changes. The confluence of these three factors built pressure up to the point that something had to give: The structure of the financial services industry imploded.

The 1997 merger between Dean Witter and Morgan Stanley marked the beginning of a seismic shift in the nature and size of banking deals. The combination raised the bar for other financial institutions: Cross-selling, size, and a retail and institutional focus had become imperatives.

In reaction, banks around the globe have begun to combine with unparalleled rapidity in some of the largest deals of all time. In the space of a little over a year, in the U.S., NationsBank has merged with BankAmerica; Travelers merged with Citicorp; Fleet has agreed to merge with BankBoston; Banc One merged with First Chicago; Norwest acquired Wells Fargo. The European banks followed, spurred into action by the 1997 merger between Union Bank of Switzerland and Swiss Bank Corporation.

In response to these external forces of technology, globalization, and regulatory change, several themes emerge. First, there is massive consolidation within sectors, particularly commercial banking and insurance. Regional banks have combined to create super-regionals; super-regionals are combining to create national banks; and banks in the same market are merging as well. Size brings with it the ability to invest in technology and to go global.

Second, mergers are blurring the boundaries between commercial banking, insurance, investment banking, and other financial institution sectors. Convergence brings the theoretical promise of cross-selling—enhancing revenues by selling each merger partner's products through the other's distribution channels. Being able to offer a diversity of products under one roof is an added convenience for customers and can induce them to choose one institution over another. Accordingly, banks are combining to achieve greater breadth of product.

International deal activity is the third trend. While early banking consolidation was almost exclusively a U.S. phenomenon, soon non-U.S. financial institutions began to feel the same pressures. European banks combined in preparation for the coming of the euro. The Deutsche Bank–Bankers Trust merger has set the stage for increased cross-border M&A activity, as other banks partner to leapfrog their competition in size and geographic reach. Japanese banks combined, in the face of widespread instability in Japan's banking sector, with the hope of creating more stable financial institutions.

In addition to these wider developments, there are several secondary trends.

First, the quest for brand loyalty is an important driver of deals. Consumers are brand-conscious, seeking out familiar names as a sign of quality and value. Financial institutions need significant size and scope to build brand names like those enjoyed by Nike and Coke, and M&A provides a quick way to bulk up. Once a strong brand is established, additional acquisitions can provide a new portfolio of products to brand, adding value for the customer.

Second, there will inevitably be a series of disappointments for many of these institutions. The concepts sound great but are difficult to execute. Furthermore, not all of these companies will be the triumphant consolidators.

Nevertheless, these deals are having a snowball effect: Announced deals are becoming larger and larger. To remain competitive after the latest big deal, banks must forge ever-larger combinations. The most attractive targets are the products of combinations themselves. Other companies will have to seek out protected niches and apply distinctive competencies to survive and prosper.

Augury of the Future

In February 1997, the marriage of Dean Witter, Discover & Co., and Morgan Stanley stunned Wall Street and shattered the world order of investment banking. The merger was an augury of the financial services future: the blurring of boundaries, the rise of the retail investor, the quest for global reach, and the creation of a strong brand name.

A Morgan Stanley–Dean Witter merger had been percolating behind the scenes for some time. Phil Purcell, chairman and chief executive of Dean Witter, and John Mack, president of Morgan Stanley, actually had been talking about the possibility of a joint venture for several years, discussions facilitated by Purcell's long-standing relationship with both Mack and Dick Fisher, Morgan Stanley's chairman and chief executive, respectively. By the fall of 1996, Purcell was ready to talk more seriously, and we were brought in to advise Dean Witter.

Purcell and his team had conducted a strategic review and decided that Dean Witter needed a broader base to compete in the consolidating global financial services business. Purcell was a visionary, understanding the effect the digital economy would have on financial institutions and wanting to be a first mover. Morgan Stanley was the right partner. Fundamentally, the merger would be a cross-fertilization of retail and institutional powers—"Class Meets Mass," as *Business Week* trumpeted. The combined company would be able to offer customers who had grown wealthy from the digital age a place to invest their money and product to invest it in. Companies that needed to raise money would have access to this powerful individual investor base.

Until recently, the institutional and retail worlds were thought of as distinct. Institutional investment banks like Morgan Stanley underwrote stocks and bonds and provided strategic advice for corporations. Retail brokerage operations like Dean Witter sold financial products—primarily stocks, bonds, and mutual funds—to individuals. Historically, the Morgan Stanleys of the world were known as the brains, the Dean Witters the brawn.

Investment banks generally viewed retail investors as not worth the trouble and therefore looked down on the brokerage houses as unsophisticated mass-merchandising operations. Rather than compete in this realm, the investment banks concentrated on their highly profitable niche business of serving corporations. As a result, investment banks did not, by and large, develop relationships with individual investors, relying instead on relatively small sales forces that focused almost exclusively on selling to pension funds, insurance companies, and other large institutional investors.

But the situation had changed by the late 1980s.

The retail side of the industry boomed. Individual investors flooded into the stock market in record numbers on the strength of a long bull market, low interest rates on money market funds, and due to the fact that many employers no longer guarantee fixed pensions. Indeed, the growing popularity of and employer support for 401(k) retirement plans, which allow employees to direct their own retirement savings, have caused billions to pour into funds. Profits for powerhouses like Charles Schwab & Co. and Fidelity soared.

The emergence of the money management product and the strong performance of banks like Merrill Lynch demolished the view that institutional and retail banking should not mix. Diversification into retail services came to be viewed as the future for investment banks.

Morgan Stanley and Dean Witter observed investors' recognition of the difference in outlook for the institutional and retail businesses. In 1997, Merrill Lynch was trading at 12 times earnings, Dean Witter at 11 times, Chase at 13 times, and Charles Schwab at 22 times. By contrast, Morgan traded at 9 times. These figures reflected Wall Street's estimates of potential and risk. The blue-chip Morgan Stanley was an institutional brand—not a household one—and its business base was narrow and volatile. Dean Witter had a strong distribution system and a money management machine. A merger would instantaneously boost Morgan's effectiveness as a banker with muscle and create critical mass in money management. A deal would also build a strong and prestigious brand.

It was against this backdrop that Purcell, Fisher, and Mack considered the possibility of a combination. Purcell saw Morgan Stanley as a source of additional products for his brokers to sell, while Fisher and Mack looked on Dean Witter as a rich trove of relatively stable earnings from asset management and Discover Card operations.

Viewing the rise of retail, Fisher and Mack already had committed themselves to expanding into the more stable, fee-generating business even before serious discussions opened with Purcell. For example, in 1996, they moved Morgan more heavily into the mutual fund business with the purchase of Van Kampen. Yet growing the asset management business was expensive, and Van Kampen lacked both critical mass and the distribution system for further customer-base expansions.

The talks between Purcell, Fisher, and Mack progressed very quickly. Morgan Stanley's own bankers were to be kept in the dark until late in the deal, with Fisher ably representing Morgan's interests himself. Furthermore, to keep word from leaking out, meetings were held in conference rooms at the law firm Cravath, Swaine & Moore, over their rather infamous soggy sandwiches. Somehow, the kitchens at Cravath have never reached the culinary standards of competitor Wachtell, Lipton.

As the negotiations came to a climax, the tension grew. What would be the role for senior managers from each company? How would the two companies be put together? The firms had very different cultures, and meshing financial services companies is notoriously difficult. Yet Purcell and Mack decided the strength of a good relationship at the top would prevail. Meanwhile, rumors swirled of Morgan Stanley bidding for PaineWebber.

Purcell, Fisher, and Mack announced their $21 billion merger of equals on February 6 in a crowded auditorium. As Fisher and Mack flashed their Discover Cards, the audience cheered. The market response to the deal was a standing ovation. Within weeks, the market price of both stocks increased 25 percent, expanding the trading multiple of the new combined company: The market value of the combination was greater than the average market value of the pieces. Purcell, the strategist, had picked the right deal. In 1998, profits surged, a triumph when compared to earnings downturns experienced by the company's rivals. Its stock has also soared over 100 percent.

Philip Purcell

Philip Purcell is not the typical securities industry executive. Unlike John Mack, a former trader who rose through the ranks at Morgan Stanley, Purcell began his career as a consultant at McKinsey & Co. A project for Sears exposed him to Edward Telling, the company's chairman, who subsequently hired Purcell to serve as an in-house strategic planner for Sears.

Purcell's first task was to advise Sears on its move into financial services; after the Dean Witter acquisition, he shifted his focus to the brokerage operation, where he was an early advocate of the Discover Card. After encouraging Sears to pump $1 billion into the start-up, Purcell made Discover into an extremely successful investment, and in 1986 became the head of Dean Witter, Discover.

Reflecting his consulting background, Purcell kept Dean Witter firmly focused on its strengths as a retail brokerage firm. Dean Witter more or less stayed out of proprietary trading and the institutional side of investment banking because Purcell perceived no comparative advantage. Instead, he concentrated on growing the Discover Card and its network of brokers, using them as leverage to build a mutual fund operation.

A strategic shift in the 1990s led Sears to divest itself of financial services. Synergies between Sears and Dean Witter failed to materialize: People were reluctant to buy their stocks at the same place they shopped for clothes. First, a minority interest in Dean Witter was sold to the public in a 1993 stock offering. Then the remaining interest was spun off to Sears shareholders later the same year. As a result of Purcell's leadership and favorable market conditions at the time, Dean Witter grew quickly. In fact the firm's growth outpaced that of the traditional Wall Street houses, putting Purcell in a position to bargain on equal terms with the venerable Morgan Stanley.

The promise of the retail channel that drove the Morgan Stanley–Dean Witter deal has come to fruition. When the success of this vision became apparent, companies began the frantic search for merger partners. What followed was an explosion of deal activity.

Prelude to the Megadeals

By the mid-1980s, economic factors and changes in technology compelled the beginnings of the restructuring and consolidation. Alternative revenue sources (the Latin American, LBO, and real estate loans of the 1980s, for example) could not paper over the fundamental competitive realities: Too many banks had built too many branches; furthermore, the U.S. has more bankers per capita than any other country except the United Kingdom, whose banking system is unionized. This excess labor capacity in the U.S. was matched by excess functional capacity as well. According to one recent study, banks had between 27 and 43 percent excess technological capacity; with the ability to process about 220 million transaction accounts, 370 credit card transactions, 4.4 million mutual fund transactions, and 750 million fund transfers annually. However, actual usage for 1995 was far below those levels.

But the bureaucracy was stultifying, and the customers not there. The U.S. banks were facing increasing competition from their much larger, global competitors. Blow after blow had left many banks tired and weak. Investors, weary of the episodic bad news, hammered bank share prices—especially the large New York money center banks. Chase and Citicorp lost 50 percent of their respective market values in 1990, while the money centers as a whole declined by roughly 35 percent. Over the same period, the S&P 500 lost only 9 percent. None of the U.S. banks ranked in the world's top ten.

The industry responded to this latest bad news with a wave of cost cutting and restructuring. Announcements of multithousand job cuts were commonplace in 1990 and 1991. At the same time, credit standards were dramatically tightened, and loans became extremely hard to come by for all but the highest-rated borrowers. Commentators wondered whether the industry might slip into a widespread collapse. Weaker banks began to partner with stronger banks to cut costs and seek harbor from the storm.

The early 1990s was an uncomfortable period for banks, as they fumbled and floundered in their quest to find solutions to their strategic dilemmas. The dominant theme of these mergers was the quest for efficiency through size. Yet other themes—quest for breadth of product, geographic expansion, and the desire to build brand loyalty—were also beginning to take shape through the visionary leadership of figures like Hugh McColl, who during this period began to assemble a super-regional bank.

With these economic factors as a backdrop, Chase Manhattan Corporation and Chemical Banking Corporation announced the intent to combine into a single banking behemoth on August 28, 1995. The new Chase—the older name survived, though Chemical executives control the new company—in 1998 had roughly $365 billion in assets, $194 billion in deposits, over 4 million consumer accounts, and the dominant retail banking network in the New York metropolitan area.

Acquirer	Target	Approximate Deal Value (in billions)	Date Announced
Travelers Group	Citicorp	$72.6	1998
NationsBank	BankAmerica	$61.6	1998
Norwest Corp.	Wells Fargo & Co.	$34.4	1998
Banc One Corp.	First Chicago NBD Corp.	$29.6	1998
First Union Corp.	CoreStates Financial Corp.	$17.1	1997
Fleet Financial Group	BankBoston Corp.	$15.9	1999
NationsBank	Barnett Banks	$14.8	1997
Wells Fargo & Co.	First Interstate Bancorp	$10.9	1995
Firstar Corp.*	Mercantile Bancorp	$10.6	1999
Chemical Banking Corp.	Chase Manhattan Corp.	$10.4	1995

Source: Securities Data Corporation, as of September 30, 1999. Starred deals are pending.

Cost savings were a clear imperative in the $10.4 billion merger of Chase and Chemical. In announcing the deal, Walter Shipley, chairman of Chemical, and Thomas Labrecque, chairman of Chase, projected a reduction in workforce of 12,000 employees and the closure of more than 100 branches. These and other moves eventually would excise $1.5 billion in annual expenses from the combined company's income statement.

The deal—while billed as a merger of equals—was a bittersweet moment for Labrecque and others at Chase. Though the stronger Chase name would be on the door of the new bank, in other respects, the once-proud, but now ailing Chase would be folded into Chemical. Chase had been founded in 1877 and later merged with Equitable Trust, growing to become the world's largest bank by the 1930s. The merger with Equitable brought cachet to Chase, as John D. Rockefeller Jr. was Equitable's biggest shareholder and therefore became highly involved with Chase. In fact, David Rockefeller, John

D.'s son, eventually took over the leadership of the bank, serving as chairman until 1981.

However, when Rockefeller protégé Labrecque became chairman of Chase in 1990, the company was a faded institution. Chase had been stung by a series of miscues, including bad Latin American loans and the crashing of a large portfolio of risky real estate loans.

Labrecque worked hard to turn the bank around, cutting costs and exiting risky businesses. But stock price failed to respond, and by 1995, Labrecque was under pressure from investors. Aggressive fund manager Michael Price of Heine Securities had taken a large stake and was agitating for more revolutionary steps. Labrecque announced a $400 million cost cutting plan, but the stock price still didn't pop. Investors were unsatisfied. Chase saw a merger with Chemical as defensive, a way to jump from number three to number one in the New York market and to placate agitated investors.

Shipley's decision to merge Chemical with Chase, on the other hand, reflected satisfaction with his 1991 $2.0 billion merger between Chemical and Manufacturers Hanover. That deal successfully combined two New York money center banks with high debt loads and fairly steep cost structures and slashed $750 million in the banks' annual expenses—$100 million more than expected.

Shipley hoped to repeat the magic with an encore deal. Again, the format was a marriage: The proclivity was a takeover.

Not all of these cost-driven mergers went smoothly. The $10.9 billion Wells Fargo–First Interstate deal, launched in 1995 and completed in 1996, is a good example. In many ways, the deal was a typical in-market merger: Wells Fargo, which sparked the deal with a hostile tender offer, had 974 branches in California at the close of 1995; First Interstate, the larger organization, had a total of roughly 1,150 locations in thirteen Western states, with 450 offices in California. The branch overlap in California provided the main opportunity for cost savings and was the key to the deal.

As outlined by Wells Fargo, the large majority of branch closings (projected at around 350) and employee layoffs (projected at around 7,200) would come from First Interstate's California operations. Moreover, redundant headquarters staff and marketing efforts could be trimmed, generating the lion's share of the projected $800 million in post-takeover savings. The integration was to take seven months in total.

While the economic logic behind the deal was strong, Wells Fargo had trouble integrating First Interstate. Technical difficulties destroyed any potential synergies—and arguably Wells Fargo itself. Integrating the two banks' computer systems was a disaster. Customers' deposits were incorrectly posted, and often checks were deposited into the wrong accounts. Wells Fargo had no choice but to credit the affected customers' accounts, but often could no longer find the accounts that had originally received the checks in error. In spring 1997, Wells Fargo announced that it was losing a whopping 1.5 percent of its accounts each month! Enormous operating losses mounted and Wells Fargo's share price plummeted—even in the face of one of the best years for the financial institutions sector in general.

In 1998, Wells Fargo finally threw in the towel, agreeing to merge with Minneapolis-based Norwest, one of the best-performing banks of the decade. It was decided that Norwest chairman Richard Kovacevich, whose background is in the retail sector, would lead the new company—to be called Wells Fargo. Kovacevich views his banks not as branches but as "stores," an attitude that has made Norwest a leader in cross-selling.

The deal was primarily defensive: Kovacevich was concerned that he would be left without a partner. Originally quite skeptical about the mega–bank mergers and their "elusive synergies," he was spurred into action only when cross-town rival US Bancorp was rumored to be courting Wells Fargo.

Norwest, which had not invested heavily in the Internet, gained Wells Fargo's Internet banking system, giving it more Internet cus-

tomers than any other bank. It is true, however, that the two cultures
to be integrated couldn't be more different. Norwest takes a people-
oriented, service-oriented approach; on the other hand, Wells Fargo
prefers to serve its customers via phone or computer. With Kovacevich firmly in charge, however, it is widely expected that the culture
will ultimately include the best of both worlds—personal service for
those who want it, plus electronic banking. But, learning from the
Wells Fargo debacle, the two banks have announced a three-year
time frame for integration to decide all those issues.

Hugh McColl: Early Visionary

While competitors fumbled, Hugh McColl, chairman of North
Carolina bank NCNB, single-mindedly pursued his strategic vision:
to grow his regional bank into a formidable national player through
aggressive acquisition activity. In this time of economic turmoil for
banks, many of his purchases were opportunistic—acquisitions of
weaker banks seeking harbor from the storm. Others were hostile
takeovers of banks that had to be dragged kicking and screaming into
McColl's banking empire. Aided by regulatory change, McColl gradually built up a collection of state banks into a super-regional powerhouse.

Valuation was the key to McColl's buying sprees: By buying
banks with lower P/Es than NCNB's, improving their operations and
integrating them, McColl supported the lofty valuation of his own
bank's stock and built shareholder value.

The buying spree began in March 1989, when Hugh McColl,
chairman of what would become NationsBank, called his counterpart at Atlanta's Citizens & Southern Bank and offered to buy Citizens. The courtly Bennett Brown, chairman of Citizens, asked for
time to consider the offer. "You have three hours to answer, or I will
launch my missiles," McColl reportedly responded.

When Brown didn't cave, McColl kept his promise. Late in the
evening of March 30, McColl had personal letters hand-delivered to

each Citizens board member detailing a hostile $2.4 billion bear hug offer. News of the offer went out over the wire services at 9:57 P.M. Not surprisingly, Citizens did not take well to the no-holds-barred approach, with Brown telling McColl to "go the hell back to North Carolina." Within days, the Citizens board declared the offer inadequate.

Three weeks of jousting in the press followed. But even in the spirited 1980s, a hostile bank takeover was prohibitively difficult. The regulatory barriers were just too great and Citizens easily could blow the favorable accounting treatment McColl wanted. On April 25, NCNB—as McColl's bank was then called—withdrew the offer for Citizens. Shortly thereafter, Citizens merged with Washington, D.C. based Sovran bank.

Spurned by Citizens & Southern in 1989, the fifty-three-year-old McColl was hardly chastened. The very next day, NCNB announced its intention to bid for MCorp, a failed Texas bank being auctioned by the FDIC. McColl would not be held back from realizing his super-regional vision.

Though McColl was one of the most voracious acquirers of commercial banks, his strategy was not unique. The tumultuous financial services environment of the 1980s was the spawning ground for vast super-regional commercial banks with multistate branch networks. Taking advantage of the gradual liberalization of regulatory boundaries within specific regions, a handful of visionaries shaped these institutions.

Other banks matched NationsBank's expansion. After building its own network of banks along the Eastern seaboard, First Union acquired First Fidelity Bancorp for $5.2 billion in 1995, adding a strong Northeastern network of banks and branches. The bank then acquired CoreStates in 1997. First Chicago NBD focused its efforts in the Midwest; Keycorp spread from an upstate New York base into the Northeast and to the west; Fleet Bank acquired Bank of New England and Shawmut to become the largest New England bank;

and BayBank and Bank of Boston merged to create BankBoston. In 1999, Fleet and BankBoston would agree to an in-market merger to create a New England super-regional.

The super-regional approach promised a number of benefits. In part, the banking industry's bloat and sluggishness created a classic consolidation opportunity—buy up competitors, slash unnecessary overlap, and boost shareholders' return on equity. Scaled-back overhead expenses could be spread across a larger operation. Size also provided a technology-oriented advantage. With larger operations, the super-regionals gained the wherewithal to support an expanded technology effort. NCNB, for example, was able to launch a $100 million plan to build an integrated computer system designed to automate nearly every retail banking task. Smaller, regional banks simply didn't have the technology budget to sustain that kind of investment and therefore lost customers who were beginning to demand technological conveniences. Indeed, this wave of deals was strongly motivated by the realization that the most efficient players would be the strongest players in the future.

The cross-border, super-regional strategy was also given a boost by regulatory changes that weakened the Bank Holding Company Act of 1956—a law that severely limited the ability of a bank to hold branches across state lines. The McFadden Act of 1927 allowed banks to circumvent this prohibition by creating bank holding companies: A New York holding company might, for example, own formally separate New York and New Jersey bank subsidiaries.

While such arrangements made considerable economic sense, allowing the combined entities to spread marketing and other costs across a larger population, the holding company structures themselves were of limited utility. Each bank subsidiary was required to maintain a separate corporate charter and was subject to state regulation in its home state.

However, even this limited form of consolidation raised concerns in Congress. Mistrust of large financial institutions remained strong, and politicians favored community control of banks and local responsiveness. The result of this concern was the Bank Holding Company Act of 1956, which further reinforced the decentralized, community-based banking model.

The act prohibited a nonbank from owning a bank. Furthermore, an acquisition could only be consummated with the approval of the Federal Reserve Board, which was directed to consider anticompetitive effects, financial and managerial resources, and community needs. A provision known as the Douglas Amendment specifically forbade approval of any cross-border acquisition unless "specifically authorized by the statute laws of the State in which such bank is located, by language to that effect and not merely by implication."

Until 1972, no state had enacted such an authorization. However, in that year, a few states began to relax the rules for certain kinds of transactions. The real break came in 1982, when Massachusetts adopted a law that lifted the interstate ban on a reciprocal basis for banks in New England. Connecticut followed suit by adopting a similar statute, so that Connecticut and Massachusetts banks could acquire each other. This selective regional approach, largely designed to exclude the New York money center banks, was challenged in the courts, but was ultimately upheld by the U.S. Supreme Court in *Northeast Bancorp*. With this blessing from the Court, a number of other states passed similar legislation.

Losses related to bad real estate and oil loans triggered a further opening to build super-regional empires. In 1982, federal legislation was passed that allowed bank holding companies to acquire failing banks in any region, providing healthy banks access to a few key markets, such as Texas, and serving the federal government's interest to increase the number of bidders for failing banks.

Hugh McColl

Dubbed the "George Patton of banking" by *Forbes* magazine, Hugh McColl is a South Carolina native with an aggressive spirit. Ever since becoming CEO of NCNB, McColl has seemed hell-bent upon acquiring every available bank between North Carolina and California. Though a fourth-generation banker, McColl doesn't fit the mold of courtly Southern banker, with his fondness for phrases like "crush the SOBs and have a nice day." Yet he prides himself on loyal support of subordinates.

NCNB's buying spree had started in 1982, when the bank's lawyers found a regulatory loophole that allowed the North Carolina bank to enter the Florida market. Because NCNB had operated a trust company in the state before 1973, it was free to buy Florida banks. McColl led the charge. In 1982, NCNB acquired Gulfstream Banks of Boca Raton; Exchange Bancorp of Tampa was swallowed shortly thereafter.

In 1983, McColl became chairman of NCNB and continued the acquisitions tear to reshape NCNB into the leading bank on the Southeast coast, from Baltimore to Miami. In pursuing that goal, NCNB would acquire dozens of banks over the course of the 1980s, ballooning from a sleepy Southern bank into a powerhouse with more than $21.7 billion of revenues in 1997. NCNB became the nation's fourth-largest commercial bank measured by revenues.

Much of McColl's tough image can be attributed to his unforgiving standards. He once called Florida bankers lazy, and showed he meant it when integrating NCNB's early Florida acquisitions into the larger bank. He sent in platoons of fired-up young staffers to overhaul the operations, and within a short time most

Sumner Redstone, tenacious and tough, has built a multibillion-dollar media empire through acquisitions. He triumphed in 1993, when he fought off Barry Diller's QVC to win the $10 billion takeover battle for Paramount Communications.

(Ron Galella Ltd.)

Barry Diller with fashion designer Diane von Furstenberg. Diller said of his unsuccessful fight for Paramount: "They won. We lost. Next." Today, Diller is transforming his HSN into a major media vehicle.

(Ron Galella Ltd.)

Cornelius Vanderbilt fought one of the first hostile takeover attempts with his unsuccessful 1868 assault on the Erie railroad.

(AP/Wide World Photos)

J.P. Morgan stood at the crossroads of American finance during the nineteenth century. One of the nation's first merger advisers, Morgan engineered a string of blockbuster deals— including the creation of U.S. Steel in 1900.

(AP/Wide World Photos)

Henry Kravis, with journalist Barbara Walters and *Washington Post* owner Katherine Graham, became a household name in the 1980s as the embodiment of billion-dollar leveraged buyouts. In the 1990s, he and cousin George Roberts continue to run KKR, the best-known LBO firm.

(Ron Galella Ltd.)

Carl Icahn, Elizabeth Dole and fiancée Gail Golden. As a high profile takeover entrepreneur, Icahn earned a reputation during the 1980s for an aggressive negotiating style. In the 1990s, he wrested control of Marvel Comics from financier Ronald Perelman.

(Ron Galella Ltd.)

Ivan Boesky, pictured outside the New York City federal
court where he pled guilty to insider trading.

(Ron Galella Ltd.)

Michael Milken and
his wife, Lori. Milken
built Drexel Burnham
Lambert into a leading
investment bank on
the strength of its junk
bond franchise, only to
see the firm collapse
after his indictment
for federal securities
law violations.

(Ron Galella Ltd.)

Boone Pickens hunted the elephants of Big Oil during the takeover wars of the 1980s, launching a series of unsuccessful tender offers. Ironically, he was pushed out of his own company by insurgents in 1996.

(AP/Wide World Photos)

Rand Araskog, chairman of ITT Corp., enjoying a light moment at a 1997 Super Bowl party. The next day, Hilton Hotels launched a $55 a share hostile bear hug offer for ITT, and Araskog was locked in 1997's corporate equivalent of the Super Bowl.

(Ron Galella Ltd.)

Richard Fisher and **John Mack** of Morgan Stanley and **Philip Purcell** of Dean Witter Discover flashed their Discover cards at the press conference announcing their companies' 1997 merger.
(Archive Photos)

Bernard Ebbers remained a relatively unknown entrepreneur until his company, WorldCom, announced a $30 billion offer for MCI. Ebbers snatched MCI from British Telecom, scoring a major strategic coup.
(AP/Wide World Photos)

Joe Flom and **Marty Lipton** have frequently faced off as legal advisers on the biggest deals of the past three decades. Flom is known for his scrappy and creative style, Lipton for his role as the dean of takeover defense.

(Photos provided by Joe Flom and Wachtell, Lipton, Rosen & Katz) of the senior staff at the bank was pushed out the door, replaced with McColl-trained people.

McColl's reputation as a tough taskmaster has sometimes hurt him, however. His unsuccessful offer for Citizens & Southern was not the first: In 1985, he had been turned away by First Atlanta Corp. Rather than merge with McColl's army, the Atlanta institution opted to accept a lower offer from the kinder and gentler Wachovia bank.

Even with the setbacks, McColl managed to translate his vision of a regional powerhouse into reality during the 1980s, while avoiding most of the serious problems that plagued banks over the course of the decade. Today, after consummation of the BankAmerica deal, McColl can claim credit for personally leading NCNB—now Bank of America—into the promised land. It has become one of the leading banks in the world.

Hugh McColl's super-regional vision became more than just a pipe dream in 1985, when a group of Southeastern states picked up on the *Northeast Bancorp* decision and enacted a regional banking compact. Effective in July of that year, banks in North Carolina, Florida, Georgia, Tennessee, and Virginia could merge together or acquire each other. South Carolina joined the group in 1986.

Very shortly after federal and state laws provided an opening, Hugh McColl spread his acquisition net to acquire banks in Tennessee, Virginia, Georgia, and Maryland, and also made an unsuccessful run at First Atlanta Bank. However, despite the regulatory openings, the McFadden Act still prohibited cross-state branching, forcing NCNB to maintain each state's operations as a stand-alone subsidiary.

Still, this limited liberalization was enough to encourage McColl and others. BankAmerica built its own stronghold in the West with acquisitions in Oregon and Washington. And after surviving its own period of troubles, the bank pushed into Nevada with the 1989 purchase of Nevada First Bank, then added operations in New Mexico and Arizona. Security Pacific—a power in Southern California weighed down by bad real estate loans—was acquired for $4.6 billion in 1992. Two years later, BankAmerica crossed the Mississippi for the first time, acquiring Continental Bank of Illinois for $1.9 billion.

After spending a few years digesting the 1985 acquisitions, McColl made a particularly shrewd move: Taking advantage of the new law allowing cross-border acquisitions of troubled banks, he entered the large Texas market. In 1988, NCNB paid a rock-bottom $210 million for a 20 percent interest in First RepublicBank Corp., a failed Texas bank that had been taken over by the FDIC. The government agreed to pick up all the costs from a $5 billion pool of bad loans and to inject $960 million of fresh capital. In addition, NCNB was granted an option to purchase the remaining 80 percent of the bank.

The media questioned McColl's move into Texas: Had he overpaid? The answer came quickly. NCNB—like Ronald Perelman in his 1988 purchase of a failed Texas S&L—was allowed to keep First Republic's tax losses, which could be used to shelter future income. Within months, it became clear that both McColl and Perelman had gotten the better of the government. NCNB's new Texas operations churned out profits, causing NCNB's stock to soar 50 percent. McColl exercised the option to buy the rest of the Texas bank less than a year later.

With First Republic integrated into its operations, NCNB renewed its acquisition streak. McColl's first deal of the decade was particularly sweet. In 1991, when Citizens & Southern–Sovran was having deep problems with bad commercial real estate loans, Bennett Brown swallowed his pride and reopened negotiations with McColl. Within a matter of weeks, the parties agreed to a $4.26 billion merger to create what would be known as NationsBank, at the time the country's third-largest bank with more than $100 billion in assets. Buying Citizens was part in-market merger: The branch networks of NCNB and C&S overlapped in South Carolina and Florida, providing an opportunity for an estimated $130 million in annual cost savings.

Perhaps the most surprising aspect of the NationsBank deal was the apparent ease with which McColl and Brown overcame the acrimony of their earlier tussle. The key, reportedly, was McColl's understated approach. Preferring one-on-one meetings with Brown—on several occasions in the casual environment of a South Carolina beach house—to large negotiations, McColl made a strong pitch for the benefits of the merger. McColl promised the senior Brown he would be chairman of the combined banks, while McColl would be president and chief executive. McColl was willing to compromise in order to get the deal done, as Citizens & Southern–Sovran would give NCNB the bulk to be a truly national player.

By year-end 1995, NationsBank was a super-regional with more than $180 billion of assets. Yet McColl was not done growing. The market imperative for consolidation remained strong: A core group of large banks had quickly coalesced which possessed the capital and scale to become global institutions. Their increased investments in technology and marketing were transforming the business of banking. Furthermore, an international race for market share was developing: The impact of the digital economy had reached North Carolina.

McColl sought to position NationsBank for this new global competition. In August 1996, aided by favorable regulatory developments, he expanded his reach into the Midwest with a $9.5 billion acquisition of Boatmen's Bancshares. The combined entity had branches in sixteen states and the District of Columbia, from Maryland to Texas, from Florida to the Mexican border.

McColl followed with the September 1997 acquisition of Florida's Barnett Banks Inc. for $14.8 billion. In capturing the deal after a quick friendly auction run by Barnett's CEO Charles Rice, McColl again showed his decisive streak. He topped the other bidders by several dollars a share to win Barnett, the undeniable jewel of Florida, and as a result gained the number one share of the lucrative market.

Bank Consolidation Charges Ahead

But McColl was not done yet. NationsBank still lacked a commercial banking presence in California. Furthermore, while the deals he completed in the 1980s and early 1990s had created a formidable super-regional, his competitors had raised the bar on the size and scope necessary to be a national leader. NationsBank was not yet truly national and was not yet large enough to be a leading global player.

McColl knew what he had to do. In April 1998, McColl announced he was tying the knot with the U.S.'s other largest super-regional and NationsBank's West Coast counterpart, BankAmerica. This blockbuster deal transformed NationsBank. The combined company has $572 billion in assets, serves 30 million U.S. households and 2 million businesses. With the deal, the greatest wish of BankAmerica founder A.P. Giannini was filled as well: to create a single bank operating from coast to coast.

One out of every twelve dollars of U.S. individual and corporate deposits are held by the combined company. At the time of closing, its banking assets were the largest of any bank in the world and the deal was one of the largest in history in terms of transaction value.

The new company was named Bank of America. McColl was to be chairman and BankAmerica chairman David Coulter was to be president and would take over the company upon McColl's retirement.

Despite all good intentions, the closing of the deal on September 30 was followed by a series of management shake-ups. First, Coulter was forced out, blamed for losses generated by BankAmerica's failed investments in D.E. Shaw's hedge fund and in Russia. Coulter had loaned D.E. Shaw $1.4 billion to invest, which turned into losses of $372 million by the third quarter of 1998. Moreover, one third of forty-five of the highest-ranking executives at the old BankAmerica have resigned or otherwise left since the announcement of the merger. Again, a marriage had become a takeover.

Other super-regional banks followed McColl's lead and began combining to ensure their place in the new global order. Coincidentally, on the same day as the NationsBank-BankAmerica combination was announced, regional banks Banc One and First Chicago announced their own $29.6 billion deal. Newly merged Banc One hopes to become a one-stop shopping center for financial services such as loans, credit, and mutual funds and will be the second-largest credit card issuer in the U.S.

Like NationsBank, Banc One and First Chicago themselves were the products of mergers. Banc One acquired First USA, a major credit card issuer, in 1997. And First Chicago NBD was the entity created by the merger of First Chicago with NBD Corp. in 1995.

Another potentially large super-regional bank combination, that of Bank of New York (BONY) and Pittsburgh-based Mellon Bank, was also announced in 1998, but never got off the ground. BONY and Mellon initially held conversations about a business combination which Mellon broke off due to fears about the two banks' very different cultures and business focuses. Specifically, Mellon was concerned that BONY's cost-cutting culture would adversely affect many of its important businesses such as asset management and could lead to the departure of key professionals.

But shortly after friendly talks broke off, in April 1998, BONY launched a $24.2 billion unsolicited offer for Mellon in the form of a bear hug letter. BONY indicated that its desire to merge was both revenue-driven—to benefit from cross-selling of financial products—and to create trading multiple expansion by capturing Mellon's lucrative asset management operation: BONY, primarily an institutional operation, also wanted a piece of the lucrative retail market. Furthermore, as in other bank mergers, the two banks would be able to make a more efficient investment in technology as a combined entity.

Reportedly, institutional holders of Mellon's stock were happy with the offer, as were research analysts who cover the stock. But Mellon rebuffed BONY's offer for the same reasons that it had broken off friendly discussions a few weeks prior: Mellon pointed out BONY's weaknesses in Mellon's three core areas: asset management/mutual funds, personal trust, and consumer financial services. The way Mellon saw it, BONY would not be bringing as much to the table as Mellon, especially given that BONY would have been in control of the combined company, with its CEO and chairman Thomas Renyi to become CEO of the new entity. Mellon had thrived and could continue to thrive as a stand-alone company. Its return on equity of 22 percent was one of the highest in the country. Because Pennsylvania's antitakeover laws virtually precluded a successful hostile takeover of Mellon by BONY, BONY was forced to withdraw its offer.

In March 1999, Fleet Financial and BankBoston announced their own regional merger. This $16 billion deal between rival New England banks will make the merged entity, to be called FleetBoston, the eighth-largest in the U.S. Cost savings are estimated at $600 million by 2001. Because FleetBoston will have a virtual lock on the New England market, both branch and ATM divestitures are expected.

Both Fleet and BankBoston have had significant experience with in-market mergers. Fleet bought ailing Bank of New England in 1991 and Shawmut National Corp. in 1995. BankBoston bought BayBank in 1996.

The two banks' operations, despite their geographic overlap, are complementary. BankBoston is strong in high-tech banking, corporate lending, and Latin America. It also has an investment banking arm: Robertson Stephens. Fleet has discount brokerage group Quick & Reilly, commercial and mortgage lending, student loan processing, and a large credit card operation. Fleet has a presence in New York while BankBoston does not. The new company plans to focus especially on international operations, such as Latin America and foreign-exchange trading.

BankBoston had become a target in late 1998 and early 1999 because its share price was hit by losses in and continued exposure to Latin America. Compared to a 16 percent decline in the bank stock index from its high, BankBoston declined 38 percent. Rather than be swallowed by a larger institution, this deal enabled its headquarters to remain in New England.

Other regionals have also combined to bulk up. In June 1999, First Security Corp. and Zions Bancorp, both of Salt Lake City, agreed to combine in a $5.9 billion deal to create the second-largest bank headquartered in the western U.S. Also in June 1999, AmSouth Bancorp of Birmingham, Alabama, agreed to a $6.3 billion deal with First American of Nashville.

THE NONBANK BANKS

Much of the competition faced by commercial banks comes from a rapidly proliferating animal—the nonbank bank. This group is populated by "monoline" credit card companies such as Advanta, home mortgage companies such as Countrywide Credit, and auto finance companies such as Olympic Financial.

Nimble and extremely aggressive, these companies stepped into the breach created by the credit crunch of the early 1990s, gobbling market share by serving customers temporarily ignored by troubled banks and thrifts. For example, four monoline credit card companies—First USA, Capital One, Advanta, and MBNA—pushed their share of the credit card market from 7.6 percent in

1991 to 17.6 percent by 1995. (First USA later combined with Banc One, which, in turn, merged with First Chicago.) The companies feature credit cards as their sole product line—hence the name monoline. First USA's loan portfolio jumped 473 percent over the same period, compared to a 73 percent increase for all cards. Auto and home mortgage companies experienced similar growth.

There is some question, however, as to the level of risk contained in this growth. Many of these new competitors pioneered the practice of loaning money to "subprime" borrowers. Lately, investors and politicians alike have begun to question whether these loans will be paid off at the rates projected by the issuing finance companies. Nonetheless, many banks appear to have embraced the consumer finance business plan.

Insurance M&A

Many of the same forces driving banking M&A have encouraged M&A activity within the insurance sector as well. Every few months, it seems, another big insurer is bought: In December 1997, American Bankers Insurance Group was the target of a $2.2 billion acquisition; the following month, St. Paul Companies bought USF&G for $2.8 billion; in December 1998, AIG bought SunAmerica; in February 1999, XL Capital agreed to buy NAC Re. Aegon agreed to buy Transamerica and Chubb agreed to buy Executive Risk. The industry is bubbling with change, affected by many of the same forces at work elsewhere in financial services.

Much of the deal activity has been taking place in two main insurance categories—property & casualty and life. Acquisition activity has been driven by a number of factors. First, and likely most influential, is that operating difficulties and poor management have weakened some companies, making them receptive to takeover. But other factors have also played a role. For instance, the insurance industry is a mature one with little prospect of organic growth. Like commercial banks who saw their revenues eroded by the advent of a strong bull market and the rise of mutual funds, insurance companies have seen sales of their retirement products fall off. M&A activity is one means for companies to grow their revenues. Many insurance companies are also overcapitalized, making attractive targets. And the restructuring of the big multiline insurers—analogous to the slimming down of the conglomerates in the early 1980s—has provided supply in the acquisitions market to feed the demand of consolidators and financial buyers.

Particular operating difficulties have varied by industry subline. Property and casualty insurers failed to reserve adequately for losses, leaving them pinched when liabilities materialized. In the late 1980s and early 1990s, environmental, asbestos, and litigation losses began to pile up, badly denting many insurers' balance sheets.

For life insurers, the main problems have been asset troubles—primarily bad real estate investments. Many insurers saw the value of their portfolios plummet when the exuberant commercial real estate market of the 1980s collapsed. Junk bonds also were a problem to a lesser extent: When the junk market crashed in the early 1990s, some regulators pressed insurers to unload their holdings at a loss, a response that was, in hindsight, an overreaction. The market soon came back up and investors who bought the paper made huge profits.

From an M&A perspective, these operational difficulties have been deal catalysts, pushing some companies to seek a white knight acquirer with a healthy balance sheet, or to sell businesses or parts of businesses. For instance, Continental Insurance sold out to CNA, the insurance subsidiary of Loews, in 1995, after being hammered by mounting property and casualty claims, chiefly for environmental clean-up. The company, forced to stop paying a dividend, found its stock off 60 percent from its August 1993 high.

Healthier companies face a less life-threatening but troubling problem of their own: As competition has heated up across the board, insurers have found it more difficult to grow revenues and earnings. Insurance investment products became a tough sell in the world of easy access to mutual funds. While people still purchase pure life insurance policies that provide death benefits, the real money in life insurance has always been in selling "cash-value" insurance, a life insurance policy wrapped around an investment vehicle: With such a product the customer pays a higher premium than would otherwise be the case, and the excess premium gains value over time. As Americans became more sophisticated about their investment strategies, however, many became convinced mutual funds provide a better investment opportunity.

AIG, one of the world's most successful insurance companies, wanted to take advantage of this trend. AIG and SunAmerica announced an $18.5 billion combination of their operations in 1998. AIG gained a foothold in the retirement investment business of SunAmerica as well as access to SunAmerica's 9,400 brokers. SunAmerica benefited from access to the 130-country international customer base of AIG. This important deal was a testament to the vision of Eli Broad, who built SunAmerica, which underwrites and sells primarily property, casualty, and life insurance products, into one of America's fastest growing companies. The deal was therefore partly insurance company combination and partly convergence of insurance and brokerage.

Another major dimension of insurance M&A has been the restructuring of the large multiline insurers—MetLife, Travelers, Prudential, and others. The multilines prospered for decades by serving all segments of the insurance market. Yet, like many large diversified companies, their diversity proved a hindrance. In many cases, top management was insulated from the front-line business units and failed to recognize impending problems. When the problems became abundantly clear, the large organizations were difficult to maneuver.

Eventually, many industry executives came to the conclusion that the companies they led needed to slim down and focus on a smaller set of markets. Prudential sold off a reinsurance business. Metropolitan and Travelers sold their health insurance units, and Aetna sold its property and casualty operations.

Consolidators and financial buyers are the final force driving insurance company acquisitions. As in other sectors of the financial services industry, changes in the insurance business have been treated as an opportunity by some: The consolidators' business plan is to combine ailing operations, slash overlapping staff, and impose rigid cost control.

Sandy Weill built Travelers by following this plan. KKR also bought into insurance. However, Stephen Hilbert of Conseco Insurance, Gary Wendt of GE Capital, and Warren Buffett of Berkshire Hathaway have been the most prominent insurance company consolidators.

Hilbert wholeheartedly followed an acquisition-driven growth plan and has been quite successful. Starting as early as 1979, he saw the vitality of the consolidation model, and the former encyclopedia salesman and college dropout began snapping up insurance companies. His early deals were primarily cash acquisitions financed with debt. As his stock rose, he favored stock deals.

But following his purchase of Green Tree Financial in April 1998, its stock price collapsed 50 percent. Hilbert's '60s-like stock performance is a cautionary tale for the giddy '90s.

Wendt's strong interest in insurance is of more recent vintage than Hilbert's. GE Capital began its insurance company acquisition spree in 1993 with the $525 million purchase of Great Northern Annuity, and over the next three years spent more than $4.5 billion to buy another six U.S. insurance and reinsurance companies. In addition, Wendt made a $2.4 billion hostile bid for Kemper (which was, however, unsuccessful) and spent $1 billion on two German reinsurers.

Berkshire Hathaway, the widely misunderstood yet wildly successful insurance conglomerate, is another consolidator. Warren

Buffett's company bought General Re for $23.5 billion, marking yet another step in the widespread combination of the fragmented reinsurance sector: Gerling-Konzern Globale had already announced the purchase of Constitution Re for $700 million; Swiss Re bought Life Re for $1.8 billion; GE Capital bought Kemper Reinsurance for $500 million; and Axa has agreed to purchase Guardian Re. Synergy with other Berkshire Hathaway insurance businesses—Geico, National Indemnity, Central States Indemnity, and Kansas Bankers Surety—motivated the Berkshire Hathaway deal. Specifically, General Re would gain access to Berkshire Hathaway's vast capital reserves, allowing it to assume more risk, and thus take in increased revenues from other insurers. Furthermore, the fact that General Re will no longer be a public company will remove concerns about earnings volatility and therefore will allow the company to write more business than it could as a publicly traded company.

Convergence

In addition to consolidation within sectors, we are now witnessing consolidation between sectors. What has resulted is a move toward the convergence of commercial banking, investment banking, and insurance. Before Morgan Stanley Dean Witter, there had been several combinations of commercial banks and investment banks. The success of the Morgan Stanley–Dean Witter deal, however, kicked off commercial–investment banking combinations on a wider scale. The model posited that a securities arm could provide the product—stock and debt offerings—to push to individual customers through established retail distribution channels and banking relationships. Spurred on by changes in the banking regulatory environment, commercial banks went on the prowl for securities firms, seeking to diversify and to offer a broader array of products. These banks were also looking to replace revenues captured by mutual funds, which, because of the booming stock market, could offer higher returns to customers.

Bankers Trust bought Alex. Brown, SBC Warburg—then a unit of Swiss Bank—acquired Dillon Read, BankAmerica teamed with Robertson Stephens, subsequently resold to BankBoston, Hugh McColl's NationsBank bought Montgomery Securities, Canada's CIBC bought Oppenheimer, Holland's ING Group acquired Furman Selz, and France's Société Générale bought Cowen & Co. As a result of the deals, there has been a significant blurring of the boundary between commercial and investment banking.

COMMERCIAL BANKS ON THE PROWL

Acquirer	Target	Price	Date Announced
Swiss Bank	S.G. Warburg	$1.4 billion	May 1995
Bankers Trust	Wolfensohn & Co.	$210 million	May 1996
Bankers Trust	Alex. Brown	$1.7 billion	April 1997
SBC Warburg	Dillon Read	$600 million	May 1997
BankAmerica	Robertson Stephens	$540 million	June 1997
NationsBank	Montgomery Securities	$1.2 billion	June 1997
CIBC	Oppenheimer	$525 million	July 1997
First Union Corp.	Wheat First Butcher Singer	$484 million	August 1997
ING Group	Furman Selz	$600 million	August 1997
Fleet Financial Group	Quick & Reilly Group	$1.5 billion	September 1997
U.S. Bancorp	Piper Jaffray	$768 million	December 1997
Société Générale	Cowen & Co.	$540 million	February 1998
Deutsche Bank	Bankers Trust	$9.8 billion	November 1998
BankBoston	Robertson Stephens	$800 million	June 1998
First Union	Everen Capital	$1.1 billion	April 1999
Chase Manhattan	Hambrecht & Quist	$1.6 billion	September 1999

While new economic realities created the impetus for commercial banks to expand into investment banking, it took a more modern banking regulatory environment for the desire to be translated into action. These changes materialized when it became clear to regulators that the post-Depression-era regulation was not appropriate for today's new economic environment.

Previously, post-1933 regulatory boundaries posed a major impediment to creating an integrated financial institution. Following the 1929 stock market crash, a banking scandal led Congress to pass the Glass-Steagall Act of 1933 and the Banking Act of 1935, which until a few years ago defined rigid boundaries between commercial and investment banking. Glass-Steagall limited commercial banks to their core function—the taking and safekeeping of customer deposits and the making of consumer and commercial loans; underwriting and brokering securities were no longer permissible for commercial banks. A new industry, investment banking, was created to fill these roles off-limits to commercial banks.

These and other regulatory reforms created a defined, segmented financial services industry in the United States. Commercial banks dominated the loan and credit business. Savings and loans collected savings deposits in passbook accounts and made mortgage loans. Investment banks underwrote and distributed securities. And insurance companies managed risks. Participants in each sector enjoyed a protected oligopoly and looked to Washington as a Big Daddy. The federal government not only defined the roles: It bailed companies out when they screwed up.

Commercial banks prospered from the long postwar economic expansion, but the enduring good times also caused them to become complacent. The commercial banking business was fairly straightforward and chiefly involved credit analysis. Described as "public utilities" or "white-collar factories," banks offered a fairly stable group of products. Institutions were hierarchical and tasks standardized, with stability and safety the focus. As Time magazine put it, "American bankers for decades operated by the 3-6-3 rule: pay depositors 3 percent interest, lend money at 6 percent, and tee off at the golf course by 3 P.M."

Of course, this world of easy prosperity could not last. More entrepreneurial, aggressive competitors emerged who found ways to work within—and to stretch—the existing framework, threatening the businesses of commercial banks. The prosperity of the new industrial era was driving the stock market up to dizzying new heights. Consumers were no longer content to invest in low-yielding savings accounts. Mutual funds and stocks were the wave of the future for the new generation. By offering these new and higher-paying investment vehicles, Merrill Lynch, Charles Schwab, Fidelity, and similar companies nabbed depositors.

These developments placed pressure on bank executives to pay higher interest rates to match those offered by their competitors and to grant riskier loans to fund the higher interest payouts. Driven by unrelenting competition in their traditional businesses, commercial banks continue to push for ways to expand and grow. The desire to break into investment banking is part of this evolution.

Today, a consensus has developed that banks do need the freedom to offer a wider range of services if they are to survive. In the last few years regulators at the Federal Reserve have taken the lead in liberalizing existing rules, triggering the wave of recent deals.

The key deal-spurring event came in December 1996, when the Federal Reserve raised the percentage of total company revenues that a bank's securities subsidiary may earn from 10 to 25 percent. Previously, the acquisition of any major investment bank would have tipped the revenue mix of most commercial banks above the 10 percent threshold. Therefore, few major deals were announced before 1996. The new rule, however, was the catalyst for a flurry of deal activity. It permitted Bankers Trust's acquisition of regional investment bank Alex. Brown, for example, whose revenues would form 20 percent of combined company revenues.

Investment banks have been quite receptive to their commercial banking suitors. High prices certainly have lubricated the process. However, a number of other considerations underlie the willingness to forsake independence. Many view having a commercial bank parent as a harbor from the storm, with size and diversification bringing stability to volatile investment banking earnings. Furthermore, commercial banks will help investment banks expand globally and adapt to the new digital economy. Global expansion is now an imperative due to the increasing internationalization of the capital markets and the increasingly multinational interest and scale of clients. There is a perception that investment banks must follow their clients abroad or risk losing them to more global institutions. Moreover, much of the world's future growth will come from emerging markets in Asia, South America, and elsewhere.

Yet going global is expensive. Even the largest investment banking institutions are relatively small when compared to commercial banks or insurance companies. Meanwhile, smaller investment banks simply lack the resources for major international pushes and have been forced to pick their spots. Many investment banks consequently look favorably on the possibility of a partnership with a capital-rich acquirer with which to share the risk of the inevitable setbacks. The crash that hit emerging markets in 1998 is indicative, significantly impacting banks with large foreign exposure—such as Citicorp and BankAmerica.

In the final analysis, post-deal implementation will determine whether the integrated financial institution model works. Some past experiments have foundered, because melding the Wall Street and Main Street cultures of different institutions can be difficult. Defection of key personnel is also an especially serious problem. When NationsBank purchased Montgomery Securities, Montgomery Securities boss Thomas Weisel defected after a policy disagreement. However, the commercial banks seem ready to commit the resources necessary to handle the transition.

The Financial Services Supermarket

The combination of commercial banks and investment banks represented one way to broaden product offerings. The creation of financial supermarkets—institutions that would converge banking, insurance, asset management, and capital markets activities—represented an even more dramatic push. The trend escalated in September 1997 when the Travelers Group announced its $9 billion acquisition of investment bank Salomon Brothers and again with Travelers' March 1998 arrangement of a merger with Citicorp, worth $36.5 billion at closing.

The notion of a financial supermarket—one-stop shopping for all sorts of customers—is not new. Several prototypes were cobbled together in the early 1980s: insurance companies, retailers, a credit card company, and brokerage firms embraced the model and rushed to translate this vision into reality. Unfortunately, implementation of the concept was more difficult than it seemed. Furthermore, customers were not yet ready for the concept; it was not until the dawn of the Internet age and the loosening of legislative barriers between banks and insurance companies that integration seemed a realistic possibility.

The Prelude: Financial Supermarkets in the 1980s

Prudential Insurance pioneered the financial supermarket concept through a 1981 acquisition of the Bache Group. The brokerage operations would provide new distribution channels for the insurance companies' mutual funds and other products and, in return, the insurance companies would provide capital for expansion and technological improvements. We and the other advisers working for Bache were thrilled to find a distinguished buyer willing to purchase a troubled brokerage company under fire from hostile raiders. Others followed Prudential into the securities business. Most prominently, between 1982 and 1984, Kemper swallowed five regional brokerage operations, folding them into its Kemper Securities unit.

Mainline American companies with existing financial services subsidiaries also latched on to the financial supermarket model. GE bought investment bank Kidder, Peabody and brought in an industrial manager to run it. In the early 1980s, Sears, Roebuck made an even more dramatic move to leverage its strong brand name and marketing prowess into a financial services unit focused on the newly prosperous middle-class Americans, with Allstate Insurance as the core of its efforts. In 1981, Dean Witter was added for $610 million; real estate broker Coldwell Banker rounded out the group in the same year. Sears forthrightly attempted to meld these three units into a single retail force. Financial services kiosks were opened in Sears stores and more than $1 billion was spent to create the Discover Card. Everything was designed around the vision of Sears as a cradle-to-grave financial services provider.

Of course, existing financial services companies were not content to cede the future to Sears and other newcomers. Merrill Lynch stepped up its own diversification efforts and, building on the 1978 acquisition of investment bank White Weld, expanded to become a major investment bank serving institutional clients. At the same time, Merrill added insurance and real estate finance to its brokerage operations. Like Sears, Merrill saw itself as the broad-based financial powerhouse of the future.

However, when it came to embracing the diversification trend, American Express was perhaps the most enthusiastic participant. Chief executive James Robinson III took over the credit card, traveler's check, and insurance company in 1977 and began an aggressive acquisition program not long thereafter. In 1981, American Express acquired brokerage firm Shearson Loeb Rhoades for $930 million, and two years later added the Trade Development Bank—a Swiss private bank—for $550 million and Investor Diversified Services for $790 million.

The IDS acquisition underscored the breadth of Robinson's vision. As a mass-market investment advisory firm, IDS was somewhat at odds with American Express' tony image. Yet the purchase fit with Robinson's goal to build a "blue box" of diverse financial services. Investment bank Lehman Brothers was folded into Shearson in 1984.

Then, after the 1987 stock market crash, Robinson paid $962 million to pick up E.F. Hutton, a retail brokerage house.

Almost without exception, the financial services conglomerations of the 1980s were failed experiments. The various units simply did not mesh together into coherent, enduring institutions. At American Express, for example, the notion of bundled services was more myth than reality. Credit card executives balked at the idea of joint American Express–Shearson statements, fearing investment setbacks might tarnish the American Express brand. For similar reasons, Shearson brokers were never given full access to the valuable American Express customer list. But likewise, customers were not yet ready for the financial supermarket concept, their choices not yet shaped by the ease of Internet commerce, which promises all services in one easy-to-access place.

American Express also had trouble managing the risks associated with its far-flung empire. Losses at the Fireman's Fund and the Trade Development Bank ran to the hundreds of millions of dollars, and Shearson made a series of bad commercial real estate and bridge loans. Robinson was forced to inject new capital into the firm.

Under tremendous pressure, Robinson cleaned up the troubled units and, reversing course, put them on the block. American Express realized roughly $1 billion on the sale of the Trade Development Bank and $2 billion for the insurance company. Robinson then stabilized the bleeding at Shearson; but this was too little, too late.

Outside directors forced Robinson to resign in early 1993, and within weeks, Harvey Golub, Robinson's successor as chief executive, had sold off Shearson's brokerage operations. The next year, American Express spun off the Lehman Brothers investment bank, marking the final unwinding of its financial supermarket. American Express' stock price zoomed.

Ironically, Robinson's vision was confirmed by subsequent events. The Dean Witter–Morgan Stanley deal, which the market reacted to with rare enthusiasm, had definite parallels to Robinson's concept. Robinson's problem, however, was the execution, not the vision.

James Robinson III

At his peak, James Robinson III, a polished, patrician Southerner, had a sterling reputation as one of America's best chief executives. He jetted around the world, overseeing the far-reaching American Express empire. His counsel to world leaders on political matters earned him the title "Corporate America's secretary of state." In the late 1980s, he championed a well-received plan to solve the developing countries' debt crisis.

Robinson was born in Atlanta and educated at Harvard Business School. Following in the footsteps of his father and grandfather, who each had served as chairman of First National Bank of Atlanta, upon graduation in 1961, he started his fast-track career at Morgan Guaranty Trust. Within six years, Robinson had risen to be special assistant to the bank's chairman. He joined American Express in 1970 and became chief executive in 1977, at the age of forty.

In the late 1980s, troubles began to mount for Robinson. American Express's Lehman subsidiary was involved in advising Robinson's friend Ross Johnson on the failed RJR Nabisco management buyout and some of Johnson's bad press rubbed off on Robinson. Then, in 1989, American Express revealed that another subsidiary's earnings had been overstated. Robinson also was forced to apologize publicly to Edmund Safra, the former head of the Trade Development Bank, after it became apparent American Express had targeted Safra in a smear campaign.

The succession of problems at American Express initially did little to dim Robinson's reputation. In fact, he became known as the "Teflon executive," with high praise given to his attractive wife, Linda, a public relations powerhouse, for keeping her husband's image intact. Curiously, it was during this period that Robinson seemed to broaden himself in thinking about the future strategy of financial services.

Eventually, though, the operating problems at Shearson became too great, and the stock price too low. Robinson publicly accepted responsibility and for a time enjoyed the continued support of his board. But investors wanted a scapegoat. Finally, the board bowed to pressure, and Robinson was allowed to lead the search for his own replacement. Robinson stepped aside, leaving American Express to Golub, his handpicked successor.

American Express was not the only company that stumbled in an attempt to transform itself into a financial services supermarket. Sears faced similar problems merging its units into a coherent whole and therefore shed Dean Witter, Discover, and Coldwell Banker in 1993, and Allstate Insurance in 1994. Even the legendary GE had enormous problems with Kidder, Peabody, whose hand-selected manager from an industrial background was mocked as a "tool-and-die" man. Kemper eventually would sell its securities business, renamed Everen Securities, to the brokerage firm's employees. And Prudential's securities business would prove a costly, scandal-ridden liability.

Resurgence

In the early 1990s, conventional wisdom held that diversified financial services companies were short-lived dinosaurs rapidly headed for extinction. However, the pessimism was overdone. In a slew of 1998 megamergers, banks embraced the financial supermarket concept once again in a search for competitive advantage. The success of the Morgan Stanley–Dean Witter combination indicated that the financial supermarket idea had come of age. A quest for product breadth and capability ensued, resulting in a flurry of deal activity.

Where originally Morgan and Dean Witter had followed the lead of Merrill Lynch, in November 1997, Merrill took Morgan's lead, paying $5.2 billion to acquire the U.K.'s Mercury Asset Management Group. One of the largest fund managers in the United Kingdom, Mercury added more than $160 billion to Merrill's assets under management.

With the coming of a new economic era, the financial supermarket model too came of age. In the Internet generation, where convenience is an imperative, diversification should allow banks to provide more services to existing clients and will therefore reduce the ability of competitors to woo existing clients with the promise of enhanced services. Diversification will also provide access to untapped markets that represent lucrative opportunities for growth.

Entrepreneur Sandy Weill had the foresight to realize that the financial supermarket would be the business model of the future, even when the idea was out of favor. Over the last decade, he cobbled together the Travelers Group, his own financial supermarket, by snapping up troubled companies and then turning them around. But in 1997 and 1998, not to be left behind in the wave of consolidation, Weill took his boldest steps ever, to transform Travelers from a strong, but more limited operator, to a financial supermarket powerhouse.

Weill's story is ironic. Having built Shearson through a series of acquisitions in the 1960s and 1970s, he sold the firm to American Express, in search of size and deeper pockets. Weill served as president of American Express for a time but then left American Express in the mid-1980s, an early veteran of the rocky financial supermarket venture, to take over a small commercial and retail finance company. From this platform, Weill fashioned his own, more successful supermarket.

The first step came in 1988 with the $1.5 billion Primerica acquisition, which brought an insurance company and brokerage firm Smith Barney under Weill's control. At the time, Smith Barney was bleeding, losing $100 million a year. But Weill turned it around, boosting return on equity to 30 percent by 1992.

Weill's next move was a homecoming. He recaptured Shearson in 1993 and folded his former creation into Smith Barney. In the same year, Primerica acquired Travelers Insurance—which was weighed down by bad real estate investments—in a $4 billion stock merger. Weill's company took the Travelers name. Aetna's property and casualty portfolio, similarly troubled, was added in 1995 for another $4 billion.

Weill's success has been the result of two factors. First, he is a disciplined acquirer with a sense for unfolding strategic developments. He bought Shearson before brokerage firms were hot properties; and he took on Aetna Property & Casualty, by consensus a toxic property. In both cases, Weill saw a different future than the crowd. He timed the market, bought the businesses cheap, and turned them around. Weill is a highly successful bargain hunter.

A relentless focus on post-deal implementation and management detail also has been key to Weill's success. By paying attention to relatively minor expenses, Weill's management team has had a large collective impact. Bloated insurance operations have been trimmed and made more efficient. Yet costs are not the only concern: Decades of working in the financial services industry have given Weill a deft touch when it comes to managing people. The bankers and brokers at Smith Barney were given enough leeway to operate effectively, and Travelers Group was rewarded with strong profits.

Even after spending over $8 billion for Travelers and Aetna's property and casualty portfolio, Weill remained openly interested in further acquisitions. As he told a reporter, "The insurance industry is consolidating, the money management business is consolidating, the securities industry is consolidating, and the lending business is consolidating. We are in all of them and we would be interested in the right thing in any of them." Weill's unabashed goal was to build a global financial services company for the new millennium, both through internal growth of Travelers' existing businesses and with additional acquisitions.

On September 25, 1997, Weill announced the $9 billion Salomon Brothers acquisition. Weill planned to fold Salomon Brothers into his Smith Barney unit, creating a financial services powerhouse to rival Morgan Stanley Dean Witter and Merrill Lynch. The new firm would be the number two underwriter of corporate debt and equities, the fourth most active merger adviser, and would field the third-largest number of retail brokers in the United States.

Much like the Morgan Stanley–Dean Witter deal, the marriage of Salomon Brothers and Smith Barney brought together an institutional power and a retail power with complementary operations. Salomon Brothers would enhance Smith Barney's global presence and add real strength in corporate debt underwriting and proprietary trading. Smith Barney, on the other hand, already had strong retail distribution and equity underwriting.

In taking on Salomon Brothers, Weill yet again demonstrated his willingness to accept challenges others found too daunting. Salomon Brothers had a reputation on the Street for volatile earnings due to heavy reliance on proprietary trading operations. Its traders were criticized as "gunslingers," routinely making large bets on market movements—some of which pay off, and some of which generate losses. This volatility, and the attendant need for sophisticated risk management, kept many potential Salomon Brothers acquirers from pursuing a deal.

Weill, on the other hand, was sanguine about the challenge posed by Salomon Brothers. He has decades of experience managing investment firms and is comfortable with the personnel issues involved in handling Wall Street stars. In addition, the new Salomon Smith Barney unit would be managed jointly by Weill's longtime lieutenant

James Dimon and Deryck Maughan, chief executive of Salomon Brothers. Weill theorized that he could dampen the volatility and acquire a world-class franchise at a favorable price. It seems that Weill underestimated the challenge, however: In 1998, huge trading losses caused Weill to curtail severely Salomon's proprietary trading operations.

But the Salomon deal was merely a prelude. In March 1998, Travelers and Citibank shocked the world by announcing what was, at that point, the largest merger in corporate history, weighing in at a hefty $72.6 billion in total deal value at the time of the announcement. News of the deal sent the Dow above the 9,000 mark for the first time ever. Both Citicorp and Travelers shares were to be converted into shares in a new company, Citigroup, which would be the first company to operate in all areas of finance throughout the world.

The creation of Citigroup was revolutionary. Its success was predicated upon the final tearing down of a law that has regulated the banking sector for over half a century: the Bank Holding Company Act. The act effectively precludes banks from engaging in insurance underwriting. A loophole in the law, however, makes it possible for a nonbank to buy a bank and apply to become a bank holding company, provided that two years after the acquisition the holding company divests itself of noncomplying insurance operations. It is also possible to apply for up to three one-year extensions thereafter. Travelers and Citibank availed themselves of this loophole in their combination, counting on Congress repealing the act within five years. Otherwise, Citigroup would have five years to divest itself of its noncomplying insurance operations, which the Fed has stated comprise 20 percent of Citigroup's revenues. In fact, Congress seems close to passing a bill allowing Citigroup to proceed.

Citicorp's explicit strategic focus over the past decade, like Weill's, had also been to build a financial supermarket, international in scope, with a worldwide retail and consumer-banking franchise and a strong corporate client base. At the core of this strategy were

Citicorp's crown jewels—international relationships that the bank has maintained for decades. Citicorp leveraged this base into a strong international branch network covering more than forty-one countries, with other operations in nearly 100 countries.

The combination was intended to facilitate cross-selling the two companies' products to each other's respective client bases. For example, Travelers' insurance, brokerage, and asset management operations sought Citibank's commercial banking clients for their products; conversely, Citibank sought to market its products to the elite group of Fortune 500 companies among the client base of Travelers' investment banking arm, Salomon Smith Barney. The combined company would offer individual customers one-stop shopping for all financial services products they might need—credit cards, personal banking, insurance, and brokerage services. Weill has set ambitious goals for the group: to capture 1 billion customers by 2010, up from 100 million today.

In the weeks before the deal was formally announced, Weill and Citibank chief executive John Reed campaigned behind-the-scenes for regulatory support. Weill made calls to President Clinton (who gave his blessing to the merger), Treasury Secretary Robert Rubin, and Fed chairman Alan Greenspan, alerting them of the merger plans. Ultimately, the deal was approved by the Fed.

The social issues created by the deal have caused more significant problems, however. Citigroup was originally envisioned to be run by co-CEOs, Weill and Reed, to whom not two but *three* corporate heads would report: James Dimon, the former president of Travelers; Deryck Maughan, head of the old Salomon Brothers; and Victor Menezes of Citicorp. But this top-heavy structure was a recipe for disaster, destined to lead to infighting and dysfunctionality. The able Dimon was the sacrificial lamb and forced to resign. Putting commercial bankers and investment bankers, whose large pay disparities are legendary, under one roof is bound to create tensions.

Between the time of announcement and closing, the value of the proposed deal eroded significantly. Large losses in Russia adversely affected the stock prices of both companies. In addition, Travelers incurred significant losses from fixed-income trading in the third quarter of 1998 and from counterparty transactions with Long Term Capital Management.

The potential for cross-selling may not be realizable in the short term, especially in light of the volatile management. Despite the company's detractors, however, Citicorp's stock has bounced back.

Weill may realize his global dream. The new Citigroup has a diverse range of financial services under its trademark umbrella—from property and casualty insurance to credit cards, from investment banking to retail brokerage, from asset management to commercial finance. It has paved the way for regulatory changes in the banking industry and other cross-industry mergers in the financial services sector.

Consolidation Goes Global

The pressures felt by U.S. financial institutions soon came to be felt around the globe as well. On Friday, December 5, 1997, two thirds of the most distinguished industrialists in Switzerland secretly gathered in Basel and Zurich to consider a groundbreaking deal— the merger of Swiss Bank Corporation and Union Bank of Switzerland to form the United Bank of Switzerland, with a market capitalization of roughly $60 billion. The third not present were board members of archrival Credit Suisse. Security for the two companies' board meeting was tight—board members and our team arrived at the Swiss Bank meeting via subterranean tunnels. As we walked through the tunnels, metal doors shut firmly behind us with the precision of a Swiss watch.

Early Monday morning, Marcel Ospel of Swiss Bank, the new chief executive, shattered European precedent by announcing that the banks would merge. The market reaction was a standing ovation as both stocks soared. At the time the new UBS emerged, it would be the world's second-largest bank, the world's largest money manager, and the leading European investment bank.

Two strategic visions sparked the deal: consolidation and globalization. As late as 1996, consolidation in the financial services industry was still principally a U.S. phenomenon. Europe's financial services market, by contrast, was balkanized along both functional and geographic lines. Individual countries and sectors were dramatically overpopulated with small to midsized players.

Pressure for change had begun to build in the middle 1990s as the shock waves from the U.S. consolidation and the effect of the new digital era radiated into Europe. Even on their home turf, European institutions now faced the increasingly sharp elbows of companies like Merrill Lynch, Morgan Stanley, J.P. Morgan, Citicorp, and others. In addition, regulatory and political developments shook the system. European Union countries were moving toward a single financial services market and a single currency.

These forces jolted European companies out of complacency. Major deals were announced with unheard-of regularity—nine multibillion-dollar deals within the space of ten months.

The potential for cost savings in the European financial services sector became apparent in the Swiss Bank–UBS deal. As a result of the deal, the two banks eliminated overlapping branches and personnel. Annual costs were slashed by over $500 million.

Globalization was the second driver behind the Swiss Bank–UBS deal. The financial services market was rapidly evolving toward the creation of a handful of institutions with the scale to support a global integrated platform. Both investment banking and asset management were becoming businesses of global distribution and branding, and this deal made UBS a leader. In addition, by combining their embryonic U.S. efforts, Swiss Bank, the owner of Warburg Dillon Read, and UBS hoped to create a platform for developing their vital American presence.

Yet the real import of the merger was not so much what it said about the present, as what it said about the likely course of future events. Just as the Morgan Stanley–Dean Witter deal had foreshadowed developments in the U.S. market, the Swiss Bank and UBS combination crystallized the inevitability of a global consolidation. The leapfrog to $100 billion in market capitalization had started.

Consolidation in Canada

In January 1998, the global consolidation fever spread to Canada, leading Royal Bank of Canada to announce plans to merge with Bank of Montreal. As a result of UBS–Swiss Bank and a number of other global banking deals, the two banks believed that bulking up into larger institutions would be essential if they were to remain players in the new world order of financial institutions. If they did not react to deals like UBS–Swiss Bank, these Canadian banks would find their businesses increasingly threatened.

Invoking the same rationale that sparked other banking mergers in 1998, John E. Cleghorn, chairman and CEO of Royal Bank of Canada, noted that the economies of scale created by the merger would allow more efficient investments in technology, an absolute necessity in today's competitive marketplace. In fact, Bank of Montreal chairman Matthew Barrett, in a particularly ironic statement made at the deal announcement, joked about "funeral arrangements" for their rival banks who had not yet planned their own mergers.

In the same spirit, in April 1998, Canadian Imperial Bank of Commerce and Toronto-Dominion Bank announced their own merger plans in what was viewed as a reluctant defensive comeback to the Royal Bank of Canada–Bank of Montreal deal.

But after the initial excitement about the two deals died down, reality set in. The two mergers were to be highly scrutinized by antitrust authorities for any hint of anticompetitive effects. Aware of the highly delicate situation, all four banks embarked on focused public relations campaigns to inform Canadian consumers about how these mergers would benefit them. Bank of Montreal and Royal Bank of Canada put together a twenty-four-page booklet detailing their motto "Two Banks. One Pledge," and placed numerous informational advertisements in daily and community newspapers throughout Canada. They stated that service charges would be reduced and front-line service staff and branch count would be increased. The banks promised the merger would lead to job creation and increased consumer access to capital. RBC chairman Cleghorn hit the road to try to sell the merger to the public.

But all the PR effort was to no avail. Finance Minister Paul Martin announced on December 14 that he would not allow any bank "megamergers" until a lengthy, comprehensive review of Canada's financial services industry was completed. The two new banks would control 70 percent of Canada's insured deposits, 70 percent of personal loans, 76 percent of lending to small and medium-sized businesses, and 61 percent of Canada's regional brokerage business, and such combination needed to be investigated.

This sobering announcement effectively killed both deals: Shortly following the announcement, both mergers were called off.

The digital age has arrived, but Canada is unwilling to acknowledge it.

Germany

Soon, the bank merger mania hit Germany as well. The merger between Deutsche Bank and Bankers Trust marks a second attempt on the part of Deutsche to enter the global investment banking business, a means for Deutsche to increase its worldwide presence. Like the Canadian banks and in contrast to Travelers and NationsBank, however, Deutsche's merger announcement was not the act of a first mover. Rather it was purely a defensive move, a last-ditch effort to enter the investment banking market in which it had previously failed miserably.

Deutsche Bank's initial foray into investment banking seemed to start out well enough, with its 1989 purchase of Morgan Grenfell, a

U.K.-based investment bank. With this deal, Deutsche thought it would become a global leader in investment banking, with operations in the U.K. and the U.S. To further build its franchise, Deutsche began madly hiring away as many experienced bankers as it could find from U.S. bulge bracket firms, wooing them with legendarily high pay packages. In 1996 the bank hired away from Morgan Stanley a group of high-priced technology bankers, including the flamboyant Frank Quattrone, in a highly publicized coup. This group was to help Deutsche rise above Goldman Sachs and Morgan Stanley to be the number one technology bank.

Soon, however, things began to go awry. The integration of Morgan Grenfell did not go smoothly, wrought with culture clashes and integration difficulties. Deutsche believed in highly centralized management and did not give the former Morgan Grenfell bankers or the newly hired bankers the autonomy they needed to be creative and respond to competition. Approximately 200 bankers left—some star rainmakers—damaging Deutsche's prospects for building a world-class investment banking practice. Quattrone and his group defected to Crédit Suisse First Boston. Meanwhile, costs were spinning out of control. The real wake-up call came when German telecommunications company Deutsche Telekom hired Goldman to assist in its privatization.

A $1.5 billion restructuring was announced, intended to encourage cooperation between commercial bankers and investment bankers. The name Morgan Grenfell was done away with and replaced with Deutsche Bank Securities. But the immediate result of the restructuring was the departure of the two top executives at the former Morgan Grenfell, Carter McLelland and Maurice Thompson. Deutsche's investment banking operations were a mess, and the conventional wisdom was that Deutsche would pull out of investment banking altogether.

In an attempt to create the investment banking powerhouse that it had originally intended, at the end of 1998 Deutsche Bank announced its intent to acquire Bankers Trust. The deal would create the world's largest financial institution. While Deutsche was paying top dollar—a 43 percent premium and 2.3 times book value—for BT, Deutsche was also sitting on top of a pile of cash, and its shareholders seemed pleased that it was at least putting that cash to use.

BT would strengthen Deutsche's weak investment banking operations, providing a particularly strong debt financing operation, an equity underwriting operation through Alex. Brown, acquired in 1997, and an M&A boutique through Wolfensohn, acquired in 1996. Deutsche would also gain the strong global custody and asset management operations of BT. It is widely believed, however, that Deutsche viewed Alex. Brown as the "crown jewel" of BT, as it would offer access to the U.S. investment banking market.

But BT was not without its own problems. In the early 1990s, several clients sued the firm for misrepresentations made in the course of overly aggressive sales practices in the firm's derivative operations. And in the third quarter of 1998, the bank lost $488 million due to bad bets in Russia and other emerging markets as well as its dealings with Long Term Capital Management. Deutsche attempted to solve its dilemma by buying a troubled financial institution. But the going will not be easy. Already Bankers Trust Chief Executive Frank Newman resigned after a series of disputes. The potential is there, and the choices were few.

France, Italy, Spain, and Belgium: Globalization Spurs Consolidation

The "shadow of the euro," as former Lazard banker and current U.S. ambassador to France Felix Rohatyn described it, has also spurred a flurry of consolidation moves in France, Italy, and Spain to create leading European banks. When the euro's transition is complete, European financial institutions will face a bruising competitive atmosphere. Customers will be able to shop around Europe for the most favorable deals, without fear of currency risk. In anticipation of this environment, European banking M&A has exploded. Significantly, these deals have been intranational rather than international in nature: In Europe, the thought of a foreign bank snapping up a crown jewel of the domestic financial institutions sector is anathema.

On February 1, 1999, French banks Société Générale and Paribas SA announced their plans to merge to create SG Paribas. But then came the real shocker: Not to be left out, Banque Nationale de Paris launched a $37 billion hostile offer for both Société Générale and Paribas in March 1999 and triggered a sprawling brawl. After a six-month highly publicized battle, no party walked away happy. Tender offer results gave only an unwilling Paribas to BNP; meanwhile SocGen has been left stranded to look for another partner.

M&A activity among Italian financial institutions kicked off with the $11 billion merger of Credito Italiano with Unicredito in October 1998 and the $10 billion merger between Isituto Bancaro San Paolo with Isituto Mobiliare Italiano in November 1998. The San Paolo–IMI merger created Italy's largest bank. After a brief lull, banking mergers in Spain—such as the January 1999 merger between Banco Santander and Banco Central Hispanoamericano—and France, sparked a new wave of activity in March 1999. UniCredito Italiano, Italy's third-largest bank in terms of assets, announced plans to acquire Banca Commerciale Italiana for $14.2 billion. The company planned to rename itself Eurobanca and was to be Italy's largest bank in terms of assets.

Just hours after the Eurobanca deal was announced, San Paolo–IMI, itself the product of the merger between Isituto Bancaro San Paolo and Isituto Mobiliare Italiano, announced its intent to purchase Banca di Roma. However, Italian regulators' rejection of the deal caused it to fall apart. The Eurobanca deal met a similar fate.

In Belgium, a bidding contest for Générale de Banque by both ABN Amro and Fortis, the Belgo-Dutch bank created through the

1990 merger of insurers Amev of the Netherlands and AG of Belgium, broke out in 1998. Originally, Fortis's offer was lower than ABN Amro's, but would have maintained Générale de Banque as a Belgian institution, creating the "Grande Banque Belge" that the government has long pushed for. ABN Amro offered a cross-border deal. In the end, Fortis' desire to capture Générale de Banque prompted it to raise its bid, which clinched the bidding war.

The combined Fortis–Générale de Banque would sell both banking and insurance products—much like the U.S. Citigroup. The deal would also pave the way for Fortis' insurance products to be sold through Générale's retail network.

The takeover marked the completion of a radical change in Belgium's banking sector. In 1996, Crédit Communal merged with France's Crédit Local to create the Dexia Group. In 1997, ING purchased Banque Bruxelles Lambert. And in January 1998, Kredietbank merged with mutual society Cera and the insurance group ABB.

Many speculate that these European deals might drive further consolidation in both the German and Italian banking sectors: Commerzbank and Dresdner Bank are widely believed to be potential merger partners, for example.

Japan

Different economic realities, of which the most significant is financial instability, have been spurring Japanese banking consolidation. While bad loans have led to widespread restructuring efforts and requests for government support, some banks have also begun to combine to create larger, and hopefully more stable, entities. Regulatory change and financial volatility are beginning to have their influence on Japan's financial institutions. Deregulation of the Japanese banking sector, the so-called Big Bang, will also create a competitive environment and lead to M&A activity.

In November 1998, Dai-Ichi Kangyo Bank and Fuji Bank announced plans to merge their trust banking operations into a jointly owned venture, which will specialize in the recently deregulated asset management sector. In January 1999, Mitsui Trust and Chuo Trust, two of Japan's largest banks, announced their merger plans.

The Japanese government has been a strong advocate of bank mergers as part of banks' restructuring efforts. For example, it encouraged Sumitomo Trust to merge with Long Term Credit Bank (but to no avail). "Only a limited number of banks will be able to go on in their present form," said Bank of Japan governor Masaru Hayami.

In August 1999, Industrial Bank of Japan, Dai-Ichi Kangyo Bank, and Fuji Bank gave regulators cause for much joy when they announced plans for a three-way merger. The combined entity would become the world's largest bank, with $1.3 trillion in assets.

There have been several deals lately involving bankrupt Japanese banking institutions. In November 1998, Chuo Trust and Banking Co. acquired the bankrupt Hokkaido Takushoku Bank. In March 1999, the Resolution and Collection Bank acquired assets of the bankrupt Saitama Shogin Shinkumi Bank. And in April 1999, Hanshin Bank merged with the bankrupt Midori Bank.

The Japanese government has embarked on a plan reminiscent of that employed by the U.S. government to solve the savings & loan disaster of the 1980s. A Japan Resolution Trust Corporation, funded with over $505 billion, will take control of ailing banks by purchasing their outstanding shares, severing strong assets from weak assets, and then transferring the restructured banks back to the private sector. M&A activity will inevitably result at the end of this process.

Foreign parties have begun to play an active role in acquiring distressed Japanese bank assets. Ripplewood Holdings, a U.S.-based buyout firm, has recently reached a preliminary agreement with the government to buy Long Term Credit Bank. GE Capital has likewise targeted distressed companies so as to secure Japanese government support and to pay a low price. Typically, the company has also tried to structure its purchases so that it will control the "good assets" of the acquired companies but will be shielded from their large liabilities. The company has purchased financial sector companies such as Toho Mutual, Japan Leasing Corporation, Koei Credit, Minebea Shinban, and Shinkyoto. More recently, GE Capital bought $11 billion in commercial loans from the Long Term Credit Bank.

The Financial Services Future

The financial services future is certain to reflect the acceleration of past trends: more competition, more blurring of boundaries, and increasing globalization. We are now just seeing the tip of the iceberg of the changes the digital age will bring. Financial institutions will be forced to adapt to the new market realities.

For the commercial banks, the fundamental trend will be toward increased size and scale. The super-regionals' gamble has been vindicated in Congress, in the form of the Riegle-Neal Interstate Banking and Branching Efficiency Act of 1994, which allowed a bank holding company to buy operations in any other state and permitted banks to convert their out-of-state activities from separate, stand-alone bank subsidiaries into branch operations. Given BankAmerica's and NationsBank's transformation from super-regional to national bank, other super-regionals will likely consolidate.

The legislation will also allow New York money center banks such as Chase to embark on the multistate acquisition strategy embraced by NationsBank, now Bank of America. In fact, Bank of New York tried to do just that with its bid for Mellon Bank.

With the historic Travelers-Citicorp combination and new legislation driving another nail into the coffin of Glass-Steagall, the pace of convergence among commercial banks, investment banks, and insurance companies will likely quicken. Chase acquired technology boutique investment bank Hambrecht & Quist and is rumored to be interested in further partnering. And as domestic companies bulk up, the independents and foreign banks will inevitably feel the pinch and embark upon cross-border consolidation. Already, the bidding spree begun for National Westminster Bank ALC indicates the world of tumultuous change Europe has embraced.

Eventually, a handful of global players will dominate the scene while profitable niches will remain for the smart and nimble.

The Telco Revolution: 12
The Story of Ma Bell,
Her Children,
and Her Rivals

Louis XVI: "Is it a revolt?"
Duc de La Rochefoucald:
"No, Sire, it is a revolution."

—Upon hearing news of the Bastille's fall

Over the past twenty years, the telecommunications industry has been fractured and transformed. Before 1981, telco was synonymous with the ubiquitous monopoly operator AT&T. AT&T was responsible for providing long distance service, universal and affordable local service, and equipment; in exchange for its investment and its commitment to provide universal service, AT&T was assured a reasonable rate of return.

For a time the system worked. But technology changed, the monopoly was deregulated, and the AT&T empire broken up.

The story of AT&T became the saga of AT&T plus its progeny—the Baby Bells. As each was thrust into a new competitive environment, it fumbled for a survival strategy. This breakup of AT&T became the catalyst for M&A activity in the telco industry. Companies scrambled to fill the vacuum left in the wake of AT&T. As the realities of the digital economy became apparent, consolidation accelerated, brought to a head by the more complete deregulation ushered in by the Telecommunications Reform Act of 1996. AT&T, struggling to respond to these changes, attempted to transform itself. Finally, in 1998, AT&T found its way, merging with cable operator TCI in a deal that would make it an integrated long distance and local service company as well as a cable, Internet, and data services provider. However, Ma Bell's rivals have been busy doing transformative acquisitions as well. New giants such as MCI WorldCom–Sprint will present a strong challenge.

Throughout the story, technological change was the only constant. Wireless, Internet, and broadband services have come to the telcos, and these, among other new technologies, sparked new industries.

The Breakup of Ma Bell

At 8:00 A.M. on January 8, 1982, representatives of the U.S. government and AT&T gathered in a Washington, D.C., office. A certain amount of hostility pervaded the room—which is understandable given the years of battling which had preceded the moment. Yet more than anything, there was a sense of disbelief. With little fanfare, the U.S. Justice Department and AT&T agreed to settle *United States v. AT&T*—an antitrust case which had limped through the courts since 1974. AT&T as the world knew it would be no more.

On January 1, 1984, America's largest private employer was split into eight separate pieces. What had been the twenty-two local telephone companies in the Bell system—reconstituted as seven independently traded regional Bell operating companies (RBOCs)—were spun off to AT&T's shareholders. The parent company kept the long distance business, known as Long Lines, equipment maker Western Electric, an installed base of millions of phones, which were leased to customers, and the world-famous Bell Laboratories.

Day One, as the breakup was known within AT&T, was not a sudden event. The process of dividing the Bell empire into separate fiefdoms had been under way ever since the 1982 settlement, and to some extent even before the settlement. Yet dividing the interconnected wires and switches of the labyrinthine telephone system into separate operating units was a technological and logistical nightmare. Dire predictions of mass failure preceded the final split. One newly anointed RBOC president picked up the phone that morning, just to check for a dial tone. To his relief, he heard the familiar buzz. However, little else of the old Bell system remained unaltered.

Path to Breakup

The drama of the moment was heightened by the long history of a unified AT&T. The Bell system could trace its roots back to March 10, 1876, when, in a Boston attic, Alexander Graham Bell articulated the first complete sentence over a telephone. By the start of the twentieth century, AT&T—affectionately dubbed Ma Bell—had already established itself as an embryonic monopoly, condemned by some for employing ruthless business practices: spurning the attempts of rival companies to gain access to the AT&T network and indirectly coercing competitors to sell out on terms favorable to AT&T.

The phone company's actions, however, did not go unnoticed by the Department of Justice, which ultimately sued AT&T on antitrust grounds. In 1919, however, an agreement was reached between Theodore Vail, then AT&T's chairman, and President Woodrow Wilson which allowed the company to go about business without government intervention. AT&T agreed to moderate its tooth-and-nails approach in exchange for the government's informal approval of the AT&T monopoly. As a result, peace reigned between the phone company and the Justice Department for the next three decades.

But AT&T's antitrust problems resurfaced in 1949, when the government focused on the fact that Western Electric, the company's manufacturing subsidiary, served as the sole supplier of phone equipment to the company's operating units. As *Fortune* later stated, AT&T "existed in a state possibly best described in terms of Zen: it was its own supplier and its own market to a degree almost unique." The company used this muscle to keep competitors out of the unregulated equipment business. To rectify the situation, the Justice Department again sued the phone company, hoping to break up this captive monopoly.

This second antitrust case endured until 1956, when AT&T took advantage of political connections to gain a settlement. AT&T signed another consent decree, allowing it to keep Western Electric in exchange for a promise to confine new business development to regulated markets. The most significant effect of the agreement was to foreclose AT&T from competing in the nascent computer business.

AT&T's critics, not yet cognizant of the full potential of computers, slammed the decree as a mere "slap on the wrist," outraged that the Bell System had remained intact. However, with the passage of time, it would become clear that the company inadvertently had made a significant concession. Ma Bell eventually would chafe under the restriction and would strive to reverse the 1956 decree.

Notwithstanding these developments, the circumstances of the 1956 settlement chagrined the career lawyers in the Antitrust Division of the Justice Department, who quietly amassed information about AT&T's activities and waited for the right time to launch another attack.

New Competition

Meanwhile new competitors were struggling to hammer open AT&T's hold on the telecommunications market. But until the 1960s, a dual system of regulatory oversight protected AT&T's monopoly. Local phone service was regulated at the state level by public utility commissions and state officials, while long distance service was regulated by the Federal Communications Commission, an agency established under the Communications Act of 1934.

Before the breakup, AT&T enjoyed a virtual lock on the long distance business. But the local market was considerably more fragmented: AT&T's twenty-two Bell operating companies monopolized local service in less than half of the United States, with more than 1,000 independents controlling the remaining markets. Major players included GTE and United Telecommunications. However, these independents had arrived late on the scene and so had conceded to Bell the most attractive, most populated markets. Yet the local independents had a cozy relationship with AT&T, whereby they shared a piece of the long distance revenues generated over their lines. For this reason, they disfavored the idea of opening the long distance market to new competitors.

Local regulators also opposed new competition in long distance because the price wars it would bring could potentially destroy the system that guaranteed individual customers cheap local service. As former House Speaker Tip O'Neill was fond of saying, "All politics are local"; therefore, in the nature of things, state politicians placed emphasis on holding local rates down. The system worked like this: Because maintaining the extensive networks necessary to provide universal local service was an extremely capital-intensive proposition, with miles of copper wire and thousands of switching stations needed, existing local rates charged to customers did not reflect the true cost of providing service. However, by charging long distance and business users monopoly prices, AT&T was able to subsidize cheap local service. Hence, state politicians and the public utility commissioners they appointed generally supported the status quo, as it benefited the local constituency.

The FCC also had been a friend to AT&T: The agency barred competitors from the telephone equipment and long distance services markets in order to protect the quality and efficiency of the phone system. However, in 1968, with some prodding from the courts, the FCC's view began to change.

The pivotal event was the invention by entrepreneur Thomas

Carter of a device to link phones and radio-dispatched vehicles: AT&T reacted against this new "CarterFone," threatening to shut off service to users of the device. Carter took his complaint to court and eventually the FCC sided with him.

The landmark CarterFone decision forced open the telecommunications equipment market for the first time in decades. AT&T made dire predictions that low-quality phone equipment would trigger widespread glitches in the phone system and therefore forced competitors to connect their equipment through an AT&T-manufactured interface, ostensibly designed to protect the system. Nonetheless, it had once and for all been decided that customers would be allowed to plug equipment manufactured by AT&T's competitors into the AT&T phone system, accelerating the development pace of new technologies, from answering machines to cellular phones. More importantly, the advent of competition set off the chain of events which ultimately led to the breakup of AT&T.

Competitors who wished to provide an alternative to AT&T long distance service also complained that Ma Bell made it unnecessarily difficult for them to obtain the connections necessary to attach customers. Under the so-called essential facilities antitrust doctrine, a company that owned unique facilities was required to allow other companies access to those facilities if the facilities would be essential to the other companies' competitive livelihoods. Relying on this doctrine, the scrappy Microwave Communications Incorporated (MCI), headed by William McGowan, filed a private suit against AT&T in 1973 seeking to force the company to provide MCI and other common carriers with the same service given to Bell System companies.

MCI began its corporate existence by agitating to build a new phone link between Chicago and St. Louis. The plan, developed by entrepreneur John Goeken, was brought to fruition in 1968 when William McGowan provided capital for the start-up and became its CEO.

The basic notion behind the early MCI application was both

simple and limited. MCI proposed to set up a system of microwave towers and sell "private line" service that would connect a single business customer's branch offices in Chicago and St. Louis. MCI proposed only to provide the "long distance" element of the connection: A call placed by an MCI customer would still travel locally over AT&T wires, and through AT&T switching stations. Once the call reached a central AT&T switching station, it would be transmitted to MCI's system, which could connect the call from St. Louis to Chicago, or vice versa, where it would be returned to the AT&T local network. MCI would pay AT&T a fee for these interconnection services.

In granting the MCI application, the FCC made clear its intention to limit MCI's scope of services to the private line variety, agreeing with AT&T that full-scale competition would harm the nation's phone system. MCI therefore would not be allowed to enter the basic consumer long distance market. However, this position ignored an inevitable reality: Once the long distance market was partially opened, competitors like MCI and others would do all they could to expand the boundaries of their operations. An almost inevitable progression of piecemeal deregulation ensued.

By 1973, MCI, having successfully used its original license as a wedge to gain approval for a broader service, had a plan in place to build a nationwide system of microwave towers. Under a new ruling, gained only after contentious fights with AT&T, the company was allowed to offer connections between a single office and any caller from a specific city. So, for example, a company might establish a "local" customer service line in Los Angeles, which customers could dial to be connected to a call center in Utah or Illinois.

Other competitors to AT&T also entered the market in the 1970s. The Southern Pacific Company, which operated the Southern Pacific Railroad, followed MCI's lead in establishing its own Sprint operation, which would become the number three long distance company. In addition, dozens of other entrepreneurs set up operations, hoping to profit from the newly relaxed regulatory barriers.

Despite these moves to weaken AT&T's power, competitors still complained bitterly about AT&T's monopoly position, citing antitrust violations. In December 1973, the Justice Department responded by subpoenaing volumes of records from Ma Bell. This investigation marked the beginning of the end for the AT&T monopoly.

Almost a year later, in November 1974, the Justice Department filed an antitrust suit against AT&T charging that the phone company had monopolized the market for telecommunications services and related equipment. While the alleged antitrust violation was one factor that motivated the suit, another equally important factor was the Justice Department's desire to refurbish its reputation for independence, which had been recently tarnished by the resignation of top Justice Department officials over Watergate. Following President Ford's promise that his administration would "zero in on more effective enforcement" of the antitrust laws, the suit sought to force AT&T to divest itself of Western Electric and to require the company either to retire from the long distance telephone business or instead spin off some or all of its twenty-two local telephone companies. By proposing a spin-off of the telcos, as they were called, the department hoped to reduce the likelihood that Ma Bell would use her monopolistic position to gain advantages in competitive markets.

While the suit was a boon for MCI, which continued to press its own antitrust case against the phone company, it was a nightmare for AT&T, for which it sparked seven years of costly court battles. On January 8, 1982, a settlement was reached whereby AT&T agreed to submit to the Justice Department within six months a plan to spin off its twenty-two local operating companies. The benefit for AT&T was that, after the spin, it would be free to enter practically any market it desired, including the computer data processing business, and would be free from regulation by the public utility commissions.

Like the oil trust, the telephone trust was busted.

The New AT&T Post-Deregulation

As AT&T had predicted, the piecemeal deregulation of the telecommunications market put a great deal of pressure on the existing structure of the phone system. The flight of long distance customers to competitors forced AT&T to reduce its rates. However, as long distance rates were lowered, the local Bell operating companies no longer had a source of subsidies for local service; therefore, local rates needed to rise. State regulators had no choice but to allow this to happen.

The AT&T breakup invigorated MCI, Sprint, and various other relative newcomers, who over the previous decade had developed both the technical ability and the marketing skill necessary to win over former AT&T customers. Specifically, in the business market, MCI and Sprint offered cost savings as well as improved products and services. In a race to sign up individual consumers, the two companies launched telemarketing and media campaigns, lobbying customers to switch long distance providers. AT&T began to see its core business eroding.

While AT&T suffered in this new competitive environment, its competition had a hard time of it as well. Deregulation had dramatically changed the cost structure of AT&T's competitors. Previously, MCI, Sprint, and other independents received substantial discounts on access charges to the AT&T system because their customers were forced to dial as many as twelve digits before a phone number to gain access. With the divestiture, however, the RBOCs would be forced to provide equal "dial 1" access to all phone companies as part of a plan to provide "equal access." The discounts were also phased out, however, creating a similar cost structure for MCI and Sprint to that of AT&T.

The Beginning of Telco M&A

This new economic reality imposed by deregulation led to a shakeout of competitors and the beginnings of telco M&A. Around the time of the breakup, more than 100 companies had entered the long distance market, including major companies like IBM, ITT, and others. However, with new higher access charges, only those with a large enough customer base to sustain continued investment and guarantee sufficient return had the strength to survive. AT&T left a power vacuum that only a sizable competitor could fill. Shaky operators began to look around for partners and industry consolidation occurred. At the end, two strong long distance competitors to AT&T emerged: MCI and Sprint.

On the way to becoming profitable, Sprint cycled through a number of corporate owners. In 1983, Southern Pacific sold Sprint to the GTE Corporation for $750 million in cash. GTE proceeded to pump $1 billion into Sprint during 1984, only to see its market share remain at a relatively paltry 4 percent. Another $1 billion investment was planned for 1985 in an effort to build an independent fiber-optic network.

But the tremendous capital drain related to Sprint eventually proved too much for GTE to bear on its own. In early 1986, GTE took a $1.3 billion after-tax write-off on its Sprint investment and agreed to merge Sprint with the long distance operations of United Telecommunications, which, at the time, was number four to Sprint's number three. United Telecommunications paid GTE $230 million, and the new company, renamed U.S. Sprint, was jointly owned by the two parent companies. Sprint now had the bulk and capital to be a viable competitor.

While U.S. Sprint enjoyed rapid growth in its first several years— its customer base ballooned from 2.7 million to 6 million—problems also plagued the unit. Customer service snafus and a continuing need for capital left Sprint with significant losses.

Finally, in 1988, GTE tired of the drag on its performance and put its Sprint interest on the block. United Telecommunications exercised its right of first refusal, buying 30.1 percent of GTE's interest and an option on the remainder. To raise cash for the purchase, United Telecommunications sold off its cellular subsidiary for $772 million.

Two years later, the decision to stick with Sprint looked shrewd. The operation had begun to generate strong cash flow and was solidly profitable in 1989. United Telecommunications therefore paid GTE roughly $500 million to exercise its option on the remaining 19.9 percent of Sprint owned by GTE and changed its name to Sprint Corp.

Like Sprint, MCI had its share of problems adjusting to the post-breakup world. The ramp-up in access charges—which accounted for as much as 50 percent of the company's operating cost—dragged MCI's operating profit margin down from above 30 percent in 1982 to as little as 5 percent in 1984. Cost cutting and revenue growth brought the margins back up over the next several years, but for a time the company's survival was not a foregone conclusion.

McGowan responded to his company's troubles by looking for a strategic partner to provide stability and a capital infusion. He put a call in to Paul Rizzo, IBM's vice chairman. Would IBM be interested in merging its budding telecommunications business with MCI? Initially, Rizzo was unreceptive. However, six months later, by June 1985, the two parties had agreed to a complex transaction. The deal gave MCI all the assets of IBM's phone subsidiary in exchange for roughly $420 million in MCI stock plus warrants to buy more stock for $15 a share. In addition, IBM agreed to invest up to $400 million over three years in exchange for further equity.

With IBM's backing and McGowan's strong leadership, MCI bounced back. Three years later, the company reported a strong profit and operating cash flow. The pace of capital investment briefly slowed to the point where MCI could afford to buy back IBM's stake in the company.

MCI's strong profitability also gave McGowan further room to expand. In 1987, MCI purchased RCA Global Communications, a telex company, from GE for $160 million; and in 1990, it bought Advanced Transmission Systems from Western Union, acquiring 700 miles of installed fiber-optic cable.

Continuing to believe that critical mass was necessary to compete against AT&T and Sprint, in 1990, McGowan then launched a signature deal in his consolidation and growth strategy, agreeing to purchase number four player Telecom USA for $1.25 billion. The deal brought MCI about 1.5 percent of additional share in the $60 billion telecommunications market and 3,000 additional miles of fiber optics. Telecom USA, itself the product of a 1988 merger between SoutherNet and Teleconnect, served roughly 500,000 customers in thirty-one states.

With the positions of MCI and Sprint firmed up, they proved formidable competitors to AT&T. The three majors carried out an unrelenting marketing war, badly bruising the former monopolist. AT&T now fumbled to find a new strategy for the future.

PROFILE

William McGowan

The ebullient William McGowan will always be remembered as the man who broke apart Ma Bell. A chain smoker known for guzzling two dozen cups of coffee a day, McGowan breathed energy and life into his company for over twenty years.

McGowan grew up in the industrial belt of Pennsylvania, the son of a railroad worker and union organizer. After a stint in the Army, he worked his way through college and then attended Harvard Business School. Upon graduation in 1954, he struck out on his own, setting up a New York City consulting business, and later tinkering with a number of somewhat successful start-ups. By

1968, McGowan had the cash and the experience to buy a controlling stake in MCI, which needed the capital to turn founder John Goeken's dream into a much larger reality. The kernels of McGowan's success were a keen understanding of the regulatory and legal process, as well as the ability to finance MCI's ambitious expansion program.

In the early years, McGowan kept MCI going more by force of will than anything else. But to grow into a profitable and viable entity, MCI needed access to a broader market than the private line business envisioned by Goeken. Regulatory issues were the primary barrier. Therefore, with cash from an initial public offering and a bank credit facility, McGowan launched a strategy of confrontation and lobbying. MCI kept a bevy of lawyers busy prosecuting antitrust suits against AT&T and other competitors, as well as lobbying the FCC and Congress. As a result, many came to refer to MCI as "a law firm with an antenna on the roof."

McGowan eventually succeeded in breaking his way into the full telecommunications market. Though he accumulated a pack of enemies at AT&T and was viewed as conniving by some in the FCC and Congress, he was a folk hero to many in the telecommunications industry.

Even so, gaining entrée to the market was just one part of the battle. Putting together the financing to build a major telecommunications network was another major hurdle. McGowan was prepared to make a major bet on the new fiber-optic technology at a time when AT&T remained wedded to copper wire, raising more than $3 billion in junk bonds to finance the revolutionary MCI network. By 1990, MCI was on the road to a 100 percent digital system, as was Sprint. When McGowan died in 1992, at the age of sixty-four, he left the legacy of a strong company and an entirely revolutionized telecommunications market. MCI's 1997 combination with WorldCom further strengthened McGowan's company.

AT&T's Fits and Starts

At first, AT&T's 1984 divestiture of the low-growth, capital-intensive Baby Bells looked like a master stroke. The parent company kept long distance and the communications equipment business, two steady cash generators. But the initial analysis proved incorrect. New competition threatened AT&T's position in its core long distance market, as did continued regulation of long distance. The FCC refused to rescind AT&T's designation as a "dominant" carrier, a designation that required AT&T, under the Communications Act of 1934, to file each proposed service and rate package with the FCC. A proposed initiative could only take effect after a minimum forty-five-day waiting period elapsed, allowing competitors a chance to challenge the proposal, and severely hampering AT&T's ability to respond to competitors' marketing initiatives.

In the face of difficulties in its core markets, AT&T targeted growth in the computer sector, both organic and through acquisition. With its experience building computerized telephone switches and the technological wizardry of Bell Labs, AT&T was projected to be a major player in the computer field. Furthermore, conventional wisdom at the time held that the computer and communications markets were converging: Clients soon would want single networks linking both computers and telecommunications. AT&T seemed just the company to provide one-stop shopping and viewed the computer sector as its new growth engine.

AT&T jumped into computers in 1984 with a $254 million purchase of a 25 percent stake in Italy's Olivetti. The companies launched a joint venture in which AT&T sold Olivetti computers in the U.S. and Olivetti sold AT&T minicomputers in Europe. The agreement was a flop. Olivetti's systems were a tough sell. Moreover, AT&T's bet on its own UNIX operating system—a software package designed to provide the basic operating architecture for computers—was a failure. The scrappy, competitive Microsoft, with its DOS precursor to Windows, significantly outmarketed AT&T. These problems were exacerbated by the fact that AT&T assigned computer sales to the same people who pushed telecommunications equipment. While this move was in line with its bundling strategy, the sales force favored the easier-to-sell telecommunications equipment.

AT&T's new computer effort racked up large losses, more than $750 million over the first two years after divestiture, and more than $2 billion by the end of 1990. Meanwhile, one reorganization effort followed another, many with major accounting charges. The company wrote off $6 billion in assets at divestiture, $3.2 billion in a 1986 reorganization, and $6.7 billion related to the switch to new digital technology in 1988.

After taking its lumps for five and a half years, AT&T finally ended the Olivetti partnership in the summer of 1989 but nonetheless stuck to its bundled "computers and communication" strategy. The company initially looked for new partners, taking a 19.1 percent stake in Sun Microsystems over a period of months, which it later sold. In June 1989, AT&T bought into another sector of the computer market with its $250 million purchase of Paradyne, a modem maker.

In late 1990, AT&T made another bet on the computer sector—its largest yet—when it announced an unsolicited $6 billion hostile bid for NCR Corp. AT&T Chairman Robert Allen—who had suddenly been elevated to the top job after the unexpected death of former CEO James Olson in 1988—still believed computers to be critical to the company's future. AT&T's own effort was in a shambles and Allen hoped to buy a fresh start.

From the beginning of the AT&T-NCR relationship, success proved elusive. Allen approached NCR's chairman Charles Exley in November 1990, but after two weeks of harried negotiations, NCR's board rejected an $85 a share bid from AT&T. Instead, Allen opted for a hostile bear hug: In a publicly released letter, AT&T stated its willingness to buy NCR for $90 a share, all in cash. The offer would only remain open for a few days.

Allen's approach was groundbreaking. Here was a staid member of the corporate establishment making use of the hostile takeover techniques so often decried by the Business Roundtable in the 1980s.

Exley was not happy with Allen's bareknuckle approach, and in a reply letter slammed Allen's plan to put AT&T's flagging computer operations under NCR's control. Effectively, Exley wrote, AT&T was looking for someone to clean up its mess. Not surprisingly, the NCR board rejected the AT&T offer. Exley stated his company wouldn't go for less than $125 a share.

Within days, AT&T demanded a special meeting of shareholders to vote on removing the NCR board. The white gloves of corporate civility had come off.

In the months before the March 28, 1991, shareholder meeting, the two sides attempted to weaken each other's position. But NCR had fairly strong defenses. Under Maryland law, where NCR was incorporated, AT&T only needed the backing of 20 percent of NCR's shareholders to call a special meeting but needed an 80 percent vote at the meeting to oust the full NCR board immediately. Without that margin of support, AT&T could only elect one third of the NCR board each year and therefore would need two years to gain a majority. In an effort to ensure that AT&T would not get an 80 percent vote, the NCR board put a block of shares into the hands of an employee retirement trust.

With the battle lines drawn, each side lobbied shareholders for support. Exley talked up NCR's growth prospects and continued to demand a minimum of $125 a share. He insisted NCR could live with a divided board for a year while the company continued to execute its strategic plan. In response, AT&T pressed the point that its offer was almost a 90 percent premium to NCR's previous trading value.

The tactical background for the proxy fight shifted in March 1991 when AT&T successfully sued to have the NCR employee trust overturned. It then became clear that AT&T would win at least four seats on the twelve-member NCR board; Exley softened his stance. Facing the realities of the situation, the NCR board authorized Exley to discuss a merger at above $100 a share.

Finally, an agreement was reached. AT&T switched its offer from cash to stock and raised its bid. Each NCR share would be exchanged for AT&T stock worth $110 at the time of the agreement, or $7.5 billion.

But almost immediately, the NCR purchase proved disastrous for AT&T. NCR failed to hit the numbers predicted by Exley and, over the next five years, NCR would lose $4 billion. Trying to salvage its purchase, AT&T poured another $2.8 billion into the business. But the mainframe computer, a mainstay for NCR, was in the process of becoming a technological dinosaur.

Part of the NCR problem was also management: The unit went through five top managers in five years. While originally AT&T had promised to let NCR management run the unit with no intervention, after two years Allen was displeased with NCR's results and instead put AT&T's own people in charge. Yet the rationale for the purchase had been to bring new management to its struggling computer business.

Meanwhile, as it became apparent that computers would not be a growth engine for AT&T, Allen placed less and less emphasis on the notion of bundled computers and communications. Instead, he shifted focus to a different variation of bundling: bundled communications services.

Allen saw that as deregulation progressed further, AT&T and the Baby Bells would be permitted into each other's markets. Bundling local with long distance service—putting the old unified Ma Bell system back together—could be a source of growth. Market participants and observers alike were projecting that customers would sign up in droves for the convenient package. In addition, new communications services like cellular and Internet access could be added, making the promise of "anytime, anywhere" communications a reality.

In essence, Allen was proposing that AT&T position itself to compete against the Baby Bells that had formerly been part of AT&T.

The Story of AT&T's Children

The January 1, 1984, breakup of AT&T left the twenty-two local operating companies largely intact and with their individual names, but reorganized them into seven regional holding companies, each of which was endowed with approximately $17 billion in assets. Specifically, the seven RBOCs were NYNEX, Bell Atlantic, BellSouth, U S West, Ameritech, Pacific Telesis, and Southwestern Bell. Each was given an exclusive territory ranging from two to fourteen states and was expected to provide local phone service but was forbidden to manufacture equipment.

According to the settlement, the regional companies received all the assets and liabilities related to local telephone service and long distance service within certain zones. AT&T was left with all of the remaining assets and liabilities related to the development, manufacture, sale, and leasing of telecommunications equipment, and to the provision of long distance service in zones not assigned to the regionals.

In an effort to breed healthy competition in the new communications market, Judge Harold Greene, the federal judge overseeing the AT&T breakup, also granted the regionals the right to sell (but not manufacture) telephone equipment to homes and businesses, and give them the right to publish and sell advertising for the Yellow Pages.

Even though the Baby Bells were well endowed with assets, the consensus at the time of the divestiture was that they got short shrift. AT&T kept the long distance and computers businesses, which were projected to be the high-growth enterprises. The Baby Bells, on the other hand, were left primarily with POTS, or plain old telephone service, and were expected to be sleepy utilities in the business of selling dial tones.

Unexpectedly, the Baby Bells quickly became extremely profitable and successful—in stark contrast to AT&T. The companies together earned $8.4 billion on revenues of $69.8 billion in 1987, and earned $8.9 billion in 1988. They also threw off a prodigious free cash flow. Meanwhile, AT&T managed to earn a relatively paltry $2 billion on $35.6 billion in revenue.

The Baby Bells' success did not come without criticism, however. Many alleged the growth was due in large part to substantial rate increases allowed by nearly all states. As AT&T had predicted when trying to defend its earlier monopoly status, without the cross-subsidy from the long distance business, local phone users were forced to carry the full burden of maintaining the local phone networks. Consumer advocates decried the effect on phone customers.

However, rising rates only explained part of the revenue growth experienced by the Baby Bells. The emergence of the digital economy also spawned a burst in telephone usage: fax machines, online services, discount long distance, paging, and cellular all contributed to a phenomenal growth spurt. By the late 1980s, total phone usage was increasing nearly three times as fast as the population.

The early successes of the RBOCs increased the pressure on their new managers. At the stronger companies, the question was how to continue the growth. At the weaker companies, management struggled to develop a new identity and shape a workable strategic and operational model for the future. In either case, managers who previously had been buried in the middle of the massive AT&T hierarchy found themselves suddenly facing all the strategic issues associated with running a large, independent public company. They now had to find their way in the world.

Further diversification into unregulated industries was almost uniformly the answer to this new strategic dilemma. BellSouth, Southwestern Bell, and others made add-on acquisitions in the Yellow Pages business. For instance, U S West alone added some twenty smaller directory publishers to its Landmark Communications publishing division. The company also pushed into real estate investment, expanding from the base of its existing holdings. Bell Atlantic spent $175 million to buy a computer services company and then bought a computer retailer. NYNEX followed suit, spending $275 million for the professional services and software businesses of AGS Computers, as well as buying IBM's struggling computer retailing chain.

These attempts at diversification turned in mixed results. Both NYNEX and Bell Atlantic ultimately shuttered their computer retailing operations. Similar operations at the other Bell operating companies also were curtailed. On the other hand, the Yellow Pages continued to be profitable for most of the seven RBOCs. But the most significant diversification effort undertaken by the Baby Bells—into cellular communications and paging—was a dramatic success.

AT&T lay in wait of an opportunity to reenter the lucrative local service market. But in the meantime, AT&T followed its children's lead, diversifying into another area: mobile communications.

Strangely, the company that invented cellular technology had, despite its initial interest, passed up the opportunity to take part in the rollout of the cellular systems after the breakup and instead concentrated on selling the equipment needed to build systems. Therefore, the early development of wireless passed AT&T by. But by 1990, Allen realized that cellular could provide the growth AT&T so desperately needed.

Early Cellular

By 1980, the technology for cellular telephony had been around for over a decade. Developed by the Bell Laboratories in the 1960s, the key to cellular technology was the application of computer technology to radiophones, which had been in use since the 1940s. The first-generation radiophones required a powerful, centrally located transmitter, and only a handful of frequencies were available for radiophone use in each locale. Because only one conversation could be carried on a given frequency, only a small number of people could use the system. For example, in New York City, no more than twenty-four conversations could take place at any one time.

The new cellular technology, which uses more frequencies and, more importantly, reuses each frequency several times in a given area, expanded the number of potential users to several hundred thousand in a city like New York. To accommodate this sharing, cellular replaces the old, single high-power transmitter with dozens of low-power transmission stations. The frequencies involved don't carry far, so that a single station covers an area—or "cell"—two to ten miles wide.

A call is picked up by the nearest transmitter and relayed to a switching station, which then ties the caller into the local landline network. When the caller moves from one cell to another, a central computer recognizes that the connection to the original transmitter has weakened and, in a fraction of a second, switches the call to a new transmitter. By hopscotching a call from transmitter to transmitter, a single frequency becomes available for multiple use, once in each cell.

Seeking to guarantee itself a cellular license in the markets it served, AT&T filed an application with the FCC in the late 1960s. The phone giant justified its right to the licenses based on its role in developing the technology and to prevent its competitors from using cellular technology as an end run around the existing local phone networks: If AT&T were excluded from this new market, competitors would be able to siphon revenues away from its local operating companies, further reducing the base of customers available to fund the local phone network.

Of course, AT&T's arguments carried little weight with McGowan's MCI and other potential competitors. The long distance companies, as well as existing radiophone and radio paging companies, recognized the revolutionary nature of cellular technology and wanted access to the new market. Here was the Dick Tracy fantasy of a phone in a briefcase becoming reality.

The generally contentious environment surrounding AT&T spilled over into the cellular area. For years, the FCC sat on the phone company's application, uncertain how to distribute licenses to the new technology. Finally, just months before the AT&T antitrust settlement was announced, the FCC settled on a compromise. Two licenses would be granted in each cellular market: One would go to a local wireline company, with AT&T presumably getting the majority of these licenses; the other license would be granted to a non-wireline competitor.

Many of the potential bidders for the second category of licenses were incensed by the decision. By guaranteeing the wireline companies access to the market, the FCC had granted them a precious head start in setting up systems. AT&T and GTE soon announced an alliance whereby they divvied up the licenses to the top thirty urban markets, with AT&T to receive twenty-three licenses and GTE seven. Given the powerful advantage presumed to go to the first mover in any market, it was not surprising that a host of players challenged the FCC ruling. However, about a month prior to the antitrust settlement, the FCC confirmed its decision. Any first-mover advantage, argued the commission, would be mitigated by a fast review process in granting the second licenses in the top thirty markets. AT&T's competitors would have a fair shot at being a close second in the twenty-three markets it would compete in, if not first.

Therefore, from the beginnings of cellular, each of the Bells—as successors to the AT&T empire—was granted a license covering its own geographic market. Soon after the breakup, however, the RBOCs raced to buy up even more licenses outside their own markets. Pacific Telesis got things started in 1985 with the announcement of its $431 million purchase of Communications Industries.

While the purchase was challenged in front of Judge Greene, the courts ultimately ruled that the Baby Bells could purchase unregulated businesses outside their markets without judicial approval.

Once the legal issue was resolved, Bell Atlantic followed with its purchase of A Beeper Corp., at the time the third-largest nationwide cellular and paging company. BellSouth spent another $710 million to acquire Mobile Communications, a cellular operator with licenses in Houston and Los Angeles. The other Baby Bells also were active. As a result of this string of deals, the Baby Bells soon were competing against each other in the relatively unregulated cellular business.

As it turned out, though, the process of distributing the second licenses in cellular markets proved to be time consuming and contentious. But despite the long process faced by competitors, the Baby Bells did not get much of a head start with their first licenses, which were tied up in red tape associated with state regulatory approval as well as administrative difficulties surrounding the breakup.

The winner of each second license in the top thirty markets was decided by a lengthy FCC review. Applicants filed detailed, comprehensive plans for service, and competitors had a chance to respond with counterfilings. Then, after hearings, the commission made its decisions and the winner was given its license free of charge.

Many parties saw the great potential of cellular. The existing radio common carriers—paging and radiophone companies—had a head start in understanding the business; but they were predominantly small organizations and lacked the capital needed to build out cellular systems. Other entrepreneurs set up entirely new companies to bid on licenses. And as word of the new opportunity became more widely known, even the financial players became involved. The result was a race to assemble the cartons of documents—feasibility studies, financial and operational plans—necessary for an application.

The regulatory game of musical chairs induced by the application process also spawned a minor acquisition wave. Existing undercapitalized radio companies got together to pool resources, and financiers and large companies bought into other radio companies as a way to bet on cellular.

The most active acquirer was John Kluge of Metromedia Inc., a company that owned radio and television stations. In April 1982, after a friend told Kluge the cellular story, Kluge investigated and decided Metromedia had to get involved. Yet with the application deadline just two months away, there was little time to start pulling together documents. Kluge instead opted to buy into companies already well along in the process.

Over a short period, Metromedia spent $112 million buying three paging companies in Boston, Chicago, and New York. The next year, Kluge added seven more companies for $169 million to gain a strong position in Dallas, Philadelphia, Washington, and Los Angeles.

By February 1984, the FCC had granted second licenses in ten cities; systems were hooked up in most of the top thirty markets by the end of the year. In the beginning, though, service was expensive and handsets cost approximately $3,000. The investment necessary to build out systems gobbled up revenues and required further capital infusions. As with fiber optics, the ability to finance the new technology was a crucial element of success.

Yet entrepreneurs continued to believe in the great promise of cellular. In fact, the FCC received so many applications for the second round of licensing—related to smaller markets—that it was forced to abandon the full-blown review process. The agency instead planned to screen out applicants unqualified to hold a license, then hold an auction among the remaining applicants. However, before this could happen, many of the applicants teamed up and split interests in most of the markets, leaving a fragmented cellular industry with many licenses jointly owned by several parties.

As had happened in countless new industries over time, a consolidation wave followed. The Baby Bells played a major role, buying up licenses in markets they did not already own. Yet the early action was dominated by individual players. Kluge of Metromedia and Craig McCaw of McCaw Cellular were the new Vanderbilt and Rockefeller, foreseeing a nationwide cellular network pieced together through acquisitions and coordinated marketing.

John Kluge's ability to spot a new technology parallels Cornelius Vanderbilt's nineteenth-century move from steamboats to railroads. Like Vanderbilt, Kluge was in his late sixties when he made the transition, in his case from television and radio to cellular. By 1985, Metromedia owned large interests in key markets: 100 percent of a Chicago license, 52 percent in Washington-Baltimore, 45 percent in New York. These and other interests positioned Metromedia as the leading provider in the country's ten largest markets.

In 1986, Kluge's consolidation strategy was dramatically vindicated. Like its fellow Baby Bells, Southwestern Bell keenly wanted to build a cellular network outside its region. Metromedia's cellular and paging interests proved an irresistible target. Southwestern Bell agreed to pay Metromedia $1.7 billion for the properties, roughly $50 per potential customer, or "per pop" as industry insiders would say— roughly double the going rate of six months earlier.

PROFILE

John Kluge

John Kluge's 1982 jump into the cellular business was the latest in a long line of entrepreneurial successes. At a time in his life when most contemporaries had retired, Kluge, age sixty-seven, made yet another major gamble on a business he viewed as a cheap investment.

Born in 1914, the son of a poor German immigrant, Kluge grew up in Detroit. By the time he was thirty-two, Kluge bought into the media business. However, rather than invest in the sexy new television medium, Kluge chose the relatively disfavored radio sector, thought by many investors to be a dinosaur that would be slayed by television. But Kluge prized the cash flow afforded by radio. Soon Kluge had a string of radio stations to fund further ventures and used the cash to purchase an undervalued billboard company on the cheap.

Finally, in 1959, Kluge acquired a television business—Metropolitan Broadcasting—and soon added seven major-market independent stations. Again, Kluge selected his investment based on his view of relative value. Many thought the independents would be driven out of business by the booming networks. But his experience in radio caused Kluge to disagree. By 1980, Metromedia was the largest independent radio and television broadcaster in the United States.

In 1982, Kluge bought his way into the cellular market by snapping up paging companies with pending cellular applications and, within a few years, was able to sell for $750 million the companies he had acquired for $300 million—while keeping the cellular licenses. Through this gambit, he effectively got the cellular licenses for free.

Around the same time, Kluge spotted another major value— Metromedia's own stock. Kluge already owned roughly 25 percent of the company, but when a series of major television flops caused Metromedia's stock to fall from the mid-50s to the low 20s in late 1983, Kluge decided to buy the remainder with his management team in a $1 billion transaction.

At the time, the highly leveraged transaction looked like a shaky gamble. Yet, very shortly, the move paid off. Kluge sold Metromedia's television stations to Rupert Murdoch's new Fox Network for $2 billion, enabling Kluge to pay off most of Metromedia's debt and still have several hundred million dollars to invest in his fledgling cellular operation. A few years later, Kluge sold the cellular business to Southwestern Bell for $1.7 billion. The remaining Metromedia businesses were then liquidated for a

> substantial profit, leaving Kluge with a net worth measured in bil-
> lions of dollars.
>
> Kluge, now in his eighties, vowed there would be no "deck
> chair" for him at the time of the cellular sale and launched a new
> venture, Metromedia International, to hold an amalgam of East-
> ern European and Asian cellular licenses.
>
> More recently, Metromedia has been building a fiber-optic net-
> work that it leases to other operators without any of the electron-
> ics needed for transmission (what is known as a "dark fiber"
> network). This medium could provide competition to incumbents'
> local networks, allowing new entrants to bypass the RBOCs' local
> loops.

In the aftermath of the Metromedia cellular deal, market watchers criticized Southwestern Bell as overexuberant and lauded Kluge
for driving a hard bargain. Soon, though, Southwestern looked to
have gotten the better deal. As the number of attractive properties
on the market declined, prices continued to be bid higher, from the
$80 per pop McCaw Cellular paid for the Washington Post Com-
pany's Florida cellular licenses to the $135 per pop Philadelphia's
Comcast Corp. paid for American Cellular Network, both in early
1988. Indeed, Kluge had not been the only buyer to identify consolidation as an appropriate strategy. At these new prices, Kluge arguably sold out early.

One of the most important and active participants in the early
cellular wars was Craig McCaw, the entrepreneur who built the first
nationwide cellular network. McCaw entered the cellular race in
1982, taking part in the FCC licensing process. At the time head of
a growing cable television company that he and his brothers inherited from their father, McCaw initially saw cellular as a logical add-
on to the company's small paging business. However, after
conducting market research, McCaw understood the huge potential

of the new technology and set out to build a nationwide network. It was this network that AT&T would later target.

McCaw began by buying interests in individual cellular licenses; however, as the consolidation wave hit, McCaw began snapping up entire competitors. In 1986, McCaw nabbed a rough-hewn gem— the cellular operations of a cash-starved MCI—for a rock-bottom $122 million. McCaw sold the attached paging business for $74 million and in the process gained 7 million pops for a little over $6 each. Like Kluge, McCaw then sold off other operations, like its cable business for $755 million, to concentrate on the campaign.

McCaw followed with a series of blockbuster moves in 1989. Toward the end of 1988, the company accumulated 9 percent of LIN Broadcasting, which controlled licenses in New York, Dallas, Houston, and Philadelphia, to "test its resolve," according to McCaw insiders. But hungry for additional capital to fund a run at LIN, McCaw next sold a 22 percent stake to British Telecommunications for $1.5 billion, or a record-breaking $140 per pop.

Five months later, on June 6, 1989, McCaw launched a hostile tender offer for LIN. McCaw attempted a preemptive bid, designed to keep the Baby Bells from bidding, of $5.9 billion, or $275 to $300 per pop. While the high price could in part be justified by LIN's presence in premium markets like Los Angeles and New York, in one fell swoop, Craig McCaw had doubled the market price for cellular properties in general.

LIN's board of directors brought us in to examine the takeover offer. The situation was particularly delicate since LIN's chief executive, Don Pels, felt strongly about his responsibility to seek shareholder value. As a major shareholder, the genial Pels was thrilled by the level of McCaw's starting bid but, after studying the terms of McCaw's offer, was freed to, along with the board, reject the offer as inadequate: LIN felt it could do better. Therefore, the company announced it would spin off its seven television stations, as previously planned, and would explore other options.

A Closer Look

Valuing high-growth businesses like cellular companies is necessarily an imprecise, subjective process. Early cellular companies
almost uniformly carried large debt burdens to finance the building of systems and the purchase of competitors, and as a consequence, few earned a positive net income. Still, both in the stock
market and in private acquisitions, these companies were highly
valued.

McCaw Cellular provides a good example. Even before the LIN
transaction, McCaw carried $1.8 billion of debt on its books; and
in 1988, the company lost $297 million on revenue of $311 million. Yet the stock market placed a value of $3.5 billion on the
company, and equity analysts estimated its breakup value at
around $4.5 billion. Even setting aside the cost of debt, McCaw
had negative operating cash flow of $7 million. So clearly, the
$3.5 billion market capitalization of its equity was not based on
its current cash flows; rather, investors were betting on future
cash flows that might be generated as McCaw increased its market penetration.

The practice of valuing cellular companies in terms of pops, or
potential customers in a company's market, was an attempt to
capture a picture of this future value. The number of pops is calculated by multiplying the population covered by the licenses involved times the percent of the licenses owned by the company.
The company's market capitalization then can be expressed in
terms of dollars per pop.

Of course, using such a rough yardstick of value poses potential problems. For example, valuing different companies based on
pops assumes that customers in New York or Los Angeles will
generate as much future cash flow as customers in St. Louis or

Minneapolis. In fact, capital costs, market penetration, rate flexibility, customer usage, and future growth have varied dramatically from market to market, thus requiring a more sophisticated
model for a nuanced analysis.

When the LIN board rejected the McCaw offer, McCaw responded by hinting it might raise its bid if a friendly merger agreement could be negotiated. Talks began but soon fell apart. LIN then
raised the stakes. Management announced the company would
agree to be acquired if McCaw came up with a firm offer to buy the
company for $6.1 billion, but McCaw couldn't support a bid at that
level, so backed off. BellSouth then entered the picture with a complicated recapitalization and merger plan. After a series of back-and-
forth bids by McCaw and BellSouth, McCaw emerged victorious.
But McCaw, strapped for cash, couldn't come up with a workable
$6.1 billion bid, and therefore allowed the LIN deadline to expire on
July 31 without a new offer.

At this point, BellSouth once again entered the picture. The Baby
Bell was extremely reluctant to do a cash deal because it would require the use of the so-called purchase accounting rules, under
which "goodwill," a metaphysical accounting asset, would have to
be amortized over a number of years. BellSouth's earnings would be
reduced each year, relative to what they would be under so-called
pooling-of-interests accounting, by the amortization charge.

To avoid the dilution problem, LIN and BellSouth developed a
complicated recapitalization and merger plan in which LIN would
pay a $20 a share dividend and then merge with BellSouth's cellular
operations. The combination would create a nationwide network
with only slightly fewer pops than McCaw's. Both LIN and Bell-
South shareholders would own 50 percent of the combined entity.
The Bell could then consolidate part of LIN's earnings on its balance
sheet without consolidating its large debt burden.

Over the next month, McCaw made a strong countermove with an agreement to buy Metromedia's share of the second New York license for $1.9 billion (the first being held by the local RBOC NYNEX). LIN, which owned the remainder of the license, had a right of first refusal to buy it from Metromedia; but to do so would dilute BellSouth's earnings.

McCaw then announced a new LIN offer—a scale-back of his earlier offer—in which McCaw agreed to purchase just enough stock to give it a controlling majority, rather than 100 percent ownership. The new offer also bumped the offer price to $125 a share, effectively valuing the total company at $6.4 billion. McCaw also proposed that an auction take place in 1994 so that it would be able to buy the remainder of LIN's stock at that time at a price per share roughly equal to what a third party would pay in an acquisition of the entire company. This innovative approach was designed to conserve McCaw's cash and to allow institutional investors to retain an interest in the cellular business.

In the face of McCaw's new bid, BellSouth swallowed hard and agreed to a sweetened merger plan. The special cash dividend was raised to $42 a share; LIN also would exercise its right to buy the Metromedia share of the New York license. Finally, BellSouth agreed to a provision similar to the McCaw auction procedure.

McCaw shot back another raise, this time to $150 a share. As negotiations progressed with LIN, McCaw finally raised its bid above $154 a share and also agreed to a tax structure favorable to LIN shareholders. The $154 a share deal valued LIN at a stunning $350 per pop, and Don Pels opened the champagne. BellSouth was priced out of the deal, but won a $66.5 million breakup fee.

After the LIN deal, McCaw emerged as the clear dominant force in the cellular market with over 60 million pops. For the next several years, Craig McCaw turned his efforts to capitalizing on the investment. A large part of the process involved reducing McCaw's debt by selling off unattractive licenses. At the time of the BellSouth deal,

McCaw already had agreed to sell 6 million pops to Contel Corp. for $1.3 billion. McCaw also focused on its Cellular One concept, a brand that brought together licenses across the country into a single national network with unified billing and marketing.

McCaw's effective withdrawal from the acquisition market, together with the recession which began in 1990, however, eventually hit the cellular industry hard. McCaw's market value dropped from $6.5 billion to $2 billion at the end of 1990; other independents were similarly hit. In the private market, acquisition prices ranged as low as $165 a pop in Southwestern Bell's purchase of Illinois properties from Crowley Cellular.

However, from an operational standpoint, cellular companies continued to thrive. The national subscriber base grew to 3.5 million in 1989, up 75 percent. And 50 percent more subscribers signed up in 1990. Growth continued at a healthy pace throughout the recession. Though per-customer monthly bills trended down, total revenues grew on the strength of the greater market penetration: By 1993, there were more than 10 million cellular subscribers nationwide. Many cellular companies had turned the corner and begun generating significant positive cash flows and earnings. Cellular looked to be on the way to delivering on its promise.

PROFILE

Craig McCaw

Betting on cellular paid off in a big way for Craig McCaw. By 1994, he would be a billionaire and each of his three brothers a centimillionaire.

The story of the McCaw family fortune begins with John Elroy McCaw, the patriarch of the family. A freewheeling entrepreneur, the elder McCaw started as a partner in the first radio station in the logging town of Centralia, Washington, a base from which he built up a small media empire. He converted New York station WINS into the country's first rock station in the middle 1950s, and within nine years flipped the station for twenty times more than he had paid. At his height, Elroy McCaw owned interests in dozens of radio, television, and cable television companies.

However, the early McCaw empire was flawed. Elroy kept terrible records of the interlocking ownership structures linking all his properties. When he died in 1969, his wife spent the next eight years putting the McCaw house in order. Just about every asset — except a 7,000 subscriber cable system in Centralia — was sold off to pay creditors and the tax man. Fortunately, Craig's father had put that business into a trust for his sons' benefit.

Upon graduation, Craig took over the family business and spent the next ten years building a small cable empire. Craig bought up "junk-pile" systems and refurbished operations. Two of his brothers, John and Keith, joined him in the business.

In the early 1980s, McCaw discovered the potential of cellular. He read a set of AT&T projections that estimated there would be 900,000 cellular customers nationwide by the year 2000. Even at that level, which proved to be remarkably conservative, cellular would be a profitable business. McCaw applied for licenses from the FCC and gained the right to operate in six of the top thirty markets in the U.S.

McCaw's next hurdle was to convince bankers to finance this new technology. The AT&T projections proved invaluable in this regard. Though McCaw didn't profess to know exactly what cellular licenses were worth, the AT&T projections made clear that they were worth far more than the going rate of $4 a pop. As a McCaw Cellular insider would later say, "The AT&T projections made it a no-brainer to go to 80 bucks a pop." The bankers bought the sales pitch and provided early financing.

From the outside, McCaw's fast-paced buying might have looked risky; but Craig McCaw always was thinking a step ahead and had an exit strategy prepared: The private acquisition market remained as a safety net. Whenever McCaw needed to raise cash, he could sell off less desirable licenses or interests in licenses.

The process of purchase and sale also was the central evolutionary mechanism used by McCaw to shape his national network. Economies of scale were crucial to the process: Clustered pops in major markets were more valuable than dispersed pops. McCaw acted on this fact by effectively swapping less desirable properties for properties near his existing major markets. He also moved to fill the major market holes in his network. By 1993, McCaw was the acknowledged master of cellular.

Since selling his McCaw Cellular, McCaw has kept busy. He founded Nextlink Communications, a local service provider that allows business customers to bypass the RBOCs' local loops, in 1994. That company owns 50 percent of Nextband, which won the Chicago rights to wireless service using the new local Multipoint Distribution Service radio spectrum. McCaw is also the biggest investor in Nextel Communications—a wireless operator geared toward business customers. Finally, McCaw is chairman of Teledesic, a satellite phone service that competes with Iridium.

AT&T Leaps into Cellular

With these early developments in cellular as a backup, CEO Allen again decided that AT&T needed to make a quick leap to gain critical mass, and therefore began looking for an attractive acquisition target in wireless. Allen very quickly became interested in a potential alliance with McCaw Cellular. Such a partnership represented the opportunity to become, in a single step, a major national player in mobile communications.

Negotiations between McCaw and AT&T were an on-again, off-again proposition between 1990 and 1992. Finally, in the fall of 1992,

AT&T rocked the telecommunications world by announcing a joint venture with McCaw under which AT&T would gain a 33 percent ownership position in McCaw. For the first time since the breakup, AT&T would be competing against the Baby Bells on their home turf. The Bells offered apocalyptic visions of what might happen. "AT&T is going to roll over everybody on the highway," predicted one of the Bells' Washington lobbyists. Immediately, the RBOCs clamored for the right to get into the long distance business.

However, the tentative AT&T-McCaw deal was far from a certainty. The parties quibbled over how their joint venture would work. Tough issues included how to share revenues on bundled long distance and cellular packages, which businesses would be part of the venture, and which technologies to develop jointly. By June 1993, the AT&T negotiating team had decided that full AT&T control was the only workable alternative. Over the course of trying to negotiate the joint venture, McCaw also had come to believe the potential of an AT&T-McCaw link would only be realized with full cooperation.

On August 16, 1993, AT&T and McCaw again shocked the telecommunications world with the announcement of a more expansive deal. AT&T would buy McCaw Cellular outright for $12.6 billion in stock. AT&T's price represented approximately $280 a pop, less than McCaw had paid for LIN, but still a full valuation. A revolution had occurred in the structure of the communications industry: AT&T was going local.

However, there was little time for celebration at AT&T. The continuing problems at NCR weighed down performance to the tune of $102 million of operating losses in 1994 and another $2.4 billion in 1995. The equipment business also faced increasing difficulties as many customers—the Baby Bells and independent cellular companies—were reluctant to buy sophisticated switching gear from the same company they competed against on a daily basis. AT&T found itself toning down attacks on competitors for fear they might cancel big orders.

Furthermore, though AT&T still controlled roughly 60 percent of the long distance market, tough competition was severely eroding margins. AT&T continued to face a strategic dilemma: Its core product was becoming a commodity, with customers willing to switch regularly for the promise of slight savings.

AT&T Restructures

In this tough environment, Allen decided it was time to jettison completely the bundled communications and computer strategy and to free the equipment business from the competitive stigma associated with the AT&T name. On September 20, 1995, almost exactly one year after the McCaw deal closed, Robert Allen announced a second major AT&T breakup—this time to enhance shareholder value. Of its own accord, the company split into three pieces—communications, computers, and equipment.

The split-up, completed by the end of 1996, represented a dramatic repudiation of much of the strategy AT&T followed in the twelve years since the original divestiture: After years of painful experience, the company had come to the conclusion that only smaller, more focused units could compete in the new competitive marketplace. In the spring of 1996, AT&T launched a $3 billion IPO—then the largest in American history—of 17.6 percent of the stock in its equipment business, renamed Lucent. In June 1996, AT&T agreed to sell its leasing unit to management and a group of investors for $2.2 billion. The remaining Lucent stock and the stock in NCR were then distributed to AT&T shareholders in the fall of 1996.

With the performance of AT&T's communications business now completely transparent, the problems facing the company could not be ignored. But increased focus on telecommunications services turned out to be no simple panacea: Long distance market share again dropped precipitously in 1996 and earnings fell short of expectations in the second half of the year. Observers raised loud questions as to whether AT&T could hold on to its core long distance franchise. A number of key executives, including Allen's assumed successor, jumped ship.

The bad news for AT&T was not just internal. After years of stagnation and bickering, Congress finally appeared close to passing a telecommunications reform bill in the fall of 1995. Revised rules would mean more competition and further commodification of long distance service. Meanwhile, the FCC was in the process of auctioning off new wireless communications licenses that would threaten AT&T-McCaw's competitive position.

The performance of Lucent has been the major bright spot since the spin-off. Even more so than projected, unleashing the equipment business from the services business gave Lucent new flexibility to go after the Baby Bells, other long distance companies, and independent cellular providers for business. Sales to the Baby Bells ramped up 18 percent in the first nine months of 1996 and the rash of new competition in the telecommunications market created new customers—all of whom needed systems, switches, and transmitters. Overall sales are now growing twice as fast as when Lucent was part of AT&T. As a free agent, Lucent profited from the cutthroat competition. Its stock price responded accordingly, increasing from about $8 to over $70 on a split-adjusted basis in little over three years.

Robert Allen

A true "Bell Head," Robert Allen started his working life at AT&T in 1957 right out of college. Over the years, he rose up through the ranks to become CEO.

Allen began his tenure as CEO of AT&T amid crisis, and enjoyed precious little respite until his forced early retirement in 1997. His elevation to the leadership role at the age of fifty-three was not a time of triumph. On the contrary, the circumstances of his promotion were downright grim. Allen's friend and mentor, chairman James Olson, had recently died after a brief fight with cancer. Two weeks earlier, in a call with directors, Olson had identified Allen as his choice to get the top job "should anything happen to me." The board promoted Allen in keeping with Olson's wishes.

From that day, Robert Allen's position was undeniably rocky, despite his lionization in the business press for bold strategic vision. Within a short time after taking the helm, he ended the failed Olivetti computer partnership, launched the assault on NCR, negotiated the purchase of McCaw, and finally, in his final major strategic initiative, split AT&T into three pieces. However, in each case, early enthusiasm waned as the promise of rejuvenation failed to materialize. Inspiration alone was not enough.

The final painful episode came in 1997. After his number two executive Alex Mandl left the prior year to join a wireless start-up, Allen agreed to retire early in order to recruit a viable successor. He then hired John Walter, a former printing company CEO, to fill the role—a choice that was panned by the market and proved a disaster for everyone involved.

A consummate salesman, Walter threw himself into the business of rebuilding AT&T. However, in 1997, rumors of a possible merger between AT&T and SBC—the parent company for the then recently combined operations of RBOCs Southwestern Bell and Pacific Telesis—hit the papers. Subsequent stories that Walter was being shut out of the talks badly eroded his position.

SBC eventually called off the merger talks when Allen initiated a public defense of the deal that wasn't. After the negotiations collapsed, the board pushed Walter out, claiming he lacked the "intellectual leadership" to take over for Allen.

The fallout from the turmoil further bruised both Allen's and AT&T's image in the market. Things went from bad to worse when it came to light that Allen had kept the candidacy of Hughes CEO

C. Michael Armstrong—considered by many to be a stronger candidate to run a technology company than Walter—from the AT&T board in the original search.

As the severity of AT&T's problems increased, pressure intensified for the board to bring in a strong outsider. However, Armstrong and other candidates demanded immediate control of AT&T, not the one-year transition favored by Allen, who had planned to retire in 1998. Ultimately the board forced Allen to resign almost immediately and gave the top job to Armstrong. Wall Street reacted with relief, bidding AT&T stock up more than 5 percent.

The Digital Age Hits Telco

As quickly as AT&T was acting, the world was changing, largely as a result of new technical innovation, regulatory forces, and globalization.

Technological Change: PCS

In 1993, as AT&T was spending $12.6 billion to buy McCaw Cellular, the world of wireless communications was changing dramatically. A new wireless technology, "personal communications services" or PCS, was on the brink of commercial application. Though PCS transmits on a higher frequency than conventional cellular and uses more closely spaced radio towers, the service capabilities differ little from conventional digital cellular.

The advent of PCS represented a revolution in the wireless market. By the fall of 1993, the FCC was preparing to auction up to five new PCS licenses for each market. Where the cellular companies—including McCaw Cellular, now AT&T Wireless—had previously operated in easygoing duopolies, they would now face the prospect of cutthroat competition. Perhaps AT&T's McCaw purchase would not prove such a blockbuster after all.

These developments had a profound effect. Investors became less willing to endorse the gravity-defying valuations placed on cellular properties. Meanwhile, the cellular companies raced to bulk up for the new competitive era: The development of a national network became the new Shangri-la. Financial capacity was one critical piece to the puzzle as companies prepared to bid in the PCS auctions, which offered an easy way to fill out holes in existing networks.

Though bulk was the general goal after the advent of AT&T-McCaw, regulators required some companies to employ unique business tactics. For example, rules promulgated by the FCC restricted the ability of a company with a cellular license to own a PCS license in the same market. Therefore, Pacific Telesis decided to split its cellular business away from its local phone companies so as to free its unregulated cellular operations from the constraints of regulation and to allow Pacific Telesis to bid for PCS licenses in markets already served by its cellular subsidiary AirTouch.

Like Pacific Telesis, Sprint butted up against this restriction as it developed its own PCS strategy. The Sprint PCS alliance—which included three cable companies, TCI, Comcast, and Cox—intended to build a national communications network that would provide local, long distance, and wireless service. To comply with the FCC's regulatory mandate, the company spun off its cellular business—with licenses mostly in a smaller cities—under the name 360° Communications. The company was later purchased by Alltel for approximately $4 billion.

MCI—another major player in the telecommunications war—had been content to remain on the wireless sidelines after it sold its original cellular business to McCaw. However, the AT&T-McCaw deal put MCI under increasing pressure to find an effective response. For a time, it pursued a PCS bidding alliance; but then, in February 1994, it settled on a $1.4 billion investment in a company called Nextel, in which Craig McCaw now holds a controlling stake. Nextel had pieced together a national patchwork of radio-dispatch systems which it hoped to convert into a wireless network. However, after MCI tested the technology and saw glitches, it got cold feet and attempted to lower the price on the investment. The deal collapsed. But today, it looks like MCI made the wrong decision. Despite initial missteps, Nextel now dominates the market for wireless business communications and is a desirable takeover target.

Other partnerships, however, proved more successful. In the summer of 1994, two major cellular alliances were formed within the space of a single month. Bell Atlantic and NYNEX were the first to get together, merging their cellular operations into a single, jointly held company with roughly 1.8 million subscribers. The new company—ranked as one of the top three U.S. cellular companies—planned to bid for PCS licenses.

Three weeks later, AirTouch—the spun-off cellular business of Pacific Telesis—and U S West announced a similar deal in which the two companies agreed to operate their cellular properties and any potential PCS systems jointly. AirTouch would acquire the U S West properties in three stages over a period of years.

The whirl of activity surrounding the PCS auctions continued as the process unfolded. Soon, the Bell Atlantic–NYNEX combination teamed up with the AirTouch–U S West combination to bid jointly under the name PCS Primeco. And Sprint found its cable partners. MCI, on the other hand, grew cautious after the Nextel fiasco and ended up sitting out the auction, betting it would be able to buy excess PCS capacity at wholesale from other providers.

When the dust settled, the winning bidders in the auction had made breathtaking bets on the new wireless technology. The ninety-nine PCS licenses sold in the first wave of auctions brought a total of $7.7 billion, with Sprint and its partners winning the most licenses and paying $2.6 billion to gain nationwide coverage. AT&T spent $2

billion and the PCS Primeco alliance $1.1 billion. However, these
numbers paled in comparison to the $4.7 billion in winning bids
lodged by newcomer NextWave Telecomm, a company that took part
in the "entrepreneurs" auction limited to "small" companies. With
favorable financing from the government, NextWave and other bidders spent an average of $40 per pop, some three times more than
buyers in the earlier auctions.

The triumph was short-lived. In fact, the government auction was
a disaster. These high prices have left many of the winning bidders
struggling to survive long enough to build their systems. Two companies have already filed for bankruptcy, including NextWave, which
had serious difficulties raising capital and was forced to cancel both
its IPO and a planned junk bond offering. Faced with the prospect
of losing the billions in licensing fees generated by the auctions, the
government has been forced to give more favorable terms to some
winning bidders and has taken back some licenses from companies
unable to make initial payments.

By the end of 1999, the drive to create a nationwide digital PCS
"footprint" reached a frenzied pitch. Megadeals abound with per pop
valuations exceeding $100. VoiceStream Wireless has cobbled together
a nationwide digital footprint by acquiring Omnipoint and Aerial; the
newly merged Vodafone AirTouch formed a wireless venture with Bell
Atlantic; and MCI WorldCom announced its blockbuster deal to acquire Sprint and its nationwide wireless division, Sprint PCS.

The Telecommunications Reform Act of 1996:
Consolidation and Convergence

The competitive landscape was redrawn again in 1996 with the
Telecommunications Reform Act of 1996, the first comprehensive revision of federal communications law since 1934. The advent of PCS
and the new Telecommunications Act amounted to a one-two
punch, shocking AT&T out of its complacency. The act redefined
the boundaries of the telecommunications industry and paved the

way for widespread convergence—that is, the integration of telco, cable, Internet, and data operations.

Under the Telecommunications Act, the local phone companies are now required to open their markets to new entrants, whether long distance providers, cable companies, or otherwise, and sell competitors access to their systems at wholesale rates. Once the local phone monopolies can demonstrate that they face competition in their home markets, they will be allowed to enter the long distance business.

For AT&T, the act embodied both a promise and a threat: The promise was the ability to enter local markets to enhance revenues and profits; the threat was the obliteration of its market share in long distance by local telcos. The Baby Bells, the children of Ma Bell, now grown up, would turn on their estranged parent. New competitors would enter.

Initially, the expected convergence did not come. A Bell Atlantic–TCI deal was in the works, but collapsed with the re-regulation of cable. The high capital costs associated with the digital revolution also moderated the trend toward integrated multiproduct telcos and cable companies: Cable companies lacked the money to pursue telephony, and phone companies were without the resources to build out digital voice and video networks. Instead, companies chose to focus primarily on relatively familiar ground. Cable companies upgraded video service, while local phone companies entered long distance telephony and long distance companies entered local telephony—at least until 1998.

More immediately, the act sparked widespread consolidation, especially among the Baby Bells, to create stronger industry players: Only the largest telcos would possess the resources and efficiencies to benefit from convergence and to compete against AT&T. First came the announcement of SBC's $16.7 billion acquisition of Pacific Telesis on April 1, 1996. PacTel had been searching for a well-heeled partner for some time, partly to rescue it from the mounting woes that began with the AirTouch spin-off, and partly in anticipation of the coming telecommunications deregulation. SBC had strong management with an excellent operating track record, and Edward E. Whitacre Jr., the chairman of SBC, was confident his team could turn around Pacific Telesis and make the investment pay off. Phone service would be the core of the company's operating plan.

If the SBC-PacTel merger hinted at the RBOCs' renewed focus on phone service, the subsequent Bell Atlantic–NYNEX merger underlined the point. This second, larger transaction hit the headlines just three weeks after the first deal was announced, also in April 1996, and was completed on August 15, 1997.

The NYNEX deal was widely regarded as a triumph for Ray Smith, chairman of Bell Atlantic, and especially welcome after the collapsed TCI deal.

NYNEX had long been one of the weakest RBOCs. Burdened with relatively older systems and an abysmal customer service record, the company was particularly vulnerable to competitors who might come into the Northeast market. NYNEX was not well positioned to go it alone in the rapidly changing telecommunications industry.

The deal promised to generate large cost savings because the two companies controlled neighboring regions. A new Bell Atlantic has emerged, astride twelve states from Maine to Virginia. With wires running up and down the lucrative Northeast corridor, the company can now service long distance calls entirely in its own network, no longer needing to pay long distance providers to connect interregional calls. Estimated savings from this change, plus other efficiencies from excising duplicative overhead, might amount to between $600 million and $800 million per year.

Smith, fifty-eight years old at the time, who had not yet designated a successor, picked as part of the merger Ivan Seidenberg, chairman of NYNEX, forty-nine. Merging NYNEX and Bell Atlantic created a combined company that had a market capitalization of nearly $100 billion, over $30 billion in annual revenue, and 141,000 employees.

U S West continued to be the most significant strategic outlier among the RBOCs. Rather than focus solely on telephony, the company continued with its dual-track cable and telephony strategy, clinging to its interest in Time Warner's cable systems and programming operations. In 1996, U S West went a step further, laying out another $5.3 billion of its cable tracking stock to buy Continental Cablevision. When, in early 1997, U S West agreed to sell its wireless assets to AirTouch in a $4.5 billion deal, it looked to be placing its growth bet squarely on cable and long distance telephony.

But the AirTouch transaction was designed around the favorable "Morris Trust" tax structure, subsequently revoked by Congress on a retroactive basis. With the invalidation of the structure—designed to allow U S West to avoid capital gains taxes—the deal collapsed. Then, in a surprising turn of events, U S West announced a plan to spin off its cable assets, which had been held in a separately traded tracking stock vehicle called U S West Media Group. The formal breakup of the two units occurred on June 12, 1998, and the U S West Media Group was renamed MediaOne.

But despite losing tax-free treatment, the AirTouch–U S West deal was not dead. In January 1998, the combination returned to life, with AirTouch agreeing to buy U S West's wireless telephone business for $5.7 billion. Subsequently, in March 1999, MediaOne announced its $58.6 billion merger with cable operator Comcast, a deal trumped by AT&T in April. Finally, in 1999, AirTouch agreed to be acquired by British wireless operator Vodafone, and in June 1999, U S West became the subject of a bidding war between 1990s high flyer upstarts Qwest and Global Crossing.

MORRIS TRUST

Closing the Loophole

Morris Trust, whose name derives from 1966 case *Commissioner v. Morris Trust,* is one of the buzzwords often heard in the deal business. Slammed by some as "corporate welfare," the Morris Trust transaction is another variation on the basic spin-off. However, this slang for a tax-free mechanism to sell a business slipped into obsolescence after Congress passed a proposal to curb the practice.

The Morris Trust mechanism allowed one company to split itself apart so that it could sell a particular part of its business on a tax-efficient basis. The first step was to spin off to shareholders the businesses which the buyer did not want. Then, in a pre-arranged transaction, the acquirer merged with the remaining business in a tax-free stock deal. Immediately after the transaction, the shareholders in the original company owned shares both in the acquirer and in the business which the acquirer did not want.

A selling company also could generate a cash return through a Morris Trust transaction by borrowing money prior to the spin-off, as in GM's sale of the Hughes defense business, which was agreed to prior to the Morris Trust repeal. The cash stayed with GM while the liability went to the buyer, Raytheon.

Reflecting perceived abuses of the Morris Trust structure, Congress passed tax law amendments in 1997 that limited application of the structure. A spin-off and subsequent sale still might be tax-free under some circumstances, but a preplanned sale no longer qualifies for favorable treatment. The talk of legislative changes to *Morris Trust* prompted a major rush to get deals done under the wire, but AirTouch–U S West was too late.

Competitive Local Exchange Carriers   Another outgrowth of the Telecommunications Reform Act of 1996 was the development of the competitive local exchange carrier (CLEC). The RBOCs—which have come to be known as incumbent local exchange carriers (ILECs)—were required by the act to offer any competitor full interconnection to their networks. Bundled services were required to be unbundled so that any competitor could lease various parts of the ILEC networks à la carte at a wholesale price that included a reasonable profit.

Under this favorable regulation, CLECs have cropped up in record numbers. Indeed, providing competition to ILECs is a quickly growing business. In 1997, CLEC industry revenues grew by 94 percent, from $1.8 billion to $3.5 billion, according to analyst estimates. But this $3.5 billion figure represents a mere 0.8 percent of the local market. There is much room left for growth.

Most CLECs offer service by reselling local service provided by ILECs. Other CLECs have begun to build out networks themselves, in a manner analogous to what MCI and Sprint did in the 1970s to compete against AT&T in long distance. Cable companies have entered the CLEC market too, gradually upgrading their systems to provide telephone service.

Teleport is an example of a CLEC that has built up its own network—it constructed local fiber-optic networks to bypass ILECs' local loops and to allow direct connection to long distance carriers. This type of network, geared to business users, allows customers to avoid paying ILECs an access fee for using their networks to tap into long distance service, providing attractive savings. Nextlink provides similar services. Such cutting-edge networks, capable of transmitting voice, data, video, and Internet data, will certainly speed convergence as well. Among the cable operators, Time Warner Communications established the first facilities-based CLEC in which telephone traffic could travel over cable lines. Subsequently, cable operators have been some of the most active entrants into competitive long distance.

While initially CLECs enjoyed lofty valuations, perceptions of slowing growth have caused CLECs' market valuations to fall. Some believe that CLECs are merely in a "hiccup" stage: They need time to catch their breath before continuing their growth. But others assert that CLECs have already captured the customers eager to switch from ILECs, the so-called low-hanging fruit.

As in other telco segments, there are benefits to scale for CLECs and M&A activity proved a viable way to build scale. For example, Brooks Fiber Properties acquired Metro Access Networks and Phoenix FiberLink, giving Brooks a presence in Nevada, Texas, and Utah. Brooks was later acquired by WorldCom, which in turn merged with MCI.

The Globalization of Telecommunications

The globalization of telecom is also accelerating rapidly. Today, a national picture of the industry is too limited.

An undercurrent of globalization has existed since 1993, when British Telecommunications agreed to buy a 20 percent stake in MCI for $4.3 billion. The investment provided much needed cash for MCI's expansion into local service and the upgrade of its systems and offered BT a window on the growing U.S. telecom market. BT had been struggling to enter into the U.S. for years, first with a failed attempt in 1988 to buy MFS Communications, then with its short-lived stake in McCaw Cellular, which was cashed out when AT&T bought McCaw.

The BT-MCI alliance also developed into an early effort at global marketing. The partners split the world geographically and developed bundled international telecommunications packages for larger international clients. The partnership gave AT&T competitor MCI something AT&T lacked: a meaningful global presence.

But BT and MCI were not alone in pursuing a global strategy. Sprint too followed the MCI model, beginning negotiations with Deutsche Telekom and France Telecom in 1994. The strategic logic for a deal was apparent: The two local monopolies faced the prospect of growing competition in their home markets and sought both marketing savvy and global scale, while Sprint needed cash to build its national wireless network. An alliance was struck in June

1995. Mirroring the MCI deal, the European companies would invest $4.2 billion in Sprint for a 20 percent stake. Though a number of regulatory roadblocks delayed the deal, it was finally launched in January 1996. AT&T opted to form nonequity alliances with a number of international phone companies in its own effort at global packaging. But it soon found itself at a severe disadvantage relative to its peers.

These early steps were, however, just precursors. In November 1996, BT and MCI announced they were giving up their alliance in favor of an outright merger. Under the original terms of the deal, BT would acquire the 80 percent of MCI it did not already own for $21 billion in stock and cash to create a new company—Concert PLC. Concert would be an instant global heavyweight, with a market capitalization of roughly $50 billion. In the U.S., MCI would gain expertise and capital for its expansion effort. Concert also would be positioned to snatch a share of the European market when national barriers come down.

However, Concert, like AT&T, also faced the daunting challenges stemming from its lack of local origination capabilities in the United States. The risks became apparent in the summer of 1997, when MCI announced that yearly losses of $800 million had resulted from its efforts to enter local phone service.

Fallout from the announcement rocked both BT's and MCI's stock prices. BT's shareholder base began to pressure the company to renegotiate the terms of the transaction. Because MCI realized it needed a partner, the company reluctantly agreed to a $3 billion lower purchase price. But this development left the deal vulnerable to a competing bid from WorldCom, a more aggressive player willing to look past MCI's immediate troubles.

WorldCom Crashes the Party

On October 1, 1997, WorldCom and its brash leader, Bernard Ebbers, became household names with a dramatic $30 billion bid to crash the BT-MCI party. In a single stroke, Ebbers reshaped the competitive landscape. If WorldCom were able to capture MCI, the combined company would offer both local and long distance services across the United States, beating the RBOCs and AT&T to the punch. This strategic vision was bold. WorldCom had just $8 billion of estimated 1997 revenue, compared to MCI's nearly $20 billion. Furthermore, Ebbers would have to navigate a number of major tactical and regulatory issues to make the deal happen.

The WorldCom story underscores just how fluid the telecom world has become. In 1983, Ebbers and three friends gathered at a coffee shop in Hattiesburg, Mississippi, and founded a start-up company later dubbed Long-Distance Discount Service (LDDS). Ebbers was originally a relatively passive investor in the operation, which planned to buy long distance capacity wholesale from AT&T and re-sell the service to business customers.

The company struggled for several years, and in April 1985, Ebbers took over as president. Under his stewardship, LDDS continued to focus on aggressive marketing to small businesses, a segment often ignored by larger providers. Ebbers also developed a passion for deals and embarked upon a core acquisition strategy that would transform LDDS into WorldCom.

LDDS initially concentrated on acquisitions of smaller long distance providers. However, in December 1992, Ebbers consummated a $560 million deal to buy Advanced Telecommunications, leapfrogging LDDS to become the fourth-largest long distance carrier in the United States. A number of smaller deals followed, including the acquisition of IDB WorldCom, which gave LDDS a new name and re-selling agreements with companies in sixty-five countries. Its $2.5 billion cash purchase of WilTel Network Services in 1995 gave World Com one of only four national fiber-optic networks.

The Telecommunications Act of 1996 accelerated the pace of Ebbers' acquisition activities. WorldCom agreed to provide long distance services for GTE and Ameritech, and was granted permission to enter the local telephone service business in California, Illinois, and Texas.

The $12 billion stock acquisition in December 1996 of MFS Communications, a local service provider over its own fiber-optic network catering to business customers and a leading Internet service provider, accelerated Ebbers' pace. After the MFS deal, WorldCom boasted a local, long distance, and data presence, but still was a relatively small player.

Ebbers' unsolicited bid for MCI shocked the telecommunications industry. How could WorldCom afford to pay $11 billion more for MCI than British Telecommunications? First, WorldCom had considerably more operational overlap with MCI than did BT. WorldCom possessed an embryonic local network and would therefore not need to make the large capital investments that MCI would require to break into local service. WorldCom and MCI also could significantly reduce overlapping overhead. While BT expected an estimated $2.5 billion of cost savings over five years, Ebbers projected at least $2.1 billion of cost savings in the first year alone.

Second, WorldCom benefited from a high market valuation. Because the company's stock was trading at approximately 90 times forward earnings estimates—much higher than MCI's—WorldCom could play the old 1960s merger game. By successfully integrating MCI's operations, WorldCom could induce the market to apply its multiple to the new EPS—approximately 20 percent higher than the pre-merger figure—creating shareholder value. Furthermore, the deal as proposed would be structured as a pooling of interests for accounting purposes. There would be no goodwill recognized from the deal on WorldCom's balance sheet, and no annual amortization.

However, despite the steep price Ebbers was able to offer, WorldCom faced a number of roadblocks in its pursuit of MCI. BT not only had a definitive agreement to acquire MCI, the company also was MCI's largest single shareholder, with a 20 percent stake. BT needed to break into the U.S. market and MCI was, therefore, a critical strategic opportunity.

Then, in another surprise, on October 15, 1997, GTE launched a $28 billion counteroffer for MCI, all in cash, which it planned to fund by taking on approximately $30 billion of additional debt. Though the bid was approximately 7 percent lower than WorldCom's all-stock offer, the theory was that MCI shareholders would prefer cash rather than potentially volatile WorldCom stock.

With two high bids on the table and a nervous shareholder base, British Telecommunications was hemmed in. The company decided against raising its offer. An auction developed between WorldCom and GTE.

Finally, MCI agreed to be acquired by WorldCom for a sweetened bid of $36.5 billion in cash and stock—for a total deal value, including debt assumed, of $43.4 billion—that offered something to both BT and MCI: In negotiations to gain BT's blessing, WorldCom agreed to buy out the British company's MCI stake for about $7 billion in cash, while the other MCI stockholders would still get WorldCom stock. Even though the cash payment to BT would prevent pooling of interests, Ebbers was willing to take on the goodwill created under purchase accounting to win the deal, an important tactical judgment. In the bull market, stock was king, much like during the 1960s boom. GTE was left holding the bag, making it vulnerable to takeover itself.

WorldCom's acquisition of MCI positioned Ebbers to do an even more dramatic deal—the $129 billion purchase of Sprint fills in WorldCom's missing telecom asset, wireless telephony.

AT&T's Strategic Shift

As Mike Armstrong took over at AT&T, he saw the need to move at warp speed. The industry was moving too fast and AT&T was being left behind.

First, he moved into data services, a business long lacking at

AT&T, by purchasing IBM's Global Network business for $5 billion. The deal gives AT&T the means to deliver voice and data services to customers in fifty-nine countries.

Coming full circle, AT&T also effected its reentry into local service. When Armstrong came to AT&T, the company was trying to move into local service by buying service in bulk from the Baby Bells. But in less than two years, this strategy had racked up losses of almost $4 billion. Armstrong knew the situation had to change, and therefore, in January 1998, purchased Teleport Communications for $11 billion. The deal provided AT&T with a network of phone lines it could use to offer local telephone service to businesses and bypass the Baby Bells completely. AT&T could bundle its new local service with its long distance product and keep the access fee it would have paid the ILEC for itself. Because Teleport established a fiber-optic system, AT&T could also provide cutting-edge Internet and data services.

In June 1998, Armstrong made an even more aggressive move to enter the consumer local telephone service market, announcing a blockbuster $70 billion merger with cable operator TCI. The deal would give AT&T access to the "last mile" of wire to consumers' homes via TCI's massive cable network, estimated to reach approximately 33 percent of homes—or 14.4 million subscribers—in the United States.

The deal was spurred on by the advent of new technology—digital cable—that promised to offer two-way communications services such as Internet and local telephone services over cable lines. The combination would expose AT&T to the world of media discussed in the next chapter.

Despite the optimistic claims of AT&T and TCI, however, up to now attempts to provide "one-stop telecom shopping" have not been successful. Indeed, at first it seemed that making the market understand the implications of the merger would be one of the most sensitive aspects of this megadeal. The enormous capital investment required to upgrade TCI's cable systems to two-way digital would effectively transform AT&T's stock from an earnings stock into a growth stock. To prevent its traditional shareholder base from selling the stock, thereby depressing the trading price, AT&T announced its intent to create tracking stocks to reflect the company's different operations. However, when AT&T's stock responded favorably to the deal, the tracking-stock plan was scrapped. After the deal announcement, AT&T's stock traded up from around $60 to $85.

Simultaneously with the deal closing, TCI combined its Liberty Media Group—a cable programming company that owns Discovery Communications and has stakes in Time Warner, USA Networks, and Fox/Liberty Networks—with TCI Ventures Group (currently a tracking stock of parent TCI) to create a new Liberty Media Group headed by John Malone, CEO of TCI. Shareholders of the new Liberty Media will be issued a tracking stock by AT&T.

This AT&T-TCI combination is a seminal event, launching a new AT&T poised to provide long distance, data services, local service, Internet, wireless service, and cable television. But AT&T was not finished. In April 1999, AT&T launched a similarly motivated $63 billion unsolicited bid for cable operator MediaOne, threatening to break apart MediaOne's purchase by Comcast. Despite Comcast's efforts to top AT&T's bid by discussing partnering with companies like AOL, Microsoft, and MCI WorldCom, MediaOne accepted AT&T's offer.

PROFILE

Michael Armstrong

AT&T chairman C. Michael Armstrong likes the role of a man of action. In short order, he cut jobs, moved AT&T into the local phone market, enhanced profitability in the wireless business, found the Internet, and became a cable company. It's premature to have a

final verdict, but Armstrong won't fail for a lack of trying. His ebul-
lience is so pervasive that one fears no one told him how difficult
it was to turn AT&T around.

Now sixty years old, Armstrong was the first nonscientist CEO
of Hughes Electronics. When Armstrong joined Hughes in 1992,
the company received more than half of its revenues from the
Pentagon. But Armstrong realized the danger in Hughes' situation, as defense spending was dropping steadily. Armstrong
therefore transformed the company from a defense products
manufacturer to a leading satellite TV and telecommunications
company. DirectTV was launched in 1994 under Armstrong's guidance. Just as at AT&T, Armstrong moved quickly to make changes
at Hughes. His actions paid off, with Hughes' stock price more
than tripling.

Armstrong graduated from Miami University in 1961 with a BS
in Business Economics. Prior to his tenure at Hughes, Armstrong
spent thirty-one years at IBM, where he rose through the ranks,
ultimately becoming chairman of IBM World Trade Corporation.

Moving Toward the Millennium

But while AT&T was undertaking its strategic changes, the telco
world continued to accelerate its development.

SBC-Ameritech   SBC and Ameritech, two Baby Bells, counter-
punched AT&T and WorldCom by announcing a $72 billion merger
in May 1998 to create a formidable global and national competitor.
The two vowed to invest a portion of the cost savings generated by
the deal to enter a total of thirty new markets, providing competition
to incumbent local telephone operators in these areas. Not only had
AT&T failed in its attempt to acquire SBC, but now the merged
SBC-Ameritech would be a strong competitor. Ironically, AT&T,

which had just announced its intent to acquire TCI, and MCI, which had recently merged with WorldCom, were some of the most vocal opponents of the deal to bulk up the already-successful SBC.

SBC, led by CEO Edward Whitacre, has the reputation as an aggressive company. In 1996, SBC bought fellow Baby Bell Pacific Telesis. A year later, SBC bought Southern New England Telephone. Whitacre is also taking steps to enter the long distance business. In February 1999, SBC announced a partnership with the communications operations of Williams Cos. in which Williams would carry SBC's long distance traffic. SBC also made a bid to buy 10 percent of Williams.

SBC is the most profitable of the Baby Bells—33 percent more so than Bell Atlantic—and its stock has averaged a 47 percent annual return over the past two years. Yet SBC understands the need to keep moving. Its once-regulated markets are quickly becoming deregulated, with new entrants threatening to lure away its lucrative business customers. This plan to merge with Ameritech is the response to the coming full deregulation—an attempt to position itself strongly to operate in a highly competitive marketplace.

AT&T and MCI WorldCom are likely entrants into SBC's local service markets. SBC needs Ameritech's bulk to compete effectively against these telco giants. The combined SBC-Ameritech would control about one third of the local lines in the U.S. and almost half of the business lines. While before SBC was able to campaign effectively to prevent rivals from entering its core markets, full deregulation is on the horizon. SBC, which has investment in only three European countries, will gain Ameritech's holdings in fifteen countries, better positioning SBC to do more international deals.

Bell Atlantic–GTE   A wounded GTE combined its Internet, data, and long distance network with Bell Atlantic's Eastern customer base in a $71 billion deal to create the nation's second-largest telephone company with 63 million lines—one third of those in the

U.S.—in thirty-eight states. GTE will help Bell Atlantic go national in phone service and therefore position it to compete against AT&T and MCI WorldCom, as Ameritech would help SBC. But most significantly, the combination is about data services: Bell Atlantic would be able to offer GTE's Internet and data services to its existing customer base. GTE has a sophisticated data network and it gained a major portion of the Internet through a purchase of BBN, an Internet founder. In short, Bell Atlantic wants GTE's data network; GTE wants Bell Atlantic's customers. Bell Atlantic's ability to offer long distance service within its own territory is limited until it indicates that its home market is competitive.

The deal indicates that, despite large acquisition premiums, it has become cheaper to buy than to build. Building a data services network from the ground up is slow and expensive; furthermore, competitors are able to cherry-pick lucrative business customers.

Both Bell Atlantic and SBC will, through these mergers, become direct competitors.

The Independents Emerge   The independents have entered the fray, chipping away at the AT&T position through M&A activity. In March 1999, Global Crossing, a two-year-old Bermuda-based upstart, announced its intention to purchase Frontier Corp. for $11.2 billion. The combination of Global Crossing's fiber-optic network with Frontier's U.S. long distance network will create the first global Internet Protocol fiber-optic networks that will provide Internet, data, and telephone service. Global Crossing had made headlines recently when it stole away a top executive, Robert Annunziata, from AT&T.

The fourth-largest U.S. long distance company also emerged when Qwest—formed in 1988 following Philip Anschutz's takeover of the Southern Pacific Railroad and laying fiber-optic cables along SPR's railroad rights-of-way—merged with LCI International in March 1998 in a deal worth $4.4 billion. The company plans to build a new 18,500-mile fiber-optic network and has already landed a partnership with Dutch operator KPN to form a 9,100-mile European network, as well as its own network in Mexico. In April 1999, RBOC BellSouth acquired a 10 percent stake in Qwest for $3.5 billion, in its own move to jump on the long distance bandwagon and is reportedly contemplating a larger stake.

Both upstarts Qwest and Global Crossing became rivals in a bidding war for U S West and Frontier in July 1999.

Global Crossing launched its bid first. Building upon its March 1999 offer for Frontier, Global Crossing proposed a $37 billion all-stock offer for U S West. The market, however, was skeptical of the strategic fit between the companies, and sent Global Crossing's stock price down sharply. Global Crossing had hoped to create another MCI WorldCom blockbuster deal. But investors balked at the idea that the growth stock they had purchased would emerge from the deal as another stodgy utility.

Undeterred by the market's reaction, Qwest weighed in with its own $55 billion unsolicited stock offer for both U S West and Frontier that valued U S West at $41.3 billion and Frontier at $13.6 billion. However, Qwest's stock price was not immune to the market sentiment that affected Global Crossing: Its stock price fell 24 percent, making its offer worth less than Global Crossing's. The fact remained that neither Global Crossing nor Qwest would be able to offer its long distance services to U S West's local customers because U S West had not shown its markets to be competitive.

As both companies contemplated revising their offers, the bidding war became personal. The battle was between two competitive former AT&T execs: Robert Annunziata of Global Crossing and Joseph Nacchio of Qwest.

Nacchio was determined to win, and raised Qwest's bids for U S West and Frontier: the Frontier offer was increased from $64.90 per share to $68 per share, $20 of which would be paid in cash. The U S West offer was upped from $65.30 to $69.00. The deal illustrates a new phenomenon stock under pressure competing with another deflated high flyer. In contrast, the market cheered WorldCom's stock offer for MCI over GTE's cash offer because synergies from the WorldCom/MCI merger were apparent to investors.

The bidding war ended abruptly. The competing CEOs divvied up the pie between themselves. Qwest got to merge with U S West and Global Crossing kept Frontier. The market took a wait and see attitude on the efficacy of these transactions.

Wireless Goes Global　As consolidation and globalization continued, the wireless segment became increasingly important. The most hotly contested asset in 1999 was AirTouch. First, acquisitive Bell Atlantic tried to get in on the action, making a $45 billion offer for the company in what would have been a dilutive deal; but it was topped by British wireless operator Vodafone's nearly $60 billion bid for the stock, the largest wireless acquisition. The new company, Vodafone AirTouch PLC, will operate in twenty-three countries with 23 million wireless customers and will be the largest wireless operator in the world. Ironically, by the end of 1999, Vodafone AirTouch had formed a U.S. wireless joint venture with Bell Atlantic valued in excess of $70 billion.

Vodafone's bid represented a bet on the future: that eventually customers will use wireless phones as their primary means of communication. In time, Vodafone AirTouch will be positioned to offer seamless wireless service to customers all over the world. The deal has shadings of the MCI wars. Vodafone, like WorldCom, had a strong stock and the willingness not to pool as its key tactical advantages.

Chris Gent

Since Chris Gent took the reins as chief executive of Vodafone in January 1997, the company has enjoyed overwhelming success. Its share price has quintupled. It trades at a price-to-earnings ratio of nearly 65 times. And the most recent deal with AirTouch promises to make it a powerful global player with a market capitalization as big as that of British Telecom.

When Gent took over, Vodafone was losing ground to new entrants like Orange and One-2-One. Since joining the company, Gent has been credited with hiring a new ad agency, redesigning the logo, and building a network of 250 company stores throughout the U.K. through which to distribute Vodafone handsets. He started selling mobile phones through supermarkets and launched prepaid service, which has been enormously successful. He also launched ventures abroad.

Appropriately enough, Gent put together the merger between Vodafone and AirTouch by cell phone while he was in Australia. But despite the approving market reaction, Chris Gent has a monumental task ahead of him.

The Creation of a European Telco Giant   Globally, the trend toward a consolidating telecom industry continues. In 1999 Olivetti—former typewriter manufacturer turned telco company—made a $50 billion hostile bid for the much-larger Telecom Italia. Olivetti planned to integrate better fixed and mobile services, as well as to insert Telecom Italia's mobile operations into a Europe-wide mobile network.

Telecom Italia, resisting the bid, embarked on a number of defensive moves, which shareholders voted down. Olivetti responded by raising its offer by 15 percent. Telecom Italia began canvassing for a white knight, and entered discussions with Deutsche Telekom. On April 22, 1999, Telecom Italia agreed to an $81.5 billion deal with Deutsche Telekom to create the world's second-largest telecommunications company. Because Deutsche Telekom is 72 percent controlled by the German government, Telecom Italia was sensitive about not ceding control to the Germans, and so DT provided an assurance that the German government would reduce its shareholding in DT in connection with a privatization move and would accept equal German and Italian representation on the new company's board. In the end, however, the majority of shareholders tendered to Olivetti due to questions about the strategic sense and regulatory hurdles of the Deutsche Telekom deal. Deutsche Telekom was the real loser, lacking an international strategy, and its partnership with France Telecom destroyed. Yet again a scrappy newcomer outmaneuvered two stodgy behemoths.

WorldCom: Challenging AT&T   By early 1999 MCI WorldCom CEO Bernie Ebbers recognized that to be a full service provider he needed to enter the wireless business. He courted Nextel but balked at the asking price and walked away. Since then Nextel's share price has almost tripled.

The only other company that could provide Ebbers with a nationwide wireless footprint was Sprint's fast-growing, highly regarded wireless business, Sprint PCS. Sprint itself, the number-three long-distance national telephone carrier noted for its high-technology fiber optic lines and the "hear the pin drop" motto of quality, would be a prize—synergies from cost savings between Sprint and MCI would be between $2 to $3 billion a year.

Sprint, while a profitable and well-run company, faced long-term strategic issues. Fifty-nine-year-old Bill Esrey, the industry's longest-serving and respected CEO of Sprint, recognized that the long-distance business was becoming increasingly commoditized. He invested heavily in technology to bring high-speed voice and data to households through a single connection, but skeptics felt Sprint lacked the financial might for widespread deployment. Meanwhile, its one-stop communications product for large corporate clients, Global One, a joint venture with France Telecom and Deutsche Telekom, was crumbling.

However, reminiscent of the GTE and WorldCom battle for MCI, RBOC BellSouth emerged as a bidder to derail MCI WorldCom's plans. BellSouth offered a higher, mostly cash consideration. Ebbers was not going to repeat the Nextel fiasco and responded by drastically increasing his all-stock bid from $63 a share to $76, even though the new price would hurt MCI WorldCom's cash EPS in the near term. The Sprint Board found Ebbers' stock strategically more compelling than a cash offer.

Together, Sprint MCI WorldCom can provide one-stop shopping for wireless, wireline, and Internet services all over the United States. The combined company will provide over a third of long-distance business and residential traffic. The company will be the leading PCS player, with a 5 million subscriber base that is growing rapidly. Its Internet operations already represent the backbone for a substantial portion of the country. Few other telecom players besides AT&T are able to match WorldCom's asset base. The merger of MCI WorldCom and Sprint, once regulatory hurdles are overcome, promises to create the new telecom giant to watch.

The Future

The digital age has brought immense change to the telco industry. New rivals such as MCI WorldCom–Sprint jostle with AT&T and the Baby Bells as they transform themselves. Technological change will continue to roll forward. We are already seeing the build-out of PCS and other new wireless services, which also may provide competition to local telephone service. Craig McCaw and others have developed and are rolling out global satellite communications networks.

In this unsettled environment, it is difficult to predict what telecommunications service will look like, even in the near future. A number of market competitors are betting that bundled telecommunications services will be the winning business model. Some companies already are providing packaged local and long distance. European deregulation could also spark both pan-European consolidation and cross-border mergers between U.S. and European telcos.

Competition in local markets, initially slow to develop, has begun to pick up. The long distance companies are not the only source of competition. Falling wireless rates have made cellular and PCS technologies viable alternatives to local landline services. But surely the big story of the next ten years will be the full emergence of broadband for video, Internet, and all voice and data communications. Deals such as the MCI WorldCom–Sprint edge toward that reality, but we are not quite there.

This pattern of chaos, consolidation, and accelerating change will continue. Ultimately, these parallel developments will bring the convergence promised in the early 1990s. Economic evolution does not, however, occur in a Hegelian progression, all forces driving toward a greater truth. There is a cycle and an uncertainty to events.

Racing Toward Cyberspace: 13
The Media and the Message
in the Age of Convergence

"Cyberspace . . . Unthinkable complexity. Lines of
light in the non-space of the mind, clusters and
constellations of data. Like city lights, receding."

—William Ford Gibson, *Neuromancer*

The revolution that transformed telecommunications has spilled over to all the other media industries. For years, the development of various "traditional" media technologies—cable, radio, TV, music, and video recordings—had run in parallel. In each technology, the players who provided content were different from those who operated the distribution system. There emerged a race to dominate the various media technologies and the content these technologies provided: As a new technology emerged, the visionaries rushed to be the leaders. Cable, radio, and television were shaped in this era. Gradually, these parallel lines began to blur. The established media became vertically integrated so as to control both distribution and content: TV networks bought TV stations; cable networks bought cable channels, studios bought movie theaters and video rental chains.

Then, in the 1990s, a new technology emerged—the Internet. In this new medium, M&A activity is only just beginning. The maturity of the Internet and the development of new distribution technology—broadband cable—are also leading to deals whose goal is convergence of Internet, cable, and telephony. All the media—cable, telephony, Internet, radio, and television—will be piped through wires to customers. In recognition of this technological change, regulation has been revamped to allow one provider to offer multiple services.

As a result of these shifts, the disparate segments that made up the media world are restructuring, coming together in a flurry of deal activity to create integrated media giants. We are now in the midst of a race toward convergence—and what a confused, halting, fumbling spectacle it is. All participants are one-legged men because there is no blueprint, no clarity, and a lot of motion. These are decisions made under uncertainty, with high stakes, incomplete data, and according to the conventional wisdom of the moment.

Some of the players in the new media race are old hands at the media business—the television networks, the big movie studios, the large media companies. But most of the key architects of the converging media and telecommunications universe are entrepreneurs.

A group of some thirty individuals have been the key drivers: Sumner Redstone of Viacom, William McGowan of MCI, John Kluge of Metromedia, Ted Turner of Turner Broadcasting, Don Pels of LIN, John Malone of TCI, Craig McCaw of McCaw Cellular, Amos Hostetter of Continental Cablevision, Bill Gates of Microsoft, Jerry Yang and David Filo of Yahoo!, Steve Case of AOL, Jeff Bezos of Amazon.com, Brian Roberts of Comcast, Gerald Levin of Time Warner, and a handful of others. Collectively this group and the people who supported them reshaped the media and telecommunications paradigms and set a model and precedent for the hotbed of Silicon Valley.

According to my partner Fred Seegal, who has worked with many of the thirty over the years, these entrepreneurs "galvanized the transition by their sheer energy. They created industries out of science fiction—by persistence."

Cyberspace and Convergence

The buzzword of the moment is convergence. The implications are enormous. A single wire—broadband—will be able to transmit voice, data, cable, video, and Internet all around the globe. The advent of this new technology is spurring the combination of cable companies, which have been upgrading their systems to broadband technology, and phone companies, which want to tap into the new technology and offer local service over cable wires. In 1998 and in 1999, the trend was validated with a string of megadeals. Cable once again had become a hot asset; the frenzy had begun. All the media titans—including the once sleepy phone companies—want to be leaders in broadband, now widely viewed as the key to the digital future.

The race to convergence started out slowly, spurred on in the fall of 1992 by two rulings from the FCC. First, the commission ruled that phone companies would be permitted to carry television programming and to buy cable operators outside their assigned service areas—a partial victory for the Baby Bells. Nonetheless, Baby Bells still were not permitted to buy cable systems in their service areas under the 1982 antitrust settlement.

The second ruling from the FCC cleared the way for cable companies to enter the telephony business, either by buying an independent local phone company, or by providing phone service over existing coaxial cable lines. But the antitrust restrictions on the Baby Bells worked two ways: A cable company was not permitted to purchase or ally with the Baby Bell that provided service in the cable company's market.

John Malone hailed the coming digital revolution promised by broadband in a famous 1992 speech in which he predicted the arrival of a 500-channel world. With the advent of broadband technology and new favorable regulation, Internet, cable TV, and telephony were one and the same.

With the regulatory groundwork laid, market participants were free to act. Initially, the hope was that existing systems would be upgraded quickly to provide added services and that cable companies and phone companies, once in entirely separate businesses, would be brought into direct competition with each other. Many companies did, in fact, embark upon a number of ambitious pilot programs around this time. However, a string of interdisciplinary acquisitions turned out to be the most visible first sign of convergence.

Participants were understandably eager to enter new markets as quickly as possible. Local phone companies saw the $20 billion cable television market as an opportunity well matched to their strengths. Though the most attractive alternative—acquisitions of overlapping local cable companies—was foreclosed by regulation, local providers hoped one day to crack that market, but in the interim began to consider entering other cable markets. For the cable companies, the potential gain was even greater. In their view, a large piece of the $90 billion a year local calling market was theirs for the taking.

Southwestern Bell's 1993 leap into the cable business was the first convergence move. The $650 million acquisition of Hauser Communications, with two cable systems in suburban Washington, D.C., raised the interest of the other Baby Bells. A few months later, U S West made a far bigger bet, agreeing to invest $2.5 billion in Time Warner's vast cable operations. Together, Time Warner and U S West hoped to build a modern cable network capable of delivering voice, video, and data. Time Warner brought its existing cable systems to the partnership, and U S West brought cash for capital expenditures and technological expertise.

The frenzy continued throughout the fall of 1993. In December, Southwestern Bell followed up on the U S West announcement with its own major cable partnership, a $4.9 billion deal with Cox Cable Systems of Atlanta. BellSouth agreed to invest in Prime Cable.

However, Bell Atlantic appeared to have cinched the first major phone-cable alliance in October 1993, when it announced an agreement to acquire both Tele-Communications Inc. and Liberty Media in a giant stock merger. The $21 billion deal promised to combine the nation's largest cable system operator, a major television programmer, and one of the most aggressive Baby Bells. Together, the companies hoped to provide voice, video, and data services on a nationwide scale. Convergence would become reality.

Bell Atlantic and the other Baby Bells also wanted to control the media content that would be pumped over the sophisticated systems they were planning to build. This new interest sparked a number of alliances and investments designed to ensure preferred access to content, the most dramatic of which came in the 1993 battle for Paramount: NYNEX backed Viacom and BellSouth sided with QVC.

The mini-boom of 1993 gave way to a temporary retrenchment in 1994, in no small part caused by the FCC. Congress re-regulated cable companies in the Cable Act of 1992 under pressure from consumers, who had seen cable rates spike roughly 60 percent since the 1984 deregulation of cable companies. In the fall of 1993, the FCC mandated a 10 percent rate reduction. The following year, the commission added another 7 percent reduction.

The steep rate cuts put a crimp in the cash flows of cable companies like TCI, most of which were already highly leveraged. Now, with less cash coming in under the new rate structure, the companies would find it more difficult to make the major capital expenditures necessary to provide new services. Convergence's future became more cloudy. With the RBOCs focused on moving away from regulated businesses into high-growth, unregulated areas, they were hesitant to dive into a business that looked to be due for more regulation.

As a result, the enthusiasm for partnering with cable companies waned considerably. In February 1994, right after the second FCC rate increase, Bell Atlantic and TCI called off their blockbuster deal in the wake of the projected 15 percent drop in TCI's cash flow. The visions of convergence faded, and cable stocks plummeted.

Southwestern Bell then also pulled back from its cable plans. The partnership with Cox Communications fell apart in April over cash flow concerns. Southwestern had been counting on the huge projected cash flows from cable to fund major technology investments; but without the cash, the deal made less sense. In September 1997, Southwestern Bell, by then renamed SBC, sold the former Hauser Communications properties for a reported $606 million.

U S West was alone among the Baby Bells in remaining committed to a high-profile cable strategy, primarily because its weak geographic footprint put it at a disadvantage relative to other RBOCs in long distance service. Despite the fact the company's alliance with Time Warner already had led to conflicts over control issues and that FCC actions threatened to make cable a less profitable business, the company continued to purchase properties. Just five months after the Bell Atlantic–TCI deal fell apart, U S West spent another $1.2 billion to acquire two Atlanta cable companies.

Indeed the events of 1993 and 1994 were a reminder that change does not usually take place along a smooth trajectory. Shifts usually occur in fits and starts, often with sputtering and retrenchment.

The other Baby Bells did not give up entirely on video services, however. Rather, they launched a number of more limited ventures designed to pave the way for future expansion. In one alliance, Bell Atlantic, NYNEX, and Pacific Telesis joined with Hollywood agent Michael Ovitz to create Tele-TV, a plan which has since been drastically scaled back. The joint venturers originally hoped to create a powerful interactive television network, providing video on demand to the three Bells' 30 million customers. This effort faced off against a similar programming alliance between Ameritech, BellSouth, SBC, GTE, and the Walt Disney Co.

Cable companies too trended toward convergence, beginning to offer local phone service. Cox Communications and MediaOne, the former cable operation of U S West, and Cablevision are examples. Cablevision in particular has been targeting high-paying business customers for its local service, extending its cable lines to industrial parks and business centers—not typical cable territories. Cablevision has also installed computerized phone switches and hired workers laid off as a result of the Bell Atlantic–NYNEX merger. More than 1,000 businesses on Long Island are currently served by Cablevision's phone services.

By 1998, the promises of convergence had regained their previous sparkle.

In 1998, AT&T announced its acquisition of cable operator TCI, hoping to use its cable infrastructure to offer a bundled package of local phone, Internet, data services, and cable. AT&T's plan is ambitious. Because TCI's strategy had been to acquire as many cable operators as possible with as little capital investment as possible, TCI's cable network is antiquated. It is estimated that AT&T will have to spend upward of $3 billion to upgrade TCI's infrastructure to support the broadband cable necessary to carry voice, data, cable, and Internet services over one wire. Yet despite its technical shortcomings, TCI's network is a valuable asset. Its cable wires reach 12 million subscribers, giving AT&T an enormous receptive audience to which it can market its services.

In 1999, the media industry moved closer to convergence when Comcast attempted to buy MediaOne, the cable spinoff of U S West, for $58.6 billion. The deal would have combined Comcast's 6 million subscribers with MediaOne's 5 million customers, creating the third-largest cable company in the U.S. Comcast would also have obtained MediaOne's 25 percent interest in a partnership that includes HBO, Warner Bros. Studios, and most of Time Warner's cable subscribers. Ambitious Brian Roberts, president of Comcast, was finally emerging from John Malone's shadow, acting to create a formidable cable power.

But the Comcast-MediaOne combination was trumped. On April

22, 1999, AT&T launched an unsolicited cash, stock, and debt bid for MediaOne worth $63.1 billion ($56 billion equity value). The deal would make AT&T, which recently acquired TCI, the U.S.'s biggest cable operator, with a total of 16.2 million subscribers. AT&T would realize substantial synergies between MediaOne and its TCI network and would also be able to use MediaOne's assets with TCI's to offer telephony, cable, Internet, data, and video services over one broadband wire.

The offer was controversial. AT&T had just acquired TCI and was only beginning to integrate it. It would be years until AT&T would realize the promise of TCI's assets. Yet AT&T was making another large acquisition—this time paying far more per subscriber than it had for TCI. The 25.5 percent stake in Time Warner Entertainment would also necessitate a negotiation with Warner. On May 3, MediaOne's board accepted AT&T's offer and gave notice that it would terminate its agreement with Comcast. Meanwhile, Comcast scrambled to put together a bidding consortium of companies including AOL and Microsoft. A frenzy over cable ensued and the media titans circled. AOL sought the super-fast broadband access that MediaOne would provide to its online service. Microsoft sought MediaOne to complement its interactive television technology. MCI WorldCom clearly saw the same promise in MediaOne as AT&T did. Time Warner wanted to assure that control over the 25 percent of its Time Warner Entertainment operation owned by MediaOne would not fall into unfriendly hands.

In the end, Comcast was paid a $1.5 billion breakup fee to back off. In return, Comcast will pay AT&T about $9 billion in return for approximately 2 million cable customers of MediaOne. Both sides have gained something in the process. AT&T will move a step closer to leadership in convergence, and Comcast was able to bulk up at a net discount. As part of the agreement, AT&T will be permitted to use Comcast's cable TV lines to offer phone service.

The Physical Infrastructure for Convergence

Cable companies hold the key to the infrastructure for convergence. Their coaxial wire backbone that connects the U.S. is upgradable to broadband technology. Phone companies, once sleepy monopoly operators, want to catch the convergence wave to expand into more lucrative and unregulated areas, like Internet, data, and video services.

The battle is also on to determine who will define the physical architecture of the new digital future in consumers' homes: the hardware that will bring about the convergence of Internet, TV, and telephony. Microsoft has been an active participant in this area, with a series of major investments designed to capture the initiative. In April 1997, Microsoft spent $425 million to acquire Web-TV, a Silicon Valley start-up with a promising software and hardware interface that allows users to access the Internet from their television sets.

Then, in June 1997, Microsoft agreed to invest $1 billion for an 11.5 percent interest in Comcast, an investment which helped the cable company with its debt load and allowed a faster rollout of upgraded digital services. But more importantly, that someone as respected as Bill Gates was making this investment triggered a broad shift in market perceptions: Gates essentially was endorsing the notion that the cable infrastructure was the best hope for wider distribution of digital products.

Indeed, Gates' reputation as a technology visionary caused investors to take another look at the disfavored cable sector. Many realized that the strategic doubts about cable had been overdone. Satellite television was not gaining converts as quickly as feared. Meanwhile, cable television companies possessed an installed base of cable that runs past 95 percent of all homes in the United States, providing a fast, high-volume pipeline. As investors began to focus on the potential, the cable companies experienced a rebound in their stock prices that coincided with the Microsoft investment.

The strategic subtext for Microsoft's investment was an unfolding battle to define the standards for mass Internet access over this cable infrastructure. Gates wanted to position Microsoft to bridge the gap between programming and consumers, whether on the Internet, on television, or through some other medium. He advocated making a version of Microsoft's core Windows software product the engine for digital cable boxes. These hardware units, known in the industry as set-top boxes because they generally sit on the top of a consumer's television, already were being developed by a number of manufacturers, who expected that new digital set-top boxes would replace the older versions and provide high-speed Internet access and interactive television.

In its plan to make Windows CE the industry standard software driver for set-top boxes, Microsoft intended to collect a fee for each unit, plus a fraction of the fees cable companies would charge for new services. The math behind this approach was straightforward: While roughly 20 million households in the United States have a personal computer and modem, more than 64 million have televisions connected to cable. Interactive digital television would be a potentially lucrative new market for Microsoft.

With the Windows CE operating system, Microsoft hoped to gain the same position in digital TV that the company enjoys in the computer industry. The conventional Windows product—the dominant operating system for desktop computers—represents a kind of annuity for Microsoft, in that the company's revenues grew in line with the penetration of computers. Furthermore, Windows is a powerful platform to introduce new products and services: Microsoft controls the gateway and can gain market share for add-ons by folding them into Windows, a practice that attracted renewed antitrust scrutiny from the Justice Department in 1997.

Web-TV's second-generation product, introduced in September 1997, provides a window on the future potential of this business. The set-top box allows a television viewer to gain high-speed Internet access and pay-per-use video, music, or games. In addition the technology allows the Internet to be accessed while viewing television in a picture-in-picture format. The promise is clear: television programming linked to Internet-based marketing tie-ins. For example, a program might be linked to a site with related products. Microsoft eventually hopes to get a small fee each time a consumer orders a movie or buys a book using its software. In early 1999, Microsoft announced that the service would be available by satellite starting in spring 1999 in a partnership with EchoStar Communications. The deal will pave the way for faster Internet access.

However, John Malone and other cable executives balked at Bill Gates' vision. They had witnessed Microsoft's rise to dominance, as well as the evolution of the VHS-versus-Betamax war, and understood the importance of controlling technological standards. Cable companies would be at the mercy of Microsoft if the company were allowed to define industry standards. So not unexpectedly, Microsoft is not the only company that saw the potential of the interactive television market. Microsoft's competitors, chiefly Oracle Corporation and Sun Microsystems, launched their own efforts. Oracle owns a majority interest in Network Computer, which is developing a television-Internet interface. Other recent start-ups such as Worldgate are also racing to develop competing systems.

At Home, now controlled by AT&T, is also working to build the hardware and software needed for an Internet access capability over the cable infrastructure. The core of the system is a private network of computers designed to parallel the Internet, only at higher speed. Initially the focus is access for personal computers, but the service is expected to expand into interactive television. In exchange for developing the technology At Home receives 35 percent of the fees generated by affiliated cable companies.

At Home's exclusive relationships with large cable operators represent the most direct challenge to Microsoft's role in the digital future. Though Time Warner is not aligned with At Home, At Home has pacts with cable companies that serve over 44 million households, placing it at the center of the debate over future technological standards. At Home will offer Internet access via TV beginning in the second half of 1999 and will introduce set-top boxes in the third quarter of 1999. AT&T's purchase of MediaOne reinforces the long-term position of At Home.

Microsoft's Comcast investment was in part an attack on the At Home consortium. Microsoft has since pursued the other major cable providers in the At Home group, as well as Time Warner and U S West.

But the cable companies have not relied exclusively on the efforts of At Home. Precisely because the development of set-top boxes is so critical to the cable industry, a consortium of cable companies including TCI established CableLabs, a research and development center charged with the responsibility for choosing set-top box industry standards to be used by the participant companies.

After the consortium considered over twenty proposals from various companies, including Microsoft, in November 1997, CableLabs decided against selecting a single industry operating system and instead endorsed an open-architecture approach, just as the Internet allows the use of various operating systems. MediaOne, for example, has chosen to use Philips' set-top box, moving away from the products offered by the dominant General Instrument and Scientific Atlanta.

As a result, the fight to design the digital future rages on. Microsoft and its competitors have now switched to marketing their systems to individual cable operators. The stakes in the continuing struggle are high and Microsoft's investment in Comcast has created a sense of urgency.

Before convergence, each of the media industries developed on a parallel course. In the 1960s, cable consolidated. Radio and TV followed. The content that today's media titans seek to pump through broadband channels also matured. These deals laid the groundwork that would make convergence possible.

Distribution Consolidation Pre-Convergence: Cable, Radio, TV, and Recordings

The Great Cable Consolidation

More than $26 billion of cable assets changed hands during the 1980s, transforming a once highly fragmented industry. Cable television—a World War II–era technology designed to transmit video signals over coaxial cable—had been a land rush waiting to happen for several decades. After the war, a number of visionary entrepreneurs promoted the new technology as the future of the television industry. Some began stringing together systems as far back as the late 1950s and already there was talk of "movies at home."

Short on capital to develop the necessary infrastructure, cable entrepreneurs picked up on the pattern followed by the electric utilities at the turn of the century, submitting to local regulation of rates and services in exchange for monopoly rights to given areas. The monopoly agreements, or franchises, typically had a term of fifteen or twenty years, with the possibility for renewal.

But in the early days, a large gap existed between commercial promise and practical profitability. For a time, basic five-channel systems were the state of the art; twelve-channel systems followed. Consumers viewed the services, which provided virtually the same channels already available free over the airwaves, as a high-tech antenna. Consequently, cable sold best where existing reception was poor.

Finally in the late 1960s, cable became more attractive due to the efforts of a handful of pioneering franchise owners to develop distinctive programming alternatives. Two of these entrepreneurs, Charles Dolan and John Malone, built up cable networks and made names for themselves as media moguls. Because of their early pioneering attempts to build up media distribution infrastructure, today they are also pivotal figures in the race to convergence. Their cable companies possess the vital coaxial link to households over which television, telephony, data, and Internet will be pumped.

Charles Dolan

Charles Dolan is one of the mavericks of cable television. He got into cable early, winning the franchise for lower Manhattan in 1965. The early years were hard. Customers were eager for the improved reception Dolan could offer, but his underfunded Manhattan Cable Television could not keep pace with demand, struggling to wire the city.

Strapped for cash in the late 1960s, Dolan sold stock in Manhattan Cable to the public, a move that kept his system going and gave him the capital to develop the unique programming concepts. His company eventually would provide the model for cable programming. Time Inc. saw the promise of Dolan's model and bought control of Manhattan Cable in the early 1970s.

However, Dolan was an entrepreneur at heart and was not prepared to be folded into the growing Time cable empire. He instead swapped his remaining 20 percent of Manhattan Cable for a handful of Long Island cable systems that Time was willing to off-load.

Over the next twenty-five years, using a three-pronged approach, Dolan built his minor beachhead in the lucrative New York suburbs into the nation's sixth-largest cable company with more than 2.5 million subscribers. First, during the late 1970s and early 1980s, he plunged headfirst into the heated bidding wars that developed for potentially lucrative urban and suburban cable franchises. Cablevision eventually won a number of spots such as

Boston, but only after committing to provide state-of-the-art services at rock-bottom prices.

Second, Dolan had a creative flair for programming. He launched the first all-sports channel featuring New York Knicks and Rangers games, as well as Home Box Office. Dolan conceived of HBO as a channel that would show unedited, commercial-free movies, for which customers would pay an added fee. Dolan's shrewd marketing and operational savvy contributed to HBO's success. He decided early on not to charge by the movie, allowing HBO to avoid the complicated technical and other problems associated with pay-per-view. He also put together a unique mix of nonmovie programming, including stand-up comedy and coverage of Wimbledon. Finally as a pioneer of the format, HBO had the leverage to negotiate favorable contracts with the studios. Notwithstanding the studios' protestations about the prices they received for broadcast rights, they had to be on HBO if they wanted to leverage their content over this additional distribution channel.

Though he ultimately lost control of HBO to Time when Time bought 100 percent of the network, Dolan still controls regional news channels as well as the Bravo arts channel and the American Movie Classics channel.

Third, Dolan recognized the consolidation trend in the industry and matched the acquisition campaigns of major competitors. Between 1980 and 1990, Cablevision spent more than $1 billion to acquire new systems, primarily on Long Island, where it built one of the largest contiguous networks of cable systems in the country. By clustering franchises, Dolan gained marketing clout and efficiency.

In 1994, Dolan made another major move, joining with ITT Corporation to buy Madison Square Garden—which owns the MSG Sports Channel, the NBA Knicks, and the NHL Rangers—for just over $1 billion. Two years later, Dolan agreed to acquire full ownership of the Garden from ITT, which came under pressure to sell assets as a result of Hilton Hotels' hostile bid.

In recent years, Dolan himself has come under some pressure. Cablevision—along with other cable companies—has been punished in the market for its steep debt burden, continuing losses, and large capital needs. In an effort to appease outsiders, the company has been pruning about 400,000 noncore subscribers to reduce debt. However, beyond that, Dolan responds that he is doing what he always has—building a valuable asset base on the foundation of strong programming. And, in fact, lately cable has bounced back.

Dolan's stubbornness is admirable, but may have cost shareholders a short-term financial opportunity. At the height of the 1994 frenzy brought on by the Bell Atlantic–TCI deal, Dolan opened talks with a number of potential acquirers. However, Dolan decided against going forward and was rumored to have turned down a bid of $120 per share. Subsequently, Cablevision traded as low as $27 per share before bouncing back.

But Dolan understands the benefits of the long-term view: His experience with Time taught him the value of retaining voting control over his company. Though he took Cablevision Systems public in the 1980s, Dolan retained a slug of supervoting stock entitled to ten votes per share. Today, he controls more than 80 percent of the Cablevision votes, effectively shielding Cablevision from hostile takeover.

His son Jim Dolan recently was appointed CEO of the company and in 1999 closed the purchase of sixteen Loews theaters in New York City for $87.5 million. Today Cablevision also provides local phone service to customers on Long Island and holds a stake in Internet service At Home, controlled by AT&T.

Even with the promise of HBO, cable continued to limp along for a number of years. Then, in 1975, the world changed when RCA launched its SatCom 1 satellite into orbit. By leasing satellite time from

RCA, HBO gained an instant nationwide distribution system. Cable operators could pick the HBO signal out of the sky with satellite dishes and pipe the channel to customers. Suddenly cable had become more than just an expensive antenna. As would happen countless times in the future, content would drive the value of the distribution channel.

As cable became more attractive, the competitive landscape shifted. The value of franchises increased and cable entrepreneurs found themselves competing against larger, more established companies. A number of aggressive companies raced to lock up rights to the remaining unfranchised territories, potentially quite lucrative areas including non-Manhattan New York City, Boston, Washington, Chicago, among other major cities. Sparked by a gold-in-the-streets mentality, the ranks of cable companies boomed in the late 1970s. When the actual building—as opposed to bidding—process began, it became apparent that success was less sure than had been expected. In the rush to grab territory, companies promised municipalities cutting-edge service at bargain prices.

These wild promises would later come to haunt many companies after they won the franchise. Competition from free broadcasters was strong and capital costs steep, particularly where operators pledged to provide then-state-of-the-art two-way interactive systems and other new technologies. For example, Warner Amex Cable, a joint venture between Warner Communications and American Express, found tough going in many of the markets it entered. The partners sunk more than $100 million into building an interactive system only to face low subscriber interest.

A consolidation wave ensued as stronger competitors bought up the weak—a pattern not unique to cable. Rather than struggle with the losses and headaches of building systems, some companies sold out entirely. Others simply narrowed their focus. For example, Warner Amex Cable brought in new management, sold off a number of systems, and raised cash by selling part of its interest in MTV: Music Television.

Meanwhile, several stronger cable companies thrived on the opportunities presented by this first-generation Darwinian shakeout. Time Inc., Cox, and Continental Cablevision all continued to be acquirers of systems; John Malone and TCI evolved into the most aggressive buyers.

By the early 1980s, TCI was already an established player in the cable business, having grown to become the nation's third-largest cable provider based on subscribers. However, Malone and TCI operated mostly below the radar in those early years. Perhaps because the company had been through a near-death experience in the early 1970s, Malone steered clear of the top-dollar bidding wars for new urban systems. Instead, he bought up old established rural systems, primarily twelve-channel, which he ran on a shoestring.

At the time, skeptics questioned Malone's approach. Multichannel, interactive systems were seen as the wave of the future, and TCI arguably risked alienating municipalities with its cash-harvesting tactic. Yet TCI's strong cash flow left it in a position to buy new systems and pick up the pieces when other operators stumbled. Following this strategy, TCI grew from just over 700,000 subscribers in 1978 to more than 2.7 million in 1983, becoming the nation's largest cable system operator.

PROFILE

John Malone—The Early Years

John Malone has been called the King of Cable, Darth Vader, and the Godfather of the Cable Cosa Nostra. An engineering Ph.D., Malone began his career as a consultant for McKinsey & Co., after which he moved to a subsidiary of General Instrument, a supplier of electronics to cable systems. In those days, most cable entrepreneurs were building systems on shoestring budgets. Malone stuck by them and earned their loyalty.

One operator in particular was quite taken with the young Malone. In 1973, Bob Magness, a former Texas rancher and the head and founder of TCI, hired Malone to run the company. Legend had it that he sold some of his cattle to build his first cable system. Since its inception in 1956, Magness had strung together operations in small towns across the West.

Magness' decision to hire Malone was a near-desperation move. TCI had raised some capital by going public in 1970, but the bulk of its financing came from borrowed money. While Magness had hoped to pay down some of the debt with another stock offering, the market for cable stocks crashed in 1972. When the thirty-two-year-old Malone joined TCI, the company was on the brink, in danger of defaulting on millions of dollars in loans.

Malone earned his reputation as a tough negotiator in those early days. Not long after joining TCI, Malone called the company's creditors to a meeting and issued an ultimatum. Either the creditors would back off or they could have the company. The brinkmanship paid off, giving TCI a measure of breathing room. Still, over the next several years, Malone continually fought a rearguard action against TCI's creditors.

At the same time, Malone struggled against local officials in a number of the communities served by TCI. For example, the city council of Vail, Colorado, wanted TCI to upgrade its service but was unwilling to let TCI boost rates to pay for the upgrade. Malone's tough competitive streak showed again. Over a weekend, he cut all cable service to the town and instead ran the mayor's phone number on the blank screen. The city capitulated.

By 1977, Malone *had* turned the company around to generate positive cash flow. A group of institutions loaned the company $77 million, and Malone was turned loose to build TCI. Like Magness, Malone had little concern for positive book earnings, which translated into a positive income tax liability. He instead focused on growing the asset base, capturing new franchises, and adding market share.

Malone avoided the franchise bidding wars of the late 1970s,

in which competitors promised to plant thousands of trees or provide ultra-high-tech service. Instead, he continued to build TCI's
cash flow and waited for the shakeout.

When values came down, Malone and TCI were waiting to pick
up the pieces. In 1984, Malone jumped into the high-density
urban and suburban franchises with a $93 million purchase of the
Pittsburgh system from the ailing Warner Amex partnership. However, Malone did not relax his disciplined operating philosophy.

Before taking over in Pittsburgh, TCI extracted concessions
from the city. TCI would not be held to Warner Amex's promises of
interactive service and would instead provide a basic system.

Though Malone had not made it onto the front pages, by the
mid-1980s, he was the recognized industry trendsetter. Magness
gave Malone the freedom to manage TCI and acquired a significant chunk of equity in the business. Further, with supervoting
stock in the hands of Magness and Malone, the two men were
free to set TCI's agenda with little concern for potential raiders.

Malone's shift to a high-density urban acquisition strategy
came at an opportune time. When the expensive realities of
building systems became apparent, cable companies began lobbying Congress for help. In October 1984, the politicians responded with a federal cable law, causing the cable landscape to
change dramatically for the better: The legislation deregulated
cable rates and restricted the ability of municipalities to revoke
systems. Basic cable rates were allowed to rise by 5 percent both
in 1985 and 1986, and, in areas covered by at least three broadcast channels, could charge whatever the market would bear
starting in 1987. Local television stations and telephone companies were barred from franchise ownership. However, after intense lobbying, newspapers managed to have removed from the
bill a provision barring their ownership of cable assets.

The 1984 Cable Act represented nothing less than a tectonic shift in the strategic landscape for cable. Higher basic cable rates meant more cash flow, and more cash flow meant increased cable values. Overnight, systems that had been trading at between $800 and $900 per subscriber now brought an additional $100 to $150 per subscriber. At the same time, the capital needs of cable companies tailed off as they completed their initial build-outs. Between 1985 and 1988, cable system prices zoomed from $1,600 per subscriber to $2,700.

But the higher prices did not dampen interest in cable. In fact, the 1984 Cable Act only accelerated the consolidation trend as the future of cable began to look somewhat brighter. The established cable companies captured most of the large deals; other players also elbowed for positions—mainly newspapers and financial buyers.

For the newspaper companies, the writing had been on the wall for a number of years. Their industry was in a long, slow decline. Even before the 1984 Cable Act, several newspaper companies had moved into cable television in a search for growth opportunities. The Times Mirror Company and the Tribune Company each had significant cable assets already. And with the passage of the Cable Act, the question of the legality of overlapping cable and newspaper ownership was resolved in the papers' favor.

The Washington Post Company promptly bought into cable, paying $350 million for Capital Cities' cable assets. Other papers added systems to their portfolios as well. However, as prices escalated, not all papers remained committed to the medium. The Tribune Company, for example, chose instead to build up its television station portfolio and therefore was required to sell off its systems in 1985. At the time FCC regulations barred cross ownership of cable, newspaper, and broadcast properties in the same area.

Cable's strong and growing cash flows also attracted the interest of financial buyers, despite the fact that cable and broadcasting companies lacked the features of a prototypical LBO candidate. Far afield from steady manufacturing companies or conglomerates with little debt, most cable companies already were significantly leveraged and were trading at healthy multiples to existing cash flows. But cable companies had great potential. These deals, however, were financial plays, not strategic plays, undertaken with a shorter-term exit strategy in mind. Consequently, in the 1990s, LBO shops have not played a significant role in the movement toward convergence.

With cable, as in other areas, KKR was a pioneer in the 1980s. Kravis and Roberts were convinced the growing cable cash flows could support the additional debt necessary to fund a purchase. Further, cable depended on subscriber payments instead of advertising revenues for cash flow and therefore seemed less susceptible to a downturn in a recession. Financial buyers also saw high valuations on the horizon for cable. They proved right: Most were able to sell their cable assets within a few years of purchasing them for a very healthy return.

KKR got its first taste of the cable business in 1984, with the purchase of a midsized conglomerate called Wometco Enterprises. Hidden among its Japanese wax museum, Miami aquatic park, vending machines, and food service operations were a pair of crown jewels— television stations and cable systems, primarily in the Southeast. KKR bought the whole package for just over $1 billion and sold everything but these two pieces. Two years later, tempted by soaring cable values, KKR put Wometco's franchises on the market. The Robert M. Bass Group, another financial buyer, bought the properties for $620 million—a stunning $1,800 per subscriber. In 1988, favorable cable valuations induced Bass to sell Wometco.

But the Wometco experience only whetted KKR's appetite for cable assets. Already by 1985, the firm had confirmed the validity of its cable strategy and was ready to make a larger purchase. The opportunity came in March of that year. A company called Storer Communications, an operator of TV stations and cable systems, was under pressure from a group of insurgent shareholders and was looking for a white knight.

KKR—in alliance with management—stepped forward with a winning $2.5 billion LBO bid. As with Wometco, KKR put Storer on the market again approximately two years later, in 1987.

Over the next several years, the value of cable distribution capacity continued to escalate and other buyers followed KKR into the cable business. In 1987, Summer Redstone made his $3.4 billion acquisition of Viacom, which included the nation's tenth-largest cable system as well as cable channels Showtime and MTV, five TV and eight radio stations. He would later grow the company into an integrated media empire. The same year Canadian entrepreneur Jack Kent Cooke, owner of the Washington Redskins and real estate interests, and an early cable investor, returned to the business with his $790 million purchase of Craig McCaw's cable assets, which he turned around in 1988.

Despite all the active consolidation activity, there was no shortage of systems on the market, especially because a number of operators continued to struggle with the high debt burdens and low earnings. For example, battling to remake itself from a lumbering conglomerate, Westinghouse put its Group W cable business on the market in 1985. Heritage Communications, a midsized independent operator, raced to find a white knight in 1987 as hostile raiders circled.

Rather, the problem for buyers was the escalating cost of acquisitions. As the industry consolidated and the smaller operators combined, the host of midsized players grew, reducing the ranks of inexpensive targets. While these midsized operators still were not large enough to possess the financial capacity or the desire to build a large-scale subscriber base, their size was however sufficient to preclude a single acquirer from digesting them whole. Moreover, these targets often owned a dispersed group of systems that did not fit with a single acquirer's existing clusters.

As a natural outgrowth of these concerns, a slew of bidding consortiums developed in which two or more of the majors would band together to purchase another operator. Each of the major deals sparked a bidding war between rival consortiums. The unit then would be operated jointly, or more often, split into pieces. In this manner, consortiums captured almost all the major properties on the market. Time, TCI, and Comcast won the Group W systems in 1985 for $1.6 billion. TCI and Comcast worked together again in their 1988 purchase of Storer's cable operations from KKR for another $1.6 billion. InterMedia Partners, TCI, and several regional operators eventually convinced Cooke to sell, but only after Cooke broke off an earlier agreement as prices continued to escalate. The combined purchase price was roughly $1.6 billion.

However, not all the big deals went to multiple parties. The larger operators also acted alone to buy up choice systems. For example, Alan Gerry's Cablevision Industries snapped up part of Wometco cable in 1988, giving Robert Bass a healthy profit on the former KKR properties. And in addition to its participation in the Group W Storer and Cooke acquisitions, TCI also did many deals alone, remaining the most aggressive purchaser in the market. After three years as a suitor, TCI bought control of United Artists Communications in 1985. The company—unrelated to the movie studio of the same name—owned the nation's largest theater chain of 2,000 screens and cable systems with 750,000 subscribers. Then, in 1987, Malone agreed to the $1.3 billion acquisition of Heritage.

FEEDING THE ALLIGATOR

Building a cable empire in the 1980s was like feeding a cash alligator. Franchises had to be won, systems built, acquisitions funded. Slow growth was not an option in the world of cable consolidation, as plum franchises were being snatched off the market month by month. While the big players had leverage to negotiate with content providers and hammer down marketing costs, other companies that failed to act feared they would be left without the scale to survive and prosper. Cash was the oxygen that kept the whole process going.

In addition to stock issuances, the high-yield market raised roughly $8 billion for TCI, Viacom, and Cablevision Systems. Weighed down by massive interest payments and huge capital expenditures that generated noncash depreciation expense, cable companies like TCI and Cablevision reported accounting losses for years.

However, the salesmanship and hustle of the cable entrepreneurs convinced investors to value cable companies not on the prevailing earnings-per-share model, but based on earnings before interest, taxes, depreciation, and amortization (EBITDA). The argument was twofold. First, using EBITDA as a yardstick was appropriate because the figure looks past a company's debt burden, allowing investors to focus on the fundamental issue of operating performance, and leaving high-debt operators the flexibility to grow. Second, an EBITDA approach strips away depreciation expenses, allowing examination of a company's ability to survive as an operating business. The theory was that, for cable companies, with their large capital needs, annual depreciation charges obscured a prodigious cash-generating potential. Eventually, these two arguments stuck, and cable investors became accustomed to looking at companies on a basis considered to be a proxy for a cash flow.

The high-debt financing model prevalent among cable companies resulted in a debt-to-equity ratio in the range of seven or eight to one: Roughly 15 to 20 percent of the value of a company belonged to stockholders and the remainder to creditors. This leverage ratio left little margin for error. Consequently, cable company stock prices were quite volatile and fluctuated widely with changes in perceptions regarding cable's future. The high-debt, low-earnings financing model also caused valuation problems for large diversified public companies with interests in cable, such as Time Inc., Westinghouse, and American Express.

But the hot market for cable properties came to a screeching halt in 1989, as continuing cable rate increases generated a groundswell of consumer discontent, and rumors swirled in Washington of re-regulation. In this environment, cable providers were unable to raise the funding necessary to buy new properties and thus saw a steep decline in cable values. For the next several years, virtually no deals of significance took place. Properties that might before have fetched 15 to 18 times cash flow (i.e., EBITDA) were priced in the 7 to 12 times range.

The great cable consolidation of the 1980s left a handful of multiple-system operators in control of a large chunk of the market. TCI's continuing acquisition frenzy sealed its status as the nation's largest cable operator, with more than 10 million subscribers as of June 1991. The next four largest operators were Time Warner with 6.6 million subscribers, Continental Cablevision with 2.8 million, Comcast with 1.7 million, and Cox with 1.6 million. Together, the top five operators controlled 44 percent of the nation's 51.6 million sub-scribers. These and other operators presided over a relatively mature, developed national cable system. It is this infrastructure that, in the late 1990s, would provide the backbone for convergence—a move-ment that would propel the second wave of deals involving both cable companies and phone systems.

Still on the Air

As cable consolidated, a separate set of entrepreneurs aimed to capture control over the distribution channels of radio and TV. This race was largely a 1980s phenomenon, because before the 1980s, reg-ulations severely limited the number of radio and TV stations a sin-gle company or individual could own.

In 1981, the FCC raised the maximum number of radio stations a single company could own from seven AM and seven FM stations to twelve each. The FCC similarly revised the television ownership rules in 1984 to permit a single company to own twelve stations, up from the previous seven, so long as their signals reached 25 percent or fewer U.S. homes. In addition, the commission indicated it would not use the requirement that it approve changes in station ownership to stand in the way of takeovers.

The rush of radio and TV deals also coincided with the rise of financial buyers and the new appreciation of the importance of cash flow versus earnings. Broadcasting had for years been an extremely cash-generative business capable of supporting significant leverage, a quality long overlooked because of the market's focus on earnings. However, private investors who understood the importance of cash flow began accumulating broadcasting assets in the 1970s; in the late 1970s and early 1980s, financial buyers entered the fray, encouraged by KKR's success with Wometco and Storer. As the strength of the station business became apparent, banks and other lenders reversed their longtime aversion to loaning money against broadcast assets.

Driven by these factors, separate but related waves of radio and television deals swept the markets, each hitting full stride a few years after the FCC acted. In 1985, 1,558 radio stations changed hands for a total consideration of $1.4 billion. The prior year, 782 properties were sold for $977 million. This deal flow compared to annual volume in the low $100 millions during the 1970s. New technologies, such as Sony's Walkman, expanded audiences and contributed to the booming prices and volume of deals.

With new freedom to operate, a new generation of radio operators emerged. Mel Karmazin of Infinity Broadcasting was one of the more successful players. In 1981, after eleven years working for John Kluge at Metromedia, Karmazin jumped ship to Infinity, a company founded by two former Metromedia executives but which owned just three stations. Karmazin was given the top spot, along with a slug of stock options.

Over the next five years, following Karmazin's thesis, Infinity bought up top stations in major cities. He wasn't shy about paying top dollar: $70 million for New York's all-sports WFAN-AM station and $116 million for a Los Angeles oldies station. Once Infinity acquired the stations, Karmazin emphasized distinctive programming, buying exclusive rights to air sporting events and backing popular shock jocks like Howard Stern and Don Imus.

The Karmazin strategy played well in the market. Following his mentor's pattern, Karmazin took Infinity public in 1986, led a leveraged buyout in 1988, and finally a second public stock offering in 1992. Shareholders prospered immensely along the way, as did Karmazin and his management team. When radio ownership laws were relaxed further in 1996, Karmazin was eager to buy CBS's radio stations, but then-CEO Michael Jordan was not a seller. In the end, Karmazin ended up selling Infinity to CBS for $4.9 billion, with the agreement that Karmazin would run CBS's radio group. Karmazin became CEO in 1998. In 1999, he merged CBS with Viacom.

PROFILE

Mel Karmazin

Mel Karmazin's story is a reflection of the American dream. His radio career began in 1967, when he took a job as an ad salesman at WCBS. Almost immediately, Karmazin was highly successful, earning so much in commissions that the studio tried to cap his compensation, a betrayal which induced Karmazin to jump ship to John Kluge's Metromedia in 1970. There he transformed the company's WNEW-FM into a highly popular classic rock station. After spending eleven years at Metromedia, Karmazin was ultimately wooed away by two former Metromedia executives who formed Infinity Broadcasting.

Karmazin was given responsibility for running CBS's radio operations after selling Infinity Broadcasting to CBS in 1997. But gradually, he began to steal control of the entire company from then-CEO Michael Jordan. His background as an ad salesman has caused him to focus his energies on CBS's advertising efforts. Karmazin set high standards for the company's advertising sales force and slashed costs. He more than doubled the number of advertising salespeople. A plaque that says "No Excuses" sits on his desk. But despite his hands-on approach to advertising sales, Karmazin has taken a decidedly hands-off approach to programming, leaving the respected Les Moonves to fill that role.

When he formally took over CBS from Michael Jordan, Karmazin acquired a lagging operation. The CBS network commands the lowest advertising rates of the big three and has the least-favorable viewer demographics. The news and sports operations are struggling. Indeed, Karmazin has his work cut out for him, but the markets have given him the benefit of the doubt and afforded him a strong currency to effect a merger of equals with Viacom.

Tom Hicks, through his buyout firm Hicks, Muse, Tate & Furst, has also been an aggressive acquirer of radio stations. Hicks, Muse built up Capstar Broadcasting and Chancellor Media into two leading radio operators and merged them in 1998 to become the largest radio concern in the U.S. The company went through a period of management and strategic dislocation. Tom Hicks himself took on the CEO mantle and renamed the company AMFM Inc. In October 1999, Clear Channel, another major radio operator, agreed to acquire AMFM Inc., for $23.5 billion in stock and debt assumed. The combined company will own 830 U.S. and 240 foreign radio stations, 19 TV stations, and a significant billboard business. Since 1996, from thousands of small, independent owner-operators, the U.S. radio industry has consolidated into two major players, Infinity Broadcasting and Clear Channel.

With the notable exception of the Clear Channel–AMFM Inc. deal, television deals have had a higher profile than radio deals, however, because more money is involved and the properties are more visible. KKR closed an early big deal in 1983 with its $280 million purchase of Golden West Television. Just two years later, in a dramatic turn of events, it sold Golden West's single station—KTLA in Los Angeles—to the Tribune Company for $510 million. In all, $1 billion of station deals were closed in 1984, $12.8 billion in 1985 and another $3.5 billion in 1986.

Many of the deals in the 1980s involved independent stations, stations unaffiliated with a network and often using lower-power UHF signals. These stations, which had been relatively cheap before the age of strong cable systems, were brought to a wider audience and made far more attractive by the advent of cable. Major examples include the KTLA sale and Westinghouse's $313 million purchase of another independent Los Angeles station from RKO.

Rupert Murdoch's $2 billion purchase of John Kluge's seven independent Metromedia stations was the blockbuster television station deal of the 1980s. That Murdoch was able immediately to resell the Boston station to Hearst Corp. for $450 million indicated the growing value of television assets.

Murdoch's move was backed by a strong strategic vision: His six new stations were to be the foundation for a fourth television network. With the help of Barry Diller, Murdoch hoped to build his newly acquired Twentieth Century Fox film studio into a television powerhouse as well.

Though Karmazin's and Murdoch's moves worked out for their respective companies, prices eventually reached an unsustainable level. A number of station deals—both radio and television—fell apart. Storer Television was one of the more prominent failures. In 1987, KKR sold the Storer stations to an entity controlled by investor George Gillett Jr. for $1.3 billion, which, at roughly 15 times 1988 cash flow, was fully priced. KKR received $1 billion in cash from the deal and also kept a 45 percent ownership interest in the stations. But very quickly, it became clear that Gillett had assumed more debt than the stations could bear. The company eventually collapsed into bankruptcy, only to be bought by Ronald Perelman, who in turn sold the Storer stations to Murdoch. Yet even with the loss on Storer Television's bankruptcy, KKR's fund showed a roughly 60 percent annual gain on its original Storer acquisition, taking into account the sale of the company's cable properties and the $1 billion from the 1987 station transaction.

Strong, well-managed companies like Infinity and Murdoch's News Corporation weathered the recession with little difficulty. They emerged in the 1990s healthy and well poised for the coming convergence.

Retail Media Distribution

The commercialization of the videocassette—first developed in the 1970s—opened another new distribution channel for content and changed the economics of the movie business.

When the Supreme Court ruled in 1984 that the taping of programs from television for personal use was not a copyright violation, the studios began to release movies to video before putting them on television so as to stimulate video rentals. This new rental market was a huge shot in the arm for movie producers: In 1987, over $3 billion of the roughly $8 billion in studio revenues were attributed to cassettes.

The videocassette boom also created a whole new retail industry. When Wayne Huizenga and his partners bought Blockbuster in 1987 for $19 million, the company had nineteen stores in a highly fragmented industry. Three years later, Blockbuster had more than 1,000 units nationwide. The chain's signature was large, well-lit stores with 7,000 titles, many more than the mom-and-pop competition. Customers loved the format. But Huizenga did not just rely on organic growth: He went on an acquisition spree, picking up ten separate video chains and Blockbuster's largest franchisee.

Huizenga eventually sold Blockbuster to Sumner Redstone's Viacom in the midst of the Paramount battle for $8.4 billion. Soon after the sale, it seemed that video stores were approaching maturity, with slower growth on the horizon. But Viacom subsequently turned the chain around, negotiating a contract with studios whereby Blockbuster would purchase video for a fraction of the price it had paid before (between $3 and $8 versus $65 and $80 before) and in return would share 40 percent of its revenues with the studios. In this way, Blockbuster was able to guarantee renters that videos would be available, boosting customer satisfaction and revenues. Reflecting this success, Sumner Redstone initiated a public offering of Blockbuster that took place in August 1999.

Similar developments swept the music business in the mid-1980s. The new digital compact disc players flew off the shelves and baby boomers rushed to replace old LPs and cassettes with the state-of-the-art medium.

The new passion for compact discs was manna for the music business. The Big Six music companies converted large parts of their music libraries to CD and began releasing new albums on this platform. With a higher retail price and fatter margins than records or cassettes, the companies enjoyed rising revenues and profits. A near-euphoria set in.

While the new DVD format for video and music is still in its infancy, it could have the same impact for the retail industry as the CD and the videocassette.

Thus, by the end of the 1980s, the media distribution channels—cable, radio, TV, and recordings—had, through their own separate trajectories, matured and been consolidated.

Satellite Television

The 1990s ushered in a new competitor to cable: satellite TV. The new satellite technology, while still in its infancy, could soon threaten cable's dominance. Satellite dishes provide customers with access to a wider variety of channels and better reception than traditional cable service. Major players in the satellite TV avenue include Echostar, DirectTV, and Primestar and BSkyB in Britain. Generally the services require users to buy a satellite dish and a set-top box—about a $500 purchase—to gain access to satellite broadcasts. Primestar customers, however, lease rather than buy equipment.

Following in the footsteps of the cable industry, the satellite TV players have also begun to combine. In January 1999, Hughes announced its $1.8 billion acquisition of Primestar, which it will combine with its DirectTV. This follows closely on the heels of its December 1998 agreement to purchase U.S. Satellite Broadcasting, a provider of satellite TV channels, for $1.3 billion. The deal will make DirectTV the third-largest subscriber TV service behind TCI and Time Warner Cable. While currently satellite TV subscribers in the United States are primarily "tech-savvy individuals," the technology is sure to gain more widespread acceptance as time goes on.

The Battle for Content

The distribution side of the media business churned throughout the 1980s, altering the balance between the supply and demand of media content. Now these new distribution channels had to be fed with product. Where a regimented marketplace had once existed, chaos prevailed. Opportunities developed over a short period, and the rewards went to companies able to bring inventive, creative product to market. Meanwhile, the value of proven content providers skyrocketed and a decade-long bidding war for control began.

The studio wars commenced with the carving up of the old Twentieth Century Fox, the maker of *Star Wars*. Oilman Marvin Davis was intrigued by the turmoil at Fox, as its top executives publicly feuded with each other, and rumors circulated of an attempted bid by Saul Steinberg's Reliance Group. Davis liked the studio's collection of assets—a Coca-Cola bottler, prime real estate in Los Angeles, Pebble Beach, and Aspen, television stations, and the movie studio. He and his partners bought the studio for $724 million, funding the acquisition largely with debt.

Over the next several years, Davis sold off television stations and spun off some of its real estate, both reducing debt and recovering most of his equity investment. However, the studio had failed to release a major blockbuster in some time and was struggling under its still-significant debt burden. Hoping to turn things around, Davis lured Barry Diller from Paramount. Meanwhile, Saul Steinberg, spurned by Fox, focused on Disney.

Though it may be hard to imagine today, in 1984, Disney was a company in decline. Yet even with its problems, the Walt Disney Company possessed a fabulous group of assets: In addition to its theme parks and movie studios, the company owned large blocks of California and Florida real estate.

Steinberg saw his opportunity when Roy Disney, son of the company's co-founder, resigned from the board in a protest over the strategic de-emphasis of animation and films. A group of investors led by Steinberg amassed an 11 percent stake in the company and launched a hostile tender offer; but Disney greenmailed the group, paying $325 million for the block of stock. Steinberg netted around $60 million on the investment, though he later returned a portion of that to settle a lawsuit filed by Disney shareholders.

Steinberg's withdrawal had predictable consequences. Disney's stock price deflated, falling as low as $45 a share; institutional investors and arbitrageurs carped. A month later, Disney management found another insurgent at its doorstep: Investor Irwin Jacobs acquired his own block of stock and began a takeover campaign. Jacobs pledged not to sell his stock back to Disney.

The Disney board responded by firing Disney's president and chief executive and recruiting Michael Eisner, who worked under Diller at Paramount, for the top job. He brought with him a Hollywood dream team including Frank Wells and Jeffrey Katzenberg, giving Disney a refurbished credibility. Furthermore, the Bass brothers of Texas, who already held a big chunk of Disney stock, agreed to increase their stake to 25 percent on a friendly basis, buying out Jacobs at a profit and agreeing not to increase their stake any further. With the Basses supporting Eisner and a newly announced stock buyback plan, Disney had defended the Magic Kingdom.

Strategic Buyers Nibble

Strategic buyers also began to shop for content in the early 1980s. One of the earliest high-profile deals came in 1982, when Coke acquired Columbia Pictures, seeing entertainment as a growth area. Coke's $692 million friendly deal was greeted with jeers on Wall Street, because it was bucking the growing pure-play trend in favor of diversification. Yet Chairman Roberto Goizueta did a great deal to silence his critics. He set the bar for Coke's new entertainment sector high, targeting 20 percent annual growth—and Columbia delivered. The studio then spent $750 million to acquire Norman Lear's Embassy Communications and Merv Griffin Enterprises. Despite weak creative output on the movie side, these strong television operations and the videocassette boom propelled Columbia to returns above 30 percent in Coke's first three years of ownership.

Australian Rupert Murdoch, whose News Corporation controls publishing assets in Australia and Great Britain, made his first attempt to expand into the electronic media in 1983 with an offer for Warner Communications. At the time, Warner Communications was reeling from $1 billion losses at its acquired Atari division. But the company's other interests—a studio, a record label, a publishing company, and the cable television joint venture with American Express—were more attractive. Unfortunately for Murdoch, Warner chairman Steve Ross refused to sell.

Ross was a survivor. He had built up Warner's collection of world-class media assets over twenty-five years, starting from a collection of funeral parlors and parking lots. Though Ross owned less than 1 percent of Warner, he was unwilling to capitulate. Like Disney, he

brought in a friend as his protector—Herbert Siegel's Chris-Craft Industries—with which Warner swapped assets. When Siegel ended
up with more than 25 percent of Warner's stock, Murdoch gave up
the battle, his dream of building an integrated international media
empire deferred. Ironically, Ross would spend the next five years
bickering with Siegel over how to manage Warner.

In 1985, the escalating value of content became abundantly clear
with Ted Turner's $1.5 billion acquisition of MGM/UA from investor
Kirk Kerkorian. Initially, Turner hoped to keep both the MGM film
library and the studio itself; however, troubles with financing led
Turner to sell all but the film library back to Kerkorian and another
group. So, in the end, Turner paid more than $1 billion for a library
of over 3,000 films.

PROFILE

Kirk Kerkorian

Kirk Kerkorian is a folksy, charming man with a commonsense investment approach. Working with a small group of trusted advisers, he controls a multibillion-dollar portfolio of investments from
his Las Vegas headquarters. The soft-spoken Kerkorian keeps a
remarkably low profile but is incredibly focused. While he was in
the news most visibly as a result of his activist investment in
Chrysler, he nonetheless remains more interested in the bottom
line than in headlines.

Kerkorian has a long history of involvement with the movie
business. However, he made his first fortune from an airline—a
charter business he started after World War II. After cashing in on
the Las Vegas gambling boom, Kerkorian sold the tiny airline—
which flew gamblers to Vegas in DC-3s—in 1968 for $107 million.

The next year, Kerkorian invested some of this cash in Western
Airlines and began a turnaround effort; but he soon became more

interested in the hotel and movie business. He announced a tender offer for 17 percent of MGM in July 1969 and took control of the board. One of his first steps was to reduce the studio's production schedule to four films a year.

Over the next twenty years, Kerkorian repeatedly shuffled the assets of MGM in an effort to maximize the studio's value, profiting along the way. He spun off the hotel group in 1978 as MGM Grand Hotels. In 1981, he acquired United Artists and raised his MGM/UA stake to 50 percent. The studio ended up a hot potato: In a surprise move, Kerkorian sold MGM/UA to Ted Turner in 1985 and appeared to exit Hollywood. But the withdrawal was short-lived: Turner kept only the movie library and sold the studio itself back to Kerkorian. In 1990, Kerkorian sold the studio again, this time to Italian Giancarlo Parretti.

But Parretti's company turned out to be built on a quicksand of bribe-induced loans and bad management. Within a few months of his taking over, MGM was in bankruptcy. Parretti's French bank forced him out and eventually installed Frank Mancuso to turn things around.

Then, in an ironic twist, Kerkorian, Mancuso, and Australia's Seven Network bought MGM from the French for the same $1.3 billion price Kerkorian had received in 1990. Though Mancuso has considerable independence in running the studio, the 1996 deal once again put Kerkorian at the heart of the market for creative content. In 1997, he and his partners completed a $600 million add-on acquisition, buying a 2,200-film library from John Kluge's Metromedia International, and then took MGM public. MGM has been struggling since, but the hope is that a joint production deal with Miramax will bolster its prospects.

The vision behind Turner's MGM deal was purely content-driven. He wanted the studio's old movies and originally hoped to have its new product as well to feed his WTBS and other cable channels. Analysts were skeptical: The Street consensus was that Turner—smarting from the CBS brush-off—had overpaid. It was a long road, but Turner proved his critics wrong.

Acquisitions of Cable Channels and TV Networks

Cable channels and TV networks serve as middlemen between content providers and distribution channels: They aggregate and package content and sell it to TV stations.

In the 1980s cable business, established brand-name channels were hot commodities. These channels had established relationships with studios and could satisfy consumers' thirst for fresh programming. By contrast, most smaller cable operators lacked the time, money, and sophistication to acquire movie rights from the studios directly. Therefore, when a major channel came on the market, buyers lined up.

Texaco's acquisition of Getty Oil triggered the first opportunity: Texaco put its sports channel asset ESPN on the block to help fund the deal, and Turner Broadcasting made a bid. However, ABC had a leg up on Turner. The network already had exercised an option to acquire 15 percent of the channel and had a right of first refusal to buy the remainder. ABC eventually paid $202 million for full ownership.

Many cable network sales were motivated by financial distress. Showtime/MTV is a notable example. Steve Ross of Warner Communications prized Warner's interest in Showtime and MTV, held through the Warner Amex cable joint venture. Unfortunately American Express wanted out of cable, and so in June 1985 agreed to sell Warner Amex to a joint venture of Time and TCI. The only way Ross could keep his prized cable assets was to exercise Warner's right of first refusal to buy American Express out. However, Ross was hemmed in as a result of the defensive measures he had taken in response to Murdoch's earlier bid: Herb Siegel of Chris-Craft didn't like the idea of purchasing more cable. Ross eventually agreed to sell off Showtime and MTV to Viacom for $100 million as a way to get the cable deal through.

Ted Turner's Turner Broadcasting was one of the most stunning cable programming successes of this period. Turner began in business at the age of twenty-four, when he took over the family billboard company after his father committed suicide. He got into television in 1970 with the purchase of a low-power Atlanta station with few prospects. Following HBO's lead, he transformed the station into WTBS and bounced its signal off satellites to local cable operators. This new "superstation" featured movies, reruns, and sports—primarily the games of Turner's Atlanta Braves and Hawks.

WTBS became extremely profitable, and its cash flow funded Turner's next bright idea: a twenty-four-hour news channel, CNN, which began operations in 1980. After five years of losses, the station turned the corner, and by 1985, Turner's two stations were the backbone of many cable systems' basic service.

Recording Companies

In music, Germany's Bertelsmann was the first mover in consolidation. The company—which already owned an interest in RCA/Arista Records—bought the remaining 75 percent from RCA in 1986. At the time, RCA Records was a down-and-out label, a money-loser, and so the $330 million purchase price prompted speculation that the Germans had been duped by their American counterparts. Within two years, however, the Germans proved the contrary. They refurbished the label, brought out a number of big hits, and used their international marketing experience to score significant sales.

Sony moved next, with the 1987 purchase of CBS Records. Again the purchase price seemed steep at the time, but soon proved cheap. In 1989, PolyGram, a subsidiary of the Dutch-based Philips Industries, followed suit with the $500 million acquisition of A&M Records. The flurry of international acquisitions left David Geffen's Geffen Records the only remaining significant independent U.S.

record company. A year later, the 1980s consolidation was completed. Geffen sold out to MCA in a $545 million stock deal, leaving just six multinationals largely in control of the music business: Time Warner, MCA, Bertelsmann, Sony, Thorn-EMI, and Philips.

In the 1990s, consolidation would once again pick up however. In 1997, Edgar Bronfman Jr.'s Seagram purchased MCA, and in 1998 purchased Polygram from Philips. In these two transactions, Bronfman created the largest record company in the world.

Vertical Integration

The parallel courses of the development of media distribution and media content began to intersect in the mid-1980s. A market consensus began to coalesce in favor of an old business model: the vertically integrated media company. With the consolidation of the various content providers and distribution channels, each was large enough to exert leverage over the other. Vertical integration would eliminate this power play between content and distribution: No longer would content suppliers be at the mercy of distribution channels, and vice versa.

Initially the trend toward vertical integration was obscured in the haze and upheaval of rapid-fire media deal flow. But Rupert Murdoch changed that in 1985 with two blockbuster transactions that created an integrated media company. First, for $250 million, News Corporation finally succeeded in breaking into Hollywood with a purchase of 50 percent of Twentieth Century Fox. Though Barry Diller had begun to turn things around at Twentieth Century Fox, the studio was still on the ropes; and rather than put more of his money into the studio, Marvin Davis agreed to sell a half interest to Murdoch. A significant chunk of the purchase price—$132 million— would go into the studio's coffers. A second deal, Murdoch's $2 billion purchase of John Kluge's seven television stations, effected the vertical integration. In this second transaction, Murdoch gained stations reaching 18 percent of the United States.

With this combination of content and distribution, Murdoch began talking about building a fourth television network. Within six months, he committed another $225 million to the vision, buying Marvin Davis out completely.

The wisdom of Murdoch's huge bet was not immediately apparent. For almost $3 billion, he had a sputtering studio with promising talent and a group of independent stations. Stitching this all together would take time. Barry Diller was the key. His content machine would turn out movies and television programs to feed the station network. While the vision was risky and ambitious, Murdoch's faith in Diller turned out to be well placed. Within a year, the studio began to rack up box office successes.

Despite early doubts about Murdoch's vision, the core logic of the vertical integration model propelled others to unite content and distribution under the same roof. Favorable placement and promotion of new releases was viewed as critical to building product, which could then be exploited in the videocassette, cable, and television distribution channels.

PROFILE

Rupert Murdoch

Rupert Murdoch, chairman of News Corporation, is a man of substance. Although demonized by some, no one can question his tenacity and imagination. He smiles a lot, but is quick to fire employees. While a student at Oxford, he boasted his own car and a bust of Lenin in his room.

Murdoch started out in his media career running the *Adelaide News,* a small paper owned by his father. He promptly fired its editor, a family friend, for waging an editorial campaign against executing an aborigine accused of murder. A few years later, he bought the British *Sun,* a trade union paper, for £250,000 and re-launched it as a tabloid. This paper, along with Murdoch's other tabloid newspapers, has gained enormous political influence. In 1988, Murdoch bought Triangle Publications, which owned a portfolio of magazines including *TV Guide*. In addition to his newspaper businesses, today Murdoch owns a movie studio, Twentieth Century Fox, and the Fox television network, as well as a global network of satellites.

The 1990s have been a new phase for Murdoch. The driving goal remains the creation of a unified global media company. As the supply of attractive media properties has dwindled, Murdoch too has focused on building new distribution and content. Some ventures have been more successful than others. The central strategic move came in late 1996, when Fox spent $2.5 billion to acquire New World Communications—with its ten Fox-affiliated stations—from Ronald Perelman. Murdoch wanted the added stations to expand the network's group of owned stations, which reached 40 percent of all homes in the United States after the deal. He also started up a Fox twenty-four-hour news channel in 1997. However, News Corporation has had difficulty finding cable operators willing to carry the Fox news channel.

Murdoch nonetheless continues to express optimism about the prospects for News Corporation, as he did during the costly start-up phase of the Fox network. Despite some setbacks, the company again has the balance sheet to weather these difficulties.

In another example of vertical integration, a number of movie studios bought into theater chains: MCA acquired 50 percent of Cineplex Odeon, Columbia bought Walter Reade, Tri-Star snagged Loews and made an abortive deal for the United Artists theaters.

Music content producers like EMI have entered distribution as well, using the Internet to reach their audience. EMI's deal with Liquid Audio will allow users to download music content from the Internet. Sony has forged a similar arrangement with Microsoft. The Internet promises to have far-reaching implications for economies of the music business.

Cable companies too began to embrace vertical integration in the mid-1980s. In the cable world, content became even more important with the deregulation of rates, as cable providers needed more channels to justify higher basic rates. Cable companies were therefore motivated to buy interests in established and developing channels.

John Malone made a major move to embrace the vertical integration model in 1987. Because Turner Broadcasting was having difficulty handling the debt from the MGM purchase, Ted Turner began shopping for an investor to provide much-needed equity. Rumors abounded that Turner would sell out to NBC or one of the other two networks. But alarmed at the prospect of having a crucial content provider in the hands of the competition, Malone, Time, and a coalition of cable providers stepped up with $563 million for a 35 percent interest in Turner Broadcasting.

The Turner investment was just a beginning for Malone and TCI. Over the next several years, TCI expanded its programming interests, with Malone eventually amassing stakes in the Discovery Channel, Black Entertainment Television, Court TV, QVC, the Family Channel, and American Movie Classics. In fact, TCI's channel portfolio grew to the point where it became a source of criticism. Competitors argued that, because new channels needed access to TCI's large subscriber base, the company unfairly used this leverage to buy interests in channels at below-market prices. Reacting to the criticism, Malone spun off TCI's programming assets as a separate company called Liberty Media in 1991. However, he remained at the head of both companies, and continues to head Liberty Media now that TCI is merged with AT&T.

Time Warner

The capstone of the 1980s vertical integration movement came in 1989 when Time and Warner Communications merged to form a $15.2 billion media company with interests in cable, movie and television production, book and magazine publishing, and the record business.

Time's executive board began to consider an expansion into the entertainment business as early as 1983. By the fall of 1987, a consensus in favor of expanding into entertainment was reached by the committee. Gerald Levin, then Time's vice chairman and chief strategist, and now chairman and CEO of Time Warner, wrote a memo to J. Richard Munro, who was then chairman and CEO of Time, in which he recommended a consolidation with Warner.

Levin's proposal rested on three considerations: First, Time wanted to control better the content provided over its cable channels, which included HBO and Cinemax; second, Time wanted to use Warner's assets as a stepping-stone to position itself for the increasing globalization of the media business; and third, Warner's key assets were simply growing faster than Time's.

We were hired as strategic advisers in Time's search for an entertainment deal. Warner became the leading candidate and negotiations began, but eventually fell apart. The sticking point was who would run the combined entity: Time's board was very concerned that any acquisition be structured to preserve Time's commitment to journalistic integrity. In essence, Time wanted to control CEO succession in the combined entity. Warner Brothers chairman Steve Ross took this as a slight and would not agree.

This temporary impasse blocked a Warner deal; so Time started to look elsewhere. However, none of these other companies were as attractive as Warner. In early 1989, Ross came around and decided to accept Time's proposed merger, perhaps motivated by a recent illness. He found Time's vision of a vertically integrated media power compelling. Time owned strong distribution assets—cable systems, HBO, book and magazine distribution. Warner also had interests in cable systems. Its primary strength, however, was in content. If Time and Warner were brought together, content from the Warner studios, record label, and publishing house could be pushed through Time's distribution channels.

The deal gathered momentum once the key governance issues were resolved with a compromise. Formally, Time and Warner would have equal board representation and the combined company would have co-CEOs: Ross and Munro initially would split duties, then Ross and Nick Nicholas, Time's CEO-designate. When Ross retired after a defined period, Nicholas would become the sole CEO. In the interim, a subcommittee of the board would be designated to govern editorial matters at Time's publications, with representatives of Time to hold a majority of the seats on this committee. This compromise opened the door, and the parties eventually agreed to a stock-for-stock merger.

Although critics subsequently charged that Steve Ross was taking over Time, in fact, Ross was fearful of dying from his recent illness and wanted to assure his legacy in the absence of an obvious successor at Warner. The deal was structured as a marriage, but the clear long-term intention was for the Time team to take over for Ross, while Warner's gifted movie division leaders, Bob Daly and Terry Semel, would continue to wield power.

To protect their deal, Time and Warner put several defensive measures in place, including an automatic share exchange that could be triggered by either company and a "no-shop" clause. Under the share exchange, Time would receive 9.4 percent of Warner's outstanding common stock and Warner would receive 11.1 percent of Time's outstanding common stock. The agreement incorporating these terms was signed, and proxies were mailed to Time shareholders, who needed to approve the merger. Their approval was expected and the deal looked to be done.

However, Martin Davis of Paramount was equally eager to get his hands on Time's assets. On June 7, 1989, just before the Time shareholders were scheduled to vote to approve the deal, Paramount announced a cash offer to purchase all Time shares for $175 per share, well above the pre-announcement price of $126.

After recovering from shock, the Time board shifted into high gear to consider the Paramount offer. The directors met on several occasions, often without management present. We then made a detailed presentation on Paramount and its offer, advising the board that Time shareholders would receive materially more than $175 per share if a full auction of the company were held. After deliberating, the board rejected Paramount's offer as inadequate.

The board next acted to preserve the Warner deal, which board members thought more attractive. Paramount responded by raising its offer for Time to $200 per share. The Time board rejected this bid too, partly because Paramount was viewed as a threat to the Time journalistic culture.

Exasperated with the actions of the Time board, Paramount and a group of Time shareholders filed suit in Delaware court. A few intense weeks of legal sparring followed. Lawyers on both sides worked around the clock to build documentary evidence. The trial was quick, and the judge ruled in favor of Time on both counts. An expedited appeal then went up to the Delaware Supreme Court, which affirmed the lower court ruling and allowed the Time-Warner deal to go forward. The gist of the ruling was that a company need not abandon a strategic merger and sell itself to the highest bidder so long as the planned merger does not constitute a change in control.

The Time-Warner deal had generated considerable criticism.

Time Warner's stock price had not performed as hoped. Adjusting for subsequent splits, Paramount's $200 a share offer amounts to $25 per current Time Warner share. While the per-share value of the offer is well below recent highs, many critics argue that because the cash offered by Paramount could have been invested in the S&P 500—which has climbed significantly since the offer—shareholders would have been better off taking the Paramount offer.

However, this decision was not the shareholders' to make: The court found that a company has no duty to sell itself when its trading value is below its sales price. Furthermore, the critics' position also ignores the fact that today's trading price is not comparable to its price at the time of the Paramount offer: The capital structure and asset mix of the company have changed since 1989. For example, Time Warner has issued many new shares in the past eight years, including the 1991 issuance of 140 million shares through a rights offering to existing shareholders. Because these shares were offered at a deep discount to the then-current stock price, the issuance heavily diluted the value of outstanding shares. This dilution was also compounded by other stock deals, including the company's 1996 acquisition of Turner Broadcasting System Inc. As evidenced by the QVC and Viacom bids for Paramount, the assets of the old Time have, in fact, appreciated with the market; but this fact is obscured because the recapitalized Time Warner is a very different and more complex company. Time Warner has assembled a premier group of assets, whose values are only now beginning to be recognized, as evidenced by its tremendous share price performance recently.

Integration Accelerates

The 1993 no-holds-barred fight for Paramount Communications ushered in a new period of large-scale vertical media combinations. By combining Viacom, Blockbuster, and Paramount, Sumner

Redstone put cable channels, television and movie production, video distribution, and publishing all under one roof—a vertically integrated media power to rival Rupert Murdoch's News Corporation. Spurned by Paramount, Diller's QVC agreed to a merger with Larry Tisch's CBS, only to have the $1.9 billion deal falter when TCI and Comcast acquired the roughly 65 percent of QVC they didn't already own.

PROFILE

Laurence Tisch

In his role as CEO of CBS, Laurence Tisch bucked every trend. Larry Tisch and his brother Robert had a long history of contrarian investments which have paid off extremely well. After inheriting a small hotel in the Catskills in the 1950s, the two picked up the Loews theater chain from MGM in 1959 when government antitrust authorities forced the studio to sell. From this base, the Tisch brothers built a small hotel and entertainment empire. Part of their genius was building hotels in Manhattan and elsewhere when others were unwilling. During the Go-Go 1960s, the Tisches diversified Loews into insurance and tobacco through CNA Financial and Lorillard, earning Larry Tisch a reputation as a sharp investor who made money bottom-fishing.

In a way, the 1986 investment in CBS was another contrarian bet. The consensus was that the networks would underperform for a number of years. Yet buying into CBS was also a dramatic shift. Controlling such a high-profile media property brought Tisch an unaccustomed level of attention.

On taking control of CBS, Tisch moved to reposition the network, slashing costs in the news division and selling off assets. Then Tisch took a page from Ted Turner's takeover plan. In December 1996, he sold the CBS music publishing business for $125 million. The magazine division went six months later in a $650 million management buyout, and Sony purchased CBS Records the following year for $2.2 billion. In a short time, Tisch had transformed CBS into a pure-play broadcasting company. He used the proceeds from asset sales to fund a $2 billion stock buyback in 1990.

At the time of each asset sale, Tisch was widely considered to have gotten beyond top dollar. The $125 million price for music publishing was a record at the time, as was the $650 million for the magazine business. But in perfect hindsight, he sold cheap. The new owners of the music publishing business resold it after three years for $337 million, management sold off the magazine business for about $1 billion within a year, and CBS Records turned in an exceptionally strong performance for Sony.

Furthermore, Tisch was subjected to unending public scrutiny of his management of CBS. Fired employees complained about being "Tisched." Staffers squealed when their expense accounts were cut. Self-anointed visionaries felt that Bill Paley's temple of media excellence was being ransacked, neglecting the fact that Paley encouraged Tisch to invest and that Tisch boosted CBS's profile by bringing in the able programmer Les Moonves. Tisch supporters would argue that he made the tough decisions necessary to groom CBS for a comeback.

In fact, the CBS investment worked out quite well for Loews, despite weak ratings at the network. After a 1994 deal to merge the network with Barry Diller's QVC home shopping company fell apart, CBS bought back another $1 billion of its stock. At this point, Loews already had recouped its investment and still owned 18 percent of the network. A year later, Westinghouse made its $5 billion deal to acquire CBS. Investors who bought CBS shares in 1986 for about $125 each ended up with proceeds of $405 if they held until 1995. Given the boom in media properties, they might have made even more if Tisch had expanded rather than contracted CBS.

> Meanwhile, Larry Tisch has returned to the large Loews em-
> pire, though a second generation of Tisches is taking a more ac-
> tive role. The family continues its disciplined investment
> philosophy, buying up disfavored assets and companies.

To a certain extent, the 1990s deal flow was sparked by the same imperatives that had prevailed in the previous decade. Yet new regulatory and technological developments defined the specific scope and dynamic of the merger market.

The geography of the content business was changed dramatically in 1995 when the FCC scrapped its financial interest and syndication, or fin/syn, rules, which since 1970 had effectively barred networks, which controlled access to 95 percent of homes, from owning studios unless they divested all interests in television production or from syndication. Starting in the early 1980s, the networks fought a running battle with the studios, trying to remove the rules. The studios, however, were not willing to give up their near-monopoly on the production of TV shows without a fight. Most disinterested observers agreed the rules made little sense in a world of cable and videocassettes. But the studios had a powerful Washington lobby. The rules came close to dying once in the 1980s until President Reagan, as a former actor, an obvious friend of Hollywood, killed the plan.

Finally in 1991, the FCC opted to relax the rules somewhat; but not pleased with the partial repeal, the networks sued in court and won. The rules were again revised in 1993, this time to repeal the fin/syn barriers completely within two years.

The removal of fin/syn, which became official in September 1995, amounted to a revolution. The networks were freed to enter the $6-billion-a-year syndication market. Talk of big network-studio mergers abounded.

The approaching footsteps of change energized the studios. Two of the big players—Time Warner's Warner Bros. and Viacom's Paramount—responded by starting their own fledgling networks. These were defensive moves designed to guarantee the studios distribution for their television product. Warner and Paramount hoped to duplicate Barry Diller's feat and create a captive distribution channel from the ground up.

The promise of network-studio mergers soon became reality. Capital Cities/ABC was the first to go in a merger with Disney. The $19 billion stock-and-cash deal, announced August 1, 1995, married one of the strongest creative talents in the media business with the number one broadcaster.

Like Rupert Murdoch's deals of 1985, the Disney-ABC merger crystallized the vertical integration strategy. The company was again a dominant entertainment power, widely hailed for its creative and marketing prowess. Michael Eisner had rejuvenated the Disney legacy. Now Eisner wanted to launch a new stage of growth.

In joining content and distribution, Eisner embraced Murdoch's model, but arguably with stronger constituent parts. When the deal was announced, ABC was the number-one-rated network. Its emphasis on family-oriented programs meshed well with Disney's focus. Disney, on the other hand, had become a programming juggernaut. Preferred access to Disney's strong slate of animated and live-action movies and television programs would give ABC an edge over the competition. Further, Disney could apply its marketing tie-in abilities to generate new viewers for the network. On the distribution side, Capital Cities also owned ten local TV stations, twenty-one radio stations, and ESPN. Disney would benefit from a guaranteed channel to distribute new television programs and other content. The network also would provide yet another outlet to promote Disney movies.

Since the Capital Cities/ABC deal closed in February 1996, press accounts of the merger have gone from glowing to skeptical. Clearly

Disney has hit some roadblocks. Ratings for ABC have dropped off considerably, and the network is fighting CBS to maintain its position.

Disney also has lost a number of top managers—the extremely capable Frank Wells, who died in a helicopter crash, Jeffrey Katzenberg, who feuded with his mentor, Eisner, and Michael Ovitz, who never integrated into the Disney system. However, the initial notion that Disney-ABC would be an overnight success was unrealistic. The broadcasting business is by nature cyclical and ABC was bound to come down from its ratings highs. Furthermore, the integration of two major media concerns just takes time. Buying ABC was the fulfillment of a dream for Eisner, but owning it has been troublesome.

Michael Eisner

When Michael Eisner joined Disney in 1984, the company was under pressure from raiders and had a $1.9 billion market capitalization. Today, the fifty-seven-year-old Eisner heads a company with a nearly $60 billion market capitalization. While the dramatic turnaround has not been without bumps along the way, Eisner is widely regarded as one of the media business's strongest CEOs.

Eisner stands out among Hollywood executives because he combines an acute sense for business with an ability to manage the creative side as well. He grew up on Manhattan's East Side, and by the time he graduated from college, had become interested in the entertainment business. A job as an NBC usher gave him a start. After spending a few years rising through the ranks at the network, Eisner sent out dozens of résumés. He ended up landing a job working for Barry Diller at ABC.

Eisner spent ten years at ABC where he and Diller drove the perennial also-ran to the top rating spot. When Diller jumped to

Paramount, Eisner followed to become president of the studio. Again, the Diller-Eisner duo worked media magic, pushing Paramount to become one of Hollywood's top performers with movies such as *Raiders of the Lost Ark* and *Saturday Night Fever.*

Diller and Eisner parted ways on leaving Paramount. Eisner wanted the freedom to run a company on his own, and the opportunity presented itself. Originally, Eisner was recruited for the number two spot at Disney but he held out for the CEO job. The company desperately needed help and gave him the offer he wanted.

In his first decade as CEO of the Magic Kingdom, Eisner avoided major acquisitions and instead focused internally. One of his first tasks was to rebuild the filmed entertainment unit, which had been lagging badly. Prior management had considered closing down the business, but Eisner and his creative team revived the operation and built it into the envy of the industry. Strong creative content was part of the story. Animated features like *The Lion King* appealed to children and families, while Touchstone and Miramax turned out more adult fare.

The content was just a first step, the raw material which propelled Disney to record earnings. Marketing was also key. Eisner's team refined the concept of marketing tie-ins to a science. For example, as *The Lion King* topped the box office in 1994, the movie also generated the number one album for the year and the best-selling video of all time. Clearly, the promise of these kinds of profitable combinations contributed to the appeal of a Disney-ABC merger.

The vertically integrated media company became the industry prototype as consolidation continued. After drawn-out negotiations, Time Warner moved even further toward this ideal with its $7.5 billion acquisition of Turner Broadcasting, a deal which grew out of Ted

Turner's frustration with the continuing role TCI and Time Warner played in his company. The two companies together owned about 40 percent of Turner Broadcasting—a legacy of the cable operators' earlier bailout—and had veto powers whereby they could block any major Turner Broadcasting deal. With their blessing, Ted Turner had managed to move TBS toward vertical integration with the purchase of two independent Hollywood studios, New Line Cinema and Castle Rock. But Turner still yearned to own a broadcast network and chafed at Time Warner's continued opposition. Starting in early 1995, he searched for a way to have Time Warner bought out.

The negotiations repeatedly hit snags. Time Warner was reluctant to sell its stock interest for cash, which would generate a large tax bite, and, in fact, hankered to control all of TBS, particularly news network CNN. The August 1995 announcement by Westinghouse that it would acquire CBS reenergized Turner. A Time Warner–TBS deal offered many of the same strategic benefits. Turner and Jerry Levin shared a similar vision, and the deal was announced in September 1995.

Over the next year, tough negotiations with John Malone and federal antitrust regulators threatened to break up the combination. Eventually though, the perseverance of Jerry Levin and Ted Turner paid off. The deal finally closed in early October 1996.

Vertical integration reached new heights by the end of 1999. Viacom and CBS agreed to merge in the largest media deal to date, combining premium content and distribution assets. The market has applauded the combination.

Vertical Integration Goes Global

The vertical integration trend also began to go global. In 1992, Sony purchased Columbia Pictures from Coke for $4.8 billion and Matsushita of Japan bought all of MCA for $7.4 billion (with assumed debt). Both deals were brokered by Hollywood agent Michael Ovitz before he joined Disney.

In movies as in music, international players were looking for content. Sony and Matsushita hoped to profit from the growing international market for American entertainment, and as equipment manufacturers, also saw strategic benefits of owning the content that consumers played on their hardware.

The idea of linking software and hardware was not new. Indeed, RCA had sold radios by setting up its NBC radio network and color televisions with NBC programs like *Bonanza*. More recently content had been critical to the videocassette recorder's success. Sony's higher-quality, higher-priced Betamax format had been an expensive flop because Sony failed to recognize the importance of the video rental business in promoting the product. When video rental stores decided to stock the cheaper VHS tapes, Sony lost the market share war. Now, Sony and Matsushita planned to use content as a source of additional marketing leverage for the introduction of new electronics.

However, the promise of this "Japanese invasion" into Hollywood has yet to be realized. Shortly after the MCA deal, Matsushita and Sony were rocked by a stock market crash that wiped out more than $2.6 trillion in value on the Tokyo Stock Exchange, along with a major recession and real estate crash. Studio chairman Lew Wasserman had agreed to sell to Matsushita partly in the hope it would provide the capital for growth and acquisitions, but the new economic realities in Japan dashed these hopes.

Matsushita's failure to back Wasserman's growth plans caused considerable friction between the parent company and MCA. Wasserman and MCA president Sidney Sheinberg pressed to buy a record company or part of a television network. However, Matsushita neither trusted Wasserman and Sheinberg to chart a strategy nor was willing to take over management directly. The feud broke into the public in 1994, deeply embarrassing Matsushita.

Sony's troubles were even more serious, as Columbia was a troubled property from the outset. Sony hired what it saw as an expert

Hollywood management team: Peter Guber, a lawyer, and Jon Peters, Barbra Streisand's former hairdresser. Sony bought their independent film company for $250 million and put them in charge of Columbia. But while Guber and Peters had produced box office hits like *Batman* and *Rain Man,* they had never run a studio and their tenure was rocky from the start. Warner Bros. sued to enforce a contract it had with the duo, and Sony was forced to settle in a deal valued by Warner at several hundred million dollars.

Guber and Peters then allegedly took advantage of their Japanese employer. They decorated lavishly and hired layers of high-priced managers. Each had a corporate jet; $175 million was spent on refurbishing the studio's Culver City lot. Most damaging, Guber and Peters made a string of expensive box office bombs like *Last Action Hero* and *Hudson Hawk.*

In November 1994, Sony accepted its black eye, then renewed its commitment to succeed with Columbia. The parent company took a $3.2 billion write-off of its Columbia investment. Guber, Peters, and their protégés were jettisoned. The next year, Nobuyuki Idei was named the new president of Sony. In an assertion of leadership, he took vigorous reins over Columbia, and hired the well-respected Howard Stringer, a former CBS executive, to head Sony's U.S. operations. He also inserted Japanese managers to play a role. John Calley became the new studio chief at Columbia.

Though Sony's Columbia investment experience was difficult, the new management team appears to have matters back on track. Columbia's box office performance has improved. Costs are coming under control, and Sony professes to remain committed to the strategic marriage of software and hardware.

Matsushita, on the other hand, chose to exit Hollywood entirely. In a way, the company was more spooked by Sony's troubles than Sony. Shortly after the Columbia write-off became public, Matsushita management decided to sell MCA to Seagram CEO Edgar Bronfman Jr., who had taken over day-to-day management of the

Canadian spirits company from his father. In the spring of 1995, Seagram announced it would sell most of the highly profitable stake in DuPont that it had received in the Conoco fight to buy 80 percent of MCA. The $5.7 billion stake valued all of MCA at over $7 billion. However, because the Japanese yen had appreciated nearly 60 percent since Matsushita's purchase, the sale triggered a significant currency loss.

Bronfman's swap of an interest in DuPont for control of MCA was a bold strategic shift, trading a large interest in chemicals and oil, the source of as much as 70 percent of Seagram's earnings, for the entertainment business. The merit of the move is not yet entirely clear. However, Bronfman has taken steps to ratchet up growth at MCA. In 1998, he bought Polygram from Philips for $10.4 billion to buttress his record business.

Wasserman and Sheinberg left MCA as part of the ownership shift. Bronfman installed Frank Biondi, brother of my partner Mike Biondi and a highly regarded professional manager who had recently parted ways with former boss Sumner Redstone, as chairman and chief executive. Under Frank Biondi's leadership, the movie and television operations were restructured across the board.

Nevertheless, in 1997, Bronfman decided he needed more help managing assets and shuffled the deck. He sold a 45 percent stake in his USA Network cable and television production operations to Barry Diller. In 1998, Seagram restructured again; Bronfman fired Biondi as well as Universal Pictures chief Casey Silver. Bronfman will take direct operating control of Universal. So far, the market has reacted favorably, with Seagram's stock price up and the implied value of its MCA stake significantly higher than the $5.7 billion invested. Nevertheless, Seagram still would have done better if it had held on to its stake in DuPont. Seagram has suffered from a string of box office flops, causing many to wonder if Bronfman's strategy is sound.

New Media and the Internet

The Internet as a media distribution channel came of age in the 1990s. Two decades ago, the Internet didn't even exist. While its predecessor—ARPANET (Advanced Research Project Agency Network)—was formed in the early 1980s by academics and the government to encourage the sharing of information, the Internet as we know it became popularized when Marc Andreessen of Netscape wrote a graphical search engine to make it easy for anyone to access this new national—now international—network. Unlike other media distribution channels, no one owns the entire Internet. Rather, the physical infrastructure of the Internet is an enormous interconnection of wires spanning the entire globe, each piece of which may be individually owned.

The Internet Age and Content

In the space of just a few years, the use of the World Wide Web has exploded. Users have been captivated by the wide array of content the Web provides in games, information, finance, chat groups, and commerce, among other things.

Commerce, because it is the most lucrative form of content, is perhaps the fastest growing area of content on the Internet: Book retailers like Amazon.com and barnesandnoble.com have created virtual stores and are doing a brisk business; home shopping is transitioning to a Web-based format.

As the Internet has evolved, thousands of new businesses have sprung up to take advantage of the revenue potential promised by the Internet. Many have already begun to combine. Internet "portals" such as Yahoo!, AltaVista, and Infoseek developed and have generated revenues primarily from advertising on their Web sites. Users are attracted to the portals because they serve as "search engines"—sites that allow users to access other areas of the Internet based on keywords they type in.

E-commerce companies are also some of the most visited sites on the Web. Amazon.com is a prominent example. The Internet bookseller has recently branched out into music, videos, and auctions as well. Its strategy is impressive and often emulated among e-commerce companies. Because Amazon.com does not operate stores, its inventory is not limited by available physical space, and therefore the company is able to offer any book a customer might want without requiring him or her to leave home. Its prices are lower than those in traditional stores due to its substantially lower overhead. Yet it also does not have the paper and printing costs that catalog retailers face. Furthermore, like Yahoo! or Infoseek, Amazon also derives revenues from advertising it places on its Web site.

While the company has yet to turn a profit, its stock trades at high levels. The company's market capitalization is more than ten times greater than that of traditional bookstore Barnes & Noble—even though Amazon is only a few years old and unprofitable. Likewise, Yahoo! trades at a forward P/E ratio of several hundred times. Such valuations either imply fantastic growth rates or that these high-fliers represent bubbles. In any event, profit is not the focus of these companies right now. Like cable and cellular companies of previous decades, these Internet companies have been pouring practically all their free cash flow into investment that will allow them to grow. The strategy for e-commerce is to develop a large market share, even if it means selling below cost. Once this base of loyal users is developed, such a high level of investment will no longer be necessary and Internet companies will therefore be able to operate at profitable levels, achieving profit through volume and efficient logistics. But without a critical user mass, the sites will not survive.

The economics of e-commerce are unlike any we have seen before. Companies, at least in theory, can sell "below cost," using advertising revenues to subsidize their product sales. Web sites like Buy.com, which vow to beat any advertised price, are indicative.

The market is no longer a geographic one—cyberspace is the new geographic frontier. In this coming world of price transparency, only the players with the most favorable economics will survive. Success tomorrow will be determined by getting the most "eyeballs"—jargon for people who view Web pages—today.

Recently, Internet companies have been attempting to capitalize on their valuations. IPOs and spinoffs of Internet operations from their parent companies promise to unlock value. For example, Barnes & Noble's initial public offering of its online bookstore barnesandnoble.com was an attempt to achieve the same type of market valuation from its Internet operations that Amazon.com enjoys. Investment bank DLJ has launched an IPO of its Web brokerage operation DLJ Direct. And Compaq sold its AltaVista Web search engine, inherited in its purchase of Digital Equipment. Many traditional and catalog retailers have announced that they are developing Web sites and have seen their stock prices jump dramatically.

One of the earliest examples of mergers and acquisitions activity involving the Internet was Microsoft's abortive deal with Intuit. The strategic concept behind the deal—online banking, interactive home-based financial services, and bundled software, all pushed through an online distribution channel—had broad application beyond the financial services arena. Though the deal crashed when the Justice Department balked over antitrust concerns, the imperative remains.

The true harbingers of the digital age came in 1995. Again, Microsoft was the messenger. While the software giant initially had underestimated the popularity and strategic import of the Internet, Microsoft, in typical Bill Gates fashion, has made up for the oversight with an aggressive development and acquisition campaign. In one high-profile investment, Microsoft contributed $220 million to a joint venture launched with NBC, forming the MSNBC cable and Internet news channel. In this vertical integration, NBC could push its content through a Web site and Microsoft could capture valuable Web eyeballs.

More recently, there has been a flurry of deal activity between Internet content companies and between Internet content and distribution companies. Deals that converge Internet, cable, and phone companies are also emerging. The popularity of the Internet as a medium and the growth of and thirst for Internet content are spurring these trends. Internet access over new broadband cable wires will allow users to access Internet content at much higher speeds than previously available. Furthermore, TV, voice, data, and Internet will run over one wire, allowing content providers to tap more fully the Internet's potential as a retail medium.

M&A activity among Internet content providers is gaining steam. Larger players are buying smaller niche players for their customer bases—bases that are almost impossible for a new entrant to cultivate after customers become loyal to the incumbent's product. Indeed, the marketing costs now required to build up a successful Web site are staggering; as in many other countries, it has become easier and cheaper to buy than to build. The acquisition of the "eyeballs" that Web sites reach—akin to viewership for television—is the lifeblood for Internet content providers. The more eyeballs a Web site has, the more advertising it can sell. In most of these deals, because the players have no earnings, the traditional concern about earnings accretion or dilution is largely irrelevant.

Two notable Internet deals involve Internet portal Yahoo! In January 1999, Yahoo! agreed to purchase for $4.6 billion Web community GeoCities—a "place" where people can set up their own Web pages and meet others with similar interests. Web communities demonstrate a great deal of commercial potential because of consumers' brand loyalty to them: Users tend to spend a lot of time there and to return often. But the Web communities have, up to now, not been attractive to advertisers because people come primarily to meet others, not to shop. A second transaction—Yahoo!'s April announcement of its purchase of broadcast.com for $5.7 billion—is intended to broaden Yahoo!'s audience. Broadcast.com is a service that supplies "streaming media programming"—radio and videos—to Internet users. As the technology for streaming media advances, the deal and others like it to come may pave the way for widespread convergence of TV, radio, and Internet.

Jerry Yang and David Filo

Jerry Yang and David Filo, founders of Yahoo!, are two visionaries of the new digital era. Born in Taiwan in 1968, Yang immigrated to the United States at age ten with his mother, grandmother, and younger brother, settling in a suburb of San Jose. He received both a bachelor's and a master's in electrical engineering from Stanford. Filo was born in Wisconsin but was raised in an "alternative community" in Moss Bluff, Louisiana, in which the Filos lived semicommunally with six other families. Filo received a bachelor's degree in computer engineering from Tulane before continuing his education at Stanford.

At Stanford, the two students launched an effort to organize the information on the World Wide Web—at that time an uncategorized mass of data accessible only via an arcane URL, otherwise known as an Internet address. Yang and Filo originally met while on a Stanford-sponsored teaching program in the early 1990s; they later shared an office at Stanford. While their faculty adviser was on sabbatical in Italy, the two established "Jerry and David's Guide to the World Wide Web," a sort of road map to the Web which they provided free to all Stanford students. This service evolved into Yahoo!—"Yet Another Hierarchical Officious Oracle"—soon thereafter.

Yahoo! became successful quite quickly. By April 1995, the high volume of traffic it generated on Stanford's network led the university to require the two entrepreneurs to move Yahoo! off campus. The two dropped out of Stanford, accepted a $1 million investment from Sequoia Capital, rented office space, and had business cards printed that described Filo and Yang as "Chief Yahoos." Strategic partnerships were key to Yahoo!'s success. In August 1995, Yahoo! began selling advertising on its Web pages. Yahoo! also teamed up with Netscape, adding a "button" on its Navigator software that linked users directly to Yahoo!, and partnered with Reuters so that users would be able to access news online by clicking a button. While the deal with Netscape was eventually altered so that Netscape featured a number of browsers, Yahoo! still is easily accessible from the popular Netscape Netcenter page.

On April 12, 1996, Yahoo! went public with an IPO. While its stock price suffered in its first year, as people doubted the promise of Internet advertising, it has since skyrocketed. Yahoo! is one of the few search engines that has actually turned a profit for the past several quarters.

The company seems to enter into new partnerships almost every day. For example, it gets a cut of any online sales made on Amazon.com. Yahoo! is also the Internet and service provider for MCI. By 1998, Yahoo! was averaging more than 850,000 hits, or views of its Web site, per day and received buyout offers from AOL and Microsoft. But Filo and Yang turned them all down. As of September 1999, the company enjoyed a market value of over $40 billion.

The Internet is one of the most active areas for venture capital activity. Venture capitalists have typically taken minority or majority positions in Internet companies in return for the start-up capital they provide. Recently, Internet investments have proved extremely lucrative due to the hot Internet IPO market: Start-ups are now going public as little as a year after their founding.

Benchmark Capital is a major investor in eBay, Critical Path, Guild.com, and Palm Pilot. CMGI, a publicly traded company, is today for all practical purposes a mutual fund, holding investments in Internet companies. One of its most successful investments, Lycos, hit the front pages of the news lately with its planned three-way merger with the Internet assets of Barry Diller's USA Networks and Ticketmaster Online-Citysearch. This deal marked Barry Diller's attempt to move toward the digital age. The company's CEO, David Wetherell, who had originally supported the merger, shortly thereafter did an about-face, speaking out about the "low" valuation assigned to Lycos (there was no clear takeover premium assigned to Lycos, but its stock had climbed more that 100 percent over the months before the deal on takeover speculation) and resigning from the Lycos board to lead a search for other combination partners. Diller had experienced firsthand the disconnect between old media and new media. The market, at least for now, would assign a lower value to Diller's combined company than it would to the separate pieces due to the fashion of Internet stocks.

Vertical integration between Internet content providers and various distribution channels—often "traditional" media companies—is a central theme. GE's NBC, one of the more successful vertical consolidators, has in addition to its MSNBC.com joint venture with Microsoft purchased 19 percent of CNET's Snap! portal (with an option that would allow it to gain a total 60 percent ownership) and 4.99 percent of CNET itself. GE also has purchased a minority stake in iVillage.com, the number one online network geared toward women, as well as a 19.9 percent stake in ValueVision.

Seeking to diversify beyond its filmed entertainment and theme park operations, Disney too has bought into the Internet trend. The entertainment conglomerate purchased 43 percent of Infoseek and integrated it into its new Go portal. Go.com provides links to other Web sites in the Disney empire, such as ABC.com, disney.com, ABCNEWS.com, and ESPN.com. But Go is still in its infancy as a portal; it is unclear whether the promised synergies between the Web site and Disney's traditional operations will materialize.

In July 1999, Disney reached an agreement to combine its Internet operations with Infoseek—the new combined entity will trade separately from Disney. It also entered into a joint venture with Earthlink, an Internet service provider, to form eCompanies, an "Internet Incubator" that will invest in Internet start-ups, following in the footsteps of companies like Amazon.com and Microsoft, which have been active corporate venture capitalists.

While CBS had a brief, unhappy stint as part owner of online service Prodigy, its recent Internet ventures have panned out well. CBS's mass viewership puts the company in a position to obtain stakes in Internet companies on favorable terms to both it and the Internet companies. Internet sites most need to build up a base of loyal eyeballs—something that CBS can facilitate through its widely viewed advertising. CBS has exploited its position, forging "equity for promotion" agreements in which both parties profit: Internet sites gain the exposure they need, and CBS gains an equity stake in Internet companies for little or no cash investment. For example, in April 1999, CBS offered office.com $42 million worth of promotion in exchange for a one-third equity stake. CBS has forged a similar deal with Big Entertainment. CBS received a 35 percent stake in the company in return for giving the new hollywood.com joint venture $100 million in CBS promotion and content. Sportsline USA (now CBS Sportsline), StoreRunner.com, and MarketWatch.com investments follow the same pattern. Fox, however, has been less successful on the Internet. It initially lost huge sums on the Delphi online service it purchased and combined into an Internet venture with MCI. More recently, Fox has effected something of a turnaround of Delphi, repositioning it as a "community portal."

AOL and the Future of the Internet

A landmark transaction in the vertical integration of Internet content and distribution was sparked by Microsoft as it shifted its focus to the Internet market. Microsoft's tactics to use its dominant Windows operating system to gain a foothold in the Internet drove one-time incumbent Netscape to run for cover, finding a partner in AOL.

At $9.6 billion, the AOL-Netscape combination could prove one of the most important for the industry. The deal promises to send shock waves throughout the computer software and Internet sectors and could very well shape the future of the Internet's development. Even giant Microsoft may not be immune to the effects. The deal will combine Netscape's content with AOL's proprietary distribution channel.

Netscape was founded in 1994 by Marc Andreessen, a former University of Illinois grad student, and James H. Clark, a former Stanford professor and founder of Silicon Graphics. While at the University of Illinois, Andreessen had already written Mosaic, the first Web browser, which he distributed for free. But Andreessen had bigger visions and partnered with Clark to start his own company. From the outset, Andreessen recognized the fast pace of development compelled by the very nature of the Internet and made it a goal to ship a new product every three months—unheard of for a software company. By placing his software on the Internet where users could download and beta test it (i.e., test it for bugs), Andreessen discovered a way to bypass one of the most time-consuming parts of the product development cycle. Netscape's IPO in August 1995 was a wild success, with its stock offered at $28 per share surging to $75 per share in its first day of trading.

Driven by Netscape's success on the Internet, Microsoft wanted to jump on the Internet bandwagon. It created its own Web browser to compete against Netscape: Internet Explorer. To boost the market share of Internet Explorer, Microsoft included it for free with all versions of Windows that it shipped and integrated it seamlessly into its operating system. Just as Netscape had risen to success on "Internet-time," Internet Explorer quickly eroded Netscape's market share by 50 percent, causing a blow to the company.

Perhaps the final straw for Netscape was AOL's use of Microsoft's Internet Explorer as its Web browser of choice. AOL and Microsoft had crafted an arrangement in which AOL users would access the Internet by clicking on an icon within AOL's interface that would launch a customized version of Internet Explorer. In return for choosing Internet Explorer as its browser, AOL received payments from Microsoft and AOL's icon received a prominent place on the Windows 98 desktop, making it more convenient to use AOL than any other Internet provider. The agreement spelled death for Netscape.

AOL—America Online—was founded in 1985 as an online link for Commodore computers called Q-Link. While only twenty-four users signed up initially, by 1995, the company (renamed AOL) went public with 200,000 customers. Its recipe for success was to provide online information to consumers who had no particular technological background. It won over customers from its more cumbersome competitors due to its ease of use, quality of service, and aggressive marketing. AOL sent out start-up disks throughout the country to encourage people to try its service. As a result, AOL became the dominant online service provider.

Microsoft, which as of late 1999 was still fighting an antitrust battle in court, argued that the AOL-Netscape deal indicates that the computer software/content industry is in fact dynamic and competitive: Government intervention is not necessary to ensure competition because market forces will act to create viable competitors. In the meantime, Microsoft seems to be the U.S. Steel or the Standard Oil of the 1990s—the high-tech operator intent on dominating its market. In striking similarity to Standard Oil, Microsoft's Windows operating system powers 90 percent of the world's personal computers.

At the same time as its transaction with Netscape, AOL agreed to purchase up to $500 million in Sun Microsystems hardware and Sun agreed to pay AOL $350 million for licensing rights to Netscape software. Both companies agreed to work together on e-commerce and new product development. Just as in the 1980s hardware manufacturers like Sony partnered with content producers, today we are also witnessing the vertical integration of hardware and content in the Internet arena.

In the process, the transaction may redefine the software/content market and create a viable competitor to Microsoft: The three-way agreement paves the way for the development of Internet applications based on Sun's Java programming language, which would run smoothly on a variety of different computer platforms using the same code.

The immediate benefits of the deal to AOL and Netscape will be in advertising. AOL and Netscape both make the lion's share of their revenues from advertiser dollars; just as advertising pays for television or magazine content, it pays for AOL's and Netscape's content as well. When users log on to AOL or view Netscape's Internet portal, they are presented with whatever advertisements AOL or Netscape choose to show them. The deal will allow AOL to drive the 14 million primarily nighttime, at-home subscribers for its proprietary distribution channel to Netscape.com's content, creating a significant new revenue base for AOL. That AOL and Netscape user bases have also been different historically will facilitate AOL's marketing of different products to niche audiences under different names. The company will control two of the most popular portals—access points—on the Internet today, attracting an estimated 58 percent of Web surfers. AOL will also gain Netscape's server software that allows companies to run Internet sites and to conduct e-commerce.

Many have argued that AOL's weak link is its failure, up to now, to provide broadband access to the Internet as At Home and Road Runner do. AOL's recent $1.5 billion investment in satellite provider Hughes, a division of General Motors, is to remedy the situation, allowing AOL access via satellite and via set-top boxes.

With well over $100 billion of market capitalization, AOL is the company to watch. If AOL buys a more "traditional" media conglomerate such as Viacom or Seagram (which have one third of AOL's market capitalization), or enters into partnership with one of the telcos as is rumored, we will see integration occur on a truly massive scale.

PROFILE

Steve Case

Forty-one-year-old Steve Case, through his commitment to bring easy-to-use online service to the masses, has become the CEO of one of America's largest corporations. With a market value of over $100 billion, Case's AOL—which he built from scratch—dwarfs traditional industrial companies like Ford and DuPont and media companies like Disney and Time Warner. But just a few years ago, industry observers were predicting the end was near for AOL. Both Microsoft and AT&T made hostile bids for the company, with Microsoft claiming that it would "bury AOL." Case, however, went on marketing his product, growing AOL to $5 billion in sales. Today, AOL reaches over 20 million users.

Born in Hawaii, Case attended Williams College where he majored in political science. He began his working life at Procter & Gamble, then moved to a job developing toppings at Pizza Hut, before ultimately joining Control Video Corp, AOL's predecessor, in 1984. Shortly afterward, the company changed its name to Quantum Computer Services and offered Q-Link online services for Commodore computers. But this service was doomed, primarily because it was too closely tied to the soon-to-become-obsolete Commodore. So Case instead focused on the Apple Macintosh, and when the computer came out, Q-Link was the service that came with it. Soon Apple realized the success of its new computer and began to impose tight controls on Q-Link, requiring that the young company achieve a technical sophistication it could not afford. Case and Apple split, and Case reinvented the service, changing the name to America Online. At that time, the service offered games, e-mail, chat rooms, news, and shopping.

Many in Silicon Valley have disparaged AOL as the McDonald's of the Internet. Indeed, Case's strength lies in his marketing ability and strong leadership, not his technological skill. Case's next challenge is combating the cable companies' fledgling online services such as the TCI-Comcast-Cox-Cablevision At Home and the Time Warner–MediaOne Road Runner. The Hughes deal is a step in that direction.

Shortly after the announcement of the AOL-Netscape deal, Internet provider At Home agreed to purchase Excite for $6.7 billion in stock. At Home is an Internet service provider via broadband cable, a connection about fifty times faster than dial-up service. Broadband, in contrast to narrow-band dial-up service, also can support video-rich advertising, increasing the revenue potential of the Internet.

Due to this hot market for Internet assets, At Home completed the purchase at about twice the market value of Excite at the time of announcement. The deal will give AT&T, which gained control of At Home after its combination with TCI, a substantial content foothold on the Internet and will allow it to provide a fuller complement of services to consumers. This vertical integration move will also give At Home a leg up on the competing broadband service Road Runner, in which Microsoft is a partner, and will make At Home more competitive with AOL, which does not yet offer broadband access. Indeed, industry observers have described the deal as "a shot of adrenaline for the cable Internet industry." Nevertheless, AOL remains the dominant force in online services, and the combined Excite and At Home still has a long way to go.

The maturing of the Internet, with its vast sums of data, made imperative the implementation of broadband, a technology that would transmit this data quickly, and the wave of broadband deals we are witnessing today. In the future, there are sure to be alliances between RBOCs and other telcos, broadband cable providers, and AOL. Broadband is one of the hottest assets, and no major player can afford to be left behind.

The Future

The geometric pace of technological change means that cable, phone, media, software, entertainment, and computer companies face a complex, exciting, but daunting future.

Over the past fifteen years, the shifting sands of technology and regulation have shaped an entirely new, unstable competitive landscape. Further changes—technological, regulatory, and financial—continue to unfold rapidly. Business models that were cutting-edge a year ago have been repudiated, and the deals continue as companies rush to catch up with developments.

The internationalization of the U.S. media business also will continue. Of course, the process is not without volatility. Matsushita pulled back with its sale of MCA; however, the sale replaced one international owner with another, Seagram of Canada. Other multinationals remain committed to the U.S. market as an important source of creative content for global distribution.

Despite skepticism about their staying power, old-line businesses remain extremely profitable. Radio has been a huge success for CBS. For Viacom, Simon & Schuster turned into one of the gems of the Paramount deal: Viacom was able to sell its education publishing business alone to Pearson PLC for $4.6 billion. Random House was sold to Bertelsmann of Germany to create the world's largest book publisher. These data points suggest a continuing vitality for "old" media formats as the market for content continues to expand.

Nonetheless, the future clearly lies with the digital technologies and the Internet. Across the spectrum of the media and telecommunications industry, companies are at the dawn of a new post-industrial age. On the edge of this frontier, the participants share a palpable sense of tremendous implications; but there is no clear crystal ball.

The digital world is here, but we are not quite ready.

The Tumultuous World of Health Care | 14

"Health is so necessary to all duties as well as pleasures of life that the crime of squandering it is equal to the folly."

—Samuel Johnson, *Wisdom and Genius*

Ten years ago, the world of health care looked remarkably different than it does today. Large insurance companies provided most health coverage, and hospitals and doctors worked as independent providers of health services. The pharmaceutical industry was fragmented, populated by extremely profitable companies not accustomed to competing based on price. The emergence of two interrelated factors, however, made this traditional model unworkable: new technology and a larger elderly population. New medical technologies have revolutionized health care and changed the way we live. Disorders that, twenty years ago, would have been fatal are now controllable with new medicines and medical devices. We are healthier and living longer.

The new medical technology and the new pharmaceuticals are expensive; while miracle drugs prolong life, the fact that they must be taken for the duration of one's life has put a significant burden on our health care system. Health care expenses as a percentage of the gross domestic product began to rise sharply and, indeed, continue to rise. By the 1980s, it became clear that some kind of structural change in the health care system would be necessary.

The fundamental dilemma has become how to find more efficient means of production and delivery for health care while maintaining quality care. Structural innovation attempted to respond to these cost imperatives. Health maintenance organizations (HMOs), physician practice managers (PPMs), pharmacy benefit managers (PBMs), and managed care organizations have all cropped up in the last two decades. And for-profit hospitals have combined into empires to reduce costs. New players and innovative entrepreneurs have emerged to implement these new business models. Even the federal government's Medicare plan is not immune; Medicare providers will be subject to a prospective payment system (PPS)— akin to the system used by managed care companies in the private sector.

These changes have not come without controversy, however. The policy tensions inherent in the system relate to the balance among three themes: social equity, economy, and quality of care. An ideal system would maximize the breadth and equity of patient care, as well as the quality of care. But these two goals in combination conflict with the need for relative economy. President Clinton's 1993 health care plan represented an attempt to mediate these concerns; but the plan was impractical and political backlash made the proposal untenable. After resistance grew, it was withdrawn. Yet the new PPS concept again has raised such issues in care for the elderly.

Many mergers in the health care industry are the result of this struggle to reduce the effective cost of maintaining health care for consumers. First, M&A gives institutions bulk, which brings opportunities for straightforward cost reductions such as the elimination of overhead and the consolidation of overlapping sales forces. Second, deals are the evolutionary mechanism by which the industry restructures and implements new business models. The activity that PPM companies and PBMs have spawned is indicative. The PPM model developed in order to reduce the cost of providing health care and was to work as follows: PPM companies would buy up numerous individual physician practices and operate them, making the physicians and nurses employees of the PPM. Costs were to be reduced through both economies of scale and improved technology. Economies of scale were to be gained from consolidation of back-office functions and through the leverage with managed care companies provided by collective bargaining. Improved technology would allow the practices to assess patient risks better and therefore to structure more favorable contracts with HMOs.

Pharmaceutical companies bought PBMs—which serve as the middleman between doctors and patients, coordinating the distribution of medications to patients and processing payments—in order to gain a captive distribution channel for their pharmaceuticals. This move toward vertical integration would in theory allow the pharmaceutical companies to steer patients to their drugs rather than to those of competitors.

But despite initial exuberance about these changes, they ultimately were failures. PPMs could not control costs effectively and the supposed actuarial technology that they brought to individual practices failed to reduce risks. Furthermore, doctors—committed to providing quality care to patients—often chafed at the fact that costs were to be reduced by lowering the quality of care. In the end, many PPMs, after a flurry of M&A activity, have collapsed under the weight of their financial woes. The idea was a good one, but the execution was lacking.

Similarly, pharmaceutical companies were prohibited from using their captive PBMs to favor their own drugs, eliminating virtually all benefit to this vertical integration. Pharmaceutical companies were stuck with these low-margin, no-growth companies relegated to performing commodity administrative functions. Indeed, the experience in the health care sector is a reminder that change is often sputtering, coming in fits and starts. Inevitably, there will be retrenchments.

The companies that have been responsible for miracle drugs and technologies—the pharmaceutical biotech, and medical device companies—have themselves been forced to respond to the new business environment that their advances created. There is now a race to innovate, in which size and scope matter. Only the largest companies will have the resources to invest efficiently in technology; a global distribution base over which the development costs can be spread is essential. The early 1990s witnessed a flurry of combination activity to build capabilities and slash costs.

By the late 1990s, the urge to consolidate had become so strong that important issues—such as business fit, social issues, and management control—were being ignored altogether. No sooner were these nuptials announced, than the bride got cold feet and ran off with another suitor. Initially American Home Products and Smith-Kline Beecham were in merger talks, but SmithKline Beecham changed its mind and instead ran off with Glaxo Wellcome. But this engagement too fell apart over social issues. In a "combination on the rebound," AHP enjoyed a brief fling with Monsanto, but the personalities of the two companies didn't mesh well. The audience still awaits a happy end to the spectacle.

As the health care industry restructures itself and new cost-saving innovations are put into practice, controversies regarding quality of HMO care and allegedly fraudulent practices at some health care companies raise the question whether economy is being accomplished at the expense of social equity or prudence. Indeed, the quest to reduce health care costs has resulted in countless scandals—U.S. Healthcare and Columbia/HCA hospitals are prominent examples—and significant hardship for those who have been treated unfairly by health care providers. Moreover, the emphasis on efficiency may reduce investment in new technologies and erode the incentive to innovate.

The dislocation that this structural change has caused on an individual level has caused many to argue that the public's stakes in the health care business are incompatible with the quest to build shareholder value. Yet the market provides the most natural mechanism for structural adjustment, and unfortunately the government's record is even worse. As a result of these crosscurrents, the health care industry continues to bubble with innovation, impressive change, and imperfection.

Aetna's Strategic Shift

Aetna's $8.9 billion acquisition of U.S. Healthcare hit the news wires on April 1, 1996. The transaction was a major signpost marking the company's attempt to transform itself into a high-growth health care company. Aetna was bursting out of its Rosen's Cube. However, the deal also had a broader significance as a dramatic extension of other recent mergers, a pointer to future consolidation, and an indication of the inevitable bumps along the road.

From the perspective of Ronald Compton, then chairman of Aetna, the U.S. Healthcare deal was the realization of a four-year strategic makeover. Compton took over an ailing company when he was promoted from president to CEO in the spring of 1992. The company's $23 billion portfolio of real estate investments was heavily peppered with bad loans, the property and casualty business was troubled, and Aetna's structure bureaucratic.

Compton and Richard Huber, then Aetna's vice chairman for strategy and finance, were determined to remake Aetna into a high-growth company focused on core businesses, with health care the number one priority. By 1990, Aetna had reorganized its health care businesses around a new managed care focus. Compton knew the transition would not be easy but hoped to extend this focus and add breadth of product offerings.

Compton also moved to lighten Aetna's load in other areas. A few months after becoming chairman, he sold American Reinsurance for

$1.4 billion to KKR. The deal—which turned into a major success for KKR—was a necessity for Aetna, providing the needed cash to reinforce its real estate portfolio. Weeks after clinching the sale, Aetna announced plans to lay off 10 percent of its workforce in an effort to boost profitability. Another major round of layoffs came in 1994.

With Aetna's operations stabilized, Compton turned to health care in earnest. The next wave of change began in early 1995 with a comprehensive strategic overview of Aetna's business portfolio. We were brought in to assist in the process. Eventually, a dramatic decision was made: Aetna would exit the property and casualty insurance business.

From an economic perspective, the decision was relatively straightforward. The property and casualty business had earned just $60 million in 1994 on revenues of $5.3 billion and would generate a $1 billion charge related to environmental cleanup liabilities in 1995. On the other hand, Aetna had been in the property and casualty business for over 100 years. Selling the operation would be a wrenching experience; but Compton eventually decided sentiment was not enough. Decisive action would be necessary if Aetna were to thrive into the next 100 years. Consequently, in December 1995, the company divested the troubled property and casualty operations to Sandy Weill's Travelers Group for $4 billion.

The Travelers deal positioned Aetna for a major health care acquisition. However, purchasing a health maintenance organization, or HMO, would be a revolutionary step, the first deal of its kind in which a major insurance company would be the acquirer. The risks were palpable, and Compton was determined to act deliberately. The threshold issue was whether the long-term strategic merit of a health care acquisition would be sufficient to outweigh the obvious short-term costs.

After considerable detailed analysis, Compton and the Aetna board decided that investors would see past the near-term costs of an acquisition to the underlying growth prospects of a stronger health care business.

The bedrock for this decision was an understanding of industry dynamics. By 1995, the health care sector was entering a second phase in its evolution toward managed care. Cost had been the driver of the first phase, which had stretched roughly from the mid-1980s to the 1994 failure of President Clinton's health care reform proposals. The second phase shifted the focus from cost to choice.

Phase One: The Early Evolution of Managed Care

Though traditional HMOs had been around for years, they began to become popular in the mid-1980s, when rising health care costs pressured employers to seek out cheaper alternatives. HMOs could provide coverage at a steep discount to what insurance companies were charging at the time, and therefore they boomed in membership and revenues.

The traditional HMO unified the financing and delivery of patient care. Central to this model was the requirement that patients stay within a tight network of doctors and hospitals, each of which contracted with the HMO to provide services according to the HMO's treatment regimen. The HMO received a set premium per patient and shifted to health care providers some of the financial risk associated with patient care. As a result, providers had an incentive to balance the cost of care against the likely benefits.

The HMO product was a reaction to the inefficiencies inherent in the health care indemnity model. Under the indemnity approach, employees were given coverage for medical expenses above a certain annual deductible. While employers sometimes took the risk of paying the future bills, generally insurance companies bore the risk in exchange for annual premiums from employers. In either case, the insurance companies were fundamentally just traffic cops in the health care system, processing claims and paying doctors and hospitals.

The indemnity model was structurally biased in favor of rising costs, as doctors knew they would be paid by insurers and fully insured patients bore none of the effects of higher costs. Under this arrangement, quality and levels of care were determined by patients and doctors, with insurers having little impact on the quality or cost of care. Any review of health care costs was principally retrospective, with little opportunity to be proactive about cost reductions.

These inefficiencies in the indemnity insurance model created an opening for HMOs. At the height of phase one, the cost differential between traditional insurers and HMOs was around 30 percent. Employers started giving employees economic incentives to enter managed care in the form of lower out-of-pocket expenses, and many employees were willing to accept a limited choice of doctors and restricted care alternatives in order to save money.

Initially, HMOs had little trouble pushing costs significantly below the norm for indemnity policies. By restricting their patients to a list of approved doctors, hospitals, and other providers, the HMOs interposed themselves as active intermediaries in the market, allowing them to aggregate patients into large pools and demand volume pricing. For example, an HMO could go to a local hospital and require a large discount over the costs being billed to individual patients under indemnity policies. The arrangement was mutually beneficial for HMOs and care providers: HMOs could offer lower rates while hospitals and doctors were guaranteed substantial patient flow. By way of contrast, because a traditional insurance company had little control over where the patients it covered would seek care, it lacked similar negotiating leverage.

Volume purchasing of supplies and medications was another easy way to reduce the health care cost structure. In addition, HMOs went a step further, deepening their relative cost advantage through the application of technology and sophisticated demographic analysis. In the traditional indemnity model, doctors made care decisions on an independent basis, generally working with limited information resources and without the capacity to track outcomes. There was little awareness of whether treatments were cost-effective. HMOs changed that: They studied each element of the health care cost structure, eliminating "unnecessary" tests and searching for other efficiencies.

It was this desire to capture efficiencies of scale that drove many phase one deals. Companies got together to increase their patient population for greater negotiating leverage with care providers and medical suppliers and to spread overhead across a larger business.

As a result of these and other measures, HMOs for a time operated under a big price umbrella, able to offer employers the option of covering employees at a much lower cost than under indemnity insurance. At the peak of phase one, the conventional wisdom prevailed that everyone would end up in a traditional HMO.

Phase Two: Choice Enters the Model

The early 1990s witnessed an important change to the HMO model: increased patient choice. The new emphasis on choice working its way into the market in the early 1990s was a watershed event. For Aetna, there were two practical implications—the rise of an alternative managed care model, known as "point of service," and the consequent segmentation of the health care benefits market.

Point of service essentially is a hybrid product that grafts choice onto the traditional HMO model. Under the new arrangement, members have the option of either staying within a company's provider network, with care delivered on the traditional HMO basis and patients paying only small co-payments for visits, or instead going outside the provider network under a discounted "preferred provider organization" network or a traditional indemnity relationship. In the latter case, the patient pays a relatively large deductible and the managed care company picks up the majority of the remaining costs.

Even as point of service developed, the indemnity model also showed continuing vitality. Defections from indemnity coverage to

HMOs began to level off, with a certain percentage of the population willing to pay more for increased flexibility and control. Earlier notions about the eventual extinction of indemnity programs turned out to be overstated. Rather, the future health care benefits market would be segmented with various product offerings.

The new business model—analogous to bundled local, long distance, cable, and wireless telecommunications services—was for a single company to provide large employers a package of different products. Both scale and breadth of product offerings were important elements in the bundle: Large employers with multiple sites in different states preferred to deal with a single benefits company for administrative convenience and cost efficiency. Yet they also wanted the ability to provide employees a range of alternatives.

This shift reinforced Aetna CEO Ronald Compton's view that a health care acquisition would be a critical element in his company's transformation. Aetna had a strong foundation to face the new health care environment, with its successful indemnity and account-servicing track record and large customer base. However, Aetna had limited experience with point of service and other managed care products, which require different capabilities than the indemnity product. Managing point of service plans requires sophisticated modeling of patient care costs and effective cost containment programs. Extending into this new field independently would have been costly and risky.

After developing a picture of the market. Compton and the Aetna board made the judgment that a combination of Aetna and an able managed care company would be necessary if Aetna were to burst out of its constraints. The acquisition analysis therefore entered a second state, with the focus on potential targets.

U.S. Healthcare was an obvious acquisition candidate for Aetna. The company had a strong presence in its home markets, primarily in the Northeast, and a reputation for efficiency, with the highest operating margins of any major player in the managed care industry. A combination with U.S. Healthcare would bring Aetna the added capabilities it wanted.

After an initial approach was favorably received, negotiations opened in early 1996. As it turned out, Leslie Abramson, chairman of U.S. Healthcare, had his own reasons to favor a merger with a company like Aetna. Realizing as early as a year before the Aetna deal that numerous competitors were beginning to crowd into U.S. Healthcare's lucrative Northeast markets, Abramson began to look for a partner to help it gain negotiating leverage over employers and providers, and thus to defend its leadership role.

Moreover, the migration toward bundled managed care and indemnity products was already taking shape in the marketplace. Travelers Insurance and Metropolitan Life Insurance had joined their sluggish health operations in 1994 to form MetraHealth. Just a year later United HealthCare—a Minneapolis-based HMO with national aspirations—bought MetraHealth for $2 billion. This joining of a managed care company and an indemnity insurance expert was a seminal phase two deal.

Abramson foresaw a market eventually dominated by five or six national players with broad product offerings. He wanted U.S. Healthcare to be one of the six, but his company lacked the resources for the fast nationwide rollout required to capture position. Nor was U.S. Healthcare experienced at managing indemnity products or multisite client relationships. Aetna, with its twenty-one-state network, offered a quick inroad to a national presence.

In summary, Aetna would bring its size, national presence, and multisite capabilities. U.S. Healthcare would bring its managed care expertise and technology. Together, the companies would have a formidable market presence and be in position to build a functional nationwide managed care network.

Under the terms of the deal, U.S. Healthcare shareholders would receive a package worth roughly $57 a share consisting of $34.20 in cash, 0.2246 of a share of Aetna Inc. common stock, and 0.0749 of a share of a mandatory convertible preferred stock for each U.S. Healthcare share. This offer represented a premium to U.S. Healthcare's trading value—the company's stock closed at just under $46 the day before the deal was announced. The price also represented roughly 20 times U.S. Healthcare's projected earnings for the next twelve months; on the low end compared to other recent HMO acquisitions. Further, most other HMO deals were basically acquisitions of additional membership. The Aetna–U.S. Healthcare deal brought Aetna both new members and management capabilities, making the price even more attractive.

However, this deal structure butted up against several of Aetna's Rosen's Cube constraints. For example, the $5.3 billion cash payment to U.S. Healthcare shareholders would cut into the cash needed to run Aetna's business. In theory, the cash made available by the sale of the property and casualty business would fund roughly $4 billion of that amount, and because Aetna's balance sheet was relatively strong and could support considerable additional leverage, the company could fund the remaining $1.3 billion through borrowing.

However, there was a problem with this approach. Because Aetna planned to remain in the insurance business, maintaining a favorable credit rating was therefore important. The interest payments from the acquisition and the capital needs of an expanded health care operation would likely consume a large portion of Aetna's cash flow, necessitating that the Aetna board either reduce the company's dividend or borrow the money. This raised a critical question: Would a dividend cut cause Aetna's shareholder base, accustomed to a relatively high dividend yield, to flee the stock?

One alternative, of course, would be to increase the $3.6 billion stock portion of the deal. However, Aetna's price/earnings ratio was considerably lower than U.S. Healthcare's ratio, making a stock deal substantially dilutive to Aetna's earnings per share.

The part-cash, part-stock deal that Aetna chose amplified this negative earnings effect with annual goodwill expense. The net effect was that Aetna would not meet its earnings-per-share targets in the immediate future. While sophisticated investors would normalize Aetna's earnings per share for the effect of goodwill, the question still remained whether investors would penalize its stock price as a result of earnings dilution.

Of course, all Aetna could do was make an educated projection of how the market would respond to a lower dividend and lower earnings per share. After exhaustive analysis, the judgment was that if the deal were properly presented, Aetna would experience a transformation in the eyes of investors from a low-growth value investment to a high-growth hot stock. If that happened, the company's price/earnings multiple would expand, offsetting any fall in earnings per share with a higher stock price. In other words, the pattern had to be broken to define a new vision.

These expectations, in fact, were realized when Aetna's trading multiple expanded as a result of its shift toward health care. In September 1995, just before the company confirmed rumors of a planned sale of its property and casualty business, Aetna traded at 9.7 times estimated 1996 earnings and 8.9 times estimated 1997 earnings. A few days after the U.S. Healthcare deal was announced, the comparable figures had risen to 13.2 times and 11.6 times, respectively.

As a reward for his vision, Aetna's vice chairman Richard Huber was selected to succeed Compton as chief executive officer at the end of July 1997, just as integration problems with U.S. Healthcare became apparent. Smoothing the transition to a unified health care operation naturally became the first order of business, though Huber continued to be interested in expanding the scope of Aetna's health care business.

The Second Phase Continues

The second phase of managed care evolution, exemplified by the Aetna deal, continued into 1997 as companies partnered to compete in a world of choice. Indeed, the managed care environment had changed substantially in the previous decade. The managed care sector was a more mature one. Organic growth opportunities had dropped off dramatically. Cost savings and growth through acquisition became key. Premium rates also began to rise.

Shortly after the Aetna deal, PacifiCare Health Systems acquired FHP, and Foundation Health Corp. merged with Health Systems International, both in multibillion-dollar deals. Again, increased size and scope were the imperatives behind these combinations. PacifiCare became the country's fifth-largest HMO, serving nearly 4 million members across fifteen states. Foundation Health Systems, the product of the marriage of Foundation and Health Systems International, topped PacifiCare with nearly 5 million members, vaulting it into position as the fourth-largest HMO.

In March 1997, insurer Cigna bought Healthsource, a troubled managed care company whose stock had dropped over 60 percent in 1996. The $1.5 billion cash deal was announced eleven months after the U.S. Healthcare acquisition and endorsed the trend toward cross-capability mergers.

Like Aetna's acquisition of U.S. Healthcare, these deals—and the promise of further consolidation—were favorably received in the market: Opportunities for organic revenue growth were viewed as limited, but potential cost savings from deals appeared as a viable counterweight.

However, in the second half of 1997, the promise waned somewhat as a series of acquirers experienced integration problems. Not only Aetna, but also Cigna, PacifiCare, and United HealthCare suffered disappointing results.

Part of the problem was endemic to the health care business—costs continued to increase at a faster rate than premiums. Problems of standardization also were significant for some acquirers: Different operating procedures, provider contracts, and computer systems all

needed to be combined seamlessly. The health care business, balkanized for decades, proved more difficult to integrate than expected.

But despite these significant setbacks, deal activity continued.
The economic realities that had driven companies together still prevailed in the marketplace. Even at companies suffering through
post-closing indigestion, executives continued to identify the acquisition of broader capabilities and wider geographic scope as critical
to survival, as only the strongest companies would have the leverage
to negotiate the shoals. It was still true that large companies had the
power to demand concessions from doctors and hospitals and the efficiencies to provide geographically diversified employers with low-
cost, one-stop shopping. In addition, larger companies have the
critical mass to sustain the necessary investment in technology that
is required to manage the broad range of products. Even though the
time might not have been right for more deals, companies feared
that if they did not act quickly and decisively their competitors
would snap up the most attractive targets. There was considerable
pressure to be a "first mover."

In the face of these opposing forces, rumors abounded in October 1997 that Prudential would be the next big insurer to reach out
for a solution to its health care dilemma: Prudential reportedly
placed its health care operations, a mixture of HMOs and indemnity
operations in forty states, on the block. Like Travelers and MetLife,
Prudential apparently decided to exit the health care business if a
suitable acquirer could be found. Interestingly, many of the same
companies having difficulty with past acquisitions were mentioned
as potential buyers, a striking testament to the perceived need for
further strategic consolidation among health care benefit companies.

In two of these second phase deals, Aetna was again the acquirer.
In March 1998, Aetna purchased New York Life Insurance's NYL-
Care managed care unit. New York Life felt that NYLCare did not
fit into the company's long-term plan to focus on traditional insurance, annuities, and mutual funds and therefore sold the opera-

tion—which included NYLCare's approximately 2.2 million HMO, point of service, PPO, and indemnity health plan enrollees—to Aetna for $1.05 billion, plus a potential $300 million payout in 2000 if certain earnings and membership targets are met. The purchase price translated into about $477 per member, far lower than the $3,179 per member Aetna paid for U.S. Healthcare. NYLCare's strongest areas—Texas, St. Louis, and Washington, D.C.—were not strong areas for Aetna, making the fit between the two companies complementary.

In December 1998, Aetna bought Prudential's health care business for a bargain-basement $1 billion. The deal added a further 6.6 million lives to Aetna's existing membership at a cost of only about $200 per member, making Aetna the number one health insurer in the U.S.

Before Aetna ultimately agreed to buy the business, Prudential attempted to sell its health care business to both Humana and Well-Point Health Networks. Neither was interested, and Prudential was forced to accept a price significantly below what it had originally contemplated. Indeed, neither New York Life nor Prudential had the scale or scope in health insurance to be profitable operators, and were therefore induced to exit the market.

The Blues

Another trend of this second phase is the merger and acquisition activity of the state Blue Cross and Blue Shield plans, the so-called Blues. The Blues, of which there are sixty-nine, are independently operated, not-for-profit corporations linked to the Blue Cross and Blue Shield Association through a licensing agreement.

Many Blues have sought buyers due to bruising competition from better-funded, publicly traded insurers like Aetna U.S. Healthcare, Cigna, and United HealthCare. The Blues, which traditionally had operated in a single state, or in a single region within a state, did not benefit from the economics of scale enjoyed by larger health insurers, and as nonprofits are unable to strengthen their balance sheets by tapping the capital markets.

Furthermore, state regulators force many Blues to serve as insurers of last resort, but have often not allowed them to raise premiums high enough to cover their risks. There is indeed a tension between affordable premiums and plan solvency. The situation has put many Blues in the precarious position of falling dangerously close to their minimum capital benchmarks, a measure of capital adequacy designated by the national association. Failure to meet the minimum capital benchmark results in a Blue's license being revoked by the Blue Cross and Blue Shield Association. The example of the New Jersey Blue plan is indicative of the dilemma. In 1992, the plan requested that regulators approve a major rate increase. The regulators would not, and instead approved a much smaller increase to ensure that the plans remained affordable. The regulator estimated that their decision to limit the rate increased the plans deficit by $38 million.

Facing these constraints, the Blues have been encountering significant financial challenges, and have resorted to M&A activity to break out of their Rosen's Cubes. For example, Blue Cross and Blue Shield of New Hampshire had debt of $30 million, as well as losses of $20 million on revenues of $600 million in 1998. Such shaky results put into jeopardy the ability of the Blue to protect its members in the face of cyclical downturns. The New Hampshire Blue is to be taken over by Anthem. And something of a battle has developed between Anthem and WellPoint over Blue Cross and Blue Shield of Colorado. The Blue had agreed to be purchased by Anthem, but subsequently WellPoint entered a bid at a much higher price.

Anthem Inc., an Indianapolis-based mutual insurance company, has been an aggressive acquirer of Blues. Previously, it merged with Blue Cross and Blue Shield of Kentucky and in 1997 it merged with Connecticut's Blue Cross plan. Upon completion of the New Hampshire deal, Anthem will insure more than 5.3 million members. WellPoint Health Networks, which agreed to merge with Blue Cross and Blue Shield of Georgia's parent, Cerulean, in July 1998, is another acquirer or Blues plans.

Blues have also begun to combine with each other to build stronger balance sheets and benefit from economies of scale. Many, but not all, of these deals resulted in a nonprofit surviving company. In 1998, Blue Cross and Blue Shield of Illinois, a mutual insurer, acquired nonprofit Blue Cross and Blue Shield of Texas after a three-year regulatory battle. Four Blues in Michigan—Blue Care Network of East Michigan, Blue Care Network–Great Lakes, Blue Care Network of Mid Michigan, and Blue Care Network of Southeast Michigan—also announced their merger to become the Blue Care Network. And in 1997, the Blues of Maryland and the District of Columbia combined.

When the independent Blues, generally nonprofits, merge with public acquirers, they drop their nonprofit status, and the sale proceeds go to a charitable health care foundation. Not surprisingly, not all state regulatory agencies have looked favorably upon these mergers between Blues and for-profit insurers. Anthem and the New Jersey Blue canceled their proposed 1997 merger due to the legal and regulatory hurdles the Blue would face becoming a mutual insurer. But many question the value of nonprofit health insurers today: If they do not have the strength to survive against their larger competitors, they will be of little benefit to the community.

The Lone Wolf on Life Support

The rise of managed care also changed the world for health care providers, both doctors and hospitals. With the number of patients joining HMOs and managed care networks on the rise, the imperative for a doctor to be part of the network was clear: The networks could assure doctors a steady flow of patients. But managed care providers' newfound scale also dramatically shifted the balance of power away from doctors and toward the managed care organizations.

HMOs, in an effort to reduce the cost of health care, squeezed doctors' profits and made their business of providing care far more risky. HMOs shifted much of the risk of care provision onto the doctors in their network, giving them a set fee per patient under a so-called capitation policy. Any excess costs of treating the patient would be borne by the doctors. For a solo practitioner, the potential downside of the arrangement is substantial: A slightly higher rate of costly illnesses can significantly reduce a year's income.

The market responded to these new realities with a new model of health care practice, the physician practice manager, or PPM—intended to bring economies of scale to doctors. These economies of scale would increase doctors' bargaining power with the managed care companies and help spread expenses across a larger base of patients.

The model works like this: A typical PPM buys the assets of many existing group practices and makes the computers and medical equipment property of a new subsidiary of the acquiring PPM. The doctors become independent contractors working for their practice group, which signs a long-term contract to provide services to the purchasing PPM.

New holding companies are set up to run the acquired practices, typically governed by a board with even representation for the PPM and the selling doctors. While representatives of the PPM have control over budget issues, the doctors control care regimens within the cost guidelines established by employers, managed care companies, and other clients of the clinic.

With the size to spread costs over a wide network of acquired practices, a PPM was to bring professional management and cutting-edge technology to the table—increasingly important in the world of capitation. Structuring effective contracts with managed care companies and employers requires an understanding of where costs come from, demographics, and how to economize. Before the advent of PPMs, most practice groups lacked the size and sophistication to handle these issues independently.

Additional economies of scale were to come from the bulk purchasing of everything from malpractice insurance to paper cups. Risk spreading is also more effective with a larger patient population, as idiosyncratic developments with one or two patients have a less significant bottom-line impact. Finally, size brings negotiation leverage, which was to put some of the money flowing to the managed care companies back into the doctors' pockets.

When stock prices of PPMs were high, the attraction of acquisitions was clear. Terms varied, but an acquiring company typically was entitled to a percentage of the acquired group's future pretax earnings, ranging from 10 to 20 percent for a primary care practice and from 20 to 40 percent for a specialty practice. Nineteen sixties–style inefficiencies in the market made this cash flow extremely valuable: Privately held group practices could be purchased for 6 to 8 times pretax cash flow, while PPMs still traded in the market at around 20 to 25 times projected earnings. Exploiting this arbitrage opportunity, a company like PhyCor—which was trading at around 40 times projected earnings for 1997—could afford to pay a premium for a group practice in a stock deal. If PhyCor paid, say, 10 times earnings for a practice, and the future earnings were then valued in the market at even 20 times earnings, the company instantly added $10 of market capitalization for every $1 of earnings purchased.

Of course, initial success bred imitation. As more PPM companies entered the market and the prime practice groups disappeared, the spread between public and private market valuations declined. Earnings-per-share growth as a result became more difficult.

Initially, concerted acquisition programs allowed the industry leaders to expand rapidly. More recently, though, it has become clear that the growth has come too quickly. PPM stocks by mid-1998 had fallen into extreme disfavor, with many PPMs collapsing into bankruptcy. The model may have been sound in theory, but no one could implement it successfully. Indeed, as a group, PPMs have performed poorly. The twenty-nine PPMs tracked by Corporate Research Group posted a total loss of a couple of hundred million dollars for 1998. The average PPM's stock was down over 50 percent in 1998 versus 1997. The experience of four PPMs—PhyCor, FPA Medical Management, MedPartners, and PhyMatrix (now called Innovative Clinical Solutions)—is indicative.

PhyCor was an early pioneer of the PPM model. The company was formed in 1988 by four former hospital executives and proceeded to acquire more than forty-seven large multispecialty practice groups, thirteen in 1996 alone. By the end of 1996, PhyCor had cobbled together more than 12,000 doctors into a single network with revenues of $770 million. But its performance was disastrous: Its stock lost approximately 75 percent of its value in 1998 after news that it was having trouble integrating the smaller physician practices it acquired into smaller groups and was taking charges against earnings. Today, PhyCor is restructuring. Yet, despite its awful performance, PhyCor was actually one of the most successful PPMs.

PPM FPA Medical Management is in even worse shape, having filed for bankruptcy protection. FPA at its height had a market valuation of a couple of billion dollars—at the end of its bankruptcy it was valued at around $100 million. MedPartners, also once a high flier, saw its shares fall over 76 percent in 1998. All told, $1,000 invested in MedPartners at the end of 1995 would have become less than $170 by the end of 1999.

The company, led by CEO Larry House, was founded in just 1993 and grew at a breathtaking pace—again, through acquisition of other PPM companies, as well as smaller independent practice groups. The company took a leap in 1996, acquiring competitor Caremark International for $1.9 billion. Many on the Street expected House to take some time in integrating Caremark into MedPartners, but he showed no sign of slowing. In 1997, MedPartners followed up on the Caremark deal with a $490 million acquisition of InPhyNet Medical

Management, a Florida-based PPM. House made no apologies for his strategy. As he said at the time of the Caremark announcement, "We want to be superconsolidators."

MedPartners' aggressive acquisition campaign appeared to pay off in October 1997, when PhyCor agreed to acquire the larger company for nearly $7 billion in stock. The deal would have created by far the largest PPM in the United States. However, initial reaction to the deal was negative. Investors worried the price was too high and the integration too difficult. MedPartners' stock fell 17 percent, while PhyCor's stock was off 19 percent. Two months later, the deal collapsed. Things went downhill from there. Therefore, MedPartners has taken a $1.2 billion charge to discontinue its unprofitable PPM operations and instead focus on its Caremark pharmacy benefits management operations. Like MedPartners, PhyMatrix has also decided to exit the PPM business.

Thus, the initial exuberance surrounding PPMs was followed by a period of retrenchment as deal after deal went sour. A severely weakened PhyCor is the only sizable player remaining in the PPM business.

The failure of PPMs likely had less to do with the model itself and more to do with poor execution. Supporting this view is the experience of some of the newly down-scaled, focused firms, which have had more success. IntegraMed, for example, is experiencing revenue growth in its business that brings together physicians specializing in reproduction. Unfortunately, however, the failure of the most visible PPMs—PhyCor, FPA, MedPartners, and PhyMatrix—caused investors to pummel the market valuations of the more successful operators as well.

Indeed, much of the problem plaguing PPMs was rising costs and poor management. While much of the appeal to doctors of PPMs was their promise to control costs and reduce risks, the PPMs often were not sophisticated enough to do so. Many PPMs had entered into so-called global capitation contracts, in which they assumed the risk for a population's entire health needs—primary care, outpatient care, hospitalization treatment, and sometimes even pharmaceuticals. But PPMs lacked the experience to manage this risk. Most lacked the actuarial expertise to predict patient costs accurately, and so costs mushroomed out of control, hammering earnings. Inadequate information systems compounded the problem. Often physicians also balked at attempts to cut costs at the expense of sound care, and a tension developed between doctors and their PPMs. Furthermore, much of the early deal activity was overexuberant and made on terms financially unfavorable to the PPMs themselves: The PPMs simply paid too much for assets that were not of the quality that would enable them to generate the returns the PPMs sought.

Despite the attention lavished on PPMs, more than half of all doctors still are self-employed and roughly two thirds practice in groups of less than three. These doctors face tremendous pressures in the new health care market. Yet only 10 percent of all physicians are affiliated with a PPM.

While the early PPM experiment was unsuccessful, the imperative remains for some type of structural change. The underlying forces that spurred the creation of PPMs remain. Managed care is here to stay, and doctors need to find a way to deal with the cost pressures managed care imposes. Physicians also need the scale to negotiate effectively with managed care companies and to spread capitation risk.

After the turmoil subsides, a second generation of PPMs will likely emerge, hopefully having learned from the mistakes of the early phases.

Hospital Empires

Doctors are not the only health care providers feeling the pinch as a result of the unfolding health care revolution. Hospitals likewise have seen costs rise and revenues decline as managed care companies and the government reduce reimbursement levels. Overcapacity plagues the system: Even successful hospitals have trouble keeping more than 40 percent of their beds filled, the national average. As with doctors, the pressures have resulted in a profound consolidation, the creation of vast hospital empires from what once were proudly independent, locally run institutions.

Most of the 5,200 hospitals in the United States are not-for-profit organizations. Yet even these institutions are not immune to cost pressures, as can be seen in the trend toward mergers of hospitals affiliated with medical schools. Prominent examples include the completed merger of Stanford University Medical Center with University of California, San Francisco (UCSF), and the merger of NYU with Mt. Sinai. Possessed of sterling reputations and state-of-the-art facilities, university hospitals nonetheless have a tough time filling beds in a managed care world. With a declining revenue base, the cost savings available from consolidation are necessary to survival.

However, the primary participants in the hospital consolidation have been for-profit, public corporations. Humana and Hospital Corporation of America were early pioneers. Columbia/HCA, which swallowed the hospitals of both of its competitors, then became the major force in the sector and now controls roughly half of the nation's 700 for-profit hospitals. Recently, though, the company has been racked by charges of impropriety and a federal investigation that is still running its course. The resulting turmoil has highlighted the significant public policy issues involved with introducing the pressures of Wall Street into the world of health care.

Richard Scott founded Columbia in 1987 with the backing of financier Richard Rainwater. Scott drove Columbia to $20 billion in revenues with a tough management style and aggressive acquisitions. At its height, the chain controlled roughly 350 hospitals, 550 home health care offices, and many other managed care businesses.

Columbia made its first acquisition in 1998—two struggling hospitals in El Paso. More deals pushed Columbia to a portfolio of twenty-five hospitals by 1993. Then, over the next two years, Scott made the leap to national player: In 1993, Columbia scooped up Galen Health Care, the spun-off hospitals business of Humana, and the following year bought Hospital Corporation of America. These two transactions grew Columbia to more than 180 hospitals.

A single-minded focus on trimming costs and reducing overcapacity—two forces that threatened to rip apart hospitals—propelled Columbia's growth. Like doctors, hospitals had become accustomed to a world where price was not an issue. Employers and the government footed the bill for health care and were relatively price-insensitive. America's health care system often adopted a "damn the torpedoes" approach to medical practice with high utilization of costly procedures, bloated hospital staffs, and a hospital in every neighborhood. Incredible overcapacity was built into the system.

Hospitals experienced a rude awakening when employers, health care benefits companies, and the government all began to cut reimbursement rates for care in the wake of the managed care phenomenon. Suddenly competition for patients became a new reality. With too much capacity, price cuts became a necessary fact of life, and many hospitals began to bleed red ink.

Columbia's strategy, and the strategy of other publicly traded hospital companies, was partly a consolidation play. The companies would buy up a number of hospitals in a city or region, shut down some and reduce staff at others. Many not-for-profit hospitals also sought out partnerships with Columbia, lacking the managerial capacity and experience necessary to survive in the world of health care competition.

When it took over operations at a hospital, Columbia brought a bottom-line approach. Scott organized the company into regions. Regional heads were given ambitious monetary targets for cost reductions and revenue growth. Managers who hit the targets were rewarded with handsome bonuses; managers who missed the targets came under intense pressure. Bareknuckle marketing was introduced to a field unaccustomed to such tactics.

From a financial perspective, the formula seemed to work. Earnings skyrocketed, and Columbia's stock price quadrupled. Yet the approach also generated considerable negative publicity. Local politicians slammed the company for practicing "Wall Street" medicine, more concerned about profits than providing care to the poor or having a positive community impact. Medical professionals complained Columbia slashed costs to the bone, and then some. Instances of understaffing were highlighted as indicative. Indeed, the quest to build shareholder value was argued by some to be fundamentally incompatible with the mission of providing health care, as it would inevitably lead to funds being diverted from patient care to shareholders' pockets.

Government investigators have begun to focus on alleged fraudulent billing practices at Columbia hospitals and in Columbia's home health care business. Critics argued these practices resulted from the market pressure on Columbia to generate favorable financial results.

Federal agents in Texas served search warrants against the company in March 1997, resulting in the indictment of a number of Columbia executives. Shareholders subsequently sued the company after its stock price dropped in response to the charges. After Columbia's board forced Scott and several subordinates to resign, Dr. Thomas Frist Jr., co-founder of HCA and former vice chairman of Columbia, was selected to replace Scott as CEO. In January 1999, the Justice Department announced that it joined a second lawsuit alleging Columbia/HCA overbilled Medicare by $9 million.

Frist pledged cooperation with the federal investigation and initiated an overall shift in strategy. Rather than be the largest, most acquisitive hospital company in the country, Frist planned to remake Columbia into a smaller operation focused on its core markets and on providing high-quality care, perhaps by spinning off as many as a third of the company's hospitals. Of course, the federal and state investigations will have to run their course before it becomes clear whether this strategic shift will allow Columbia to survive and prosper once again.

Even before the Columbia scandal broke into the open, there generally was an increasing resistance to the sale of nonprofit hospitals to for-profit companies. When a nonprofit is sold, the proceeds typically go to the creation of a new charitable foundation. Columbia and other profit-making hospital companies argue that this benefit, plus future tax revenues generated by a switch to for-profit status, more than outweigh any social costs of converting a local hospital. Critics disagree. The main concern has been the commitment of providing care to uninsured patients and support to the community.

Yet the economic logic for consolidation of hospitals remains considerable. Too many beds and too much brick and mortar remains in place. Not-for-profit hospitals can only afford to run at a loss for so long before they must begin to look for alternatives.

Other for-profit consolidators besides Columbia remain in the market today. Tenet Healthcare is one of the largest challengers. The company, formerly named National Medical Enterprises, went through its own near-death experience in 1993, in which 600 federal agents descended on the company's Santa Fe headquarters in the culmination of an investigation into the billing practices of National Medical's psychiatric division. Board member Jeffrey Barbakow stepped in to take over operations and he paid out more than $500 million in fines and settlements, ultimately refocusing the business on its core hospital operations.

But a series of acquisitions have rejuvenated Tenet. The company purchased National Medical Holdings for more than $3 billion in 1995, doubling its hospital portfolio to near seventy-five. And in 1997, Tenet acquired OrNda, the nation's third-largest hospital company.

Though Tenet now has over 125 hospitals, it nonetheless remains a distant number two to Columbia.

In the aftermath of the Columbia scandal, Tenet and Columbia were rumored to be in merger talks. Reflecting Columbia's troubles, Tenet management was expected to take over if a deal occurred. However, when Dr. Frist assumed the CEO job at Columbia, he put the merger negotiations on hold. A deal still may happen, but probably not until the financial impact of the Columbia investigation becomes more certain.

HealthSouth has also been an aggressive acquirer. The company's strategic vision is to create "integrated service plazas" that are slightly smaller than traditional hospitals and focus on less serious problems. These centers provide patients with "one-step health care shopping," primarily in the areas of rehabilitation and outpatient care.

In May 1998, HealthSouth agreed to buy thirty-four surgery centers from Columbia/HCA for $550 million. And just two weeks later, the company agreed to acquire forty surgery centers from Chicago-based National Surgery Centers for $590 million. These surgery centers will fill in HealthSouth's "product line" and make HealthSouth the dominant player in the surgery center sector. Today, the company has operations in all fifty states, the U.K., and Australia.

Hospital ownership will continue to concentrate in the future, with the pace and scope of consolidation shaped by regulatory and political developments. Eventually though, the cost savings possible with consolidation will push the trend forward.

The Government and Structural Change

The government too has had to react to the effects of rising health care costs imposed by its Medicare providers. The so-called prospective payment system (PPS) is the result, imposing new restrictions on nursing homes and home care providers that are reimbursed by Medicare. Under the system, nursing homes will be given a flat fee to pay for all the care needed for each patient, much like the private sector capitation model. These facilities will, under PPS, be responsible for negotiating the best possible deals with ancillary service providers and deciding what services are truly necessary for their patients. Financial risk will shift away from the government, to be increasingly borne by these facilities. Previously, nursing homes were reimbursed by Medicare for the services they provided, which the government alleges led to over $9 billion of fraudulent reimbursements annually.

PPS is also being applied to home care providers. During the period between 1990 and 1997, the number of home care visits per Medicare beneficiary more than doubled. The government has attributed this rise to the failure of the cost-based payment system to provide an economic incentive for Medicare patients not to abuse the system.

The impact of PPS is sure to be staggering. Most nursing homes and home care providers do not have sufficient leverage to negotiate favorable deals with ancillary service providers; most do not even know what these service providers' costs are. Furthermore, nursing homes are responsible for serving the sickest, most expensive patients. Balancing the competing goals of providing quality care while cutting costs will be exceedingly difficult. And even though care is being conducted in their facilities, it is doctors that ultimately control the level of care—not nursing homes.

The advent of PPS is sure to elicit a response from nursing care and home care providers. Many will likely combine to achieve economies of scale and negotiating leverage with ancillary providers, to spread risk, and to make more efficient investments in the technology necessary to control cots. PPM-like players may also emerge.

Medical Device Industry

The medical device companies are also beginning to consolidate. The impetus for the trend has been two-pronged. First, the collapse of the market for small-capitalization device companies in June 1996 drove them into the arms of larger, more stable partners. Second, managed care created an environment which favored the further expansion of the larger companies to provide one-stop medical device shopping.

Prior to June 1996, there were two classes of medical device companies. The first tier consisted of the large-cap, established players: Johnson & Johnson, Boston Scientific, U.S. Surgical, and Medtronic, for example. The second tier consisted of smaller players, many recently founded based on the promise of a single product: Cordis and Heart Technologies fell into this category.

For many years, the overall industry had been a stodgy one, with little attention paid to this first tier of companies. But in the early 1990s, great technological advances made by the smaller players thrust the industry into the spotlight, creating tremendous market demand for the start-ups. A "class of 1996" IPO was launched amid great fanfare. These companies, in general, possessed wonderfully promising technology that would revolutionize the way patients received care. Two companies, Cardiothoracic Systems and Heartport, are indicative.

These two companies had developed minimally invasive cardiac surgery technology, intended to provide a higher level of patient comfort at a lower cost than traditional bypass surgery. Using the new technology, a device could be inserted through the patient's side or between his ribs, with which computer-assisted microsurgery would be performed.

But two problems sank the procedure and ultimately the share prices of the two companies. First, while the procedure had enormous promise, convincing doctors to adopt it was more difficult than expected. Second, clinical trials suggested that the new procedure might have a higher mortality rate than the traditional procedure. In a minimally invasive procedure, the doctor relies on a computer image to perform the microsurgery. If there are unexpected problems, the patient still needs to be opened for traditional surgery, and in the meantime his condition may deteriorate.

Other companies ran into similar difficulties. They overestimated their ability to push products through the approval process as well as their ability to market the products. Based on the dismal experience of a few of these second tier companies, institutional investors bolted from these small-cap players. By June 1996, the capital markets for the start-ups had dried up, and venture capital funds lost interest.

Indeed, this trend strongly parallels what had happened in the biotech industry a few years before. Many of these companies who had sought IPOs as exit strategies or had relied on continued access to the capital markets to raise money were either forced out of business or had to look elsewhere for capital. As in biotech, the first tier players began to play the "rich uncles" to the second tier, making strategic investments in promising start-ups so as to benefit from the new technologies they are developing.

Acquiring these smaller players has also provided a way for the first tier companies to solve their own strategic dilemmas created by the managed care environment. In this environment, hospitals, forced by insurers to reduce costs, have come to favor the providers that can offer both the lowest prices and one-stop shopping. As a result, the big medical device companies have sought combinations both to reduce their manufacturing costs through economies of scale and to create a wide-ranging portfolio of products. Several players have taken the lead in a recent move toward consolidation: Tyco, Boston Scientific, Medtronic, and Guidant.

Tyco, a diversified conglomerate and relatively recent entrant into the medical device arena, has employed a sector roll-up strategy. Most recently, in November 1998, Tyco acquired Graphic Controls Corp. for $460 million. Previous acquisitions included the $3.2 billion purchase of U.S. Surgical, a minimally invasive surgical products company, the $1.8 billion purchase of Sherwood-Davis & Geck, and the 1994 purchase of Kendall International. U.S. Surgical had, for some time, been languishing in a highly competitive environment. The deal with Tyco gave it the bulk to be a more effective competitor.

Boston Scientific bought Schneider Worldwide in September 1998, building upon previous acquisitions, including its 1995 purchases of EP Technologies, Meadox Medicals, Heart Technology, SciMed Life Systems, Cardiovascular Imaging Systems, and Vesica, and the 1997 purchase of Target Therapeutics, a maker of catheters and other medical equipment used in minimally invasive medical procedures. The SciMed acquisition provided Boston Scientific with the immensely popular coronary balloon catheter.

Medtronic, a company primarily active in the cardiovascular surgical devices market, has been another aggressive acquirer. In March 1999, the company purchased Avecor Cardiovascular. In January 1999, it purchased stent maker Arterial Vascular Engineering for $3.6 billion and neurological and spinal equipment maker Sofamor Danek Group for $3.6 billion, deals which followed closely on the heels of acquisitions of defibrillator maker Physio-Control International and neurosurgical instrument maker Midas Rex.

This flurry of combinations transformed Medtronic, literally doubling the size of the company over the course of a few months, and furthering the company's goal of becoming a one-stop shop for medical devices. Before the diversifying acquisitions, the company dominated the worldwide market for implantable pacemakers and was the number two player in implantable defibrillators.

Guidant has also pursued growth through consolidation. In January 1999, the company acquired Sulzer Medica's cardiac rhythm management business for $810 million, and in 1998, it acquired the company's electrophysiology business. Both acquisitions were contemplated so as to gain a technological lead over Medtronic. Also in 1998, the company served as rich uncle acquirer to a trial defibrillator maker InControl, which had depleted its cash reserves in clinical trials.

Several of the companies these tier one players purchased were portfolio companies of the big pharmaceutical players. In the 1970s, when broad diversification was in fashion, the pharmaceutical companies saw difficult years ahead and price pressures on their core drug business. They viewed diversification as a hedge against this risk and therefore purchased companies outside their core areas, including medical device companies. But in the 1980s and 1990s, the trend began to reverse itself. The medical device business proved to be a much slower grower than the drug business: 10 to 12 percent per year, versus a potential 20 to 30 percent per year growth in drugs. Because the medical device companies were not pulling their weight, pharmaceutical companies began to put them on the block. For example, in September 1998, Pfizer sold its Schneider Worldwide catheter business to Boston Scientific for $2.1 billion, and in December 1998 it sold its Howmedica orthopedic business to Stryker for $1.65 billion. The Schneider Worldwide acquisition marked one of the first combinations in a long time for Boston Scientific and has been accompanied by significant indigestion.

American Home Products too has been selling off some of its medical device operations. Boston Scientific also purchased Symbiosis from American Home Products in 1996. And Sherwood-Davis & Geck, a division of American Home Products, was bought by Tyco.

Big Pharma

By almost any measure—aggregate dollar volume, global scope, or otherwise—the pharmaceutical deals have been the most significant aspect of the unfolding health care evolution. Over the past ten years, the big pharmaceutical companies have taken part in a mammoth merger wave with two major peaks, first in the late 1980s and then in the mid-1990s. These deals have had a major economic impact, driving the combined market share of the top ten companies from 25 percent in 1988 to 53 percent in 1997.

The merger wave in the pharmaceuticals industry began in earnest in the late 1980s. In 1988, an attempted hostile takeover by Roche, a Swiss company, of Sterling Drug ended when Sterling fell into the arms of white knight Eastman Kodak for $5.1 billion. Similarly a bidding war erupted the same year for A.H. Robins Company. American Home Products ended up the winning suitor, leaving Sanofi of France disappointed. This consolidation was triggered by an industry-wide drive to fill out sales and marketing capacity. The pharmaceutical industry was going global, and companies were doing deals to catch up. Even in the purely domestic deals, the desire was to gain more capacity to build market share.

More recently, however, consolidation attempts have some aspects of opera buffa. From the outside, one day partners announce their marriage, only to cancel it the next day, when the infidelity of one of the players is revealed. As if that weren't enough, when it is announced that the groom is leaving his bride to join his mistress, that partnership too collapses over "social issues." Of course, these machinations are reflections of subtle but quite deep business issues, where the theoretical benefits of mergers sometimes clash with the practicality of running companies.

TOP TEN WORLDWIDE PHARMACEUTICALS COMPANIES

Company	(Billions of Dollars as of September 1999) Market Value
Merck & Co.	$162
Bristol-Myers Squibb	$147
Pfizer	$142
Glaxo Wellcome	$ 97
Novartis	$ 89
Roche	$ 82
Schering-Plough	$ 74
AstraZeneca	$ 74
Eli Lilly & Co.	$ 73
American Home Products	$ 61

The First Wave

The first merger wave crested in 1989 with two big deals—the $16 billion merger of SmithKline Beckman and Beecham, followed shortly by the $12 billion merger of Bristol-Myers and Squibb. In many ways, the SmithKline-Beecham deal was indicative of industry trends.

By and large, the 1980s were boom years for the pharmaceuticals business. Companies were able to raise the cost per prescription at rates faster than inflation and a number of breakthrough drugs inflated into billion-dollar-a-year revenue machines. As a consequence, even though the industry remained highly fragmented, the pharmaceuticals business was the most profitable sector of the American economy. Returns on equity outpaced the median for Fortune 500 companies by roughly 50 percent. Success motivated entrepreneurs to enter the industry with new start-up companies.

However, as the decade came to a close, things had begun to deteriorate somewhat. Patent protection was about to expire on many of the blockbuster drugs that had propelled earnings growth and stock market appreciation over the prior decade. In addition, escalating competition had shortened the profitable life of new drugs. Companies piggybacked on each other by turning out modifications of existing drugs. For example, when ulcer medication Tagamet became a billion-dollar-a-year drug for SmithKline Beecham, Glaxo countered with its Zantac formulation, which claimed fewer unfavorable interactions with other drugs. Strong marketing also pushed Zantac above the billion-dollar mark in annual revenues.

The shorter life cycle of these and other drugs caused experts to predict diminishing returns from this kind of incremental innovation. Drug companies needed to develop entirely new blockbuster drugs, but few such innovations were in the lengthy approval pipeline.

This was precisely the pressure faced by SmithKline. Rumors that the company was a takeover target began to circulate toward the end of 1988, largely because of uncertainties surrounding the future of Tagamet. While the company had risen to star status on the strength of this product, no successor had been developed despite spending hundred of millions of dollars annually on research. Sales of Tagamet were already declining and patent protection would expire in much of Europe by 1992. The American patent would last just a few more years, until 1994.

Beecham, on the other hand, owned a portfolio of strong over-the-counter brands like Tums, and had several promising new drugs in the pipeline, including a heart attack medicine and an arthritis remedy. However, the U.K. company wanted to beef up its U.S. marketing presence.

SmithKline's stock price shot up on continuing merger speculation, and the pressure grew. Within two weeks, matters came to a head and the Beecham deal was announced. The two companies would join in a stock-for-stock merger of equals. SmithKline's chairman, Henry Wendt, would become chairman of the combined entity; Beecham's chairman, Robert Bauman, would be the chief executive.

Bauman—the first American to run the British Beecham—saw increased size and breadth as critical to Beecham's future success. Increased research and development, which constitute a higher percentage of revenues for drug companies than other kinds of companies, would be necessary to fuel drug discovery: Indeed, the expectation was that a major drug company would need to spend more than $500 million a year on research to be successful, with R&D spending to grow 10 to 15 percent higher each year. But few companies in the industry could afford such a high level of expenditure on their own. Beecham and others faced an unattractive choice: Either gamble on a few seemingly promising areas, or work more slowly on a broad range of projects. In either case, there would be dry spells where no significant developments emerged.

Many companies found neither alternative attractive. Growing large through mergers, on the other hand, would allow the surviving company to support a larger combined research effort. The best projects from each company could be backed fully and discovery time slashed. By pursuing several research efforts simultaneously, companies would be diversified and thus less dependent on the success of one particular venture.

However, research costs were just part of the impetus for the SmithKline-Beecham deal. The merger also had a broader strategic resonance. Many of the largest companies in the industry were European players—Glaxo, Roche, Sandoz, Beecham. While these companies were successful, they lacked a strong presence in the U.S. market, which today accounts for roughly 40 percent of worldwide pharmaceutical sales. Building a beachhead in this market was particularly important because drug prices were unregulated in the United States, unlike in other countries, and as a result, U.S. sales of a drug could effectively subsidize non-U.S. sales.

Hence, the international players had a donut hole to fill. They needed to crack the U.S. market, and acquisitions were one way in the door. Financial fluctuations—particularly the dollar's decline to postwar lows and the U.S. stock market swoon of 1987—lubricated the process.

The trend in favor of European suitors for U.S. companies first became apparent in the Sterling Drug bidding war. Initially, Roche made a play for the U.S. maker of Bayer aspirin and various prescription medications. However, Sterling Drug soon found white knight Eastman Kodak, a company interested in diversifying away from reliance on the photographic business. Sanofi had a similar experience with its failed bid for A.H. Robins. Beecham was the first company to succeed in jumping into the U.S. market, perhaps because it was led by an American.

Eastman Kodak's struggles with Sterling, however, demonstrated the importance of having a global presence. Because Kodak lacked the global drug distribution network to boost international sales, in 1991, Kodak fashioned a global alliance with Sanofi. Then, in 1994, Kodak got out of the drug business entirely, selling the prescription pharmaceuticals operations to Sanofi for $1.7 billion, the over-the-counter lines to SmithKline Beecham for $2.9 billion, and the diagnostic businesses to Johnson & Johnson for $1.0 billion.

As the 1980s came to a close, the cross-border imperative remained strong. In 1990, Rhône-Poulenc, a French chemicals and pharmaceuticals company, paid over $2 billion to acquire the Rorer Group, a U.S. drug company that owned over-the-counter brand Maalox and various prescription businesses. Glaxo, Sanofi, Sandoz, Roche, and others continued to shop for merger partners. While the downturn of the early 1990s slowed the process, in time the European invasion would accelerate again during the second merger wave of the 1990s.

On the domestic front, the SmithKline-Beecham deal opened the consolidation floodgates. Shortly thereafter Dow Chemical announced a multibillion-dollar deal for Marion Laboratories in which Dow would acquire control of Marion in stages over several years, with the first 39 percent acquired immediately for cash. Bristol-Myers and Squibb followed with their marriage. Each successive deal increased the pressure on competitors. Even companies like industry-leader Merck, which avoided major acquisitions, agreed to a joint venture with DuPont, which had spent more than $2 billion on pharmaceuticals research over the previous few years.

However, the deals of the 1980s were just a first step in the consolidation of the global pharmaceuticals business. Even with all the billion-dollar matches, each of the top five companies in the industry had less than 5 percent of the total market. The pharmaceuticals business remained highly fragmented and ripe for further consolidation.

The Biotech Future

Intersecting with the consolidation among main-line drug companies, biotech companies—the hot stocks of the previous decade—also came under pressure when revenues and earnings failed to meet expectations for fast growth. The large pharmaceutical deals slowed to a trickle, as one by one, the crippled biotech companies were swallowed by healthier acquirers. However, these deals were relatively small compared to the multibillion-dollar pharmaceutical mergers, and only obscured the larger undercurrents in the market. Biotechnology was essentially a sideshow, though an interesting one.

The pressure on biotech companies built up amid years of predictions about a coming revolution. Biotech companies were routinely vaunted as the heirs to the future; their ability to identify and map genes, and engineer new drugs from plant, animal, and human proteins, promised to unlock cures for cancer, heart disease, and other ailments. Biotech also had potential applications to agriculture and livestock breeding.

By 1990, the promise of biotech remained, but developments were taking longer than hoped. Time and again throughout the early part of the decade, the approval of a biotech company's hot new drug would get held up by the FDA and its stock would plummet.

Biotech companies also faced an escalating cost for research, but lacked the stable cash flows of the big pharmaceutical companies. When the biotech start-ups stumbled, they began to look for cash-rich partners to fund their immediate research needs.

A smattering of such deals began to appear in 1986. Targets included Connaught Biosciences, Hybritech, and Genetic Systems. However, none of these deals was large enough to generate much attention. But the deal flow really accelerated in 1990 with the landmark alliance between Genentech and Roche.

Genentech's situation was a classic example of the pressures imposed when financing an early-stage venture on Wall Street. Genentech founder Robert Swanson had turned to the public markets as a means to finance the realization of his vision—an integrated, independent pharmaceutical company built on the strength of biotechnology. He was not shy about advertising his ambitious goals for the company: Genentech, he projected, would generate $1 billion in annual revenues by 1990.

Setbacks, however, contributed to Genentech's increased need for capital. The FDA approval process for the company's heart drug TPA had taken longer than originally expected. Moreover, initial sales of the drug, which came in at about $200 million in 1989, fell well short of expectations. The company had projected more like $400 million in annual sales for 1988, with annual increases thereafter.

By 1989, Genentech was looking for an escape valve, hoping to bleed off some of the pressures that had built up. The company also had identified more promising research opportunities than it could afford to fund. Basically Genentech needed a stable, patient source of capital.

Roche, on the other hand, was still hoping to realize its U.S. ambitions, and found the highly creative, entrepreneurial Genentech an attractive partner. We began negotiations in the fall and a deal was announced in February 1990. Under the agreement, Roche would pay $2.1 billion for 60 percent of Genentech.

In a two-step transaction, Roche would buy 50 percent of the 84 million outstanding Genentech shares from shareholders and subsequently would buy another 22 million shares newly issued by the company. The issuance of new shares to Roche would provide roughly $500 million in fresh capital to Genentech. Roche also would have an option to acquire the remaining 40 percent of the company in the future. The option, originally set to expire in 1995, was later extended to 1999. In the summer of 1999, Roche exercised that option, took Genentech private, and innovatively and profitably took the company public again.

The Genentech deal was viewed in the market as an endorsement of the industry's future at a time when investor sentiment had soured. Large pharmaceutical companies began to exhibit interest in finding biotech partners. A rush of activity ensued, fueled by the fear that the few prime properties would be swallowed.

About a year after the Genentech deal was announced, American Home Products followed suit with its own acquisition of Genetics Institute. Seeking to bolster its pharmaceuticals operations, AHP paid a steep premium in the $666 million deal. Again, the acquirer bought part of its initial stake from the public and part from the company itself. AHP, like Roche, would end up with an initial 60 percent stake and an option to buy the remainder of its target. Unlike Roche, though, American Home Products exercised its option in 1996, buying the remaining 40 percent of Genetics Institute for another $1.25 billion.

The Genentech and Genetics Institute deals set intriguing strategic precedents: The operational marriage of biochemical and biological research promised access to a fuller range of new products. Other deals followed. Many kept to the earlier pattern, that is, large pharmaceutical buys struggling biotech company. For instance, drug and chemical company American Cyanamid bought a controlling stake in Immunex.

However, not all deals involved an established pharmaceutical company as acquirer. Strong biotech companies also sought out partnerships as a way to consolidate their positions. Chiron's acquisition of Cetus Corp., in which financial distress again triggered the seller's interest in a deal, is the primary example.

Cetus owned a gene mapping technology known as PCR, but otherwise had been unable to convert promising technologies into marketable products. The company hit a wall in 1990 when the FDA delayed approval of its interleukin-2 cancer treatment. Shortly thereafter, with our help, Cetus began looking for a partner. Chiron emerged as the winning suitor. Because it lacked the cash for a stock purchase, the deal was structured as a stock swap, with additional capital to be raised through the sale of the PCR technology to Roche.

While this deal bought some time for Chiron and Cetus, in 1994 the combined companies turned to much larger Ciba-Geigy for a cash infusion. The Swiss company bought slightly less than 50 percent of Chiron at an almost 100 percent premium to the prior trading price of Chiron stock. In addition, Ciba-Geigy committed to provide financial backing for future research.

A few fortunate biotech companies were able to survive or even thrive as independents. Amgen was the most successful, effectively stepping into Genentech's shoes as the standard-bearer for the publicly traded biotech companies. The company had what others lacked—two approved drugs, Epogen and Neupogen, generating significant revenues. In fact, the company was sufficiently flush with cash so that it could acquire a smaller rival, Synergen, for $262 million in a 1994 deal. The following year, the company weathered rumors of an impending takeover by Bristol-Myers Squibb.

By 1996, Amgen, along with the broader biotech industry, was back in favor. Amgen generated $2.2 billion of revenues, primarily on the strength of its two approved blood therapeutics. As a result of the strong performance, the company has today been rewarded on Wall Street with an overall stock market capitalization of almost $40 billion. Its 1998 revenues were $2.6 billion.

Notwithstanding Amgen's relative success, the shakeout in biotech was to be expected. The frenzy to snap up the next big thing had led to a large number of publicly traded companies with little more than an idea and start-up capital. A number of these companies were bound to stumble. Some failed. Others still had strong science and just needed a boost.

The consolidation wave of 1990 to 1994 was indicative of a broad market realization that few companies could afford to go it alone. By and large, the new model has become a semi-independent entity within a larger company. The core of this model is the continuing expectation that biotechnology is the best hope to produce the next generation of blockbuster drugs. However, the equity market capitalization of the top biotech companies is just a fraction of that of the top pharmaceutical companies. Biotech may be the future, but its promise is not yet fully developed.

The lackluster performance of many biotech firms has induced many venture capital companies to divert funds away from biotech and instead to infotech companies and Internet companies.

Given this dearth of start-up capital, bigger biotech companies are increasingly partnering with smaller ones to provide "corporate venture capital." Amgen, for example, spends about one third of its R&D budget on start-ups and alliances with universities. In March 1999, the company announced it paid $100 million for the development and commercialization rights to Praecis Pharmaceutical's prostate cancer drug. Indeed, such partnerships have recently been responsible for increasing the stock prices of the large biotechs.

Recapturing the Distribution Channel

In the early 1990s, conventional pharmaceutical companies were much healthier than the biotech companies and had the capacity to act as "rich-uncle" strategic acquirers. Nevertheless, they faced their own set of troubles, driven by both the managed care trends and by political reaction against high drug prices. Both forces threatened to contain drug prices and thereby reduce drug companies' profits.

While companies struggled to fend off what they saw as a political threat, the desire to regulate drug prices, they also began to look for new ways to compete in the managed care world. Understandably, managed care companies tried to use their leverage to induce drug companies to reduce their prices. One response drug companies explored was to purchase pharmacy benefit managers (PBMs).

A concept only a few years old, PBMs acted as middlemen between employers and managed care companies, aiming to reduce the cost of providing prescription drug benefits. Costs were kept down in two ways. First, the pharmacy benefit managers bought drugs in bulk, and therefore were able to negotiate and pass on favorable discounts to HMOs. Second, the PBMs maintained lists of preferred drugs for given conditions, with cost the primary determinant of a preferred drug. Doctors in a managed care plan were then encouraged to select drugs from the list. If they instead selected a more expensive drug, the PBM might have its employees call in an effort to encourage a switch to equally effective but cheaper drugs.

Merck was the first mover in the PBM acquisition spree, agreeing in 1993 to pay $6.6 billion for distributor Medco Containment. The next year SmithKline Beecham announced a similar $2.3 billion deal to pick up Diversified Pharmaceuticals Services, and Eli Lilly bought PCS Health Systems, the benefits division of McKesson Corp., for $4.1 billion. Three other drug companies—Pfizer, Rhône-Poulenc Rorer, and Bristol-Myers Squibb—formed a strategic alliance with managed care company Caremark International.

The rationale behind this rash of deals was simple: Drug companies saw their control of the distribution channel for pharmaceuticals slipping away, along with their favorable margins. By acquiring the big pharmacy benefits companies, with which the HMOs deal, the drug companies would have a channel through which they could aggressively push their products. Analogous to movie studios buying video chains, PBMs vertically integrated the drug companies.

This new environment contrasted sharply with the drug environment during the 1980s. Before the advent of HMOs or managed care, the key was the ability to market directly to doctors. If a company won over doctors to its products, it won market share. Once the doctor prescribed a particular drug, patients were unlikely to switch. For chronic conditions, a single prescription could mean a long-term revenue stream.

Therefore, before the advent of PBMs, pharmaceutical companies focused their marketing effort on doctors themselves. Salespeople were hired and trained to push products in one-on-one sales calls. Studies were commissioned to highlight the benefits of a particular product and presentations made at medical conferences. Many busy physicians lacked the time or inclination to do their own research regarding the latest developments in drug research. As a result, the drug companies themselves were often the source of information.

A doctor would wade through the competing claims of drug companies and select what seemed the best medicine. Though decisions generally were made aboveboard, abuses did occur. For example, one drug company designed a controversial, and ultimately withdrawn, program under which doctors could receive frequent flyer miles for prescribing a particular drug.

All this activity became increasingly less relevant with the rise of managed care, which often transferred prescription decisions away from doctors and put them in the hands of the pharmacy benefit managers. By buying control of the PBMs, the drug companies hoped to recapture the ability to encourage doctors to favor their drugs.

Unfortunately for the acquiring drug companies, however, antitrust issues limited their ability to benefit from their captive PBMs. The first two deals—Merck-Medco and SmithKline-Diversified—gained government antitrust approval fairly easily. However, by the time of the third deal, political pressure had mounted. Lilly was forced to consent in advance to maintain an "open formulary" or a relatively liberal list of favor drugs for its PBM, PCS; competitors' drugs could not be excluded from the list. Moreover, Lilly was required to set up a "fire wall" between it and PCS so that it would not receive information regarding what other pharmaceutical companies charged for their drugs. The FDA too has attempted to crack down on PBM promotions and kickbacks between drug makers and PBMs.

The Lilly restrictions eventually whipsawed Merck and Smith-Kline. Government antitrust officials reviewed their deals a second time, after the fact, as is permissible under antitrust regulations. Merck and SmithKline ended up accepting the same restrictions as Lilly.

Partly because of these limitations, the PBM deals have turned in almost uniformly unfavorable results. Furthermore, PBMs acquired by pharmaceutical companies were in their very nature low-growth, low-margin businesses that underperformed relative to pharmaceutical companies' core drug businesses. PBMs already provided services for approximately 75 percent of all employed people, leaving little room for organic growth. And the low prices at which they sold drugs left little room for profit. In an environment where regulation impeded pharmaceutical companies from pushing their products through captive PPMs to the exclusion of other products, PPMs added no value to pharmaceutical companies, instead dragging down profitability. Lilly has fared the worst. In June 1997, the company cut the original $4.1 billion book value of PCS by $2.4 billion, taking a large one-time charge in the process, a tacit admission that Lilly had overpaid for PCS. Then in November 1998, PCS was sold to Rite Aid for a mere $1.4 billion.

In 1999, recognizing PBMs' disfavor in the market, SmithKline Beecham also agreed to sell its PBM, Diversified, to Express Scripts for $700 million. Merck, on the other hand, has had success with Medco. Since acquiring the company in 1993, Merck has reportedly increased its distribution of Merck products by 50 percent. The company has gained market share and roughly $400 million of annual profitability not even counting the separate profits of

Medco. Analysts attribute the recent growth in part to Medco's influence.

Given the regulatory and managed care environment, pharmaceutical companies' PBMs are by and large just pharmacy claims processors now. A commodity business, the PBM receives a claim for a product electronically, examines the claim to determine patient eligibility and the appropriateness of the drug, and then pays the pharmacy. Because it is so easy to provide this service, PBMs today compete almost solely on price, which has further hurt their market and acquisition values.

But PBMs have been more attractive to pharmacies like Rite Aid, which is combining PCS with its own PBM, Eagle Managed Care. A PBM promises to provide pharmacies with four benefits: 1) greater leverage with manufacturers, 2) economies from the combination of retail pharmacy and PBM computer systems, 3) the ability to bring additional services to their patients, leading to 4) more customers coming into their stores. Significantly, PBMs can help pharmacies track all the drugs a given patient takes to ensure they will not interact unfavorably with each other. Undoubtedly, this service could induce a patient to direct his business to a pharmacy partnered with a PBM. If more traffic is driven into a pharmacy, the store can then cross-sell its other higher-margin products to the pharmacy customers. Furthermore, automated mail-order processing is a strength of PBMs that pharmacies can exploit.

In the end, managed care was not the threat that it at first seemed. Prescription drugs are playing a large role in managed care budgets because they are highly effective preventative measures against serious illness. A long-term course of preventative drugs is generally much less expensive than letting a medical situation escalate to the point that a more radical solution like surgery is warranted. Furthermore, managed care companies are passing on the increasing cost of drugs in the form of higher premiums, rather than limiting services.

Jan Leschly

Since taking over as chief executive of SmithKline Beecham in April 1994, Jan Leschly has been at the epicenter of the pharmaceutical consolidation wave. An affable Dane, he began his professional life not in the executive suites, but on the tennis courts, where he rose to be the tenth-ranked player in the world. When his tennis career came to an end, Leschly joined Danish pharmaceutical company Novo and began a fast-track rise to the top of the pharmaceutical industry.

Leschly moved across the Atlantic in 1979 to take a job at Squibb, where he quickly stood out as a marketing and management expert, overseeing the introduction of Capoten. This hugely successful heart drug eventually grew into the second-biggest-selling prescription medication in the world.

By 1988, Leschly was president and chief operating officer of Squibb and was often mentioned as a likely successor to CEO Richard Furlaud. However, at that point, Furlaud decided to sell Squibb to Bristol-Myers. Leschly was given the opportunity to stay on, but felt the odd man out. Instead of staying, he resigned and spent a year at Princeton University studying philosophy and religion. Eventually, though, Leschly missed the action and excitement of running a business and in 1990 joined SmithKline Beecham to run its pharmaceuticals division.

Having been through an acquisition in which one party predominated over the other, Leschly was determined to integrate the SmithKline and Beecham operations on an even basis. Remarkably, sales and profit growth remained strong through the 1990s recession and transition of Tagamet to over-the-counter status.

The payoff for Leschly came in 1994, when he took over as

CEO of the parent company. In keeping with his determined, aggressive style, he moved quickly to act on his strategic vision. Looking across the spectrum of the pharmaceuticals industry, Leschly saw a clear trend: Size and global scope were becoming critical. Only five or ten truly international players would emerge with the assets and capability to discover innovative new products.

SmithKline's acquisitions and divestitures of 1994 were the first steps toward preparing the company for this future. The acquisitions of Diversified Pharmaceuticals, subsequently sold, and the over-the-counter businesses of Sterling Winthrop were intended to expand dramatically SmithKline's global distribution network. Although Diversified Pharmaceuticals didn't work as expected, Sterling Winthrop brought strong international over-the-counter brands and, more importantly, an experienced international sales force to supplement SmithKline's overseas efforts.

Leschly followed the two acquisitions of 1994 with a couple of major divestitures. Part of the Sterling Winthrop business, mainly U.S. OTC products including the rights to the Bayer name, were sold to Bayer AG of Germany for $1 billion. Bayer had long been after the American rights to its flagship brand, which it lost after World War I. The Bayer deal was followed by the $1.5 billion sale of Smith-Kline's animal health division.

Leschly subsequently stumbled with the abortive moves for AHP and Glaxo-Wellcome. He soon recovered his balance, refocused the company with divestitures of low-growth businesses, and launched SmithKline on aggressive growth targets backed by a promising product pipeline.

The Second Wave

The biotech and PBM deals obscured for a few years the impact of cost pressures and the shifting competitive landscape. But in the early 1990s, even with higher unit volumes, prices for branded prescription drugs were falling due to the wide availability of generic substitutes. Mergers were seen as a solution, designed to build broader product lines with opportunities for cross-selling and to reduce the cost of drug development and delivery. As a consequence, a second major pharmaceuticals merger wave—a sprint of multibillion-dollar deals—kicked off in 1994.

The desire to reduce costs, especially marketing and R&D costs, was, as before, a significant driver of many of the second-wave mergers. Furthermore, companies whose drug patents were to expire within a few years, with the next blockbuster not to come for several years after that, have sought companies with a complementary drug pipeline to bridge the gap.

M&A has also come as a response to new technologies, such as combinatorial chemistry and gene mapping, which promise to alter the fundamental economics of the pharmaceuticals industry. The traditional method to develop drugs was to look for naturally occurring organisms that would accomplish a specific goal. But more recently, combinatorial chemistry has allowed pharmaceutical companies to combine molecules so as to form a compound that will interact in a specific way—with a particular bacterium, for example. This new technology allows researchers to develop literally thousands of different chemicals in a very short time, promising to speed up the drug development process.

The second innovation, gene mapping, seems equally promising. The Human Genome Project—a project to map the entire human gene sequence—began in the early 1990s and is expected to be completed in a few years. Already, the project has impacted the pharmaceuticals industry significantly. Because scientists now know the composition of specific genes, they will be able to develop gene therapies—often using combinatorial chemistry—that will interact with those genes to correct a variety of disorders. There is widespread acknowledgment that genetic capabilities will be essential to a drug company's success in the future. The quest for capability in this area is now—and will continue to be—one of the imperatives for consolidation.

Genetic capability has also led to the creation of the life sciences field—the production of genetically engineered crops and crop protection products. Now a growth area, companies are faced with the strategic decision of whether to expand their business lines into life sciences. Companies active in life sciences include AHP, AstraZeneca, Aventis, BASF, Bayer, DuPont, and Novartis. The market until recently has been willing to apply the higher pharmaceuticals multiple to the earnings generated by the life sciences business of drug companies. Stagnation in crop protection sales and consumer worries about genetically modified crops are causing pharmaceutical companies to reevaluate their life sciences portfolios.

Finally, broadening the product mix was also seen as an important goal. Managed care companies and other providers of health care benefits were themselves increasingly focused on efficiency and cost savings. Drug companies with wide product lines possessed a marketing advantage because they could offer one-stop shopping to the PBMs that served as gatekeepers. Higher volume with single customers could translate into volume pricing for the customer and more efficient distribution for the manufacturer.

The twin gods of cost and capability were widely recognized across the spectrum of pharmaceutical companies. The companies that would thrive in the future would be the very large, global players and the small focused players. Those in between would slip through the cracks. As a consequence, competition for merger partners intensified. Success came to companies willing to be creative, to break through the boundaries of conventional industry norms.

American Home Products, under the leadership of Chairman Jack Stafford, demonstrated such a willingness in its 1994 pursuit of American Cyanamid. Stafford defied convention on two accounts: First, in the normally clubby pharmaceuticals business, he launched a $9.2 billion hostile bear hug offer for Cyanamid; and second, he put a slug of goodwill on the combined company's books as a result of the all-cash deal structure.

AHP made its offer in August 1994. Stafford had been considering a deal with Cyanamid for some time. In fact, he and Cyanamid chairman Albert Costello had scheduled a meeting for the end of the month. However, Stafford was pushed to act more aggressively when word leaked of negotiations between SmithKline Beecham and Cyanamid of a multibillion-dollar swap of SmithKline's vaccine and animal health business for Cyanamid's prescription drug and consumer products businesses.

Of course, it was precisely Cyanamid's prescription and consumer products brands that Stafford wanted: Cyanamid, which had divested most of its chemical business in 1993, was an attractive fit for AHP. The company's generic business would fill out AHP's prescription lines and position it better with managed care providers. In addition, Cyanamid's over-the-counter and consumer brands had received relatively little marketing and promotion attention. Stafford calculated that his company's sales force could pump up sales of these products.

The tactical situation required AHP to make a strong bid or no bid at all. Consequently, AHP's initial offer was $95 a share, all in cash, or a 50 percent premium to the previous closing price of Cyanamid's stock. Normalizing for the run-up in Cyanamid's stock price as a result of deal rumors, the premium was even higher. Yet the Street endorsed Stafford's strategy, bidding AHP's stock higher on news of the offer.

AHP's bid was widely viewed as an attempt to preempt other potential acquirers. The approach worked. Cyanamid's board pursued talks with SmithKline and others, but no other company was willing to top the bid. The price was full and few American companies were willing to consider taking on the amount of goodwill that would be created.

Still, Cyanamid's takeover defenses gave it some negotiating leverage. By continuing to stall and look for potential white knights, Cyanamid eventually teased an additional $6 a share out of AHP. Two weeks after the AHP bear hug, the parties agreed to a $9.7 billion friendly deal.

The potential for cost savings was a critical foundation for Stafford's willingness to bid at such a high level for Cyanamid. Within the year, AHP announced plans to lay off 4,300 of the combined company's 74,000 total employees. Annual cost savings were estimated at $650 million, or 11 percent of combined overhead.

The benefits of these cost savings, and strong merger implementation, have powered American Home Products in the stock market. Adjusted for a subsequent split, American Home Products' stock was trading at $14 before the bear hug letter was made public in August 1994. By August 1998 the stock traded up to approximately $100 a share for a 63 percent compound annual growth over the four years. Since then, concerns about its life sciences business and product liability exposure have held back stock performance.

Significantly, AHP's performance came despite the fact that the goodwill created by the Cyanamid deal initially reduced AHP's earnings per share. The market saw the underlying economic sense of the deal, as Jack Stafford had predicted. The dollars-and-cents benefits of consolidation were underscored, only increasing the competition for merger partners.

Globalization Accelerates

Much of the pharmaceutical mating dance of the early 1990s took place on an international scale, stemming from the imperative to globalize.

The pace of cross-border consolidation picked up in 1994. Many of the deals were sparked by the continuing focus among international drug companies on entering the U.S. market. Roche followed its Genentech investment with another big deal, buying Syntex, a troubled California drugmaker, in a $5.3 billion deal in 1994. The next year, Germany's Hoechst ended Dow Chemical's unsuccessful foray into the pharmaceuticals business by acquiring Marion Merrell Dow for $7.1 billion. Pharmacia cracked the U.S. market in a merger-of-equals with Upjohn.

In addition to European companies' desire to expand into the U.S., international differences in accounting rules also led U.S. targets to end up with foreign acquirers. Despite AHP's pioneering willingness to take on goodwill, most U.S. drug companies resist the earnings dilution that results from goodwill. Many European companies, on the other hand, are governed by more favorable accounting rules in which goodwill is written off immediately and does not flow through the income statement. There is therefore no earnings impact, giving European acquirers a bidding edge.

However, the biggest drug company deals of the past five years have been purely European affairs. Starting in 1995, each successive year brought another multibillion-dollar European pharmaceuticals deal. In 1995, Glaxo launched a successful $15 billion hostile takeover of fellow British company Wellcome to create the world's leading pharmaceutical company in terms of market share.

At the time, the deal created the largest U.K. company by market capitalization and was the second-largest combination in history. The immense combination also opened a Pandora's box of social issues—primarily revolving around job cuts. A delicate balance needed to be achieved between economy and fairness. In addition, despite the fact that Glaxo was the acquirer, enough key Wellcome employees had to be kept on to justify the deal. That the deal was hostile marked a watershed event for pharmaceuticals, an industry in which social issues are of paramount importance. Zeneca and Roche were approached as white knights but neither entered a bid. Nearly 82 percent of Wellcome shareholders tendered to Glaxo, among which was 40 percent holder Wellcome Trust.

Glaxo chief executive Sir Richard Sykes became chief executive of the new Glaxo Wellcome. His company would operate in four product areas whose sales exceeded $1 billion annually: gastrointestinal, respiratory, antiviral, and antibiotic. Both companies, however, were heavily dependent on their top-selling drugs: Glaxo derived 40 percent of its sales from Zantac; Wellcome derived more than 33 percent of its sales from Zovirax. Both drugs faced patent expiration issues. The deal promised expense cuts that could counteract this potential loss in revenue. Despite Glaxo Wellcome's size, however, it still holds less than a 5 percent market share in pharmaceuticals today.

Ciba-Geigy and Sandoz followed in 1996 with a friendly $36 billion merger to create a new company named Novartis, which became a number two to the new Glaxo Wellcome in market share. The deal was, however, the largest corporate combination at the time. Like the Glaxo Wellcome combination, this merger aimed to reduce costs: Fourteen thousand jobs were to be slashed.

Roche kept pace with its own $11 billion acquisition of Germany's Boehringer Mannheim, announced in May 1997. Roche's purchase transformed it into the leading business in diagnostics—a $19-billion-a-year business which provides equipment to test patients for disease—overtaking Abbott Laboratories. However, diagnostics is a low-margin business, in which sales have recently been flat. The managed care phenomenon and government reimbursement cut-backs have, in large part, been responsible for this trend.

The deal was not the one the market was expecting. Cash-rich Roche was rumored to be in the market for a major pharmaceuticals player—not a diagnostics business. The deal made clear that Roche, in contrast to its Swiss competitor Novartis, was embarking upon a very different course. Boehringer Mannheim's business does, however, complement Roche's diagnostic business well, a business that before the transaction already owned the PCR technology (poly-merase chain reaction). This valuable asset allows diagnosis of viruses or other foreign DNA in the human body.

Of the European deals, the Novartis merger most dramatically underlined the tremendous changes taking place in the global phar-maceuticals business, and in the European view of corporate merg-ers and acquisitions. The cost savings central to these European deals represented a dramatic shift. Until recently, European execu-tives resisted mergers as a mechanism for corporate restructuring, with the pressure on maintaining full employment rather than boost-ing profitability. Over the last few years, however, European compa-nies, like their American counterparts, have started to feel growth concerns and cost pressures. The merit of mergers has become ap-parent.

Mergers have had a powerful catalyzing effect in the European pharmaceuticals industry, creating the opportunity for huge savings. The Novartis deal is indicative. As part of the deal, Ciba-Geigy and Sandoz projected $1.5 billion in annual cost savings from reduced overlap, news which almost immediately added $12 billion to the combined company's market capitalization, which rose to $76 bil-lion. Between March 1996, before the deal was announced, and July 1999, the combined market capitalization appreciated by more than 100 percent.

Novartis was not the only case of major cost savings driving a Eu-ropean cross-border merger. Similarly, Glaxo and Wellcome promised over $1 billion of annual cost savings by 1998. As has been true for U.S. pharmaceuticals mergers, research capacity and diversification opportunities are also key issues. In 1997, adding to its life sciences business, Novartis picked up an insecticide and fungicide business from Merck for $910 million.

While these European deals were successful in helping the combining companies cut costs, they did not address one of the most pressing strategic concerns: building a presence in the U.S. The U.S. is a larger and more lucrative market. Any pharmaceuticals company that wants to be a global leader will have to build a significant presence in the U.S. But no such deal has yet come.

Nineteen ninety-eight ushered in a new era for pharmaceutical companies. Breaking out of several years of price stability, drug prices rose in 1998. Mylan Laboratories was largely responsible for this trend, having raised prices on its generic drugs; other generic and branded makers followed.

Indeed, the pharmaceuticals industry is in a new period of prosperity. And unlike in the early 1990s, the future outlook is rosy. The rate of drug spending is expected to increase in the future, rather than to fall, driven by the aging of the population, increasing life expectancies, and large untreated patient populations which can benefit from new drugs. A new class of blockbuster drugs has emerged, driving incredible revenue growth. Drugs like Viagra, aggressively marketed to patients themselves, rather than just doctors, promise a bright future for the companies that developed them. A new generation of painkillers that block the COX-2 enzyme, such as Monsanto's Celebrex and Merck's Vioxx, also promise to be strong performers. The impact of gene therapy will be especially dramatic.

Deal activity in 1998 was as much about the deals that failed to happen as those that did. In February 1998, American Home Products and British drug maker SmithKline Beecham were in merger discussions to create what would have been the largest maker of prescription and OTC drugs. Furthermore, the merger promised operational synergies: With a reported sixty potential new products in the pipeline, AHP was excited by SmithKline's pharmacy benefit management operations (now sold).

In an offstage act between meetings, however, SmithKline Beecham CEO Jan Leschly got a phone call from Sir Richard Sykes, chairman of Glaxo Wellcome, who proposed revisiting merger talks between SmithKline and Glaxo—talks that had been abandoned the year before. Such a deal would create a company far larger than the combined SmithKline-AHP and would not expose SmithKline to AHP's potential exposure to product liability lawsuits.

Leschly beat a hasty retreat from AHP, boarding the Concorde and flying to New York to hammer out the details of the deal. The two companies quickly came to terms and, amid much fanfare, announced a merger to create the world's largest drug company. AHP, still working out the details of its deal with SmithKline, found itself abandoned.

The market was abuzz with details of the deal. When SmithKline Beecham announced its annual results, Leschly projected great enthusiasm about the combination. But problems soon cropped up. Sir Richard, in the announcement of his firm's annual results, was unexpectedly silent about the deal. Glaxo then tried to define the terms of the deal into what would be essentially a management takeover, much like BP-Amoco or the Daimler Chrysler deal. The disagreement was more fundamental than simply who was to get what job: SmithKline Beecham's strategy was to build a well-rounded health care company while Glaxo Wellcome's focus has been primarily on drugs. The top executives could not agree on how the new company would be run and what its focus would be. Furthermore, there was a growing realization that the cultures of the two companies were very different: Glaxo Wellcome is a decentralized operation, while SmithKline Beecham is run firmly from the center.

With talks deadlocked, SmithKline Beecham issued a press release saying that Glaxo's conduct had "inevitably strained relations" between the two companies. The deal soon fell apart. Understandably, institutional shareholders were irate that these differences were not ironed out before the merger announcement was made. Smith-Kline Beecham executives became concerned that the deal would turn into a hostile takeover, now that the market was expecting a deal. But no hostile offer came.

Later in 1998, spurned AHP bounced back, announcing a deal with Monsanto. It was to be one of the largest combinations ever in the pharmaceuticals industry—$33.5 billion—and would create a life sciences giant. AHP is best known for its drug and over-the-counter health care products—Advil, Robitussin, and Chap Stick—and Monsanto makes Nutrasweet, Roundup herbicide, and agricultural biotech products.

Analysts noted that the combination would enable AHP to double its annual research spending to approximately $3 billion per year and strengthen its genetic engineering effort. The combined company also would have a deep pipeline of new drugs. At the time of announcement, Monsanto had five drugs that were to enter the final stage of trials and AHP had several more. If some of these drugs were not to pass Phase III trials, the combined company's greater product diversification would better enable it to withstand the shock than could two stand-alone companies.

Other synergies were to come from cutting of duplicative costs, such as overlapping administrative and research functions, and use of AHP's drug distribution network to market Monsanto's products.

But this merger announcement was also premature. The antitrust waiting period gave the couple more time to get to know each other. The two CEOs—John Stafford of AHP and Robert Shapiro of Monsanto—found they couldn't see eye to eye. The deal was soon called off.

In pharmaceutical companies, the intellectual capital of a drug company is its greatest asset. If researchers are not happy, a deal will fail—no matter how financially compelling it may look on paper. The role of management is less clear.

Four other companies, however, did manage to get together at the end of 1998. Germany's Hoechst announced a cross-border combination with France's Rhône-Poulenc, and Swedish Astra combined with Zeneca.

Hoechst–Rhône-Poulenc

In December 1998, the German Hoechst and the French Rhône-Poulenc announced a 50-50 combination to create the second-largest drug company in the world measured by sales and a leader in life sciences. The company, to be headquartered on the German-French border, in Strasbourg, France, would be called Aventis. The deal's strategic imperative was to accelerate top-line growth. In contrast to the deals that weren't, this combination was proceeded by a very long courtship.

Originally, the two companies planned to spin off their non-life-sciences units before the completion of the merger in 2001. The resulting Aventis Pharmaceutical would incorporate prescription pharmaceuticals, vaccines, and biologicals, while Aventis Agriculture would comprise crop science, animal nutrition, and animal health. Yet a later plan, intended to move up the schedule for the deal's closure to 1999, dropped the complicated spin-off plans.

Despite Aventis's strong pro forma sales, the deal will merge two companies that face serious strategic dilemmas. Hoechst and Rhône-Poulenc also share the same fundamental weakness, primarily the lack of a meaningful U.S. presence. While Aventis will be the world's second-largest drug company, it will rank only twelfth in the United States by sales. Furthermore, many expect Aventis's rankings to fall, as neither Hoechst nor Rhône-Poulenc has blockbuster drugs in their pipelines. Yet this deal could pave the way for a new wave of pharmaceutical combinations.

Zeneca-Astra

Zeneca Group PLC of the U.K.—the former agrochemical and drug arm of ICI—and Astra AB of Sweden moved to create the third-largest pharmaceutical company worldwide by sales—Astra-Zeneca—shortly following the announcements that Hoechst and Rhône-Poulenc would merge to form Aventis and that French pharmaceutical companies Sanofi and Synthelabo would combine. The merger will allow the two companies to increase their combined R&D budget to $2 billion after proposed cost cutting, significant in light of the imminent expiration of patents on Astra's Losec anti-ulcer treatment—the best-selling prescription drug in the world—and on Zeneca's heart drug Zestril.

Zeneca had planned its merger with Astra for three years, with contact first made in 1996. But it was not until the joint venture between Astra and Merck—one in which Merck was entitled to market all of Astra's products in North America—was unwound in the summer of 1998 that Astra and Zeneca could seriously entertain the possibility. The split of the partnership between Astra and Merck will result in Astra paying Merck at least $4.4 billion over the next ten years.

The Future

Across the health care spectrum, the need to consolidate will not go away. In the last several years, health care costs have continued to escalate at rates in excess of general inflation, and the trend seems likely to continue. While in the area of health care services there have been some setbacks and failures, economic and structural conditions favor combinations. New models will inevitably be developed. The tension among equity, quality of care, and technology remains unresolved.

In the pharmaceuticals, biotech, and medical device sectors, the cost of technological innovation also continues to favor business combinations.

Part Three | # Doing the Deal

"Nothing astonishes men so much as common sense and plain dealing."

—Ralph Waldo Emerson, *Essays*

A Guide to the Players

15

*"It is better to be making the news than taking it;
to be an actor rather than a critic."*

—Sir Winston Churchill,
The Malakand Field Force

The process of translating a strategic concept into a successfully executed deal can be incredibly arcane and difficult. Even the best concepts can founder on the rocks of poor execution. Spurred on by a combination of high stakes and complexity, an industry of takeover advisers has developed over the last thirty years.

The intensity of big-deal M&A draws individuals who thrive under the pressure, while otherwise highly capable people find they have no taste for the roller-coaster binges of intellectual effort. The best people at this business are indeed very capable and the overall dedication and professionalism in the industry is high.

Unfortunately, the process also attracts its share of hustlers and swaggering mediocrities who think that aggressive posturing is a substitute for talent. Moreover, the bundled services offered by large financial institutions don't necessarily promote excellence.

If you hang around the deal business long enough, you become accustomed to the cycle of boom and bust. A flush of adrenaline is generated when a deal is fresh. But if you lose the sense of excitement and curiosity, it's time to leave the business.

Lawyers and investment bankers are the highest-profile outside merger advisers, but many other professionals play important roles. Included in the mix are accountants, proxy solicitors, public relations professionals, and even private investigators. In addition, institutional investors, arbitrageurs, and business journalists are key players in determining which strategy appeals to the "market."

The Lawyers

Lawyers have been midwifing corporate combinations as far back as the nineteenth century. In 1891, for example, John R. Dos Passos, the author's father, reportedly earned a $500,000 legal fee for setting up a sugar trust.

Today, the legal team working on a large friendly merger or acquisition may have as many as fifteen or twenty lawyers, including corporate or M&A lawyers and specialists such as tax, environmental, employee benefits, real estate, and intellectual property lawyers.

The split between M&A lawyers and specialists reflects the nature of mergers and acquisitions. Specialists advise with respect to the regulatory frameworks involved in a deal. M&A lawyers, on the other hand, have a more general expertise. They help to negotiate the contractual agreement between the buyer and seller and act as an interface with the regulatory world.

If a deal becomes hostile, the legal team involved necessarily gets larger, especially when litigation is used as a takeover tactic. A target company may file various lawsuits in an effort to stave off a hostile acquirer. Or a hostile bidder may use litigation to force a target to relax its antitakeover defenses. Common grounds for litigation include antitrust, securities law, state antitakeover statutes, and general state corporate law regarding the fiduciary duties of board members. In the most actively contested deals, it is not uncommon for a single takeover contest to generate several lawsuits in various locations.

With the high level of mergers and acquisitions activity, corporate lawyers have prospered. In 1998, for example, the top ten M&A law firms in the United States, ranked by gross revenues, brought in more than $4.1 billion of M&A revenue according to a survey by *The American Lawyer* magazine. The same survey shows that partners in each of the top ten firms, this time ranked by profits per partner, on average earned more than $1.4 million in 1998.

In a large merger or acquisition, speed is critical. To serve this need for speedy action, a handful of firms, primarily located in New York, have developed into leading players in the M&A advisory business. According to *Corporate Control Alert,* the top ten M&A firms, ranked for 1998 by frequency of involvement in M&A transactions, were:

TOP TEN M&A FIRMS

Firm M&A Volume Rank	Profits Per Partner*	1998 Revenues*	# of Lawyers*
1. Skadden, Arps, Slate, Meagher & Flom	$1,380,000	$890,000,000	1,187
2. Sullivan & Cromwell	1,645,000	426,500,000	454
3. Simpson Thacher & Bartlett	1,495,000	386,000,000	490
4. Dewey Ballantine	860,000	250,000,000	417
5. Shearman & Sterling	1,045,000	425,500,000	683
6. Wachtell, Lipton, Rosen & Katz	3,105,000	269,000,000	143
7. Davis Polk & Wardwell	1,530,000	435,000,000	464
8. Cravath, Swaine & Moore	2,050,000	334,000,000	334
9. Fried, Frank, Harris, Shriver & Jacobson	760,000	225,000,000	393
10. Jones, Day, Reavis & Pogue	700,000	530,000,000	1,164

*Source: *Corporate Control Alert* and *American Lawyer*. Reflects total revenues and profits.

However, these statistics are misleading because they don't differentiate between the roles actually performed by the firms and the individual lawyers in each firm. And while not on the top ten list, many other firms, including regional powerhouses, play important roles in the deal process.

Perhaps the most has been written about Skadden, Arps, Slate, Meagher & Flom, founded in 1948 by Marshall Skadden, Leslie Arps, and John Slate. The date on which the firm was founded—April Fools' Day—reflects something of the firm's early character: irreverent, unconventional, ambitious, yet a bit unsure of itself. From the start, Skadden had something to prove. Each of its founding members had been passed over for partnership at an old-line Wall Street law firm. When the three recruited Joseph Flom, fresh out of Harvard Law School, as their first associate, they described their joint venture as a "flier."

Notwithstanding the principals' enthusiasm, the early years at Skadden, Arps & Slate were lean. With only ten lawyers, the firm took on proxy contest work spurned by the more established partnerships. During this period, Flom emerged as the driving force at Skadden, having worked on a series of high-profile contests that put the firm on the map (such as the successful defense of American Hardware Corporation against an insurgent stockholder who owned one third of the company's stock).

These proxy contests of the 1960s foreshadowed the hostile tender offers to come in the 1970s and 1980s. From a lawyer's perspective, a critical moment in the rise of the tender offer came with the passing of the Williams Act in 1968, designed to regulate the tender offer process. Providing federal rules and regulations, rather than curbing tender offer activity, seemed to legitimize tender offer tactics, creating an entirely new field for takeover lawyers who now had a set of rules to interpret.

Lawyers with proxy contest experience were well positioned to take advantage of this potential market. Therefore, Flom and Skadden jumped into the budding M&A market without reservation in the 1970s, while other more established law firms hesitated. Flom in particular was sought out by investment bankers at Morgan Stanley, who felt their regular lawyers didn't have enough experience in the area. For example, he was hired by Morgan Stanley to advise Inco on the 1974 takeover of ESB, a deal whose success led to a series of engagements, which in turn propelled Flom and Skadden to the forefront of the takeover movement.

The results were dramatic. Largely on the back of its M&A expertise, Skadden grew from ten lawyers in 1960 to over 1,000 lawyers in 1999. Along the way, Flom and his partners advised one side or the other in the large majority of blockbuster deals during the 1980s and 1990s.

As the firm grew, it branched into other practice areas outside the field of takeover work. Flom leveraged the retainers Skadden received from takeover clients to perform legal work in other fields, and then persuaded stars with large client networks in these non-takeover fields to join the firm. Flom thus created his vision of the multioffice, multipractice firm of the future.

The early 1980s were heady times for Skadden. Takeover litigation was the legal frontier, and Skadden was one of the most aggressive implementers of scattershot lawsuits as a tactical maneuver. Consequently, the firm earned a reputation for being willing to take the gloves off for its clients.

One of Flom's more famous episodes was his advisory role to oil company Conoco on its 1981 defense against Seagram. Under his guidance, Conoco sued to enjoin the liquor company's bid in North Carolina and Florida where state laws arguably barred a liquor company from owning gas stations. In this way, Conoco managed to get several local judges to delay Seagram's bid. While the effort was ultimately futile—Seagram had the injunctions overturned—the tactic added to Skadden's reputation for creative advocacy. In the end, Conoco agreed to be acquired by DuPont in a friendly deal.

The latest upswing in deal activity has demonstrated once again the immensely profitable nature of Skadden's core M&A franchise. According to *American Lawyer*, in 1998 the firm earned gross rev-

enues of $890 million and had average profits per partner of
$1,380,000. Reflecting this success, the culture of Skadden is hard-
charging. Lawyers and support staff routinely work through the
night. And when Friday rolls around, associates joke about being
happy that only two more days remain in the workweek. On top of
this, the firm has a high ratio of associates to partners, allowing each
partner to benefit from the revenues of several other lawyers.

Yet there is a sense of camaraderie at Skadden among all its
lawyers who have been through the wars together. Flom's leadership
and personality and the mix of ambition and creativity ooze through
the pores of the firm. Skadden has beaten much of the white-shoe
Wall Street legal world and is proud of it.

Today, Flom is in semiretirement, but his four key disciples control the bulk of the M&A deal flow: Peter Atkins, Roger Aaron, Morris Kramer, and Finn Fogg. Each has a different personality. Aaron
and Fogg are the consummate client counselors and handholders,
Atkins a smooth, immaculately groomed adviser to boards, and
Kramer a buzzsaw of creativity and energy.

Skadden's reputation as a tenacious, powerful M&A presence is
stronger than ever today. Or, as Flom puts it, "We're very strong.
We're permanent. We're an institution." Flom is not only a distinguished lawyer but a business prophet.

Fried, Frank, led by Arthur Fleischer Jr., is similar in structure to
Skadden but lower-key. The firm seems to recognize that being less
intense has its attractions, and takes pride in its client relations.
Fleischer, known for his professional erudition and biting humor,
sports three-piece suits and colorful patterned English shirts. In
fact, the M&A legal business's version of *Crossfire* is Skadden's Morris Kramer negotiating with Arthur Fleischer. In the opening gambit,
Fleischer lectures precedent while Kramer attacks. They beat each
other to a pulp, seeming to enjoy the sport. Then their partners do
the deal.

Skadden's main competition for the title of premier takeover law firm has come from Wachtell, Lipton, Rosen & Katz. Wachtell was founded a generation after Skadden, in 1965, by Herbert Wachtell, Martin Lipton, Leonard Rosen, and George Katz, four classmates from NYU Law School. The firm's founders made an effort to develop a collegial environment: Only the best young lawyers were hired, and, unlike at other firms, the expectation and hope was that every associate who remained committed to the firm would make partner. In exchange, lawyers were expected to work very hard and treat the firm as family, the center of life.

Indeed, this sense of community at Wachtell results in an intensity level even higher than at Skadden; but the anxiety about making partner is less. Wachtell, Lipton has chosen to remain small and to focus almost exclusively on takeover and bankruptcy-related legal work. Wachtell's staff consists of approximately 140 lawyers, compared to Skadden's 1,000, and its single regional office, in Chicago, is home to only one lawyer.

Wachtell has distinguished itself from Skadden in ways more substantive than its small size, however. For example, throughout the 1980s, Wachtell refused to represent hostile acquirers, a position that proved an excellent marketing tool. The firm's lawyers inveighed against the "hostile, two-tier, leveraged, bust-up" acquisitions of the time, lobbying in Congress, writing articles, and giving press interviews to advance their views. The effort positioned Wachtell well with corporate CEOs worried about losing their companies to a takeover, and helped make Wachtell the preeminent hostile defense firm.

Along with Herb Wachtell, its senior litigator, Marty Lipton is the star of the firm. Born in 1931 to a middle-class family in Jersey City, New Jersey, Lipton spent a year working for a judge after graduating law school, then joined Selig & Morris as a junior associate, where he worked on his first takeover.

By the middle 1960s, Lipton had already developed a reputation in proxy contests. In the same year he founded the Wachtell, Lipton firm with his three friends, Lipton worked on the contest for Illinois Central Industries. Later, the Tisch brothers hired Lipton for a series of high-profile deals in the 1970s, including the hostile fight for CNA Financial Corp., a financial services company. The network of friendships Lipton built from the contacts made in the early deals created a wide web of clients. Lipton has become the first-call takeover defense lawyer for many CEOs.

Lipton's masterstroke came in 1982, when he developed the poison pill defense: a mechanism to make hostile takeovers too expensive to be contemplated. The technique required that existing shareholders be given special securities that would convert into a high number of target company shares if a raider accumulated the stock of, and tried to merge with, the target. Because under the scheme the raider's securities would not convert into common stock, the raider would be left with a significantly lower percentage of the target. Over the next several years, Lipton evolved the strategy, and when the Delaware Supreme Court blessed the approach in 1985, Lipton and the pill were in great demand.

Wachtell, Lipton proved itself incredibly adept in takeover contests again and again throughout the 1980s, with the combination of Lipton and an all-star litigation team headed by Wachtell its comparative advantage. The Wachtell lawyers also emphasized their willingness to cooperate with local firms, whereas Skadden, with its network of offices, was in competition with them. Though relatively small, its concentration on takeovers allowed the firm to throw a dozen or more lawyers on a hot deal.

The firm often takes on clients for fees based on the size of a transaction rather than hours billed, a further testament to the quality of Wachtell, Lipton's work. Wachtell lawyers argue they are integral to the successful resolution of the matters on which they work and should earn fees commensurate with the intense, complicated nature of the transactions.

The deals flooding through Wachtell's doors and its billing practices have made the firm among the most profitable in America on a per capita basis. Though the latest *American Lawyer* survey puts Wachtell at number twenty-seven in terms of gross revenue—generating roughly $269 million in 1998—the firm brought in more than $1.9 million in revenue per lawyer and profits per partner averaged $3.1 million.

Lately, Wachtell has relaxed somewhat its stricture against representing hostile acquirers, mainly for large corporate clients. In 1991, for example, the firm advised AT&T in its fight to acquire computer company NCR. However, Marty Lipton's phone still routinely rings with calls from CEOs under fire.

Compared to Skadden and Wachtell, Cravath, Swaine & Moore has embraced a more traditional approach. Cravath—which can trace its roots back to 1819—has a premier reputation attributable to two characteristics. First, the firm has perhaps one of the most blue-chip client lists in America: Longtime Cravath clients include IBM, Chemical Bank (now Chase Manhattan), CBS, Time Warner, and Bristol-Myers Squibb. Second, the firm has been able to develop legal stars who excel on high-profile matters, such as litigator Bob Joffe and dealmakers Alan Stephenson, Allen Finkelson, and Rob Kindler.

The Cravath System—to institutionalize the practice of law—was first declared by Paul Cravath in the early 1900s. Under his system, lawyers were to be selected based on merit rather than bloodline. Senior lawyers were to mentor and guide junior lawyers. Steady, capable advice was the goal. Partners would be added only through internal promotion, and lawyers passed over would be asked to leave. In this way, a strong bureaucracy was built up, and Paul Cravath grabbed the bulk of his firm's profits.

During the 1970s, and early 1980s, Cravath played a relatively small role in the rough-and-tumble world of hostile deals. While many other old-time firms resisted becoming involved in such deals for fear of alienating clients, Cravath rarely faced the issue: It simply lacked the necessary staffing to handle takeover litigation because of its heavy involvement defending IBM against a government antitrust case. However, when the IBM case settled in 1982, Cravath came charging back. Today, the firm routinely is involved in major M&A transactions such as the WorldCom-MCI merger and the Viacom-CBS merger.

Cravath has approximately 390 lawyers, 83 of whom are partners—a revered status. The firm is still unique among its peers. It eschewed frenetic growth in the 1980s, though to a lesser extent than Wachtell. And unlike most other firms, where new associates are assigned work out of a pool, new Cravath associates spend the first several years working directly for a series of partners, each for an extended period.

This Cravath System survives today, more or less as handed down, and has served the firm well. In the 1998 *American Lawyer* survey, Cravath enjoyed profits of over $2.1 million per partner.

Sullivan & Cromwell, whose most famous leader was John Foster Dulles, is the quintessential Wall Street law firm, often representing investment bankers such as Goldman Sachs. Regarded historically as somewhat stuffy, S&C has worked hard to modernize its practice by building up a specialized M&A team. Including such skilled senior partners as Benjamin Stapleton, S&C also boasts expertise in international deals and a premier practice in financial institutions led by Rodgin Cohen.

Simpson Thacher, led in recent years by former Secretary of State Cyrus Vance, has grown in visibility and prestige in the past decade. Presiding partner Dick Beattie, a former Marine Corps carrier pilot known for plain talk and sharp insight, has played a major role in the evolution. Beattie's early focus was on LBOs: During the 1980s, he often served as counsel of choice to KKR, most famously on the RJR takeover. Beattie has used this experience with KKR as a wedge to tout his firm as a dealmaker, an effort which has translated into a leading M&A practice.

Shearman & Sterling used to be dominated by its relationship with Citibank. Today, however, the firm has become a major player in the mergers business on the strength of relationships with bankers such as Merrill Lynch, Morgan Stanley, and CSFB, its very strong international client base, and the deal savvy and mature judgment of presiding partner Steve Volk. Clients have been receptive. Volk represented Morgan Stanley in the Dean Witter deal and his firm has been involved in many other major deals of the 1990s—Bell Atlantic–NYNEX, Sandoz–Ciba-Geigy, and the fight for MCI, for example.

Recently, New York firm Paul, Weiss, Rifkind, Wharton & Garrison has become another major contender for merger work. The firm's corporate practice was built on business relationships developed by the firm's legendary senior litigation partner Arthur Liman, who recently passed away. His disciple Toby Myerson currently leads the firm's growing corporate practice, which is known for its international expertise and long-term client focus.

The New York takeover bar captured a commanding share of the M&A advisory business in the 1970s and 1980s. Proximity to the capital markets and investment professionals was partly responsible. Morgan Stanley fed business to Flom and then to Steve Volk. Henry Kravis came to depend on Beattie. Lazard became close to Marty Lipton. A perception that the New York law firms had unique capabilities in the takeover field also contributed to their dominance.

Yet regional strongholds like Vinson & Elkins of Houston and Jones, Day of Cleveland crop up in major deals on a regular basis. These firms used long-standing relationships with the major corporations on their home turf to break into the deal business.

Vinson & Elkins, for example, has long enjoyed a national presence. The firm was founded in 1917 by James Elkins Sr., a Texas native known as "The Judge," and William Vinson, and soon developed a thriving practice representing local oilmen. Swept along in the Texas oil boom, Vinson & Elkins bloomed into the nation's third-largest firm in the late 1970s. And when the Oil Wars flared, the firm naturally became a frequent M&A adviser. Though Vinson & Elkins' relative size has recently declined when compared to other large firms, it retains a strong position in Texas and is poised to take advantage of the next oil patch merger boom.

Jones, Day is no longer a regional firm. With more than 1,000 lawyers, the firm is a global institution, the third-largest law firm in the U.S. by revenue. Still, Jones, Day's foundation is its status as a fixture in Cleveland and the greater Midwest, and its strong relationships with major industrial companies in the region. Bob Profusek, its lead dealmaker, has used this base to build a formidable national practice.

Investment Bankers

As far back as J.P. Morgan's U.S. Steel deal of 1901, bankers have been involved in an advisory capacity in major corporate transactions. Because Morgan worked before the creation of the Glass-Steagall wall separated investment and commercial banking, he could wear several hats. Morgan loaned money directly to clients—what we now think of as the commercial lender's role. He raised capital in the markets, mostly debt and some equity, by arranging the syndication of securities—the corporate finance function of modern investment banking. And he provided strategic advice to deal participants. Today, regulatory changes have allowed his successors at J.P. Morgan to fill these roles once again. While still primarily a commercial bank, J.P. Morgan is beginning to build up its investment banking and M&A operations.

However, the bank regulatory framework created in the 1930s for a time divorced commercial and investment banking. During the Great Depression and Second World War, Wall Street became a relatively quiet place. In the immediate postwar years, investment bankers stayed busy raising the capital to fund the great American industrial expansion then under way. The American M&A advisory business again quieted during the 1950s and early 1960s, booming again in the frothy stock market of the late 1960s, and continuing to be strong into the early 1970s. In the process, the first M&A power-house was born—Lazard Frères & Co.

The story of the Lazard Houses dates back to the mid-nineteenth century, when three Lazard brothers emigrated from France to America to found a clothing store in New Orleans. After their store was gutted by a fire that swept the city, the brothers picked up and moved to the boomtown of San Francisco, where they established themselves in the dry goods business. Soon, however, they shifted to the more lucrative area of trading gold and currency. Eventually, the brothers founded three independent but affiliated merchant banks with the same name: Lazard New York, Lazard London, and Lazard Paris.

Because none of the three Lazard brothers had a son, control of the firm passed to David David-Weill, the son of Lazard cousin Alexandre Weill, who had joined the brothers early on in San Francisco. Under the guidance of David-Weill and others, the Paris bank grew into a major force. But the New York bank was not as success-ful, known into the twentieth century chiefly for bond underwriting. Everything changed, however, in the 1940s. Among those fleeing Hitler's approaching shadow were André Meyer, a brilliant young partner from the Paris bank, and Felix Rohatyn, whose family came from Austria to New York via Casablanca and Rio de Janeiro—fig-ures who would be pivotal in the transformation of Lazard New York.

In 1943, Pierre David-Weill—David's son—asked Meyer to take over management of the New York bank. Meyer, who had known Ro-hatyn's stepfather in Paris, later gave the young man a summer job, and Rohatyn stayed on to become Meyer's chief protégé.

Perhaps before anyone else, Meyer saw that an investment bank could earn high margins by focusing on the M&A business, a sector which required little committed capital. One of Meyer's first direc-tives was to shutter the firm's retail operations: Bond salesmen and the like were fired. Then, with an iron fist, the autocratic Meyer set about implementing his vision. By the mid-1960s, the transformation was complete. Lazard had earned a reputation as the "merger house" and, in 1968, Meyer was called "the most important investment banker in the Western World" by *Fortune* magazine. The three houses have historically been affiliated but independent; in June 1999, however, after a period of management turnover, Lazard announced a restructuring in which the three houses would merge and be brought under common control.

Felix Rohatyn

The conglomerate wave of the late 1960s launched the rise of Felix Rohatyn. Born in Vienna in 1928, the son of prosperous Jewish brewery operator Alexander Rohatyn, Felix and his family grew increasingly fearful of the Nazi presence in Europe in the early 1940s and fled to America in 1942.

Upon arriving in the United States, Rohatyn enrolled in high school and from there earned his undergraduate degree in physics at Middlebury College. Rohatyn described his college experience as undistinguished: "The physics faculty and I both reached the conclusion that I did not have a future in the sciences."

Fortunately, Rohatyn had been working for investment bank Lazard Frères during the summer and, after catching the eye of André Meyer one evening, was offered full-time employment. After a number of years as an apprentice, Rohatyn developed a reputation for technical financial skill and negotiating prowess. But more importantly, he learned to deal with Meyer's explosive temperament. The two men—both expatriates—developed a strong working relationship.

While Meyer gave his young disciple an entrée into the world of finance, Harold Geneen would make Rohatyn into a superstar. Geneen started sending ITT's work to Lazard in the early 1960s. Then, in the course of the 1965 transaction in which ITT bought Avis from Lazard, Geneen became greatly impressed with Rohatyn, and from then on used Rohatyn as ITT's investment banker. At the height of the relationship, Rohatyn worked side by side with Geneen—he would visit ITT's offices almost every day, and he attended Geneen's brainstorming sessions at the Waldorf Hotel. Rohatyn advised on almost every major deal ITT did in the 1960s and 1970s: Bobbs-Merrill Publishers, Sheraton Hotels, Levitt & Co., Hartford Insurance. Like Geneen, Rohatyn was attacked over the Hartford Insurance affair but was ultimately exonerated.

Rohatyn's reputation was further enhanced in the mid-1970s, when he teamed up with attorney Marty Lipton on the pro bono committee that saved New York City from insolvency. At the time, New York faced a budget shortfall of hundreds of millions of dollars, the culmination of years of spending more money than it was taking in. Banks refused to honor the city's bonds, and New York was on the verge of declaring bankruptcy. The governor brought onto the scene Rohatyn and others, under whose guidance New York City slowly got back on its feet.

Meanwhile, Rohatyn's relationships served him well. When takeovers surged again in the 1980s and 1990s, he emerged as the dean of the profession. Although he publicly questioned the advisability of the leveraged transactions which were taking place, he was fully immersed in the new wave of activity. In the 1990s, he has retained a unique position as a distinguished public figure and the statesman of the business. He retired from investment banking in 1997 to become the U.S. ambassador to France.

While Rohatyn and Lazard profited heavily from advising M&A clients, the major investment banks generally shied away from the business in the 1960s. Each had only a few professionals assigned to the field, and the firms rarely charged clients for advice. Firms tended to view the M&A practice as a tool to maintain underwriting relationships, a loss leader to bring in more corporate finance business.

However, by the early 1970s, M&A bankers at several of Lazard's competitors began to see the fee-generating potential of the advisory business and fought, both within their organizations and in the marketplace, to develop the business.

Morgan Stanley's M&A unit wanted to outdo Lazard. Its opportunity came in 1974 when the bank was approached by Inco, a client who sought advice on its planned hostile bid for ESB. But Morgan Stanley, like many investment banks at the time, had a policy of not handling hostile acquisitions, fearing that to do so would alienate the firm's roster of blue-chip underwriting clients. Therefore, for a time, debate raged within Morgan Stanley. The M&A camp made three main arguments. First, Inco had come to Morgan Stanley for help. Offering advice was a matter of client service. Second, the underwriting business was suffering from declining margins. Fixed brokerage commissions, long a staple of New York's big investment houses, were on the way out. Third, and perhaps most importantly, hostile takeovers were an inevitable trend. If Morgan Stanley refused to assist clients in this area, its competitors would take up the slack. These pro-M&A arguments carried the day and Morgan Stanley began to build up its M&A business. Today Morgan Stanley plays a leading role in M&A and is known for its particularly aggressive team.

In a symbiotic way, Goldman Sachs benefited from Morgan's inroads: Goldman used its wide web of corporate relationships as the foundation for the leading takeover defense group. Steve Friedman, the gracious and intellectual banker who built up the firm's M&A

practice and who eventually became the firm's chairman, made Goldman an attractive, safe choice for corporate executives. As a result, Goldman has become the leading force in the M&A, advising on 28.6 percent of all deals completed in 1998.

When the M&A effort at First Boston seriously began in the late 1970s, we questioned how to crack the Lazard-Goldman-Morgan oligopoly. The solution was simple: First find the holes in the market, and then raise the stakes by outprofessionalizing the competition. While Goldman focused primarily on divestitures and defenses, we went after the buy side for their clients. And while fair or not, we prospected a good number of Morgan's clients who had become dissatisfied with the firm due to conflicts, because they had lost a bid, or because Morgan's aggressive manner chafed them.

The second step was to professionalize the business. We expanded our M&A group, added industry specialties such as energy and insurance, formed an idea-creation unit, and focused on products such as divestitures. Eventually, the old First Boston became one of the three M&A leaders. Our competitors built up as well, and the industry was thus transformed. I am very proud that many of my former colleagues have landed as the leaders of the M&A practices on Wall Street: Chuck Ward at First Boston, Joe Perella and Garry Parr at Morgan Stanley, Bob Cotter at Salomon, Mike Koeneke at Merrill, and Nick Paumgarten and Mark Rosoff at J.P. Morgan, among others.

Among the large leading firms today are Morgan Stanley, Goldman Sachs, Crédit Suisse, First Boston, and Merrill Lynch, and among the smaller banks Lazard and Wasserstein Perella. A number of commercial banks also have M&A practices: Citigroup's Salomon Smith Barney, J.P. Morgan, and Chase Manhattan.

M&A bankers provide a number of services, including:

- general strategic advice
- presentation of acquisition ideas

- tactical know-how
- negotiation support
- valuation and fairness opinions
- technical execution and coordination, and
- the structured sale of a business.

There is a significant difference in the quality of service offered by firms, and even within the same firm—especially the larger ones—as different bankers have varying merit. The small firms argue that they can provide excellence and focus, while the large firms sell market power and breadth of product. Quality does matter, as does attention. Some advisers go through the mechanical motions and others make a contribution.

Do bankers really make a difference? Often not. The role can be prophylactic, to insulate a board, or routine. However, sometimes bankers act as the creative generators of the concept of a deal, a nerve ending in an informational web, or the catalyst in the implementation of a transaction. The best bankers have a large databank of comparative experience and can draw on it to ask the right questions to help executives make their decisions.

An interesting recent phenomenon is the development of industry-specific M&A bankers. These professionals are advantaged by their in-depth knowledge of a business. However, because tactical and even some strategic considerations know no industry bound, such a narrow background can also be limiting.

THE GESTATION OF THE BIG DEAL

Big corporate transactions have many fathers. Financial and strategic buyers each go about the process in a different manner. Financial buyers, by definition in the business of buying and selling companies, are constantly on the lookout for potential targets. They are peppered with suggestions daily and tend to look opportunistically for the valuable "special situation."

Corporate acquirers, on the other hand, go through a more idiosyncratic process. A corporation may have been thinking about a potential deal for some time but will only act when prompted by a specific circumstance. The DuPont-Conoco deal is a case in point. DuPont had been considering vertically integrating into oil for some time, but Conoco was not a specific target until the Seagram imbroglio triggered an interest.

Philip Morris' move into the food business followed a different pattern. The company used us to prepare a broad analysis of the food industry, which eventually focused on specific targets. Dozens of candidates were screened based on both fundamental and financial factors. The process culminated first with the acquisition of General Foods in 1985 and then of Kraft in 1988.

Some deals are generated by a ricochet effect. An initial deal in an industry ripe for change will trigger shock waves: Competitors reassess strategy and a rush of deals results. For example, the Dean Witter–Morgan Stanley deal focused attention on the new structure of financial services. As a result, a sequence of deals followed, including the Salomon–Travelers Group transaction, the Travelers-Citicorp transaction, and the NationsBank-BankAmerica transaction, among others.

Finally, some deals arise because they are promoted by investment bankers. The better bankers realize their long-term interest lies in presenting deals with a strategic logic. For ultimately, the investment banking business is about building a long-term trusting relationship with clients. But of course, some push deals for the sake of deals. Few are effective in this approach. In the end, management makes the decision; an investment banker only provides advice and offers options.

Accountants

Accountants provide three primary services in the mergers and acquisitions area: tax structuring advice, financial structuring advice, and due diligence assistance. The Big Five accounting firms are PricewaterhouseCoopers, Andersen, Deloitte & Touche, Ernst & Young, and KPMG. Each firm has M&A SWAT teams whose members are able to handle issues in all three substantive areas and who are experienced with the rapid-fire timing of a major transaction.

In the area of tax structuring, good accounting advice is vital, as the formal structure of a deal determines how it will be treated for tax purposes. The same substantive economic result often can be accomplished in many different ways, with dramatically different tax results.

The structure of a transaction also impacts the reported earnings of the combined company. Accountants attempt to navigate the complicated rules so as to preserve pooling accounting treatment where possible (at least until pooling's demise in 2001).

Finally, accountants can be helpful in performing due diligence review, which is closely analogous to the audit function and takes place prior to the closing of a friendly merger or acquisition. Very little, if any, due diligence can be performed in a hostile acquisition. Rather, the acquirer must rely on publicly available documentation. A review is designed to examine a potential merger partner's operations and finances. Site visits, management and employee interviews, and document reviews are typical. Lawyers and investment banks play a role, as do accountants, who typically review financial documents.

Proxy Solicitors

Before the hostile takeover became an accepted part of the corporate arsenal, the proxy contest was the only way to wrest control of a company from incumbent management. Today, the proxy contest remains an important tactical option, sometimes used as a cheaper alternative to a full-scale bid or to clear the way for a hostile bid. As part of the process, both an insurgent shareholder and incumbent management often hire one of the handful of firms, known as proxy solicitors, that specialize in lobbying shareholders.

In a proxy contest, an insurgent shareholder nominates a slate of directors and sends out an alternate proxy solicitation. The shareholders must then decide which slate to favor, the insurgent's or management's. The candidates who receive the most votes, whether cast in person or by proxy, will be elected to the board. If the insurgents win a majority of the board, the board in turn can replace incumbent management.

A proxy contest is a political campaign, with the attendant questions of "spin" and expenses of mailings and advertisements. The process is made somewhat easier when a takeover is involved because for most takeover targets the bulk of shares generally will be held by a relatively small number of institutional investors and arbitrageurs. Still, at large companies, a significant proportion of shares may be held in small lots by individual investors, with whom communication may be difficult.

A relatively small number of firms operate in this specialized field: D.F. King & Company and Georgeson & Company are the most notable: Both firms have established the infrastructure necessary to conduct mass mailings to shareholders and concerted calling efforts. While this machinery is most often used to collect votes in regular, uncontested annual shareholder votes, it also plays a significant role during proxy contests in which "fight letters" are mailed to shareholders.

Another of a proxy solicitor's tasks is information gathering, generally known as a "stock watch" program, to determine the beneficial ownership—the stockholders who have control over voting rights—

of a company's stock. Such activity can be critical in a contest because each beneficial owner has the right to vote a share.

It is not always easy to uncover shareholders' identities, as many shareholders' stock is often held by various brokerage houses in agents' names. Major investors want their identities concealed while they accumulate a stock position to keep others from mirroring their actions and thus driving up the company's stock price. Furthermore, financial institutions are expected to keep their clients' trading positions secret and are usually unwilling to supply the information requested by proxy solicitors.

Private Investigators

Potential takeover targets as well as corporate raiders may use private investigators to extract comprehensive financial data, detailed biographies of executives, and information about any possible wrongdoing on the part of their opposition. Investigators who handle this kind of work are not, however, the Sam Spade, rumpled-trench-coat type. Rather, a number of discreet, professional firms, staffed largely by former prosecutors, FBI agents, and investigative journalists, have sprung up to serve corporate clients. Kroll Associates and Investigative Group Inc. are two of the largest.

New York–based Kroll Associates, founded by Jules Kroll in 1972 and acquired by O'Gara Co. in 1997 for $101 million, earned a reputation in the 1980s as Wall Street's private detective. In the early days, his firm worked mostly for financial printers, ferreting out improper conduct by employees. When the takeover boom hit in the 1980s, however, Kroll recognized the value of information to takeover targets. Capitalizing on this profitable business, Kroll Associates has grown, now employing several hundred employees in thirteen countries, excluding the hundreds of regular subcontractors. The company has more than $50 million in revenues.

Though the firm prides itself on discretion, involvement in a number of high-profile takeover contests during the 1980s generated considerable publicity for Kroll. In the 1984 contest for Phillips Petroleum, for example, a court ruling—later reversed—temporarily barred Kroll from gathering information on Boone Pickens. Kroll Associates had amassed a thick file on Pickens, a copy of which the firm reportedly would sell to any Pickens target for $500,000.

Kroll had a major triumph in the United Kingdom when it contributed to the successful defense of ICI from Hanson PLC, a major conglomerate. Kroll uncovered the fact that Lord White of Hanson bought a string of racehorses with company money, an embarrassing revelation that took some of the wind out of Hanson's bid. The offer was eventually withdrawn.

Several years later, in 1989, Kroll Associates reportedly helped Avon Products defend against Amway Corp. and financier Irwin Jacobs. Six days after filing its original bid, Amway did a dramatic about-face, withdrawing its offer. According to newspaper accounts at the time, Kroll had uncovered a number of pending lawsuits against Amway and possible insider trading by two of the company's executives.

Kroll Associates uses two basic investigative techniques in the takeover field. First, the firm's computer analysts, largely recent college graduates with strong technical training, delve into public and proprietary databases of information. The goal is to build a complete picture of a subject which can be used to assess the ability to raise capital for a bid and to anticipate tactical maneuvers. A survey also might turn up information regarding a raider's past bankruptcy, criminal conviction, or other embarrassing misdeed.

Second, Kroll employs former FBI and CIA agents, investigative journalists, and the like for field investigations. These investigations can involve calling former employees or acquaintances, various forms of surveillance, and locating assets. Of course, if abused, any detective system can easily backfire. Overall, detective firms are best used for due diligence.

The Market

The parties to a deal and their advisers attempt to structure the most advantageous, appealing transaction possible. For the buyer, or for merger partners, the goal is a transaction that will be applauded by shareholders and the market. More specifically, the hope is that current shareholders will grant any approvals necessary to execute the deal. Furthermore, all parties to a transaction hope the market price of the surviving company will rise, both in the near term and the long term—the ultimate blessing for a deal.

For most large companies engaged in a merger or acquisition, the base of shareholders is made up of two key groups: institutions and arbitrageurs. The perceptions of these and other shareholders are shaped in part by the business press.

Institutional Investors   Institutional investors control a major portion—often a majority—of the stock in America's Fortune 500 companies. For example, institutions own roughly 52 percent of GE's outstanding common stock and 56 percent of IBM's. In the aggregate, institutional shareholders own more than 40 percent of the publicly traded corporate equity in the U.S. These large stakes, combined with a number of developments over the past fifteen years, provide institutions with significant influence over the future of most corporations.

The world of institutional investors is well populated and diverse. However, the players can be arranged into four main groups: the public employee pension funds, the private pension funds, mutual funds, and insurance companies. Public employee pension funds were the most visibly active in the 1980s. For example, the giant California Public Employees' Retirement System, known as CalPERS, developed a reputation as a tough and independent shareholder. Not content to act alone, CalPERS and similar funds were instrumental in forming the Council of Institutional Investors to advance their interests.

With a fiduciary duty to serve the interests of pension holders and few loyalties or ties to corporate America, the public pension fund managers tend to focus on short-term performance. They push companies to maximize shareholder value and often pressure management to accept merger proposals if a concrete better alternative is not on the near-term horizon.

PROFILE

The Council of Institutional Investors

The Council of Institutional Investors has been a driving force to encourage strong performance. The group was formed in 1984 at the behest of California state treasurer Jesse Unruh and other leaders who oversaw large public pension funds. Now with more than 100 pension funds as members, the group speaks for institutional investors with more than $1 trillion under management.

During the 1980s the council actively battled against greenmail and other defensive tactics used to entrench poor management. For example, the council flexed its muscle in the battle over the Phillips recapitalization, grilling Pickens, company representatives, Icahn, Boesky, and others in advance of the shareholder vote. The sessions contributed to the feeling among pension funds that the plan was unfair and led to the defeat of the original recapitalization proposal.

In the 1990s, the council has targeted companies on its annual list of underperforming companies, with publicity and voting power its primary weapons. No CEO wants his or her company to appear on the council's list of target companies. Newspapers generally run stories on the list, and CEOs who appear more than once rarely last long. The council also takes a more active role in

> specific situations, in the past coordinating attempts to oust man-
> agers or reform corporate governance provisions.
>
> Because the council sometimes opposes incumbent manage-
> ment, its membership tends to be heavily weighted toward public
> employee pension funds and university endowments.

Corporate pension plan managers tend to be more supportive of incumbent management than their public employee and union counterparts, a trend generally attributed to the relationship between the funds and their corporate parents. A corporate fund manager often faces direct or indirect pressure from senior management not to vote with outsiders or sell stock into a hostile tender offer: CEOs, frustrated by the market's short-term view, have directed their captive pension plans to take a more long-term approach. While the Labor Department has recently put pressure on corporations to take a more active role in managing their pension funds, corporate pension plans still lean toward management on controversial questions.

Mutual funds and other asset managers hold a growing share of America's financial assets. These institutions tend to fall somewhere between the public and private pension funds in their level of shareholder activism. Mutual fund families that serve individual investors tend to be more focused on near-term performance than corporate pension funds. However, with the rise of 401(k) retirement plans, corporations often have the ability to favor particular fund families by designating them as providers for the plans. Other asset managers often depend on corporate pension plans for direct investments and consequently have tempered their activism to avoid alienating their clients.

The constant inflow of capital to institutional investors in the 1990s has increased the pressure on money managers. With fresh billions to manage each year, it becomes more challenging to deliver strong investment returns. Beating the market is difficult when investing on the scale required of managers at CalPERS and other groups. Funds like Fidelity's Magellan—with approximately $84 billion under management—are so big that almost any significant action they take moves the market.

Rather than actively trading stocks, many investment groups now focus on trying to improve company performance through active shareholding. The institutions are, in other words, attempting to reunite ownership and control, repairing the divide observed sixty years ago by academics Berle and Means. Of course, like a single individual shareholder, a single institution rarely carries enough weight to impact a large corporation. A handful of institutions, on the other hand, may have the combined voting power to be decisive but until recently were hampered in their ability to act together. Under federal securities regulations, an institutional shareholder was required to file a proxy statement with the government and mail it to all fellow shareholders before seeking support from other institutions. These rules were changed in 1992.

The new proxy rules allow shareholders to cooperate without filing any proxy materials, requiring a proxy filing only when one shareholder is seeking proxies from other shareholders or when a shareholder owns a large percentage of a company's stock. Shareholders may also announce how they intend to vote on a matter and advertise their position without first mailing materials.

The impact of the new rules became apparent soon after they were implemented. A series of boardroom coups in 1993 and 1994—in which Westinghouse's, Sears', and IBM's CEOs were forced out—were widely attributed to increased pressure from activist shareholders.

With their new power, institutional shareholders play a major role in corporate strategy. Advisers and executives lobby them in proxy battles and pay particular attention to their response to a proposed merger or acquisition. In hostile deals, institutions often sell their stock after the initial run-up in price, happy to take the sure gains. Increasingly, however, institutional investors hang in until the end, and are therefore of great importance in determining the outcome of a deal. This is especially true in the large stock-for-stock deals of the 1990s, where institutional investors want to make sure the stock they will hold in the surviving company is worth as much as possible.

Arbitrageurs   The practice of risk arbitrage is buying the stock of a takeover target after a deal is announced. Unless the market expects a higher bid, stock in a company with a deal pending often trades at some discount to the offering price, reflecting the risk that not all tendered shares will be accepted. Arbs buy the stock, and if the deal goes through, they make a profit off the spread. Even with narrow spreads, the profits can be significant under the right circumstances. First, the faster a deal closes, the higher the returns. Second, returns can be enhanced further with leverage. Third, if another bidder comes along with a higher price, the arbs make even more money.

By the end of a successful offer, a large portion of the trading float is in the hands of the arbitrageurs: In a medium-sized deal it may be as much as 50 percent of the shares. Thus any offer must be structured to contemplate the needs of the arbs. In addition, if a competing bid is made, the arbitrageurs often play a decisive role in determining its success.

Arbs are the ultimate short-term investors, focused on maximizing the value of their investment over the briefest period possible. Each day a deal is open, interest accrues on their margin loans and returns fall. As a result, when a company's stock is concentrated in the hands of arbs, they begin to put pressure on management to deliver fast results, barraging managers and advisers with phone calls, working the press, and doing everything they can to advance their narrow self-interest. The key, from management's perspective, is to understand the goals of the arbs and keep in mind that much of what they say often is nothing more than bluff and posturing. On the other hand, in some situations, the arbs do carry the deciding vote. Therefore, it can be dangerous to ignore their presence.

For an arb, success depends on the ability to judge how quickly a deal will go through and whether a new bidder will emerge. Information gathering and analysis are therefore critical elements of the process. Arbs provide liquidity for institutional shareholders and others who would rather have a guaranteed return than a chance at a slightly higher return. The more arbs in the market, the narrower the spreads become.

During the 1980s, few deals fell apart and bidding wars often erupted, making risk arbitrage extremely profitable. The market became crowded with arbitrage funds, set up as investment partnerships, and most investment banks rushed into the arbitrage game. Estimates put the total money invested in deals as high as $18 billion.

Risk arbitrage received bad press after Ivan Boesky's arrest. A tough period of low deal flow followed in the early 1990s. Then, in the latest merger wave, the prevalence of stock deals has made the business more complicated. As a result, arbitrage is once again a profitable but relatively quiet corner of the market. Total arbitrage money in the market has been put somewhere between $3 and $4 billion.

PROFILE

Robert Rubin

While Ivan Boesky chose a flashy style, most successful arbs operated below the public radar. Their names rarely appeared in the press and they almost never granted interviews. Rather, they were content to ply their trade out of the public eye. Before moving to Washington D.C., Robert Rubin, former treasury secretary under President Clinton, was the classic arb.

Rubin was born into a New York City family with long Democratic party traditions. He graduated near the top of his class from Harvard University and then studied at the London School of Economics for two years. On his return, he attended Yale Law School, graduating in 1964.

After two years as a Wall Street lawyer, Rubin definitely decided the law was not his calling and instead landed a job at Goldman Sachs in the equity arbitrage department. There he worked under the tutelage of legendary Goldman chairman Gus Levy, the man who professionalized arbitrage.

Rubin proved to be a gifted arbitrageur. Highly analytical, Rubin would pore painstakingly over deal documents. A yellow pad was a constant companion. There were always questions. What was the chance the bidder would raise the cash needed? Would the government block the deal on antitrust grounds? Rubin would constantly question his co-workers and search through the documents for answers.

By 1974, Rubin was Goldman's chief arb, running a desk that took positions in as many as 250 deals a year and was recognized as one of the most professional. Most deals worked well, but some did not. In one month in 1979, his traders reportedly ran up losses that exceeded the firm's entire profits in its best year. On balance, though, the small arb operation was tremendously profitable—regularly the second most profitable at the firm, behind the M&A department. Therefore, the arrest of Rubin's partner, Robert Freeman, for securities law violations was a shocking event. Throughout, however, Rubin's personal reputation remained untarnished.

In 1984, Rubin moved from the arbitrage desk to oversee Goldman's foreign exchange and options trading operation. He promptly turned the business around, winning respect within the firm.

Outside Goldman, I served with him on the takeover legislation panel advising Congress. He always promoted reasoned dialogue, though an undercurrent of firmness was evident. He seems to have a rare facility for using dry humor as a means of contesting ideas and defusing tension.

These skills as a consensus builder eventually led his partners to elevate him to co-chairman of the firm. He served in that position for two years before joining the Clinton administration, where he served as the most effective treasury secretary in recent years.

Public Relations

Public relations experts are having an increasing impact on M&A transactions. In the world of M&A, maintaining a strong, consistent story serves several purposes. First, it can help convince investors and research analysts that a prospective friendly deal will be beneficial. Perception can be as important as reality, and getting the story out early may allow the participants to define the terms of debate.

Second, in a contested situation, image can have an impact—especially in a hostile situation. A public relations campaign launched by a target to discredit the bidder can be effective, as the image of a bidder is important in stock deals or deals subject to regulatory approval or litigation. Shareholders naturally are concerned to know the character and history of the people whose performance will determine the future value of their stock. Nevertheless, all the public relations in the world will rarely deter a well-funded, determined bidder willing to pay cash.

Morale is also crucial to a takeover fight. As in any contest, a defense team functions best when the members believe in the worth of their struggle. Furthermore, regulatory bodies and courts do, as a practical matter, keep an eye on the media, and the "rapacious villain" role is not desirable. Image is important, especially on issues of how long a court should extend a pill.

In an effort to get favorable coverage, public relations professionals sometimes selectively "leak" information to the media or grant "exclusives" to a journalist the night before a breaking event. Although often attractive to the PR adviser, who gets points with the reporter who is given the story, there are serious issues. First, of course, are the legal and ethical issues. Second, other reporters may be alienated.

Overall, a number of potential pitfalls exist in implementing a public relations program. Consistency of message is sometimes a problem, as company executives may have different views than public relations people. The key is to ensure that the public relations professionals' agendas match those of the company. Tone is also a matter of concern. Like all advocates, public relations people can lapse into the hyperbolic in defense of their clients' interest, an approach which can backfire. Ideally, a communications program should be ongoing so as to develop a trusting strong relationship with the institutional investors and other major shareholders who hold the critical votes in a takeover contest. Such a relationship can provide powerful defensive leverage.

From a bidder's perspective, public relations can serve to defuse potential roadblocks. Political opposition can make it harder to close a deal. If not careful, a bidder can be cast as a carpetbagger, a liquidator of businesses, or a threat to local communities. On the other hand, these images can be countered with an effective communication plan.

Grand Metropolitan's 1988 hostile bid for Pillsbury provides a classic example. Under the tutelage of Linda Robinson, Grand Met—a British company—launched its bid from Minneapolis, home base to Pillsbury, rather than from New York or London. The announcement was followed by a round of meetings with local reporters and politicians. Designed to convey Grand Met's commitment to maintaining a strong presence in Minneapolis, the strategy played well. Local newspapers ran favorable stories under banner headlines. Pillsbury, the hometown team, felt outmaneuvered.

Robinson received positive reviews for her work with Grand Met, but was faulted for her handling of Ross Johnson's RJR bid, a deal in which she took a particularly active role. Failure taints all participants and Robinson was, therefore, attacked for the terrible press Johnson received, particularly a *Time* magazine cover story that cast his bid as "a game of greed." Unfortunately, visibility is a double-edged sword. Limited publicity is sometimes the best policy.

Kekst & Company, founded in 1971 by Gershon Kekst, is often cited as the leader in the field of financial PR firms, which includes Hill & Knowlton, Robinson Lerer & Montgomery, hotshot newcomers Sard Verbinnen & Company, Abernathy MacGregor Frank, and crisis intervenor Clark and Weinstock. Since an essential part of offense tactics is to crack the willpower of a board, Kekst and his competitors are experiencing a boom.

PROFILE

Gershon Kekst

Gershon Kekst—the dean of the financial public relations community—is an anomaly in his business. With an understated approach and discernible aversion to press clippings, Kekst is far from gregarious. He speaks in hushed, barely audible tones and describes himself as shy. Yet he has played a role in many of the major deals of the last twenty years. Memorable clients have included Henry Kravis in the RJR Nabisco takeover, Martin Davis in Paramount's defense against Viacom, and Louis Gerstner in IBM's takeover of Lotus Development.

Born to Hebrew school teachers, Kekst retains an intellectual, professorial air. He happened into the field of financial PR by something of a coincidence: The firm's first office was in the same Manhattan office tower as Skadden's offices, and Kekst managed to get a number of early referrals from Joe Flom.

The first such referral involved a company called Sterndent, a maker of dental equipment. A group of investors—including the heirs of a well-known Jewish philanthropist and some Arab partners—made a takeover offer for the company. Flom was hired to defend the company and brought in Kekst. Together, the two came up with a strategy that became known as "the Jewish dentist defense": Reasoning that many dentists, Sterndent's customers, would not want to be involved with a company partially owned by Arab investors, they conceived an advertisement that played up the investors' ethnicity. Sure enough, complaints poured in. The approach also drew some criticism as xenophobic, but is credited with helping to turn back the bidders.

Kekst keeps his edge by offering broad strategic advice and maintaining a bond with corporate chief executives. To be iconoclastic, when he competes for business his advice is often "Do nothing," as his competitors frantically scramble for nonviable creative ideas.

Corporations keep Kekst on retainer. As with Flom and Wachtell, the money buys corporations a kind of double insurance policy: Kekst is available to them if needed but would be conflicted out of working on behalf of a potential hostile bidder. If a big deal is in the news, Kekst is quite likely at the center of the action.

The Press

The business press acts as an increasingly ubiquitous interface between shareholders and investors. As in politics, the first story about a deal often defines the terms of debate and can have a significant impact on how institutional investors and arbs view the transaction. To an even greater extent, the business press shapes the view of individual investors who often lack the time or inclination to dig below the surface.

The rising tide of mergers in the 1980s and a long bull market brought an increased interest in business news. More competition crowded into the field and television became a factor with the advent of CNBC. Meanwhile, the mainstays—*The Wall Street Journal, The New York Times, Business Week, Forbes,* and *Fortune*—upgraded their coverage of mergers and acquisitions. Professionals turn to *The Daily Deal,* in which we have an investment.

Today, even more news outlets exist. CNN and others have added channels to compete with CNBC. Online business news reaches more homes each month. For strength of impact, though, *The New York Times* and *The Wall Street Journal* still predominate, although *The Financial Times* is often better on international stories.

Of the two papers, *The Wall Street Journal* has the stronger combination of professional reporting and in-depth, sophisticated business news. The *Times,* with more limited coverage, tends to cover stories on a more focused basis. Both papers receive their share of criticism, however. But friction is understandable: Being the subject of press scrutiny is a rather remarkable experience, even for someone sympathetic to journalists.

Much of the criticism is attributable to misunderstandings on the part of interview subjects, and for this reason, very clear ground rules are extremely helpful. Terms of art like "for background" or "not for attribution" mean different things to different people. An interview subject should understand their meaning in context before proceeding. Furthermore, reporters sometimes will conduct an interview, then use quotes months or years later.

To a certain extent, though, friction cannot be avoided. Journalists and those they cover simply have different agendas and perspectives. In the nature of things, a series of positive stories is likely to cause some reporter to gun for a negative story as a contrarian "scoop." Trading favors such as access or information for favorable coverage may not be the answer because a company's competitors will lobby reporters just as hard as the company. A strong relationship with reporters therefore is never bulletproof. Moreover, reporters don't necessarily control their final product. Editors can change the meaning or slant of a story with a headline or new opening paragraph.

Norman Pearlstine

Norm Pearlstine, currently the editor-in-chief of Time Inc., is the father of modern business journalism. Before joining Time in 1995, Pearlstine spent twenty-three years at *The Wall Street Journal,* first as a reporter, then as managing editor and executive editor. He guided the paper's editorial staff during the heyday of the 1980s merger boom and was responsible for reshaping coverage of the M&A business.

Pearlstine cut his teeth as a reporter working out of the *Journal*'s Dallas office and subsequently spent a number of years living the itinerant life of a rising star reporter—first in Detroit, then Los Angeles, then Tokyo. Pearlstine was appointed the Tokyo bureau chief in 1973 and became managing editor of *The Asian Wall Street Journal,* a paper that he helped found. After a two-year intermission as an executive editor of *Forbes,* Pearlstine was lured back to become the *Journal*'s national news editor. He rapidly rose to become managing editor, a job he held from 1983 until 1991.

Pearlstine left a considerable mark on the *Journal*'s pages. He organized the paper into an innovative three-section format in 1988 and expanded news coverage. But, most of all, he professionalized the paper. Page-one special reports became a regular feature and beat reporters were encouraged to develop the expertise necessary to cover complicated economic and business issues. The best of the *Journal* was second to none. Jim Stewart's reporting, for example, on mergers and the insider trading scandal was recognized as the best in the business.

As the *Journal* rejuvenated, a star system developed, with the key reporters becoming celebrities and the lesser reporters resentful, creating internal friction. Critics contended that this desire for fame at times eroded some of the paper's objectivity, as reporters looked for notches in their belts rather than a balanced story. Pearlstine, however, deserves considerable credit for pushing the paper to a new level of excellence and excitement.

Pearlstine left the *Journal* in 1992 to try his hand at media ventures. But in 1995, he was lured back to journalism by Time Inc., where he has editorial responsibility over a powerful magazine portfolio, including *Time, Money, Fortune, People,* and *Sports Illustrated.* Under Pearlstine's tutelage, the magazine group was shaken up and many of the editors replaced. Today, the business is thriving.

The goal from the perspective of management and their advisers is to maximize the chance that a company's story will receive a fair hearing in the press. In this process, it is important to keep in mind the constraints faced by journalists. Print journalists have deadlines and are under constant pressure to turn out material. Television journalists face an even shorter time frame. In such an environment, there sometimes is little time for research and goodwill can often be generated by providing background material to journalists. But this approach is sure to backfire if the material is biased or hackneyed. Journalists are by nature skeptical and are likely to uncover the other side. Full disclosure or no disclosure usually is the best policy.

The first story on a subject can have a large impact. And once first impressions are formed, news cycles can take a day or longer to turn. It is important, therefore, for a company to have its position reflected in the early story. While reporters generally are good about giving the affected parties a chance to respond for the record, the nature of most print deadlines is such that journalists are likely to call during hours when most businesses are closed. Making a contact available after hours therefore can be critical. In fact, the more negative the story, the more likely a call will come in around 6:00. If there are errors in the story, editors almost always fiercely defend their reporters.

Like all professions, journalism has its mixture of dedicated professionals, superficial sensation seekers, and people who miss the point. As always, the thrill of a scoop is exhilarating, and the dream of being the next best-selling author an objective. Therefore, treating reporters with respect but caution is most professionals' advice.

The Price | 16

*"What is a cynic? A man who knows the price of
everything, and the value of nothing."*

—Oscar Wilde, *Lady Windermere's Fan*

The ultimate decision in evaluating a deal is whether to pay the price. To rationalize their bids, buyers go through a bevy of pyrotechnics, with reams of paper consumed in obscure calculations—all designed to answer a simple question: What price should the bidder pay? The pressure becomes particularly intense in a competitive process with more than one bidder.

Buying companies is like participating in an art auction. The losers think the winner overpaid and, if there are ten potential buyers, the bidder in fifth place seems the most reasonable. But of course, that bidder hasn't bought anything. Meanwhile, the losers often spend time denigrating the wisdom of the buyer.

Truth, here, is not only elusive, but intensely subjective. It may well be the price paid by the buyer makes perfect sense for it and none at all for the fifth-place finisher due to potential synergies or other strategic considerations that the winner will enjoy. For example, Shell Oil could pay more than its competitors for the Belridge Oil properties because Shell had superior recovery technology.

To further confuse the calculus, it usually takes a long time to figure out whether a buyer overpaid. A large part of success comes not only from the price at which an asset is bought, but how it is em-

ployed in the future and how well the subsequent opportunities the
deal provides are exploited. If a lagging business is turned around
and becomes much more valuable, the price paid might prove a bargain, in retrospect. No one can foretell the future and every business
is different. The best a bidder can do is to collect the data and make
a judgment about the appropriate price. To maximize the chance for
a positive outcome, a buyer tries to understand the dynamics of a
company, analyze its characteristics, and then finally look at future
value.

Fundamentals

A common mistake buyers make is to leap into the morass of
evaluation without first thinking about context. The first three rules
of merger valuation are: fundamentals, fundamentals, fundamentals.
First, the overall timing of a potential investment needs to be
thought through. Are we at the peak of a bull market or the bottom
of a bear cycle? Even if the target is a great company, a purchase in
September of 1929 may not have been wise. Second, a review of industry fundamentals is important. A good company in a bad industry is likely to be dragged down to the level of its peers. Finally, a
thoughtful analysis of each key market and product in which a company participates goes a long way. What really drives the business?
Particular issues worth considering include:

- the business environment and applicable government regulations
- the impact of the business cycle on the business and a recognition of the current stage
- geographical spread and country risk
- cost structure, including materials and labor
- the ease of financing the business and the permanence of capital availability

- state of facilities and capital investment status and requirements

- competitors and potential entrants, with an eye on comparative strengths

- channels of distribution and outlook for change

- characteristics and needs of key customers

- price flexibility, inflationary expectations, and margins

- strength of management, ages, experience, and depth

- technological position and record of research and innovation

- brand support, advertising, and promotion

- legal risks and potential liabilities

- opportunities for expansion

The process of fundamental analysis deserves more than lip service. Quantification without a clear articulation of premises is absurd, merely a garbage-in, garbage-out exercise in eighth-grade math.

Quaker Oats provides a good example of the role of these fundamental drivers. In 1984, the company purchased Stokley–Van Camp for $220 million. Some analysts called the price too generous, but by 1990 the deal would be hailed in a *Business Week* article as one of the "standout acquisitions" of the 1980s. Gatorade proved the hidden gem in the deal. Stokley had sold the sports beverage line mostly in the Southeast and lacked a coherent marketing strategy. But, looking at the fundamentals, Quaker saw an opportunity.

CEO William Smithburg saw a strong but underutilized brand, room for geographic expansion, and channels of distribution similar to Quaker's other lines. Gatorade was a brand he could grow. Therefore Quaker bought Stokley and proceeded to sell all the brands other than Stokley's pork-and-beans line and the Gatorade brand, reducing Quaker's net purchase price to $95 million.

Smithburg concentrated on distribution and marketing the acquired brands over the next five years. Quaker bumped ad spending, and in particular targeted sports promotions and athletic endorsements as key opportunities. The acquisition paid off phenomenally well. Sales grew at a 30 percent annual rate through 1989 and in that year, Gatorade's operating profit of $125 million accounted for roughly one fifth of Quaker's total. Competition from Coke and Pepsi emerged in the 1990s, but Gatorade remained a billion-dollar global brand.

The Gatorade deal stands in stark contrast to Quaker's more recent Snapple acquisition, which may go down as one of the worst deals of the 1990s: Quaker bought the business in 1994 for $1.7 billion and sold it two years later for just $300 million. In the interim, Quaker absorbed $100 million of losses from Snapple, and Smithburg quit as CEO.

Of course, hindsight is perfect, but a number of fundamental problems with the Snapple business made it an unlikely target for a repeat of the Gatorade success. Snapple's juice and tea beverage concept had exploded in popularity over the past several years. However, around the time Quaker bought the business, sales growth was slowing and competition growing. In fact, Quaker bought Snapple on a downward blip in its stock price following a horrible third-quarter earnings report.

Further, the plan to integrate distribution of Snapple and Gatorade presented tough challenges. The two beverages were distributed through different channels: Quaker focused on grocery stores and other large outlets, while Snapple on convenience stores and gas stations. Mastering each channel required different skills.

Comparing Gatorade to Snapple underscores the extent to which fundamental operating issues define the success or failure of a transaction. Clearly, price cannot be understood in isolation. Problems cannot always be foreseen, but a fundamental analysis can go a long way.

The Body Count

Within a context, financial numbers do sing a song to the sensitive listener and are an important tool in a fundamental analysis. Yet accounting is limited and flawed, notwithstanding its central role in business. The accounting rules are part good-faith best effort to describe economic reality and part counterintuitive arcana, full of vagaries and inconsistencies. The challenge is to filter the bad information from the good, to uncover the buried bodies: Why are the numbers presented in this form? What was the objective of the management? How do these numbers relate to the fundamental analysis of the company? Then the numbers and ratios need to be cross-compared to those of competitors.

To begin to understand a company, one must first assemble a databank—information provided by the company, all public filings, including exhibits, all news articles for the past several years, and all recent security analysts' reports about the company and its competitors. For financial information, a buyer should start by reading the footnotes, which contain highly relevant information such as revenue recognition and depreciation and amortization policies. The notes often will also contain a company's explanation of restructuring and other one-time charges, debt repurchases, and the like.

Once a buyer develops a preliminary feel for the numbers, the question becomes whether any buried bodies remain hidden. The three deceits of buried body accounting are overstated earnings, managed earnings, and hidden assets and liabilities. Recognizing these patterns, accounting figures can be massaged into useful data.

Pumping Up the Bottom Line   Because so much attention is paid to reported earnings, pumping up the so-called bottom line is common. A company can use one of three basic techniques to accomplish this goal. Revenues can be boosted; expenses can be pushed off into the future; or one-time gains can be triggered.

BOOSTING REVENUES.   If expenses are held constant, higher revenues trickle down to the bottom line on a dollar-for-dollar basis. Current revenues can be boosted either by shifting future revenue to the current period or by fabricating additional revenues.

Under U.S. Generally Accepted Accounting Principles, or GAAP, revenues can be recognized only when they have been both earned and realized. Revenues are earned when a company provides goods or services to its customer. Revenues are realized when the customer in return provides cash or another asset, such as a binding promise to pay that is likely to be fulfilled. Fuzzy areas abound; for example, when refunds are available or when the obligation to pay doesn't have much bite.

This revenue recognition test is highly subjective. As a result, a continuum exists. Some companies take a conservative stance, understating their revenues. Other companies take an aggressive approach, overstating their revenues. The most common blowup is when shipments to customers who distribute a product are pumped up so that the pipeline is filled to overflowing. Eventually, there will be excess returns, but by then the company will already have been sold.

PUMPING SALES

The MiniScribe Fiasco

The now-defunct MiniScribe Corporation is a classic example of a company that got too aggressive with its recognition of sales. MiniScribe was a high-flying technology company of the late 1980s, run by "Dr. Fix-It," as Mr. Q.T. Wiles was known. Wiles, who also served as chairman of high-tech investment bank Hambrecht & Quist, had come to MiniScribe in 1986 while the company was in the midst of a deep crisis. It had just lost IBM's business and was suffering through a major industry slump. As a result, the company was hemorrhaging cash and losing customers.

Notwithstanding the difficulties, Wiles parachuted in and quickly turned MiniScribe around, at least as far as the outside world was concerned. In October of 1988, MiniScribe announced its thirteenth consecutive quarter of record-breaking sales.

However, problems lurked not far below the surface. Seven months later, the company jolted the financial community by announcing that its record sales growth was pure fiction. The books had been cooked. It wasn't just that the company had inflated inventory figures or aggressively booked sales. Not satisfied with such manipulations, company employees actually shipped ordinary bricks to distributors and booked the shipments as disk drive sales. They also tried to convince outside accountants to book as sales the cargo on a freighter that supposedly had set sail in late December of 1986. The accountants refused, and the cargo and the freighter, apparently a fiction, weren't mentioned again.

Other employees were apparently unwilling to accept no as an answer from the accountants. When the auditors uncovered discrepancies, these employees broke into locked trunks to change the auditors' work papers. Despite all these irregularities, Coopers & Lybrand, the company's accounting firm, issued clean audit reports to the company and reportedly overlooked questionable practices such as the back-dating of sales. What's more, Coopers approved a decrease in MiniScribe's bad-debt reserve even as accounts receivables ballooned.

Ultimately, the accounting shenanigans led to MiniScribe's bankruptcy, liability payments for Hambrecht & Quist and Coopers & Lybrand, and a criminal conviction for Wiles.

Other more recent instances of accounting fraud, while perhaps not as outrageous as that exhibited by MiniScribe, are worth mentioning. Two illustrative examples are provided by Livent—a producer of Broadway shows such as *Ragtime, Kiss of the Spider Woman,* and *Showboat*—and Cendant—a conglomerate that owns the franchise operations of Avis, Century 21, and Coldwell Banker, as well as membership club operations.

Livent was a powerful producer in North American theater, commanding approximately 18 percent of the box office for Broadway shows. The company also owned theaters in Chicago, New York, Vancouver, and Toronto. Yet Livent's apparent financial success was really a sham.

Garth Drabinsky—former chairman and CEO—along with the former president and director, Myron Gottlieb, had concocted a scheme to inflate revenues, earnings, and assets reported in financial statements to the SEC and the public. Top Livent executives masked losses and shifted costs using a custom-tailored accounting package that they had created to allow them to carry out their fraud. Losses from failed shows were shifted to costs of shows in development.

The cost of advertising the show *Ragtime* was reclassified as a construction cost for Chicago's Oriental Theater. Drabinsky and Gottlieb arranged for two friends to purchase $381,000 worth of tickets for the Los Angeles production of *Ragtime* so that the show would appear to meet minimum ticket sales as required by the theater's owner and to make the show look successful before its Broadway run; Livent reimbursed these individuals. The CFO also kept hidden from auditors the fact that Livent had to pay certain fees for the rights to perform *Showboat*, fees that would have increased reported liabilities. Favorable results were cooked up in anticipation of a public bond offering.

The result of all this manipulation was a record of steady profits. Even some of the most prominent figures in finance were fooled.

The board of directors and major shareholders consisted of buyout specialist Thomas Lee, Canadian entrepreneur Jim Pattison, and newspaper magnate Conrad Black. But in fact the company was generating losses.

In early 1998, however, Livent's facade began to crack, as the board became more aware of its financial difficulties. The board removed Drabinsky from day-to-day management; former Disney president Michael Ovitz invested $20 million (Canadian) in the company and took over day-to-day management. Roy Furman, of Furman Selz, was appointed chairman. But the extent of the financial difficulties was not yet apparent.

The scale of the manipulations was so exhaustive that the company kept two sets of books so as to be able to distinguish between the real and the phony numbers. But the sham came crashing down when the new management team headed by Ovitz began asking questions and then discovered the accounting irregularities. Livent subsequently filed for Chapter 11 bankruptcy protection to reorganize its financial affairs and find a way to pay millions of dollars in bills.

Cendant, the company formed with the 1997 merger of conglomerates HFS and CUC, also was guilty of widespread accounting fraud. HFS was a conglomerate consisting of franchising companies—such as Days Inn, Howard Johnson hotels, Avis, Coldwell Banker, and Century 21—and CUC was a membership club operator that CEO Walter Forbes called a "virtual business" and whose 70 percent membership renewal rate gave it an "annuity-like" earnings stream. The $14 billion deal was a blockbuster, joining two highly successful companies into a powerful conglomerate. The market reacted extremely favorably to the deal.

But then the accounting irregularities on CUC's books were revealed. Cendant's new chief accounting officer Scott Forbes (unrelated to Walter Forbes) discovered that members of CUC's accounting department, which Walter Forbes insisted remain independent from HFS's, attempted to shift excess merger reserves into income to meet Street consensus earnings estimates. He was even more horrified to discover that it had been done before. Henry Silverman, former CEO of HFS and current CEO of Cendant, forced out those responsible for these accounting irregularities.

But the story only kept getting worse. Eight days later, two midlevel CUC accounting executives described in detail the widespread fraud that had taken place at CUC. CUC had, quarter after quarter, met Street earnings estimates by making numbers up. Casper Sabatino, CUC's vice president of corporate accounting, described one night in which he stayed up until 1:00 A.M. preparing seven pages of fictitious accounting entries. Fictitious revenues had been concocted since 1995. Accounts receivable were made up, with no corresponding customers or services. All in all, CUC had created more than $500 million of phony profits.

Cendant's share price fell from about $41 to less than $10. Silverman was irate and held Walter Forbes personally responsible. Forbes disclaimed all knowledge of the fraud, but eventually agreed to step down as chairman of Cendant.

UNDERREPORTING EXPENSES. The underreporting of expenses is most often accomplished by moving expenses from the current period into the future.

The GAAP rules regarding depreciation and amortization afford the most straightforward opportunity to shift costs. GAAP generally requires that the depreciable value of a long-lived asset—measured as the difference between acquisition cost and predicted salvage value—be expensed over its useful life. The portion of the total that is written off each year will depend on the depreciation method selected. Under the straight-line method, the depreciable value is written off ratably over the asset's useful life. Other accelerated depreciation methods front-load the process, with more expense recognized in the early years.

GAAP depreciation standards leave open three possible cost-shifting strategies. First, a company can inflate an asset's predicted terminal value, which reduces its depreciable value. Second, a company can inflate the useful life of an asset: A longer useful life results in a reduced annual depreciation expense. Third, a company can select straight-line rather than accelerated depreciation.

For example, prior to a 1993 accounting change, Delta Airlines depreciated its Boeing 727s on a straight-line basis over a fifteen-year period. TWA, on the other hand, depreciated its 727s over a twenty-year period. As a result of the different depreciation periods chosen by Delta and TWA, Delta's 1992 earnings were understated by approximately $35 million when compared to TWA's. Therefore, if the same valuation multiple were applied to the earnings of both companies, Delta's value as a company would be understated relative to TWA's. Perhaps for this reason, Delta lengthened its depreciation period in 1993 to the now-industry-standard twenty years.

This phenomenon of differential depreciation is by no means uncommon. General Motors provides another example. A *Forbes* magazine article pointed out the impact of GM's alteration of its depreciation policy for tools and dies: When in 1987 the automaker GM stretched out the depreciation period to match that used by Ford and Chrysler, EPS increased by more than 33 percent.

The classic cautionary tale, however, is that of Leasco. Based on his Wharton thesis, the creative Saul Steinberg set up a company which leased IBM computers. IBM took the conservative position that its computers would become obsolete fairly quickly and accordingly offered customers short-term leases at high rates and depreciated machines over a short time frame. Steinberg, on the other hand, bought machines on credit and offered longer, noncancelable leases at lower rates. Leasco effectively was betting the machines would be useful over the longer period.

For a time, the assumption held, and Steinberg cleaned up. The initial lease rates covered most of the cost of buying equipment. As customers signed on, Leasco's earnings popped because of the significant spread between the rental terms and the stated depreciation on the machines. Results were great, and Steinberg was a hero. But then IBM came out with a new line, making Leasco's machines obsolete even though not fully depreciated. The company's stock price crashed. But Steinberg had the tenacity to bounce back and prosper with what eventually became Reliance Insurance.

The decision of whether to capitalize costs in the first place affords a more fundamental opportunity for cost shifting. Capitalizing a cost, to be depreciated over a set term, reduces earnings by a steady amount over a set period, whereas expensing a cost creates a large, one-time hit to earnings. A guiding premise is that a cost should be capitalized only if it will provide future benefit. If not, the cost should be fully expensed in the current period. Examples of borderline expenses that are sometimes capitalized include advertising, research and development, and start-up costs.

Shoe and apparel manufacturer L.A. Gear is a good example. The company, initially a hot growth prospect, began to falter in the late 1980s. Then, in 1988, L.A. Gear capitalized a portion of its advertising expenditures, a gimmick that caused earnings to increase a record 377 percent over the prior year. The company continued the practice into the first quarter of the new year, capitalizing $3.9 million of $7.2 million in total ad spending. Soon, however, the reality regarding L.A. Gear's boosted earnings became widely recognized, and the company's stock price deflated.

Ultimately, the capitalization question comes down to basic common sense: Will the claimed asset associated with an expenditure really provide future benefits?

The treatment of capitalized R&D expenses by acquirers has been the focus of much SEC scrutiny lately in the M&A context. Acquirers, particularly in the technology sector, have aggressively written down capitalized R&D costs, taking a one-time hit against their income statements. The theory is that this one-off charge will be ignored in the mass of merger-related expenses, but after the deal, the combined company's earnings will not be negatively impacted by the amortization of capitalized R&D.

Writing down R&D allowed tech companies to overpay for targets, and was therefore widely employed. The SEC's steps to limit this practice are likely to have a dampening effect on tech company M&A.

Companies also attempt to shift retirement and health care costs to future periods. Theoretically, a company should expense such costs over the working lives of covered employees, with complicated actuarial formulae used to estimate the cost that should be attributed to a given year. But the predictive nature of this process gives a company some leeway to shift costs by taking an aggressive stance with respect to projected liabilities, the projected return on invested cash, and so on.

Even with all the accounting gimmicks in the world, though, bad news cannot be put off forever because the cumulative effect of expense shifting is to reduce future reported net income. Some companies attempt to mitigate this reality by periodically cleansing their financial statements: Expenses are piled together into one period in the form of a restructuring or other one-time charge and are justified as costs associated with a strategic shift. This "big-bath" accounting gets all the pain over with at once, so that future earnings will not be handicapped. Analysts often "back out" or ignore these ostensibly one-time charges in their valuations, further encouraging these questionable practices.

The New York Times has cited AT&T as an example of a company that has used big-bath accounting. The telephone company recorded four "one-time" restructuring charges during the decade ending in 1996. These charges totaled $14.2 billion, an amount almost 50 percent greater than the company's entire reported earnings over the same period.

NONRECURRING GAINS.   The selective triggering of nonrecurring gains provides another opportunity to manage earnings. Such gains theoretically should be ignored from a valuation perspective because, if truly one-time gains, they are unrelated to the company's operational performance. The problem, however, is that "one-time" income items, if occurring repeatedly, act as a kind of white noise, and can be ignored as such and instead viewed as part of normal earnings.

A nonrecurring gain often comes when a company sells an asset with a low book value. Real estate, inventory, and debt are common sources of one-time gains. In the case of real estate, the incipient gain generally results from the simple passage of time: The real estate appreciates in value, while the book value remains fixed at historical cost. The difference can be recognized as revenue if the property is sold.

THE MAGICIAN

Harold Geneen Manages ITT's Earnings

ITT chairman Harold Geneen was an accounting Svengali. In 1971, the burgeoning conglomerate acquired Hartford Insurance, a deal that, at the time, Geneen reportedly crowed gave ITT an "opportunity to have programmed earnings."

The key to the strategy was Hartford's large portfolio of stocks, bonds, mortgages, and other investment reserves. These reserves had a certain amount of built-in gain—that is, there was a positive difference between the market value of the investments and their historical cost. So, whenever ITT needed a boost to make an earnings target, it could simply sell some of these assets.

In 1974, for example, Hartford's entire portfolio was $241 million underwater. Nonetheless, through judicious asset sales, Geneen was able to generate $22 million in after-tax gains. This careful management prompted one former ITT executive to remark that "the Hartford portfolio was played like a violin."

A company which sells inventory in the ordinary course of business generates operating profit. It is possible, however, to manipulate one-time inventory sales using the last-in, first-out (LIFO) inventory valuation method; gains from this type of transaction, however, should be segregated as nonrecurring. The LIFO method, sanctioned by GAAP, charges the most recently purchased inventory cost against current sales in calculating gross profit. This is in contrast to the first-in, first-out (FIFO) method, where the first inventory purchased is charged against current sales. As a result, in an inflationary environment, a company's inventory on hand may have a book value per unit that is much lower than the current unit cost under LIFO. The aggregate difference between book value and current cost—called the LIFO reserve—represents a built-in gain. This gain can be recognized by liquidating the inventory.

The flip side of the inventory income generation maneuver is the failure to recognize the real value of the inventory in write-downs. Stale inventory of finished goods is quite common.

A company also may be able to generate one-time gains by repurchasing its outstanding debt at a discount. Debt will trade at a discount when market interest rates exceed the bond's coupon rate. Depending on the terms of a particular debt instrument, the issuing company may have the right to repurchase the debt at market value. According to GAAP, the difference between this market value and the principal amount of the debt is booked as a one-time gain even if the debt is replaced by new instruments carrying the higher rate.

Income Smoothing   Like efforts to boost the bottom line, income smoothing is symptomatic of the emphasis placed on reported earnings. However, income smoothing has more to do with trends than with the absolute amount of earnings.

Income is smoothed by creating reserves for future expenses as a way to shift "excess" earnings into the future. These earnings are banked for a rainy day, and can be released in a tough year. *Forbes* singled out oil companies in particular as "champions of income smoothing," implying they manage earnings by selectively booking environmental clean-up expenses. For example, in 1990, Amoco had an extraordinary gain of $471 million from settling claims related to asset seizures during the Iranian revolution. But in the same quarter, Amoco added $477 million to its reserves for environmental damage, thereby giving itself future earnings flexibility.

Hidden Assets and Liabilities   Book value is defined as the difference between the value of assets and liabilities as shown on a company's balance sheet. Generally speaking, however, book value is a flawed measure of assets' worth.

ASSETS.   Balance sheet asset values rarely match current market values because GAAP values certainty over accuracy. This ethos dictates that assets generally should be recorded on a company's books at historic cost. There are exceptions, of course, such as marketable securities, the book values of which are marked up or down to current market value. The divergence of book values from market values can have dramatic results.

For example, in the fall of 1988, Northwest Airlines' stock was trading in the low 50s, creating an equity value of roughly $1.5 billion. The company then disclosed that it had rejected a Japanese investor's offer to buy Northwest's Tokyo residential compound for $200 million. The news came as a pleasant surprise to investors because they had not realized that Northwest held this and several other pieces of extremely valuable Japanese real estate. None of these properties, which together were worth roughly $500 million, had been separately disclosed in the company's financial statements. When we worked on the takeover bid for Northwest, the Japanese real estate was a key factor in the valuation.

While real estate is the most commonly undervalued asset on company books, other hard assets, such as plants or production facilities, may also be similarly undervalued. Unfortunately, though, assets may be buried in such a way that their true value cannot easily be discovered.

LIABILITIES.   With liabilities, problems may arise because claims are not recognized on a company's books at all, or have been shifted off the books.

There are a number of circumstances in which companies may fail to record a liability when they arguably should. Companies which receive payment up front for goods or services that will be provided over time sometimes record the entire payment as current revenue; however, the more appropriate treatment would be to record the amount related to future goods or services as a liability because the services have not yet been provided. Naturally, this situation arises most often in industries where up-front payment is common, like franchising, magazine publishing, or prepaid vacation sales.

Companies also may fail to report contingent liabilities that arise due to litigation or other disputes. According to GAAP, a company should record a liability when a loss is more than likely and the amount can be calculated with reasonable certainty. But with litigation, there is a lot of room for discretion.

The practice of shifting liabilities off the balance sheet is even more widespread, and in recent years, companies have developed sophisticated financial engineering tools specifically for this purpose. For example, a common securitization strategy is to pool receivables which are then sold to third parties. The selling company will even in some cases go so far as to guarantee that the receivables will be paid, receiving what is essentially a secured loan. Though the existence of the guarantee typically is disclosed in financial statements, companies have some flexibility to account for the transaction as an outright sale. In that case, it can come as quite a surprise if the company is forced to make good on its guarantee.

Uncovering the Bodies

The fiction of artificial earnings can only hold up for so long before the underlying reality becomes apparent. Of course, the key is to uncover problems before they are disclosed. Only then is the knowledge valuable.

Outright fraud unfortunately is difficult to detect. However, in other cases, financial ratio analysis can act as an early warning system. Attention to three key ratios—inventory turnover, accounts receivable turnover, and the cash ratio—will tell a great deal about the quality of a company's earnings.

A company's inventory turnover ratio equals its cost of goods sold for a period divided by its inventory (including the so-called LIFO reserve if any). A declining inventory turnover means a company is building inventory faster than sales. Rather than address the fact that sales are declining by scaling back inventory, the company ignores reality and continues production or purchasing at its former pace. Eventually, some of the added inventory will likely need to be written off, causing a decline in future earnings.

A company's accounts receivables turnover equals its sales divided by its accounts receivable. A declining turnover ratio means a company is taking longer to convert sales into cash and perhaps is loosening credit standards to boost sales. If some of the sales are never converted to cash, current earnings and assets will have been overstated.

Finally, a company's cash ratio equals its cash items divided by current liabilities. A declining cash ratio indicates an impending liquidity crunch. This ratio provides another window into the accounts receivable problem mentioned above, but can also indicate other cash management problems. The fact that a company's revenues are increasing but cash is decreasing may indicate an overly aggressive accounting posture. The company may be booking shipments as sales or may not be writing off an appropriate percentage of accounts receivable.

These three ratios provide a good start for analysis. However, ratio analysis must also be supplemented with a careful reading of the footnotes to a company's financial statements as well as a real-world sanity check.

Spotting the Value

Success in the merger business comes from spotting the underlying value. Henry Kravis and George Roberts are masters of the art, as evidenced by their highly successful purchase and sale of Duracell.

KKR's involvement with Duracell began in late 1987, when Kraft Inc. decided to sell the business. The battery operation, which Kraft had picked up as part of its earlier merger with Dart Industries, was not core to Kraft's other food businesses, and therefore stockholders had been pressuring John Richman, Kraft's chairman, to divest the business. Moreover, worried by the rumors of an impending Kraft takeover floating around, Richman believed a Duracell sale might stave off the hostile attack.

When bidding opened, Richman expected the sale would bring a bit more than $1 billion. Therefore he was pleasantly surprised when a bidding war erupted among a handful of financial buyers. Ted Forstmann eventually tried to preempt the action by offering a $1.5 billion exploding bid.

Kravis responded to Forstmann's move by approaching Richman. KKR was prepared to go higher, but had to know the next round of bidding would be the last. Richman agreed and KKR bettered its first-round bid of $1.2 billion by $600 million. Expecting another round of bidding, Forstmann, Clayton & Dubilier, and Gibbons Green all came in lower. At $1.7 billion, Forstmann was the next highest bidder and demanded a chance to top KKR. But Richman kept his word to Kravis.

Kravis and Roberts had become interested in Duracell almost as soon as they saw the descriptive memorandum. What did they see in Duracell that made it worth $1.8 billion, almost $800 million more than Richman had expected? The fundamentals of the business were strong: In a market with few competitors, Duracell was second to Ralston Purina's Eveready in the battery market, and led the booming alkaline battery segment. Furthermore, the inexorable miniaturization of electronics equipment continued to drive demand higher. Operating income margins were over 10 percent.

In addition, Duracell's president Robert Kidder and the company's other managers chafed under Richman's leadership and were primed to lead a buyout. As the bidding process unfolded, Kidder identified a number of areas where costs could be reduced. He also made a strong case that the business could be expanded.

With the fundamentals and management looking good, KKR turned to the numbers. Kidder's projections for Duracell showed growing cash flow. Therefore, KKR agreed to fund the Duracell acquisition with just over $350 million in equity for a debt-to-equity ratio of four to one. Inserting Kidder's numbers into an LBO consequences model showed KKR that Duracell could successfully carry the $1.45 billion in debt that would be used in the deal without any asset sales. If Duracell hit its projections, KKR, its investors, and Duracell management would earn a solid return on the equity.

Skeptics regarded the $1.8 billion price put on Duracell as a stretch. Some reports chalked it up as another case of LBO guys needing to spend the money they controlled. The price represented roughly 14 times Duracell's 1987 earnings before interest and taxes (EBIT) and 11 times EBITDA (EBIT plus depreciation and amortization, a measure of operating cash flow). This offer came at a time when Gillette—a somewhat comparable consumer products company—traded in the market at 10 times 1987 EBIT and 8 times 1987 EBITDA. But the key to the valuation was KKR's vision of the future value in Duracell. KKR liked Kidder's enthusiasm and believed his projections.

As it turned out, Duracell soared. Kidder and his team trimmed administrative costs, increased R&D spending, and grabbed market share from Eveready. Innovations like a disposable battery tester and strong international sales drove cash flow above the original projections, and Duracell was able to repay $224 million of senior debt ahead of schedule.

By 1991, things were going so well at Duracell that KKR took the company public, using the offering proceeds to reduce debt even further. In one of the year's hottest IPOs, Duracell issued $450 million of stock priced at $15 a share, which was then bid above $20 within the first few days of trading. Meanwhile, the KKR group, which didn't sell any stock in the offering, retained a 73 percent stake in Duracell. Stock purchased at $5 was trading in the market for four times that amount. Over the next several years, KKR would capitalize on this run-up through a series of stock sales which reduced its stake to 34 percent.

The ultimate takeout came in 1996, when Gillette purchased Duracell in a stock-for-stock deal. The merger of Gillette, a strong international marketer, and Duracell, with limited international presence outside Europe, wowed investors. In the two days after the deal was announced, Duracell's stock rose 27 percent in the market and Gillette's rose 8 percent.

The Gillette deal was finalized in December 1996, closing an extremely successful investment for KKR. Taking into account Gillette's stock price at closing and KKR's earlier stock sales, the firm's original $350 million investment had grown to more than $3 billion. As can only be seen in hindsight, the Duracell purchase price had been a bargain.

The Valuation Framework

The Duracell story is indicative of the valuation process. Having analyzed the fundamentals of a company and its financial history, a bidder can forecast a company's future performance and come to a point of view of its worth.

All valuation methods have their flaws, but they are very useful as cross-checks. The new science of valuation, with quantitatively derived answers, is almost laughable in its simplicity—despite the ostensible precision. Sophisticated companies don't pay the same attention to theoretical financial models as newly minted MBAs.

Essentially, every five years a bright business school professor or economist comes up with a new twist on corporate finance theory and publishes it in the *Journal of Finance* or some other academic periodical. It filters down, often through consultants and bankers, to corporations who adapt variant forms of the theories. But it's all theoretical as hell, so naturally the models get adapted and tangled. As long as it's all taken with a grain of salt, the exercises are worthwhile.

There are three generic types of valuation methods: discounted cash flow models, comparable companies analyses, and consequences impacts.

The Discounted Cash Flow Model

According to the discounted cash flow model, or DCF, the value of a company should equal the present value of its future cash flows. Constructing the model is formulaic. First, cash flow projections, which exclude the effect of any debt, must be developed. Second, a terminal value—the value of the enterprise at the end of the last year for which projections are developed—is determined, generally by applying some multiple to EBITDA or EPS. Third, the appropriate discount rate must be estimated. Finally, the present value of each year's cash flows as well as the terminal value is calculated using the hurdle rate to "discount" the values. The resulting present value number reflects the operating value of the firm. Because the value is independent of its capital structure, the technique can be used to compare several different operating businesses, if desired. The value of a company's common equity then can be determined by subtracting the value of debt and other non-common-equity claims.

Two main concepts underlie the DCF model. The first is that projected cash flows, not earnings, are the appropriate stream for discounting because cash flows better reflect economic reality. It is the cash flows, rather than the accounting earnings, that are available to be paid out to shareholders. Earnings are more of a metaphysical construct, calculated according to somewhat arbitrary accounting principles.

The second foundation is the time value of money: A dollar of future cash flow is worth less than a dollar of current cash flow because a dollar of current cash flow can be invested at some rate of return. At a 5 percent interest rate paid annually, for example, a dollar invested today becomes $1.05 a year from now.

However, because DCF analysis is more theoretical than the other valuation models, a dose of common sense is critical to its use.

Cash Flow Projections   The "cash flow" in DCF projections does not refer to the number reported at the bottom of a company's cash flow statement, a figure that includes cash paid and received from financing and investment activities. Rather, the DCF model uses a different cash flow concept, known as "unlevered free cash flow"— the amount of cash generated by the operating business in a given year.

Net income is a starting point to calculate free cash flow. Depreciation and amortization are then added back to net income because they are noncash expenses. This step also allows one to compare the valuations of companies with different depreciation practices. Increases in working capital and capital expenditures—which consume cash but are not incorporated as expenses in the net income figure—are subtracted.

The final step is to unlever the cash flow by adding back any interest expense on a tax-adjusted basis. To tax-adjust the interest expense, one must subtract the tax shield provided by the tax-deductible interest payments.

Once interest is excluded, the resulting balance is free cash flow to the unlevered firm, the basic building block of DCF analysis.

The Projections   The DCF model requires that unlevered free cash flow be projected for some number of years into the future. There are two sources where one can find the data to build these projections: management and research analysts.

The typical time horizon for projections is five to ten years. For cyclical industries, however, the forecast period should capture at least one full cycle, which may in fact be longer than ten years. DCF projections in the outer years are understandably very subjective. Indeed, the easiest way to "jigger" a DCF analysis is to defer or underestimate new capital expenditures or research and development expense or, for a consumer company, marketing expenses. But it is precisely those outer-year earnings figures which are capitalized to create the all-important terminal values. Therefore, particularly for growth companies which do not generate positive cash flow in early years, DCF can become mere gut feel cloaked in science.

To counteract this problem, the base case needs to be tested. Margins and growth rates should be scrutinized. Does the picture presented comport with the industry's strategic dynamic? Any divergence from industry norms deserve particular attention. For example, expanding margins in a competitive industry must be justified. Likewise, continued growth in a stagnant industry needs to be explained. Sensitivity analyses are often run to examine the effect of "downside" scenarios.

Novell Buys WordPerfect

Consideration of the worst-case scenario—and its impact on value—should also be part of a DCF analysis. Of course, the worst case sometimes happens, as was demonstrated by Novell's experience after it bought WordPerfect in 1994, a stock deal initially valued at $1.4 billion.

The WordPerfect deal ran into trouble from the start. Investors dumped Novell stock when the diversification was announced. The price plunged from $24 to $15.25 by the time the deal closed, driving Novell's effective acquisition price down to $855 million.

The problem was Microsoft. The world changed for other software companies with the introduction of a vastly upgraded Microsoft Windows operating system in 1990. With an approachable format, this new package became a marketing sensation. Microsoft began to bundle various applications in a single unit whose selling price was not much more than that for a single application.

By the time of the 1994 Novell purchase, the privately held WordPerfect was being routed. Marketing blunders compounded by the slow introduction of a Windows-based product drove sales down. The company's two owners were ready to sell.

Novell saw two possible alternatives for WordPerfect's future. In one, sales would continue to decline, margins erode, and profits evaporate. In the other, with new stronger management, WordPerfect would rebound and become a strong number two to Microsoft. With its purchase, Novell clearly endorsed this latter vision.

Unfortunately, the worst case happened, probably to an even greater extent than Novell might have imagined. Novell bundled WordPerfect with the spreadsheet Quattro (purchased around the same time from Borland) in its own package. But Microsoft continued to out-innovate and out-market the WordPerfect business. And Novell's sales force—accustomed to selling networking software—proved incapable of pushing the new products. Margins vaporized and more than 4,000 of WordPerfect's employees had to be laid off. Finally, in 1996, Novell sold both WordPerfect and Quattro to Corel, a Canadian company, for about $125 million, creating an $875 million loss in less than two years.

Novell clearly bet on the wrong technology. In business, companies necessarily take risks. The trick is to take calculated risks and avoid gambles.

Terminal Value   Once projections have been made, one must then calculate the value of cash flows generated in the years beyond the projection period—the gross terminal value. One common method is to determine the multiple at which comparable companies trade or have been acquired and apply the multiple to the company's earnings in the last year of projections. So, for example, if comparable companies were to trade at 10 times EBIT, the 10 times multiple might be applied to a company's projected EBIT of $10 in the final year for which projections were made. The terminal value would then be $100. Obviously, however, the scope of discretion allowed and the sensibility of applying today's ratios to tomorrow's projections are somewhat questionable.

The other methodology for calculating terminal values, which superficially looks more scientific, is to capitalize the final projections based on some perpetual growth rate. The terminal value is then equal to a perpetual stream of cash flows growing at a constant rate each year. Because nothing grows forever, it is rare that a high growth factor is used at the terminal point.

The Discount Rate   In theory, a company's weighted average cost of capital (WACC)—the weighted average of a company's equity and debt costs—is the appropriate discount rate to use in the DCF analysis. An estimate of a company's cost of debt generally is calculated based on the yields implied by the trading prices of its outstanding debt. The cost of equity capital is based on the premium above the "average market return" investors demand for investing in the company's stock.

As a practical matter, cash flows of mature companies are generally discounted at the 12 to 13 percent level depending on the riskiness of the target's business. However, in today's relatively more stable economic environment some theorists are arguing that a 9 to 11 percent rate is more realistic.

CALCULATING THE WACC

Over time, a fairly standard method for calculating a company's WACC has evolved.

THE CAPITAL STRUCTURE.   Despite its potential flaws as an indicator, a company's existing capital structure—which is assumed to remain static over the life of the projections—is the starting point for analysis. This assumption, of course, is an oversimplification, as a company's capital structure often shifts with time. For this reason, the WACC is based not on a company's current structure, which may be anomalous, but rather on some target capital structure—often derived from examination of industry averages.

THE COST OF COMMON EQUITY.   The next step is to calculate the cost of equity capital. Most commonly, practitioners use the Capital Asset Pricing Model (CAPM). The model's premise is that the cost of equity—the return to investors who hold the company's stock—equals the "risk-free return" plus a risk premium, which compensates investors for market risk, plus any adjustment to it necessitated by the systematic risk associated with the target company's equity. This risk in a target's stock over and above market risk is the company's *beta*.

While at one time there was no risk-free rate, as even three-month T-Bills had some interest rate risk, the advent of the inflation-adjusted U.S. Treasury Bill has created a nearly risk-free benchmark (as the default risk on U.S. government securities is practically nonexistent). The market risk premium represents the difference between the return on a diversified "market" portfolio and the risk-free rate, a figure which has historically been between 5 and 7 percent. Of course, what constitutes a "market" portfolio is a subject of debate. Theoretically, the market should be so diversified as to include all asset classes, including foreign securities, real estate, precious metals, commodities, and so on. But in practice, people often use the S&P 500 for simplicity.

A company's *beta,* like the market-risk premium, most often is drawn from a third-party database. A company called BARRA compiles predicted *beta*s for over 6,000 publicly traded companies. Mathematically, the *beta* is the variance of the return of a security from the return of the market. A *beta* of one indicates perfect correlation with the broader market: If the market returns 10 percent, the security will also generally return 10 percent. A *beta* of zero indicates no correlation with the market. A *beta* of negative one indicates that the stock is perfectly negatively correlated with the market: If the market returns 10 percent, the stock will generally return –10 percent and therefore is countercyclical. In practice, very few stocks have negative *beta*s. Because a *beta* also reflects the riskiness of a company's capital structure, if a different capital structure is used to calculate WACC, the *beta* must be adjusted.

Real-world evidence challenges the predictive power of market *beta*s. Based on empirical research, various academics have argued that other factors—such as company size, degree of leverage, and equity book-to-market ratios—provide more accurate measures of the risk premium. Still, CAPM remains the most functional measure of the cost of equity.

Potential Pitfalls DCF analysis, with its complex calculations and forecasts, seems to be very precise. Yet the DCF model is something like a sausage factory: A number of different ingredients—the assumed capital structure, projected cash flows, the cost of capital—come together in the final result. But when the casing is peeled away, it becomes clear that each of these ingredients can be of varying quality. A testing of each critical assumption is helpful. But there is little question this is an imprecise tool.

DCFs are most useful when a mature company with a predictable capital structure buys a similar target. On the other hand, three situations are particularly difficult to analyze with the DCF technique.

One is a company with so-called hockey stick projections—a firm with a mediocre historical performance that is projected to undergo a dramatic turnaround. Though rebounds do happen, the timing, scope, cash impact, and long-term stability of this kind of turnaround plays havoc with the DCF technique.

Similarly, a company in a cyclical industry doesn't neatly fit conventional patterns. If the company is in the middle of a downturn, the projections closest to the present may show declining or stagnant cash flow for the early years. If the company is on the upswing, the projections in the near future may show increasing cash flows. The danger of the DCF method is that the impact of a part of the cycle closest to the present is exaggerated by the discounting technique: Near-term cash flows are given greater weight than cash flows in outer years. Therefore, a DCF would value more highly a cyclical company in the upswing part of its cycle than a company in the downswing part. But regardless of where a company is in its business cycle, it should maintain the same intrinsic value. This is a serious flaw of the DCF.

DCF valuations of high-growth or start-up companies are also difficult. These companies often have negative cash flow in the early years. Even assuming a company will be a success, however, projecting the nature of the company's subsequent performance can be extremely dicey. In addition, the cost of capital generally must be calculated based on industry comparables, of which there might not be any.

Ultimately, making an appropriate valuation is still a question of judgment.

DCF Becomes EVA® Though DCF valuation is an imprecise tool, a variant recently has gained popularity as a management tool. Rechristened "economic value added" by consulting firm Stern Stewart, which holds a trademark on the acronym EVA, this theoretical approach is designed to help management and investors assess corporate performance. The basic notion of EVA is derived from the DCF framework—a company that does not earn its cost of capital is shortchanging capital providers.

A company's economic value added for a given year equals its operating cash flow minus its dollar cost of capital for all capital held on the balance sheet. In this context, operating cash flow means net income plus certain adjustments designed to convert GAAP figures into useful real-world figures. The dollar cost of capital is calculated by multiplying a company's WACC times its capital base (again adjusted from GAAP to reflect economic reality, rather than arcane GAAP rules), thereby creating a "line item" expense for capital on the balance sheet. In essence, then, the WACC is treated as a hurdle rate and the cost of capital like any other income statement expense. Economic value added is positive when a company earns more than all of its expenses, among which is its cost of capital.

Arithmetically, given a set of projections, the economic value derives precisely the same value for a business as DCF. Indeed, the theoretical foundations of the two models are the same. Still, EVA has become a popular tool because companies can use it as a benchmark for incentive compensation programs and as a tool to judge internal investment decisions. Research analysts are beginning to report EVA as another measure of company performance. Even some investors are following the calculation.

The chief difference between DCF and EVA is one of presentation and focus. By highlighting the fact that capital has a cost, EVA spotlights the importance of capital budgeting decisions. EVA also provides a transparent period-by-period tally of a company's performance and value-creation or value-destruction activity. DCF, on the other hand, returns an overall valuation range for a business, but does not provide a period-by-period tally of the excess of operation income over cost of capital.

Of course, EVA faces some of the same challenges as DCF. First, the cost of capital is difficult to measure with precision. Second, projections of future performance are inherently uncertain. However, this latest version of management science is helpful because it highlights increases in a company's value on a period-by-period basis.

Comparable Companies Valuation

Given the difficulties with DCF, buyers often revert to a simple comparable companies valuation, an approach with strong intuitive appeal. From real estate to cars to consumer goods, it is natural to value things in terms of what similar products might cost—a practice that translates easily into the valuation of companies. The United States has an active public market and strong disclosure laws; as a result, a significant amount of quantifiable data exists. Because comparable companies analysis relies on publicly available information, the method is fairly easy to use.

The basic approach is to develop a database of companies that are comparable to the company being valued and to determine the ratio between their public market value and various profitability measures. For example, if a group of consumer products companies has an average EBITDA multiple of "13 times," the value of a comparable company might then be estimated at 13 times its EBITDA. Such multiples can be calculated both based on the subject company's historical accounting data and from consensus projections of results.

Multiples of net income, EBITA, and EBITDA are the standard drivers of comparable companies analysis. These alternatives can be thought of as the points along a spectrum, with operating cash flow (EBITDA) on one end, net income on the other, and EBITA in between. Though all three measures are often explicitly reported in a particular model, one of the three generally is considered most relevant, depending on the situation. As a rule of thumb, EBITDA multiples are preferred for companies in more capital-intensive industries in which depreciation is a significant factor, because such multiples correct for the impact of different depreciation policies, or in industries where there have been extensive acquisitions and the amortization of goodwill distorts the picture. Net income multiples are used for less-capital-intensive industries.

Each of these methods may hide a problem, however. For example, valuing a company based on EBITDA alone ignores potentially inefficient, intensive capital spending because the increased depreciation that results from unexpected expenditures is not included in EBITDA. Net income, however, must be carefully scrutinized for purity and may have to be adjusted to exclude the effect of one-time and restructuring charges, one-time gains, and other mechanisms companies use to "manage" their earnings.

Net income multiples and EBITA and EBITDA multiples also differ from an important computational standpoint. Because payments on debt are deducted from operating profits to arrive at a company's net income, which represents the profits to the common shareholders, net income multiples are calculated as a ratio to the company's stock market capitalization. The measure of value is matched to the stream of earnings—the value of a company's common equity is compared to the profits attributable to the common. EBITDA and EBITA multiples are broader operational measures, however. Interest on the debt has not been deducted from these operating statistics and therefore both creditors and stockholders have a claim on these earnings streams. As a result, the multiples are calculated based on so-called adjusted market value or enterprise value—the value of both equity and debt.

Another ratio, the book value multiple, is often reported in a comparable companies analysis, but generally only given weight when applied to specific industries: Financial services companies—banks, insurance companies, finance companies—are the classic examples. The same concept of matching applies to the calculation of a book value multiple. Book value is a measure of common stockholders' equity in a company. Hence, market capitalization is the appropriate measure to use in calculating a book value multiple.

In certain industries, these standard four multiples have been supplemented with industry-specific rules of thumb. Cable companies, for example, are valued in terms of subscribers, cellular companies in terms of the population in the region covered by their licenses, and soft drink bottlers in terms of cases shipped.

Practical Issues The discretion inherent in the comparable companies analysis again underscores the important role common sense plays in the merger process, both in constructing the analysis and in using the results. Obviously, the result of the analysis depends on which companies are selected as comparable. Take one top performer off the valuation list, and a particular multiple might drop by a point.

Furthermore, comparable companies analysis is based on *trading* multiples, which are tied directly to, and fluctuate with, stock prices. Timing issues therefore can have a major impact on the multiples, especially in industries with volatile trading. Multiples might drop significantly over the course of a single week if the relevant sector is trading poorly. But a company's "true" or intrinsic value arguably should not change so drastically from day to day. Moreover, the multiples of companies in a cyclical industry will vary over the course of the cycle. Attention to these timing issues is necessary to ensure that comparable companies analysis is not misused.

In addition, comparable companies analysis does not incorporate the control premium that is typically paid in private market acquisitions. Usually, a control premium of 30 to 50 percent is added to trading value to determine acquisition value—another exercise in discretion.

Comparable Acquisitions Valuation

In the comparable acquisitions method, the database of comparable companies is restricted to those which have been acquired or have been merged into another surviving entity. Both the equity market value and adjusted market value of comparables are calculated based on the purchase price paid in the relevant transaction and therefore already incorporate a control premium. Then, as with comparable companies analysis, various multiples are calculated and applied in some fashion to the company that is being valued.

The problems are obvious. One must ask how comparable the precedents are in terms of the companies involved, the prevailing market conditions, and the transaction structure. Nevertheless, this technique is a necessity because everyone wants to understand the terms of the other deals in the industry.

Sometimes this analysis also is used as the basis for a "breakup" valuation of the pieces of a company, a necessary exercise if a low-earning asset such as real estate is buried in a company. Theoretically, the value of a company in pieces should be the same as the value of a company as a whole; a breakup valuation determines how much each individual piece of a company could be sold for and provides a cross-check against the other valuation techniques.

Consequences Model

Finally, a company thinking about a deal also wants to know the pro forma impact of doing the deal. Will earnings be diluted? What will happen to the stock price? Will management get jeers or applause? Modeling the impact on earnings, cash flow, the balance sheet, and market valuation multiples under alternative transaction structures is a necessity.

The process of creating a merger consequences model—sometimes known as an accretion/dilution model—is similar to that for building projections for a DCF valuation. The goal of the exercise is to construct an income statement for several years after the transaction to examine the transaction's impact on earnings, and, by applying combined company earnings to a range of multiples, the impact on post-deal stock price. An assumption about how the transaction will be funded—with debt or equity, or some combination of both—is made. Other key variables are the cost of funding the debt and the appropriate tax rate.

The earnings provided by the combined business is the output of the model. Of course, the hope is that a transaction will be immediately accretive, or additive, to earnings per share, given that the EPS figure is one that investors—rightly or wrongly—focus on.

However, for sophisticated acquirers, the immediate earnings impact is not the critical focus. Rather, they want to know the impact over a longer period, because often the pattern of the deal's impact on EPS reverses. A transaction that is dilutive in the first year may nonetheless be accretive in later years. Therefore, the markets now generally give companies a year of grace. The long-term earnings and cash flow impact is more determinative of how a deal will be perceived.

In modeling the impact of a deal beyond the first year, it is imperative to normalize the capital structure. If a transaction is financed with debt, one must examine the impact of future debt reduction on earnings per share. Alternatively, if a stock-for-stock merger is contemplated, the resulting company may be overcapitalized. Therefore, a merger consequences model should account for any planned share repurchases, although care must be taken not to violate pre-2000 pooling eligibility guidelines.

Income statement impacts from debt reduction or stock repurchases are determined by creating a balance sheet and cash flow statement integrated with the income statement. Cash expenses not reflected on the income statement, such as capital expenditures, dividends, and stock repurchases, are included on the cash flow statement, whose ultimate goal is to determine the cash generated or used by the company during the year. This cash flow, if positive, can be used to pay down debt or repurchase shares; if the cash flow is negative, additional debt needs to be added to the balance sheet. A decreased debt balance (or increased cash balance) will lower net interest expense, thus increasing EPS. Similarly, fewer shares outstanding also may increase earnings per share. Thus the relationship between the three financial statements is a highly circular one: Net income—an income statement item—is dependent on interest expense, which is dependent on yearly average debt and cash balances—balance sheet items—which in turn are dependent on cash flow, a figure whose calculation begins with net income. Modern spreadsheets are able to solve the complex systems of equations implied by these circular relationships to create an integrated financial model.

Like any model of the future, key assumptions such as the interest rate, projected growth rates, capital needs, and so forth need to be tested and their impact sensitized. An awareness of the sensitivity of outcomes is the raw material for the exercise of an informed judgment regarding a proposed transaction. Nevertheless, the final result should always be viewed with some skepticism.

Of course, even if there is earnings dilution, a deal may make sense. First, free cash flow—the money that could in theory be paid out to shareholders—could increase as a result of a deal even if accounting earnings were diluted. Secondly, while investors are fixated on EPS, the number is again just an accounting fiction. A deal could create value—that is to say, have a positive net present value for shareholders—according to the EVA model even if it were dilutive to EPS. A deal in which a company with a low P/E multiple buys a company with a higher P/E multiple and successfully integrates the operations of both companies could derive the benefit from the target's higher growth rate and therefore higher P/E, increasing the company's stock price, and building shareholder value. If a cement company buys an Internet company, for example, EPS would almost certainly be diluted. But the deal could make sense from a strategic repositioning perspective. After all, M&A is about strategy—not simple mathematics.

AGAIN, THE FUNDAMENTALS

Forstmann Little Scores with Topps

Strip away all the fancy mechanics, and the valuation process is really about the fundamentals. What one thinks of the multiples, the projections, the DCF model—it all ends up as a question of basic business judgment. Is the company a strong business that can thrive with the planned capital structure? The answer to that question can only be investigated in the present and is determined in the future.

An acquisition or merger essentially is a calculated gamble that a particular vision of the future can be made to come true. Forstmann Little's 1983 acquisition of Topps Company is a case in point.

The trading card company, controlled by the Shorin family, had a long history. Founded by four Shorin brothers in 1938, the Topps Gum Company expanded into baseball cards in 1952 and enjoyed a monopoly on the Major League Baseball card business until 1980, when Fleer busted Topps' hold on the market through litigation.

By 1983, chairman Arthur Shorin—a son of one of the founders—was interested in selling the business. He put a value of $100 million on Topps and wanted us to find a buyer who would fall in love with the idea of owning the baseball card company.

Topps proved to be a tough sell. We pitched the business to a number of corporate strategic buyers, but they all balked. Topps lacked the identifiable, stable growth and defined cash flow which could be easily fed into a model. No good comparables for the business existed, making it tough to value.

Still, having watched the trading card business cycle over a number of years, Shorin knew a new fad would come along and Topps would capitalize on it. He didn't know what it would be, but he knew it would happen. In addition, Shorin saw great potential in the baseball card business, which eventually would bounce back to popularity. We worked with Shorin to develop a creative sales pitch based on the potential growth in the business.

Topps simply was the kind of business which required an imaginative, entrepreneurial buyer. Forstmann Little eventually agreed to pay $95 million—just short of Shorin's original asking price—financed with $10 million of equity and $85 million of debt.

Over the next decade, Shorin's instincts—and Forstmann Little's inclination to trust those instincts—proved remarkably on target. The next big thing for Topps turned out to be its phenomenally successful Garbage Pail Kids line; baseball card sales also surged dramatically. Overall sales more than doubled and debt was paid down early.

Forstmann Little sold a small stake in Topps in a 1987 IPO. Success continued, and with a significantly reduced debt load, Topps was able to borrow $140 million a few years later to fund a special dividend to shareholders. Forstmann Little continued to reduce its stake with stock sales, then, in 1991, distributed its remaining 53 percent interest to the original investors who funded the deal.

The trading card boom eventually flattened, taking Topps' stock price down—along with the value of Ron Perelman's Marvel. However, by that time Forstmann Little and its investors had been vastly rewarded for their willingness to think outside the formal valuation box. All told, the firm grew the original $10 million of equity in the deal more than seventy times over.

Models and Muddles

With computer time cheap, there is a tendency to provide valuation wisdom by the pound. A thick book of backup materials is presented to justify a particular number or range. The level of detail can be overwhelming; valuation can devolve into a mechanistic averaging of the outputs from various seemingly sophisticated models.

A better approach is to view valuation as a triangulation process. The outputs of various models are assessed with an understanding of the limitations of each technique and what assumptions were used as inputs. Even if the models are perfect, the room for fundamental error is huge because models assume a projection of future value based on the world of today. In addition, the terminal value in the DCF model, and the comparable companies in that analysis, reflect today's market value.

Obviously, many of the deals of the 1980s and 1990s have turned out well simply because of the dramatic rise in the market. Of course, during some periods, markets go down as well. In the end, the question of price is one of judgment.

Structuring the Deal | 17

*"Achitecture begins when you place
two bricks carefully together."*

—Mies van der Rohe

The architecture of a deal must be designed with the complex mosaic of corporate law, the tax code, and accounting rules firmly in mind. The impact of these issues ripples through the process, defines the tactical possibilities, and must be carefully reconciled with corporate objectives. Each possible structure has its unique tactical, legal, and financial benefits as well as defects which need to be carefully weighed. All of the considerations are interrelated, somewhat complex, and yet, vital to any understanding of the deal process.

Form and Function

In mergers, form does have a function, a point underlined recently by developments in the merger of Bell Atlantic and NYNEX. The deal, billed as a "merger of equals," was originally cast in the form of a combination: A new holding company was to be created, which would then issue shares in exchange for the outstanding stock of both NYNEX and Bell Atlantic.

While this structure served the objective of preserving the

"merger of equals" format it also created roadblocks to completing the deal. Because the ownership of both NYNEX and Bell Atlantic would shift under the plan, regulatory authorities in each of the thirteen states served by the two companies would need to approve the deal. The parties quickly decided the marginal benefit of a transaction structure enshrining the merger of equals concept was less important than a smooth review process.

For this reason, the merger agreement was revised so that Bell Atlantic was the acquirer whose ownership would not shift under the plan and would remain over 50 percent in the combined company. By avoiding a separate approval process in each of the seven Bell Atlantic states plus the District of Columbia, potential pitfalls were minimized.

Corporate Mechanics

Getting a big deal like the NYNEX–Bell Atlantic merger done, therefore, necessarily involves a certain amount of logistical maneuvering. Skillful navigation can be critical to a deal's success.

Large M&A deals break down into two primary transaction types—the merger and the stock purchase. Each has unique attributes. While the specific steps in the process vary from state to state, Delaware law governs the majority of major U.S. corporations and is in many ways indicative.

The Merger   A merger essentially melds two corporate organizations into one pursuant to the terms specified in the merger agreement. In particular, the agreement typically outlines the mix of consideration to be paid in the merger (cash, securities, or otherwise), the conditions under which the transaction will become effective, any representations made by the parties, and the effective date. On the effective date, the acquiring entity issues cash or securities in the appropriate ratios to the target's former security holders. The target's assets, contract rights, and liabilities, disclosed or not, pass automatically to the surviving company unless otherwise specified in the merger documents.

The merger mechanism has a number of advantages. First, the procedure is flexible. The parties can define the consideration involved however they like: Target shareholders can be given stock, debt securities, cash, or any other form of payment for their shares. The automatic transfer of assets and liabilities from the target to the acquirer without complicated documentation is another benefit. The old target corporate entity no longer exists.

Finally, once a merger has the necessary approvals, there is a so-called cram-down effect. That is to say, target stockholders who voted against the merger must either accept whatever payment is offered or seek remedy in court, through appraisal rights. Thus a key advantage of the merger is that no minority stockholders remain; all stockholders will have been forced out in exchange for cash or an interest in the acquirer. This effect allows the acquirer to run the target free of the legal and operational complications that sometimes crop up with minority shareholders.

However, the merger process can have unwanted side effects for the companies involved. For instance, the flexibility in choice of payment sometimes leads to shareholder discontent with the payment to be received. Most state statutes provide shareholders with a remedy for this discontent in the form of appraisal rights. However, companies can rest assured that there are limitations to the applicability of this procedure. Under the Delaware statute, for example, there are no appraisal rights for a stockholder in a public company if the stockholder is receiving stock in another public company. And even if the right to appraisal exists, appraisal procedures must be handled quite gingerly: The methods of evaluation used by courts can differ considerably from market value. For example, in Delaware, market value, book or liquidation value, and dividend yield are all weighed as factors in the valuation analysis.

The automatic transfer of assets and liabilities in a merger also can be troublesome because the acquirer will be subject to liabilities of the target that may not have been disclosed. Furthermore, some contracts—leases and rights to use intellectual property, for example—specifically provide that they do not pass to a successor, a provision that can raise serious obstacles to a merger.

Even in the best of circumstances, the merger procedure is somewhat unwieldy. Under Delaware law, for example, a merger generally must be approved by the directors of each company and then be submitted to the target company's stockholders. So, if the target's directors are recalcitrant, the merger route obviously doesn't work. Mergers rarely work as the first step in the hostile takeover context, for example.

Most big mergers also require the approval of the acquirer's shareholders. While legally no vote is required if any stock to be issued in the transaction has already been authorized by shareholders, the New York and American Stock Exchanges both require a shareholder vote if the stock to be issued in the acquisition equals more than about 18.5 percent of the acquirer's outstanding voting stock.

Where the approval of shareholders is required, state law typically provides that the approval be in the form of a majority vote. However, a company's bylaws or certificate sometimes require a higher margin for merger approvals.

One way to smooth the merger process is to structure a deal as a so-called triangular merger: The acquirer creates a special merger subsidiary, funded with the consideration to be given in the merger. The subsidiary and the target then merge. Either the subsidiary or the target can be the surviving entity. The main advantage of the triangular merger technique is that it may eliminate the need for the acquirer to hold a shareholder vote. Because the acquirer is the sole shareholder of the new special-purpose subsidiary, the approval process may involve only the subsidiary's board of directors, which can be the same as the parent company board. However, the 18.5

percent rule of the stock exchanges still may force a vote of the acquirer's shareholders.

Holding the target as a separate subsidiary also may help insulate the parent from the liabilities of the target, a potentially significant advantage where the target is in a business with high litigation or environmental exposure. However, again, in certain cases the parent may nonetheless be held liable despite the separate corporate formalities.

Regardless, all the structuring sophistication in the world can't avoid a simple truth: Potential booby traps abound in the merger process. A Clausewitzian view of deal tactics would stipulate that delay is an enemy to a deal; but unfortunately mergers take a lot of time. For instance, holding a stockholder vote can be a source of delay. And if it isn't time for the annual meeting, the expenses of calling a special meeting for a public company are high as well. The public stockholders must be provided with a proxy statement describing the transaction and a prospectus outlining the terms of the securities which they are going to receive, which must be both filed with and approved by the SEC—a notoriously long process.

The proxy statement is filed with the SEC for review like any other registration of securities. The SEC sometimes has comments and changes must be made. But the biggest delay is in the preparation of the document itself, especially if the combined financial statements, or pro formas, are complicated. During this lengthy delay process, a deal is very vulnerable.

Five months is the typical time period between deal conception and closing. Aside from giving stockholders adequate notice of a stockholder meeting (usually about thirty days in advance), a registration statement, which is required if securities are to be issued in the deal, must be cleared through the SEC before these documents can even be sent (just as is true for the proxy).

The Mechanics of Time Warner

The importance of corporate mechanics to the deal process was illustrated all across the front pages in the merger of Time and Warner. Just before this friendly merger was to be consummated, Paramount pounced. The parties defended their deal by shifting its structure.

Initially, the combination of Time and Warner was to be structured as a merger, an attractive alternative both for accounting reasons and because the consideration was to be all common stock. Under the accounting rules, a stock-for-stock merger would allow Time Warner to avoid goodwill charges, which otherwise would reduce future accounting earnings. Time also wanted to avoid the added interest burden that comes with debt.

Days before the shareholder vote to approve the deal, Paramount came in with a higher cash offer for Time. The Time board preferred to stick with Warner for strategic reasons but, as structured, Warner's deal would have required a Time shareholder vote to go forward. However, several Time directors felt shareholders might not see the long-term strategic value in the Warner deal: If a vote were held, the Warner merger probably would be rejected in favor of the immediate cash payoff offered by Paramount.

Therefore, Time and Warner went back to the drawing board. The deal was restructured as a two-tiered tender offer by Time for Warner stock, to be paid in cash on the front end and stock on the back end, and would not require a vote of Time's shareholders until after Time had control of Warner. In the first step, Time would buy 51 percent of Warner's stock for $70 cash per share, a relatively low premium, and would borrow between $7 and $10 billion to fund this purchase. Later, in a back-end merger, the remaining Warner stockholders would receive securities worth roughly $70 a share.

With this relatively simple change, Time shifted the entire tactical landscape. Paramount's only recourse was to sue Time and Warner in an attempt to block the deal. When the suit failed, Time's deal for Warner went through before Paramount could— following tender offer procedures—buy Time.

The Stock Purchase   As demonstrated by the Time-Warner deal, a stock purchase—typically followed by a merger—is an alternative to an outright merger. Payment for target company stock can come in the form of cash, stock, debt, or other property. The main advantage of this approach from a corporate law perspective is the lack of required formalities, which explains why Time turned to a stock purchase of Warner when its merger was attacked. Neither the target company board of directors nor shareholders must formally approve a stock sale. Of course, target company shareholders have de facto approval rights in the sense that they can decide whether or not to sell their shares. And while the acquirer's board usually approves any major purchase, a vote of acquirer shareholders is generally unnecessary if the deal is to be funded with cash or debt securities, significantly reducing the time between offer and purchase. For this reason, hostile takeovers most often involve a stock purchase through a tender offer.

Another advantage of a stock purchase is that it allows the acquirer to maintain the corporate existence of the target, thereby retaining in the acquired company any valuable contract rights, such as franchises, which cannot be assigned. However, there are sometimes "change of control" provisions in instruments that void this advantage.

The preservation of the corporate shell does not, however, result in the "squeezing out" of minority shareholders, a disadvantage relative to a merger. Therefore, to eliminate minority shareholders, companies often effect a clean-up merger sometime after an initial stock purchase. If the acquirer purchases majority control in the front end of the deal, the back-end merger vote becomes a formality. Recognition of this fact obviously impacts the position of target company shareholders when faced with a decision whether to sell their shares in an offer. Taking the up-front money may be far more attractive than waiting to see what happens on the back end.

In fact, for the back-end merger, an acquirer may be able to use a "short form" procedure which does not require a stockholder vote at all. For example, in Delaware, once an acquirer owns 90 percent of the outstanding shares of target company stock, the acquirer's board of directors may approve a short-form merger of the target into the acquirer with no vote of the minority holders required. However, the minority stockholders may be entitled to appraisal rights.

Issuing Stock or Securities as Consideration

The federal securities laws regulate the issuance of stock or securities as consideration in a corporate merger or acquisition. In particular, two Depression-era statutes govern the issuance of securities: The Securities Act of 1933 and the Trust Indenture Act of 1939.

The Securities Act In the context of a business combination, the 1933 act requires that, absent an exemption, any shares or other securities offered to target company shareholders must be registered. This process can take months.

The SEC has created a special form to be used for securities issued as part of a business combination or exchange offer. For large public companies, this Form S-4 is attractive because it allows an abbreviated presentation. Rather than detail all the financial information required in the longer Form S-1, a company can incorporate such information by reference to previous company filings.

Alternatively, in a case where the target company's shareholders must vote to approve the transaction, the proxy statement also can serve, with modification, as a registration statement for any securities offered. The Form S-4 in essence wraps around the required proxy statement, which is then also used as a prospectus.

Under the so-called Aircraft Carrier proposal (because it is nearly 600 pages long), made by the SEC in 1998 however, the Forms S-1 and S-4 would be replaced by a new Form C. Most of the requirements in Forms S-1 and S-4 would still exist in the new Form C; however, the requirement that a prospectus or proxy statement be delivered at least twenty days before the date of the vote or expiration of the exchange offer when incorporated by reference would be removed, because documents incorporated by reference are easily available on the Internet. And a new Schedule TO would combine Schedules 13E-4 and 14D-1, allowing tender offers and going-private disclosures to be combined into one document. Furthermore, the SEC proposes that security holders be permitted to tender securities for a limited time after the initial offer—including all extensions—has been completed, effectively creating a "subsequent offer period." This rule would afford shareholders the opportunity to tender into an offer after the bidder discloses the results, rather than wait for a back-end merger or have to sell shares into what could be an illiquid market. The proposals are not expected to take effect until sometime in 2000.

For greater flexibility, corporations frequently involved in acquisitions often use a technique called "shelf registration," which limits the need to file a new registration statement with every merger or acquisition. Generally, securities can be registered only if they will be distributed in the near future. However, SEC regulations permit a large company engaged in a continuing program of acquisitions to register a reasonable number of securities for future offerings and "put them on the shelf," with the registration statement being periodically amended after its filing to keep it current.

The appeal of a shelf registration is that, if an acquisition opportunity arises, the already registered securities can be used without the delays of first commencing a registration process. Absent the shelf, stock and securities generally will not be available in time for use in the front end of a two-tiered offer. Of course, even with an active shelf, if a stockholder vote is required, a proxy statement is still necessary.

The Aircraft Carrier release, if adopted, would change the shelf registration procedure somewhat. Companies eligible under the proposal to offer securities using Form B—in general, those that have 1) previously registered securities on a form that did not become effective upon filing, 2) a one-year reporting history and have filed at least one annual report, 3) a public float of at least $250 million, or at least $75 million and an average daily trading volume of $1 million or more—will find in the form many of the benefits of shelf registration. Because Form B will not be subject to pre-effective review by the SEC, an issuer can designate the time for its registration to become effective and then, as is true for the current shelf registration system, time offerings to take advantage of favorable market conditions.

However, there will be several differences from the current system in the use of Form B. Current rules permit an issuer to file a prospectus supplement up to two business days after a "shelf takedown." With a Form B offering, transactional information must be filed at or before the first sale. Companies not eligible to file using Form B would have no means by which to effect shelf registrations.

Trust Indenture Act   When debt is being issued in a deal, it will become subject to the Trust Indenture Act. The act requires that publicly held debt be issued pursuant to a contract, called an indenture, which contains specific provisions to protect the public. For each debt issue, there must be a trustee whose obligation in the event of a default on the debt is to protect the public debt holders as if the trustee were a "prudent man" acting on his own behalf.

The 1939 act also specifies the wording of certain provisions of indentures, particularly those dealing with events of default and the responsibilities of the trustee. As most indentures are structured, the trustee must notify the holders within ninety days if there is a known default.

Once there has been a default, the trustee must act prudently. The holders of a majority of the securities may take control from the trustee if the trustee's costs are covered. However, without the consent of each individual holder, no right to principal repayment may be waived, and most indentures do not allow any waiver of interest.

One might ask why a trustee is required for debt instruments but not for equity securities. Most would answer that, as a general proposition, debt securities are more complicated than stock and therefore require additional administrative oversight. First, debt requires the payment of principal and interest, which is obligatory rather than discretionary like stock dividends. There are also various prepayment rights (which are, however, also often used in preferred stocks). The debt indenture might also place restrictions on the issuer's actions, which need to be continually policed. Finally, debt indentures contain default provisions, while equity securities generally have none (although, again, sometimes preferred stockholders are entitled to appoint directors should certain events occur). A trustee is needed to guide bondholders through this maze of mechanical complications.

THE ASSET DEAL

Large corporate transactions rarely deviate from the merger or stock purchase alternatives. However, in some cases, an acquirer might opt to pursue an asset deal, a transaction in which the acquirer purchases—for cash, stock, or other payment—a specified group of assets.

Under Delaware law, a majority shareholder vote is required for the sale of all or substantially all the assets of the company; conversely, it may be possible, then, to sell 35 percent of the company without shareholder approval. Unlike in a merger, however, stockholders objecting to the asset transfer have no appraisal rights under Delaware law.

The ability to select carefully the liabilities being assumed is one key advantage to the acquisition of assets. For example, if the target company previously sold defective products or broke its contracts with impunity, the acquiring company has the option of not assuming the contingent liabilities; in contrast, when stock is purchased, the acquiring company actually owns the target, including both its assets and its liabilities. Therefore, the asset deal structure may be attractive if an acquirer has concern about undisclosed liabilities. Asset purchase treatment may also have favorable depreciation consequences for the acquirer because assets are depreciable over the course of their useful lives. The resulting depreciation expense reduces taxable income and therefore a company's tax liability.

However, not assuming the old corporate shell can make the acquisition of assets quite cumbersome, as every asset has to be specifically assigned, including every contract. There can be literally thousands of documents. Furthermore, many contracts have clauses which state that they may not be assigned without the consent of the other party, which can create enormous burdens. And quite often the problems are not merely administrative: For example, a key supplier with a no-assignment clause may well see the asset deal as a perfect opportunity to renegotiate the contract on more favorable terms to him. These large hurdles, as well as the enormous tax liabilities created by gains on the sale of assets, are the reasons that large, fast-paced acquisitions rarely take the form of asset deals.

Tax Issues

The tax law adds another layer of complexity to a transaction. A merger or acquisition may be structured as either a tax-free, partially tax-free, or taxable transaction, with dramatically different consequences for sellers and purchasers. The tax law can have a substantial economic effect on a transaction and may represent a decisive factor in formulating a deal's structure or in deciding whether to do a deal at all.

Purchase of a Parent Company: Tax Implications   When purchasing a public parent company, a merger or stock purchase followed by a merger are the structures typically contemplated. Depending on the circumstances, a merger or stock purchase will either be tax-free or taxable.

A merger will be tax-free to selling shareholders if a "continuity of business enterprise" and a "continuity of interest" test are satisfied: Under the continuity of interest test, the selling stockholders must receive stock in the surviving entity equal in value to about 40 percent (or more) of the value of the stock surrendered. Under Treasury regulations, sales of stock received (other than to the acquirer or a related party) don't count against continuity of interest. Furthermore, under certain acquisition formats, "substantially all" of the target's assets must be acquired. In a merger, if selling shareholders received any nonstock consideration, gain is recognized to shareholders to the extent of such nonstock consideration.

A stock purchase will qualify as tax-free if at least 80 percent of the company's shares by vote are acquired and exchanged for voting shares in the acquirer. No "boot"—any security other than common or participating preferred stock—may be exchanged. The continuity of interest test must also be satisfied.

A continuing interest includes any form of stock—including nonvoting preferred. Long-term debt, however, is not considered to be a continuing interest even though the interests of a long-term debt holder are very similar to those of a holder of nonvoting preferred stock. Under current law, nonparticipating preferred stock, though supplying continuity for purposes of qualifying a merger as tax-free, may be considered taxable boot to the recipient.

In applying the continuity tests, courts also tend to integrate a series of transactions and consider them as one deal. This "step-transaction doctrine" lets courts look beyond the form of a transaction and examine its substance. So, if stockholders receive cash to redeem their stock immediately before or after a merger, a court may deem the payment to be part of the merger terms and count the cash against the stockholder in applying the continuity of interest tests.

As a result of these rules, target company shareholders who exchange their shares as part of a merger or sale of 80 percent or more of parent company stock generally will not recognize a tax gain or loss to the extent they accept acquirer stock as payment. Instead, a shareholder's basis in his target stock is transferred to the acquiring company stock. When the new stock is eventually sold, the gain or loss on that transaction equals the difference between the price received and the seller's original "basis," or investment in the target company stock. A target company recognizes no gain or loss upon its merger into the acquirer in a tax-free transaction. The acquirer takes a carryover basis in the assets it acquires in the merger.

In a taxable transaction, the buyer pays selling shareholders with cash, nonvoting securities, or some combination of the two. The selling shareholders recognize a capital gain or loss equal to the difference between their respective tax bases in the shares and the value of the property received in exchange. The acquirer then has a basis in the target company's shares equal to the purchase price paid.

There is generally no step-up in asset basis in the acquisition of a top-tier public company (there sometimes can be an asset step-up in buying a subsidiary or division); but in a taxable transaction, there is a step-up in the basis of the purchased *stock*, which can reduce the acquirer's tax on a subsequent disposition.

Viewing this summary of tax implications, it is easy to see why selling stockholders generally prefer tax-free transactions. If a stock has run up in price—as most stocks have over the past two decades—the tax-free transaction allows the owner to defer taxes on the transfer of the old stock. However, notwithstanding this benefit, some sellers prefer a taxable transaction for one of two reasons. First, if there is a loss rather than a gain on the security being sold, stockholders would want a recognition event so that the tax loss can be used to shelter other income. Second, the seller may be a tax-exempt investor, such as a pension fund, that would rather have immediate cash liquidity than the ongoing investment required in the stock-for-stock tax-free deals. Even for taxable investors, cash is often more highly regarded than a security, which may or may not be worth its estimated value.

If an acquirer contemplates a two-step transaction, in which cash is offered in the front end and stock is offered in the back end, the consideration received by selling stockholders in the front end will always be taxable. In general, the stock consideration received in the back end will be taxable as well, unless the back end provides sufficient overall continuity of interest. However, there is one exception. By employing the "Top Hat" or "Double Dummy" structure, the consideration received in the back end can be tax-free. After target shareholders receive the cash front-end portion of the merger, both acquirer and target are combined into a new holding company in a tax-free reorganization. Traditional reorganizations permit a maximum cash payout of approximately 60 percent to shareholders; the Top Hat structure, however, circumvents this rule by invoking Section 351, which permits the back-end stock portion to be received tax-free if the companies contributing their assets to the new holding company maintain at least 80 percent control over the holding company. The rule counts all simultaneous contributors toward this 80 percent figure, which would therefore include both the acquirer and target. Under the Top Hat structure, the target and acquirer own 100 percent of the newly created holding company, making the stock portion of the transaction tax-free.

Purchase of a Subsidiary: Tax Implications Three structures are possible when the purchase of a subsidiary is contemplated. The acquirer can purchase the stock of the subsidiary, the assets of the subsidiary, or purchase the stock but elect to have the deal treated as an asset purchase. In the case of a subsidiary sale, the selling stockholder is the parent company that holds the subsidiary. Whether a subsidiary purchase is taxable or not is, in general, subject to the same rules as a parent company purchase.

In a taxable purchase of the stock of a subsidiary, the tax basis of the subsidiary's assets will not be stepped up (except in the case of a special election); rather, the acquirer will receive a carryover basis in the subsidiary's assets. In a taxable purchase of a subsidiary's assets, however, assets are stepped up to fair market value (while they are not in a tax-free purchase). Goodwill (the excess of the price paid over the fair market value of the assets) in an asset purchase can, for tax purposes, generally be written off over fifteen years, reducing a company's tax base. By contrast, goodwill in a stock deal is not tax-deductible. Finally, an election can be made to treat a taxable purchase of the stock of a subsidiary as an asset sale, a structure that provides the aforementioned tax shield to the acquirer, but possibly at some additional cost to the seller.

If such an election would, in fact, increase the cost to the selling parent company, the acquirer will generally have to pay the seller more. Indeed, the buyer and seller generally must decide how to split the benefits that the step-up provides.

Lawyers and accountants use shorthand references derived from the relevant subsections of the International Revenue Code to describe the standard tax-free deal structures.

The straight merger of a target into an acquirer where at least 40 percent of the consideration is acquirer stock is an "A reorganization" or "A reorg," named after Code Section 368(a)(1)(A). The triangular merger is either a forward or reverse triangular reorganization depending on which corporate shell survives—forward (known as an "(a)(2)(D)") if the special merger subsidiary survives, reverse (known as an "(a)(2)(E)") if the target company survives. A tax-free stock swap without a merger is a "B reorg." A tax-free asset deal is a "C reorg," and a spin-off may involve a "D reorg."

Tax Rulings and Opinions

A company planning a merger, acquisition, or spin-off that is meant to be tax-free sometimes will seek an advance ruling from the IRS regarding the tax-free status of a deal. Alternatively, the parties can rely instead on an opinion from tax lawyers. A private letter ruling provides greater certainty regarding the tax treatment of a transaction, especially for tax-free spin-offs to shareholders which involve complex, subjective tests. Several countervailing concerns exist, however.

A private letter ruling is a formal document provided by the IRS to a taxpayer that can be relied on as binding. This assurance has value, particularly in a large transaction where the potential tax liability might be quite significant.

Yet certainty is elusive. Private letter rulings generally are based on a factual description of the contemplated transaction provided by the relevant taxpayer, as well as a number of assumptions. If any of these assumptions or facts change, the ruling is no longer binding.

Another problem with seeking a ruling is the cost, time, and energy required to secure the document. First, a written ruling request is filed with the IRS, perhaps preceded by a preliminary conference. The issue then is assigned to someone in the IRS's Chief Counsel office who calls with a preliminary response roughly three weeks after assignment. There are then opportunities for further submissions to address concerns. If the IRS lawyer indicates an inability to grant the ruling, the taxpayer is entitled to a conference with a supervisor. Assuming a decision is made to issue the ruling, a letter is drafted and sent to the taxpayer.

The entire ruling process generally drags out over five or six months, but sometimes can take longer. Some lawyers specialize in the rarefied practice of shepherding clients through the gauntlet. At times, it seems as if the IRS is looking for magic words from some prior ruling or case. If a ruling request fits the mold, approval is granted. If not, the review is much more painstaking and the IRS's ruling guidelines in certain areas are more strict than the law would seem to require.

Furthermore, politics plays a role in the process. The mood of the moment might favor tightening up to reduce merger flow or loosening to allow a more active merger market. A transaction that does not pass muster with the IRS might be ruled tax-free in the courts if it were contested. But going down that avenue is unlikely, given the time delays and negative public exposure associated with a court battle.

A tax opinion, on the other hand, can be obtained quite quickly. Moreover, expert tax counsel can reflect on the full scope of the law.

A tax opinion is a letter from private tax counsel, usually from a major corporate law firm. In the context of a spin-off, for example, a tax opinion might state that the contemplated spin-off "will" be treated as tax-free. However, there are a number of gradations to opinion standards. The issuing law firm might only state that the transaction "should" be tax-free, or that it is "more likely than not" that the transaction will be tax-free. These are terms of art intended to capture varying levels of certainty.

A tax opinion provides comfort on two levels. First, top-notch firms guard their reputations closely. A strong opinion therefore is a good indication that a sound position in favor of tax-free status exists. Second, an incorrect opinion may provide grounds for malpractice litigation. However, any eventual malpractice liability payments are likely to pale in comparison to the resulting tax liability. Clients nonetheless joust with counsel attempting to force a stronger opinion, mainly to ensure that lawyers are willing to stand up for the advice they are giving.

Of course, even the strongest opinion is just an opinion, which is why the large majority of public companies contemplating a spin-off—a particularly complicated and subjective area of the law—condition the transaction on the receipt of a favorable ruling.

Accounting Treatment

Accounting treatment, like tax law, is at the heart of the merger business. How a deal will be priced, the consideration involved, and how the market will react are often driven by accounting. Historically, when one company acquired another or when two companies merged, the corporate combination could be accounted for as either a pooling of interests or as a purchase. This choice of purchase versus pooling had absolutely no impact on a company's underlying health or performance. However, from a financial accounting perspective, the survivor's earnings differed dramatically depending on which approach was taken. Because many investors are focused on earnings, companies often hesitate to take on dilutive transactions.

But a recent pronouncement from the Financial Accounting Standards Board (FASB), the private sector entity that governs the GAAP rules, would eventually eliminate pooling of interests treatment. For much time, the FASB has believed that most deals which, economically speaking, are purchase transactions—that is to say, where an acquirer can be easily identified—receive pooling of interest accounting treatment nonetheless. Furthermore, acquirers to which pooling is available are able to bid more than those for whom pooling is not available, because pooling does not have a dilutive effect on earnings per share. The FASB argues that purchase accounting increases transparency, demonstrates more clearly to shareholders the effects of a company's M&A activity, and levels the playing field for potential acquirers.

Therefore, the FASB has proposed that pooling be eliminated by late 2000. The elimination of pooling, however, will not be retroactive. The FASB also proposes requiring that the maximum goodwill amortization period be reduced from forty to twenty years.

Until 2000, both pooling and purchase remain as options.

Purchase Accounting   If a firm buys a piece of equipment for cash, the cost of the asset is reflected on the company's books at its purchase price. Similarly, when a company purchases another company's stock for cash, the total price paid is reflected under the "purchase" method of accounting. However, the price paid often is above the fair market value of the target company's tangible assets. The difference between the purchase price and the tangible asset value is known as goodwill.

In order to reflect the full cost of the transaction, the buyer enters both the value of the acquired firm's tangible assets and the related goodwill on its balance sheet. For example, if a company has tangible assets worth $10 and it is purchased for $15, $5 would be goodwill. Goodwill is almost universal in purchase-accounting acquisitions because earning power and growth opportunity usually make a firm worth more than the value of its tangible assets.

The critical question then is how the frequently arising goodwill should be treated. As a general default rule, U.S. companies must amortize goodwill over not more than forty years (tangibles such as plant and equipment are depreciated, intangibles such as patents and goodwill are amortized). This amortization is recorded as an expense on the income statement and therefore reduces earnings. But accountants now often require amortization over a shorter period. For example, if a firm with a tangible worth of $40 million and earnings of $10 million a year before taxes were purchased for $80 million, the amortization of the $40 million in goodwill could well have a dramatic impact. If the goodwill were amortized over, for example, twenty years, annual earnings would be lower by $2 million.

As the result of a 1993 tax law revision, goodwill generated in an asset purchase may in some cases be tax-deductible, allowing net income to be increased by the applicable tax rate multiplied by the yearly amortization. The tax law requires deductible goodwill to be amortized over a fifteen-year period.

Naturally, executives actively involved in either selling or buying companies have opposed the amortization of goodwill for financial reporting purposes. The theoretical basis for this position is that goodwill is not a wasting asset—it lasts as long as the company exists. For added support, executives point to the U.K., which until 1998 allowed companies to write off acquired goodwill directly against shareholder equity. Such a write-off does not flow through the income statement, increasing reported income relative to what it would be using U.S. reporting standards. This procedure arguably gave U.K. companies an edge over U.S. companies when attempting an acquisition. But under new rules implemented in 1998, U.K. companies will be required to carry goodwill on their balance sheets and amortize it over time (ordinarily twenty years) unless they can show the goodwill has not declined in value. Companies of truly comparable size—where the split between their market values is no greater than 60-40, may be eligible to use merger accounting—akin to pooling in the U.S. But to be able to do so, target shareholders may not receive an acquisition premium or boot in exchange for their shares.

Wells Fargo Busts Pooling

Wells Fargo Bank's 1995 hostile takeover of First Interstate was a rare exception to the rule in the banking world. Wells Fargo & Co. chairman Paul Hazen, in the top spot just a year, made the decision to go hostile.

Hazen's predecessor had long pined over First Interstate and had made several unsuccessful approaches to First Interstate management. Therefore, when Hazen took over, he knew private talks were not the answer. With a reputation as "the king of the hardball bankers," Hazen considered taking a tougher stance. Winning First Interstate was not the problem; Hazen was confident that could be managed. Rather, the accounting rules for mergers were the main stumbling block.

Bank mergers were almost uniformly accounted for as poolings of interests. The consensus before Wells Fargo launched its bid was that the market would punish a bank with goodwill on its books. In addition, if Wells Fargo wanted to try for pooling, it would have to suspend its share repurchase program, a critical part of Hazen's strategy to boost Wells Fargo's share price.

After consideration, Hazen decided there was much to gain from playing the maverick. He was confident he could convince the equity analysts who followed Wells Fargo to look past the artificial impact of the resulting goodwill. Plus, a hostile takeover was the only way to nab First Interstate. So, on October 18, 1995, Hazen announced his tender offer for First Interstate. Under the plan, Wells Fargo would pay $10.9 billion in stock for its target.

Hoping to avoid being swallowed by its cross-town rival, First Interstate rushed into the arms of a white knight: First Bank System, a Minneapolis bank with far fewer overlapping operations, agreed to merge with First Interstate in a stock deal valued at

$10.1 billion. Unlike Wells Fargo, First Bank was expecting to account for the deal as a pooling of interests.

Over a period of three months, Hazen traded barbs and lawsuits with his two counterparts. Ultimately, though, the market decided the contest. Because both deals on the table involved stock as consideration, the relative values fluctuated with the banks' stock prices.

Hazen and his team traveled to New York and wowed analysts. At the time, Wells Fargo was turning in a strong performance, and Hazen promised to turn his bank's tough cost cutters loose on First Interstate. The market responded by bidding up Wells Fargo's stock price.

As a result, First Bank's friendly deal was hanging by a thread. Then the SEC ruled that First Bank would be barred from buying back any shares for two years if its merger with First Interstate were to go through. Like Wells Fargo, First Bank viewed share repurchases as critical to its effort to make its stock more valuable. But First Bank was not willing to embrace the maverick purchase accounting approach. Rather than continue the fight, First Bank took its $200 million breakup fee, and Wells Fargo emerged the winner.

However, First Interstate's former management enjoyed a measure of vindication in the months after declaring defeat. First Interstate's top managers almost uniformly took their golden parachutes and moved on. Meanwhile, Wells Fargo had great difficulty integrating the two banks. A host of customer service problems, sparked by the post-deal brain drain and difficulties in meshing computer systems, plagued Wells Fargo. Depositors pulled their money from branches and Wells Fargo's stock price fell 20 percent, while other banks enjoyed a boom.

Hazen responded to the integration problems with an aggressive turnaround effort, which began to take hold in the fall of 1997. But it proved too little, too late. Wells Fargo, in an admission of defeat, sold out to Norwest in 1998.

Pooling   Accountants have felt that the purchase method is not appropriate for all merger transactions, especially stock-for-stock merger-of-equals transactions. Pooling is an alternative accounting concept under which, in certain limited circumstances, the purchase of a company is ignored for accounting purposes; rather, the two independent concerns involved are treated as though they had always been together. The purchase price is not reflected on the acquirer's balance sheet because the assets of the companies are pooled. The loose conditions required for pooling, however, led to widespread abuse and the ultimate elimination of pooling of interests for most transactions in 2000.

If a company with assets of $30 million book value purchases a company with assets of $20 million book value for $30 million in voting stock, conventional purchase accounting would state that goodwill of $10 million would be present in a combined company with $60 million in assets. Under pooling, however, the goodwill would be ignored, and the total assets on the surviving company's books would be equal to the sum of the book value of assets of both companies: $50 million. Hence, pooling—which avoids the creation of goodwill—can make an important difference in earnings results.

The original theoretical foundation for the pooling approach was that two companies of roughly comparable size involved in a stock-for-stock purchase should be treated as though they joined one another. Over the years, however, because of the favorable earnings impact provided by pooling treatment, companies of grossly disproportionate size have used the pooling method. The American Institute of Certified Public Accountants (AICPA) came out with study after study over a period of twenty years that suggested criteria to limit the use of pooling, including rough comparability of size among companies.

At the height of the 1960s merger wave, critics, including the Federal Trade Commission, argued that pooling increased the incentive to merge by jacking up earnings relative to companies that had used purchase accounting. The SEC finally brought pressure on the AICPA to reform. In a first-draft opinion, the AICPA did, indeed, state a comparability-of-size test for pooling, but the howl from the nation's leading companies and their accountants was overwhelming. As a result, a rough compromise was fashioned in the final AICPA opinions. These governing rules are vital to any merger analysis.

In order to be eligible for pooling treatment pre-2000, a merger was required to meet a number of somewhat arbitrary rules. For example, each of the combining companies had to be independent and could not have been a division or subsidiary of another company in the two years prior to the merger; the deal would need to be completed within one year in one transaction; and the consideration provided to target shareholders had to be voting common stock for substantially all of the target company's voting stock. The surviving company also generally was required to refrain from share repurchases in excess of 10 percent of the stock to be issued in the pooling combination, for the two years before the transaction, and was forbidden from repurchasing the shares issued in the transaction. The SEC disallowed pooling where the agency believed a share repurchase completed within two years after a transaction was contemplated at the time of the transaction.

If pooling is eliminated as proposed, many predict a chilling effect on M&A activity. EPS-sensitive companies would have a harder time justifying dilutive deals. Companies might also be less inclined to bid at large premiums to their targets' trading values, as a bid premium would be reflected in goodwill, an asset whose amortization depresses earnings. Yet the proposal could also induce the market to move to value companies on a cash flow basis. Increasingly, companies are reporting, in addition to regular EPS, a "cash EPS" figure, which excludes the effect of non-cash expenses, such as goodwill amortization. As the market gains comfort with cash EPS for valuation purposes, companies may be encouraged to ignore the dilutive effect of goodwill.

THE BATTLE OVER GOODWILL

Fundamentally, whether a merger is accounted for as a purchase or pooling shouldn't matter. The annual goodwill expense consumes no cash and is unrelated to the underlying operating performance of a business. A sensible approach would be to add back goodwill amortization to the earnings of all companies with goodwill on their books, normalizing the presentation for comparison purposes, unless the value of the assets was impaired.

As a practical matter, though, investors do follow earnings per share, and the presence of goodwill may have at least a psychological impact on perceptions of performance. As a result, companies in the past have been reluctant to enter into deals that generate considerable goodwill.

However, lately, investors are becoming more sophisticated about discounting the real-world impact of goodwill charges. Moreover, there is growing recognition that the avoidance of goodwill has a cost: acquirers' issuance of more stock than optimal to fund deals. From an economic perspective, with low interest rates and the tax-deductibility of interest expense, financing with debt may be otherwise more beneficial. Of course, shares may eventually be repurchased, but only after the passage of time required by the pooling requirement.

Wells Fargo and several other high-profile companies have seized on this fact and consequently have demonstrated a willingness to do deals under purchase accounting, despite the large slugs of goodwill involved. Bell Atlantic's short-lived deal with TCI, for example, also would have generated goodwill—roughly $20 billion worth, for $2 billion a year of goodwill amortization over ten years—an amount greater than TCI's earnings, making the deal highly dilutive for Bell Atlantic. However, Bell Atlantic chairman Ray Smith was focused on cash flow, not earnings: Before the FCC lowered cable rates, TCI was projected to have a strong and growing cash flow—money that could be used to pay down debt or upgrade TCI's systems to digital technology. Furthermore, like Smith, investors were willing to look past the goodwill to see the logic of the deal. Bell Atlantic's stock climbed almost eight points on the announcement of the deal.

The Bell Atlantic–TCI deal ultimately fell apart, but others have picked up the banner for purchase accounting deals. Disney's acquisition of ABC was accounted for as a purchase and created more than $18 billion of goodwill. Aetna's purchase of U.S. Healthcare created $8 billion of goodwill. Both deals were favorably received on Wall Street, though Disney has since had operating problems with ABC.

Notwithstanding these exceptions, companies generally seek to avoid goodwill. However, there are inklings of a wider shift percolating through the system.

The Leveraged Recapitalization   In the days of the classic LBO, financial buyers cared little about the intricacies of purchase versus pooling. Goodwill amortization was an accounting fiction with an Alice in Wonderland quality, and was therefore ignored. Cash flow was the focus, and private market sales to like-minded acquirers the anticipated exit strategy.

In recent years, financial buyers have been capitalizing on the hot IPO market by taking portfolio companies public as quickly as possible. Indeed, the high prices they pay are justified as a variant of momentum investing. Therefore, financial buyers have begun to focus on strong earnings as an important marketing tool.

Purchase accounting is one critical barrier to strong reported earnings. The problem of goodwill amortization can be circumvented by the leveraged roll-up strategy: A public company is purchased and then used as a vehicle for further stock mergers. However, in most cases, financial buyers need to invest cash.

Facing the dilemma of how to invest cash without creating good-will, financial buyers developed the leveraged recapitalization structure. The typical transaction has two steps. First, the target company borrows enough money to create a leveraged capital structure, say with a four-to-one debt-to-equity ratio. This cash is paid to existing shareholders as a dividend or in a stock redemption. Second, the financial buyer or other acquirer buys shares in the target, either from the target or from its shareholders. The end result is a leveraged company, up to 80 percent of which is owned by the acquirer and 20 percent owned by original target company shareholders.

Curiously, with careful structuring, the accounting rules treat such a transaction as a recapitalization of the target. No goodwill is created at the target level, enhancing earnings. Because financial buyers typically use special-purpose dummy companies as acquisition vehicles, it is these companies rather than the target that record the goodwill arising from the purchase. The goodwill of a dummy shell is immaterial to financial buyers and potential purchasers. The only cause for concern would be if the target itself—owned by the special-purpose company—were required to record the goodwill on its books. So-called push-down accounting would require this action, but generally only if the financial buyer were to own more than 80 percent of the target or if the continuing shareholders were to own 5 percent or less of the company.

Deal structure, therefore, has important tactical implications during the deal process and financial implications after the deal closing. Being flexible during negotiations may be necessary to get the deal done, but the second order consequences of a flawed structure can be long lasting.

Implementing | 18
the Deal

". . . But were you effective?"

—Brian D. Young, LBO Specialist

Implementing a deal requires a blend of psychology, business judgment, and technical dexterity. While taxes, accounting, and corporate law provide the skeletal frame for transactions, it is through the negotiating process that the deal actually gets done. In-depth knowledge of deal tactics and the inherent pitfalls in various transaction structures is essential. Conceptualizing a deal is quite different from executing it.

Negotiation Tactics

Successful negotiation tactics are partly instinctual, but also rely on accumulated insight and interpersonal skills. Unlike litigation—where one side wins and the other loses—negotiated deals necessarily involve working with another party to arrive at a mutually satisfactory resolution of the issues. Experts on the strategy of negotiations stress the need for a cooperative approach. In a truly successful bargaining session, everybody can feel some satisfaction: Negotiation need not be a zero-sum game.

In complicated deals, the ability of the negotiator is paramount for two reasons. First, the terms negotiated can substantially alter the economics of a transaction. Second, and more importantly, the negotiator may be the determining factor in whether the deal is consummated at all. Unless skillfully handled, a myriad of small issues sometimes builds into mutual antagonisms. Out of this accumulation of irritation, the building up of lethargy, disorganization, and lack of creative problem solving, many a deal that should have lived has died.

Objectives

Before entering into any bargaining session, well-advised parties engage in some preliminary reflection. The first, and perhaps the hardest, task is determining objectives. One reason for the difficulty is that the different parties representing the principal often will not share the same perspective or, even worse, will not have thought enough about the main issues. A key challenge is, therefore, coordinating the parties on one's own side and focusing their energies. To consider techniques independent of a clear set of objectives makes little sense.

One dramatic example when two parties' objectives failed to intersect can be seen in the failed merger of SmithKline Beecham and Glaxo Wellcome. The deal, announced in 1998, was to create the world's largest drug company. Originally, it seemed as if both companies shared the same objectives: to cut costs and help spread drug development risk over a larger capital base. The intellectual capital of both companies would be pooled to create a formidable competitor.

But one of the key objectives had not been addressed: the operating strategy of the combined company. SmithKline Beecham's historical strategy was to build a well-rounded health care company while Glaxo Wellcome's focus had been primarily on drugs. The top executives could not agree on how the new company would be run and what its focus would be. The parties had failed to define the most important objective: What would the new company look like and how would it be managed?

Because of this failure to define objectives, the megadeal fell apart, angering shareholders and shocking industry analysts.

Preparation

Extensive preparation gives a negotiator a competitive edge. Not only is it desirable to research the issues, but knowing as much as possible about the other side's representatives and its current position and techniques is invaluable. Likewise, determining the needs of the other side, both personal and economic, is fundamental to successful negotiation.

Financial modeling can also be helpful. If a party is likely to focus on the earnings-per-share impact of a deal, understanding the impact at various transaction values and with different structures can provide a sense of the practical negotiating range and answers to questions such as: What are the projected earnings per share for the first couple years after a deal? What is a likely trading price? How much can the other side afford to give?

Likewise, modeling the cash flow impact of a deal at various prices and with different capital structures gives insight to the perspective of a financial buyer. Of course, if the party on the other side of the table is using different assumptions in modeling the transaction, the results will vary.

Just as important to the flow of a negotiation is an understanding of the mannerisms, personalities, and reactions of each side's representatives. Sometimes, there is a clear mismatch of styles or personalities. Skillful negotiators step in and smooth the irritation to keep the deal on track.

Despite conventional wisdom, it is often helpful if the other party is being represented by a sophisticated advocate. When the other side at the bargaining table does not have a knowledgeable team, it may feel disadvantaged and insecure, creating an atmosphere of suspicion and delays. Knowledge provides the confidence to be flexible. For example, when Warren Buffett agreed to a warrant issue—a security to which he had a philosophical aversion—in the Capital Cities acquisition of ABC, he had the credibility and the sophistication to understand that the strategic imperative of the deal was worth the trade-off. When it makes sense, the strong can afford to be weak.

By contrast, the natural reaction of someone in over his head is to be recalcitrant. To take a typical situation, if a buyout of a small company has complicated tax implications, it is extremely difficult to persuade someone who does not understand the tax laws to devise a structure that uses those laws to maximum advantage.

Techniques

Techniques are mechanisms to obtain objectives. Obviously, the appropriate technique depends on the particular objective. There are, however, some universal guides:

Control   A key element in negotiation is retaining control. For example, negotiators try to keep control over the master document and do the drafting. When parties are making comments around the table, the copy that will be sent to the typist is the one the negotiator controls. Naturally, this position of control gives the negotiator a good bit of leverage. First, the negotiator usually has the choice of redrafting a comment later rather than inserting language during the course of negotiations. Second, if the negotiator feels that debate on any point should continue, the issue can be kept open simply by not writing anything down or bracketing conflicting language.

Pace is also key. Good negotiators never let a deal get away from them; if substantive issues are being discussed too rapidly without careful thought, haste may haunt the negotiator later. The ideal way for a negotiator to control pace is to be the host for the meeting: The negotiator then controls when the documents are distributed, when breaks are taken, and often what the time pressures are. It is very important, however, to be cordial and accommodating so that the adversaries will want to return. For example, Wachtell, Lipton works hard to be a gracious host by offering extensive support services and lavish lunches and dinners. Just as in sports, where the home team usually performs better in its own stadium, a negotiator often obtains improved results by bargaining in friendly territory.

On the other hand, it is also the responsibility of the negotiator to make sure the pace of issue resolution is such that the deal survives. Long hours, lists of key issues, and constant prodding may be necessary, but a deal is like a soufflé; timing is of the essence.

Sam Butler: Mr. Friendly Deal

Lawyer Sam Butler, the recently retired presiding partner at Cravath, looks like a former Harvard football player, which he was, crossed with a fraternity president, which he also was. Always smiling, always gracious, Butler is a nice man whose avid hobby is theater. Yet Butler was also an editor of the *Harvard Law Review,* a U.S. Supreme Court clerk, and has a crack legal mind with a unique instinct for compromise. Behind the amiable facade, Butler knows how to move deals along, a maestro of the deal process. He will cut fools to ribbons if they bluff, but remain gracious to those who go along. If Marty Lipton is Mr. Defense, Sam Butler is Mr. Friendly Deal.

Butler's natural ability is supplemented by an ingrained sense of the power of small incremental advantages. When negotiating a document, he lives by his rule "Control the master." He also prepares agendas and lists of open points in a negotiation. Controlling these administrative details allows him to shape the process. Butler's focus and discipline shine throughout it all.

The Butler legend is that when he was an associate up for partnership, he finished the bound volumes of documents for a big deal—which usually memorialize a transaction six months after the event—by the closing, an astonishing feat.

His skill, experience, and wisdom put Butler in high demand. Though his press profile may be lower than that of Marty Lipton or Joe Flom, Butler has led numerous high-profile deals to closing. For example, he handled the corporate law side of the 1989 Time-Warner deal for Cravath client Time Inc. and in 1995 advised Geico when Warren Buffett bought out the minority stake he didn't already control. Also in 1995, Butler simultaneously represented both Capital Cities/ABC and CBS in their respective sales. He helped Cravath maintain its status as one of America's leading corporate law firms before passing the torch to Bob Joffe as the new presiding partner.

Credibility It is very important to establish credibility early in a negotiation. Often credibility is automatically accorded some negotiators because of their reputation, and unless they demonstrate otherwise, they have no further need to prove themselves: A senior partner in a major law firm or investment bank is usually assumed to be skilled, but a young colleague may not be assumed to have that credibility. For the less-experienced negotiator, preparation is essential to establish credibility. Demonstrating an awesome familiarity with the documents and making a few obviously salient points earn respect.

A related issue is that of firmness. Although negotiating is a cooperative process, most parties are prepared to pick the other's pockets if the opportunity presents itself. If one side thinks that the other is an easy mark, the negotiations will inevitably degenerate. Therefore, the tendency of inexperienced negotiators, often due to their insecurity, is to be too belligerent and inflexible. When these negotiators realize that the goal is to close on reasonable terms rather than to bulldoze the other side, this overindulgence is soon toned down. But the art of not being too pliant is a more delicate one, depending in large part on the situation.

One way to handle overbearing advocates is to take one issue as a test case and spend extra time resolving it. The goal is to make the other side desist from bullying behavior by demonstrating that such behavior will be firmly resisted. Sometimes the other side will be represented by someone who is obstinate for obstinacy's sake. If all else fails, experienced negotiators try to make sure that the clients on both sides watch a performance in person. Often, the principal will rebuke an unnecessarily obstinate advocate, and behavior will change with surprising quickness.

Then, of course, there is the occasional pathological bully. Some people just can't help themselves and rant and rave with red-faced demonstrations of temper. My favorite response is to speak softly and say, "Everybody else in the room can scream too. We can resume business when you're done." The bully craves sensible limits.

Sensitivity   Because negotiation is necessarily a cooperative process, both sides have to be reasonably happy for the deal to work. A little psychology is required on the part of the negotiator. It is therefore important to be reasonable, although not obsequious, and, ideally, to give the other side enough so that its advocates feel that they have made a positive contribution and do not feel resentful. After all, if a negotiator does not feel this way, his presence wasn't required.

It's not that all parties need be equally happy with the results of a deal; it's just that everyone should have some limited solace. Courtesies, such as specifically marking changes, providing extra copies of documents, and giving personal assistance, may also bear important dividends, especially if the parties are to have an ongoing relationship, such as in a joint venture. When a side has bargaining strength, it sometimes becomes giddy with power. Maintaining perspective is important because one day the tables may turn, and a loss of dignity is seldom forgiven or forgotten.

In addition to these universal techniques, other strategies are very much dependent on the situation:

Confusion Versus Clarity   Generally, it is advisable to articulate a clear, concise position. Sometimes, however, there is great advantage to confusion, especially if time is running against the other side. For example, in buying a company with a tax-loss carry-forward, an acquirer can claim that operating managers have difficulty understanding or caring about after-tax impacts, since incentive compensation is based on pretax results. Such an excuse is frustrating to a seller, but much less bothersome than stating that those rights are valuable and then refusing to pay for them.

Similarly, confusion often simplifies bargaining by limiting flexibility. For example, an advocate may assert that though there is great merit in the twenty modifications sought by the other side, the client is a large organization with standard policies and it would require months of delay and myriad committee decisions to alter the documents as suggested. Confusion, whether just apparent or real, gives the other side a rational reason for accepting proposals which are irrationally unfair. But even if one does not care to use this confusion gambit, it should be recognized in the techniques of others.

Emotions   The Russians historically have developed a reputation as negotiators who kick and scream over every comma. Pretty soon, the other side becomes immune to the dramatic effect. But there are negotiators who can skillfully turn on righteous indignation at precisely the right point and be extremely effective. Certainly, control over feelings is useful and histrionics are seldom persuasive. But all anger need not be repressed. Especially if one has been cooperative and reasonable throughout the process, a show of anger at a key moment may well be an effective tactic.

Support   As a general rule, experienced merger negotiators like to have some balance between the number of representatives on their side and the other side at a meeting. With fewer representatives than the opposing side, a negotiator—especially an inexperienced one—may feel overpowered. Conversely, however, if a negotiator overwhelms the other side with numbers, he may well be greeted with obstinacy instead of willingness to make reasonable concessions.

On the other hand, the lack of full representation gives a negotiator more personal control and more chance to ferret out information from the other side without a quid pro quo. Furthermore, the more people from the negotiator's side present, the more likely that negotiation planning will be upset. For example, in a large conference, it is common for two businesspeople to begin talking directly to each other instead of going through the negotiators. To prevent such a circumstance, it usually makes sense to develop a small team with the negotiator as the authorized spokesperson. The spokesperson can then turn to the others on the team as appropriate. Some coordination is required, or else the team will act as a jumble of individuals with contradictory ideas and techniques. Such a situation cannot help but weaken a side's bargaining position.

Agents Versus Principals   For sessions to be productive, the negotiators must have the bargaining authority, subject to their principals' comments, to compromise on the less-material issues. A more fundamental question, however, is whether a principal should always be present to make major decisions. Without a doubt, proceedings are expedited if disputes can be resolved immediately, but there are serious drawbacks to keeping principals so heavily involved—most importantly, the loss of time for reflection and the opportunity to keep the various outstanding points in balance. Furthermore, principals often get impatient with discussions of details which may be cumulatively important.

In general, it is helpful to have the principals present at early meetings to discuss fundamental terms and then let their staffs attempt to implement the agreed-upon principles. If, as is usual, there is a list of major items which cannot be agreed upon by the staffs, the principals can meet again to resolve them.

One common tactic used when principals are not present is for a negotiator to try to elicit concessions from the other side and then refuse to make corresponding compromises because of an alleged lack of authority. If this technique is allowed to succeed, the result is a one-way give-up. One must either insist that principals attend negotiations or agree that the concessions are points the negotiators will each recommend, but both sides can in good faith revise their positions.

PROFILE

Carl Icahn

Carl Icahn is a tough negotiator. Whether he ultimately buys a company, motivates a white knight to buy the company, or sells his stock back to the target or in the market, one thing remains constant: Icahn is never content to split the difference—he wants to win on every point.

One of Icahn's tactics in the 1980s was to get a full night's sleep the day before a negotiation, perhaps even take a nap in the afternoon of the negotiating day, and then show up late to the meeting. He would stubbornly drag the debate into the early morning hours. Since he was well rested and his adversaries presumably were not, Icahn figured he would have the advantage.

In his early days, opponents underestimated Carl. He speaks in a circular, rambling style with no attempt to get to the point, sometimes affecting a thick New York accent. When clients found out that he was a Princeton graduate and extraordinarily sharp, they used to be shocked. Now the corporate community knows Carl is a serious player who doesn't scare easily. U.S. Steel, Texaco, and RJR have all felt Carl's bite.

The most effective opponent to Icahn we represented was the chairman of U.S. Steel, David Roderick. Icahn bought an interest in Roderick's company in late 1989 and began to agitate for a breakup of the company's oil and steel businesses. The two men eventually sat down to try and work something out. Roderick, who was used to labor negotiations, liked to spin a yarn as much as Icahn. He kept talking and talking. Finally, a reasonable settlement was achieved. Each party had tired the other out.

Contract Issues

Legendary Hollywood producer Sam Goldwyn reputedly once said, "A verbal contract isn't worth the paper it's written on." This may be hyperbolic, but in the context of a merger or acquisition, documentation is important. A detailed negotiation regarding the terms of a deal reduces the likelihood of future disagreement. Though every eventuality cannot be anticipated, comprehensive documentation focuses attention on the major issues.

A contract can allocate the risk of economic loss from undisclosed defects in the target company and provide protection in the case of a later disagreement. These protections have limits, of course, but can provide significant and sometimes decisive leverage in any dispute. A contract might even specify dispute resolution procedures.

Many executives understandably get bored with the legal byplay on drafting provisions. In the end, however, the wisdom of the conference room discussions is unimportant; it is the wording and clarity of the contract that counts. The slip between verbiage and paper is a recurring and often serious problem in deals.

The Five Pillars of Contract

The variety and number of issues that arise in big-deal negotiations are virtually limitless, but a certain amount of order can be introduced to the process. A typical merger or acquisition agreement covers five basic areas, each of which raises issues for negotiation. These five pillars are: pricing terms, representations, covenants, conditions, and indemnifications.

Pricing   Pricing, which on its face should be one of the most straightforward parts of a deal, is often the most elusive. The form and terms of consideration (cash or stock), their tax impact, assumed liabilities (present and contingent), the assumption of costs, and closing adjustments are all major items that often receive less attention than they deserve. Lawyers all too often are fuzzy on these subjects because they are technical business matters that are specific to each deal.

For example, the closing adjustments related to noncash working capital alone can be a multimillion-dollar item. Noncash working capital consists of current assets other than cash, chiefly accounts receivable and inventory, less current liabilities such as accounts payable. A clause providing for working capital adjustments must be made to guard against the possibility that a seller will convert current assets to cash and slow down payment of current liabilities. If the cash generated is drained from the business between the time a deal is signed and closes, the buyer can end up with a crippled company.

One approach to protect against this eventuality is to prohibit the payment of cash dividends between signing and closing. Another approach is to establish a "peg" balance sheet at signing and adjust the purchase price based on working capital fluctuations. If working capital is higher at closing, then the buyer pays the difference; but if working capital declines, the buyer reduces its purchase price by that amount. The seller then has no incentive to convert working capital to cash. Of course, for a business like retail, some provision also may need to be made for seasonal fluctuations.

Even with a no-dividends provision, however, a buyer often argues for a purchase price adjustment mechanism to shift some of the operational risk to the seller. Because a deal can take months to close, a buyer's purchase price based on current projections of operating performance and cash generation may in retrospect prove too high or too low if operational performance changes. The buyer often will argue that the seller should bear the risk, since it is the seller that will control operations until closing. Conversely, the seller will argue the buyer should take the business as is. A purchase price adjustment typically is the mechanism for risk sharing.

Representations   Representations are contractual assertions as to the state of affairs at the time a contract is signed. While buyer and seller typically both make representations, the seller's representations regarding the target company and its operations are key.

The primary representations a seller makes are that the information contained in its financial statements and other information materials provided is correct and without material omissions. These two provisions often are supplemented by a representation that no "material adverse change" has affected the business since the date of the last financial statements. This so-called MAC clause is often resisted by sellers on the ground that a buyer should make its decision based on the existing facts and other terms of the agreement. A MAC clause nonetheless is often included, though what constitutes a "material adverse change" may be narrowly defined so as to exclude changes brought about by wider economic shifts.

Other common representations include detailed provisions regarding environmental matters, copyrights or patents licensed or owned by the company, major real estate and equipment, key leases and contracts, pending litigation, tax liabilities, and so on. Theoretically, all representations other than those regarding the informational documents and the financials should be irrelevant because if they in fact were material, they would have been reflected in the documents. However, it is generally preferable from a purchaser's point of view to go through the litany of more detailed representations for two reasons.

First, the detailed representations, in effect, define what would be material under the contract. For example, if the company represents that all employee contracts for salaries over $100,000 a year are listed in Exhibit X, presumably $100,000 is the cutoff level of materiality for employee compensation. Defined representations also have the ancillary benefit of providing a number of triggers that can be used as closing conditions. In general, the more representations provided by the buyer, the more leverage the seller has to adjust the price at the closing.

Second, and equally as important, there is solace in detail for the buyer. Specificity increases the probability that a buyer will ferret out material facts. Generalizations are easier to ignore than specifics; if, for example, a company has to list all loans to officers, it may well stumble over some which should have been described in the draft of documents provided to the purchaser but weren't. Specific lists also indicate to the purchasers which documents they or their representatives should examine before investing. Of course, for the seller, an anal buyer who insists on a lot of representations is a nightmare.

Representations can be more or less favorable to a buyer depending on how they are drafted. For example, one common way to water down a representation is to add a reference to knowledge or materiality: A seller's representation that the target company has filed all tax returns, for example, might be altered by limiting the coverage to "material" tax returns or conditioning the representation on the seller's knowledge regarding any failure to file. If knowledge is used as the qualifier, a contract typically will state whose knowledge counts—anyone at the selling company, or only its directors or officers, for example. Adding knowledge and materiality qualifiers gives the seller wiggle room in any future dispute, allowing the company to argue that a problem was not material and that it had no knowledge of the condition.

The strength of representations ultimately depends on the extent to which they survive the closing. At one end of the spectrum, a pro-buyer agreement might provide that representations survive indefinitely. In a pro-seller contract, however, the representations would evaporate at closing. At stake in the difference is the buyer's ability to recover for a breach of the representations under any indemnity provision or otherwise. Tactically, a seller may be willing to represent everything under the sun as long as it doesn't survive. A common middle ground solution is to have the representations survive, but only for a short period, perhaps six months. Certain representations, such as those regarding taxes and environmental matters which involve third-party claims, often are carved out and given a longer life.

Naturally, the public company deal is documented somewhat differently than a private company deal. Unless one shareholder group holds a large controlling stake in the target, it is unusual to have representations survive the closing.

Covenants   Sellers provide both pre-closing and post-closing covenants, or promises. Common pre-closing covenants include the seller's guarantee that it will operate the business in "ordinary course" and provide access to the purchaser. The target also often agrees to maintain life insurance policies on the key executives, facilitate the transition, and comply, at the option of the investors, with the information requirements of the federal securities laws. Common post-closing covenants include the sellers' promises not to compete with the target after the sale, to preserve the confidentiality of information and to provide transition assistance.

Conditions   Conditions—or prerequisites to closing—protect the parties to an agreement. When a condition is breached, the aggrieved party typically has the power to cancel a transaction. A loosely drafted condition that favors the buyer, for example, effectively transforms a "binding contract" into an option agreement: If the buyer does not like the target company's prospects at the time of closing, a breach of a loosely defined condition can provide justification for termination. Alternatively, tight conditions enhance the likelihood that a buyer will follow through on its commitment to purchase. Conditions are, therefore, an important pressure point.

One powerful condition found in many agreements stipulates that the representations are true as of the closing date, and the seller is in compliance with the covenants. From the buyer's perspective, this "bring-down" provision serves several purposes. First, where a document will be signed far in advance of closing, the bring-down motivates the seller to put time and effort into operating the target company. Otherwise, the target may breach a condition, letting the buyer off the hook.

Second, with favorable representations—particularly a MAC clause and a bring-down—in place, the buyer maximizes the chance it will have an out should it find substantial problems through later pre-closing due diligence. Even if the buyer doesn't terminate the deal, a MAC clause provides leverage for renegotiation of price.

Sellers often receive the same type of protection in a stock-for-stock merger: The seller will not be required to close and will face no breakup fee penalty if there has been a material adverse change in the buyer's business. However, if controlling shareholders have already made an agreement to support the deal, the MAC provides added protection and can be used as a tool for renegotiation.

An "antitrust out" is another common condition. Such a provision might give the buyer the right to terminate a transaction that is challenged by either the government or a third party on antitrust grounds. Here, as elsewhere, an agreement can be drafted to favor buyer or seller. A pro-buyer version of the condition would have a hair-trigger: For example, the condition might require that no lawsuit or other proceeding be pending which might lead to an unfavorable antitrust ruling. A more limited condition might be triggered only if an actual ruling has been rendered that blocks the consummation of the contemplated transaction on antitrust grounds.

In either case, a buyer is also usually protected by a condition triggered if the government's antitrust review process remains open as of the closing date. Whether the antitrust out was used in good faith was the cornerstone of the suit by Cities Service against Gulf over the 1982 cancellation of their merger.

Conditioning the closing on the buyer's securing of financing obviously favors the buyer and therefore often is excluded from contracts. In an auction of a division or a company, for example, it has become increasingly common not to accept a financing condition; in that case, buyers typically arrange for financing sources to "bridge" the period between closing and the obtaining of long-term financing. Sometimes, however, the condition is included, along with a good-faith representation to obtain the money. Sellers have to beware, of course, that the buying entity isn't an unfunded shell.

A consents condition typically requires a seller to secure all third-party consents necessary to allow the transfer of assets and contracts. Valuable leases, for example, may require the lessor's consent if they are to be transferred from seller to buyer. This condition often presents an opportunity for a holdup: The lessor who thinks his consent is valuable often asks for a renegotiation of terms which could adversely impact the economics of the entire deal.

Finally, both sides to a transaction often will require a legal opinion from the other side's outside lawyers as a condition to closing. Such opinions state the lawyers' conclusions as to the valid and binding effect of the pertinent agreements and their enforceability, that the federal securities laws were not violated, and that the lawyers' clients have the power and authority to carry out the contemplated transaction.

The opinion of the counsel to the company can be expanded to be more comprehensive. Counsel will resist any expansion fiercely—after all, lawyers sensibly don't want added risks if they can avoid it. But the intent is not to sue the lawyers if they are in error; rather, it is hoped that the responsibility of an opinion will goad the lawyers into doing a more thorough job of diligence.

The key is that investors should be aware of any problems in the target business before entering into a deal. In addition to requiring a statement that no known agreement made by the target is violated by the deal, buyers should also request an affirmation that the target's counsel is not aware of any material misstatements or omissions in the relevant deal documents. However, learned counsel often insist that they give opinions only on law rather than on fact.

While conditions afford both parties the ability, should a breach occur, to cancel what would otherwise be a binding contract, such an extreme remedy is not the only possible outcome. Under most contracts, an aggrieved party also has the power to waive a breached condition in writing, a provision that allows the party affected by the breach to decide whether the deal still makes sense in light of the new developments or to negotiate for some price adjustment. Alternatively, a contract may give a breaching party the power to cure. In this case, an aggrieved party is required to give notice to the party in breach, who has a specified period of time to remedy the breach. Only if the breach remains unresolved does the aggrieved party have the power to terminate the agreement. While allowing cure may encourage repeated breaching and curing of breach to extend the period before closing, a drop-dead date solves this problem: Either party is allowed to cancel the contract if the deal has not been closed by a specified date some time after the original planned closing.

Indemnities   Indemnities specify the circumstances and the manner in which an injured party to a contract will be reimbursed or seek damages.

Sellers typically moan and groan quite a bit before indemnifying a buyer. Nonetheless, an indemnity is sometimes forthcoming, usually in the context of an asset deal or the sale of a subsidiary.

Because every dollar of undisclosed liabilities paid by a buyer constitutes an additional dollar of purchase price, a cautious buyer instead will in the absence of an indemnity assume there exists a certain amount of undisclosed liabilities in its valuation analysis. This assumption will lead the buyer to pay a lower up-front price for the target than it would if given the assurance it would not be responsible for any hidden liabilities. With an indemnity in hand, however, a buyer will value the target on the basis of zero undisclosed liabilities. If no such liabilities materialize, granting the indemnity costs nothing—in theory. However, indemnities are yet another source of contention, and experience has indicated the fewer indemnities granted, the lower the risk for a seller.

The time period during which an indemnity claim can be raised is determined by the extent to which the representations survive the closing. Sometimes, a seller will refuse to indemnify the buyer at all, with the contract stating the transaction is on an "as-is" basis.

If granted, however, the seller will want to be notified if the buyer becomes involved in court proceedings or some other controversy that may give rise to an indemnity claim against the seller. The seller often will also demand the right to appear in and control the proceedings, a request supported by the fact that in the typical indemnity, the seller must pay for all reasonable expenses related to a claim, including attorneys' fees. If the seller is on the hook for the expense, it will argue, it should be able to dictate how the claim is litigated and when it is compromised.

The buyer, on the other hand, may fear that the seller will take undue risks in litigation, risks that might have a secondary impact on its reputation or operations. A possible middle ground is for the buyer to retain basic control, with approval rights on any settlement going to the seller.

Often, an indemnity with a "basket" is used to bridge this gap between buyer and seller. With such an indemnity, the basket must fill up to a specified amount before the buyer can recover anything. In this way, the basket immunizes a seller from the bother of relatively minor damages, while protecting the buyer from major problems.

However, an indemnity provides little protection unless the indemnifying party has the ability to pay a claim. Indemnified parties therefore often seek to backstop the indemnity with an escrow or a setoff against any deferred payments due.

The Documents

In structuring a deal, the fundamental principles are first informally discussed and, perhaps, later itemized in an incomplete term sheet. However, parties must be careful when drawing up any sort of documentation before they announce a deal. For if the deal is of material size to either party, an agreement in principle, or even a handshake, may trigger required disclosure before the parties are prepared for publicity.

A term sheet summarizes the key points of a deal. Usually, letters of intent are not legally binding and are subject to both the approval of the respective boards of directors and the drafting of an acceptable definitive contract. However, these letters do have the advantage of limiting the scope of debate in the negotiations, morally if not legally. After all, if a term sheet says a debt instrument will have a stated sinking fund, it's rather difficult to raise the point as a fresh issue in negotiations.

The problem with spending too much time designing letters of intent is that as they become more detailed, the time and energy exerted could better have been spent working on the definitive contract. Because letters of intent are not legally binding, spending too much time on their details can become a dangerous delusion. Such letters create a sense of progress, but provide no impediment to a competing bidder from scooping up the prize. Conversely, if they are not detailed enough, allegations may be made that some essential point was not discussed.

When it comes to the actual binding contract, different documents are used for the various forms of negotiated transactions.

The Stock Purchase Agreement   In a stock purchase agreement, the buyer agrees to buy and seller agrees to sell a defined package of stock for a specified price. A stock purchase agreement—whether to be paid in stock or cash—is only practical when the selling company is owned by a limited group of shareholders whose significant ownership stake an acquirer wishes to have explicitly committed to a deal. Otherwise, a tender offer is used.

A stock purchase agreement generally covers the five pillars—price, representations, covenants, conditions, and indemnifications. The key question associated with such agreements is under what circumstances the selling shareholder has an "out." For example, if the sellers own 30 percent of a company and agree to sell and another company bids, who keeps the profit?

Our experience with the sale of Maybelline provides an example of one approach. Our partners owned roughly 30 percent of the company, acquired through a leveraged buyout which was subsequently taken public. We were very pleased when, after weeks of intensive private negotiations, L'Oréal, the French cosmetic company, agreed to pay $35 per share for Maybelline. Then we got to negotiating the contract.

L'Oréal wanted us to sell them our shares for $35 each pursuant to a stock purchase agreement, regardless of whether a higher offer materialized. But we had not shopped the company to other potential buyers and were, therefore, reluctant to make such a commitment. After much wrangling, we split the difference. L'Oréal offered to pay $36.50 for the company in return for their receiving half our profit above $36.50 if there were another bid. If L'Oréal itself raised its price, the increase was ours.

L'Oréal's archrival, German cosmetics giant Benckiser, eventually came in to top L'Oréal's bid, and after a series of counterbids, L'Oréal finally won at $44. Luckily, our partners got to keep the increase.

The Merger Agreement   Where a target company is a division with a single corporate shareholder or a privately held company with few shareholders, a merger agreement can be very similar to a stock purchase agreement—with the addition of the mechanics of the merger. If the target company is publicly traded or has many shareholders, however, the nature of the merger agreement necessarily changes.

A public company merger agreement typically has only limited representations which do not survive the closing. Normally, no indemnity is provided. Two factors account for this arrangement. First, considerable information regarding the past performance of a public target company is available in SEC filings, theoretically reducing the need for aggressive due diligence, and making representations less critical as a disclosure mechanism. Second, upon consummation of the merger, the consideration paid by the buyer will be dispersed broadly to the target's shareholders, raising the logistical issue of exactly who it is that will provide the indemnity. Though an escrow might be used to protect the buyer, this approach is rarely adopted. As a result, a large public company merger is often legally less complicated and faster to execute than an acquisition of a division or a private company.

The Asset Purchase Agreement   The asset purchase agreement mirrors the stock purchase agreement with a few important exceptions. First, where the target company is selling the majority of its assets and intends to liquidate shortly thereafter, the same indemnity problem found in a merger may arise: There is no large shareholder block to grant the indemnity. But if the target is closely held, a purchaser might demand an indemnity from the target's shareholders, or an escrow arrangement might be decided upon. Oddly, there seems to be less resistance to the use of an escrow when a public company sells its assets than when a merger is involved.

Second, the assets that will pass at closing must be identified, a task far more difficult than it sounds. A large business may have multiple operations, various legal and other intangible property rights, and numerous fixed and mobile assets. As has been discussed, the list of items requiring individual transfers may be extensive and could result in the generation of thousands of individual documents. When consents are needed to effect certain transfers, a key issue to be addressed in the document is whether the closing will occur if permission hasn't been obtained. Unless all the assets are being sold in a bulk transfer, the parties must specify what goes and what stays behind, as well as which related liabilities are being assumed.

Defending the Deal

Depending on the circumstances, both a buyer and a seller may have good reason to worry that a third party will bust up an existing deal. Paramount's attempt to break apart the Time-Warner deal and QVC's run at Paramount illustrate the reality of the fears.

A buyer will likely have invested a great deal of time, effort, and expense to develop a transaction, which might be particularly attractive—and not replicable. Therefore, a seller will inevitably favor some sort of defensive measure to encourage the deal to go through. Such defensive measures may also provide a negotiating carrot for the seller, inducing a buyer to offer full value or make other concessions. Perhaps less cynically, the buyer may have a genuine strategic interest in preserving the original deal.

The parties to acquisition and merger agreements, acting on the desire to defend their transactions, have implemented a number of defensive mechanisms: Prominent examples include stock and asset options, bust-up fees, and no-shop and window-shop agreements. These mechanisms can be implemented together or on a stand-alone basis, but are often weakened by the inclusion of a fiduciary out for the seller.

REVLON AND LOCKUPS

Lockups—agreements to acquire valuable assets of a target—are an obvious pressure point for a hostile bidder attempting to bust apart a friendly deal. Hostile bidders often sue to block these provisions in cases where an entire company is being sold, arguing the favorable terms are designed to protect the interests of incumbent managers rather than shareholders. There is no bright-line rule regarding the propriety of the various available mechanisms; rather, the courts generally examine an arrangement based on the particular circumstances.

Revlon is the seminal sale-of-control case involving a lockup arrangement, decided by the Delaware Supreme Court in 1985. The case centered on Ronald Perelman's bid to take over Revlon. Because Perelman was persistent in his pursuit, Revlon concluded it should seek out a white knight. Forstmann Little was selected, and an agreement was negotiated. In its final form, the agreement provided Forstmann with a crown jewel lockup option to buy certain Revlon assets at an attractive price, as well as a breakup fee and other concessions designed to preclude an acquisition by Perelman.

Perelman challenged the agreement between Revlon and Forstmann Little, arguing that Revlon's directors had breached their duties to shareholders by agreeing to the lockup. The Delaware Supreme Court agreed and invalidated the lockup and breakup provisions of the agreement and in the process created what have come to be known as the *"Revlon* duties" applicable to a sale of control.

Revlon duties are triggered when a sale of control or breakup of a company becomes "inevitable." In the *Revlon* case, the board's approval to negotiate with potential white knights was the final "recognition that the company was for sale." Once the sale-of-control threshold is crossed, the duty of a board "change[s] from the preservation of Revlon as a corporate entity to the maximization of the company's value at a sale for the stockholder's benefit": The directors became "auctioneers" rather than defenders of the corporation and its policies.

The implication of *Revlon* is that a board involved in a sale of control may favor one bidder over another only as a means to encourage an active bidding process. Accordingly, defenses that preclude another bidder from offering a higher bid are inappropriate and invalid under *Revlon*. In other words, the court developed a "smell test" of reasonableness. However, the courts have subsequently limited the circumstances where a *Revlon* duty is triggered, especially in stock deals.

While most states analyze lockups under a *Revlon*-type analysis, some do not. Pennsylvania, for example, has a state statute that allows the board more latitude to protect nonshareholder constituencies.

Stock Options

As a defensive tactic, a target company sometimes gives a buyer a lockup stock option to purchase authorized but unissued shares. The Time-Warner merger agreement, for example, included cross stock options through which each party could purchase approximately 10 percent of the other company's common equity. Typically, the exercise price for such defensive options is set at the share price to be paid in a stock purchase or at the market price in a merger.

The lockup stock option serves two purposes. First, it gives the buyer an opportunity to influence the outcome of any target company shareholder vote by exercising the option and voting the shares. Second, an option allows a prospective buyer to profit should a higher bidder come along—a kind of compensation for the original bidder's efforts, which arguably induced the new bidder to materialize.

Lockup stock options have received mixed reviews from courts. As a general rule, options are permissible if granted to induce a favorable transaction. Options may not be used, however, to cut off bidding. A corollary of this rule is that an option is viewed more favorably when demanded by a buyer than when suggested by a seller. Moreover, the longer the period between the signing of a definitive agreement and a planned closing, the more receptive a court will be to a significant lockup. A longer period imposes greater risk and cost on a buyer for which it should be reasonably compensated.

Asset Options

The asset option, or "crown jewel lockup," affords the prospective buyer the option to buy an especially attractive asset—frequently a key subsidiary or division which is less than approximately one third of a company's value. The option price generally is an approximation of fair market value, though often toward the low end, and is triggered by a specified event. The asset option is a powerful tool because the asset in question is strategic to the buyer: Even though the price may be full, the buyer is happy to walk away with its prize. Common triggers include another bidder's accumulation of a certain percentage of target company stock or the target's failure to consummate the planned transaction by a given date.

An asset option is another means to compensate a bidder for taking the risks associated with negotiating a transaction. However, the option also may discourage other bidders whose primary objective is to gain control of the asset under option. Taxes can also compound the defensive nature of an asset lockup. While in theory another bidder may be willing to pursue an acquisition absent these assets, the taxes a target may have to pay on any capital gain from the asset sale may depress earnings, making the target even less attractive.

This defensive potential makes courts skeptical of crown jewel options. Courts often will disallow options whose strike price is less than the full market value of the asset in question or if the agreement appears to preclude other bids. *Revlon* is one of the most well-known examples of a court overturning a crown jewel lockup. In that case, Revlon CEO Michel Bergerac and the Revlon board granted Forstmann Little a $525 million lockup on the company's National Health Laboratories and Vision Care businesses, exercisable if another bidder ended up with 40 percent of Revlon's shares.

The option terms were the focus of some bargaining: Ted Forstmann insisted on the lockup as part of his firm's agreement to raise its outstanding white knight bid. However, the fact that the purchase price was some $100 to $175 million lower than the value placed on the businesses by Revlon's bankers at Lazard caused the option to flunk the Delaware court's smell test, leading the court to toss out the option as part of its larger ruling in favor of Perelman.

The *Revlon* case presented a unique set of facts. In the typical situation, the precise measure of full value can be difficult to determine. Courts will make relative judgments based on expert testimony, the parties' own valuations, and the extent of arm's length negotiations involved. However, even in the face of tough arm's length negotiations over price, courts remain skeptical.

For example, in the 1982 takeover fight for Marathon Oil, a federal district court judge, applying Ohio law, upheld a crown jewel option granted to white knight U.S. Steel, only to be overturned on appeal. The agreement in question granted U.S. Steel the right to buy Marathon's half interest in the valuable Yates oil fields of West

Texas for $2.8 billion if an acquirer other than U.S. Steel were to buy more than 50 percent of Marathon's common stock.

U.S. Steel's lockup right had considerable defensive teeth: The Yates field, which produced 100,000 barrels of oil daily, was the key Marathon asset sought by both U.S. Steel and other bidders. Mobil argued that the Yates interest was worth roughly $1 billion more than U.S. Steel was to pay under the option agreement. But the district court rejected Mobil's argument and upheld the option, largely because Marathon was able to show that the price had been the subject of tough haggling. U.S. Steel initially wanted the option price to be set at $2 billion, but Marathon had held out for the $2.8 billion "even if it was a deal breaker." This stance, and U.S. Steel's original unwillingness to pay $2.8 billion, supported the price as fair. The Marathon board also had considered detailed valuation reports on Yates field before approving the option.

Despite these facts, however, a federal circuit court overturned the lower court's ruling on appeal, finding that the Yates field option constituted an impermissible "manipulative" practice under the federal securities law. Fundamentally, the court was worried the option circumvented the "natural forces of market demand" for Marathon stock.

So, even with extensive negotiations and good facts, a crown jewel lockup necessarily opens a board to criticism over price. Stock options raise some of the same issues, but are more favored as a defensive mechanism because publicly traded stock is much easier to value. A premium to the stock's recent trading value is easier to support than a crown jewel agreement.

Bust-up Fees

Bust-up fees provide a somewhat more direct, and consequently more obvious, defensive mechanism: The target agrees to make a payment to a prospective buyer if the parties' transaction is not consummated. Another variation of the mechanism triggers the payment at some earlier point, perhaps even when another bidder appears on the scene with a higher offer. Fees might also be due if the target's stockholders fail to approve the transaction or if the deal does not close by some specified "drop dead" date.

Generally, a bust-up fee is designed to cover a buyer's expenses and to provide some additional return. For a large transaction, the typical fee is in the range of 1 to 3 percent of the transaction value, including the value of any stock options granted. Bust-up fees in smaller deals ($50 to $500 million) tend toward the higher end of the range.

Like other defensive mechanisms, a bust-up fee is subject to judicial review. A fee that by itself exceeds 2 percent of transaction value is particularly suspect in a large deal, whereas a fee under that threshold generally will be allowed. The standards are somewhat more flexible in smaller deals. To reduce the risk that a breakup fee will not be upheld, it is preferable to position the fee as compensation for a bidder's efforts rather than as a defensive mechanism.

No-Shop Clause

While lockup options and bust-up fees usually are implemented as part of a definitive and binding agreement, a no-shop clause is sometimes agreed to earlier, often as part of a letter of intent.

Under the typical no-shop clause, a target company may not seek or encourage a third-party offer, nor may it provide information to or negotiate with other bidders. This prohibition is subject in most cases to a fiduciary out—the board of directors may break the terms of the clause if not doing so would violate its fiduciary duties to stockholders. The window-shop provision is a variation on the same theme, giving the target company the freedom to provide confidential information to and negotiate with *unsolicited* bidders but not browsers. The art form is in limiting the size of the window to real new bidders, not browsers.

Like other defensive mechanisms, a no-shop or window-shop

clause must be reasonable or it will not be sustained under a court challenge. Courts have found no-shop clauses particularly troublesome where they bar the target company from discovering the value and terms of a prospective offer.

A modern innovation has tightened no-shop clauses without running afoul of court oversight: A common approach is to include a provision that requires a selling company to notify the acquirer five days in advance of accepting any offer from a third party, effectively creating a right of first refusal for the acquirer. Such an agreement reduces third parties' willingness to bid. In addition, no-shop clauses now commonly require any third-party offer to be fully financed before the selling company can accept, further limiting the number of potential bidders without precluding other offers.

Fiduciary Outs

The fiduciary out is designed to protect the directors of a target company from having to choose between violating their fiduciary obligation to shareholders and violating a purchase agreement. Under a fiduciary out, the directors need not take some action if they determine that to do so would constitute a violation of their fiduciary duty. So, for example, a board might be able to negotiate with a third party notwithstanding the existence of a no-shop clause. Other obligations that are often waived include the requirement that a board recommend a merger to shareholders prior to their vote on the matter. As a check on the invocation of the fiduciary out clause, an agreement often requires the target to receive an opinion of outside counsel stating that the required action or the prohibition involved in fact would constitute a fiduciary violation. However, few law firms will agree to provide such a document.

To prevent an overly broad fiduciary out clause, acquirers will sometimes identify expressly in the no-shop provision specific circumstances that will allow the target board to invoke the fiduciary out. Potential triggers may include a requirement that the third-party proposal be in writing, that it offer for more than some threshold percentage of the target's stock or assets, or that the proposal be fully funded.

The fiduciary out will customarily only allow the target to provide or obtain information, but not solicit or otherwise facilitate a competing bid. Depending on the agreement, if the target board, exercising its fiduciary out provision, chooses to recommend what it deems to be a superior proposal instead of that provided by the original bidder, the target may or may not be required to terminate its agreement with the original bidder. Some agreements may even require termination of the original agreement before the board withdraws its recommendation for the original transaction.

What makes these provisions so difficult to negotiate is the competing objectives of buyer and seller. The acquirer will typically prefer a broad no-shop provision and a narrow fiduciary out. The target, conversely, will want to preserve its options and will seek the opposite.

As with options and lockups, *Revlon* limits the scope of no-shop clauses that will be permissible, as a company's board must be in a position to maximize the price paid once the company is in play. Some courts, though, have acknowledged that a strong no-shop provision and a weak fiduciary out may be necessary to induce an acquirer to enter into an agreement in the first place and therefore to maximize the price obtained. In fact, in stock-for-stock merger agreements it has become increasingly common to drop the fiduciary out clause.

There are two points in time when a board's actions may be judged with respect to a no-shop clause. First, when the target enters into the agreement, courts may ask if the board had obtained sufficient data to determine that the provision would maximize shareholder value (e.g., by performing a market check). Second, when a competing bid is made, if the no-shop provision is so broad that it prevents the board from ever examining the proposal, the court may consider whether the board breached its duty of care.

Raising the Cash

Of course, a deal won't get done unless the acquirer can finance the purchase. Issuing stock or other securities is one option for corporate acquirers, but necessitates a lengthy registration process. However, a deal that involves all or partial cash consideration raises a different set of issues.

Cash on hand—generated from operations, asset sales, capital markets activities, or in the case of financial buyers equity under management—is one obvious source of funding. But in most cases, cash on hand is insufficient to fund an entire deal. Financial buyers shy away from financing solely with equity because they target the higher returns on equity associated with a leveraged deal. Therefore, both corporate and financial buyers might look to finance a deal with some debt.

Leveraged acquirers, whether financial buyers or less established corporations, tend to use three types of debt: bridge loans, banks loans, and high-yield bonds.

Bridging to the Deal

In the context of takeover bidding wars, or even in heated friendly auctions of companies or divisions, the ability to provide assurance of financial capacity can be critical to winning the target. Shareholders will discount an offer made contingent on financing and therefore fully funded bidders are more likely to prevail. However, raising money from banks or through a high-yield offering takes time. Therefore, bridge loans have evolved to gain the advantage of a fully funded offer on short notice.

For an acquirer, a bridge loan is expensive short-term financing meant to fill the gap until other, cheaper debt can be raised. Lenders—investment banks, commercial banks, or other financial intermediaries—tend to look at bridge loans as a necessary tool to win more lucrative bank and high-yield finance business. The risk of the bridge financing is reduced by syndication: arranging for third parties to provide part of the loan in exchange for a share of the fees involved. In fact, a number of investment banks have raised bridge loan funds from third parties in order to guarantee fast response time on potential bridge loan situations.

The terms of a bridge loan are designed to reinforce the loan's short-term nature. Economic incentives encourage the borrower to repay the loan with the proceeds from other borrowings. The lender commits to provide bridge financing in exchange for an up-front fee. Another funding fee, also around 1.5 percent, must be paid if the money is actually drawn down. Bridge loan interest rates are high. Furthermore, if the loan is outstanding for longer than a few months, the rates begin to ratchet up, providing companies with a strong incentive to find other financing and compensating the bridge loan funds for the increased risk.

Fundamentally, a bridge loan is uneconomic to draw down and therefore acquirers try to avoid using the money. The time between an offer and a closing, which must be at least twenty business days in the tender offer context but can be longer, is used to negotiate bank loans, or raise high-yield, convertible, or equity capital. Even if the bridge loan is drawn down at the closing, having long-term financing commitments in place ensures that the bridge will be paid down in short order.

Bank Loans

Compared to bridge loans, bank loans are a cheaper and longer-term source of financing. Most bank loans have variable rates, defined in terms of some variable base rate—most commonly the London Interbank Offered Rate or LIBOR, plus a certain amount. The spread over the base rate depends on the acquirer's credit history, asset quality, and market conditions at the time the loan is negotiated.

The usual acquisition bank loan comes in the form of a credit facility with both a term loan component and a "revolver." A term loan is used to fund the acquisition and must be repaid after a fixed period, typically ranging from five to seven years. The revolver, on the other hand, is meant to fund the working capital needs of the acquired business and can be drawn upon and paid down at the discretion of the company, as long as the company is in compliance with the covenants set out in the bank loan agreement. For example, seasonal working capital buildups can be funded with the revolver, which then is paid down once the working capital is converted to cash.

Both the term loan and the revolver are structured to be senior to other borrowings: The bank will be paid before other lenders in the case of insolvency. If the loan is secured, the bank has a right to look to specific assets for repayment.

Today, banks syndicate most credit facilities. The lead bank arranges for other banks to provide part of the capital in exchange for a share of the fees and interest. Of course, the lead bank grabs the biggest share of the fees in exchange for organizing the process.

There are four main pitfalls associated with bank financing. First, banks require an acquirer to agree to tight covenants—rules about how the business can be run, how much additional debt can be borrowed, and when dividends can be paid. Bank loans also include maintenance tests that require the borrower to maintain a certain amount of cash flow to cover its interest payments. Attention to the covenants is crucial—a violation of a covenant may put the borrower into default, which may cause the loan to become due.

Second, depending on the circumstances, a bank may require the borrower to begin paying off the principal of a loan before the end of its term. These cash payments can be a drain on the underlying business, making the amortization schedule a common sticking point in bank loan negotiations.

The variable nature of bank loan interest rates also can pose problems. If the LIBOR rises, a company can get pinched. Some companies use derivative contracts to hedge this risk, but these agreements can be quite complex and expensive.

Finally, because bank loans must be repaid in fairly short order, some thought must be given to how the loan will be replaced. If the acquired company will be held for the long term, it may be more prudent to find a longer-term funding source. Of course, if the plan is to sell off assets quickly, a bank loan may be the appropriate funding vehicle.

PROFILE

James Lee Jr.

Despite the traditional feel of its paneled offices, Chase Manhattan Bank has emerged as the most aggressive bank lender to leveraged borrowers in the 1990s. Jimmy Lee is Chase's point man in leveraged lending and, as a Chase vice chairman, is leading the charge to convert Chase into an investment bank.

Known for his silver-dollar suspenders and blue shirt with white cuffs, Lee is a gregarious banker who joined Chemical Bank out of college and rose through the ranks. Though charming, Lee thrives on competition. He headed Chemical's loan syndication unit during the early 1990s crunch and earned goodwill and loyalty by staying in the market—continuing to lead syndicates and make loans—when others would not. In particular, Lee forged strong relationships with the leading leveraged buyers. The bank emerged in 1996, after the Chase merger, with an astounding 20 percent of the $888 billion syndicated loan market.

Today, Lee is looking to build upon this foundation. Chase has capitalized on its leadership in the senior bank debt business to gain a share of the junk bond market. Lee's troops have even built a presence in the corporate finance and merger advisory businesses. The ability to provide one-stop shopping is the goal.

Competition in each of the markets Lee has targeted is fierce, but he has made significant headway. In one high-profile example, Chase scored a clean sweep of business in the E32 billion acquisition of Telecom Italia by Olivetti: Chase led a syndicate of banks to provide E22.5 billion in senior secured credit facility to fund Olivetti's acquisition, joint led E9.4 billion of high-grade bond offering, and was one of the acquisition advisers to Olivetti.

Lee appears committed to gaining more of this kind of lucrative assignment. His investment banking unit continues to build staff, hiring bankers away from the competition at double the salary for multiyear contracts. Recently, Chase bought technology boutique investment bank Hambrecht & Quist for its equity underwriting capabilities. Lee's challenge is to knit the pieces together into a coherent whole.

High Yield

High-yield bonds, popularly known as junk bonds, provide the final layer of financing. Over $450 billion of high-yield bonds currently are traded in the market with nearly $150 billion issued in 1998. These instruments generally have a fixed rate and a seven- to ten-year term and are subordinated to bank loans. That junk is subordinated requires its yields to be higher than those provided by bank debt of an equivalent term from the same borrower.

For the issuer, the main advantages of high-yield debt are its long term, fixed rates, and less onerous restrictions than bank debt. In particular, high-yield instruments generally do not have maintenance covenants—which require the borrower to maintain a certain ratio of cash flow to interest payment—or principal amortization requirements, affording the borrower somewhat more flexibility on the downside. Attention must nonetheless be paid to the remaining covenants to make sure they do not unduly restrict the issuer's flexibility.

The call provisions in a high-yield indenture provide the borrower with additional flexibility, affording the right to repay the bonds early. This option could prove attractive if rates were to fall in the market or if the issuer's financial circumstances were to change. Of course, lenders discipline the process and require some compensation on a conversion.

The high-yield issuance process varies depending on how quickly capital is needed. If an acquirer has sufficient time, the bonds are registered with the SEC in the same way stock is registered prior to a public offering: An offering document is filed for review and once completed, the bonds are issued to investors and publicly traded.

In more urgent situations, high-yield bonds can be privately placed with sophisticated investors. Under an exception to the federal securities law known as Rule 144a, bonds need not be registered, but cannot be publicly traded. As a result, the purchasers typically demand that the issuer conduct a follow-up registration of bonds, which are then exchanged for the original bonds, providing investors with a publicly traded instrument. Issuers prefer this process because the follow-up registration can take place after the acquisition is closed. In fact, during the recent bull market in high-yield securities, the 144a route has become increasingly popular, with little or no penalty to the issuer.

Even with a Rule 144a offering, however, raising high-yield money takes some time: An extremely accelerated process involving public companies whose information is already available might only take a few days; but if the target company is not public, the process might take eight to twelve weeks.

In the interim, an acquirer sometimes obtains a "highly confident" letter from the investment bank that will act as underwriter, affirming that the deal can be financed. However, while highly confident letters are viewed by most investment bankers as a credible indication of the ability to finance a deal, such letters are not legally binding and therefore are not nearly as valuable as a commitment letter or bridge loan. On the other hand, highly confident letters are much less expensive than commitment letters.

The Takeout

The common theme in financing a deal is that an acquirer should match its book: Long-term cash needs should be met with long-term financing sources, short-term needs with short-term sources. Otherwise, an acquirer builds a house of cards that can be easily blown over when the re-funding date comes.

Offense: 19
Battlefield Tactics

"These things are rather bloody, you know."

—Thomas Mellon Evans,
a veteran of
corporate takeovers

The mist clears. All the analysis, calculation, and frenzy comes to this. The deal is launched. Pressure builds. An avalanche of calls, rumors, and demands sweeps away any semblance of tranquillity. The sputter of the crowd is incessant. In the midst of the mayhem, the distinguishing mark of the skillful bidder is an inner sense of calm. This equilibrium is achieved through preparation, preparation, and more preparation.

What are the pitfalls? Where are the ruts? What can go wrong? Of course, inherently, decisions are made under conditions of uncertainty, but it is possible to anticipate the range of the risks. Most important in the process is to maintain a strategy. The tactics used need to be consistent with the strategy and well executed.

Crafting the tactical staging of a deal is a delicate matter: Aside from economic and legal considerations, it is an art, not a science. Recently, large corporate bidders have preferred preemptive bids because they make an offer inevitable, reduce the fuss and the controversy, stun the target board, and crack the feasibility of resistance. On the other hand, there is much to be said for the notion of satiation: A target so exhausted by defending itself may be vulnerable to a raised bid. This strategy, however, requires patience, time, and a thick skin.

Deciding which route to travel requires a profound understanding of both the target's psychology and the bidder's own strategic imperatives. There are three fundamental strategic options: attempt to negotiate a friendly transaction, use the bear hug approach, or simply launch a hostile tender offer. Each of these alternatives has both its attractions and drawbacks.

The Friendly Approach

A negotiated deal trades a friendly solution for the loss of strategic advantage associated with a surprise offer. An attempt at negotiation tips the acquirer's hand and provides some warning as to possible hostile intent. Furthermore, by seeking a friendly negotiation, an acquirer may jeopardize a later aggressive deal.

When a friendly dialogue is started, the target will often ask a potential acquirer to sign a standstill—an agreement that prevents one signatory from pursuing a merger or acquisition with the other, except on friendly terms. The agreement allows the target to negotiate with a potential bidder without the coercive threat of a potential unwanted pursuit. The willingness to sign a standstill also serves as a kind of litmus test, an indication of the bidder's true intentions.

For a determined bidder, a poorly drafted standstill agreement does not necessarily pose a barrier to a later offer, a reality demonstrated by Ron Perelman in his 1986 and 1987 dealings with Gillette. Using Revlon as his vehicle, Perelman made a bid for Gillette; the company responded with a plan to sell a large block of convertible preferred stock to a white squire, a shareholder who will vote his shares in management's favor in a hostile situation, which would effectively foreclose a successful Revlon hostile bid. Perelman therefore agreed to sell his shares back to Gillette, making a $35 million profit. Yet Perelman soon came to feel the decision was a mistake:

Gillette's white squire never materialized, and the company remained an attractive target. However, Perelman had signed a ten-year standstill when selling his Gillette shares. Searching for a way around the standstill, Perelman approached Gillette with a new $4.7 billion friendly offer conditioned on the elimination of the standstill, later increasing the pressure by raising his offer to $5.4 billion. All the while, he insisted Revlon would only do a friendly deal in keeping with the standstill.

Eventually, Perelman gave up the pursuit. But in the process, he had created a precedent for circumventing a standstill agreement. Gillette subsequently was forced to fight off another takeover attempt—this time waged by Coniston Partners—with a major leveraged recapitalization and stock buyback. Ultimately, Gillette became a high-performing stock of the 1990s (with some recent hiccups) with the launch of its new Sensor and later Mach III shaving systems.

The mid-1970s were the years of the lightning-fast hostile tender offer. With a slump in stock prices, American and foreign companies saw an opportunity to acquire fundamentally healthy firms or firms with high potential on the cheap in a bear market. Tender offers were quick and effective. Without warning, a chief executive could wake up in the morning and find a huge two-page ad in the paper announcing a surprise attack. These Saturday Night Special deals could be completed in as little as seven days.

But things have changed since then. A state and federal regulatory framework now impedes the rapid takeover. For deals of any significant size, federal antitrust laws require a minimum fifteen-day waiting period. Furthermore, federal securities law requires that a tender offer be held open at least twenty days and several states require shareholders to approve certain kinds of offers.

Management had also become increasingly adept at rapid response. Many large corporations have a takeover preparedness plan in place. And with the advent of corporate delaying devices such as poison pills, a hostile offer usually drags out for months.

Given the new legal environment, the advance notice provided by a friendly overture preceding a hostile offer may not significantly weaken a bidder's strategic position. However, where the target company's management has a known antipathy to the possibility of an acquisition or merger, as was true for Rand Araskog of ITT, the chances of a successful negotiation may be slim.

Yet there is still a case to be made for the surprise bid. First, many litigators feel it is imperative to obtain the right jurisdiction for the inevitable flood of litigation. Furthermore, bidders like to offer a premium, which is easier to do before the trading price of the target is affected by news of a pending deal. A negotiation poses a higher risk of a leak and a subsequent spurt in prices. Thus, the tactical advantage gained from surprise could then weigh in favor of a different approach.

The Bear Hug

A bear hug is a formal acquisition proposal made to the board of directors as a nudge toward a negotiated transaction, and is typically used either if the friendly approach is deemed inappropriate or after an unsuccessful friendly approach. Such an offer calls the board to address its fiduciary responsibilities to shareholders, and is particularly effective where the target company has a sizable constituency of institutional investors. The boisterous pressure from institutional shareholders and arbitrageurs is designed to crack the will of the board.

In some cases, the bear hug strategy has been adopted by investors who have accumulated a stake in a target on the open market and seek to stimulate potential acquirers to buy at a premium to the investor's cost. When a bear hug becomes public, the arbitrageurs will often step in and add to the pressure. The technique, therefore, may put a company in play.

This tactic was commonly used by Icahn, Pickens, and other takeover investors of the 1980s, who viewed public agitation as an in-

tegral part of their investing process. With a host of well-financed acquirers in the market and relatively undeveloped takeover defenses,
the strategy often proved effective: Pickens pushed Gulf into the
arms of Chevron, and Icahn forced Phillips Petroleum to sweeten its
recapitalization plan.

Though the advent of the poison pill has reduced the sting of the
bear hug, the tactic remains part of the modern takeover arsenal. For
example, in June 1997, investment partnerships associated with the
Bass family made a formal offer to Fisher Scientific, a Fortune 1,000
distributor of scientific equipment 10 percent owned by the Bass
Partnerships. After discussions with Fisher management, the partnerships, including the Trinity Fund and the Texas Pacific Group,
sent a letter to the Fisher board laying out a proposed leveraged recapitalization plan. At the time of the offer, Fisher stock was trading
at around $37.50; the plan would have provided shareholders a sug-
gested price in the range of $47 to $48 a share.

With the pressure of a premium offer on the table, the Fisher
board rushed to find a friendly suitor and in August inked a $51 a
share deal with buyout shop Thomas H. Lee Co. One month later, a
major UPS strike negatively impacted Fisher sales and market share,
and the acquisition price was revised to $48.25 a share. Nonetheless,
the bear hug letter had served its purpose, sparking a deal. Although
the Bass partnerships may have preferred to acquire Fisher, the
Thomas Lee deal brought Fisher shareholders liquidity at an attractive price.

Within the broad category of bear hug letters, the specific tactics
employed can vary considerably. Including a price in a bear hug has
the advantage of increasing the pressure on a hesitant board: Directors who vote to reject such an offer must face the possibility of
stockholder lawsuits. If the offer is at a significant premium to the
target company's current trading price, dissatisfied stockholders can
argue the rejection of a higher offer constitutes a violation of the directors' fiduciary duty.

Sometimes, as an inducement to negotiation, the bidder will state that it will offer "at least" a specified dollar amount or indicate that upon the receipt of additional information, it might consider a higher price. This was the approach Bass took in its offer for Fisher. The difficulty with this technique, however, is that the target always knows there is more money in the bidder's pocket. On the other hand, leaving money on the table protects the bidder from the preemptive strike of a competing friendly offeror, who might bid a higher price in exchange for lockups and thereby preclude the initial bidder from putting his best foot forward.

To have maximum effect, a bear hug letter usually needs to be in a form which requires disclosure. Alternatively, the bear hug offer may be made conditional, so that it does not require disclosure. While the target knows that the offer might be disclosed at any time, the initial show of restraint allows for the private friendly decision without the hubbub generated by disclosure.

BAXTER CRACKS THE BOARD

The bear hug is a flexible tactical weapon. In 1985, for example, Baxter Travenol Laboratories used a bear hug to crack apart a merger between Hospital Corporation of America and American Hospital Supply.

HCA and American Hospital announced their merger—effectively a takeover of American Hospital by HCA—in June 1985. As a hospital company, HCA had few obvious overlaps with American Hospital, and thus relatively little potential for cost savings. Rather, the deal was a vertical integration of customer and supplier. This type of combination, however, posed a problem for many of American Hospital's customers, who threatened to pull business from the company because it would be part of a direct competitor. Reflecting these concerns, both HCA's and American

Hospital's stocks declined in value on the announcement of the deal.

Almost immediately, Baxter became interested in pursuing an alternate deal with American Hospital. The motivation was clear: Both companies had operations in hospital supply and medical equipment, a competitive market in which the opportunity for cost savings would be appealing.

The difficulty for Baxter was that HCA's $3.6 billion stock swap with American Hospital included defensive mechanisms such as reciprocal stock options which would make a hostile deal for American Hospital prohibitively expensive. Yet the agreement was nonetheless vulnerable: American Hospital had a large constituency of institutional investors, many of whom failed to see the logic of the deal and were looking for a better alternative.

Despite potential institutional support for a bid he might offer, Baxter faced the practical dilemma of how to break apart a done deal. Baxter's key advantage relative to HCA was that its businesses offered greater potential synergies with American Hospital, giving it room to outbid HCA.

Baxter crafted a strategy to play on this strength. The company bear-hugged the American Hospital board, topping HCA's $36.50 per share offer with a $50 offer. Because Baxter was not ready to pursue a hostile deal, as it made clear in its letter to the American Hospital board, it needed a much stronger offer which would put the American Hospital directors in a fiduciary bind. Therefore, this wide margin was critical to the success of the approach.

HCA refused to raise its bid for American Hospital because a higher stock bid would be too dilutive to its earnings and a cash deal would kill pooling. Eventually, the board cracked under the pressure from investors and arbs, including Carl Icahn, who had accumulated a large stake. Furthermore, the investment banker to American Hospital threatened it would have to revoke its fairness opinion in light of the higher Baxter bid. Eventually, American Hospital agreed to a slightly sweetened $51 a share offer with Baxter. Baxter meanwhile settled with HCA, paying a breakup fee but gaining a lucrative supply contract. HCA agreed, in return for a breakup fee, not to exercise its options to buy stock in American Hospital.

After the deal closed, Baxter faced a difficult task bringing its two hospital supply divisions together into an efficient whole. Integration problems proved to be a costly distraction. In 1996, the company spun a significant chunk of its hospital supply operations off as a stand-alone business, now called Allegiance Corp. Baxter International, the renamed parent, retained American Hospital's lucrative cardiovascular equipment business.

Going Hostile

Mounting a hostile offer can be expensive. Of course, the willingness to pay a premium price is critical to success, but price is rarely enough to guarantee victory. The likelihood of a successful campaign also depends on a number of key nonfinancial factors, which potential bidders analyze with extreme care.

Stock Ownership   The identity and sentiment of a target company's stockholders is a critical issue in any hostile takeover, as are their feelings about incumbent management. Generally, an acquirer begins its analysis by determining the ownership by management, officers, and employee benefit programs whose investment decisions are controlled by management. Related, but distinct, is the block owned by all other employees. Employees may or may not have strong feelings of loyalty to present management, but officers almost always will.

Next, a breakdown is compiled of the types of other key holders: For example, what percentage are institutions versus individuals, what are their average holdings, and how long have they held the securities? The objective is first to determine the "float" in the market—the trading shares that will easily flow to the highest bidder—and then those which can be acquired with a little more work.

Some companies are very hard to attack: Those where management owns a high percentage of the stock, employees are loyal, stockholders have held the stock for years and have prospered, and the trading float is thin pose problems for the hostile acquirer. Following financial reverses, however, stockholder loyalty often disappears. For this reason, tender offers are often made to companies which are underachieving. A disillusioned stockholder is usually willing to sell and a defending management merely seems protectionist.

Corporate Structure   The corporate structure of a target firm can be a key factor in determining the success of an offer. Therefore, a potential acquirer must study the provisions of the target's bylaws and corporate charter (sometimes called a certificate of incorporation), paying special attention to provisions for a staggered board, the inability to remove directors without cause, or high quorum requirements for approval of mergers—all of which could make life very difficult for the would-be acquirer. On the other hand, the lack of a staggered board—as in ITT's case—or the ability of shareholders to call a special meeting can be pressure points. Provisions such as cumulative voting can be a double-edged sword: They make entry onto the board easier but make elimination of minority opposition more difficult.

Analysis of Possible Defenses   Possible defenses to a tender offer will be discussed in detail later, but obviously an acquirer should analyze all likely strategies. For example, are the executives signed to long-term contracts, is a poison pill in place, are there substantial authorized but unissued shares available for defensive mergers, will there be a competitive bid, and so on?

An acquirer also must be aware of the weaknesses in its own position: sensitive and blurry disclosure issues, antitrust and regulatory hurdles, state antitakeover laws, and the company's own record. A key issue can also be made out of the consideration offered. Cash is cash: It is very difficult to litigate the value of a cash deal. But when securities such as common stock are being offered as part of the transaction, litigators and PR firms load up for target practice.

Martin Sorrell—Pushing the Envelope

On June 11, 1987, Martin Sorrell, chief executive of WPP Group, rocked Madison Avenue with a $45 a share hostile tender offer for JWT Group, the parent of ad agency J. Walter Thompson and public relations company Hill & Knowlton. Two weeks later, JWT Group's chairman capitulated. Don Johnston signed an agreement endorsing a sweetened $55.50 a share deal, and the first successful hostile takeover in the advertising business was sealed.

Sorrell's dramatic coup pushed the envelope on hostile deals, shattering the conventional wisdom that a hostile attack on a services business is unworkable. Skeptics pointed out that the chief assets of an advertising or public relations agency, namely its top people, could easily walk out the door, leaving little of value behind.

Sorrell was well equipped to challenge this view, however. A graduate of Harvard Business School who returned to his native London after graduation, he eventually became finance director of advertising firm Saatchi & Saatchi, where he worked for nine years, and was the chief financial architect of the global expansion plan that transformed their firm into the world's largest.

In 1986, Sorrell left Saatchi looking for his own show to run. He bought Wire & Plastic Products, a tiny manufacturer of wire shopping carts with a mere $5 million in annual revenues, and set out to transform WPP into a marketing powerhouse.

The makeover began with acquisitions of a number of small advertising and marketing companies. A bullish London stock market subsequently allowed Sorrell to raise more equity and pursue larger deals. With this critical mass established, Sorrell was positioned to benefit from a strong British pound and lofty valuations in the U.K. market when pursuing what interested him most: potential U.S. acquisitions.

WPP's 1987 J. Walter Thompson deal, a $566 million purchase, was his first U.S. deal. However, that was just the start. In 1989, Sorrell approached a second major target in the rapidly consolidating U.S. advertising business—Ogilvy & Mather—with a bear hug intended to pressure Ogilvy's management into a friendly deal. After an acrimonious campaign of mudslinging and two raises from WPP, Ogilvy finally acquiesced, again in two weeks. Sorrell had his second target in an $860 million deal.

WPP's two major acquisitions demonstrated that unfriendly approaches can work in the services context. There were some hiccups, of course. Staff members of one J. Walter Thompson subsidiary bolted and set up a rival shop, while the employees ultimately paid WPP a $10 million settlement. The defections cost the firm prospective business.

But overall, the J. Walter Thompson acquisition was a success. Sorrell adopted a hands-off approach, installing top management with the freedom to run operations. Most creative people stayed with the firm, and relationships with key clients had deep institutional roots. Sorrell contributed financial discipline to the mix, balancing staff costs and revenues, and managing the financial side. JWT's margins increased from a dismal 4 percent of revenues to a more normal 9 or 10 percent.

> Ogilvy was a more difficult integration. WPP struggled through the recession of the early 1990s, burdened with its heavy Ogilvy debt. However, Sorrell successfully restructured the debt, issuing equity in its place. The firm emerged from the recession strong and intact, with Sorrell still at the helm. In 1998, WPP had revenues of approximately $3.1 billion and net profit of $230 million. Sorrell had stymied the critics.

Before the Hostilities

It used to be that a potential bidder would accumulate a block of stock before making an offer. But regulatory changes have since changed the tactical landscape dramatically. A meaningful accumulation above $15 million is almost impossible today without public disclosure.

The temptation to buy a pre-offer block of stock is obvious. In an active merger market, a third party might make its own, more attractive offer for the target company and the original potential acquirer could find itself a loser in a bidding war, with nothing but a pile of legal and other expenses to show for its efforts. Buying stock in the market at pre-offer prices can reduce the sting of this situation, providing the losing bidder with a gain on the stock to offset expenses and perhaps provide a net profit on the transaction.

A sizable block of target company stock can also provide valuable leverage in an eventual takeover contest. Most directly, the bidder can benefit from the voting power associated with the shares it owns. Such voting power can prove critical at various stages of a fight for control, which may involve a proxy fight, shareholder approval under a state takeover statute, or the election of directors.

However, federal antitrust law is the main barrier to a secret preannouncement accumulation. Generally, if a stock or asset purchase falls within the so-called Hart-Scott-Rodino framework, seen at work in the DuPont-Conoco deal, the purchaser must report the transaction to the federal government and must observe a waiting period before making the purchase. These rules apply to transactions over $15 million where the acquirer has more than $100 million in assets or annual sales, and where the target has over $10 million in assets, with one exception: An exemption from the antitrust reporting requirements and waiting rules will cover the purchase of up to 10 percent of an issuer's voting stock if the stock is held "solely for the purpose of investment."

The $15 million rule—a relatively low one in today's M&A environment in which so many deals are in the billions—has recently come under some attack. Senator Orrin Hatch has recommended that the Justice Department save money by raising the standards for review so as to reduce the need to examine so many mergers. Originally, the rule was intended to require advance notification of no more than 150 mergers a year and was to be a "notice-and-wait" process for only the largest mergers. HSR was to provide enough time to enable enforcement agencies to convince a court to enjoin a merger pending a full trial on its merits. But in 1998, parties to more than 4,000 transactions were required to make HSR filings.

Furthermore, SEC rules, to be discussed later, prevent any acquirer from buying more than 5 percent of a target's stock without disclosing its beneficial ownership within a ten-day period. Therefore, unless the initial purchase is in total less than $15 million, the purchaser must make full public disclosure of its intent before a tender offer is formally announced.

Certain state laws similarly restrict the ability to accumulate shares. For example, responding to perceived takeover abuses during the 1980s, a number of states enacted control share provisions requiring that a purchaser receive approval from current target company shareholders before acquiring stock in excess of a specified limit. In addition, the conventional poison pill of the 1980s prevents an accumulation of more than 10 or 15 percent of a target's stock.

The combined effect of federal and state disclosure laws is to make a "creeping acquisition"—the purchase of a controlling block of stock in the open market—effectively impossible. When the purchaser's intentions become public knowledge, the target company's stock price will be bid up. As a result, a bidder often times its tender offer to coincide with the first disclosure of its stock holdings and hostile intention.

Fighting by Proxy

Once the decision is made to pressure for a deal, tactics take center stage. The proxy fight—the main arrow in the 1960s insurgent quiver—has again become an important weapon as defensive mechanisms have proliferated and become more effective. High-profile examples abound: IBM's successful assault on Lotus; Kirk Kerkorian's proxy threat in his running battle with Chrysler; Hilton Hotels' proxy attack on ITT; and AlliedSignal's proxy fight for AMP. Similarly, Carl Icahn's long fight to force a split-up of RJR Nabisco featured one failed proxy contest and a second ongoing one.

Takeover-related proxy fights can either be the main weapon or a clearing action for a tender offer. In the first instance, the insurgent seeks control of the target's board by running a slate of candidates against the incumbent directors up for reelection; the shareholders then choose which slate should govern. This approach has a decided appeal for a dissident investor. Waging a proxy fight is expensive, but a winning proxy fight can give effective control with far less capital than an outright purchase.

This was Carl Icahn's agenda with RJR Nabisco. In 1995, Icahn followed Bennett LeBow into RJR. Icahn put together a 7 percent stake, buying on margin, then launched a proxy fight together with LeBow in the fall of 1995 to take control of the board and break RJR into separate food and tobacco companies. Their chances initially looked good after the two narrowly won a preliminary nonbinding vote in favor of splitting up RJR (though, technically, the tally went against LeBow's Brooke Group if votes submitted after its self-imposed deadline were excluded).

LeBow then made a huge tactical blunder. In a stunning move, LeBow engineered a settlement of tobacco litigation against Liggett, a small, flailing tobacco company which he controlled. As part of the settlement, Liggett made admissions that would be damaging to RJR and agreed to help plaintiffs' lawyers. RJR shareholders went ballistic. Icahn tried to recover by dumping LeBow's name from the slate, but it was too late. The insurgents lost.

Still, for the next ten months, Icahn continued to press RJR. He prepared for a second proxy fight, this time without LeBow, appearing ready to keep up the struggle. However, not one to get emotional over a stock position, Icahn ultimately decided the proxy contest was a losing battle. Because RJR's stock price was up from his average cost per share, he sold his stake in a block trade for $730 million, netting a reported $130 million gain and an annualized return in the 40 percent range.

But in late 1998, Icahn returned, accumulating a 5 percent stake by December 1998, which he raised to 8 percent in February 1999. Again, he sought to split the food business from the tobacco business. In March 1999, RJR Nabisco reacted, announcing a plan to split off its U.S. cigarette business and sell its international tobacco business to Japan Tobacco.

A proxy fight can also be used to clear the way for a tender offer. Many modern takeover defenses—such as the poison pill or application of a state antitakeover law—can only be removed through a shareholder vote or by the corporate board. Alternatively, the proxy fight might attack new defenses proposed by management.

IBM used a proxy contest when going after Lotus in 1995. The deal was groundbreaking—the first ever hostile bid from blue-chip IBM and the first hostile deal in the software industry. IBM's team—led by Chairman Louis Gerstner—saw Lotus as a critical piece in its shift toward a higher profile in the software business. Numerous friendly overtures were made, but Lotus CEO James Manzi refused to negotiate. Gerstner worried Manzi would find another partner. Taking a calculated risk, IBM chose the hostile route.

This approach was fraught with peril. In software, as in advertising, people are the chief asset, and an acrimonious takeover fight might drive them to the exits. Gerstner hoped to minimize the risks with a swift knockout punch: IBM bid a full $3.3 billion price to discourage a bidding war. IBM's public relations team fanned out in the market to explain the strong strategic fit between the two businesses and Lotus employees were lobbied to back the deal, including over the Internet.

Finally, capitalizing on a major hole in Lotus's defenses, IBM launched an accelerated proxy fight. Because the Lotus certificate of incorporation allowed an insurgent to solicit consents directly from shareholders rather than wait for a vote at the annual meeting, IBM filed documents with the SEC to conduct a campaign to replace the Lotus board. Within sixty days, its candidates could be in place.

Seven days after the IBM offer, Lotus crumbled under the pressure. A deal was negotiated and Lotus became part of Big Blue.

Fundamentally, a proxy fight is defined by an issue and a meeting date. The issue is control of corporate policy. A meeting date nominally determines when shareholders will gather to vote on the various proposals. However, rather than attend the meeting in person, many shareholders vote in absentia, granting a right, or proxy, to someone else, who then votes the shares. A shareholder generally will give its proxy either to management or the insurgent, depending on which side the shareholder favors.

Soliciting proxies amounts to an election campaign governed by SEC rules. Lately, institutions have become much more sophisticated and proprietary about these contests which they often decide. The sight of corporate executives deferring to them seems increasingly to be a process they enjoy. Furthermore, the efforts of institutional investors have been aided by the SEC's revision of the proxy rules, which now allow investors to confer without having to file a proxy statement.

In this new environment, even the threat of a proxy campaign can expedite the solution to a dispute over corporate policy. Kerkorian's battle with Chrysler—now merged with the German Daimler—is a case in point. A classic contrarian, Kerkorian began building a large Chrysler stake in 1990 as the company slumped along with the auto industry. By 1994, Chrysler was on the rebound, and Kerkorian controlled nearly 10 percent of the company's shares. Kerkorian—who bought in at $12 and $18 a share—was sitting on a significant paper gain. But, shortly thereafter, the stock again skidded and Kerkorian grew disenchanted. He even made an offer to buy the company in a friendly deal which was promptly rejected.

After his deal fell through, Kerkorian hired both Jerome York— formerly the CFO of Chrysler and then CFO at IBM—to lead the next charge and Wasserstein Perella to help present his views. Kerkorian's main problem with Chrysler was its growing cash hoard—nearing $7 billion. As an active investor, Kerkorian wanted change.

Specifically, Kerkorian wanted Chrysler Chairman Robert Eaton to pay a chunk of the company's cash out to shareholders. Kerkorian also hoped to purchase a larger Chrysler stake but was blocked by a poison pill. Eaton countered that Chrysler needed its cash to ride out the next recession.

Jerry York turned up the pressure, encouraging Chrysler management to raise its dividend and increase its stock buyback program. York also wanted a number of defensive measures removed: In particular, he wanted the threshold on Chrysler's poison pill raised to 20 percent so Kerkorian could safely buy more stock.

Eaton and the Chrysler board remained adamant for a time, but York indicated a proxy fight was in the works, hoping to shake things loose. Kerkorian bought more shares through a tender offer to add muscle to his threats. The strategy worked. Eaton eventually came to the table with a favorable proposal which gave Kerkorian a representative on the Chrysler board. Chrysler also agreed to double its 1996 share repurchase program to $2 billion and buy back another $1 billion of stock in 1997. In exchange, Kerkorian agreed not to raise his Chrysler stake for five years.

Curiously, Chrysler appears to have embraced Kerkorian's platform even more so than required by the settlement agreement. The company continued to increase its dividend and voluntarily doubled its 1997 share repurchase to $2 billion, thus endorsing York's original position that the company could afford $2 billion in annual buybacks.

Kerkorian, who until the merger with Daimler was the largest holder of Chrysler stock, had a paper gain of more than $3 billion on his investment.

The Tender Offer

The tender offer is the most direct weapon in the takeover arsenal. Rather than confront the corporate board directly, the battle is waged on shareholders' turf: Shareholders are given the option to hold on to their shares or sell to the bidder. A premium offer provides a powerful inducement to act.

In the early 1980s, the tender offer was virtually unstoppable. Selling out to a white knight bidder was one of the few defenses to a fully funded tender. Yet there is a dynamic to the development of takeover tactics: New weapons eventually spark new defenses. And indeed, with the rise of the poison pill, the force of the tender offer attack was blunted. Shareholders today rarely can be pushed into a rapid response to a tender.

Still, the tender offer remains an important tool, and strategies for implementing the tender offer have evolved to meet the new realities. When combined with a proxy contest, a premium tender offer can splinter a company's defenses, as in the IBM takeover of

Lotus. Even without an imminent proxy contest, the premium offer pressures a board to act.

A tender also can be a powerful way to bust up an existing friendly deal, evidenced by Paramount's plan in attacking the Time-Warner merger and QVC's plan in bidding for Paramount. Once a sale of control is initiated and the *Revlon* duties triggered, a board can no longer rely on the pill to fend off a tender offer.

Consequently, when a bidding war erupts, as in the battle for Paramount, shareholders are often presented with dueling tender offers. In that contest, each party laid out the terms of the various offers in long and complicated tender documents. And with each revision to the offer, an amended document was released to shareholders. At the same time, QVC and Viacom lobbied shareholders in full-page advertisements featuring pithy headlines and bulleted key points.

Tender offers need not be unfriendly, however. A firm can tender for its own shares. Furthermore, a friendly deal might be structured as a tender offer for timing, tax, accounting, or other reasons.

The Dynamics of a Tender Offer

Offers can be for cash, or for another security—in which case they are referred to as exchange offers. The common denominator is that both cash tender offers and exchange offers are made directly to all public security holders of a company. By contrast, a merger is, in effect, carried out between the corporations themselves.

Federal securities law imposes a number of reporting, disclosure, and antifraud obligations on a bidder who launches a tender offer. A bidder may not, for example, purchase any shares in a target company once a tender offer has commenced other than through the mechanism of the tender.

The Securities and Exchange Commission takes the position that the term "tender offer" covers more than the formal solicitation of offers through public announcements or mailings directed at shareholders. According to this view, privately negotiated and even open-market purchases may, under certain circumstances, constitute tender offers.

THE SEC TEST

As guidance regarding what constitutes a tender, the SEC has suggested an eight-factor test, which also has been cited with approval by several courts. The factors are:

- Active and widespread solicitation of public shareholders;

- Solicitation for a substantial percentage of the issuer's stock;

- The offer price constitutes a premium to the prevailing market price;

- The terms of the offer are firm rather than negotiated;

- The offer is contingent on the tender of a fixed number of shares;

- The offer is open for a limited time;

- Stockholders are pressured to sell stock; and

- Public announcement of a plan to purchase shares that precedes or accompanies rapid accumulation.

Not surprisingly, the definition of what constitutes a tender offer has generated considerable litigation. Although the SEC has taken the contrary position, no court has held that open-market purchases by themselves constitute a tender offer. To the contrary, a court has held that a series of open-market purchases did not qualify as a tender offer where the total shares purchased were less than 5 percent of the outstanding shares. Another court held that an attempt to gain voting control through a series of open-market purchases did not constitute a tender offer. Even street sweeps—large block purchases of an issuer's stock on the open market over a short period of time— have been found not to be tender offers by several courts. Hanson Trust PLC made dramatic use of the mechanism in its 1985 attempt to take over SCM Corporation.

When SCM announced a defensive restructuring, Hanson withdrew its tender offer and bought 25 percent of SCM's outstanding shares on the open market, which, together with Hanson's existing holding, allowed Hanson to block SCM's restructuring. Because SCM's stock was largely in the hands of arbitrageurs, Hanson accomplished this coup with just six purchases.

After reviewing the purchases, a federal appeals court ruled that Hanson's maneuver did not constitute a tender offer. Factors cited by the court included the fact that the purchases took place at the market price and did not involve pressure or secrecy. Of course, today, the ability to carry out a street sweep is limited by antitrust laws unless a bidder has already received antitrust clearance.

However, courts have ruled that open-market purchases combined with privately negotiated transactions can constitute a tender offer. These cases generally seem to hinge on whether the "pressure-creating characteristics of a tender offer" are present. Pressure is created, for example, where a public announcement precedes a rapid series of purchases. On the other hand, where no such announcement was made and the purchases occurred more slowly, a court ruled no tender offer had occurred.

Courts are generally divided with regard to whether privately negotiated transactions alone can be tender offers. Some privately negotiated transactions will qualify as tender offers, but most will not, with the test apparently one of intent: "Any privately negotiated purchase that interferes with a shareholder's 'unhurried investment decision' and 'fair treatment of . . . investors' defeats the protections of the Williams Act (described in the next section) and is, most likely, a tender offer."

For example, in *Wellman v. Dickinson,* a bold sneak attack was planned by Sun on Becton-Dickinson, a massive distributor of medical supplies. A subsidiary of Sun made secret offers to twenty-eight of the target company's largest shareholders, who together held 35 percent of the target's stock. The parent company's identity was not disclosed. Each shareholder was given a short period of time to consider the offer—ranging from one half hour to overnight.

On these facts, a court held that a tender offer had taken place, citing the eight-factor test. Even though the approach may have been conceived of masterfully as a legal matter, the actual performance of some of the overly enthusiastic solicitors fouled up the deal. Moreover, the fact the subsidiary was called LHIW, for "Let's hope it works," couldn't have thrilled the court.

Obviously, the subject of what constitutes a tender offer is a legal tightrope, since superb execution by the numbers is difficult to achieve in an open-market purchase.

The Tender Offer Rules

In reaction to the rising tide of takeovers in the 1960s, Congress adopted the Williams Act in 1968. The act, named after Senator Harrison Williams, was later amended to expand its coverage and has been implemented in SEC rules that govern the structuring of a tender offer.

Section 13(d)—the basic protection against silent accumulation of a target's shares by an acquirer—requires beneficial owners of securities (stockholders who have control over the voting rights of securities) to report their ownership once they have crossed the 5 percent threshold. But an investor is not restricted from making further purchases during the ten-day lag period between crossing the 5 percent threshold and the filing date. As a result, investors can, in theory, accumulate considerably more than 5 percent of a company's securities by the date of the 13D filing, when the beneficial owner's current ownership must be revealed.

In addition to the percentage of stock owned, the Schedule 13D also discloses the purchaser's background, the manner in which the securities were acquired, and the purchaser's future plans with respect to the target. This last point is key: A 13D filer must state whether it intends to seek control of the relevant company. If the filer subsequently increases its ownership by more than 2 percent or if there are other material changes in the information disclosed, an amendment is required. For example, a purchaser who originally disclosed a passive investment strategy must disclose a change to a more active strategy.

These requirements cannot be avoided by dividing an investment among affiliates or by acting with a group of ostensibly separate purchasers. The disclosure rules of the 1934 act are broadly worded and interpreted so that the holdings of a group of related purchasers will be aggregated.

Passive investors owning between 5 and 20 percent of a public company's shares are permitted to use the short-form Schedule 13G rather than the longer Schedule 13D. Investors who change their investment strategies from passive to active or acquire more than 20 percent of a company's shares must file a 13D within ten days, though. In addition, such investors become subject to a "cooling off" period in which they are prohibited from acquiring additional shares or voting their shares beginning on the date of change in investment purpose or acquisition of 20 percent of securities until ten days after the 13D is filed. The investor can once again file a 13G if its ownership falls below 20 percent as long as he remains a passive investor.

In summary, rule 13(d) forces potential acquirers to reveal their plans earlier than they might like, but gives shareholders information material to their decision to hold or sell.

Section 14(d) covers tender offers and provides the same sort of protection with respect to cash offers that the stock registration process provides in exchange offers. Specifically, the act mandates that any person making a tender offer that will result in the offeror owning more than 5 percent of any class of equity security must file a Schedule 14D-1 and all solicitation material with the SEC. If a position of over 5 percent has been accumulated in the last ten days and a tender offer is being announced, a combined Schedule 13D and 14D-1 is usually filed.

Having required these disclosures, the law attempts to assure their accuracy. Section 14(e) is an antifraud provision which specifically provides that the disclosures required under 14(d) may not contain an untrue statement of a material fact or omit to state a material fact. In addition, Rule 10b-5, the general antifraud provision of federal securities law, is also applicable.

The 1998 Aircraft Carrier release from the SEC proposes several notable changes to the tender offer rules. Under current rules, other than with a self-tender, a bidder who publicly announces a cash tender offer triggers the obligation to file a tender offer statement within five days of the original announcement. Under the new proposal, a bidder would not be required to file a tender or exchange offer statement until the bidder first disseminates instructions to security holders on how to tender into an offer, marking the "commencement" of an offer. Communications could be made prior to this commencement, relying on a new "safe harbor" provision, so long as the communication advises security holders to read the tender offer material when it becomes available. A new Rule 14e-8 would clarify that announcing a tender or exchange offer without the intent or ability to follow through would be fraudulent and therefore prohibited.

The Aircraft Carrier also proposes to put cash and exchange offers on more equal footing. Currently, exchange offers cannot commence (i.e., the required twenty-business-day offer period cannot commence) until the registration statement has been declared effective after what is often a lengthy SEC review period. By contrast, cash tender offers commence immediately upon filing the tender offer statement: No SEC review is necessary for the twenty-day offer period to commence. Therefore, the SEC proposes to allow exchange offers to commence upon the filing of the registration statement (or a later date, if desired by the bidder).

The release also proposes a mandatory "subsequent offer period" after the initial offer. During this period, all security holders who did not tender into the initial offer would be permitted to tender, allowing security holders the right to change their minds after the results of the tender offer are announced. This change would prevent these nontendering shareholders from being forced into a back-end merger or from having to sell their shares into what would be an illiquid market.

Finally, the schedules required to be filed would be changed. Schedules 13E-4 and 14D-1, used for issuer and third-party tender offers respectively, would be combined into a new Schedule TO. This new schedule would therefore be used for both tender offer and going-private disclosures. To facilitate comprehension of the schedules by investors, the SEC also proposes that a "plain English" summary of the proposed transaction be provided. The forms S-4 and F-4, currently used for business combinations, would be replaced with a new Form C, which would require substantially all the same disclosures.

After comments on the release are approved by the SEC, the release is expected to be effective sometime in 2000.

A series of statutory sections and regulations limit the actions of the offeror during the tender. Among the most important of these provisions are the following:

Directors   If, pursuant to any arrangement or understanding, a majority of the directors of the target company are to be elected or designated other than at a shareholder meeting, the rules require a full-fledged proxy statement to be sent to shareholders at least ten days before such persons can take office. The objective is to provide to the public full disclosure about such backdoor arrangements.

Other Purchases   Once an offer is announced, a purchaser may not buy any security subject to the offer except pursuant to its terms. This rule is intended to prevent preferential deals once the tender is under way. Accordingly, if an acquirer desires to pick up large private blocks outside the terms of the offer, it must do so before or after the tender, but not during.

Terms of Offers   The rules contain a number of technical provisions to protect the public from unfair or coercive offers. A bidder must allow shareholders to withdraw tender shares so long as the offer remains open, and offers must be kept open a minimum of twenty days. Another rule provides that if more securities are tendered than are offered for, each tendering shareholder will be allowed to tender the same percentage of his shares. And any increase in the price during a tender must also be paid to shareholders who have already tendered.

Finally, in response to the *Unocal* case, in which T. Boone Pickens was defeated by Unocal's discriminatory self-tender, the SEC recently enacted the "all holders" rule, which forbids discriminatory tender offers by either an issuer or third party.

THE SCHEDULE 14D-1

The Schedule 14D-1 is the principal tender offer regulatory document. Reflecting its role as an information source for shareholders, the 14D-1 contains background information on the issuer and key business highlights. In general, the following must be disclosed:

1. Any transactions (including contracts) between the bidder and the target.

2. Any contacts, negotiations, or transactions in the past three years between the bidder and the target concerning a deal.

3. The source and amounts of the funds being used for the offer.

4. The purpose of the offer, including any plans to acquire control, liquidate, sell the assets of or merge the target, or to make other major changes in the business or corporate structure of the target, including any changes in dividend policy, capitalization, directors, or listing of securities.

5. Any target company shares owned by the officers and directors of the offeror and their associates and any trading done within the past sixty days.

6. A description of contracts or understandings with any person regarding the securities.

7. All persons retained to make solicitations for the securities and the terms of their employment.

8. Any other material relationships between the bidder and the target and a description of any regulatory requirements, the applicability of the margin, and legal issues.

The Offer to Purchase

The actual offer to holders of the target's securities is not made through the 14D-1, but rather through an Offer to Purchase, which is mailed directly to the record holders and incorporates the important information in the 14D-1. Traditionally, a summary advertisement has also been published in national newspapers.

The first part of the Offer to Purchase usually states the terms of the offer, including the price, and if applicable, the minimum shares required, the maximum commitment, the withdrawal dates, the date through which the proration obligation applies, and the mechanics for tendering. Care is taken in this section to state explicitly whether the offer may be extended or amended.

General information is then provided about the offeror and the target. In most instances, the information about the target is quite straightforward, usually a brief capsule of financial information, a summary description of the business from the annual report, and sometimes a quote from incumbent management about the company's prospects.

If the offeror, however, has any nonpublicly available information from the target such as projections, such material, even including projections, must be disclosed to avoid liability for the failure to state a material fact—although a disclaimer is usually put in stating that the offeror cannot attest to the information's accuracy. This is one of the most interesting sections of the Offer to Purchase.

Among the most difficult sections to write in the Offer to Purchase are those dealing with the purpose of the offer and the future plans of the offeror. The instinct of most offerors is to be as vague as possible; but federal securities law specifically requires a detailed statement about these items and mandates that they be included in the Offer to Purchase. Unlike the rather cursory general financial disclosures, courts have been insistent that the description of future intent be specific, particularly in the case of offers for less than all the shares. The theory behind this requirement is that security holders have a right to know the offeror's intent with respect to untendered shares and what will happen to the company if they remain shareholders. Even in a limited offering, there will necessarily be a continuing relationship between the stockholders who do not sell and the offeror, which requires full disclosure.

The most pertinent question regarding future intent is whether the acquirer desires control and whether, if the acquirer became a controlling shareholder, it would effect a merger. In one case, *Mis-*

souri Portland Cement, the U.S. Supreme Court ruled that an offeror for 50 percent of the outstanding stock should have explicitly stated that the purpose of the offer was control. Similarly, if the primary purpose of the offer is to frustrate a takeover by another party in a defensive alliance, full disclosure must be made.

Perhaps the most difficult disclosure situation occurs when the offeror's management has studied a series of alternative possibilities but has not made any definitive commitment. In the *Otis* case, the court held that a plan should be disclosed if there were evidence of its adoption, explicit or implicit, by high corporate officers. Specifically, in that case, a study was presented to the board of directors regarding a tender offer followed by a merger. The board explicitly approved the tender but did not act on the merger. Nevertheless, the court held that the merger possibility should have been described. On the other hand, more recently courts have recognized that the purposes point has become a key target for dilatory litigation by target companies and consequently have discounted the protestations of incumbent management accordingly.

Arrangements or understandings regarding the company's securities are often very simple to describe: Usually, there are none. Sometimes, however, large holders will hold options or there will be in place voting-trust agreements. These, of course, must be fully described.

Finally, if there are any regulatory hurdles to implementation of a contemplated deal or other required governmental approvals (including those of foreign governments), they also must be described. The antitrust status of the transaction should also be indicated and the following questions answered: Was clearance sought; were any antitrust difficulties expected; was there notification of government antitrust authorities? The implications of the offer, if any, on the listing status of the target company's stock on the exchange on which the stock is traded should be described.

State Regulation

State legislation is playing an increasingly important role in the tender offer field. Under pressure from local businesses, state officials have reacted to the large number of tenders by passing laws which, in effect, act to delay hostile tenders but which, by their terms, are inapplicable to offers recommended by the target's management. State antitakeover laws generally apply to companies which are either incorporated in the state in question or which conduct a substantial part of their business in the state and generally include one or more of the following provisions: a fair price rule, a merger moratorium, a control share rule, and a cash-out rule.

A fair price rule curbs unfriendly coercive two-tier bids by forbidding a back-end, squeeze-out merger between a bidder and a target unless the consideration paid is the same as that paid to acquire securities on the front end. A merger moratorium similarly blocks a bidder from merging with a target for a period of time after initial stock purchases absent approval from a supermajority of stockholders or the target board of directors.

Control share rules require shareholder approval before a bidder can acquire more than a specified percentage of target company stock. Depending on the state, the rules either simply forbid further acquisitions or strip any shares acquired of voting rights.

Like the fair-price rule, a cash-out rule is targeted at two-tier tender offers and gives shareholders a right to sell their shares to a bidder at the same price and on the same terms as the acquirer's initial purchases. The rule is triggered when an acquirer buys a certain percentage of target company stock.

Two states provide interesting examples for antitakeover status: Delaware and Pennsylvania. The Delaware statute is particularly important given the high concentration of major companies incorporated in that state—roughly half of all NYSE-listed firms.

Under the Delaware procedure, a hostile bidder who buys 15 percent of a company's outstanding voting stock may not complete a business combination with the company for three years after the bidder acquires the 15 percent interest, a rule that effectively bars the back-end merger. Three exceptions apply, however. First, a combination can take place if the board approves the transaction prior to the bidder's crossing the 15 percent threshold. Second, there is no limitation if the bidder acquires 85 percent or more of the company's voting stock in the front-end deal. Third, a business combination can go forward if approved by the company's board and a two-thirds majority of its shareholders (excluding stock held by the bidder). A company can, however, choose to opt out of any of these provisions through board action by amending its bylaws within ninety days of the effective date or at any time through a charter or bylaw amendment supported by a majority of the outstanding shares. The shareholder action will not be effective for twelve months and shall not apply to any person holding 15 percent of shares at the time of the vote.

The Pennsylvania law is generally considered the toughest state antitakeover law in the country. The statute limits the voting rights of a bidder who acquires 20 percent or more of a covered corporation's voting securities. Pennsylvania also has a business-combination rule and a cash-out rule. In addition, a board of directors is expressly allowed to consider constituencies other than shareholders in deciding whether to accept a takeover bid.

Most important, though, Pennsylvania has adopted a so-called disgorgement approach in which a "controlling person or group" may be forced to return certain short-term profits to the target company—in particular, profits on shares sold within eighteen months of the date on which the 20 percent threshold was crossed. A controlling person or group is defined to include a single investor or group of investors acting in concert who hold at least 20 percent of the company's vote as well as anyone who discloses the intent to acquire control of a corporation by any means. Under the law, the target company, and in certain cases shareholders, have standing to sue a controlling person or group.

States other than Pennsylvania and Delaware have similar anti-takeover laws. Because each state law has its own variations and complications, and it can be argued that a corporation does a substantial portion of its business in any one of a number of jurisdictions, hostile bidders have learned to spend considerable energy studying the applicable statutes before launching a takeover attempt.

THE U.K. TENDER OFFER RULES

The notion of a hostile takeover is not uniquely American, but the rules vary in other countries. In the United Kingdom, for example, the mechanics and procedures of a takeover offer are primarily determined by the nonstatutory Takeover Code. The code is enforced and administered by the Takeover Panel, a nongovernmental organization whose members are drawn from various sectors of the U.K. takeover community, and aims to ensure that all shareholders, particularly minority shareholders, are treated equally in the takeover context. While the code does not have the force of law, it is considered binding by most market participants.

A number of rules regarding the purchase of stock are incorporated in the code, which explicitly contemplates open-market purchase programs. Important provisions include the following:

- If a bidder has purchased 10 percent or more of the target company's stock in the twelve months before the offer, the offer must be for cash or have a cash alternative at the highest price paid in that period;

- If a bidder purchases 30 percent or more of a target company, then a bid must be announced immediately which is conditional only on obtaining 50 percent of the votes and approval by antitrust authorities;

- In general, no more than 10 percent of a company's share can be purchased in any seven-day period if the purchase, when aggregated with the purchaser's other holdings, will carry 15 percent or more, but less than 30 percent, of the voting rights of the company; this condition will be waived if the acquisition is in connection with an announced tender offer;

- Once an acquirer crosses the 3 percent ownership threshold, purchases have to be disclosed to the market within forty-eight hours (or sooner under certain circumstances); and

- Defense techniques are limited.

The tactics in hostile takeovers of British companies are determined both by these and other rules of the code and by its non-statutory nature. British courts recognize the role of the Takeover Panel as arbiter and are seldom asked to interfere in the bid process. Rather, U.K. takeover bids are fought on the basis of economics, and skillful exploitation of the opportunities for purchasing shares in the open market often is determinative. For example, in Wal-Mart's $10.9 billion deal for British supermarket retailer Asda in 1999, in which we advised Wal-Mart, one key feature of the tactics of the deal was the purchase of 15 percent of the Asda stock within twenty-four hours of announcing the bid.

Crafting the Offer

A tender or exchange offer—whether friendly or hostile—is a fast-paced, complex, and highly charged situation. The consequences of a mistake in judgment can be much greater than merely the failure of an offer, for liability for damages and expenses in suits can be staggering. With a top-quality team in place, a bidder can turn to the terms of the offer.

Stock Deals   Two kinds of market risk arise in a stock deal—pre-closing risk and post-closing risk. Pre-closing risk derives from the fact that a selling shareholder often must decide whether to tender its shares a considerable time before payment will be received. During the period between the tender or signing of the merger agreement and the actual closing of the transaction, the promised securities may decline in value, leaving the selling shareholder with a lower return than expected.

This issue of pre-closing risk is illustrated in the proposed British Telecommunications–MCI merger. Like most major deals, the BT-MCI pairing had to progress through a long regulatory process before it could close, a delay further compounded by the fact that it was a cross-border deal. By July 1997, the approvals were in process and the deal almost done. Surprising news from MCI, however, then blew apart the original transaction.

When MCI announced that losses from its efforts to enter local phone markets could reach $800 million for the year—double prior estimates—both the BT and MCI stock prices were hit hard. BT shareholders began to question the wisdom of joining their fate to MCI. They pressured the company to renegotiate terms, but MCI had a favorable contract which specifically excluded local phone losses from status as a "material adverse change." Though this language arguably gave MCI a strong negotiating position, BT shareholders ultimately were able to push part of the pre-closing risk onto MCI shareholders and the deal was renegotiated at a $3 billion lower price. Of course, the BT shareholders ultimately paid a price for the revision when World-Com snatched MCI for itself with a $37 billion offer.

Post-closing risk derives from the fact that the securities received may underperform the market and may not prove as valuable as originally expected. This risk is particularly troublesome where the selling shareholder must commit in advance to hold its shares for an extended period of time to receive favorable tax treatment.

Reflecting the reality of pre-closing and post-closing risks, buyers have come up with several approaches to minimize these concerns for sellers. The idea, of course, is to smooth the acquisition process.

Pricing Formulas and Pre-Closing Risk   In a contested bid, an acquirer has a strong incentive to reduce pre-closing risk; but a selling company also may demand such protection in a friendly deal. When the acquirer is offering securities, it sometimes puts a "safety net" underneath its bid: Although the variations are numerous, the primary mechanisms include the floating exchange ratio, the collar, the fixed exchange ratio within a price collar, and the walk-away.

The floating exchange ratio—in contrast to the fixed exchange ratio—attempts to address the value risk faced by the target. With a fixed exchange ratio, the number of acquirer shares to be exchanged for each target share is set at the time the offer is made or the definitive agreement is signed. The arrangement allows an acquirer to know with absolute certainty how many shares it will need to issue in a deal and thus the deal's pro forma impact on earnings per share: The mechanism eliminates the EPS dilution and ownership risk for the acquirer. From the perspective of selling shareholders, however, a fixed exchange ratio presents significant pre-closing risk: Any decline in the value of the acquirer's stock will translate into less value received by the seller. For these reasons, acquirers tend to favor and sellers may dislike fixed exchange ratios.

In contrast, the floating ratio shifts this pre-closing risk from the seller to the buyer by providing a set value to the seller. The exchange ratio is allowed to "float" to whatever number will guarantee the seller the agreed-upon value at closing. Calculations of the exact exchange ratio often are based on an average market price prior to the deal announcement. The acquirer takes the risk that its stock price will decline between the time deal terms are set and deal closing, which would require the issuance of more shares, but could also benefit from any appreciation in the value of its stock.

A floating ratio exposes an acquirer to the possibility of unanticipated EPS dilution—the more shares it has to issue, the lower EPS will be. This situation is usually unpalatable for an acquirer, particularly since a stock price decline may be temporary and may reflect broad market factors not specific to the acquirer. Not surprisingly, acquirers tend to resist floating exchange ratios.

An acquirer can limit the risk posed by a floating ratio by capping the maximum number of shares to be issued. As a trade-off, acquirers often agree to issue a minimum number of shares as well. This arrangement—an upper and lower limit on the number of shares to be exchanged—is known as a collar.

Alternatively, the standard fixed exchange ratio can also be combined with a price collar. This formulation provides a fixed exchange ratio so long as the acquirer's stock trades within a given price range. For example, if the acquirer's stock is trading at $50 when an agreement is signed, the parties might agree to a one-to-one exchange if the stock remains within a 10 percent band (that is, between $45 and $55 per share). But if the stock moves above or below the outer limits on the price collar, the exchange ratio is allowed to float so that the seller receives stock with a value equal to the nearest end point on the price collar.

Typically, the floor and ceiling are within a specified symmetrical range—usually 10 percent or 12 percent. However, the width of the band is usually subject to much negotiation.

A double-trigger collar protects the acquirer from being penalized by volatility in the broader market. In a fixed exchange ratio deal, such a collar might state that a target has the right to adjust the ratio only if two conditions have been satisfied: 1) the average trading value of the acquirer's stock drops a certain amount; and 2) the drop was some given factor greater than the drop in the broader market.

In the merger between XL Capital and NAC Re, a deal on which we worked, such a provision was utilized. In the event that both the average trading price for the ten days prior to closing were 15 percent less than the price on the first trading date after issuance of the press release describing the deal and the NYSE composite index fell by less than 15 percent over the same period, the acquirer could choose to adjust the exchange ratio in a fashion specified in the merger agreement. If the acquirer chose not to do this, the target could terminate the agreement.

A walk-away reduces pre-closing risk in a negotiated transaction, and allows either party to cancel a deal under certain circumstances. For example, a seller might negotiate for the right to walk away from a deal with a fixed exchange ratio if the acquirer's stock price declines below a certain level. Or, an acquirer might seek the ability to walk away from a floating exchange ratio if its stock price declines too much. While reducing pre-closing risks for an acquirer, a walk-away adds uncertainty as to the deal happening.

MARKET DYNAMICS AND THE COLLAR

In a fixed exchange ratio deal, some form of a collar is very compelling from a seller's point of view because the value of an acquirer's stock may decline during the pendency of a deal. Should this happen, investors may become concerned about the value they will receive and thus vote against the deal. But in a floating ratio deal, there might be concern that earnings will be diluted in the short term, or simply the technical concern that too many shares being issued will cause an overhang on the market.

Indeed, this was the dynamic in the Paramount battle. As the bidding climbed toward $10 billion, investors in the market began to discount the stock of whichever bidder was perceived as more likely to win. The effect was pronounced after Sumner Redstone announced the Blockbuster deal, when it became increasingly apparent that Viacom would be victorious. Between January 10 and February 15, 1994, when Viacom finally won, QVC's stock price climbed from $39.25 to $50.25, an almost 30 percent increase. Over the same period, Viacom's class B stock declined over 20 percent, from $38.25 to $28.00.

Without a collar, under a floating exchange ratio, a bidder is forced to issue more shares as its stock price declines. Unfortunately, this can be a self-perpetuating phenomenon. If investors in the acquirer know that additional shares will be issued, diluting EPS, they will further discount the acquirer's stock price, causing even more shares to be issued. From the perspective of a tendering shareholder, this feature makes it extremely difficult to judge the relative values of competing offers.

Conversely, if under a fixed exchange ratio arrangement the acquirer's share price rises dramatically between the deal signing and closing, the seller will receive more value than expected. The economics of the deal are unaffected from the perspective of the buyer. Gillette's stock purchase of Duracell is one example of this situation. The deal—struck at a fixed exchange ratio of 0.904 Gillette shares for each Duracell share—was a hit on Wall Street. Gillette's shares appreciated from $65.13 on the day before the deal was announced to $77.75 on the day of closing, making the deal even more beneficial for Duracell.

Derivative Securities and Post-Closing Risk   Tactical pressures also sometimes press an acquirer to minimize post-closing risk through arrangements most commonly called "contingent value rights" (CVRs). For instance, a version of the CVR was the "Diller killer" of the Paramount fight.

A CVR is designed to provide the selling shareholders assurance that the acquirer shares they will receive will be worth at least some specified amount. However, unlike the fixed-value exchange, the assurance is keyed off post-closing share prices. If the acquirer's stock trades below a set price for a defined period of time, the selling shareholders will receive some additional compensation in the form of cash, stock, or securities, often at the acquirer's option. The acquirer also may have the right to extend the period of the CVR. Of course, the extension comes with a price—an increase in the protection offered.

In Paramount, each Diller killer CVR represented the right to receive, in cash or securities of Viacom (at the option of Viacom), the amount by which the trailing sixty-day average trading value of Viacom Class B common stock was less than $48 per share. The initial measurement date for the CVR was the first anniversary of the transaction closing, and the CVR had a floor of $36 per share if Viacom chose not to exercise its extension rights. Under the extension rights, Viacom could push the measurement date forward one or two years. For each year of extension, the target price and the floor would be increased.

The advantage of a CVR is that it gives the acquirer's stock time to recover from any decline associated with the announcement of the deal. If the acquirer's stock price increases to a point above the CVR price, the CVR costs virtually nothing. However, if the acquirer's stock does not perform as planned, a CVR effectively requires the acquirer to pay more for the related acquisition. In the Paramount deal, Viacom ended up paying $82 million to retire the CVRs.

Cash Versus Securities   Each form of payment has its tactical advantages in the context of an offer. Cash offers historically have been much more sudden and a more effective surprise attack than exchange offers because the securities involved in exchange offers must be registered with the SEC. The Aircraft Carrier would, however, put tender and exchange offers on equal footing with respect to timing. Furthermore, the value of securities offered is often subject to a debate and even a target for litigation.

Indeed, the decision of whether to offer selling shareholders cash or stock is a crucial tactical one that can determine the success of a bid. Increasingly, unsolicited bidders have been using stock as the acquisition currency for big deals. The success of these over cash offers is dependent on whether the strategic benefits are immediately understood by the selling shareholders.

For example, in the battle between GTE and WorldCom for MCI, GTE calculated that it could offer less than WorldCom because MCI shareholders would prefer the value certainty that its cash offer would provide. GTE, however, underestimated investor faith in WorldCom's strategy; MCI shareholders overwhelmingly chose WorldCom's higher all-stock offer. To them, the deal made compelling strategic sense, and the synergies were both immediately realizable and significant, at 5 percent of the deal value. A similar pattern emerged again in WorldCom's winning stock bid for Sprint over BellSouth's cash offer. Likewise, high-flyer Vodafone's stock rose on news of its merger with AirTouch. The business fit was clear, and Vodafone's willingness to use some cash provided AirTouch shareholders with additional comfort.

When synergies and strategic fit between acquirer and target are not immediately achievable or transparent to outsiders, shareholders have sought the certainty of cash. In the case of British supermarket retailer Asda, which had committed itself to a stock deal with Kingfisher, shareholders bid down Kingfisher's stock price, which allowed us to advise Wal-Mart to enter the fray with an all-cash offer. Wal-Mart proceeded with the largest-ever U.K. cash tender offer and knocked out Kingfisher. Similarly, in the contest between Qwest and Global Crossing for Frontier and U S West, the market's pummeling of both bidders' share prices induced Qwest to add a cash element and a collar mechanism to its offer. Market jitters about strategic benefits of mergers and fear of earnings quality dilution can be fatal to a stock deal.

RECENT DYNAMICS IN CASH VS. STOCK OFFERS

Bidders	Target(s)	Deal Effect on Bidder's Stock Price	Outcome
Bell Atlantic (stock) Vodafone (cash and stock)	AirTouch	Down Up	Vodafone merged with AirTouch
Deutsche Telekom (stock) Olivetti (cash)	Telecom Italia	Down Unchanged	Olivetti received over 50 percent of Telecom Italia shares
GTE (cash) WorldCom (stock)	MCI	Down Up	WorldCom acquired MCI
Global Crossing (stock) Qwest (stock revised to cash/stock)	Frontier, U S West	Down Down	Qwest added cash element to offer; Qwest to buy U S West, Global Crossing to buy Frontier
Kingfisher (stock) Wal-Mart (cash)	Asda	Down Unchanged	Wal-Mart acquired Asda

A part-cash, part-stock transaction also allows an acquirer to satisfy various constituencies. Some selling shareholders may prefer the immediate liquidity provided by an all-cash payment. Other selling shareholders may wish to gain the tax-deferral benefit available in an all-stock exchange. By allowing shareholders to choose between these alternatives, an acquirer may gain support for its offer.

The pricing structure of a part-cash, part-stock deal is even more complex than in a pure-stock deal. An acquirer must determine both the type and value of the exchange ratio to be used and the proportion of cash and stock to be offered in the package. How these two questions are answered can have dramatic effects on the dynamic among selling shareholders.

For example, one possible approach is to offer the option of stock at a fixed exchange ratio per share or a fixed amount of cash per share. Given the fixed exchange ratio, the value of the stock offered by the acquirer will fluctuate: If the acquirer's stock price goes up, selling shareholders will be induced to tender for stock. If the price goes down, the cash portion becomes more attractive. This approach is therefore inappropriate where the acquirer wishes to allow selling stockholders to decide between cash and stock on the basis of their favored tax treatment.

As an alternative, a floating exchange ratio—which will hold the relative value of cash and stock constant—can be paired with a fixed cash price. Selling stockholders are therefore free to choose between cash and stock on the basis of their tax concerns.

An acquirer must also decide how to allocate the cash and stock components of its offer among tendering shareholders. Straight proration—in which each tendering shareholder receives a fixed percentage of cash and stock—is one option. The receipt of cash likely will trigger some capital gains tax for each shareholder. As with the fixed-exchange ratio, this option does not afford selling stockholders the choice between cash and stock on the basis of their favored tax treatment.

Minimum Requirements   Acquirers often dictate a minimum requirement—the lowest number of shares that must be tendered for an offer to become effective. There is a danger, however, associated with setting a minimum requirement.

A minimum that is too high may discourage arbitrage. If the deal announcement causes the target's market price to rise above its pre-offer level but the minimum number of shares are not tendered, the deal will fall apart and the price will once again decline to its old level. Any stock purchased by arbs at post-offer levels will have declined in value and the arbs will have lost money. This high potential for risk discourages arbs' incentive to pick up the float.

However, a low minimum also can be problematic, as the acquirer will not be assured of control over the target. An acquirer rarely wants to be stuck with the securities of a company in which it has less than majority control. For example, a hostile offeror with 15 percent of a target company is in a no-man's-land: There is no control and a rival bidder or insider may obtain a larger block. Further, the market for resale of the acquirer's large—but not majority—block may be illiquid and registration may be required of the securities involved—all in all, not an enviable position. A minimum control level may also be necessary in order to qualify a deal as tax-free, for accounting purposes, or to satisfy loan covenants. Finally, a rival bidder may get 50 percent and merge the 15 percent holder out with unwanted securities.

The latter is what happened to Seagram in its bid for Conoco. Seagram ended up with 32 percent of Conoco's stock, but DuPont was the winning bidder, and forced out Seagram in a back-end merger for stock consideration. Seagram ended up with a 20 percent stake in DuPont and professed to be happy with the deal. In Seagram's case, the minority investment worked out well: The DuPont stake proved quite profitable and eventually provided the capital for the purchase of movie studio MCA in 1995.

Pricing Tactics   The heart of any deal is the pricing. However, within the pricing band to which the bidder limits itself, the issue of how to present the bid to best strategic advantage is perhaps the most difficult aspect of structuring the deal, particularly given the range of possibilities and the dollars involved. Acquisition premiums to the market price in tender offers vary from hardly anything to more than 100 percent. According to *MergerStat*, the average premium has ranged from a high of 50 percent in 1974 to a low of 25 percent in 1968, when the firm started keeping statistics. The average premium paid over the four weeks prior to closing price was 34 percent in 1998. Of course, merger premiums—particularly for marriage transactions—were substantially lower than tender offer premiums.

Pricing strategy depends on the circumstances of the bidder and the nature of the offer. A contested offer with potential rival bidders, for example, is likely to result in a higher premium than an uncontested deal. Pricing is designed not only to placate the tendering stockholder but also to preempt a rival from entering into a bidding contest.

Pricing is complicated by the possibility that a bidder may amend an offer: The first offer is not the final offer. It may seem that one could test a low bid and raise it later, if necessary. However, an unsuccessful low bid will usually attract a competing bidder, creating a risk of "sudden death": a lockup created by another bidder. Therefore, to play the "test the market" game, a bidder needs to be particularly humble and willing to bid against himself when concerned with competitors.

Some tacticians believe in the concept of satiation—that it makes sense to bid a couple of dollars low so that everyone can be a hero when a settlement comes. But lately, preemptively priced deals by large industrial companies have been the vogue, such as IBM's bid for Lotus, for the reasons discussed.

Designing a bid in the tender offer context can also present difficulties. For example, despite all precautions, it is not uncommon—especially in friendly tenders—for the market to anticipate a tender, causing a run-up in stock price. This circumstance may not in fact reflect any conspiracy, but rather a widespread belief that a company is a likely tender target or simply common knowledge that the target has had many visitors from other companies lately. A tactic often used to deal with such a situation is to let the speculation die down by delaying the offer. Another is to tender at a low premium on the theory that the securities are readily available at that level because the assumed premium is already reflected in the price. It is for this reason that keeping a bid secret before announcement is imperative.

Hamish Maxwell

Hamish Maxwell, former chairman of Philip Morris, is a deft tactician with a natural gift for takeover maneuvers. The son of a third-generation tobacco leaf dealer in London, Maxwell came to Philip Morris in 1954 and rose through the ranks on the strength of operating skill. Eventually, he was given responsibility for Philip Morris' international tobacco business, which he shaped into a major growth engine. He became chairman of the company in July 1984.

As chairman, Maxwell proved to be a bold strategic thinker and was the guiding hand behind Philip Morris' diversification into the food business, launched soon after Maxwell took the lead job. First came the acquisition of General Foods in 1985, then the takeover of Kraft in 1988. Throughout these landmark deals, Maxwell was always one step ahead.

The General Foods bid germinated in the spring and summer of 1985. Maxwell had initiated a broad strategic review of Philip Morris and found that the company was quite strong and its tobacco operation was a cash machine with improving margins. The real problem was what to do with the cash generated by the business, other than just repurchase stock. After a thorough review, Maxwell and his board decided to diversify into the food business, and we were hired to assist.

The food business in particular was selected for two primary reasons. First, the industry distributes through the same channels and markets products in about the same way as tobacco, complementing Philip Morris' strength as a marketer of consumer packaged goods. Philip Morris could leverage its experience in consumer goods in a foray into foods. In addition, Maxwell saw stable cash flows and room for improved performance.

The General Foods campaign opened on September 23, 1985, when the Philip Morris board authorized Maxwell to approach his counterpart at General Foods. Maxwell was authorized to bid $115 a share for the stock, which was then trading around $85.

Maxwell understood the subtleties. Institutional investors controlled General Foods' stock and, as a result, the General Foods board would face considerable pressure in the face of a premium bid. Philip Morris' strong balance sheet also put it in a good position to capitalize on the sentiment of arbs and institutional investors with a cash bid. Yet the General Foods board would want to feel it had fought the good fight. Everyone needed a sense of victory for the deal to proceed quickly.

Maxwell opted for a classic bear hug. He called James Ferguson, chairman of General Foods, and offered to do a friendly deal in the $110 to $111 a share range. He told Ferguson to shop the company quickly to the most likely buyers, and Ferguson would see that Philip Morris had the strongest bid. The iron fist also glinted from beneath the velvet glove. Maxwell told Ferguson that Philip Morris was prepared to launch a hostile bid if Ferguson didn't respond positively after shopping.

Ferguson hired investment bankers who scrambled to find a white knight. KKR looked at the business, but didn't see a bid above $110. The board also considered taking on a slug of debt to pay a special dividend, perhaps in conjunction with a defensive acquisition. Ultimately, though, Maxwell cracked the board's resolve to fight. He met with Ferguson and raised the Philip Morris bid to $115, at the same time making it clear a hostile bid would be forthcoming shortly if the parties couldn't come to terms. The board decided the Philip Morris bid was the best thing for shareholders and accepted. Maxwell had a victory.

Philip Morris spent the next three years digesting General Foods and running its businesses. But Maxwell wanted to build further critical mass in the food business.

Therefore, Maxwell launched the Kraft tender offer on October 17, 1988, just weeks before Ross Johnson would move to take RJR Nabisco private. Again, Maxwell understood the need for satiation. KKR and other potential rivals also stood in the wings, making a quick resolution important. Furthermore, Kraft had a poison pill and other takeover defenses in place.

Philip Morris initially bid $90 a share, a 50 percent premium to the recent $60 trading price in an offer designed to be high enough to put pressure on the Kraft board, but low enough to raise if necessary to get a deal done.

Kraft conducted a short defense, developing a recapitalization plan which it valued at $110 a share. The board then told Philip Morris that $110 was the minimum price it would accept. Maxwell opened negotiations and eventually raised to $106. Eleven days after the initial offer, Philip Morris and Kraft agreed to a friendly deal.

Maxwell rounded out Philip Morris' food business in July of 1990 with the $3.8 billion purchase of the Swiss company Jacobs Suchard.

From a tactical standpoint, both the Kraft and General Foods acquisitions were successes. The price paid in the end was exactly what Maxwell expected to pay. He just played his cards well.

The shift into food has also been a substantive success. Philip Morris has performed well under the tutelage of Maxwell and his successors, despite the overhang of litigation risk related to the tobacco business. In fact, adjusting for splits, the price of Philip Morris stock has climbed from around $3 in July 1984 to roughly $35 today, slightly less than 18 percent per year on average.

The Resurgence of Unsolicited Deals   A flurry of recent hostile bidding wars illustrates the resurgence of hostile takeover attempts in the late 1990s. The first involved U.S. companies AlliedSignal,

Tyco, and AMP. The others—unusually—involved European companies, marking the newfound acceptance of unsolicited bids on the
Continent.

First, on August 4, 1998, AlliedSignal, a maker of aerospace and
automotive products, launched a $44.50 per share cash hostile bid
for AMP, the world's largest maker of electrical equipment and con-
nectors. The offer represented an approximate 55 percent premium
to AMP's share price at that time, but nonetheless was spurned by
management, who regarded the offer as a lowball bid. With its ability to tender for AMP limited by AMP's poison pill, which would not
expire until November 1999, AlliedSignal announced that it would
initially purchase a mere 18 percent of AMP's stock. But if it were
not successful in removing AMP's poison pill, AlliedSignal, as a non-
majority shareholder, would not benefit from synergies or strategic
advantage. AlliedSignal's initial offer had the added disadvantage of
requiring AlliedSignal to nearly double its existing debt load. In fact,
were AlliedSignal to buy the entire company as it eventually intended, its debt-to-capital ratio would rise from approximately 21 to
67 percent.

AlliedSignal went to court to have AMP's so-called dead-hand
poison pill—a defense that cannot be removed unless a majority of
directors who implemented the pill vote to revoke it—removed. At
the same time, AlliedSignal waged a proxy fight to install its own
slate of seventeen board members. But AMP too went to court and,
for a time, successfully blocked that action by filing a conflict-of-
interest suit: The AlliedSignal-appointed directors owed a duty to
AMP, but had a conflict of interest due to their association with AlliedSignal. However, after AlliedSignal's director slate formally acknowledged their conflict and their fiduciary duty to AMP, the judge
allowed AlliedSignal to continue with its proxy fight.

By November, AMP had found a white knight—an acquirer that
would be acceptable to management and that would top AlliedSignal's bid. Industrial conglomerate Tyco International offered $51 per

share in stock—$11.3 billion in total—to AMP stockholders. While the Tyco deal clearly provided the higher price for AMP shareholders, the offer had two other added benefits. First, the stock offer would not require AMP shareholders to pay capital gains taxes, in contrast to the AlliedSignal cash offer. Furthermore, Tyco is domiciled in Bermuda and will be able to reduce AMP's tax rate by as much as 5 percent. The AMP-Tyco deal illustrates the advantage a company has with a high-multiple stock.

In June 1999, AlliedSignal bounced back with a $13.8 billion deal with aerospace equipment maker Honeywell. The creation of this new company, to take the name Honeywell, was cheered by analysts. The question of CEO succession at AlliedSignal would be settled with Honeywell CEO Michael R. Bonsignore to become CEO of the new Honeywell. The company would become the leader in aerospace electronics.

The other takeover battles are being waged on the European continent. In March 1999, Olivetti—formerly a typewriter and computer manufacturer, now a telecom company—made a $50 million unsolicited bid for Telecom Italia. The psychology of the 1980s in the United States had come to Europe: Telecom Italia was an undervalued asset, and Olivetti saw an opportunity to snatch it away from incapable management and a new, unproven CEO, relying on shareholders' desire to increase their wealth. Before these battles of 1999, hostile bids were virtually unheard of in the clubby world of the European business elite. But now the gloves have come off. Significantly, the scope of this bid put the takeover into the ranks of the largest deals ever.

Telecom Italia defended vigorously against the Olivetti bid. Olivetti had expressed the intent to integrate the operations of Telecom Italia Mobile—60 percent owned by Telecom Italia. Telecom Italia offered to buy the 40 percent of TIM that it didn't already own. By using debt to effect the purchase, Telecom Italia would be highly levering itself, making it a far less attractive target for Olivetti, who also planned to use $24.5 billion of debt to fund its bid. Telecom Italia would likely not be able to support the debt burden from both the TIM buyback and the Olivetti takeover. Indeed, this bid seems to have taken a lesson from the LBOs of the 1980s. Second, Telecom Italia motioned to convert its nonvoting savings shares into common shares.

Olivetti shot back with a 15 percent increase in bid. However, Olivetti specified that it would drop its bid if Telecom Italia's plan to convert nonvoting savings shares, which Olivetti had not tendered for, into common shares was approved. Telecom Italia shareholders voted down the company's takeover defenses, however. Then in April 1999, Telecom Italia agreed to merge with white knight Deutsche Telekom. But Telecom Italia's shareholders discounted the likelihood of a deal closing with Deutsche Telekom due to regulatory and other hurdles and tendered over 50 percent of their shares to Olivetti.

A second hostile battle has been taking place in the once-staid French banking sector. On February 1, 1999, banks Société Générale and Paribas announced their plans to merge in a $17 billion deal. But soon after, Banque Nationale de Paris entered the fray, making a $37 billion hostile bid for both Société Générale and Paribas in a move to consolidate significantly the French banking sector. Société Générale and Paribas issued an initial rejection of the BNP bid, and refused to talk to BNP. The government encouraged all three parties to talk, but the talks quickly collapsed. The final tally of the simultaneous tender offers gave BNP control of Paribas but not SocGen. The regulators have asked BNP to dispose of the SocGen shares tendered to it. SocGen will have to find a new partner.

A third European hostile deal revolves around luxury goods maker Gucci Group. For several weeks, rumors swirled that LVMH Moët Hennessey Louis Vuitton would launch a hostile bid for Gucci. Slowly, LVMH was increasing its stake in Gucci. Eventually it acquired about 34 percent of the company's shares.

Gucci reacted by forging an alliance with French retailer Pinault-

Printemps-Redoute in an agreement in which PPR would immediately accumulate a 40 percent stake in Gucci. Under the deal, which valued all of Gucci at $7.31 billion, Gucci issued 39 million new shares which were to be purchased for $75 each by PPR.

But there were further complications for LVMH. In January 1999, Gucci had undertaken a 37 million share issue to its employees that would increase its outstanding shares by approximately 40 percent in order to deter against a creeping takeover by LVMH.

LVMH did, in fact, launch a hostile bid for the shares it did not already own that valued the company at $7.4 billion. LVMH also went to court to have Gucci's defensive moves overturned.

Subsequently, LVMH sweetened its offer, issuing a raise to $8.67 billion, which it made conditional upon the cancellation of Pinault's purchase of 40 percent of Gucci. But Gucci rejected the new offer as inadequate due to both its value and its condition that the Pinault agreement be canceled. In June 1999 LVMH filed two more lawsuits against Gucci in an attempt to take control.

Stodgy British financial institutions initially felt immune to the rough-and-tumble hostile M&A activity taking place in continental Europe. Then beleaguered National Westminster, Britain's fourth biggest bank, became the first victim of a hostile bid, and, even more interesting, from a smaller Scottish rival, the scrappy Bank of Scotland. NatWest had a history of poor earnings performance and disastrous forays into investment banking. The last straw was its intention to acquire Legal & General, Britain's seventh-biggest life insurer—investors felt that, once again, NatWest was overpaying for a deal that had little strategic merit. Bank of Scotland's bid set off a domino-like scramble that affected the strategic thinking of all of Europe's major financial institutions.

Defense: 20
Fight or Sell?

*"Firstly, on the moment of his awakening, the
thought occurred to him: 'Why do I lie here? The
night is wearing on, and at daybreak it is likely
that the enemy will be upon us.'"*

—Xenophon, *Anabasis*

The threshold question is when to fight, and when to sell. Sometimes the time comes to sell. Eloquence of execution, then,
becomes the key issue. Disgruntled shareholders, lack of clear management succession, adverse business prospects, and the strategic
benefits of a combination or a blowout price may all impel a sale.

But there are sales, and there are sales. A forced sale to an unde-
sired buyer under time pressure is very different from a carefully
honed private process. Of course, some sellers purely interested in
price prefer the frenzy of a public auction. For many companies,
however, the prospect of an untimely sale is most unattractive. The
competing rights of short- and long-term shareholders, managers,
and the community make up the vortex which generates the most
passion about deals.

If directors decide a strategic shift is timely, they consider the relative merits of three alternatives—some sort of sale or merger, a corporate spin-off, or the issuance of a targeted stock. Once the

decision has been made, implementation takes center stage. Every deal has its own life. The stakes are high, with the future of a corporation up for grabs. In this context, cookbook solutions are for bookstores.

Selling a Division

A sale of a subsidiary may be the most attractive solution. The sale process can be completed more quickly than a spin-off, and can satisfy immediate cash needs. While some cash can be harvested through a spin-off by having the subsidiary take on debt to pay a dividend before the transaction, a sale of the business is the most direct way to convert equity interest in the subsidiary to cash; spin-offs, on the other hand, may not be feasible if the disposed operations lack the size or critical mass to survive as a separate stand-alone business.

Tactical concerns related to defending against a hostile bid may also weigh in favor of selling a division. An outright sale of the business sought by a bidder, much like a crown jewel lockup, is one way to reduce interest in a takeover of a multidivision company. Alternatively, the cash from a sale might be the war chest for defensive maneuvers such as an acquisition or the payment of a special dividend to shareholders.

These potential benefits must be weighed against the relative costs of a sale. Some of the pitfalls are familiar. Taxes can be one significant problem, though structuring alternatives may minimize the impact. The cost of retained corporate overhead—which will be spread over a smaller business—must be factored into the equation, as in a spin-off or split-off.

Careful execution of the process is of the utmost importance. Once a sale process begins, word may leak out. An unsuccessful or "busted" sale marks the unit involved as damaged goods and can reduce its value for the near term. While a full IPO of the subsidiary is another alternative, a failed or weak IPO undermines value if a sale is later contemplated.

In a cash sale, the value of lost earnings is another concern. If a parent company is trading at a higher multiple to earnings or cash flow than it receives on the sale, the market could regard the sale as a value-destroying action. For example, a parent might be trading at 20 times earnings but only receive 15 times the subsidiary's earnings in a sale. In an efficient market, this difference would not be a problem, because investors would value the parent company based on its constituent parts: If a multiple of 15 were appropriate for the subsidiary, that multiple would be imbedded in the parent company's price and the 20 multiple would be the blended average of the multiples for the parent's various business units.

Yet markets are not efficient. It is possible that the parent's trading value assumed something more than a 15 multiple for the subsidiary's earnings, implying a lower value for the rest of the company. It is due to this market inefficiency that such a sale might be a value-destroying action from the parent company's perspective.

The defensive sale raises other concerns. A sale must be completed quickly to have any tactical impact; but a sale under duress probably will not result in a full price paid. Selling too cheaply opens the board to charges of breach of fiduciary duty, while selling too slowly can result in no sale at all.

Marketing a Business Selling a company is like selling any other product. The fundamentals are important, but positioning and presentation can be just as much so. Sizzle sells. A sense for the target market audience to a considerable extent determines the approach taken. The world of potential private market buyers can be broken into two main categories—financial buyers and strategic buyers.

A financially oriented buyer generally is more concerned with price, financial structure, projected returns, and management quality than with the intricacies of operations. For this reason, a financial buyer often retains the existing management. However, these buyers, instead, are sometimes partnered with free-agent management teams.

Unless the company in question is an "add-on" to an existing publicly traded company—part of a roll-up strategy—financial buyers tend to favor transactions structured as cash purchases or leveraged recapitalizations. The cash sale is straightforward. A leveraged recapitalization is really just a partial cash sale in which a seller retains some interest, perhaps 20 or 30 percent, in the divested subsidiary. Under this scenario, the seller gains cash but also keeps a portion of any upside from the business; the buyer gains control and runs the business. Furthermore, if push-down accounting can be avoided, no goodwill is created.

On the other hand, a strategic buyer looks for companies which might be combined profitably, and focuses more on operations, strategic fit, and post-deal integration. Potential cost savings give a strategic buyer the opportunity to generate higher incremental profits than a financial buyer on the same revenue base. As a result, strategic buyers tend to place higher values on most companies, although companies with high cash flow and low reported earnings are common exceptions. That being said, however, financial buyers are increasingly taking a strategic approach to acquisitions with roll-up strategies, bringing the objectives of financial and strategic buyers closer.

With stock more commonly available as an acquisition currency, strategic acquirers also have available to them more structural alternatives than financial buyers. In a stock-for-stock transaction with the divested company, the selling company is left with an interest in the combined company. The seller can either retain the interest as a passive investment or distribute the stock to shareholders in a taxable distribution.

The Importance of Good Grooming   Ideally, the decision to sell a business is made a year before the business is put on the market, allowing time for the all-important grooming process.

Grooming a business for sale requires a delicate balancing act. Top management must consider the trade-offs involved in the whole range of management decisions. For example, increased capital expenditures might be put off in favor of higher returns on capital. Increased marketing might be put off in favor of higher margins. But in general, operational improvements should be made where possible.

At the same time, little is to be gained from operating a business too far outside the ordinary course. Purchasers are likely to see through short-term improvements, especially in the face of wide disparities in spending compared to historical practice. It also can be difficult to sell a business that has peaked recently because buyers are more interested in a growth story than in a rebound story. Likewise, if all the cost savings have been wrung out of a business and every expansion option exploited, little room is left to pitch the upside.

Of course, the natural inclination for potential buyers is to be skeptical about any business the owner no longer wants. Therefore, the challenge is to package an opportunity. As is true when marketing any product, the key is to figure out sales points, which may include projected revenue growth, improving margins, potential cost savings, or a consolidating industry. Why does the seller want to dispose of the business? is the first question asked. Lack of strategic fit is sometimes persuasive. But modesty is also effective: Selling the notion that somebody with a different skill set is needed to take advantage of latent opportunities works and is flattering to a buyer.

Another imperative in dressing a business for sale is to motivate and retain key executives throughout the sale process, as top-flight management talent can add considerable value to a business and smooth the divestiture process. Therefore, retention plans with "stay" bonuses, golden parachutes, and other arrangements are commonly put in place for such individuals. Of course, such arrangements need to be disclosed to potential buyers, especially where the company may be on the hook for a material amount of additional compensation expense.

Once the actual sale process begins, even in the preliminary stages, managing the information flow is important. If news of a pending sale leaks, employee morale, customer and supplier support, and market perception can erode. To avoid these undesirable consequences, the number of people involved in deliberations should be kept to a minimum and the sale completed as swiftly as possible.

The IPO Alternative   An IPO can be an attractive divestiture mechanism, particularly when the new-issues market is frothy. Three factors typically drive a company's IPO analysis—valuation, the story, and implementation.

Generally, the most important question is how much a company will receive upon issuance. Comparable companies' trading multiples are the main data source used to answer this question, typically applied as a valuation benchmark to the results of the business to be offered. Normally an "IPO discount" of 10 to 15 percent is taken from comparable companies' multiples to arrive at the issue price, reflecting the common investment banking practice of issuing shares at a discount to their projected trading value. The bargain price "greases" the distribution channel, making initial investors more willing to buy up the stock. The market will then equilibrate supply and demand to come up with a market-clearing price which implies a value for the company.

But equally important as valuation is the marketing of an IPO. How the story is told, how a stock is positioned, can have a great deal of impact. For example, we worked on a public offering for American Pad and Paper—a company that makes paper-based office products and at the time was majority-owned by financial buyer Bain Capital. In taking AmPad public, there were two stories that could be told. One would have positioned AmPad as a paper company and another would have positioned AmPad as a "consumer products" paper company. The latter approach was chosen because the "consumer products" sector benefited from higher multiples than the paper sector. Thus, by successfully telling the consumer products story, Bain floated shares in AmPad at a significantly higher price than otherwise would have been possible.

The urge to be creative, however, is constrained by two factors. First, the market can be a skeptical, incredulous animal. The AmPad pitch only worked because it was grounded in reality. Second, federal securities law and regulations enforce honest disclosure. The IPO registration process is much like the process necessary to distribute stock in a spin-off. A lengthy registration statement and proxy must be drafted by the issuer and approved by the SEC. The "red herring"—a preliminary version of the document with only the price left blank—is distributed to potential purchasers. The final version goes out with the shares.

Whether an IPO or a private-market sale will be more favorable cannot be determined with scientific certainty. A judgment must be made based on available information. Public-market trading multiples can be compared to private-market acquisition multiples for some guidance. Yet, as with all decisions as to price, value is a metaphysical concept that can only be estimated.

It is possible that the registration statement filed as part of the IPO process may trigger interest among bidders, who might preempt a planned IPO with a premium offer to purchase the entire company.

Xerox benefited from this dynamic on the sale of its Van Kampen asset management unit. As part of an ongoing effort to refocus, Xerox filed for a public offering of up to 38 percent of Van Kampen's stock in 1992. However, as the deal approached market, buyout firm Clayton, Dubilier & Rice swooped in with a $360 million offer to buy the whole company. Xerox was ecstatic with the price and accepted. Clayton, Dubilier ended up holding Van Kampen for less than four years, selling it to Morgan Stanley in 1996 for a nice gain.

Tactical Considerations   The private-market sale is a more varied animal than the IPO. A spectrum of approaches exists. Nonetheless, it can be helpful to think of the range of possibilities in terms of two ideal types—the classic two-step auction and the negotiated sale. The basic demarcation between these alternatives is the scope of the marketing effort: A negotiated transaction may involve just one other party besides the seller, while an auction may be opened up to dozens of bidders.

Neither approach is intrinsically superior. Each serves different objectives. A wide-ranging auction generally maximizes value, particularly since the "best buyer" on paper is not always the party who eventually pays the highest price. Furthermore, the presence of multiple bidders builds natural tension into the process and generates more energetic bidding. The absence of secrecy or speed is the main downside to an auction. Meanwhile, a negotiated sale may not wring the last dollar from a property, but generally will bring a faster result and maximize secrecy. A defensive sale therefore is more likely to be conducted as a negotiated sale.

The Classic Two-Step   The classic two-step auction starts with the drafting of an offering memorandum that describes at some length the business for sale. A list of potential buyers is created along with the offering document. The identity of the prospects influences the contents of the document.

Once the offering memorandum is prepared, prospective purchasers are contacted. Those who express an interest are asked to sign a confidentiality agreement before they receive materials. Copies of the offering document then are distributed to prospects and a follow-up program carried out.

Interested parties might be given more information at this stage based on requests. At some predetermined date, potential buyers who wish to proceed must submit nonbinding preliminary indications of interest. Such indications usually state a price range.

Based on the ranges and other factors, a number of prospects will be asked to enter a second round of bidding. Top management usually makes a presentation to these potential purchasers; a tour of facilities also might be arranged and a "data room" filled with documents regarding the company's business organized and made available. The well-run data room can make an important difference in the bid process because in a rigid two-step, buyers are expected to complete their due diligence review prior to the final bid date. Not only can easy access to data help bidders, but issues on the sale can be addressed at an early point.

As the bidding process nears its climax, a bidding procedures letter, which generally outlines the nature of acceptable bids, is circulated to the final bidders along with a sample purchase agreement. On the final bid date, bids are received and a winner is declared.

Price often is the determining factor in an auction; but other issues sometimes make a critical difference. For example, one bidder might offer a high price, an unfavorable contract, and no concrete details regarding financing. Another bidder might be willing to pay less, but offer a "clean" contract and quick closure.

Once a winner is selected, the contracts are negotiated and executed. The transaction will typically close one to two months after a definitive purchase agreement is signed, though in large public-company deals, the process can take significantly longer.

The garden-variety two-step auction is also known as a sealed-bid auction. A "dripping wax" auction is a variation on the two-step in which the "final bids" are not really final. Instead, the seller goes back to the few highest bidders, with the high bid used as leverage over the others in an attempt to force a raise. If successful, the new prices can be used against the former high bidder. However, this kind of trading tactic can backfire. If the seller has a reputation as a dripping wax auctioneer, potential buyers may underbid initially as a protective mechanism.

Running an Auction   Though the two-step procedure is by now standard practice, running a successful auction is an art, like writing a suspense novel. There must be a frame to the story, a formal skeleton to the process. Spontaneity must be managed so the story is not lost in the confusion. Yet pressure must run throughout.

The auction format naturally creates tension—especially the blind auction, in which bidders are not told how many other parties they are competing against. Information on other bids is released selectively. If the auctioneer is able and the integrity of the process is maintained, even a single bidder can be induced to enter a "full" bid.

However, structural stress is not the only motivating factor in a well-run auction. If the process is managed correctly, bidders will be pulled along by the desire for more data. For example, the offering memorandum might describe the business and industry, with some limited projections. Further detail might be released in several later stages, such as after indications of interest are in and during the management presentation. A subtle touch is required to maximize the effect.

THE AUCTIONEER'S RULEBOOK

1. Always have more information than the buyer.

2. Understand the buyer's focus.

3. Control pacing.

4. Sell an opportunity.

5. Provide realistic projections.

6. Have a professional data room.

7. Describe problems; have answers.

8. Radiate the integrity of the process.

9. Be flexible.

Naturally, sophisticated bidders will do their best to circumvent the auction format. For example, bidders frequently attempt to wheedle whatever additional information they can out of the auctioneer or seller. Information leaks all too easily and undermines the process. More dramatically, a prospect might make a preemptive bid which explodes if not accepted by a certain date, just as Forstmann Little did in Kraft's Duracell auction. The reaction to such tactics depends on how steep the bid is and how critical it is to the bidder to maintain the process. With many interested bidders, Kraft felt able to shop the offer, and therefore approached Henry Kravis, who, like Forstmann, attempted to short-circuit the process. He offered to make one more raise so long as he had a guarantee that it would be the last round. This extra knowledge proved decisive.

Sometimes a bidder will raise his bid after the final deadline, despite the rules. The auctioneer is then in a quandary and sometimes invites another round of bids. Obviously, the original "winning" bidder will be furious.

The true challenge of running an auction is maintaining the integrity of the process. Rules must constantly be defended from encroachment. Prospective buyers must be motivated to continue in the process, but can't be pushed too hard or a sense of desperation will develop. Above all else, flexibility must be maintained.

The Negotiated Deal   A negotiated sale process can involve just one prospective buyer, who is approached and, if interested, signs a confidentiality agreement. Information is exchanged and negotiations open. Neither party wants to be the first to name a price, but a price can be coaxed out of an aggressive bidder. The momentum of a bidder's ambition can be used as a tool to gather information for a seller. If the parties agree to a price, a letter of intent might be signed, followed by contract negotiations and an eventual closing.

The most common mistake sellers make in negotiated transactions is granting a prospective buyer the exclusive right to negotiate a purchase for a period of time. Buyers often will request this right based on little more than a preliminary nonbinding bid and, after performing due diligence, will come back with a much lower offer, claiming to have discovered problems. At that point, the buyer has leverage over the seller. If the deal falls apart, the company on the block is viewed as damaged goods by other prospective purchasers.

A seller can avoid this circumstance by refusing to grant an exclusive. Moreover, a seller might decide to conduct a limited auction even though one particular prospect appears to be the likely buyer. Having just one other real bidder in the picture gives the seller negotiating leverage and can improve the outcome considerably. Of course, a unique buyer or the strong desire for a quick execution may dictate the exclusive arrangement.

After a Busted Sale   Even in a full-blown auction, there is the real possibility that no bidder willing to pay the seller's minimum price will emerge. A party also might be selected as the winning bidder and then later back out of the transaction. While contractual language can be drafted in the attempt to avoid this outcome, the risk cannot be eliminated.

Of course, a busted sale becomes more likely as the number of bidders in the picture declines. A smart bidder who perceives itself to be the only player in negotiations may force matters by making a lowball offer or refusing to bid.

A seller can rebound from a busted sale in one of three ways. First, it can accept a sale on a distressed basis: taking a lower price than would result from a more patient approach in exchange for being able to move on in its corporate life. Second, the seller can remove the property from the market with the intention of remarketing in a few months or years. Or third, it can remove the business from the market and commit to managing the business.

BUYING OFF A BUSTED SALE

A busted sale can be a buyer's gain. If the seller needs cash or has unalterably decided to divest the particular business, a buyer may be able to scoop up a rough-cut gem at a bargain price. Maybelline's buyout followed this pattern.

In 1989, Maybelline was owned by Schering-Plough Corp., a large pharmaceuticals company, which decided to put it on the market. The cosmetics company was perceived as a dowdy brand under pressure from competition. Despite Maybelline's problems, analysts placed its value at around $500 million.

Schering-Plough's auction did not proceed smoothly. Strategic buyers showed no interest and Schering eventually settled on a $320 million offer from a financial buyer. Two months later, the deal stumbled as the buyer wanted to slash the price.

Through an investment buyout fund, we had been in the Maybelline bidding early on, and had researched the company. On hearing reports of the busted sale, we offered $305 million for the company with a time fuse for acceptance. Schering-Plough accepted the offer.

As things turned out, Maybelline was a bargain purchase. When we purchased the company, its brands were sold primarily in the domestic market. One of our initiatives was to expand the company's international exposure beyond the few international markets Maybelline dabbled in. The strategy was not to demonstrate strong profitability overseas—the company lacked the resources. Rather, the idea was to show that the Maybelline brands were extendable.

In 1996, L'Oréal saw the opportunity and grabbed it. They bought Maybelline for $761 million, including $158 million of assumed debt, and melded it with their existing international personal care business. Taking into account several prior dividends and the cash received in a prior recapitalization, this amounted to a return of $623 million on the $160 million of equity originally invested in the Maybelline buyout by our fund.

Selling the Entire Company

Selling an entire company is in many ways similar to selling a division. Grooming the business for sale can have a big impact; keeping employees on the job and maintaining morale are just as difficult. Both an auction and negotiated sale are possible approaches.

However, there are also a number of differences between the two tasks which influence the nature of the process and tactics used.

The mechanics of deal implementation are different in a sale of an entire company than in a divestiture. A vote of shareholders in both the target and acquirer may be necessary to approve a stock-for-stock merger, while friendly cash deals typically are accomplished by way of a tender offer. In either case, the reaction of shareholders and other constituencies is of immediate import, which is usually not the case in sales of divisions or subsidiaries.

Perhaps the most significant difference between a divestiture and a corporate sale is the larger role played by the board in a sale. Directors have an undeniable responsibility to affirm or reject a plan to sell their company and then decisions are more likely to be challenged with the stakes so high. Consequently, throughout the process, directors pay close attention to their legal and fiduciary obligations.

The Business Judgment Rule   Courts generally will not second-guess the business judgment of corporate directors, a deference embodied in the so-called business judgment rule. As articulated in the Delaware courts, the rule holds that "directors' decisions are presumed to have been made on an informed basis, in good faith and in the honest belief that the action taken was in the best interests of the company." Normally, in a sale, a decision of the board will not be overturned unless a plaintiff is able to carry a heavy burden of proof.

Specifically, the plaintiff must show that the board failed to meet either its duty of care or its duty of loyalty.

To prove that duty of loyalty was breached, a plaintiff must show that directors were grossly negligent. Yet the duty of care doctrine is not without teeth. In 1985, the real possibility of personal liability was underscored for corporate directors by the case *Smith v. Van Gorkom*. Most directors are protected by liability insurance, but the Delaware court's sharp rebuke of the Trans Union Corporation board in *Van Gorkom* dramatically sensitized directors to their responsibilities.

Trans Union was a company with large investment tax credits and no way to use them on its own. In 1980, Jerome Van Gorkom, the company's chairman and CEO, decided to sell the company. Having done almost no financial analysis, Van Gorkom approached the Pritzkers, the prominent Chicago investors, and suggested they buy Trans Union for $55 a share. The Pritzkers were quite interested and negotiations proceeded quickly. Van Gorkom called a board meeting on one day's notice. Trans Union's investment bankers were not invited and most of the company's directors and officers knew nothing of the deal until the meeting.

At the board meeting, Van Gorkom gave a brief verbal presentation on the deal. Then the directors were advised by the company's CFO that the deal seemed at the low end of what would be fair. Van Gorkom assured the directors that Trans Union would be able to accept other offers for ninety days under the terms of the Pritzker deal, but the actual merger agreement was not presented. After a two-hour discussion, the deal was approved.

Four years later, a Delaware court found the Trans Union directors to have been grossly negligent. While the price received in the merger represented a significant premium over the company's trading price and no other bidders had emerged, the court said the directors did not live up to their duty of care. As particular flaws, the court highlighted the lack of valuation data and the failure to review the merger agreement.

Van Gorkum underscores that a key aspect of duty of care is the process involved. Directors who "inform themselves of all information reasonably available to them and relevant to their decision" are not grossly negligent. Furthermore, directors may reasonably rely on information and opinions provided by qualified third parties, such as company lawyers, executives, and investment bankers, without breaching the duty of care. If the process is duly deliberative, directors are unlikely to be considered grossly negligent.

A breach of the duty of loyalty is equally tough to prove: A plaintiff must show that the board engaged in "self-dealing"—using the company on whose board the directors sit to further a transaction in which they have a direct financial stake, such as in a management buyout, or where the directors stand to gain some improper financial benefit.

Courts use an amorphous, fact-specific analysis to decide whether the self-dealing of a single director or a small group of directors rises to a level that calls an entire board's actions into question. If the duty of loyalty is breached, the business judgment rule will no longer apply. Instead, the burden shifts and the board must prove the "entire fairness" of the deal.

FAIRNESS OPINIONS

As part of the deliberative process, a board often will hire an investment bank to give a fairness opinion regarding a planned transaction. The opinion itself is a relatively brief document which states that, in the investment bank's opinion, the transaction is fair—from a financial point of view. Accordingly, shareholders are the only constituency considered in the opinion. Although a lot of analysis is done, the conclusion is one of art—not science—taking into account all of the data considered.

A fairness opinion not only helps insulate a company and its board from liability to shareholders but also helps inform directors about a transaction's financial and strategic impact. With more information, directors presumably can make better decisions.

While a fairness opinion itself is short, considerable backup analysis and documentation is prepared as foundation. Fairness is, after all, a subjective quality and the fairness inquiry must be contextual. The question is: Fair under what circumstances, at what point in time?

In preparing a fairness opinion, a feeling for past performance and strategic situation is critical. Then, both the subject company and the consideration to be received in the transaction (if not cash) are valued using various methodologies.

With a number of analyses assembled, the valuation comes down to a cumulative judgment. For example, most firms require a fairness opinion committee composed of senior professionals with broad experience and perspective to approve any opinion. A give-and-take exchange takes place regarding the merits and a consensus is reached.

The fairness opinion process at times draws fire. Some of the more heated criticism has come when an investment bank grants a fairness opinion and its client completes a deal even though another higher offer is on the table or the market price exceeds the offer. How can the lower offer be fair?

The answer lies in an understanding of what a fairness opinion signifies. Fairness does not mean the reviewed transaction matches some objective sense of intrinsic value, nor does it mean the target will receive the highest auction price attainable. Of course, if an all-cash offer is matched with another all-cash offer, it is difficult to endorse the lower-priced deal, unless there is substantial risk the higher offer will for some reason not be consummated. However, if the terms are different or if the consideration is different, the situation changes. For example, an all-stock tax-free deal with upside continuity for the shareholders may, indeed, make more sense than an all-cash deal. Sometimes an offer price will be below market price due to frothy market speculation rather than fundamentals.

Some have criticized the fairness opinion process, saying that bankers have a built-in incentive to find transactions fair due to their "success fee" arrangement. Critics argue a banker in this position is biased in favor of granting a fairness opinion. As a result of the perceived conflict, companies sometimes negotiate for the investment bank to handle the fairness opinion for a flat fee. Bankers, however, do take pride and care in their opinions because their reputation is on the line.

Obviously, the more extensive the analysis and unbiased the bank, the more valuable the opinion. For this reason, a company sometimes will hire a second investment bank—in addition to the bank providing broader strategic advice on the transaction—for the sole job of providing an opinion. This arrangement leaves little room for the argument that the bank giving the opinion has a stake in the deal.

The *Unocal* Standard　In certain circumstances, courts have found the traditional deference shown to the business judgment of directors to be misplaced. Company insiders who also serve as directors may tilt board decisions in favor of arrangements which ensure continued employment, no matter the consequences to shareholders. Second, directors who are ostensibly independent outsiders may act in a similar fashion out of loyalty to corporate insiders and to preserve access to the perks associated with being a director.

These concerns came to light in *Unocal v. Mesa Petroleum,* the case in which the Delaware Supreme Court reviewed Unocal's defensive response to Boone Pickens' takeover bid. As part of its defensive strategy, Unocal initiated a self-tender for its shares at a substantial premium to Mesa's hostile offer but excluded Mesa from the offer. Pickens sued to have the discriminatory self-tender invalidated.

In *Unocal,* the Delaware Supreme Court recognized the "inherent conflict" facing a board when deciding whether to pursue a defensive maneuver and found, as a result, "an enhanced duty which calls for judicial examination at the threshold before the protections of the business judgment rule may be conferred."

This enhanced scrutiny involves a two-pronged analysis. A board must show that it had "reasonable grounds for believing that a danger to corporate policy and effectiveness existed," and that defensive measures were "reasonable in relation to the threat imposed."

These two burdens can be satisfied largely by showing that a reasonable investigation was undertaken prior to the decision to adopt defensive measures. Courts have paid particular deference when decisions are approved by a majority of independent directors, especially if these directors have been counseled by outside legal and financial advisers.

However, cases subsequent to *Unocal* make clear that the purported threat must be specific and defined. Specific threats so far recognized as acceptable include the coercive nature of a two-tiered hostile tender offer, general inadequacy of the offer in comparison to perceived intrinsic value, and timing concerns related to arranging counteroffers. Moreover, the defense of an existing, defined corporate strategy such as in *Time* qualifies as a valid defensive motivation.

Indeed, "the nature of the threat associated with a particular hostile offer sets the parameters for the range of permissible defensive tactics," according to *Unocal.* Reasonableness in the context of this proportionality inquiry is defined as a range, not a single value, and defenses which are not preclusive or coercive generally will be shown some deference.

Courts in particular disfavor responses which force a transaction favored by management on shareholders. Yet the measure of what is preclusive is legal, not practical. The fight for Wallace Computer Services makes the point. In the summer of 1995, Moore Corporation made an all-cash tender offer for the outstanding shares of Wallace with completion of the offer conditioned on the redemption of Wallace's poison pill. At $56 a share, the offer represented a 27 percent premium over the trading price of Wallace stock before the announcement. Moore subsequently raised its offer to $60 a share.

Notwithstanding the market premium, the Wallace board considered the offer and declined, citing the inadequacy of the price in light of the company's improving operating performance. The board—in a decision supported by a Delaware federal court—therefore refused to redeem Wallace's pill despite the fact that 73 percent of the company's shareholders tendered into the offer. Essentially, the *Wallace* court was satisfied that the poison pill under review did not preclude the bidder from waging a proxy contest.

From a practical standpoint, though, the Wallace pill effectively precluded a successful takeover, because in addition to its poison pill, Wallace also had a staggered board. Thus, while Moore was free to contest a proxy contest, the company would need at least two years to gain control in this fashion. Moore indeed pursued a proxy contest and won a block of board seats in the first election, but gave up before the second election.

The Sale of Control   The *Unocal* standard governs if a board is determined to fight off a hostile bidder and remain independent. However, in many cases, a company responds to a hostile tender offer by seeking out a white knight to buy the company on more favorable terms, a strategy that raises concerns similar to those addressed in *Unocal:* Directors might favor one bidder over another out of self-interest. Consequently, the courts formulated an appropriate standard for director behavior during the sale of control: The *Revlon* rule states that directors must maximize shareholder value in a sale.

The problem for the Delaware court, however, has been that *Revlon* could be read too broadly, preventing strategic corporate combinations because of their tactical vulnerability. If any merger were viewed as a sale of control, only the strongest of companies would initiate a transaction. Therefore, the scope of *Revlon* was nipped in the landmark *Time* case, in which the court held that the proposed strategic Time-Warner merger did not involve a change of control and, therefore, did not trigger the *Revlon* duties. In essence, then, *Time* is the godmother of corporate marriages.

In *Time,* the court found the Time-Warner merger to be in keeping with Time's long-term strategy of creating a "vertically integrated video enterprise" while at the same time preserving the "Time culture" of journalistic integrity. This type of strategic merger would not trigger *Revlon* duties. Rather, two circumstances trigger such duties—first, when a corporation explicitly initiates an auction, and second when a corporation "abandons its long-term strategy" in response to a hostile bid and instead seeks a white knight.

However, in *QVC,* the pendulum swung back the other direction when the Delaware court limited the scope of *Time.* The *QVC* case revolved around Barry Diller's hostile bid for Paramount, to which Viacom and Paramount responded by renegotiating their merger contract. As part of the deal, Paramount agreed to keep the stringent defensive measures in place to protect the Viacom merger, and Viacom agreed to raise its price.

Even though the Viacom-Paramount merger was styled as a strategic merger, the court held it was in fact a change in control that triggered *Revlon* because Sumner Redstone would have 40 percent of the common stock and 70 percent of the voting stock in the new entity and therefore could determine its corporate strategy going forward. As a result, the merger constituted a sale of control that entitled Paramount's shareholders to receive the control premium associated with an auction. The court basically was not convinced the Paramount board had acted "reasonably to seek the transaction offering the best value reasonably available to the stockholders."

Justice Andrew Moore

For twelve years, Justice Andrew G.T. Moore refereed America's corporate legal battles. As a justice of the Delaware Supreme Court, he was the author of many of the leading legal opinions which form the basis for modern takeover law, including *Revlon* and *Unocal*. He also sat on the panels that decided the *Time* and *QVC* cases. Justice Moore may well have had more of an impact on modern corporate law than any other individual.

A native of New Orleans, Moore was stationed in Delaware while in the military. He returned to the state after law school to clerk for the chief justice of Delaware's Supreme Court, and remained in the state to become a corporate litigator at Connolly, Bove, Lodge & Hutz, of Wilmington, Delaware. In 1982, after eighteen years at the firm, he was appointed to the Supreme Court.

While on the court, Moore developed a reputation for pragmatic judgment or, to be more practical, the use of a flexible "smell test." He seemed philosophically opposed to hostile takeovers by junk bond raiders; yet he argued that the quality of corporate directors also needed to be improved, and came down hard on any lack of corporate propriety.

Much of the takeover litigation coming across Moore's desk involved the fundamental question: How much leeway should a board be allowed in moving to stave off raiders? Moore usually took a balanced view. For example, in *Unocal* he wrote an opinion upholding a controversial defensive technique. Yet in *Revlon* he held that a board's response to a hostile takeover attempt must be reasonable.

Moore came up for reappointment in 1994. Despite widespread support among both institutional investors and members of the takeover bar, he was not offered a second term. The decision generated an uproar in Delaware and was rumored to be political in nature.

Today, Moore is a senior managing director at Wasserstein Perella, where he specializes in corporate defense work and provides advice to boards. He also teaches as a visiting professor at various law schools.

Nonshareholder Constituencies The *Revlon* case makes clear that a board's duty in Delaware lies with the shareholders it represents and not other constituencies such as bondholders, workers, or the community at large. As the court put it:

> A board may have regard for various constituencies in discharging its responsibilities, provided there are rationally related benefits accruing to the stockholders. However, such concern for non-stockholder interests is inappropriate when an auction among active bidders is in progress, and the object no longer is to protect or maintain the corporate enterprise but to sell it to the highest bidder.

However, the view is different in states other than Delaware. For example, a Pennsylvania statute clearly contemplates the weighing of varied interests and the 1997 litigation surrounding the hostile fight for Conrail illustrates that the Pennsylvania courts will go out of their way to protect local corporations.

The Fine Art of Corporate Marriages

The process of merging two companies is a very delicate one. Dramatic stories in the news continue to remind companies and M&A practitioners of the dangers of poorly executed mergers.

Recent Health Care Deals   The string of announced health care mergers which faltered in early 1998 illustrates the importance of considering social and management issues. No sooner were these deals announced, than they fell apart due to disagreements about issues that were not—but should have been—considered prior to announcement. The megamerger announced between SmithKline Beecham and Glaxo Wellcome died a quick death because the executives at the two companies could not decide how the new company would be run and what its focus would be. Furthermore, executives could not reconcile the cultural differences between the two companies. The announced deal between American Home Products and Monsanto followed the same pattern. The desire to seek approval from the market inspired the premature merger announcement.

The Cendant Disaster   While the merger of CUC and HFS into Cendant, unlike the recent health care deals, ultimately went through, it was a disaster. The top executives at HFS and CUC did not see eye to eye on almost every issue, but nevertheless allowed their combination to go through anyway, trusting that the "minor details" would somehow be sorted out in the end.

Both CEO of HFS Henry Silverman and CEO of CUC Walter Forbes had agreed to a merger of equals. They had further agreed that Silverman would serve as CEO immediately after the merger, with his team to run the combined companies, while Forbes served as chairman. They would switch roles in January 2000. But quite quickly it became clear that it wouldn't work.

Someone had to go because the cultures of HFS and CUC were fundamentally incompatible, largely due to the radically different management approaches employed by the two chief executives: HFS was highly organized and hierarchical, while CUC was more entrepreneurial and haphazard. One victor had to emerge to impose cultural unity upon the organization if the merger were not to be a complete failure. Battling between the Silverman and Forbes fiefdoms had made Cendant dysfunctional following the merger. The company was not integrated. Accounting departments and managerial staffs were kept separated.

Silverman's employees then discovered widespread accounting fraud on CUC's books. Silverman acted quickly to force Forbes out. The company's share price dropped by over two thirds.

The Cendant experience is not an isolated example. A host of mergers have occurred with management scuffling:

Citigroup   The newly formed Citigroup was to have two co-CEOs, Sandy Weill and John Reed, to whom three investment banking executives would report: Deryck Maughan, James Dimon, and Victor Menezes. But the top-heavy structure was unwieldy and doomed to fail. Soon executives complained of unfocused and ineffective leadership. Operations suffered. Weill dealt with the problem by sacrificing the talented Dimon and eventually taking the reins on the business side from Reed.

Bank of America   At the new Bank of America, former chairman of BankAmerica David Coulter was forced out over losses at his firm from transactions with hedge fund D.E. Shaw, as well as losses in Russia. Hugh McColl liked running his own show in any event.

Other deals that were pitched for public relations as mergers of equals have turned out to be quite a different experience.

BP Amoco   John Browne, chief executive of BP, is calling the shots at the new company and his managers dominate the executive ranks. Thousands of Amoco employees have been fired in a wave of cost-cutting activity.

DaimlerChrysler   Similarly, in the Daimler-Chrysler deal, both Chrysler and Daimler were to have been partners; but now that the deal has been complete, Daimler chief executive Juergen Schrempp has firmly grasped the reins. While the company nominally has two headquarters—in Auburn Hills and in Stuttgart—decisions are being made increasingly by Stuttgart. In the management ranks directly beneath the two co-chairmen, Schrempp and Eaton, nine of the eleven executives are German. Eaton himself is on a retirement track and has agreed to step down three years after the merger closing at the latest. High-level Chrysler departures have accelerated.

Morgan Stanley Dean Witter   Even the highly successful Morgan Stanley–Dean Witter combination has not been without its difficulties. John Mack, COO of Morgan Stanley Dean Witter, who was next in line for the top spot at Morgan Stanley before the merger, attempted to become co-CEO with Philip Purcell. But his bid was unsuccessful, partly because of the well-written governance agreements.

The experiences of these companies must be clearly kept in mind when deciding whether to enter into a corporate marriage.

Factors to Consider in Marriages

If directors do make the decision to sell, an auction typically maximizes value. However, a company may be unwilling to sell itself to the highest bidder for valid strategic and business reasons, and in this situation must be careful not to trigger an auction. Again, if a *Revlon* auction is triggered, the selling company loses control of the process and price becomes the only question. Of course, for hostile bidders, the trick is to force a board into the *Revlon* mode.

Under the *Time* analysis, the strategic merger is the most effective tool for a selling company to control its own fate. An agreement to merge with a strategic partner is far more defensible against interlopers than a cash transaction. However, the deal still is somewhat vulnerable because shareholders of both companies must vote to approve a corporate marriage. This necessity leaves an obvious point of attack for an outsider gunning for the deal.

The modern bias in favor of strategic mergers has a practical impact on the way a company is shopped. Often, a company will hire an investment banker and announce an intention to study "strategic alternatives." Potential merger candidates consider this an invitation to make an offer. At the same time, though, the company is not put up for sale and technically avoids a *Revlon* auction.

A secret negotiated merger of equals is another common tactic to avoid *Revlon*. But the greatest danger in this approach is that word of negotiations will leak out. If nothing then comes of the discussions, pressure can build to do some alternative transaction.

Recent examples of major transactions structured—at least nominally—as marriages include the Exxon-Mobil deal, the Daimler-Chrysler deal, the Dean Witter–Morgan Stanley deal, the Chase-Chemical merger. Merger of equals deal terms vary. However, several defining characteristics can be identified. A corporate marriage involves a merger between two parties of roughly comparable size where the exchange ratio is set approximately at market-to-market pricing. Executives from both companies share the management roles in the combined entity.

The three main issues in negotiating a marriage are the exchange ratio, corporate governance, and post-deal integration. With regard to the exchange ratio, the working hypothesis at the outset is that neither company's shareholders should receive a premium. Having said that, however, the parties inevitably posture over the appropriate ratio. Relative trading values vary over time, so the period selected can alter the result. For example, an exchange ratio of two to one may have been marked-to-market over the average of the preceding thirty trading days, but not at the deal signing. The impact of unusual events, leaks regarding the deal, or sharp fluctuations all can be debated as well. A party may argue that an independent valuation would be a more appropriate measure of the exchange ratio.

For these and other reasons, the ratio announced with the terms of the deal sometimes deviates from the no-premium norm, with the smaller company sometimes getting a slight premium. Once the ratio is set, the parties must determine whether to use a fixed or floating exchange ratio, with or without a collar.

Agreement on the key corporate governance issues is another critical sticking point. The big questions are board makeup, executive representation, headquarters location, and corporate name. Both parties generally are reluctant to cede board control; one solution is to have an evenly divided board. In other cases, board representation might be traded off against other issues.

Certainly, executive representation is a concern for top management, because for a merger of equals to work, the parties have to be willing to share power. A common solution is to have the chief executive of one company become the chairman of the combined entity's board and the other chief executive retain the title of CEO. Then, after some period of years, the chairman agrees to retire, and the CEO takes over the top spot as well. This was the intended procedure in the NationsBank-BankAmerica deal, before David Coulter was forced out. A variant is for the older CEO to remain in that position and the younger to be president for a short period. The committee structure of the board also is carefully crafted to assure balance.

Headquarters location and the corporate name can also be particularly emotional issues. A large company often has a major presence in its community and management and other employees may be unwilling to move across country. Compromise is often necessary. In the Ultramar–Diamond Shamrock merger, for example, Connecticut-based Ultramar agreed to move the combined corporate headquarters to San Antonio, Texas.

The name of the combined entity is held important mainly for its signaling effect: In a true merger of equals, neither party wants to appear to have sold out. For this reason, the combined entity will often carry the name of both formerly independent companies, as in the Morgan Stanley–Dean Witter deal, or as in Daimler-Chrysler. As the previous action indicates, while a transaction may, from a financial perspective, be structured as a merger of equals, one party to the deal may—intentionally or unintentionally—come to dominate the new company. Despite the fact that DaimlerChrysler has two CEOs and two headquarters, it is a German company.

Post-closing integration determines whether a transaction advertised as a merger of equals turns out to be one. Matters sometimes fail to go as smoothly as envisioned. Veterans of one corporate culture may come to dominate the surviving company. The danger, of course, is that infighting will damage the prospects of the combined company. The Travelers-Citicorp deal provides an example of just how damaging such infighting can be.

The Spin-off

The notion of a spin-off is deceptively simple: A parent company distributes shares in a subsidiary to shareholders; afterward, the shareholders own interests in two stand-alone businesses. Yet the spin-off process in practice can be complicated, due to a thicket of tax rules.

Three specific transaction structures fall under the generic spin-off rubric. In a basic spin-off, the stock in a subsidiary business is distributed pro rata to shareholders. No sale is involved; rather, the spun-off entity becomes a completely separate company with its own board of directors, management, assets, liabilities, and owners. However, immediately after the transaction, the original parent company shareholders own both the spun-off entity and the remaining company.

A second alternative is to precede a spin-off with an equity carve-out, as when Sears sold a minority interest in Dean Witter to the public prior to its 1993 spin-off. A portion of the stock in the subsidiary is sold to the public in an IPO and the remaining interest is then distributed to parent company shareholders, as in the basic spin-off. Both the IPO and the distribution can be structured as tax-free transactions. However, to qualify for tax-free status, no more than 20 percent of the subsidiary may be carved out prior to the spin-off.

Finally, there is the split-off. Like the basic spin-off, this is a non-sale transaction. However, in this case, shares in the subsidiary business are not distributed pro rata to shareholders. Instead, an exchange offer is made, giving shareholders the option to turn in all or part of their old shares for new shares in the subsidiary in what amounts to a share buyback, with shares in the subsidiary as the consideration. At the end of the day, some shareholders own an increased interest in the remaining company. The other shareholders own an interest in the new company.

THE TANGLED WEB

Qualifying a Spin-off

Once the business issues are settled, the requirements for a non-taxable spin-off must be satisfied. For example, prior to distribution, the parent must control at least 80 percent of the stock of the entity to be spun off; the parent must distribute at least 80 percent of the stock in the spin-off; and both the parent and the spun-off entity must have been engaged in an active trade or business for at least five years. Parent company shareholders also must maintain a continuity of interest going forward and the spin-off must be accomplished for a valid, corporate-level business purpose.

The IRS has issued extensive interpretive regulations and rulings on each of these requirements while the courts have added considerable precedent as well. Few cases ever reach litigation. As a result, the IRS has become more or less the final arbiter on issues of interpretation, and fulfilling its requirements is like tiptoeing through the tulips.

Much of the uncertainty surrounding the status of a proposed spin-off stems from the business purpose test. The test is amorphous and requires a fact-specific inquiry; arbitrary distinctions and hair-splitting are par for the course. For example, increasing shareholder value is not an acceptable business purpose but achieving cost savings is. Lawyers make careers interpreting the IRS's rather idiosyncratic views.

Other business purposes recognized by the IRS as valid include: providing an equity interest to employees, facilitating a stock offering or borrowing, resolving management or other problems arising from operating two different businesses, resolving competitive conflicts with customers or suppliers, facilitating an acquisition of or by the company, and insulating one business from the risks associated with another business. Once a valid business purpose is identified, the taxpayer has the burden to show that a spin-off is the only practical and efficient way to achieve that purpose.

Advantages   A spin-off offers many potential advantages. Perhaps most importantly, the disaggregation of diverse businesses is applauded in the market. After a spin-off, investors and research analysts have an enhanced ability to follow the distinct businesses; the creation of formally separate companies gives the full benefit of pure-play trading values.

Another effect is to unleash entrepreneurial potential that may be stifled as part of a larger company. As part of a larger business, a smaller subsidiary often succumbs to the rich uncle syndrome in which the parent company protects the subsidiary in lean times and may not force the subsidiary to live up to its potential.

While many of these same benefits can be captured through a sale, a spin-off also has several special advantages. The most important difference involves tax treatment. A spin-off is tax-free both to the company and to recipient shareholders, while a sale may trigger a significant tax liability, both at the corporate and individual level: The company would be taxed on any gain realized on the sale, and if receiving a special dividend from the sale proceeds, stockholders also would face a tax liability.

A spin-off also allows shareholders to retain their interest in the business and therefore to benefit from future growth. Some empirical evidence suggests that both spun-off companies and their former parents tend to outperform the market in the years following the spin-off. Many explain this phenomenon by noting that many spin-off candidates are conglomerates, and the market expects a takeover bid after the spin.

Although the spin-off is an invaluable tool for strategic planning, the long time fuse involved limits its value as a response to an immediate hostile threat. However, the announcement of a planned spin-off may be enough to make a company's share price pop and placate shareholders.

Preceding a spin-off with an equity carve-out has a number of additional advantages. First, the sale of stock in the subsidiary generates cash, which, if generated from the sale of less than 20 percent of the total subsidiary stock, can then be distributed to the parent tax-free. In addition, by floating shares in the subsidiary, a trading market is created—important in the case of a large spin-off.

AT&T's 1996 spin-off of Lucent illustrates the technique. With a projected market capitalization in excess of $17 billion, Lucent would be among America's largest companies. Inevitably, however, the distribution of a large block of Lucent shares would temporarily depress the share price. Hoping to counteract the downdraft, AT&T chose to offer almost 18 percent of the company to the public in what was then the largest IPO in U.S. history. The remaining stock was distributed only after this initial chunk had been trading in the market for several months. An active trading market, research coverage, and other after-market support minimized the negative impact of the sudden float following the spin-off. Of course, this advantage can be counterbalanced if the shares sold in the carve-out trade at a discount in anticipation of the subsequent spin-off.

A split-off similarly reduces the pressure on a divested entity's stock price because the shareholders who exchange their stock in a split-off do so by choice. As a result, they are less likely to look for a quick sale immediately following the exchange. A split-off also may be preceded by an equity carve-out, which creates a trading value for the subsidiary that can be used to set an exchange ratio for the split-off. From the parent company's perspective, a split-off also enhances earnings per share by reducing the number of outstanding parent shares.

VIACOM SPLITS OFF CABLE

Viacom's 1996 split-off of its cable operations, which were then acquired by TCI Cable, is indicative of the complexities and potential rewards of the transaction structure.

The gist of the transaction was that Viacom raised $1.7 billion in cash by borrowing against its cable business, retained the cash, and divested the business in a split-off. Specifically, Viacom shareholders were given the option to exchange a portion of their Viacom common for stock in the cable business. Once the split-off was completed, TCI injected $350 million of equity into the stand-alone cable unit in exchange for control, and the cable company shares that Viacom shareholders had received in the split-off exchange were converted automatically into a preferred stock interest.

This deal structure—negotiated and agreed to before the split-off—walked a high wire in terms of the requirements for a tax-free split-off. The fact that when the transaction was completed, Viacom shareholders had no common stock interest in the

former Viacom cable business did not cause a continuity of interest problem because under established precedents, preferred
stock qualifies as a continuing interest. However, that shareholders also relinquished voting control over the cable business made
the tax treatment a closer question.

Ultimately, the IRS granted a favorable ruling in June 1996,
after considering the prospect for almost a year. The transaction
was completed shortly thereafter.

The cable split-off was a coup for Sumner Redstone's Viacom.
Following the Paramount and Blockbuster deals, the combined
company had a heavy debt burden. The $1.7 billion cash payment
in the TCI deal helped ease the burden and the unique transaction structure allowed Viacom to unload noncore assets at a favorable price, enhanced by the absence of tax. The number of
outstanding common shares also was reduced, beefing up Viacom's long-term earnings-per-share potential.

Disadvantages   Perhaps the chief criticism of a spin-off is that it
often represents nothing more than a paper shuffling of assets. Unless management improvements go along with the change, a spin-off
may not significantly enhance shareholder value. The troubles experienced by ITT after its spin-off underline a fundamental truth: A
spin-off can be a catalyst for change, but is not by itself the be-all
and end-all of improved performance.

Another potential disadvantage of a spin-off is that any cost savings related to size are lost. The spun-off entity may need to add additional administrative layers and may face a higher cost of capital
than it did as a part of the larger entity. Similarly, the distributing
company, now managing a smaller operational base, may be left with
unneeded overhead. An operational restructuring at the parent company level may be necessary to maximize the positive impact of a
spin-off.

The complex tax and legal process to accomplish a spin-off or split-off is the main implementation hurdle. Where the consequences of failing to qualify for tax-free treatment are significant, a spin-off rarely goes forward without a favorable advance ruling from the IRS, a process that can take six to nine months, involves steep legal and accounting costs, and consumes valuable management time. Other legal aspects of a spin-off add further costs and complexity.

Structuring Issues A spin-off or split-off also creates many difficult structuring issues. If the business to be spun off has not been operated as a separate subsidiary, a decision must be made as to the appropriate segmentation. Assets and liabilities must be divvied up and new legal structures created.

Considerable thought also must be given to the corporate governance of the subsidiary to be spun off. Issues include where the company should be incorporated, what kind of takeover defenses the company should have, the makeup of its board, and management structure. If the business has been operated as a separate subsidiary, existing practice can be used as an appropriate starting point. However, a spin-off is also an opportunity to revisit past practices, which may not be appropriate for a stand-alone entity.

For example, the allocation of debt is a key business issue. The subsidiary may not have its own separate debt, yet part of the parent's borrowing may be attributable to the subsidiary's cash needs. It may be appropriate to assign a portion of the parent company debt to the subsidiary, or to have the subsidiary issue debt and pay a dividend to the parent. The goal in allocating debt is to balance benefits to the parent with the viability of the subsidiary. A desire to leave the subsidiary with a strong credit rating usually acts as the practical ceiling on the amount of debt the company can bear.

Implementation Generally, no shareholder vote is necessary to accomplish a pro rata spin-off, whether preceded by an equity carve-out or not, and a company's board in most cases has the authority to distribute a dividend so long as the company will not as a result become insolvent. Therefore, a spin-off is often implemented through the relatively simple process of distributing shares to existing shareholders. Shareholder approval may, however, be needed if more than half the assets are being distributed.

As is true in any IPO, the shares in the subsidiary also have to be registered with the SEC prior to distribution. Once the registration is finalized, a company can simply dividend the shares out in a spin-off or proceed with a formal exchange offer to effectuate a split-off. If an exchange is pursued, the offer must be held open for a minimum of twenty business days, as with any tender offer. Furthermore, if the exchange is to be tax-free, 80 percent control in the subsidiary must be distributed.

In a split-off, the central issue is the exchange ratio between new subsidiary shares and parent shares. If a preliminary carve-out has been completed, the trading value can be used as an indication of the appropriate relative valuation. In other cases, the company must estimate the appropriate value and set the exchange ratio—a high-stakes art form. If the ratio is miscalculated, the whole deal fizzles in the sunlight of the public market.

Targeted Stock

The targeted stock alternative has become increasingly popular. Proponents argue that targeted stock is the happy medium between divesting and retaining a diverse business portfolio. Critics counter that targeted stock merely papers over the negative side effects of diversification.

A targeted stock is a separate class of stock issued by a company with multiple business units and is designed to provide a return to investors which reflects the performance of a defined business unit. However, the targeted stock is not a stock in the separate business unit but rather stock of the parent company. It is a modern creation—in effect, "virtual" common stock.

By definition, then, a company with a targeted stock will have at least two classes of stock. One will track the targeted business, the other will track the remaining businesses. For example, before effecting a spin-off of its media group, U S West's media stock targeted its cable and cellular assets, while the other class of U S West stock tracked the performance of the company's conventional telecommunications assets.

Advantages   Some corporate managers and directors find targeted stock appealing because of the hybrid nature of the mechanism: Targeted stock allows a company to straddle the boundary line between pure-play and diversified companies. While historically targeted stock issuance did not trigger corporate tax, unlike most sales, a 1999 proposal could make targeted stock issuance taxable.

With a separate stock for each distinct major business line, a diversified company becomes a virtual pure play and is positioned to capture some of the benefits that flow from conforming to the new market orthodoxy. Wall Street research analysts can provide separate coverage for disparate units. For example, by using a targeted stock to acquire EDS, GM avoided having automotive analysts cover the technology business. Instead, automotive analysts could follow the "regular" GM stock, and technology analysts the GME stock.

Furthermore, the universe of potential investors interested in holding a company's stock can be expanded as a result of a targeted stock issuance. Some major investors, such as mutual funds, may limit their field to certain industries. A targeted stock—and the separate financial reports generally provided for each business—allows investors to value and invest in each targeted business separately.

Targeted stock may allow a company to close the gap between current trading value and the projected trading value of its businesses as stand-alone, pure-play entities. If a company's trading value implies a discounted value for a particular business, a targeted stock issuance might generate the same multiple expansion associated with a spin-off.

Another benefit of being a notional pure-play company is that management incentive programs can be refined. The pay of managers at the targeted company can be tied more directly to the stock market performance of the business they control. Entrepreneurial incentives can be strengthened to encourage superior economic results and increased shareholder value. This goal was integral to the GM-EDS story and one of the motivating factors in issuing the GME stock.

At the same time, a targeted stock issuance does not involve a true corporate fission. Some of the positive aspects of operating as a single consolidated business remain. The parent company retains full ownership of and control over the targeted business, allowing the operating businesses to share overhead expenses. Because the businesses remain combined, borrowings may be structured so that creditors of one business can look to the earnings of the other business for payment, improving borrowing costs and capital availability versus a spin-off. The bulk of the combination may also enhance takeover defenses. The combined company can still file a consolidated tax return. Earnings from one business thus can be offset with losses from another for tax purposes, reducing the overall tax bite.

Finally, keeping the businesses together preserves flexibility to unwind the arrangement at a later date. For example, General Motors has revisited the structure of both its Class E and Class H stocks, as has U S West with its MediaOne stock, now spun off. By way of contrast, once a company is spun, it's gone.

Disadvantages   The targeted stock approach is not without disadvantages. The targeted business remains under the control of existing management and investors do not have a direct claim on the assets of the business. As a result, the targeted stock may trade at some discount to what would be the stand-alone value if the "moral" credit of the parent company is in doubt. Theoretically, targeted stocks should have no effect on aggregate valuation. That being said, during the 1990s bull market, letter stocks have traded very well.

Furthermore, in some situations a targeted stock may be unworkable. There is the potential problem of liability overhang because the targeted business is not legally separated from the remaining company. A large claim against the remaining businesses may still impair the assets or profitability of the targeted business, making it difficult to convince investors that a targeted stock is attractive. RJR Nabisco faced this issue in 1993 when it was forced to withdraw a proposed targeted stock linked to its Nabisco food operations, partially because investors raised concerns regarding the potential legal liabilities associated with RJR's tobacco business.

Targeted stock also introduces considerable complexity into a corporate ownership structure. The typical implementation process is time consuming and can take as long as four to six months. The parent board must deal with two classes of stock and investors, each with its own interests. Balancing these interests raises inevitable conflicts. For example, the capital allocation decision can be a zero-sum game—more money for one business means less for the other. But a board bears a fiduciary responsibility to all shareholders, and the friction associated with a targeted stock may induce additional shareholder litigation.

The legal structure of the target stock also can hamper flexibility. A back-end exchange is sometimes necessary if the company wishes to unwind the targeted stock arrangement. This reality can act as a barrier to a restructuring or the sale of the company. However, careful drafting of the targeted stock documents can circumvent most such problems, and, on balance, the targeted stock can be a helpful innovation which allows a company to arbitrage inefficiencies in the market.

Implementation Issues   Structuring a targeted stock involves a number of business, legal, tax, and accounting issues.

First, an issuer must decide on a division of business units. Because the targeted business group need not be segregated in a distinct legal entity, there is a great deal of flexibility and room for creativity. Assets, including goodwill, and liabilities, including debt, must be allocated.

In carrying out this process, thought must be given to the profile of the new hypothetical companies. For example, the targeted business might be structured as a high-growth business that will be valued primarily on a cash flow basis. The remaining business grouping might contain the more mature operations that will be valued on an earnings basis. To facilitate such a split, noncash expenses such as goodwill need to be divided thoughtfully.

The relative rights that will be attached to the different classes of stock must also be defined. There is a tension to this process, however. While more separate, defined, and unalterable rights inherent in a targeted stock increase its marketability, targeted stock must be structured as a stock of the parent company rather than a subsidiary for tax reasons. If the targeted stock were treated as stock in a subsidiary business for tax purposes, the parent company might be taxed on the issuance and the distribution treated as a taxable dividend. The targeted stock shareholders therefore make a number of concessions to ensure favorable tax treatment.

Dividend policy is another area of concern. Targeted stock shareholders usually prefer an ironclad guarantee that they will receive a fixed payout from the targeted business; but this arrangement would make the targeted business appear too separate for tax purposes. Therefore, dividends on the targeted stock usually are set as some percentage of the targeted business's net income, with the parent company's board retaining the sole discretion to adjust the amount, as with all dividends.

Targeted stock dividends are also subject to the same legal limitations which govern the payment of stock dividends generally. In other words, if the combined company becomes insolvent, the targeted stock's holders will not receive a dividend. This effective link between targeted stock dividends and the parent company's overall earnings argues in favor of treating the targeted stock as stock in the parent.

The treatment of dividends plays an important role in defining the virtual company underlying the targeted stock. For example, in designing its Media Group targeted stock, U S West broke with tradition and included no dividend on the stock. This approach, however, was in line with the company's objective of creating a high-growth profile for the business, because like actual cellular and cable companies, this virtual company would keep its cash flow for investment. By forgoing the dividend payout, U S West indicated to the market how the business should be valued.

A letter stock agreement also specifies how future sale proceeds will be treated. A number of alternatives exist. Under one common approach, if the targeted business is sold, the company is required to pay some portion of the net proceeds to the letter stockholders. Alternatively, the company might have to convert the targeted stock to regular common stock at a premium.

Letter stock typically has voting rights, though there is no requirement that letter stock be voting stock. The usual approach is for the letter stock to have a number of votes per share that floats with the relative value of the targeted stock and regular stock. This approach has two advantages. First, it allows voting power to reflect the underlying economic reality. Second, it avoids the situation where "cheap votes" can be acquired. A fixed voting ratio, on the other hand, may cause the votes attached to one class to be cheaper than the votes attached to the other should relative valuation change from relative voting ratios.

The relative value of votes is important because in most matters, such as the election of directors, the two classes vote together. However, where the outcome of a vote would have a special effect on the targeted business, the targeted shareholders may need to approve the action in a separate class vote.

Many of these legal issues also have a financial reporting impact. The targeted business remains consolidated with the parent company business for accounting purposes and, consequently, the parent still must prepare consolidated group financial statements. But in addition to the consolidated group financials, a parent also prepares audited financials for the targeted business, often appended to the parent company financials and sent out as a unit.

Mechanics   A shareholder vote is necessary to incorporate the terms of the letter stock in the corporate charter. At the company's option, either a special shareholder vote is called or the issue is brought up at a regular shareholder meeting.

The final implementation step is distribution. There are several possible approaches. First, the company can simply distribute the letter stock to existing shareholders in a tax-free dividend or exchange offer. Second, the company can use the letter stock as an acquisition currency, giving it to selling shareholders. Third, the company might sell the letter stock to the public in an initial public offering. The particular context and needs of the issuer determine which alternative is selected.

Several conglomerates—most notably GM and AT&T—have chosen to issue letter stocks as part of their self-restructurings.

General Motors and AT&T Try Alphabet Soup

Unlike ITT, Westinghouse, and the other conglomerates, General Motors was a fairly focused company during the 1970s. A relatively small percentage of its earnings came from defense contracting, financial services, and other nonautomotive activities. Above all else, GM manufactured cars, trucks, and buses.

Generally speaking, GM's operational performance remained

strong during the 1970s. A quick response to the first Oil Shock in 1973 gave the company a competitive advantage over Ford and Chrysler, and by 1978, GM was turning out smaller, more fuel-efficient cars. Customers loved the product. The statistics are stunning—sales of $63 billion, record earnings of $3.5 billion, market share approaching 50 percent.

Buoyed by this strong performance, GM formulated an ambitious plan to stay on top, making a dramatic bet on new technology. The company would spend some $40 billion over seven years to undertake a radical redesign of every car line and retooling of every factory. By the middle 1980s, GM would be turning out smaller, high-quality, fuel-efficient cars.

Of course, history did not progress as GM had planned. Oil prices crashed and customer interest in larger cars was renewed. GM, with its focus on new, fuel-efficient models, was hamstrung by dated models as foreign competition, especially from Japanese manufacturers, grew even more intense. The benefits of the capital spending program proved more elusive than hoped for.

By the middle 1980s, the wear and tear definitely was beginning to show. GM's U.S. market share, which had hovered at 48 percent in 1979, eroded to 41 percent in 1986. Profits were lower than in 1978, even though revenues were significantly higher. Moreover, the new models rolling out of GM's factories were the butt of jokes: Regardless of the nameplate, all the cars looked alike, a fact that competitors hammered home in effective advertisements.

GM chairman Roger B. Smith responded to these circumstances with a number of operational and financial initiatives. As part of this program, Smith decided to look outside GM for technological expertise, acquiring Ross Perot's Electronic Data Systems for $2.5 billion and Hughes Aircraft Corporation for $5.2 billion.

The EDS transaction was to bring high-tech thinking into GM and to rationalize and update GM's computer and communications systems. Hughes Electronics would bring additional technical expertise to the table, which GM hoped to transfer to the carmaking business. Furthermore, both EDS and Hughes were extremely profitable, high-growth businesses, which could allow GM to diversify away from the mature, cyclical auto business. GM used letter stock to facilitate the market's full valuation of the exciting growth opportunities provided by the new businesses.

GM introduced Class E stock as a low-cost way to fund approximately $500 million of the $2.5 billion EDS purchase. Though not legally bound to do so, GM pledged to pay an annual dividend on the Class E shares equal to approximately 25 percent of EDS's annual operating profits. The Class E shares also served as a means to motivate EDS employees, who were accustomed to being compensated partly in stock. In fact, a majority of the original 13.6 million Class E shares were held by EDS employees. Another 15.4 million shares eventually were distributed as a dividend to GM's existing shareholders and 3.1 million shares were sold to the public, raising $190 million for GM.

The Class E stock traded extremely well. Originally valued at around $44 a share, it zoomed up roughly 150 percent in the first eighteen months. Pleased with the reception, GM relied even more heavily on letter stock to fund the 1985 Hughes acquisition: Newly issued Class H shares represented roughly half of the $5.2 billion purchase price. GM pledged to pay a dividend on the shares based on the earnings of Hughes and to distribute additional shares to the public within three years of the acquisition.

In a sense, GM's foray into letter stock was a success. These special issues allowed the company to tap the glamour associated with its new subsidiaries. The growth opportunities inherent in these acquired companies were put into the spotlight, rather than buried within a large diversified company. Technology analysts, who would not have followed GM stock, began to follow GM Class E and Class H stock, boosting their share prices.

However, the acquisitions of Hughes and EDS were not without their difficulties. Tough integration issues, particularly with EDS, kept GM from realizing many of the hoped-for strategic benefits. And even though EDS and Hughes prospered, the transactions diverted management's focus. GM suffered through a difficult patch in the recession of the early 1990s, much of which CEO Jack Smith—who took over in 1992 after a boardroom revolt (and who is not related to his predecessor, Roger Smith)—blamed on the Hughes and EDS deals.

Likewise, EDS and Hughes suffered negative side effects from being owned by GM. GM's direct competitors constituted a large part of EDS' and Hughes' potential markets, and therefore hesitated to provide confidential business information and revenue to GM.

For these reasons, Jack Smith and the GM board ultimately decided to reverse the EDS and Hughes acquisitions. In 1996, GM contributed its block of Class E shares to its pension plan and then spun off EDS (after taking a $500 million dividend). The Hughes defense electronics business was sold outright to Raytheon for $9.5 billion.

From a financial perspective, both acquisitions and subsequent divestitures were very lucrative for GM. GM's $2.5 billion investment in EDS was converted into approximately $9.2 billion: the $190 million raised in 1984 through the letter stock offering, the $500 million dividend, and the satisfaction of roughly $8.5 billion in obligations to the GM pension fund. In addition, GM shared in the cash flow from and benefited from the services of EDS and Hughes over a period of years.

Having sold Hughes' defense electronics business to Raytheon, GM is currently considering spinning off the rest of Hughes to shareholders. GM also recently completed a spin-off of Delphi Automotive Systems (which it had merged with its AC Delco automotive electronics business).

AT&T too had planned to issue a tracking stock in connection with its 1998 merger with TCI to ensure full valuation of the company. AT&T's stock has long traded on the basis of its earnings. But the TCI deal would create both goodwill, whose amortization reduces earnings, and require the issuance of more shares, diluting earnings per share; AT&T was concerned that these two factors would cause its share price to fall.

Therefore, a plan was conceived to issue tracking stock, onto which most of the accounting changes could be off-loaded. Because that stock would track the company's high-growth, no-earnings businesses, including cable TV assets, it was thought the stock would trade, as cable TV stocks tend to, on the basis of EBITDA (earnings before interest, taxes, depreciation, and amortization), and so these accounting charges wouldn't reduce its price. Furthermore, because AT&T shareholders would exchange some of their shares for the new tracking stock, the number of AT&T shares would be reduced, increasing EPS, and thus AT&T's share price.

But there was a snag. Long distance phone service would be one of the most important elements of the tracking stock—and long distance generated profits.

So AT&T then contemplated a stock to track just cable TV and wireless operations. But this plan led to operating, accounting, and personnel issues. Fortunately, the market solved the problem for AT&T, understanding the logic of the TCI combination, and sending AT&T's stock up in value. AT&T did, however, issue a letter stock to track the operations of Liberty Media, a cable programming company headed by TCI's Malone.

Investment bank DLJ has also jumped on the tracking stock bandwagon to capture the sky-high valuations afforded to Internet stocks. Its new letter stock trades the operations of its online brokerage operation DLJ Direct.

We are all still on a journey of exploration with tracking stocks and do not have the wisdom of extensive experience. To date, there have been a series of issues which were misguided at conception or bungled in execution. In general, the record has been exceptionally positive; but the 1999 Clinton budget proposal has made the future of tracking stock uncertain, threatening to make the issuance of tracking stock taxable. The tax-free nature of tracking stock transactions has been one of its primary benefits. If the proposal is ultimately adopted, tracking stock's role may be limited.

Defense: Building the Battlements | 21

"Force is never more operative than when it is known to exist but is not brandished."

—Admiral Alfred Mahan

When a company falters, the carrions of prey circle. A low stock price relative to underlying asset values, an aging CEO without a successor, a weak board, a cash-rich balance sheet, and obvious opportunities for cost reductions all attract attention and put a company squarely in the takeover crosshairs. A target not in motion is a sitting duck.

The key to defense is advance preparation. Few companies are immune to attack, and size is not necessarily an insurmountable barrier. Nor does a healthy balance sheet guarantee protection. The best prophylactic is a resolute management and board of directors, a high stock price, and good shareholder relations. Keeping a board informed and resilient is one of the key responsibilities of a CEO. Because directors get bombarded with lawsuits and pressure during a deal, building a bond with them before it all starts is invaluable.

Most companies have some sense of their vulnerabilities, but a disciplined analysis crystallizes the intuitions. Working from this foundation, a company can build effective defensive battlements, reducing the vulnerabilities.

Shareholder Analysis

Shareholder analysis is to a takeover contest what polling is to a political campaign. These data can be extremely helpful in crafting a defensive strategy and in opening a channel of communication with shareholders. Relevant considerations include the geographic distribution of share ownership and the breakdown of share ownership by individual investors, institutions, employees, customers, and suppliers.

For example, shareholders who live where a company has sizable operations may be more likely to side with management. Likewise, individuals and employees are generally more favorably disposed toward management than institutional investors. On the other hand, shares controlled by fiduciaries such as trustees or mutual fund managers are more likely to be in favor of a hostile raider.

The frequency with which company shares trade can have significant defensive implications. A high shareholding turnover may signal a disenchanted shareholder base with a short-term investment horizon, while a more stable base of shareholders may bode well for management. Furthermore, companies attempt to estimate the tax basis of major shareholders because a low tax basis, which reflects a large built-in capital gain, may make major shareholders relatively more unwilling to sell their shares for cash given the resulting high tax liability.

Systematic communications with major shareholders can enhance a company's chances of winning a proxy fight or of fending off an exchange offer because shareholders who are part of a dialogue are more likely to be receptive to management. A shareholder relations operation also creates proxy fight machinery.

Early Warning

Trading activity in a company's stock sometimes spikes upward in advance of a takeover attempt. To monitor trading activity, many

companies have initiated "stock watch" programs designed to uncover stock accumulations or stock price movements that reflect
possible leaks regarding a deal. The company's transfer agent, who
handles the administrative details involved in transferring ownership
of shares, is one key source of information, and is admonished to
prepare timely transfer sheets and report any unusual movements.
Though shares often trade in the "street name" of brokers, the
bunching of large block trades can indicate a potential hostile bidder
is accumulating shares.

If properly cultivated, the specialist or market maker—the member of a stock exchange who is responsible for making an orderly
market in a company's stock—can also be valuable. Market making
consists of buying and selling stock for one's own account when
there is a market imbalance or maintaining a trading market for a
company's stock if it is traded over the counter, such as through the
NASDAQ system. Specialists and market makers often will be the
first outsiders to know about large block trades.

A stock watch program includes routine surveillance of government filings, such as 13D securities filings. However, because hostile
bidders are aware of the various filing requirements, they often
structure their activities so that an actual hostile bid follows quickly
on the heels of any public filing. And since the revisions in the Hart-
Scott-Rodino requirements have made rare the secret accumulation
of more than $15 million, a stock watch program can occasionally be
helpful but is rarely a silver bullet.

Even without insider trading, rumors of impending deals often
circulate. As a natural law, the larger the team, the higher the
chances word will get out. Often the leaks are inadvertent—the executive who cancels his well-known plans and the adviser who, to
avoid legal liability, "restricts" his research and trading divisions
from being active in the stocks. A bank loan has been a prime
source of rumors because the number of people in the know mul-
tiplies.

Defensive Overview

Large public companies often conduct reviews of their takeover defenses. An annual presentation to the board can provide the catalyst for discussions of a company's current defensive posture. Such meetings serve a dual purpose. First, a board presentation jogs the corporate memory and motivates a careful defensive review. Second, a presentation educates directors about "state of the art" takeover defenses. This process is critical given the central role played by directors in any takeover contest.

The starting point for defensive analysis is a strategic overview of corporate policy. A company's defensive position is enhanced greatly if the board of directors has a standing, conscious policy of keeping the company independent: Both the *Time* and *Wallace* cases underline that the board has the power to determine corporate policy, and strategic decisions will be respected, absent unreasonable or improper behavior.

Once corporate policy is established, a thorough defensive overview involves an analysis of defensive provisions in a company's charter, bylaws, and loan agreements. The terms of any poison pill are also important. In addition, the relevant state antitakeover statutes and case law should be studied for their defensive implications, as should applicable regulatory frameworks. Finally, on a more substantive level, a review of corporate structure can provide insights regarding business strategies that reduce the likelihood of an attack.

Because the state of the art of takeover defense is constantly evolving as hostile raiders develop mechanisms to counteract existing technology, companies should regularly update their takeover defenses. But building an insurmountable barricade is not necessarily the goal, as a court will invalidate abusive defenses. Rather, the objective is to build enough friction into the system so that management and shareholders will have the time to make informed decisions about the strategic alternatives. If a sale is the right answer, shareholders will get a higher price from an orderly process.

The Approach

Bidders often approach a company informally, with a casual pass in the form of a call to a board member or executive. These discussions are the first opportunity to establish a firm defensive posture. Unfortunately, this opportunity sometimes is squandered because the recipient of the call is unprepared to respond with a forceful rejection. An ambiguous response can be misread as an indication of interest and generate an unwanted suitor. The classic example is Conoco CEO Ralph Bailey's waffling response to the Dome Petroleum offer, which spawned a takeover bid.

As part of the defensive review process, the board should authorize the CEO and other executive officers to discourage any casual overtures. For maximum effectiveness, the policy should be conveyed to managers down the line. The recipient of a takeover solicitation should be encouraged to notify the CEO. Of course, any formal offer requires a careful, thorough board review.

Companies generally resist disclosing casual passes out of concern that to do so will put them in play. Negotiations of a friendly deal also can be extremely sensitive, and parties tend to prefer to wait until a concrete agreement has been reached before making disclosure. There has been much focus on just how concrete negotiations must be for an obligation to arise. Both the SEC and the Supreme Court in *Basic v. Levinson* have taken the position that a company's disclosures must be accurate and complete in all material respects. The Supreme Court said that a company has an obligation to make nonmisleading statements once it has commented on a situation. However, the Court also stated that a company's reply of "no comment" would be treated as silence and, therefore, not misleading.

Accordingly, the practical result for most companies is never to comment on pending merger discussions until an agreement in principle is reached. Up to that point, anything other than "no comment" will only cause problems, as when former AT&T CEO Robert Allen publicly defended the embryonic AT&T-SBC merger of 1997, which proceeded to fall apart under the glare of media attention.

Preventive Defense

The state of the art in the defense field has evolved through a Darwinian process of attack and response. As attacks became more potent, an array of defense devices were developed that parried the thrusts and created a more balanced system.

Three major categories of defensive mechanisms have been developed: poison pills, structural devices generally referred to as shark repellents, and golden parachutes. The cumulative effect has been to make a hostile takeover more difficult and more costly.

The Poison Pill

A kind of spring trap, the poison pill makes an unfriendly takeover prohibitively expensive. The idea is simple. A corporation issues a new class of securities to shareholders that have no value unless an investor acquires a specified percentage of the company's voting stock (typically 10 to 20 percent) without prior board approval. If an investor crosses the threshold, the securities activate in a way that devalues the investor's stake in the company.

A poison pill serves two possible purposes. First, it is a vehicle to slow the attack and give directors and shareholders a reasonable period of time to consider a takeover bid and, if appropriate, develop alternatives. Certainly, the pill can counter the arguably coercive nature of two-tiered offers. Second, the pill might be used as a means to preclude takeovers altogether.

In *Household International,* the Delaware Supreme Court expressly confirmed the authority of a board to issue a poison pill as a preventive defensive measure. The court also held that the business judgment rule would apply to the decision to enact a pill so long as the *Unocal* reasonableness test is satisfied. This position was reaffirmed in *Revlon,* where the court approved Revlon's initial implementation of a poison pill as a reasonable means to counter Ronald Perelman's two-tiered bid. The frontier of the poison pill debate thus focuses on when, if ever, a board should be required to pull the pill.

Early Evolution   The first-generation poison pill was developed by Marty Lipton in 1982. This type of pill, which evolved out of a series of "special power" preferred stock called "blank check preferred," involved the distribution of a preferred stock as a dividend to shareholders. In a takeover of the issuer in which the issuer was merged into the acquirer, each share of preferred stock would be converted into forty shares of the acquiring company, thereby substantially diluting the ownership interest of the acquirer.

As originally conceived, preferred stock plans had several disadvantages. First, the preferred stock generally could only be redeemed after an extended period of time, typically ten years. This feature severely limited the flexibility available to an issuer if it later decided to pursue a merger. Second, the preferred stock had a negative impact on an issuer's balance sheet because credit rating agencies sometimes treated it as long-term debt when assessing a company's strength.

The second-generation pill—called a "rights plan" or "flip-over pill"—was designed to address these problems. Under a flip-over plan, a company would issue rights to its shareholders which, if the company were involved in a merger or other business combination not approved by its board, entitled its shareholders to purchase stock in the surviving company at a substantial discount. The target shareholders could thus flip over to become acquiring shareholders, diluting the acquirer in the process.

A major weakness of the flip-over pill was dramatically demonstrated by Sir James Goldsmith's takeover of Crown Zellerbach Corporation. Ironically, Goldsmith became interested in the San Francisco–based paper company when it put its pill in place. Less than six months later, Goldsmith was revealed as a major buyer of Crown Zellerbach stock when he filed a 13D with the SEC. And within another seven months Goldsmith had purchased voting control of Crown Zellerbach.

How did Goldsmith manage to overcome the Crown Zellerbach pill? Quite simply, after purchasing voting control on the open market, he stopped short of a back-end merger. Without tripping this doomsday trigger, the Crown Zellerbach rights never became active in the sense of allowing a bargain purchase of stock. The rights never flipped over.

Patience was the key to Goldsmith's strategy. He was satisfied to hold 51 percent of Crown Zellerbach's outstanding stock and hold off on a back-end merger until the rights could be redeemed. In fact, Goldsmith was able to turn the pill to his advantage. By crossing the initial ownership threshold that made the rights nonredeemable, he severely limited Crown Zellerbach's options. The board—unable to redeem the rights—found it hard to find a white knight willing to step in and buy the company. The problem was that, like Goldsmith, any such white knight would have to swallow Crown Zellerbach's pill if it wanted to gain full control.

Flip-In, Flip-Over Pill   A third-generation pill—the "flip-in, flip-over"—was developed in reaction to Goldsmith's victory and is the most common form of poison pill currently in use. Though endless variations exist, this type of pill generally has certain standard features.

The pill is implemented through a special dividend of one stock purchase right per outstanding common share which lies dormant until a triggering event—typically the acquisition of 15 percent of the company's voting stock without prior board approval or a hostile tender for 30 percent or more of the company's voting stock.

When the rights activate, all holders (except the investor who triggers the rights) become entitled to purchase additional stock in the issuing company at a substantial discount. This is the flip-in.

Also, if the issuing company takes part in any business combination or asset sale after the triggering event, all rights holders other than the triggering investor may buy voting securities of the surviving corporation at a substantial discount. In certain circumstances, this right allows target shareholders to buy stock in the bidder. This is the traditional flip-over.

In most cases, the rights can be redeemed at any point prior to a triggering event for a nominal amount such as $.02 per right. The board may amend the rights at any point prior to a triggering event.

Two features make the flip-in a potent defense against a Goldsmith-type acquisition. First, the flip-in right is fully activated by a single step—the acquisition of stock in excess of a specific amount. Second, the flip-in rights are discriminatory. The acquirer who triggers the flip-in is not given the opportunity to purchase target company stock on the cheap.

Both the flip-in and the flip-over impose considerable dilution on a hostile raider. If the threshold is crossed and the rights are exercised, the value of the raider's investment will drop precipitously.

Why retain a flip-over when the flip-in protects against the circumstances covered by the flip-over? The main reason is that the legal status of the discriminatory flip-in was unsettled for a time. Hence, the flip-over was retained as a backstop to provide what protection it could. However, the flip-over has become largely unnecessary given that, since *Household,* at least twenty-four states have adopted statutes that permit corporations to adopt discriminatory flip-in, flip-over pills.

The modern poison pill can be, and is typically, put in place by the board of directors without a shareholder vote. The rights—usually with a ten-year life—are then issued as a dividend on the common stock, effectively "stapled" to the common stock so that the rights and stock trade together until a triggering event. However, upon the occurrence of a triggering event, the rights can be traded separately; the issuer then will mail separate certificates to shareholders.

OSCAR WYATT UNHORSED

The power of the pill was put on dramatic display in the 1989 battle for Texas Eastern, with Oscar Wyatt of Coastal Corporation pitted against his old nemesis Dennis Hendrix. Wyatt's $2.5 billion cash offer put Texas Eastern in play, but a well-designed pill gave the board the time to conduct an orderly auction. As a result, Texas Eastern shareholders instead received $3.2 billion in cash and stock in the Panhandle Eastern buyout.

Wyatt had a history with Texas Eastern and its CEO Dennis Hendrix. As the head of Texas Gas in 1983, Hendrix had turned Wyatt away by agreeing to sell out to white knight CSX, whom we represented. Then, in 1984, Coastal had bought a block of shares in Texas Eastern, but the rumored takeover attempt failed to materialize. However, Coastal retained a nearly 5 percent stake in the company.

Finally, in 1989, Wyatt decided to pursue Texas Eastern. The takeover attempt did not begin auspiciously. Coastal announced its intention to bid on Martin Luther King Day, January 16, 1989. Wyatt's team apparently forgot about the relatively new holiday. At the last minute, Coastal discovered that the SEC was closed, so the company could not file its tender offer. Coastal was forced to wait a day to make a formal announcement, a tactical gaffe that gave Hendrix an extra day to prepare Texas Eastern's legal defenses.

On January 17, Coastal made a $42 a share, $2.5 billion offer official. The market responded by dramatically bidding up Texas Eastern's stock, which closed above $46 a share. Over the next few days, the price floated up even further, touching $48. Apparently, investors believed Wyatt had lowballed the company, and that some deal would go through at a higher price.

Considering the history, Hendrix naturally was loath to have his company folded into Wyatt's empire. But Hendrix quickly realized that Texas Eastern would not survive as an independent company, and investor pressure was fierce. The defense team, which included us, calculated that we needed some maneuvering room. We kept Texas Eastern's pill in place, but provided a board commitment to remove it on March 15 to allow time for an orderly auction without the risk of a court removing the pill.

Ultimately, Panhandle Eastern topped Wyatt's $42 a share cash bid with an offer of $53 in cash for 80 percent of Texas Eastern and stock worth roughly $53 in a back-end merger. The pill facilitated the month-long process of soliciting a large group of bidders, providing information in a Houston data room and gathering bids.

Effect   Considerable research has been conducted on the effect of poison pills. Some studies analyze the stock-price impact of installing a pill; other studies investigate the pill's effect on takeover premiums. While not all research is uniform in conclusion, the consensus seems to be that the implementation of a pill has a slight negative effect on a company's stock price, while the presence of a pill increases the premium a company receives in a takeover. The net effect on shareholder value is unclear, but likely positive.

Redemption   By the late 1980s, the poison pill defense had evolved into an effective stopgap measure which could delay the most determined suitor. Even though a pill might not permanently thwart a raider, it halted any stampede. However, the pill is by no means insurmountable. The board's ability to redeem a pill—a common feature—opens the way to attack. A hostile bidder can take advantage of this feature by launching a tender offer that is conditioned on the redemption of the pill. If the bidder offers a substantial premium, the board is placed under pressure to vote in favor of redemption.

The previously described dead-hand pill, however, prevents a bidder from gaining control of a target company's board through a proxy fight and then removing its pill.

Dead-hand pills are rare, mainly as a result of *Bank of New York v. Irving Bank,* a 1988 case in which a New York court invalidated a dead-hand pill under New York law. In more recent cases, a Pennsylvania court upheld but a Delaware court invalidated the poison pill defense. The dead-hand pill was upheld in 1998 by a Pennsylvania court in the *AlliedSignal v. AMP* case. However, in a case in Delaware—where many U.S. corporations are located—*Carmody v. Toll Brothers,* Vice Chancellor Jack B. Jacobs ruled against the dead-hand pill because any limitations on the power of directors, or attempt to create two separate classes of directors—which the dead-hand pill effectively does—must be set out in a company's charter, which they were not. So-called slow-hand pills, pills that cannot be redeemed for a certain period after an offer, have not yet been widely ruled on. The particular facts of the situation in the *Mentor Graphics v. Quickturn Design Systems* case caused the Delaware Court of Chancery to find the slow-hand pill invalid under the *Unocal* reasonableness test. But on appeal, the Delaware Supreme Court found the slow-hand pill statutorily invalid in general.

Regardless, the possibility of a proxy contest raises an obvious question: Why adopt a redeemable rather than a nonredeemable pill? The answer is twofold. First, in approving the poison pill as a defensive measure, the Delaware courts have placed considerable weight on the redemption feature. In *Household,* for example, the

Delaware Supreme Court cited the possibility of redemption as supporting its view that the pill does not preclude a takeover. Rather, the court found, the pill simply redressed the previous power imbalance between bidder and target.

Second, the redemption feature provides necessary flexibility to an issuing board. By including a redemption feature, a board retains the ability to adopt positive transaction alternatives, as was the case in the Texas Eastern defense. An unredeemable pill simply may alienate institutional investors in a proxy fight.

Under Delaware law, once a bid is launched, the decision whether to retain a pill is subject to the same fiduciary test applied to other defensive measures—the *Unocal* standard. *Unocal* and *Household* require that the board show both procedural and substantive reasonableness with regard to the decision to keep a pill in place rather than accept a specific tender offer. Hence, the board must show good-faith investigation of the offer and other alternatives and keeping the pill in place must be reasonable in relation to the threat posed by the offer.

Given the inherently fact-specific nature of the *Unocal* inquiry, it should not be surprising that the courts have yet to develop a simple consensus regarding when a pill can be retained. Rather, the courts conduct a wide-ranging analysis and analyze pills on a case-by-case, fact-specific basis. Important factors include the perceived coerciveness and financial adequacy of the offer and the characteristics of the alternative advanced by the board. Courts are particularly skeptical where a board uses a pill to protect its own preferred transaction.

The most fundamental redemption issue is whether a board should be required to pull a pill in the face of an all-cash, all-shares offer. Even on this point, the law remains divided. Some cases have found no threat to shareholders under those circumstances and have required the pill to be pulled, for example in the 1988 battle for Pillsbury.

The Pillsbury battle began on October 4, 1988, when Grand Metropolitan, a British company, announced a surprise tender offer at

$60 a share, all in cash. Pillsbury's stock had been trading at $39 the day before. Given the over 50 percent premium, the food and spirits conglomerate was widely viewed to be looking for the quick knock-out. Of course, the bid was conditioned on the redemption of Pillsbury's poison pill.

From the perspective of a target's board, an all-cash, all-shares bid creates the most pressure to redeem an existing pill, with the arguably coercive aspects of a two-tier offer missing. In this situation, the main goal becomes using what leverage the pill provides to obtain the highest bid possible. Shareholders then can decide whether to tender into the offer.

This was the predicament that faced Pillsbury CEO Philip Smith and the Pillsbury board. The company launched a series of litigation maneuvers to hold off Grand Met, and almost immediately the board came to the conclusion that Pillsbury would have a tough time remaining independent. However, Grand Met had implied it might raise its bid, and the board wanted to get as much as it could for shareholders.

The problem, of course, was that Pillsbury needed a credible alternative to tease a higher bid out of Grand Met. Seeking to encourage other bidders, the Grand Met offer was rejected as inadequate. A number of potential white knights were pursued, but Grand Met's preemptive bid kept most from getting involved. Smith and the board decided to pursue a recapitalization as the next best alternative. A plan was drafted to spin off Pillsbury's Burger King, pay shareholders a special dividend, and sell a number of other businesses.

All this activity was really just a prelude to the final negotiation. Matters came to a head in early December 1989. Pillsbury had won an earlier battle in Delaware court when a judge refused to force the company to redeem its pill, reasoning that Pillsbury should have time to pursue other options that might benefit shareholders.

In December, a second hearing was held in Delaware court. Pillsbury had already managed to get a higher bid—$63 a share—out of Grand Met, but the second round in court went to Grand Met.

Using a *Unocal* analysis, the court found the only major threat to shareholders to be an economic one. The all-cash, all-shares offer was not coercive and the shareholders should be allowed to decide the issue of value. Pillsbury would have to redeem its poison pill.

Little negotiating leverage remained. Pillsbury quickly came to terms with Grand Met and a merger agreement was signed. Even so, Grand Met raised its final bid to $66 a share. Pillsbury's aggressive defense had forced a 10 percent increase in an already fully priced bid.

At the time Pillsbury was decided, legal experts generally read it to mean that a bidder could force a pill redemption with an all-cash, all-shares premium bid. However, the waters have since been muddied by *Time, Wallace,* and *AMP.*

For example, in *Time,* the court refused to force Time to delay its tender offer for Warner so that shareholders could accept the Paramount offer. While not directly a pill redemption case, the court expressly rejects the idea that the only threat from an all-cash, all-shares offer is that the price may be too low. Rather, the court implies that other concerns might reasonably keep a board from allowing shareholders to accept an offer. This aspect of the *Time* case has since been stretched to a point where *Time* arguably overturns the lower court decision in *Pillsbury.*

Wallace, in particular, makes a more direct attack on *Pillsbury.* The federal district judge in *Wallace* expressly ruled that the company need not withdraw its poison pill and thus barred shareholders from accepting Moore's all-cash tender offer. In justifying this outcome, the judge applied a *Unocal* reasonableness analysis and relied on *Time* for support. He determined that the Moore offer reasonably could be construed as a threat because shareholders might accept the offer without a full understanding of Wallace's future prospects. While in *AMP* a Pennsylvania judge ruled that AMP did not need to redeem its poison pill in the face of an all-cash, all-shares offer from AlliedSignal, this decision was highly dependent on the unique position Pennsylvania law takes with respect to takeovers.

However, notwithstanding the outcomes of *Wallace* and *AMP*, the fact remains that an all-cash offer puts considerable pressure on a board. If the board stands behind its pill and rejects such an offer, it likely will find itself the subject of litigation and a proxy fight. In *Wallace*, the judge expressly recognized that there is a point at which a board will have a fiduciary duty to redeem a pill. Precisely when that duty arises will remain murky until the Delaware Chancery Court revisits the issue directly on a different set of facts.

THE DELAWARE PRISM

Trying to predict how the Delaware Chancery Court—Delaware's business law court—will resolve a particular takeover challenge is like tracking a beam of light through a prism. One can calculate the course of light as it bounces through based on the size and position of the prism's faces. Similarly, takeover decisions of the court are a pragmatic response to many different factors. By weighing the totality of the circumstances in a given case, the outcome is easier to predict.

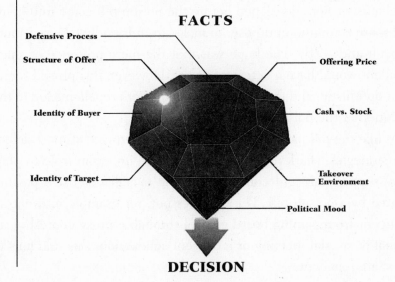

FACTS

Defensive Process

Structure of Offer

Offering Price

Identity of Buyer

Cash vs. Stock

Identity of Target

Takeover Environment

Political Mood

DECISION

A number of issues in particular seem to animate the Delaware case law. These are the facets of the Delaware prism: the premium offered, the process involved, the structure of the deal (two tiers or one), the personality and reputation of the buyer, the form of consideration (cash or securities), the personality and reputation of the target and its board, the takeover environment, and the political mood regarding deals.

So, for example, *Unocal* went against Boone Pickens because, though he offered a premium price, the deal was two-tiered; he had a reputation as a raider; the back-end consideration was a package of securities of uncertain value; Fred Hartley was a member of the business establishment; and there was a growing backlash against hostile attacks.

Shark Repellents

Corporations and their advisers have identified a number of defensive mechanisms—loosely referred to as "shark repellents"—that can be embedded in either a corporate charter or bylaw. These mechanisms were developed before the poison pill came into being and share a common purpose: to make an unfriendly takeover more difficult and costly. The hope was that the mere presence of shark repellent would have a deterrent effect. However, this proved somewhat optimistic, and the mixed success of shark repellents led to the evolution of the poison pill.

While the pill has developed into the centerpiece of most defensive strategies, shark repellents still have an important role to play: They supplement and contribute to the overall defensive posture created by a poison pill. The pill does not, for example, prevent an insurgent from gaining board control through a proxy contest at an annual or special meeting or a consent solicitation; this role falls to the shark repellent.

There are fundamental distinctions between the way different types of shark repellents must be implemented. Some require shareholder approval, while others can be put in place by the board of directors without shareholder approval. This distinction generally parallels the split between provisions that must be enacted through charter amendment and those that can be enacted by amendment of the bylaws.

The law of the state in which a company is incorporated, along with its existing corporate charter and bylaws, determines what may be enacted as a bylaw without shareholder approval. Generally, only the more procedural rules may be accomplished through bylaws; but because most forms of shark repellent require amendments to a company's corporate charter, they require a shareholder vote.

The decision to implement shark repellents is not without risk. If a company is already in a precarious position, seeking shareholder approval for defensive measures may prove disastrous. An unwelcome proxy contest may result, and the shareholders may reject the shark repellent. Not only would this leave the company unprotected, it would likely generate unwelcome attention from hostile bidders, as a shareholder defeat effectively communicates the lack of shareholder support for incumbent management.

A company considering the use of shark repellent should spend time analyzing its shareholder base and voting history. Although it can be difficult to predict the course of a shareholder election, certain general trends are apparent. As mentioned previously, individual shareholders tend to side with management; institutional investors, on the other hand, have a known antipathy to most forms of shark repellent. Some institutional investors actually have adopted a policy of voting against them. With the help of an experienced proxy solicitor and these general observations, a company can get a good sense for the prospect of shareholder approval.

Almost endless variations exist within the category of shark repellent. The most typical varieties include staggered board elections, restrictions on shareholder action, antigreenmail provisions, super-voting stock, and various debt-based repellents. ·

Reinforcing the Board of Directors   Control a company's board of directors, and you control the company. It is therefore no surprise that the board is often a hostile raider's prime target. This fact makes reinforcing the board an important part of any defensive package.

Common board-related defensive measures include a staggered board and limitations on cumulative voting and the removal of directors. These provisions can frustrate a raider's attempts to take control of a company through a proxy fight. In contrast, a poison pill provides no protection against a proxy fight.

A staggered board—in which directors are divided into a number of classes, with only one class up for reelection each year—is created by amendment to the charter. So, for example, a nine-person board might be divided into three classes. Directors in each class would serve a three-year term, with one class elected each year. The defensive virtue of this arrangement is that a raider who holds a majority of the stock theoretically still must wait for two elections to capture board control.

As a practical matter, though, a board may not be able to hold out against a major stockholder, and instead may bow to the inevitable in the face of pressure from the stockholder, whether exerted through litigation or by other means.

Careful design can maximize the protective capacity of a staggered board. Limits must be placed, for example, on the ability to increase the size of the board to prevent an insurgent shareholder from simply adding seats to the board so as to elect a majority at a single meeting.

Under cumulative voting, a shareholder can cast all its votes for a single candidate. So, for example, a shareholder with 100 shares would have 300 votes in an election for three open seats and could cumulate all 300 votes for a single candidate. This provision maximizes minority shareholders' board representation.

In the context of a takeover contest, cumulative voting cuts both ways. The provision may allow a hostile bidder who is a minority shareholder to gain board representation and thus access to confidential company information. However, if a hostile bidder becomes a major shareholder, cumulative voting, like a staggered board, can also delay its assumption of control.

From a defensive standpoint, then, the ideal arrangement would be to allow cumulative voting only once a single investor or an affiliated group of investors acquires a major stake in the company. A less favorable approach would be to avoid cumulative voting altogether.

Depending on where a company is incorporated, its ability to adopt either of these alternatives may be limited. Some states permit cumulative voting, others require it. States which take the permissive approach generally set up a default rule and then require a corporation that wishes to take the opposite position to do so through a provision in the charter or bylaws. While a company that is incorporated in a permissive state theoretically can rid itself of cumulative voting once it is in place, this may prove difficult to accomplish if a supermajority vote is mandated by state law.

In addition to other board reinforcement mechanisms, a provision specifying that directors can only be removed "for cause" or under certain specified circumstances enhances the defensive posture. To give such a provision teeth, it should also be supported by a supermajority requirement for amendment or repeal.

Restricting Shareholder Action   Defense of the board becomes somewhat superfluous if shareholders have the power to bypass the board and gain direct control of their corporation. A number of companies have experienced this, much to the chagrin of insiders.

Attention to a number of details can compensate. In particular, a company can limit the ability of shareholders to call special meetings and act by consent, and can require advance notice of shareholder proposals for action. Finally, the approval of a supermajority can be required for certain transactions.

Unless a company's certificate of incorporation specifies otherwise, many states require a corporation to call a special shareholders' meeting if the holders of a specified percentage of the corporation's outstanding shares so request. A special meeting poses a number of potential problems for corporate insiders on the defensive.

First, if the board is not properly reinforced, an insurgent shareholder may be able to use a special meeting to take control by expanding the number of board seats and electing new directors or by removing sitting directors if they are not protected by "for cause" language in the bylaws or charter.

Second, an insurgent shareholder can use a special meeting as a forum to contest a proxy fight. An unfavorable vote can weaken the corporation's defenses in a number of ways. A majority of shareholders might vote in favor of a nonbinding resolution to remove a poison pill. The board can then be faced with the prospect of either surrendering to the insurgent or ignoring shareholder wishes.

For these reasons, companies often restrict the ability of shareholders to call a special meeting. The relevant corporate statute in each case regulates the possibilities. At the extreme, the right to call a special meeting can be reserved solely to the board and the CEO. Or shareholders might be permitted to call a special meeting, but only if a supermajority agrees. The possible agenda items at a special meeting might also be restricted.

Consent solicitations pose another problem. Under some state statutes, a company may permit shareholders to act by written consent, without a meeting. A raider can use this power to take control of the board or enact some other change on an expedited basis, although a consent solicitation must generally abide by the disclosure requirements and procedures applicable to proxy contests. The process might be completed as soon as documents are filed with the SEC and holders with the requisite number of shares sign the consent.

Two approaches have been used to limit shareholder consent rights. Some companies have proposed charter amendments that restrict the ability of shareholders to act by consent. However, a shareholder vote is required to enact them. Consequently, other companies have favored bylaw revisions, which can be adopted by a board without shareholder approval. While bylaw revisions have this advantage, courts have subjected restrictive bylaws to tough scrutiny, fearing that they might be used to circumvent the required shareholder approval process.

As an added defensive measure, a corporation may enact a bylaw that requires advance notice of shareholder proposals and board nominations. Provisions vary as to the length of notice required, but sixty days is not uncommon. The receipt of notice serves several defensive purposes. First, it gives a board sufficient time to consider the appropriate response or to select its own slate of candidates. Second, a long notice period tends to reduce the likelihood of challenge because an insurgent shareholder may simply overlook the deadline and by the time another meeting comes around, the challenge may have died.

Supermajority rules provide another effective barrier to a hostile takeover. The general approach has been to require a higher level of approval for a merger or other transaction involving an "interested shareholder." While different standards are used, a 5 or 10 percent ownership threshold is commonly used to measure "interest."

Various mechanisms qualify as supermajority provisions. For example, 80 percent shareholder approval might be required for a merger with an interested person. Or the approval threshold might be set on a sliding scale—the higher the interested person's shareholding percentage, the higher the required supermajority. Another alternative is to require approval from a majority of the shares other than those held by the interested shareholder.

A supermajority rule, like other preventive defenses, should be supported by a suitable amendment provision. In other words, a similar supermajority vote should be required to amend the supermajority rule. Otherwise, a hostile raider might circumvent the requirement.

ON THE BATTLEFIELD

Johnson & Johnson Goes for the Heart

Two 1995 takeover contests demonstrated just how gaping a hole the consent solicitation leaves in a company's defensive structure. First there was IBM's one, two punch of a premium bid for Lotus backed by a consent solicitation. Then, later the same year, Johnson & Johnson adopted similar tactics in its takeover of Cordis Corp. of Florida, a maker of heart instruments.

Johnson & Johnson had made friendly overtures to Cordis early in the fall of 1995, but Cordis management refused the offers. In the eyes of Ralph Larsen, CEO of Johnson & Johnson, the strategic imperative for a deal was strong. Johnson & Johnson had a hot cardiac product known as a stent, an implant used to clear blocked arteries. Yet Johnson & Johnson lacked a broader line of cardiology devices. This segment of the industry was divided among a number of smaller competitors like Cordis, and Larsen saw an opportunity for consolidation.

On October 19, 1995, Johnson & Johnson launched a $100 a share hostile tender offer for Cordis that provided a fairly slim premium of 16 percent over the latest close. However, the Cordis stock price had been bid up on takeover rumors and Johnson & Johnson's bid represented a 30 percent premium to the closing price thirty trading days prior to the deal announcement. In total,

Johnson & Johnson was offering $1.6 billion in cash. The company also left the door open for a friendly stock deal at $105 a share.

Like IBM, Johnson & Johnson backed up its bid with an immediate SEC filing of materials for a consent solicitation. Once the materials were approved, Johnson & Johnson could begin soliciting consents from shareholders. If 50.1 percent backed Johnson & Johnson, it could replace the Cordis board.

Cordis rejected the $100 offer and began an accelerated search for white knights. For a time, it looked as if Cordis might try to hold off Johnson & Johnson with a controversial dead-hand poison pill put in place only a few days prior to the Johnson & Johnson bid. (This variant of the pill can only be redeemed by the actual directors who voted on the original plan, or their hand-picked successors.) The idea was to circumvent the consent solicitation process by keeping a hostile bidder from being able to redeem the Cordis pill even if it gained control of the board.

As part of its assault, Johnson & Johnson immediately sued to have the dead-hand pill revoked. The consensus of legal observers was that Johnson & Johnson had a strong case in light of an earlier court decision in which such a pill was revoked. Cordis management apparently agreed. When no white knights stepped forward, the company capitulated, though it was able to get Johnson & Johnson to sweeten its bid to $109 in stock.

Antigreenmail Provisions   Greenmail refers to the practice of repurchasing shares from a hostile bidder at a premium to the current market price. In the mid-1980s, the prospect of receiving greenmail was a major motivation for hostile raiders to profit immediately from a hostile bid.

Acting on the theory that if you take away the honey, you can avoid the bees, many corporations have enacted antigreenmail provisions. These provisions typically involve charter amendments that restrict the corporation's ability to repurchase shares at a premium. Another provision might require shareholder approval before stock can be repurchased from a shareholder who holds more than a specified percentage of stock. Waivers are generally included that cover open market purchases and purchases at the market price (which still can profit a raider, if the market price exceeds his purchase price).

The popularity of antigreenmail provisions has declined with the introduction of a federal greenmail tax. In addition, companies have come to realize that a strict antigreenmail provision might actually reduce the flexibility needed to deal with a hostile bidder.

Supervoting Stock   Placing a supervoting stock in friendly hands is attractive from a defensive perspective. By giving certain shareholders more voting power per share than others, an incumbent management and board can ensure that friendly shareholders will be in control, effectively precluding the possibility of a hostile takeover. The tactic is most commonly used where a founding individual or family holds a large block of stock. Notable examples include Sumner Redstone's block of supervoting Viacom stock, John Malone's TCI stake (now sold to AT&T), and most newspaper companies (such as the New York Times and Dow Jones), which have two classes of stock.

However, there are limits to the use of supervoting stock as a defensive mechanism. First, implementation generally involves some form of recapitalization, with the approval of existing shareholders a necessary precursor. But shareholders in many cases may be unwilling to disenfranchise themselves. Second, supervoting stock is only useful as a defensive measure where its ownership can be concentrated in the hands of pro-management investors. Third, the creation of a new supervoting class of stock is generally forbidden under the uniform Voting Rights Policy of the NYSE, the AMEX, and the NASD.

Several exceptions to the Voting Rights Policy, arising from the history of the 1994 Voting Rights Policy, explain the continuing existence of supervoting stock among public companies. Between July of 1988 and June of 1990, the Securities and Exchange Commission had a so-called one share/one vote rule in place that grandfathered dual-class voting structures put in place before July 1988. Then, on June 12, 1990, a federal appellate court overturned the SEC rule as outside the scope of the agency's authority, and the Voting Rights Policy was developed as a response. The policy allows the continuation of any supervoting arrangements permitted under the prior SEC rule and also grandfathers arrangements put in place between the time of the court ruling and the enactment of the new uniform policy.

This somewhat idiosyncratic history means that a company with an existing supervoting arrangement can continue to issue supervoting shares of the same class, but most other public companies cannot adopt a defensive supervoting structure.

Debt Instruments　Shark repellent–type provisions also can be incorporated in debt instruments. After a flurry of popularity, however, they are losing their appeal because they result in a lack of flexibility for the company.

Employee Severance Arrangements

Employee severance arrangements with change-in-control provisions can supplement a company's defensive posture. The Chrysler Corporation, for example, put a so-called golden parachute plan in place in response to Kirk Kerkorian's 1995 takeover attempt.

Severance arrangements can allay concerns among covered employees and encourage them to remain with a company. This protection is important because recruiters besiege key employees with alternative job offers during the pendency of a deal.

Severance arrangements can also ally the interests of top management with shareholders: The theory is that management will not be as recalcitrant if its downside is protected.

Common change-in-control severance plans can be grouped into two categories: golden parachutes and silver or tin parachutes. The chief distinction between the two categories is the percentage of employees covered.

Golden Parachutes   Large contractual compensation payments to management triggered upon a change in control and popularized as golden parachutes were a controversial element of the 1980s mergers boom. For example, in the 1989 RJR Nabisco takeover, CEO H. Ross Johnson lost his job and earned an estimated $53 million in the process. Executive Vice President John Martin earned roughly $18 million.

A golden parachute plan covers the few dozen key employees of a major company. Such agreements obligate the company to make a lump-sum payment to employees who are terminated after a change in control. Some golden parachutes have a fixed term, such as a year; others are "evergreen." An evergreen agreement has a one-year life but is automatically extended for a year if no change in control occurs during the year.

Compensation under a golden parachute is calculated as a multiple of recent compensation. So, for example, an agreement might provide for a payment equal to three times the compensation earned by a covered executive in the most recent year. The payments are due whether the termination is voluntary or involuntary.

A change in control is usually defined to take place when an investor accumulates more than a specified percentage of stock. The threshold is often set in the 25 to 30 percent range, but some companies have also adopted parachutes with a much lower threshold. Exemptions can be built in for friendly transactions, a merger or reorganization which results in substantial continuity of shareholder interest, or other particular situations. However, these exemptions may erode the ability of a golden parachute to address employee retention concerns.

Silver or Tin Parachutes   A silver or tin parachute functions like a golden parachute, but covers more employees. At the extreme, a tin parachute might cover all full-time employees. Like a golden parachute, these arrangements usually guarantee a lump-sum payment, and perhaps continued employee benefits, to a covered employee. The lump-sum payment is typically measured as a multiple of length of service.

A tin parachute in most cases is triggered by an employee's termination after a change in control, unless the termination was "for cause." The definition of cause is delineated under the terms of the plan, and is usually fairly narrow.

Implementation   Employee severance arrangements can be implemented by a board of directors without a shareholder vote. Board approval may not even be necessary for a tin parachute that excludes top management, but is certainly advisable.

The decision to implement golden parachutes, if made prior to a specific takeover threat, will generally be protected by the traditional business judgment rule. However, where a golden parachute is a response to a specific threat, courts will apply the *Unocal* test, requiring the board to show that it conducted a reasonable and good-faith investigation of the perceived takeover threat and that the parachute plan represented a reasonable response.

Outside the courts, golden parachutes have sparked considerable criticism. Opponents argue that such plans represent self-dealing by managers who control the adoption process. These arguments were particularly heated in the late 1980s, when several instances of large parachute payments occurred. Reacting to these criticisms, most large companies now have established compensation committees made up of outside directors to examine these benefits.

Tax Implications   In 1984 and 1986, the federal tax law with respect to parachute payments was revised to curb the practice. The new law imposes tax penalties on certain parachute payments. In particular, an "excess parachute payment" is subject to a dual tax penalty. First, such payments are not tax-deductible to an employer. Second, a recipient must pay a 20 percent excise tax in addition to normal income tax. The definition of an excess parachute payment for this purpose is extremely complicated, but creates a penalty if the chute exceeds three times an executive's average compensation for the last five years. In deals, buyers give "gross-ups" to managers to insulate them from the taxes.

Reincorporation as a Defensive Strategy

A wholesale defensive strategy is also available—reincorporating in a state with laws more favorable to takeover defense. A company might, for example, reincorporate in Pennsylvania to take advantage of its tough antitakeover statute. Historically, this happened when many major corporations originally incorporated in New Jersey moved to Delaware.

A particular state may be attractive for a number of reasons. The takeover-related provisions of the relevant corporate statutes are, of course, important. Particular issues include the treatment of poison pills, cumulative voting, staggered boards, and hostile tender offers. In addition, the attitude of the courts, particularly regarding the fiduciary duties of corporate directors in the takeover context, is critical.

Tactical issues must also be considered. Because reincorporation requires the creation of a subsidiary in the new state, followed by the merger of the parent into the subsidiary, shareholders must approve the merger of the parent. A company therefore must analyze its shareholder base (as it is advised to do before implementing shark repellents through corporate charter amendments). Reincorporation should be pursued only if a company expects to win the necessary shareholder approval.

Reincorporation should be pursued before a specific bidder has emerged. But the strategy can be used as a reaction against an offer. In 1983, Gulf Oil tried reincorporation in order to defeat Boone Pickens. When Pickens began to circle, Gulf was incorporated in Pennsylvania, a state whose corporate law had several unattractive features: required cumulative voting and a low threshold allowing 20 percent of a company's shareholders to call a special meeting. Pickens already had 9 percent and would likely be able to find another 11 percent to call a meeting.

In an effort to boost Gulf's defensive posture, the company's board of directors approved reincorporation in Delaware. Management narrowly won the contested vote. While the new rules applicable to Gulf may have slowed Pickens somewhat, the shift amounted to only a tactical victory. The company got a bare majority, an expression of relative shareholder discontent. Three months later, the Gulf board agreed to a friendly deal with Chevron.

Perspective on Defenses

All of these defensive devices have their limits. The battlements can become their own Maginot Line, holding in an undeserved complacency. Strong operational performance is the best defense.

Defense: 22
Battlefield Tactics

"Isn't the best defense always a good attack?"

—Ovid, *The Loves*

Takeover contests are fast-paced, draining affairs. A company must file its response to a hostile tender offer at the SEC within ten days. Major tactical decisions must be made and responses implemented very quickly.

The corporate boardroom is the epicenter of the action, the place where critical strategic decisions are made. How should the target respond to a hostile bid? What path should a business take? The questions can be agonizing and decisions are not reached lightly.

Adding to the pressure, directors face the specter of shareholder lawsuits. In the context of a takeover fight, directors can be sure that virtually any defensive response will draw some sort of litigation. Insurance coverage protects against personal liability, but the annoyance and potential for damage to personal reputation cannot be avoided. Almost as bothersome is the incessant criticism from shareholders and the press, the feeling of being in a glass fishbowl.

Defending Against an Unsolicited Offer

An unsolicited offer can manifest itself in several ways. The first hint of impending trouble may come in the form of an apparent stock accumulation. A company might learn of accumulation through a variety of channels: a stock watch or market surveillance program or a Hart-Scott-Rodino or Schedule 13D filing from the accumulator.

Alternatively, notice of an impending offer can come directly from the offeror in the form of an expression of interest. The expression can vary in terms of formality. An interested party might simply make an "informal pass." Or, a formal bear hug letter might be sent to the target's board. In either case, the contact may or may not contain a forthright expression of hostile intent.

Third, the indication of interest might take the form of a full-blown tender offer. In this case, the hostile bidder will have shrouded any market accumulation in secrecy and announced the bid prior to crossing the Hart-Scott-Rodino and Schedule 13D filing thresholds.

Once a target company becomes aware of a potential takeover threat and determines to fight, the first step is to review the existing framework of preventive measures. Certain of these measures can be usefully revised even with a tender offer on the table. Beyond a review of structural defenses such as the poison pill or staggered board elections, a number of specific responses are available to a target company. These responses range from passive to active and entail varying costs and risks. Though no list can be exhaustive, the main alternatives are as follows:

- The "just say no" defense;
- Negotiating a standstill agreement;
- The payment of greenmail;
- The Pac-Man defense;
- Finding a white knight or white squire;
- A recapitalization or restructuring;
- Issuing shares to an employee pension trust;

- A defensive acquisition; and

- A litigation and public relations blitz.

A universal is to keep the team well rested. Terrible decisions are made by exhausted people, and after a couple of weeks of incessant meetings and belligerent pestering from arbs, even the feistiest defenders simply get tired.

Overall, there is no paint-by-the-numbers approach to takeover defense that can be applied in every case. The intent here is to describe the range of possibilities.

Just Say No   Faced with an unsolicited offer, a board may simply fortify its defensive barricades and decline the bid. Of course, both the addition of new defenses and the refusal to redeem an outstanding poison pill must pass muster under *Unocal,* the Delaware case that set a two-prong test for the conduct of boards on defense. The first *Unocal* prong, which focuses on the defensive process, is fairly easy to satisfy—a well-founded board determination that the offer is inadequate and represents a threat to existing corporate strategy generally will suffice. The second prong requires proportionality between the remedy and the threat, but will not cause problems for defensive measures unless it is deemed "preclusive" or "draconian."

So, under *Unocal,* common structural defenses such as the poison pill are generally safe if properly implemented, except perhaps in the face of an all-cash, all-shares offer. A larger question remains: Will the just say no defense work? The *Time* and *Wallace* cases, both under Delaware law, suggest it can.

However, the just say no defense is certainly not impregnable. For example, Moore had already gained three of nine Wallace board seats through the proxy machinery when it gave up its fight for Wallace. If Moore had continued, it might have gained a majority of the board, giving it the power to redeem the Wallace poison pill.

Even in the absence of a successful proxy fight, a well-financed and motivated hostile bidder can place considerable pressure on an incumbent board. An offer that represents a significant premium can create difficulty for a board under *Unocal*. The higher the premium involved, the more likely shareholders are to agitate in favor of acceptance. In addition, a board may find it hard to characterize an all-cash offer at a significant premium to market as a "threat to the corporation or its shareholders." To the contrary, the Delaware courts have expressly stated that "at some point, the failure to redeem a poison pill can constitute a fiduciary breach."

DOA

Loewen Says "No" to Service Corp.

A vital poison pill is not essential to a successful defense, as indicated by the Loewen Group's fending off a $2.9 billion hostile bid from Service Corp. International. The two companies—number one and number two in the "death services," or mortuary, business—battled to a draw after four months, at which point Service Corp. decided that withdrawal was the better part of valor.

The fight began in September of 1996. On the same day Loewen was switching from the NASDAQ stock listing to the New York Stock Exchange—normally an auspicious occasion for a company—Service Corp. announced a bear hug bid for its competitor. Even before the bid, the companies shared bad blood. The funeral service business had been undergoing rapid consolidation for a period of years, and Loewen and Service Corp. had grown to be the primary competitors.

Raymond Loewen, chairman, CEO, and founder of Loewen, almost immediately vowed to fight Service Corp.'s initial $43 a share offer. Even when Service Corp. sweetened the bid to $45 a share, Loewen remained defiant.

In a certain sense, the Loewen Group was a vulnerable target. The company had been forced to settle two breach-of-contract cases in 1995, for a total liability payment of $205 million. Furthermore, while Loewen had a poison pill in place, under the applicable Canadian law, courts tend to force pill redemption after sixty to ninety days. The board could say no only for so long.

Recognizing this reality, Loewen still had a number of strong defenses. Foremost was the fact that Raymond Loewen, his family, and associates controlled 20 percent of the company's stock. British Columbia law—which applied since the company was incorporated in that province—required that 75 percent of the shareholders approve any deal; and with Loewen staunchly opposed, Service Corp. would need nearly all of the remaining shareholders to agree.

Loewen was not content to rely on this structural barrier to a takeover. The company also continued on its own acquisition spree, buying up over $325 million in other death services companies. Top employees were granted fairly generous golden parachutes. Finally, government antitrust officials were lobbied to oppose any combination as anticompetitive.

Ultimately, though, Service Corp.'s failed bid had more to do with price and financial structure than anything else. The $45 bid, all in stock, just didn't excite the largely institutional shareholders who owned most of Loewen. Without a stronger bid, the shareholders stuck by management. High leverage and poor operations eventually forced Loewen to seek bankruptcy protection, wiping out shareholder value.

Greenmail and the Standstill Agreement   The practice of paying a potential acquirer to go away was common in the 1980s. Texaco bought a block of stock back from the Bass brothers for $1.2 billion, or roughly 3 percent above the previous closing price; Disney bought

Saul Steinberg's stake for $325 million plus a $28 million expense payment; the Belzbergs of Canada sold stock back to USG.

Greenmail is a payment to repurchase shares at a premium price in exchange for the acquirer's agreement to forgo a hostile offer. It is typically accompanied by a contractual standstill agreement that 1) specifies the amount of stock, if any, that the acquirer can accumulate or retain; 2) restricts the circumstances under which the acquirer can sell any retained shares, often including a right of first refusal for the target company; 3) restricts how the acquirer can vote retained shares, such as by foreclosing the acquirer from participation in a proxy contest; and 4) states a specified term for the agreement.

The point is to craft an agreement which effectively forecloses future agitation on the part of the potential acquirer. Naturally, a potential acquirer is unlikely to agree to such stringent terms without inducement. Hence a target sometimes will agree to pay greenmail, either in the form of a direct share repurchase or a more indirect benefit.

From the perspective of incumbent management, a greenmail payment may be viewed as a small price to pay to avoid the turmoil and expense of a prolonged takeover contest. Critics argue, however, that the payment of greenmail unfairly discriminates against other shareholders and represents a bald management-entrenchment device. In the mid-1980s, such criticisms developed into a consensus against the practice. Consequently, managers and board members must be prepared to deal with negative publicity if greenmail is paid to a potential acquirer.

Litigation is another frequent by-product of greenmail payments: Shareholders will often sue board members in a derivative capacity on behalf of the target company, asserting that the approval of such payments constitutes a breach of fiduciary duty. These kinds of claims generally have received short shrift in Delaware courts. Following a *Unocal* analysis, the courts have found greenmail to be a reasonable response to the threat posed by potentially disruptive hostile raiders. Courts in other states, California in particular, have taken a far less favorable view, however.

For instance, the Disney greenmail payment to Saul Steinberg and companies he controlled generated years of litigation. Shareholders sued under California law, arguing the Disney board had breached its fiduciary duty to shareholders by granting preferential treatment to Steinberg. Two California state courts agreed. The trial judge in the case granted a preliminary injunction in the favor of the shareholders and an appellate court upheld the decision.

Finally, in 1989, the Disney case was settled, with Steinberg's Reliance Group agreeing to pay about $21 million in damages. Disney itself was liable for $22 million in damages, though its insurers picked up most of the tab.

More troubling than the litigation threat is the prospect that the payment of greenmail may be tactically counterproductive. The presence of a potential acquirer in the market generally will push the price of target company stock higher. On news of a greenmail payment and standstill agreement, the stock price may fall back to previous levels. In that case, a new acquirer may come on the scene, hoping to take advantage of the target's apparent willingness to pay greenmail. This dynamic can result in a continuous stream of hostile investors, as St. Regis discovered in 1984. After St. Regis paid off two successive major shareholders, a third greenmailer took a stock position in the company. St. Regis saw no end in sight and agreed to be acquired by a white knight.

The receipt of greenmail payments can also have unfavorable tax consequences: Under federal tax law, a greenmail payment triggers a 50 percent tax on the gain associated with its receipt. The law, enacted in 1987, defines a greenmail payment as money or other value paid to acquire stock from a shareholder who made or threatened to make a tender offer for the payor's stock and who held the stock less than two years, but not paid to any other shareholders.

These various drawbacks have severely reduced the attraction and use of greenmail payments as a defensive tactic.

The Pac-Man Defense   A more aggressive approach is to go on the offensive. In other words, a target of a hostile bid can turn around and bid for the bidder. This tactic was used on several occasions in the early 1980s—Cities Service counteroffered for Boone Pickens' Mesa Petroleum in 1982; Houston Natural Gas did the same for Coastal States Gas in 1984; American Brands swallowed KKR's Beatrice spin-off, E-II Holdings, in 1988.

The fundamental message of a Pac-Man counterattack is that a particular combination in fact makes strategic sense, but in the reverse direction. Sometimes, the issue is the target's higher management quality. For example, Cities Service management could make a plausible case that it was better prepared and suited to managing a business of the size which would result from a Cities-Mesa merger.

There is also a defensive element to the counteroffer: The tactic sends a strong message that the original hostile bid will be opposed at all costs. In addition, the possibility that the bidder may itself be put in play can encourage the bidder to withdraw. Of course, to proceed with a Pac-Man defense, a target company must actually have the capacity—stock or debt—to buy the bidder.

The Pac-Man approach, if carried out to the end, is a doomsday machine. If both sides proceed with their offers, shareholders of each company receive cash for their stock, squeezing the equity out of the companies. The result will be two companies with infinite debt-to-equity ratios, and insolvency is the inevitable by-product.

Timing is another critical issue. The first mover has an advantage in most takeover contests because its tender offer will expire first. This advantage allows the first mover to purchase control of its opponent before the opponent can counter. In light of the importance of procedural issues, an understanding of the tender offer rules and other statutes is critical.

However, the real question is which corporation can effectively control the other first. The answer generally reveals itself in a perusal of the relevant state corporate law and a thorough review of each company's corporate governance provisions. Staggered boards, delayed shareholder meetings, and the like can keep a company from capturing effective control.

If the Pac-Man threat is carried out and the initial aggressor doesn't blink, a circular ownership structure will result. The question then arises, who controls whom? Under many state statutes, including the Delaware corporate law, a subsidiary is not permitted to vote stock it holds in its parent: Therefore, neither side can control the other. By this reading, the stock essentially becomes nonvoting and any remaining stockholders attain control.

SWALLOWED BY PAC-MAN

The Bendix–Martin Marietta Fight

All these issues played out in the classic Pac-Man battle, featuring four aggressive managers and four major corporations—Bendix, Martin Marietta, United Technologies, and Allied Corp. The principal protagonists were William Agee at Bendix, J. Donald Rauth at Martin Marietta, Harry Gray at United Technologies, and Ed Hennessy at Allied Corp. Agee and his advisers at Salomon Brothers got the whirling corporate slugfest started on August 25, 1982, with a $43 a share bid for Martin Marietta.

The most controversial aspect to surface during the ensuing battle was Agee's relationship with Mary Cunningham. Agee was a native of Idaho and graduate of Harvard Business School, and had risen quickly through various corporate jobs to become Bendix chairman at age thirty-eight. Cunningham—also a Harvard Business

School graduate—had joined Bendix as Agee's executive assistant in 1979. Infatuated with the "science" of strategic planning, Cunningham was a business school zealot. Her relationship with Agee developed into a romantic one, and she eventually was forced to resign. She was hired into the Seagram planning department, then married Agee in 1982. Her role as Agee's most trusted adviser in the Martin Marietta bid drew considerable resentment.

Martin Marietta was advised by investment banker Marty Siegel, who plugged himself as the Minister of Defense, and convinced Rauth to launch a counterbid. Throughout the ensuing contest, Rauth stuck to his guns. Marietta strengthened its position even further when Harry Gray bid for Bendix as well. Matters had escalated.

The situation came as something of a shock to Agee, although members of the Bendix camp had considered and rejected the possibility of a Martin Marietta counterbid. Compromise became the focus as the parties tried to avoid the disastrous consequences of Bendix buying Marietta and vice versa.

Yet no compromise had developed by the deadline for the Bendix tender. Agee went ahead and bought up the tendered Marietta shares, giving Bendix a timing advantage. But a feature of the Maryland law that specified that a shareholder had to wait ten days to call a special meeting made Bendix unable to take control of the Marietta board. Bendix, on the other hand, was governed by Delaware law, which allowed a majority shareholder to take board control almost immediately.

Bendix neutralized the timing advantage provided by the Maryland statute to a certain degree by convincing a Delaware judge to enjoin Marietta from voting any Bendix shares it might purchase, relying on the fact that Marietta technically was a subsidiary of Bendix.

This opening gave Bendix time to find a way out of the complicated mess, though Agee lost his top spot in the process. Ed Hennessy of Allied—who had learned the acquisition business under Gray at United Technologies—had developed a competitive relationship with his former mentor. We were brought in by Agee at this late stage to persuade Hennessy to bid for Bendix as a white knight. Hennessy topped the Marietta and United Technologies bids, but Marietta went ahead and purchased shares in Bendix. The resulting ownership structure was spaghetti.

Ultimately, the cross-purchases were unwound. Bendix—now controlled by Hennessy at Allied—and Marietta swapped the shares they had purchased in each other. The Marietta stake held by Bendix was more valuable, so that Bendix ended up keeping some Marietta stock. Agee became president of Allied, but lasted only a few months in the job, until June 1983.

Eventually, Agee's black eye from the Martin Marietta fiasco healed and he landed on his feet as chairman of the struggling Morrison Knudsen. Yet he and Mary continued to generate a lot of controversy. The turnaround effort at Morrison Knudsen collapsed amidst recriminations in 1996, and Agee was again out of a job. Martin Marietta meanwhile prospered and eventually merged with Lockheed in 1995. Agee had the concept right, but the resentment over his image overwhelmed any appreciation for his business insights.

Finding a White Knight   A white knight transaction, in which a target company merges with or is acquired by a friendly suitor, may be the best alternative for a company faced with a well-financed and motivated bidder. Though the white knight strategy necessarily involves a loss of the target company's independence, it may nonetheless be preferable to the alternative. A white knight may pay a higher price, promise to retain target company employees and management, or support the existing corporate strategy.

With a hostile bidder banging down the door, the process of finding a white knight is necessarily urgent. An investment banker conducts the search, canvassing various alternative suitors. Many companies often hesitate when offered the opportunity to act as a white knight out of fear that a costly bidding war will develop. As a result, an interested white knight generally will demand protective provisions in any acquisition agreement with a target.

For example, a prospective white knight might demand a stock or crown jewel lockup, as Forstmann Little did in the fight for Revlon. A stock lockup option gives the white knight the right to purchase authorized but unissued shares in the target company. From a white knight's perspective, such an option has two advantages. First, the white knight can exercise the options and vote the shares in favor of the proposed transaction between the white knight and the target. Second, the options provide a hedge against the possibility that another acquirer will pay a higher price for the target. If that happens, the white knight can exercise the options and sell the shares to the eventual acquirer for a profit.

A crown jewel or asset lockup gives a white knight the right to acquire key assets from the target under specified circumstances. The acquisition price is set at a level that is fair, but the deal is strategic for the white knight. If the assets covered by the lockup are viewed as critical or central to the target company's operations by other holders, a lockup arrangement reduces the likelihood of intervention.

Revlon may pose a problem for any defensive provisions in an agreement between a target company and a white knight, unless the auction was fully explored. Because of the risk of judicial challenge, lockups are not used as frequently as they were during the 1980s.

The White Squire   A company can also issue new shares as a defensive maneuver and place them in the friendly hands of a so-called white squire.

A white squire investment can have three defensive benefits. First, the white squire presumably will vote in line with management. Second, a standstill agreement can be structured so that the white squire shares will not be tendered into a hostile offer, making the hostile bidder less likely to obtain the minimum number of shares needed to complete its offer. However, unlike with a white knight, control of the company is usually not ceded to a white squire, who owns only a portion of the shares.

Finding an appropriate white squire can be difficult, however. With a potential hostile acquirer in the wings, a squire must be willing to face the possibility of becoming a minority shareholder in an unsettled situation. In addition, from the target's perspective, a number of restrictions are necessary to ensure the squire remains friendly. A squire therefore must be willing to make a sizable long-term investment with limited prospect for control.

Even once a squire is identified and negotiations are concluded, issues of implementation remain. The stock can be issued directly from the target only if it has sufficient authorized but unissued shares available. Otherwise, either the target company will have to amend its charter to provide for additional shares, which requires shareholder approval; or the squire will have to purchase shares in the open market.

An issuer must receive adequate consideration and must issue the securities for a proper purpose. If a white squire arrangement is initiated in response to a particular takeover threat, the board must satisfy the *Unocal* analysis.

The particular security issued to a white squire varies. However, convertible preferred stock is favored because the preferred dividend provides a certain cash flow to the white squire and the conversion feature will allow the white squire to vote the stock, if necessary. Alternatively, many companies have so-called blank check preferred in place that can be used for this purpose. Blank check preferred—provided for in a corporation's charter—is authorized but unissued preferred stock, the terms and conditions of which can be established by the issuer's board without further shareholder approval.

Shareholder approval may be necessary even if a company has authorized but unissued shares available to sell to a white squire. The New York Stock Exchange requires such approval if shares are to be sold to officers, directors, or significant shareholders, or if the shares to be issued have or are convertible into voting rights equal to 18.5 percent or more of the voting power previously outstanding.

THE WHITE SQUIRE IN ACTION

Buffett and Salomon Brothers

Warren Buffett is the most renowned white squire investor of the past decade. His 1987 purchase of a large block of stock in investment bank Salomon Brothers illustrates how he structured these investments.

For Buffett, the Salomon Brothers drama began in the summer of 1987, when Buffett got an urgent call from John Gutfreund. Buffett had developed a relationship with Gutfreund, head of Salomon Brothers, over the years, and the two chatted fairly regularly about the prospects for Salomon.

Minerals and Resources Corp. (Minorco), a 14 percent stakeholder in Salomon, was unhappy with its investment and had hired Felix Rohatyn to find a buyer. Word spread and Ron Perelman became interested.

Rohatyn ratcheted up the pressure on Gutfreund by negotiating a tentative deal with Perelman, an unpleasant prospect for Gutfreund. But, in fact, Perelman only wanted to do a friendly transaction and to get two board seats along with his Salomon stake.

Gutfreund nonetheless was cornered. Salomon Brothers could not afford to repurchase Minorco's shares at the $38 price offered by Perelman, roughly a 20 percent premium to the market price. So Gutfreund turned to Buffett. The two men met in Wachtell, Lipton's offices, and within a matter of hours, Buffett agreed that Berkshire Hathaway would purchase a $700 million block of convertible preferred from Salomon. The securities would carry a 9 percent guaranteed yield and could be converted into Salomon common stock at an effective price of $38 per common share.

In structuring his Salomon investment, Buffett intended to create an instrument that would give Berkshire Hathaway a 15 percent overall return, estimating that the 9 percent coupon plus appreciation on the underlying common stock would accomplish that goal. From Gutfreund's perspective, the capital infusion would allow Salomon to buy out Minorco.

Salomon has had its problems since 1987. The stock market crash in that year, plus a Treasury trading scandal and management turmoil, contributed to an unstable performance. However, as the bull market of the 1990s heated up, Salomon prospered. The 1997 acquisition of Salomon by Sandy Weill's Travelers Group converted Berkshire Hathaway's roughly 30 percent Salomon stake into a 3 percent stake in Travelers. Buffett, a frequent home run hitter, characterized the deal's $80 per share valuation as a "scratch single" for Berkshire Hathaway.

Recapitalizations and Restructurings   A company can initiate a wide variety of financial and operational changes in response to a potential bid. Common strategies include a leveraged recapitalization, the assumption of additional debt, the issuance of new shares, the purchase of outstanding shares, or a spin-off or split-off.

Using a leveraged recapitalization as a takeover defense requires the target company to assume new debt to fund a dividend payout or share repurchase. Just as in financial-buyer-sponsored transactions, the company is recapitalized as equity capital is replaced with debt and, as a result, the target company's debt-to-equity ratio is increased. This was the type of defense Telecom Italia attempted when faced with a hostile bid from Olivetti in 1999: It planned to buy the 40 percent of Telecom Italia Mobile it didn't own, highly levering itself in the process. Shareholders, however, voted down the plan.

Leveraged recapitalizations can have several defensive benefits. First, the assumption of additional debt reduces the target company's debt capacity, posing an impediment to using the target's surplus debt capacity to fund the acquisition of control. Likewise, if partially funded with existing cash balances, a recapitalization can remove a source of funding for a hostile bid.

Second, the payment of a large special dividend should significantly improve the disposition of target shareholders toward management. A major share repurchase likewise offers liquidity to shareholders who might otherwise have tendered into a hostile offer, reducing the percentage of "dissatisfied shareholders" in the marketplace and thus target company resources that might be used by a hostile bidder to fund an acquisition. Furthermore, if insiders choose not to sell shares into the repurchase plan, their ownership percentage will be concentrated.

The federal securities law limits a target company's ability to purchase its own shares after a third party has made a tender offer for the company's stock. So long as a third-party tender offer is open, the target company must file a statement with the SEC before repurchasing any shares that sets forth the following information: a description of the securities to be purchased, the purpose of the repurchase, the method of repurchase, and the source of funds for the transaction. In addition, the issuer must send a statement containing the same information to shareholders, unless such information has already been provided within the previous six months.

The chief tactical distinction between an open-market purchase plan and a self-tender offer has to do with timing and flexibility. Once the issuer disseminates the information required by the securities regulations, open-market purchases can be initiated. Alternatively, an open-market plan can be drawn out over a period of months or even years.

A self-tender offer, on the other hand, is subject to rules that basically mirror the third-party tender offer rules. Under the self-tender rules, an issuer must file a statement with the SEC in conjunction with the commencement of an offer which must remain open for at least twenty days from the date of commencement. If the price offered is increased or decreased, the offer must remain open for an additional ten days. Tendered shares must be accepted on a pro rata basis where the issuer will purchase less than all such shares.

The third defensive benefit to recapitalizations is that the interest payments on new debt provide a tax shield for the target company's earnings that is not available from recurring dividend payments. In addition, a high debt load may increase management's incentives to improve operations, providing benefits similar to those associated with a leveraged buyout.

The combined effect of the provisions of a recapitalization, if well designed and implemented, may be to increase the value of shareholders' target company holdings. Of course, a recapitalization will be most effective as a defensive measure when it provides greater value to shareholders than a proposed hostile bid.

A target also can take on additional debt without paying a special dividend or carrying out a share repurchase and can use the cash generated to fund operations, make acquisitions, repurchase shares, and so forth. Again, the issuance of debt will reduce the target's debt capacity and may deter a raider intent on funding an acquisition with a target company's own borrowing capacity.

Debt can be added to a company's balance sheet either by issuing publicly traded bonds or by borrowing money directly from a bank or other lender in a private transaction. While publicly traded debt may be more cost-efficient due to lower interest charges, the necessity for time-consuming SEC registration may make its issuance impractical for a defensive restructuring. If a company anticipates the use of publicly traded debt in this context, it may, however, shelf-register debt securities so they can be drawn down on a moment's notice. The SEC Aircraft Carrier rule release may limit the ability to shelf-register, however, for less-seasoned issuers.

Cash from operations and additional debt are not the only available sources of funding for a recapitalization. Target companies can also sell assets or operations, or partially or completely liquidate as a defensive response. Alternatively, rather than pay a large cash dividend, some targets choose to spin off operations into the hands of shareholders.

The sale of divisions or assets can serve two purposes. First, the sale of a particularly attractive asset—a crown jewel sale—may discourage a potential bidder intent on acquiring the company. Second, the proceeds from the sale can be used to fund various recapitalization alternatives.

However, an asset sale is difficult to accomplish in a short period of time. Furthermore, a rapid sale may not maximize the selling price. Indeed, a target company board of directors must be careful in this regard because if an asset sale is defensively motivated, the *Unocal* test may apply. Particularly if the price received on the sale is low, the transaction may be enjoined and the directors may be charged with having violated their fiduciary duties.

A partial or total liquidation is another possible defensive strategy. A partial liquidation involves the sale of assets and payment of the proceeds to shareholders as a dividend. In a total liquidation, the company is broken up and sold piecemeal with the expectation of generating a higher return than promised by a hostile bidder.

Both alternatives face the same timing dilemma as an asset sale. Furthermore, a liquidation of all or substantially all of a target's assets must be approved by shareholders. Thus, while a liquidation may promise a higher return to shareholders, the drawn-out process involved and the associated uncertainty may make the option sufficiently unpalatable to shareholders and therefore unrealistic as a defensive alternative.

If a target is unable to find a buyer for assets, it can instead carry out a spin-off. This approach has the advantage of focusing market interest on each entity as a separate piece and can cause the combined value of the pieces to increase relative to the target's pre-spin-off value. Like an asset sale or liquidation, however, a spin-off can take some time to accomplish. For instance, Pillsbury floated the idea of spinning off Burger King as part of its Grand Met defense, but, as expected, shareholders proved too impatient for this approach. As a result, a company that is contemplating a spin-off will often complete the transaction before a raider appears on the scene, hoping that the preemptive action will reduce the likelihood of a hostile offer.

The range of defensive options expands if a pill and other defensive structures are in place. A well-defended company may have time to pursue defensive strategies not available to the unprotected company.

ESOPs The employee stock ownership plan, or ESOP, provides a valuable alternative to the white squire as friendly shareholder. Regulated in the U.S. under federal employee benefits and tax law, an ESOP is designed to hold company stock as an undiversified retirement investment for employees. The chief defensive benefit of placing a block of shares with an ESOP is based on the presumption that employees will tend to vote against a hostile bid that might jeopardize jobs. However, this result cannot be guaranteed through a standstill agreement. Rather, the employee beneficiaries of an ESOP generally must be given the freedom to control the shares in an ESOP, with the protection of confidentiality.

Notwithstanding this drawback, an ESOP can have considerable defensive force, particularly in conjunction with state antitakeover laws. Under the Delaware statute, for example, a hostile bidder who acquires more than 15 percent of a company's stock cannot complete a back-end merger with the company unless either a two-thirds majority of shareholders other than the bidder approve or the bidder acquires at least 85 percent of the target company's stock. An ESOP that owns as little as 15 percent of a company therefore may have the power to block a bust-up transaction that is predicated on the acquisition of 100 percent control.

Another advantage of an ESOP-based defense is the speed with which it can be implemented. A company can either issue shares directly to an ESOP or the ESOP can purchase shares on the open market; the dilutive effect of issuing new shares to the ESOP can be offset by open-market purchases, if desired. Under applicable regulations, the ESOP may borrow up to 100 percent of the cost of acquiring company shares and may use the company's credit guarantee for this purpose; the company then may make tax-deductible contributions to the ESOP to fund the loan payments.

In setting up an ESOP, care must be given to the price paid by the ESOP for company securities. If the ESOP overpays for the securities, the purchase and sale will constitute a "prohibited transaction" under federal employee benefits laws. If, however, the ESOP is allowed to purchase the securities at a bargain, the company's officers and directors open themselves to a claim that they violated their fiduciary duties to other shareholders.

There is a major distinction between putting shares into an ESOP and selling shares to a white squire. While a white squire pays for its shares, an ESOP is funded by the target company and therefore becomes part of a company's overall compensation expense structure. Because simply adding an ESOP without reducing other benefits provided to employees could cause a substantial increase in compensation expense, a company may need to reduce other benefits when creating an ESOP. Setting aside takeover-related issues, such a shift in compensation structure can have implications for employee morale.

In the recent hostile bidding war for Gucci, that company chose to issue shares to an ESOP as a defense as well. In January 1999,

Gucci issued 37 million shares to an ESOP, diluting the stakes of would-be acquirers Prada and LVMH.

Ashland Avoids a Repeat

Management at Ashland Oil learned a quick lesson when the Belzberg family of Canada bought a 9 percent stake in the company. By March 1986, when the stake came to light in an SEC filing, the Belzbergs already had a reputation as successful takeover specialists. Samuel Belzberg, chairman of First City Financial, made his first big strike in the early 1980s with an investment in Bache Group; when Prudential Insurance bought the company, Sam Belzberg pocketed a large gain.

Fearing their company would be put in play, Ashland managers at first refused to comment on the offer. However, behind the scenes, the company opened talks with the Belzbergs. An agreement was reached quite quickly. Ashland agreed to buy the Belzbergs' stock back at $51 a share, the takeover-inflated market price, and the Belzbergs reportedly made just over $15 million on the transaction before taxes.

The Ashland board was glad to be rid of the Belzbergs, but understood the 1980s market dynamic. Their company was now in play. However, the board came up with a package to pull Ashland off the market: a stock buyback program covering up to 23 percent of the company's stock was implemented and asset sales were considered. The central feature was a powerful new ESOP. Funded with bank loans, the Ashland ESOP would purchase shares in the market.

By January 1999, the ESOP controlled 10 percent of Ashland's outstanding common stock and the continuing presence of the block helped ward off repeat attacks.

Going Private When faced with a determined hostile bidder, target company management may conclude that, in one form or another, a sale of the company is inevitable. But this does not mean the company must be sold to a third party. Taking the target company private in a leveraged buyout may provide an attractive solution both for shareholders and management. Public shareholders will receive a premium price for their shares and management will retain control of the target company.

The prospect of going private in a management-led buyout raises various financial structuring issues as well as concerns about self-dealing.

Management must comply with specific federal securities disclosure requirements applicable to a going-private transaction. As reflected in Delaware case law, the heightened role for corporate directors in a going-private transaction reflects a commonsense view of shareholders' rights: There is always the worry that the self-interest of managers will motivate the board to push through a sweetheart deal. And the slightest appearance of impropriety likely will generate shareholder lawsuits, with all the attendant unpleasantness. Of course, when competing bidders are already on the scene, even an entrenched management may find it difficult to structure an advantageous deal.

In any lawsuit that does develop, the behavior of directors will not be measured under the forgiving business judgment rule but rather under the far more demanding "entire fairness" review that applies to transactions which involve self-interested directors. The entire fairness review requires a far-reaching judicial inquiry and places particular emphasis on both procedure and price. If a challenged management buyout is to go forward, the court must be satisfied that shareholders are treated fairly.

These concerns are often addressed by establishing a special committee of independent outside directors, not affiliated with management, to assess the merits of a going-private transaction. This was the procedure when Ross Johnson proposed a management buyout of RJR Nabisco: A committee of outside directors was established, which took charge of the process, hired its own financial and legal advisers, and solicited additional bids for the company. The special committee eventually selected KKR as the winning bidder.

If carried out properly, the special committee process can restore the protective shield of the business judgment rule to a transaction.

The possibility of triggering an entire fairness review is not the only hurdle in the way of a management buyout. The SEC's going-private rules also impose significant obligations with which management must comply before a transaction that will leave the issuer with 300 or fewer shareholders or result in the issuer being delisted from a national securities exchange can be consummated. In general, the SEC takes the position that its going-private rules will apply to a leveraged buyout with management involvement where managers will participate in the deal on a basis that leaves them owning 10 percent or more of the surviving company. As a result, the going-private rules apply to almost every management buyout.

The substantive going-private rule has two components. First, an acquirer must satisfy certain mandatory reporting rules by filing a schedule with the SEC that details the purpose of the transaction, the transaction structure, and alternatives that were explored. An in-depth defense of the transaction's fairness must be included and any reports from third parties must be fully disclosed. Second, an acquirer must wait a minimum of twenty days between the time of filing and the first purchase of stock.

The going-private rules, and in particular the extensive disclosure obligations, magnify the importance of deliberate board consideration of any management buyout. In the fast-paced environment of a takeover contest, it can be easy to lose sight of this fact. However, with full disclosure required and entire fairness as the standard, even the appearance of impropriety can scuttle an otherwise well-conceived management buyout.

The Defensive Acquisition   Defensive acquisitions are another option for a company with a strong stock price or borrowing capacity. The idea is twofold. First, by increasing its debt load, a company derives many of the defensive benefits of a leveraged recapitalization: Bidders are less likely to be attracted to a company that has already utilized a significant portion of its debt capacity.

Size and scope can also be advantageous in a defense. Simply by becoming a larger concern, a company raises the stakes for a bidder seeking to acquire the new, larger company. More cash must be raised, more stock issued.

The 1979 defense of Daylin is a classic case of a defensive acquisition used to advantage. W.R. Grace bid to take over the company, knowing there were no white knights in the wings. Daylin CEO Sandford Sigoloff then decided to bid for a third company, Narco Scientific, in an effort to force a higher bid out of Grace. In fact, the premium bid for Narco worked. Grace raised its offer, and Sigoloff accepted.

Of course, the kind of defensive acquisition used by Daylin now may need to pass muster under *Unocal*. A thorough analysis and reasoned approach are critical to supporting eventual acquisition decisions. While the board has the authority to set strategic policy under *Time,* the acquisition process should be above impeachment so that a court will have no reason to enjoin or overturn such moves.

Timing can also be an issue. Just as with a sale, an acquisition requires considerable time and energy from start to finish. However, for defensive purposes, it may be sufficient to sign a definitive agreement binding the company to future action. In any event, the perceived propriety and ease of execution are likely to be enhanced where an acquisition has been under consideration for some time.

Litigation and Public Relations Blitz   Litigation and public relations remain important aspects of a full defensive strategy, but rarely are decisive factors. Courts have become skeptical about most kinds of legal claims related to takeovers and outright abuses will be curbed. Yet the courts are not prepared to be the arbiters of every takeover contest. As a result, rules of standing and other procedural barriers have been erected to limit overzealous litigators.

Common categories of takeover litigation include antitrust matters, securities law violations, breach of fiduciary duty cases, and breach of confidentiality cases. Antitrust law is the only area where a consistent possibility of delivering a decisive blow exists.

The public relations story is slightly different. With the preponderance of strategic stock-for-stock deals, pitching the story of a deal to the markets is increasingly more important. Clearly, there is a role for public relations professionals in the merger process.

In addition, in situations with multiple or hostile bidders, attack advertisements are often used. These full-page advertisements, placed in *The New York Times, The Wall Street Journal,* and newspapers circulated in major cities, are essentially short position papers, typically featuring pithy headlines and bulleted text, and intended to influence shareholders' perceptions of a takeover situation.

The Hotel War—Hilton Versus ITT

One of the most highly publicized hostile takeover battles of the 1990s—that between Starwood, Hilton, and ITT—induced the target ITT to attempt to mount one of the most complicated and formidable defenses to date. Even the strongest defense, however, must pass the judicial smell test. ITT's failed.

On January 27, 1997, Hilton Hotels Corp. launched a $55 a share bear hug offer for ITT Corp. Many themes of the takeover arena—both strategic and tactical, on offense and defense—were reflected in the eleven-month battle.

The roots of the ITT battle stretch back to the conglomerate days of the 1960s when Harold Geneen diversified the company away from its traditional telecommunications base. Rand Araskog—the West Point graduate most responsible for unwinding Geneen's legacy—already carried several battle scars from past defensive campaigns. After a series of spin-offs, he had focused the company on core hotel operations, adding a gaming business with the acquisition of Caesars in a play to build a strategic legacy, a premier "destinations" company. But ITT shareholders reacted skeptically. Both the strategic design and the execution were called into question as ITT Corp.'s stock gave back the gains from the 1995 spin-off plan.

The continuing problems at ITT triggered the interest of Stephen Bollenbach, a gifted corporate dealmaker who had recently taken over as head of Hilton Hotels. Before joining the company, Bollenbach earned acclaim on Wall Street as chief financial officer for the real estate businesses of Donald Trump, Marriott, and Disney. In the process, he helped Trump avoid bankruptcy, guided Marriott through a highly successful split into two businesses, and orchestrated the financial aspects of Disney's Capital Cities/ABC acquisition.

Bollenbach came to Hilton with a mandate to turn around the conservative hotel company. He opened with a bold stroke—a $3 billion acquisition of casino company Bally Entertainment. Then, in the fall of 1996, Bollenbach became interested in ITT.

For Bollenbach, ITT looked like a company in trouble. ITT's Planet Hollywood strategy seemed misguided: ITT had agreed to put up all the cash to build Planet Hollywood casinos—more than $1 billion—but would pay Planet Hollywood 10 percent of the cash flow as a license for using the hip brand name. Bollenbach likened this to "Coca-Cola leasing A&W Root Beer." ITT had its own strong casino brand in Caesars and less costly opportunities for growth.

Bollenbach began planning a bid for ITT in October 1996. The initial question was how to approach, whether by friendly offer, bear hug, or outright hostile tender. Although Araskog had repeatedly demonstrated his antipathy to being taken over, Bollenbach decided to make an attempt at a friendly deal.

Throughout the fall, Araskog rebuffed several informal offers to negotiate a deal. Finally, in January 1997, Bollenbach gave up and launched a tender offer at $55 a share, a 26 percent premium over the trading price prior to the announcement of the offer.

Araskog immediately put ITT into alert mode. This veteran of the takeover skirmishes of the 1980s—the subject of a self-congratulatory book entitled *The ITT Wars*—found himself again arguing a raider was trying to snatch ITT "on the cheap." Though ITT had significantly underperformed the market during Araskog's tenure, Araskog and the ITT board rejected the offer as inadequate and launched an aggressive defense. Planned capital expenditures were slashed and an extensive asset sale program triggered. The annual shareholder meeting—normally held in May—was delayed until November.

Many on Wall Street agreed that the Hilton bid was low. Indeed, Bollenbach had faced the modern dilemma of takeovers: Either be preemptive with a high bid or face a grueling duel. Bollenbach opted for a drawn-out test of wills in an attempt to keep the price down. Of course, the strategy left Araskog with time to respond.

But Bollenbach had seen the chink in ITT's defensive armor: Because the company lacked a staggered board, all of its current directors were up for election at the next annual meeting. As part of its bid, Hilton announced its intention to nominate a slate and conduct a proxy fight. Bollenbach assumed shareholders would have an opportunity to decide the contest by November at the latest—the latest date to which ITT could delay its shareholders' meeting. Bollenbach chose to take an option on a low-price deal rather than pursue the more likely success of a higher bid.

Araskog then took aggressive steps to forestall any shareholder vote. He unloaded the recently acquired Madison Square Garden and several other properties for a profit. In May 1997, ITT agreed to sell five hotels as part of its larger divestiture strategy. And the company also began to entertain bids for some of its marquee properties. ITT was not, however, getting out of the hotel business; rather, the company retained the contractual right to manage the hotels for a fee. Araskog was counting on the fact that Hilton wanted the hotels and likely would not purchase ITT without them.

These hotel sales had embedded in their related management contracts an additional defensive aspect—change-of-control provisions allowed the new hotel owners to discontinue the management arrangement should the ITT hotel company get bought out. This language, while relatively common in management contracts, amounted to shark repellent in the takeover context. If Hilton were to take over ITT, it would face the risk that part of the value of the company it had purchased would simply walk away.

In what was meant to be a knockout punch, ITT next announced a two-step restructuring plan. The first step would be another breakup of ITT into three separate companies, a hotel and casino operator, a technical school company, and a publisher of telephone directories. Afterward, the Yellow Pages company—the successor to the "old" ITT—would buy back $2.1 billion of its stock in a $70 a share tender offer, well above Hilton's initial $55 offer.

For a time, it looked as if Araskog's maneuvers had effectively foreclosed a Hilton takeover. The spin-off and subsequent restructuring amounted to a two-tier, front-end-loaded self-tender offer. ITT shareholders would receive some cash on the front end and a package of stock in the three new ITTs on the back end. Moreover, each of the two spin-off companies—including ITT Destinations, the hotel company that Hilton wanted—would be restructured with full takeover defenses.

Two features in particular looked to give ITT Destinations impenetrable armor. First, the terms of ITT Destinations' board members would be staggered, so that Hilton would not be able to gain control for several years. Second, the spin-off of Destinations would, through compliance with a set of complex tax rules, be tax-free to ITT shareholders; but a subsequent purchase of ITT Destinations by Hilton arguably would not have the tax-free status. Hilton would then be on the hook for $1.4 billion of taxes, a hidden poison pill that would likely make Destinations too toxic to be taken over.

But the ITT team had overdone it. They were effectively disenfranchising their shareholders with a staggered board where none previously had existed and foreclosing the possibility of a takeover. The strategy was vulnerable to legal attack.

Bollenbach sensed ITT's vulnerability and in August 1997 ratcheted up the Hilton bid to $70 a share. The terms of the new bid called for Hilton to buy a majority of the shares for cash and the remainder for Hilton stock. At the same time, Hilton filed a challenge to ITT's restructuring plan in a Nevada federal court, using its raised bid to add pressure. Six weeks later, on September 29, 1997, Hilton won a court order that required ITT to put its restructuring plan to a vote. The Nevada judge rejected ITT's arguments that its plan amounted to a simple dividend of stock in ITT Destinations and the technical school company. To the contrary, the judge ruled that the ITT restructuring plan had "as its primary purpose the entrenchment of the current board."

The ruling in favor of Hilton dramatically eroded ITT's position and required ITT to hold a shareholder vote by November 14, 1997. After months of dogged resistance, Araskog's complex defenses had crumbled. ITT suddenly faced the prospect that Hilton's slate of directors might be elected, ensuring Hilton a victory.

Both ITT and Hilton rushed to lobby shareholders for support. Each company placed a stream of full-page advertisements in *The New York Times* and *The Wall Street Journal*. A certain amount of mudslinging broke out as Araskog and Bollenbach pressed their points. In a published *Barron's* interview, Araskog called Bollenbach "a drive-by financier who has held four jobs in five years and has a lot less impressive business career than people give him credit for." Bollenbach shot back: "What Araskog has shown ever since we made our first offer in late January is that he will do anything just to try to fend us off and preserve his own job."

Bollenbach's statement proved to be only half right. Araskog was committed to defeating the Hilton bid, but he would sacrifice his job in the process. With the clock ticking toward the November ITT shareholders' meeting, ITT made a dramatic late October announcement. The company had found a white knight who seemed to be willing to top Hilton by a considerable amount: Starwood Lodging, a hotel and real estate company, had agreed to acquire ITT in a friendly deal valued at $82 a share, or $9.8 billion. Starwood was a paired-share real estate investment trust (REIT), a legal status that advantaged the company in the bidding process. REITs are exempt from taxation so long as they pay out 95 percent of their cash flow as dividends. Paired-share REITs like Starwood can also shield their income from non–real estate operations—such as room rental and gambling—from taxation. For most companies, paired-share status was abolished in 1983. But REITs that enjoyed paired-share status prior to 1983 were grandfathered. In addition to Starwood, there were only three other paired-share REITs.

The Starwood deal represented an ironic turn of events for ITT. Starwood was a high-growth, high-multiple company with relatively little earnings. Measured by stock market capitalization, Starwood was a much smaller company than ITT. Yet Starwood's high-priced stock gave it the currency to go after the larger company. In an ironic twist, a high flier of the 1990s would be buying the remnants of a high flier from the 1960s in a deal that would be massively accretive to Starwood's earnings thanks to Harold Geneen's old earnings-per-share game of the 1960s. If the market priced the combined company at a higher multiple than the blended average of the two stand-alone companies, as initially appeared to be the case, the merger would create value for shareholders. As it happened in WorldCom-MCI, and Tyco-AMP, the high-multiple stock was the winner in a bull market, just as in the 1960s.

In any event, Araskog again looked to have delivered a knockout punch. While Starwood was offering a 1960s-style stock deal, Hilton was offering 50 percent cash. Each raise would drain some of the company's borrowing capacity, make a deal less accretive, and reduce post-deal operating flexibility. Starwood's $12 per share premium to Hilton's offer appeared to have priced Hilton out of the fight. Bollenbach applauded Araskog for doing "the right thing" for ITT shareholders and essentially conceded defeat. Hilton was not "going to chase the deal."

The only chance for Hilton would be if Starwood's stock price dropped considerably before the deal was approved. ITT's shareholders were partially protected against this eventuality by a price collar included in Starwood's offer, in which shareholders were guaranteed to receive $82 in cash and Starwood stock so long as Starwood's stock traded in a band between $53.26 and $61.26 per share. This collar discouraged shareholders from discounting the Starwood stock in its offer.

But on October 27, 1997, a single-day 554-point drop in the Dow average dramatically changed investor psychology. People began to question the value of high-flying stocks such as Starwood. Bollenbach jumped at the opportunity and again raised Hilton's bid.

Under the new bid, Hilton would pay ITT shareholders $80 per share, 55 percent in cash (up from 50 percent) and the remainder in Hilton stock. Hilton also included a contingent value right (CVR) that would pay ITT shareholders an additional amount if Hilton's stock failed to trade at an average of $40 for any twenty-day period in the following year. The $40 target price would make the two Hilton shares given to ITT shareholders on the back end of the Hilton offer worth the same $80 as the cash paid on the front end. If the stock didn't reach the $40 level, Hilton would pay holders of the CVRs up to $12 per share. In the worst case, this guarantee would cost Hilton more than $600 million.

These terms compared favorably to Starwood's offer, which included only $15 in cash and $67 in stock. ITT's board finally budged. Exercising the fiduciary out provisions in the merger agreement with

Starwood, the company announced it would auction itself off to the highest bidder and established a special board committee of outside directors to evaluate competing bids.

Meanwhile, Starwood faced pressure to raise its bid. If at the ITT shareholder meeting Hilton's slate of directors were elected, the contest would be over. But Starwood instead hoped ITT shareholders would back the company's incumbent board one last time. To encourage shareholders to vote for the ITT slate and keep the auction going, Starwood raised its bid to $85 per share and increased the cash portion in advance of the meeting.

ITT shareholders dramatically rewarded Starwood for its generosity. An estimated 72 percent of the shareholders backed ITT's incumbent slate of directors, and within twenty-four hours after the meeting, the ITT board had endorsed the revised Starwood offer. Though the new merger agreement included a fiduciary out for ITT, any new offer would have to top Starwood's price and be fully funded or possible to finance. Hilton meanwhile withdrew its offer. Bollenbach conceded the price for ITT had gotten too rich: "Once it was clear the market would treat [Starwood's] stock like cash, I think it was a lost cause."

Though Araskog had his victory, it was bittersweet. Araskog would walk away with an estimated $55 million lump-sum payment. However, his efforts to keep ITT independent had failed. The Starwood deal would mark the final death of the conglomerate built up by Harold Geneen. In addition, Araskog would relinquish both his board seat and the top job to Starwood's Barry S. Sternlicht.

Araskog couldn't resist one last barb at Bollenbach even as the Hotel War wrapped up. In interviews after the shareholder vote, Araskog said the outcome would have been different if Hilton had bid $75 per share for ITT at the outset rather than $55. Then, Araskog asserted, the ITT board would have felt obliged to negotiate with Hilton.

Of course, it is impossible to know what would have happened, but Bollenbach rejected the idea that a preemptive bid would have cracked the ITT board. In his view, the board was never prepared to sell control of ITT until forced to do so. An original bid of $75—at the high end of what Hilton could afford to pay—would only have priced Hilton out of the fight from the outset, according to Bollenbach. Critics, however, disagreed.

Bollenbach took a philosophical approach to the episode: "In thirty-five years I have been through lots of deals and I usually lose. That's the deal business. This is part of what I do for a living." Ironically, the status as a paired-share REIT that gave Starwood a bidding advantage over Hilton was revoked shortly after the deal closed, when Congress eliminated the grandfather clause that allowed paired-share REITs to put new acquisitions into the paired-share structure. Starwood has since become a normal, tax-paying C-Corporation and its share price has suffered significantly. The shares in Starwood that investors treated like cash revealed their volatility. In April 1999, Richard Nanula, the number two executive at Starwood who served as president and COO, resigned—a further indication of the turmoil at Starwood. Lofty multiples don't necessarily last forever.

The Government | 23
Intervenes

"The great corporations . . . are the creatures of the state, and the state not only has the right to control them, but it is in duty bound to control them whenever the need for such control is shown."

—Theodore Roosevelt, in a speech at Providence, Rhode Island, August 1902

The influence of the government pervades the deal process. The impact of various government organizations is felt in securities and tax laws, industry regulations, and sometimes even through direct intervention. This all-pervasive giant of government affects the structure, pace, and scope of transactions.

Other than mandated public filings, antitrust law is the most direct interface between government and deal participants, a costly web that can entangle even the most sophisticated acquirer. The perceived risks of an antitrust challenge can have a determinative impact in a hostile situation, such as the 1990s bidding war for Conoco. Alternatively, in the friendly deal context, if the government decides to launch an antitrust challenge, the acquirer must either back out or subject itself to lengthy litigation. A dealmaker therefore needs to understand both the substantive and procedural rules of antitrust before entering a contest.

The Renewed Power of Antitrust

Antitrust challenges to mergers and acquisitions were relatively infrequent during the Reagan and Bush years. The major antitrust milestone of the period was the breakup of AT&T; however, most deals sailed through the antitrust review process.

Lately, the winds have shifted, and government authorities have shown a renewed interest in challenging proposed transactions. The 1997 challenge to the Staples–Office Depot merger was a particularly dramatic showstopper, a sign of regulators' new assertive posture and of the courts' willingness to block a deal. In 1998, the FTC successfully blocked the mergers between AmeriSource Health Corporation and McKesson and between Bergen Brunswig and Cardinal Health—the four largest drug wholesalers in the U.S.

Win, Lose, or Draw   Antitrust has in recent years been reinvigorated by strong personalities like Justice Department antitrust chief Joel Klein and his special prosecutor David Boies. In the Microsoft antitrust trial, Boies ripped Microsoft's defense to shreds, calling into question the credibility of Microsoft's twelve key witnesses. Boies also exposed a flawed Windows 98 demonstration, intended to show that Internet Explorer ran slowly when detached from Windows: The tape that was supposed to have been made with one computer really was made by splicing together demonstrations conducted on several computers. As a result of Boies' work, the judge refused to rely on the tape and Microsoft's credibility was called into question.

Joel Klein has been an even more visible figure over the past few years. Revitalizing the role of the Justice Department in antitrust enforcement, Klein envisions a leading role for the agency in the "new economy" of globalization and information. Indeed, antitrust enforcement has not been so vigorous in the past thirty years as it is today under Klein, who took over as head of antitrust enforcement at the Justice Department in 1997. The son of a postman, Klein graduated from Columbia University and Harvard Law School. Before assuming his current post at the Justice Department, Klein had been President Clinton's deputy counsel.

Detractors have asserted that Klein has politicized antitrust and that his attacks on big business are based more on class warfare than on sound economic principles. Indeed, Klein has made it his mission to take on big business like Intel, Microsoft, and Staples. But that is not to say that Klein is "anti-business." In fact, Klein's middle-of-the-road pro-business views—epitomized by his refusal to mount a challenge to the 1996 merger of Bell Atlantic and NYNEX—almost prevented his appointment.

The government's growing interest in placing antitrust limitations on mergers has been in the headlines for several years. Microsoft was one of the first companies to feel the sting. When in 1994, the software giant agreed to acquire Intuit, the maker of the financial software Quicken, the Justice Department attacked the deal as anticompetitive and would not back down, forcing Bill Gates to pull the plug on the deal.

But Microsoft's situation is the classic story of the self-inflicted wound. The proposed deal followed closely on the heels of the settlement of a four-year antitrust battle between Microsoft and the Justice Department which was roundly criticized by Microsoft's competitors as too soft. So, when Microsoft announced the Intuit deal, the Justice Department faced political pressure to toughen up.

Unfortunately for Microsoft, as part of their review, Justice Department officials came across several unfavorable documents. Naturally, the government became fond of quoting Scott Wood, Intuit's chief executive officer, who referred to Microsoft as "Godzilla" in internal memos and who also predicted in writing that the combination of Microsoft and Intuit would leave financial institutions "one clear option" for financial software and would eliminate a "bloody [market] share war." In a separate memo also cited by the government, a Microsoft executive wrote, "as a combination, [Intuit and Microsoft] would be dominant."

Relying on these statements and more substantive arguments, the Justice Department challenged the Microsoft-Intuit transaction and shortly thereafter the deal collapsed. The lesson is that, even in internal, preliminary documents, salesmanship must be tempered with realism so that any materials which end up with the government present a balanced picture.

Less than two years later, another major transaction suffered a similar fate. The Federal Trade Commission (FTC) challenged Rite Aid's agreement to purchase Revco for $1.8 billion, arguing that together the two drugstore chains would have the power to keep health care groups from negotiating lower prices for prescription medicines. Rather than fight, Rite Aid dropped the deal and instead acquired Thrifty Payless. CVS then acquired our client Revco in 1997.

While Microsoft and Rite Aid were signposts pointing to a more skeptical government review process, the Staples case had a wider impact. Not only did the government challenge a major transaction—once a rarity—but the government actually won a preliminary round in court.

The concept of a big-box retail store devoted entirely to office products was relatively unheard of as late as 1990. Staples founder and CEO Thomas Stemberg and his rivals at Office Depot pioneered this retail format and quickly rolled out stores across the country. By the fall of 1996, the two chains together had over 1,000 stores with more than $10 billion in annual revenue.

A simple vision animated the office superstore business plan—low-cost office supplies for the small business and home office markets. Before the superstores came on the scene, these markets were served by the highly fragmented stationery industry. But Stemberg prided himself on his ruthless competitive nature, and by constantly finding ways to lower prices, he grabbed a large market share for Staples.

In September 1997, Staples and Office Depot announced a plan to merge in an approximately $4 billion stock swap. The combined company would be the largest office superstore and Office Max—with 503 stores and $3.3 billion of revenue—would be its only remaining competitor.

Of course, Stemberg and David Fuente, the chairman and CEO of Office Depot, anticipated that the merger of the number one and number two players in a three-company industry would attract some government attention. However, they believed that the relative lack of geographic overlap between the two companies' stores weighed in favor of the deal. Furthermore, the companies had a strong history of lowering prices for consumers, which Stemberg and Fuente underscored by standing in front of a banner that read "Save Even More" when they announced the deal. According to the companies, the merger would bring $4 billion of projected cost savings, part of which would be passed on to consumers in the form of lower prices. In the final analysis, Stemberg and Fuente expected these factors would convince government lawyers to approve the deal.

This forecast proved to be wrong. In March 1997, the FTC voted to challenge the deal despite the fact that the two office superstores would control less than 6 percent of the total office supply market. Nor were government lawyers swayed by the fact that the tremendous growth of the office superstore format had come as a result of these chains' strategy of undercutting mom-and-pop competitors on price.

Critics lambasted the FTC's decision, arguing that a merger of Staples and Office Depot would pose no danger to consumers. Members of the takeover bar expected the government to settle, especially after Staples agreed to divest sixty-three stores in overlap markets to Office Max.

However, the FTC was not persuaded. The commission argued the superstore segment of the office supply business represents a market unto itself and that a combination of the number one and number two competitors in that narrow niche would be anticompetitive. For support, the FTC relied on a pricing study which showed that Staples charges somewhat higher prices in markets where it lacks a superstore competitor. The combination with Office Depot would dramatically increase the number of markets without a second store.

Unlike Rite Aid or Microsoft, Staples decided to fight the FTC, going to court to defend the deal. Commentators gave the companies a good chance of prevailing, primarily because the government's narrow market definition seemed to fly in the face of reality. The notion that customers would buy a particular group of widely distributed products only from a particular class of stores was relatively novel.

Yet again the predictions were wrong. On June 30, 1997, federal district judge Thomas Hogan ruled in the government's favor, granting a preliminary injunction blocking the merger. Hogan was persuaded by the government's pricing studies—largely an analysis of scanner data from checkout counters—and by evidence that the office superstore chains priced differently in markets without another superstore. In addition, there was evidence that Staples and Office Depot thought of each other, and Office Max, as their primary competition. The antitrust proceedings uncovered a graph created by Staples in 1996 that showed it anticipated competition from Office Depot in 76 percent of its markets by 2000, compared with 46 percent in 1996.

Within days of this stunning upset, Staples and Office Depot dropped their plan to merge. Arbitrageurs—who had been listening to lawyers predict a Staples victory—lost large sums on their investments. Takeover professionals were left to speculate whether the case represented a new dawn of restrictive antitrust enforcement. But they took some solace in the FTC's contemporaneous approval of the $14 billion merger of Boeing and McDonnell Douglas Corporation. Meanwhile, Stemberg and Fuente went back to being competitors after having spent months anticipating a deal. Antitrust enforcement was alive and kicking.

Procedural Rules

The subtlety of antitrust is that both procedural and substantive aspects play vital roles. Two branches of government administer the antitrust laws: the Antitrust Division of the Justice Department and the Bureau of Competition of the Federal Trade Commission. The agencies coordinate their activities, with one of the two designated to review each particular transaction.

This bifurcated authority on its face makes no sense, although a host of legal articles solemnly argue that nothing could be more appropriate than some competition in enforcement of antitrust laws. A more sophisticated defense advanced by supporters of antitrust enforcement is that the two existing bodies have more political clout separately than when combined. Reformers have, to no avail, periodically pointed out the inanity of it all—split resources, duplication, lack of coordination, and so forth. So diffuse government policy in this field probably will remain institutionalized.

Certainly, the Federal Trade Commission is the more colorful of the two branches. The FTC was established in 1914 as an independent regulatory agency to combat the abuses of businesses. At various times over the years, it has been a vigorous and imaginative enforcement agency; but it has also been a phlegmatic repository for political cronies. Every few years, another reform group springs up to salvage the FTC, but the impact of the reports of these groups has historically been fleeting. Recently, however, the influence of the FTC has taken an upswing.

As an administrative agency, the FTC brings complaints which have first been recommended by the staff and approved by the commission. Each complaint is heard by one of the FTC's hearings examiners, and the commission as a whole then votes whether to accept or reject the hearing examiner's findings. The decision of the commission can be appealed in the federal circuit courts.

In theory, because its hearing examiners and commissioners specialize in the trade regulation field, the FTC should be able to make more sophisticated and better decisions than the courts. This was the cutting edge of economic planning theory circa 1914.

But among the problems faced by the FTC in fact is that many of its commissioners and hearing examiners are not of the highest caliber. In addition, there is an inherent systematic tension created when commissioners who decide, on the basis of staff recommendations, whether or not to bring complaints later judge the merit of their own decisions in an investigation.

The FTC approval process from complaint to final commission ruling historically has taken years. Recently, however, the FTC has implemented new fast-track rules that commit the commission to make a final decision on a complaint within thirteen months. But this new process is untested.

The Antitrust Division, by way of contrast, uses the federal court system as the venue for its proceedings. Since the days of the FDR administration, when Thurman Arnold reinvigorated the division (after the Supreme Court indicated that the president's alternative program of economic regulation—the price-fixing codes of the National Recovery Act—was unconstitutional), the Antitrust Division has generally had the more professional reputation of the two enforcement branches. The FTC has generally had more populist intent.

PROFILE

Robert Pitofsky

Robert Pitofsky is the man most responsible for reviving the moribund FTC and sparking the revival of antitrust law. Pitofsky took over as chairman in 1995, returning to the agency from a stint in private practice. The former dean of the Georgetown University's law school and a Carter administration FTC commissioner, Pitofsky was very helpful years ago when I was part of a Ralph Nader team examining FTC merger policy.

As an academic, Pitofsky developed a reputation for a relatively tough antitrust stance, emphasizing the political importance of antitrust. To Pitofsky, large business entities posed a democratic as well as economic threat that regulators should curb. Media conglomerations were a particular concern because such combinations might put too much power to control the public debate in the hands of a few businesses.

Yet, as chairman, Pitofsky has not taken a uniform "big is bad" position. The FTC has instead adopted a more nuanced—and somewhat confusing—approach. At times, Pitofsky has taken a tough stand against mergers which pose little real anticompetitive threat, while on other occasions he has expressed a willingness to recognize potential efficiency gains as a countervailing justification for some deals.

In fact, Pitofsky is a bundled package of instincts: He is certainly bright and professional; he is a populist by inclination; he has a romantic faith in the purpose of the FTC as a viable institution guiding America's economic future; but he is also an astute politician whose agenda is to please the president.

Pitofsky's political grandstanding was reflected in his challenge of Time Warner's acquisition of Turner Broadcasting. Pitofsky fought hard with the Justice Department to get jurisdiction over the deal, and after winning that battle, the FTC requested box after box of documents—more than a million pieces of paper. For almost a year, the FTC's staff sorted through all the paperwork and hemmed and hawed about the deal.

Finally, after long negotiations, the case was settled. Time Warner agreed to relatively light concessions, which was not surprising since the legal issues were minimal. But Pitofsky saved face by declaring a victory.

The agreement capped TCI's ownership in Time Warner and drew some blood from TCI, at the time one of the least popular companies in Washington circles. Time Warner also guaranteed that it would carry an independent all-news channel on its cable systems. Curiously, though, many of the requirements of the settlement were already part of the Telecommunications Act of 1996.

Despite the controversy surrounding the drawn-out Turner process and subsequent Staples challenge, Pitofsky continues to take aggressive positions in particular cases while attempting to find a middle road. He favors allowing U.S. companies to combine if to do so would allow them to become more competitive in a global marketplace. And he has generally not challenged large defense industry mergers necessitated by declining government budgets. Moreover, in 1997, Pitofsky's FTC joined with the Justice Department in endorsing new antitrust guidelines which recognize potential efficiencies as a factor to be considered in reviewing deals, although the substance of these initiatives is not yet clear.

While Pitofsky has succeeded in raising professional standards at the FTC, the conflicting signals coming from the agency have made the merger review process a bit of a crap shoot. Even antitrust experts have trouble predicting where the FTC will come down on a particular deal. Of course, that might be precisely the result Pitofsky wants. Uncertainty is a powerful regulatory hurdle for a practical populist.

Reporting Requirements   In late 1976, Congress passed the Hart-Scott-Rodino Antitrust Improvements Act, which requires firms involved in acquisitions of more than $15 million in voting stock or assets to file notification forms with both the Federal Trade Commission and the Antitrust Division of the Justice Department. The parties must also provide substantial information about the transaction to the government. Substantial penalties—as much as $10,000 per day—may accrue if a company fails to file.

There are four principal exceptions to the filing requirement. First, filing is not required if the acquirer purchases less than 10 percent of the target's voting stock and intends only to be a passive investor. Second, the filing requirement does not apply to the purchase of options, warrants, or other securities convertible into voting stock unless the purchase is deemed a device for the avoidance of filing. Of course, the conversion of the securities into voting stock may trigger a later reporting responsibility. Third, certain acquisitions involving foreign targets or acquirers are also exempt from filing.

Before the law was passed, two companies could merge without giving the government an opportunity to review the transaction in advance. But because a completed transaction is more difficult to unwind than a proposed transaction, the government was put under considerable pressure to overlook marginally anticompetitive deals.

There is, however, a loophole for newly formed partnerships and corporations. A partnership or corporation which has not yet prepared a balance sheet showing $10 million or more of assets need not file, as long as no single party controls 50 percent or more of the entity, measured by the right to assets or profits. Furthermore, there must be a business purpose for purchasing through the entity, other than just avoidance of the Hart-Scott filing requirement.

After both parties notify the government of an intended transaction, the parties are subject to a waiting period of thirty days (fifteen days for cash tender offers) before the deal can be consummated. In the case of a tender offer, the target company must file a notification form within fifteen days of the acquirer's notice (or within ten days in the case of a cash tender offer). Included in the extensive information required by the notification form are a description of the transaction, all background studies relating to it, detailed product-line breakdowns, a listing of competitors, and an analysis of sales patterns.

During the waiting period, the government may ask for additional material and, based on the responses, may request a twenty-day extension (ten days for cash tender offers) of the waiting period from a federal district court. In the event the government reacts adversely to the information it receives, the act describes a procedure for facilitating the immediate federal court hearing of a preliminary injunction motion.

Implications   Hart-Scott reporting requirements make it virtually impossible for hostile acquirers to build a substantial stake in a company in secret prior to a tender offer. While in the 1980s, hostile acquirers often used the passive investment and partnership exceptions to avoid Hart-Scott filings, the government attacked many of these cases as abusive. Such tactics are no longer permitted.

Due to increased enforcement of the rules, deal documents generally are drafted with an eye toward possible antitrust problems.

In the friendly-deal context, executives often feel pressured to overstate the case for a particular transaction, both internally and externally. Internally, certain executives may need to lobby ultimate decision makers, and in the process may be tempted to use unrealistic superlatives to describe the potential benefits. Likewise, an acquirer has an incentive to convince external observers and investors that a transaction will be beneficial to consumer welfare.

The problems faced by Jimmy Ling demonstrate the importance of including in deal documents what is known as an "antitrust out"— the ability to pull out of a deal should there be an antitrust challenge or an unfavorable antitrust ruling. Reacting in part to the howls of the other large steel manufacturers, the Justice Department challenged LTV's 1968 takeover of Jones & Laughlin, a large but sluggish steel company. Pending determination of the suit, LTV was not allowed to exercise control over J&L, tying up vast amounts of LTV's cash in J&L stock without allowing LTV to receive offsetting cash flow from dividends. Soon cash to pay interest on LTV's pyramid of securities became scarce and the LTV house of cards began to topple. LTV eventually reached a negotiated settlement with the Justice Department in which LTV agreed to spin off some other subsidiaries but keep J&L. It was, however, too late; the time delay brought about the eventual downfall of Ling.

This kind of antitrust proceeding can be incredibly expensive, because it is so time- and resource-intensive. Furthermore, the FTC or Justice Department may even challenge a merger after the notification period has run and the deal has been consummated. If fully litigated, a government merger suit can take eight to ten years to be finally resolved. Expense, however, cannot be thought of merely in terms of legal bills; the drain on management time and energy can dwarf those fees. In addition, if a successful private suit is brought, a company will face paying treble damages.

Ongoing antitrust litigation may result in a loss of corporate flexibility. Even if an injunction is not issued as part of the litigation, it is difficult for a firm to do the most elementary planning when its asset structure is seriously in doubt. Furthermore, investors and creditors will naturally reflect the ambiguity of the situation in their decisions.

Although the risks are substantial, they can be exaggerated. First, even if sued, a company may well settle the case without a significant divestiture, or may win in court. Furthermore, even if an acquisition is lost after a suit, much of the economic benefit of a good investment will have accrued, and, probably, a sizable profit can be made on resale. Second, very few antitrust suits are actually filed. So a theoretical antitrust problem may not be a real litigation risk.

In addition to negotiating an antitrust provision in the deal documents, an acquirer should be prepared to spend considerable time and energy on the review process. Like DuPont, an acquirer should not treat the review process as a black box that will take care of itself. Rather, the acquirer should seek to create an ongoing negotiation with the reviewing agency.

An alternative to the whole process under Hart-Scott-Rodino is for the parties to a deal to negotiate a voluntary settlement with the government. Such settlements typically are reached during the review process and result in the government filing a complaint together with a proposed consent decree. Though a consent decree must be approved by a federal judge, the court in most cases merely validates the terms of the existing agreement.

The government typically either requires the merging parties to divest overlapping businesses or restricts potentially anticompetitive conduct. In the recent Time Warner–Turner consent decree, for example, the government required the combined entity to guarantee competitors access to its cable systems. Understandably, buyers who are risk-averse often prefer to seek a consent decree rather than face a challenge. Otherwise, they bear the risk that one day after the deal is consummated, the acquisition will be challenged.

PROFILE

Robert Joffe

Bob Joffe, a partner at law firm Cravath, Swaine & Moore, is a master of the complicated antitrust process for mergers. Joffe has distinguished himself as an adept, smooth courtroom presence with an effective behind-the-scenes negotiating style and took over as Cravath's presiding partner when Sam Butler retired at the end of 1998.

Joffe graduated from Harvard Law School in 1967 and spent the next two years on a fellowship in the newly independent African nation of Malawi, where his responsibilities included helping the country rewrite its laws. Joffe then joined Cravath in 1969.

Very quickly, Joffe gravitated toward antitrust matters, cutting his teeth on drawn-out cases for Kellogg and Westinghouse. By 1978, he was a partner at the firm and began to develop a relationship that would define much of his career: The client was Trime Inc.'s HBO subsidiary.

In 1980, four movie studios teamed up with Getty Oil to launch a cable channel called Premiere and, as part of the venture, the studios agreed not to license their films to HBO. If allowed to stand, the arrangement would have given Premiere a distinct competitive advantage over HBO. But Joffe convinced the government that this agreement constituted unacceptable anticompetitive behavior. The Justice Department sued and Premiere fell apart.

Joffe's Premiere victory sealed his relationship with HBO. Soon, he grew into the lead antitrust litigator for all of Time. In 1989, the merger of Time and Warner propelled Joffe to even greater prominence. First, Joffe successfully shepherded the deal through the Justice Department's antitrust review. Then, when Paramount tried to bust the deal apart, Joffe teamed up with Herb Wachtell to defend the deal.

In a hearing broadcast live on CNN, Joffe made a widely acclaimed presentation defending the authority of Time's board to make a strategic decision and stick to it. Time won the case, and the deal was done.

Though less heralded, Joffe accomplished another triumph in 1996, when he negotiated the settlement with the FTC which allowed the Time Warner–Turner deal to proceed. At the outset, Joffe faced a thicket of problems, including FTC chairman Robert Pitofsky's concern about large media deals. The Turner acquisition, which would bring together two of the largest cable channel operators—one of which (Time Warner) was also a major cable system operator—was just the kind of deal to excite Pitofsky.

And TCI's partial ownership of Turner Broadcasting only exacerbated the situation because TCI's John Malone has had a long history of run-ins with federal antitrust regulators. As a result, not only was the government predisposed against TCI, but the combination arguably would give TCI an incentive to favor Time Warner–Turner channels on its cable systems.

Because Time Warner's Jerry Levin publicly promised the Turner deal would go through, there was a lot of pressure on Joffe to deliver. But Joffe's negotiating power was constrained, as the terms of Malone's deal with Ted Turner allowed him to veto any settlement Joffe might negotiate with the government.

The process began with the Hart-Scott-Rodino filing and subsequent information requests, quarterbacked by Joffe. When the FTC expressed reservations about the deal, he opened negotiations on a settlement, a process that dragged on for months. Joffe laid out an assertive position: He had a strong case and would go to court if necessary. Time Warner was willing to work with the FTC, but would only go so far to settle. The trick, according to Joffe, is to "draw a line in the sand" only where a strong legal foundation exists for the position.

The approach paid off. Three days before the FTC was scheduled to vote on the deal, the government blinked. Time Warner and the FTC reached a settlement which amounted to a win for Joffe and his client but also allowed the FTC's Pitofsky to declare victory.

The Substantive Law

While procedural rules are important, the actual teeth of antitrust resides in the substantive law. Yet antitrust is probably one of the most uncertain areas of the law, and, therefore, one of the most frustrating to corporate executives. In the merger field, there are few bright-line rules, only guidelines from precedents.

For legal purposes, mergers are analyzed in three categories: horizontal (between competitors), vertical (between customers and suppliers), and conglomerate (between firms in unrelated industries). The law is most developed in the horizontal area and most uncertain as applied to conglomerates. However, because conglomerate mergers are relatively rare, most of the interplay surrounds horizontal and vertical deals.

In all three cases, Section 7 of the Clayton Act is the starting point for antitrust analysis. As amended by the Celler-Kefauver Act of 1950, Section 7 provides that "no corporation . . . shall acquire, directly or indirectly, the whole or any part of the stock . . . [or] the whole or any part of the assets of another corporation . . . where in any line of commerce in any section of the country the effect of such acquisition may be substantially to lessen competition, or to tend to create a monopoly."

In examining any merger, the scope of the relevant market must be defined both geographically and by product. The answer to this threshold question is often critical, as was demonstrated in the Staples–Office Depot case. Procter & Gamble's 1991 acquisition of Max Factor provides another example. Prior to the transaction, Procter & Gamble's Cover Girl—America's leading brand of mass-market cosmetics—controlled 23 percent of the mass cosmetics market. Max Factor had roughly 7 percent of the mass market.

The proposed deal would further concentrate the mass market for cosmetics, arguably reducing competition. However, the market can also be defined more broadly to include cosmetics sold through department stores such as Estée Lauder, and direct sale products like Avon. Employing this market definition, the market shares of Cover Girl and Max Factor would plunge. Market definition, therefore, involves a complex, multifactor inquiry. When the government embraced a broader definition, the deal sailed through.

Horizontal Mergers   In the 1960s and 1970s, courts adopted a tough quantitative test to judge the legality of horizontal mergers. In the 1980s and 1990s, however, they began to relax their restrictions.

The early, quantitative approach to market definition began with the first major case decided by the U.S. Supreme Court under the amended Section 7, *Brown Shoe,* which centered around the merger of the Brown and Kinney shoe chains. Although the Court in its 1962 decision considered many factors, the merger analysis focused primarily on post-deal market share. Significantly, the Court indicated that even a 5 percent level of market control after a merger could, under certain circumstances, be regarded as anticompetitive.

In its 1963 decision in *Philadelphia National Bank,* the Supreme Court went a step beyond *Brown Shoe* and articulated its presumption that high market shares resulting from a merger will reduce competition. The Court held that such an increase in concentration would be enjoined in the absence of evidence clearly showing the merger was not likely to have anticompetitive effects. *Brown* and *Philadelphia National Bank* were breakthrough cases because the Court spurned the previously invoked "rule of reason," an analysis which considered issues on a case-by-case basis, and instead accepted the "bright-line" test. The stated reason for rejecting a rule-of-reason test in *Philadelphia National Bank* was that permitting too broad an economic investigation would defeat the congressional intent of limiting the increase in concentration.

After *Philadelphia National Bank,* and until recently, courts became increasingly specific about what would be considered unacceptable concentration levels. In the 1964 *Alcoa-Rome* decision, the Court firmly established the principle hinted at in *Philadelphia National Bank:* In a concentrated industry even slight increases in market share may be considered illegal. Thus, Alcoa's acquisition of Rome was deemed in violation of Section 7, even though it added only 1.3 percent to Alcoa's approximately 28 percent control of the national aluminum conductor market. A later appeals court case, *Stanley Works,* established the converse proposition: A firm with 1 percent market share could not acquire the leading firm with 24 percent of the market.

In *Von's Grocery,* the Supreme Court in 1966 expanded the *Philadelphia National Bank* quantitative standard to firms with relatively small market shares if the industry was exhibiting a trend toward concentration. Noting that the number of single-store groceries was declining in the Los Angeles area, the Court held that a merger resulting in a firm with a total of 7.5 percent of the Los Angeles market was illegal.

However, in more recent times, both the courts and the enforcement agencies have relaxed their tough quantitative approach to merger policy. While the courts continue to enjoin mergers on the basis of a projected increase in market share, they tend to do so only in cases where the existing market shares and the impact of the merger on concentration are considerable. Otherwise, courts have given increasing weight to evidence that merged firms will be unable to raise prices even though they may have an increased market share. This evidence generally relates to ease of market entry or projected efficiencies from the proposed merger.

Perhaps most notably, regulators approved the recombination of the former Standard Oil of Ohio (BP) with Standard Oil of Indiana (Amoco) into BP Amoco. The combined company, on a pro forma basis, sells 12 percent of the gasoline used in the U.S. Ironically, it was Standard Oil that sparked the creation of antitrust laws.

And if regulators approve the currently pending Exxon-Mobil merger, a combination of the former Standard Oil of New York with Standard Oil of New Jersey, the antitrust tide will really have turned.

The telco industry has also witnessed the approval of the recombination of the so-called Baby Bells, created in the 1984 antitrust breakup of AT&T. Bell Atlantic has merged with NYNEX and SBC has merged with Pacific Telesis and Southern New England Telephone. Furthermore, a deal is pending between SBC and Ameritech and between U S West and Quest which, if consummated, will leave BellSouth as the only remaining independent Baby Bell.

What has been responsible for this significant turning in the antitrust field? In the case of oil mergers, regulators likely realized that oil is a global market: Due to the large number of global players, not even the combined firms will be able to control prices. Furthermore, if these combinations were not permitted, the high cost structures of U.S. oil firms would cause their competitive positions relative to foreign firms to erode further, putting U.S. consumers in a position of even greater dependence on foreign oil. In the case of the telco industry, the companies put forth a strong case that an increase in scale, effected through a combination, would be necessary to become global players and to make efficient capital investments. The market is now a global one and U.S. companies are facing a new competitive reality. Fortunately, regulators have evolved with the times.

Companies in industries that are easy to enter are less able to raise prices than those with high barriers to entry. For example, in *United States v. Gillette Co.,* a lower court in 1993 refused to enjoin the merger of two fountain pen manufacturers because the court reasoned that the combined entity would be unable to raise prices: The relevant manufacturing technology was readily available to potential competitors and no regulatory or legal barriers barred potential entrants from the market. Thus, no significant barriers to entry existed.

In other cases, courts have identified the following as potential barriers to entry: high capital expenditures, large sunk costs, long lead time, a large minimum scale for efficient production, the need for specialized knowledge or technology, regulatory barriers, and brand loyalty.

HORIZONTAL MERGERS — GOVERNMENT GUIDELINES. In the early days of the Clinton administration, joint guidelines were issued to indicate which mergers would likely be challenged by the Justice Department and the Federal Trade Commission. Although the guidelines are not definitive, they do provide a rough feel for issues the government considers.

The calculation of a projected post-merger market share—based on either the total sales or the production capacity of all market participants—is the starting point for analysis under the guidelines. Both existing market concentration and the extent to which concentration will increase after a merger are stated in terms of the so-called Herfindahl-Hirschman Index. This particular measure of market concentration was selected in part because it weights firms with large market shares heavily and is sensitive to increases in the size differences between firms. The index is calculated by adding the squares of the two companies' post-merger market shares. Relative to adding market shares without first squaring, the Herfindahl-Hirschman Index weights large market shares more heavily.

The following example demonstrates the difference between the pure market share approach and the Herfindahl Index. Under a pure market share approach, three companies with a combined 45 percent market share, split evenly, would be treated the same as three companies with a combined 45 percent share where one company had 43 percent and the other two 1 percent each. Both 43+1+1 and 15+15+15 equal 45. The Herfindahl Index distinguishes between the two cases. In the first situation, the index would total 675 (15^2 times three); in the second situation, it would be 1,851 ($43^2+1^2+1^2$). This attempt at high science is obviously quite primitive, but it is important to be in on the jargon.

The guidelines indicate that a separate index will be calculated for each market in which either of the merging companies participates, both pre- and post-merger. The guidelines then provide the following decision rubric:

Post-Merger Market Concentration	Ordinarily Not Subject to Review	Potentially Anticompetitive	Presumed Anticompetitive
Unconcentrated (HHI <1,000)	Yes	N/A	N/A
Moderately concentrated (HHI between 1,000 and 1,800)	HHI increases less than 100 points vs. pre-merger	HHI increases more than 100 points vs. pre-merger	N/A
Highly concentrated (HHI >1,800)	HHI increases less than 50 points vs. pre-merger	HHI increases between 50 and 100 vs. pre-merger	HHI increases more than 100 points vs. pre-merger

As the next step under the guidelines, the reviewing agency will conduct a broad analysis of a particular merger's anticompetitive effect relative to two basic concerns. First, a merger may make coordinated interaction, such as price fixing, more likely or more successful. Second, a merger may create market conditions that allow participants to benefit from anticompetitive unilateral action such as raising prices.

However, the guidelines allow ease of entry and increased efficiencies from mergers to counterbalance other negative merger effects. With regard to ease of entry, the guidelines provide three factors that will be considered: the time lines of entry, the likelihood of entry, and the sufficiency of entry. The efficiency analysis is free-ranging, but the guidelines indicate the government generally will reject claims of efficiencies if comparable savings could be achieved by some means short of a merger. Efficiency claims also must be substantiated.

While the presence of mathematical guidelines appears to give the antitrust review process a grounded scientific basis, the process is not nearly so simple. In fact, how regulators view combinations is very much influenced by political climate, lobbyists, and key personalities. A striking example is that of the consolidation in the oil industry. During the 1981 takeover contest for Conoco, fear of antitrust scrutiny drove Conoco shareholders to favor DuPont over Mobil. At that time, Mobil and Conoco were the nation's second and ninth largest oil companies, respectively. The political climate was such that their combination rang the alarm bells in Washington, a factor that DuPont used to its advantage. When the Justice Department cleared DuPont to buy Conoco but slapped Mobil with an information request, shareholders tendered to DuPont—even though its offer was significantly lower than Mobil's.

But by 1998, the climate had changed dramatically. That the number one and number two oil companies in the U.S.—Exxon and Mobil—could even contemplate a negotiated merger of equals demonstrates the seismic shift in regulatory attitude that has taken place over the last twenty years. Size alone is no longer feared. That Exxon Mobil would be the largest company in the U.S. is not per se bad. Cost savings and industry efficiency are now key considerations. While regulators are still examining the deal, most expect that it will be approved.

HORIZONTAL MERGERS — MARKET DEFINITION. Given the focus on market shares and the index, product and geographic market definitions are critical in the determination of the legality of a merger. *Brown Shoe* defines a product market as follows: "The outer boundaries of a product market are determined by the reasonable interchangeability of use or the cross-elasticity of demand between the product itself and substitutes for it."

The cross-elasticity of demand between two products posits a change in the price of one product and measures the impact on demand for the other product, indicating the extent to which one product would, in fact, be substituted for another.

With respect to geographic markets, the Supreme Court adopted a "pragmatic, factual approach" in *Brown Shoe*. Moreover, in that case, the Court indicated that every city with a population of 10,000 might be considered a geographical market. Subsequent decisions have split as to whether a particular small town fit the "section of the country" standard in Section 7, but the general principle remains true that geographical markets may be determined on quite a localized level.

More generally, in *Philadelphia National Bank,* the Supreme Court defined a geographic product market as "the 'area of effective competition . . . in which the seller operates, and to which the purchaser can practicably turn for supplies.'" Lower courts have identified a number of factors relevant to this inquiry: actual sales patterns (i.e., localized versus national), transportation cost, regulatory barriers, and industry practice. As with product markets, the guidelines repeat the "small but significant" price increase analysis to define geographic markets: Would a small but significant price increase induce a consumer to purchase goods elsewhere?

In the case of both product and geographic markets, the courts have broken broad product categories down into more narrow submarkets. Starting with *Brown Shoe,* the Supreme Court indicated that in defining submarkets it would consider as important factors industry or public recognition of a submarket as an independent economic entity and the product's characteristics such as uses, required production facilities, customers, and sensitivity to price changes in competing products. Thus, the Court in *Brown Shoe* held that there were separate submarkets in men's, women's, and children's shoes; in *Alcoa-Rome,* aluminum and copper cable were treated distinctly; and in *Clorox,* household liquid bleach was deemed to be a product with no close substitutes.

Some federal lower courts have in the past extended the Court's narrow interpretations of markets even further: For example, florist aluminum foil has been recognized as distinct from other lines of aluminum foil, and paper-insulated power cable has been deemed different from other cables. Recently, however, some courts have examined more seriously assertions of cross-elasticity—that the supply, demand, and pricing of one product, such as oil supplied to utilities, will produce an effect on demand and price of another product, such as coal.

However, despite some broadening of the definition of product and geographic markets and the application of less strict quantitative standards, horizontal mergers are still judged by fairly tough criteria.

Lately, the government has advanced a so-called differentiated products theory to define markets. This theory—used in *Staples* to limit the relevant market to just office superstores—states that merging companies are in the same market if a significant percentage of their customers would not switch suppliers in the face of a small but significant price increase. However, this theory lends itself to narrow market definitions tailored to the parties in a deal. Once a narrow market is defined, a deal will significantly concentrate that market, almost by default. Furthermore, preventing a merger based on this criterion can be ludicrous if consumers' responses are not economically rational but rather conditioned by force of habit.

Only time will tell whether the differentiated products theory gains widespread acceptance in the courts. However, in the modern regional, national, and global economy these narrow definitions of market and of potential competition are increasingly archaic. Decades from now, the standards will become more sophisticated. The new reality of international trade as well as Internet commerce is a looming presence over the 1950s world of antitrust market definitions.

Vertical Mergers   The law covering vertical mergers has undergone considerable change in recent years. Initially, courts' basic concern in vertical mergers was that an acquisition by a supplier of an outlet for its products would foreclose the supplier's competitors from a segment of the market.

Over the years, through a string of vertical transactions cases, courts have developed multiple criteria to determine whether a particular vertical merger could potentially foreclose competition. The *Brown Shoe* decision stated that the size and nature of the market foreclosed to competitors by a vertical merger was a significant but not dispositive factor in such a transaction's legality. Trends, the actual economic effect on competitors, and barriers to new entry, all should be considered in vertical integration situations, according to the *Brown* Court.

More recently, both courts and the Justice Department have reversed field somewhat and questioned the fundamental notion that vertical mergers might be anticompetitive. Several courts have highlighted the potential efficiency gains from a vertical combination and have rejected the idea that market foreclosure leads to increased market power. Picking up on this trend, the 1982 guidelines, which still govern vertical mergers, state that the Justice Department is unlikely to challenge a vertical merger unless the relevant market is highly concentrated (i.e., has an index above 1,800).

Following these standards, the government challenged relatively few vertical mergers during the Reagan-Bush years. In fact, a new era of lax scrutiny was ushered in when President Reagan's antitrust chief canceled the Department of Justice's thirteen-year investigation of IBM. However the Clinton administration has demonstrated renewed concern about vertical mergers. Three major vertical telecommunications acquisitions were challenged by the Clinton administration in 1994: the AT&T–McCaw Cellular deal, the British Telecommunications–MCI deal, and the TCI–Liberty Media deal. All three challenges resulted in agreements between the parties and the government designed to address potential anticompetitive effects. The message seems to be that vertical deals are permissible if the government can claim some concessions.

In perhaps the most dramatic vertical antitrust challenge in years, the Justice Department has once again launched a broad-based antitrust investigation of Microsoft, which has resulted in a long, ongoing trial. The allegation is that Microsoft is using its dominant position in operating systems to foreclose competition in software and the Internet through anticompetitive practices such as making its own software and Internet applications work more smoothly with its Windows operating system than those of its competitors. Government investigators have found incriminating memos in which Bill Gates and other Microsoft employees devised strategies to drive their competitors, such as Netscape, out of business.

The government's allegation of Microsoft's absolute market power may have been somewhat weakened by the merger between AOL and Netscape: Many observers felt the merger demonstrated that industry participants will always find some way to compete. However, political sentiment against Microsoft is strong. And since the antitrust process reflects the political consensus, it is possible that the outcome will involve some limitations on Microsoft.

Conglomerate Mergers   The most vexing area of merger law concerns conglomerate deals. Piercing through the rhetoric of the case, one key area of concern is simply the overall tendency toward economic concentration. But neither the statutes nor the case law explicitly addresses this problem: There is no clear legal basis for the position that bigness or overall concentration is per se bad. Instead, the few early cases overturning conglomerate transactions cited two perceived problems: First, conglomerate mergers can entrench the position of a dominant firm and second, conglomerate mergers create the opportunity for reciprocal dealing between business units.

Perhaps the leading case in the conglomerate field is the Supreme Court's 1967 *Clorox* decision. Clorox held some 48 percent of the national sales market for liquid bleach before being acquired by the nation's largest advertiser, Procter & Gamble. Interestingly, the Court found that Clorox had achieved its dominant position primarily through advertising, since, in fact, all liquid bleaches are chemically identical.

In light of Procter & Gamble's advertising dominance, the Court reasoned that the merger would discourage competitors from entering the bleach business. Furthermore, because Procter & Gamble was regarded as the most likely potential entrant into the market, and the Court felt that this loss of potential competition exacerbated the entrenchment of Clorox's position, Procter & Gamble was therefore ordered to divest Clorox. Yet years later it was allowed to buy Max Factor with no challenge.

The 1965 *Consolidated Foods* decision is the leading reciprocity case. In *Consolidated*, the Supreme Court held that the acquisition by Consolidated, a wholesale and retail food marketer, of Gentry, a garlic and onion powder supplier, was illegal because buyers of garlic and onion in the food-processing business would favor Gentry so as to gain better overall terms from Consolidated, reinforcing Gentry's leading role in the market.

However, recently, conglomerate mergers have received little attention. Such mergers are no longer as fashionable. Furthermore, the implicit recognition is that the legal case against them was thin anyway: The guidelines make no mention of conglomerate mergers.

Special Situations

The Failing Company   Although the guidelines clearly state that the economics of a transaction will not ordinarily be considered in evaluating a merger, failing companies are an exception. If a target company is clearly failing with no reasonable prospect of remaining viable and no offer of acquisition has come from a noncompetitor, the government may forgo a challenge to a deal it might otherwise attack.

This appears to have been one reason for the light review given to the Boeing–McDonnell Douglas merger of 1997. McDonnell Douglas had been routed by Boeing and Airbus in the commercial aircraft market. Though not yet failing, McDonnell Douglas' strong downward trend in this key overlap market made approval easier.

Private Suits   Under Section 16 of the Clayton Act, private parties are entitled to file antitrust suits under Section 7 and recover treble damages. Recently, private claims have become popular in response to tender offers. Courts have questioned, however, whether competitors or target companies have standing to sue. Standing requires an antitrust injury, and the Supreme Court has emphasized that competitors often benefit from the ability to increase prices presented by an anticompetitive merger. But litigators like the tactic anyway.

Cross-Border Deals

When a merger or acquisition crosses international boundaries, new layers of antitrust complexity result, as the review processes of countries other than the U.S. may be implicated. Antitrust policy in Japan and Europe, two of the most active participants in cross-tender deals, is discussed below.

Japan The Japanese antitrust framework, created in the aftermath of World War II, was consciously modeled on the U.S. system but has evolved to include a few key differences. As in the U.S., the parties to a merger must receive consent from the Japanese equivalent of the FTC. A filing is required and the government initially has a thirty-day period to review antitrust implications of a planned merger (which can be extended by another sixty days if required).

One of the key differences between Japanese and U.S. antitrust policies is that in the U.S. both mergers and stock purchases require a Hart-Scott filing, but, in Japan, the acquisition of shares is not reviewed in advance. The Japanese government will provide guidance but rarely makes a definitive judgment before the purchase takes place, believing that a stock purchase can be easily unwound. After a stock purchase takes place, the government has ninety days to raise an antitrust challenge.

Japanese antitrust regulators focus on market share as the touchstone of their analysis. The basic rule of thumb is that a combined market share below 25 percent is acceptable. A market share above that threshold is not automatically disallowed but will draw more careful scrutiny.

This focus on market share, as in U.S. policy, makes the question of market definition crucial. Obviously, the larger the relevant market, the less likely a merger will face negative scrutiny. As in the U.S., acquirers try to broaden the market definitions to include somewhat similar products and international markets. Ultimately, most deals above the 25 percent threshold come down to a negotiation between the parties and the government, and, as in the U.S., the parties and the government usually reach some compromise.

Europe   The European antitrust regulation is a patchwork of an overarching European Union regulation combined with the various rules of individual states. However, most large cross-border deals are picked up under the EU Merger Regulation.

The EU Merger Regulation gives the European Commission exclusive authority to review the antitrust implications of deals with a "Community dimension." A merger or acquisition has a Community dimension if 1) the aggregate worldwide sales of the resulting entity exceed roughly 2.5 billion euro (approximately $2.7 billion) per year; 2) at least two of the parties have EU-wide revenue of at least 100 million euro (approximately $107 million); 3) the parties have combined revenues of at least 100 million euro in each of three separate EU member states; and 4) at least two of the parties individually have revenues of 25 million euro (approximately $26 million) in three member states. But even if all four tests are not satisfied, the EU merger guidelines will be involved if 1) the parties have aggregate worldwide revenues of 5 billion euro (approximately $5.3 billion) and 2) at least two of the parties have aggregate community-wide sales of 250 million euro (approximately $267 million). However, a transaction is not covered if each party generates over two thirds of its Community revenues in a single country. A deal which impacts the "legitimate interests" of one particular EU country, such as national security or media diversity, may also be referred to the country's antitrust authorities.

As in the U.S., the parties to a deal covered by the EU Merger Regulation must notify the EU's minister of competition before proceeding. A three-week waiting period is imposed, with a possibility for extension. The commission must decide whether to open an investigation within one month of receiving the notification, and must decide within five months whether to approve the deal.

The EU's standard of review is whether a deal is "compatible" with the European common market. That is to say, officials determine whether a deal would "create or strengthen a dominant position as a result of which effective competition would be significantly impeded in the common market or in a substantial part of it." The EU's antitrust case law is relatively underdeveloped, but the commission seems to conduct a wide-ranging contextual economic analysis. With some notable exceptions, few deals have been challenged by the EU antitrust authority to date.

CORPORATE DIPLOMACY

The Boeing–McDonnell Douglas Deal

Over the past two decades, many industries have become global in focus and international in scope. As a result, international merger rules can be implicated even in a deal involving two U.S.-headquartered companies. This new reality was dramatically demonstrated in 1997 when the European Union challenged Boeing's plan to acquire McDonnell Douglas.

Boeing and McDonnell Douglas announced their $14 billion stock merger in December 1996, yet another step in the wider post–Cold War implosion of the defense industry. Yet it was the commercial aviation market, not the concentration of the U.S. defense industry, that was the main concern for EU regulators. The commercial aviation business has been dominated by three companies—Boeing, McDonnell Douglas, and Europe's Airbus consortium: In 1996, Boeing captured roughly 65 percent of the market for commercial jets, Airbus 31 percent, and McDonnell Douglas 4 percent.

Standing alone, the Boeing deal posed little realistic threat to Airbus. McDonnell Douglas already was a troubled competitor relegated to the margins of the commercial market, and there was some question whether its efforts in the market would continue. However, the deal coincided with a new aggressive Boeing marketing campaign which had already raised European hackles: In the space of a few months, Boeing tied up long-term exclusive contracts with American Airlines and Delta Air Lines, and negotiations continued in a similar deal with Continental Airlines, all of which threatened to close Airbus out of the lucrative U.S. market for twenty years.

EU competition commissioner Karel van Miert branded the Boeing–McDonnell Douglas deal as "totally unacceptable" under the European merger regulation. Despite howls from Boeing, the EU issued a "statement of objections" on May 21, and van Miert promised to block the deal unless concessions were made. He backed up the threat by pointing to a treaty which gives the EU the authority to block a deal where it finds "an abuse of market position." If Boeing had flouted the EU's concerns, van Miert could have imposed fines of up to 10 percent of the combined companies' annual revenues, or $4 billion, and could have seized Boeing's planes in Europe to enforce any fine.

Boeing initially talked tough, calling the EU's antitrust position an inappropriate attempt to extend its reach outside the borders of its territory. President Clinton and other U.S. politicians lobbied for the deal. However, eventually Boeing settled the controversy rather than get sidetracked with an extended battle.

The company agreed to forgo enforcement of the exclusive contracts with American and Delta Air Lines, and to keep Douglas Aircraft as a separate unit. But the contracts themselves were kept in place. As a result, the airlines had large outstanding orders with Boeing but could theoretically also purchase planes from other suppliers. But the general expectation in the marketplace was that Boeing's relationships with the airlines would continue on an exclusive basis even without the exclusivity clause.

The subtext for the Boeing controversy was the ongoing struggle between the U.S. and Europe over the relative competitive positions of their state-supported aerospace companies. Still, the flare-up demonstrated the growing importance of international antitrust policy even for what might be thought of as purely domestic transactions.

Regulated Industries

Antitrust is not the only regulatory framework relevant to mergers. A wide array of U.S. federal agencies govern regulated industries such as broadcast communications and commercial banking. In each case, an agency is typically responsible both for ongoing oversight and for approval of any corporate combinations. The ostensible overlap of these other regulatory frameworks and the antitrust law raises two questions. First, with respect to the various regulated industries, there is the question of which agency or agencies have the authority to review a merger. Second, there is the question of what standard applies to the review of a merger in each particular industry.

Generally speaking, the existence of an industry-specific regulatory framework does not exempt industry participants from the antitrust laws. But in rare cases, however, Congress has exempted a specific industry from antitrust oversight, supplanting an alternative framework. Rail mergers, for example, are subject to the exclusive supervision of the Surface Transportation Board (formerly the Interstate Commerce Commission).

The standards used in considering mergers generally mirror the statutory antitrust provisions. However, regulatory bodies are often specifically granted more flexibility to consider factors other than competitive effects in analyzing a proposed transaction.

Defense Industry   Over the past five years, the defense industry has gone through a domino-toppling consolidation in one deal after the next. More than $75 billion in defense-related transactions have taken place since 1992. Two factors have triggered the sudden rush. The end of the Cold War brought defense cutbacks, and as opportunities for revenue growth narrowed, cost savings became the critical profit driver. The new Clinton administration's 1993 relaxation of antitrust review for defense deals spurred the consolidation to begin in earnest.

Lately, the defense merger wave has accelerated as the remaining properties dwindled. Lockheed and Martin Marietta joined in a 1995 merger agreement. The next year, the new company bought most of Loral for $7.0 billion. Boeing acquired the defense and aerospace businesses of Rockwell International. And Raytheon bought the defense assets of Hughes Electronics and Texas Instruments for a combined $8 billion.

A contest developed between Boeing and Lockheed, each racing to be the largest defense contractor. Boeing's $13.3 billion deal for McDonnell Douglas raised the stakes. And in July 1997, Lockheed followed with its own $11.6 billion Northrop Grumman merger, which however failed to be consummated due to antitrust challenge and Pentagon disapproval.

The Pentagon played an active, behind-the-scenes role in bringing these deals together. In fact, the government actually agreed to pay part of the costs of consolidation on the theory that the government would benefit from cost reductions and should encourage the process. Lockheed Martin, for example, was to receive about $1 billion in reimbursements related to the merger that created the company.

Government inducements to consolidate have not been only economic; the antitrust review process has also played a part. Technically, defense mergers are governed by the antitrust laws and are subject to Hart-Scott review. However, both the FTC and the Justice

Department essentially have deferred in many of the recent transactions to the Pentagon's view that a market with two or three strong contractors would generate more active, productive competition than a market with five or ten weaker contractors. Besides, in a world of declining budgets, there seemed to be little choice. Less defense infrastructure can be supported, and mergers are an effective way to squeeze out costs and redundancy. Despite these trends, the Pentagon, along with the Justice Department, in fact argued against the Lockheed Martin–Northrop Grumman merger on antitrust grounds.

Antitrust review of the defense industry is, therefore, rather cutting-edge. The major focus has been on costs and efficiency, with an undercurrent of political concern for layoffs. Transactions which the government might challenge in other sectors have, with some exceptions, passed muster largely because the government is paying the bills and any cost savings have a tangible political benefit.

Banks and Bank Holding Companies Banks are subject to both Section 7 and regulatory agency oversight. In reaction to the *Philadelphia National Bank* decision, Congress passed the Bank Merger Act of 1966, which, aside from legalizing past bank mergers, mandated that any merger not challenged by the attorney general within thirty days of its approval by the pertinent regulatory agency could not be challenged under Section 7. In addition, the 1966 act also stated that anticompetitive effects could be outweighed by a finding that the deal meets the "convenience and needs" of the community to be served. However, this defense is not applicable to the acquisition by banks of nonbanking businesses.

Three different agencies review banking mergers, depending on the parties involved. The comptroller of the currency has responsibility for transactions where the "acquiring, assuming or resulting bank" is a national bank. The Federal Deposit Insurance Corporation oversees mergers where the acquiring or resulting bank will be a federally insured state-chartered bank that operates outside the Federal Reserve System. Finally, the Board of Governors of the Federal Reserve System reviews transactions where the acquiring or resulting bank will be a state bank within the Federal Reserve System.

In all three cases, the relevant agency conducts its own review, but also considers a review provided by the Justice Department, which applies a slightly modified Herfindahl index to bank mergers. Under this rubric, the Justice Department generally will not oppose a bank merger unless it results in an index over 1,800 and an increase of more than 200. Notwithstanding this input from the Justice Department, the parties involved in a transaction covered by the Bank Merger Act are not required to file notifications under Hart-Scott-Rodino. The Fed also announced in 1997 that it would expedite its own review of bank mergers whose post-merger index would be less than 2,200 and which would increase less than 250 points from its pre-merger level.

Railroads   Railroad mergers are governed by the Surface Transportation Board, which is the direct descendant of the now defunct Interstate Commerce Commission. Under the ICC Termination Act of 1995, a transaction approved by the Surface Transportation Board is exempt from the antitrust laws. Instead, the STB applies a five-factor test to determine whether a specific transaction should be approved. They are:

- The effect of the proposed transaction on the adequacy of transportation to the public;
- The effect on the public interest of including, or failing to include, other rail carriers in the area involved in the proposed transaction;
- The total fixed charges that result from the proposed transaction;

- The interest of rail carrier employees affected by the proposed transaction; and

- Whether the proposed transaction would have an adverse effect on competition among rail carriers in the affected region or in the national rail system.

The overarching question considered by the STB is whether the combination in question is "consistent with the public interest."

In exchange for approving a transaction, the STB may also impose conditions, such as the divestiture of parallel tracks or the granting of track access to competitors. When faced with conditions, the parties to a transaction may either accede or may forgo the deal. Hence, an interplay between the parties and the STB may result, with a negotiated settlement the outcome.

Despite the exclusive grant of authority to the STB, the Justice Department is not shut out of the review process. Rather, the parties and the STB must file notices with the Justice Department, which is given an opportunity to contest a deal at STB hearings. Standard antitrust principles therefore do carry some weight. However, objections from the Justice Department are not decisive, as was seen in the case of the Union Pacific–Southern Pacific merger: In that case, officials from the Antitrust Division of the Justice Department opposed the deal, which was nonetheless approved by the STB.

THE GOLDEN SPIKE

As the referee of railroad takeover fights, the Surface Transportation Board has tremendous power to shape outcomes. The saga of the consolidation of the railroads has been part of American economic life since the Civil War, and finally has come to fruition with the creation of two national systems—in effect designed by the STB.

The epic saga again flared publicly in October 1996 when our client CSX agreed to merge with Conrail. Under the terms of the original deal, CSX offered $92.50 in cash for 40 percent of Conrail and stock for the remainder. Less than a week later, Norfolk Southern declared war, launching a rival all-cash bid of $100 per share.

Reminiscent of Vanderbilt's pursuit of the Erie, the Conrail fight featured the three major East Coast roads: Conrail, CSX, and Norfolk Southern. Conrail—a direct descendant of the Erie—was formed in 1973 out of the wreckage of the Penn Central bankruptcy. To ensure its health, the railroad was given a stranglehold on the valuable Northeastern market. Both CSX and Norfolk Southern saw parts of Conrail as the vital piece needed to form a competitive rail network.

Conrail had talked with both roads over a period of years about potential combinations, and CSX and Norfolk held extensive negotiations with each other as well. The situation was this: CSX wanted the old New York Central and Norfolk wanted the old Pennsy plus half of the New York Central. Conrail originally wanted to stay in one piece.

CSX got the jump on Norfolk by persuading Conrail chairman David LeVan and the Conrail board that a deal with CSX offered greater benefits. First, CSX chairman John Snow had built a first-class network throughout the Southeast and Midwest. And a combination of CSX and Conrail made strategic sense in a world of multiple transportation alternatives: Together, the two companies could offer shippers one-stop shopping for transportation services over a wider geographic region. Equally important, John Snow also promised to keep the company's headquarters in Philadelphia and minimize layoffs of Conrail employees. Although CSX was willing to split Conrail, neither Norfolk nor Conrail would do it in the manner CSX desired.

Knowing Norfolk Southern was a potential suitor, Snow and LeVan wanted a tight deal with strong breakup protections. We were brought in along with Marty Lipton to help package the deal. While Conrail already had a poison pill in place, a $300 million breakup fee was added in the merger agreement, and Conrail granted CSX stock options at $92.50 a share. Finally, Conrail and CSX agreed to a no-shop provision under which neither side could talk to other potential merger partners.

These strong deal protections were, as usual, subject to court challenge. But, based on Wachtell, Lipton's review of Pennsylvania corporate law, the parties were confident the protections would stand. Under Pennsylvania law, enacted in response to Boone Pickens' attack on home-state favorite Gulf Oil, a board can weigh the interests of employees, the community, and other constituencies, along with the effect on shareholders, in approving a merger. Essentially, a board has no obligation to auction a company to the highest bidder and, therefore, a company like Conrail could agree to a strategic merger without putting itself in play—in theory.

Indeed, on the strength of the Pennsylvania law, a federal court judge upheld Conrail's agreement with CSX. However, another provision of Pennsylvania law limited the impact of the court victory: An acquirer which purchases 20 percent or more of a target company's stock must provide the same consideration to all shareholders in a later acquisition of the whole company, although target company shareholders are permitted to waive this requirement in a shareholder vote.

Because the CSX offer included both cash and stock, the deal required shareholder approval to proceed. A shareholder meeting, originally scheduled for December 1996, was held in the middle of January.

A temporary stalemate resulted. CSX owned 19.9 percent of Conrail after completion of its first-stage tender offer. But in a ploy to win the shareholder vote, Norfolk Southern had promised to buy 9.9 percent of Conrail for $115 after the vote. CSX calculated that it would lose the first vote because shareholders would have to vote no to get the $115. But after the first vote, CSX thought it eventually would win because the present value of Norfolk's offer was much lower than its own for the remaining 90 percent of Conrail's stock: The breakup provisions of CSX's agreement were still in place and shareholders would probably not be allowed to receive Norfolk stock for two years, although Norfolk was vigorously squirming to fight this result.

At this point, Norfolk Southern was offering $115 a share in cash, or $10.5 billion, and CSX had raised its front-end offer to $110 cash and had included additional securities in the back end. Many arbs argued the CSX offer was fundamentally inferior, but CSX and Conrail retained the winning position. Presumably, shareholders would eventually tire of the fight and take the CSX offer, because technically, CSX was poised to buy the company at a lower price once the court upheld the terms of the agreement.

But at this point, the STB stepped into the fray. STB chairwoman Linda Morgan expressed a strong suggestion that all three parties to the fight sit down and negotiate a settlement so as to preserve balanced competition in the East. If either party captured all of Conrail, the winner might potentially dominate the market and limit the possibilities for creating two balanced East–West lines.

In the end Conrail was split, with CSX buying the old New York Central lines and Norfolk the Pennsy. Linda Morgan controlled the deal.

Cable Television   The cable television industry is an example of a federally regulated industry where the oversight agency—the Federal Communications Commission—has expressly stated it does not consider itself primarily responsible for antitrust enforcement. Consequently, the Justice Department and FTC retain primary responsibility for reviewing cable company transactions.

The Voting Trust

An acquirer considering a stock purchase may wish to go ahead with the transaction while regulatory review is pending—especially when the review process is extended (as with the STB and rail merger oversight, which typically takes more than six months) or where the acquirer is sure it will receive approval and is willing to contest any adverse ruling.

The voting trust mechanism is fairly simple. An acquirer purchases the securities in its target company, then places them in a trust with an independent trustee, who often is required to vote the shares in proportion to the vote of all other target company shareholders. The major exception is that if and when the merger or acquisition is eventually approved, the trustee must vote in favor of approving the transaction.

There are two primary advantages of a voting trust: tactical leverage and economic benefit. First, a voting trust may give a bidder an edge in a competitive bidding situation because selling shareholders can be paid for their shares without contingencies.

The 1995 battle for Santa Fe Pacific railroad illustrates the importance of this tactical leverage. Union Pacific bid for the company in an effort to bust apart a deal with Burlington. However, the Street consensus was that the Union Pacific bid, though significantly higher than what Burlington promised, would not be enough: Shareholders feared the government would block the deal and were unwilling to give up the Burlington offer for a riskier Union Pacific deal.

To stay in the contest, Union Pacific lowered its offer but guaranteed the purchase with a voting trust mechanism, effectively taking all the risk that the deal might fall apart. Union Pacific ended up losing the fight anyway, but the voting trust kept it competitive longer than would have otherwise been the case.

Second, a voting trust may allow an acquirer to receive economic benefits from a target company. While the trustee retains the voting rights associated with the target securities, any economic benefits, such as dividend payments, can flow through to the acquirer as beneficiary.

The major and obvious disadvantage of a voting trust is that considerable capital can be tied up for an extended period during which the acquirer has no ability to control the target. This situation can cause severe problems in the case of a target company in need of restructuring, as was the case with LTV's acquisition of Jones & Laughlin in the 1960s. Likewise, the lack of control can be a problem in an acquisition premised on the assumption that target assets will be sold to pay down debt.

Postscript

We are at the beginning of an inflection point in our economic history, the dawn of a digital age. Amidst the euphoria and chaos, a recognition of the role of corporate restructuring of assets through mergers and acquisitions in the evolution of our economy is appropriate.

At the turn of the century, Admiral Alfred Mahan, a naval historian, reflected on political events and concluded that seapower had a broad impact on the course of history. His seminal book, *The Influence of Sea Power upon History, 1660–1783,* stated an obvious but underappreciated thesis that changed the perception of the naval role.

The impact of mergers and acquisitions has a similar quality. While not claiming any exaggerated significance for the M&A process, the buying and selling of companies has been a critical and undervalued force in the history of American economic development.

Over the past two decades, the pace of economic change has been staggering, the volatility overwhelming. In industry after industry—media, telecommunications, health care, oil, financial services—fissures in the economic foundations have jolted the competitive landscape.

There has been pain, dislocations, and blunders. Perhaps some of these jolts reduce the pressure along the fault lines of our system, without which the economy would spasm into more convulsive eruptions. The turbulence involved in running some of America's leading businesses is daunting. AT&T, one of America's most distinguished corporations, managed to make itself the butt of ridicule as it rocked from one debacle to another. Yet decisions have to be made in the face of tremendous uncertainty and some will inevitably be wrong.

Who would have thought ten years ago that the local and long distance markets would be reunited? Or that oil prices would fall back to earth and stay there for over a decade? Or that computers, movies, and phones would become a vast interrelated business? Or that our traditional banks would disappear? Or that the stock market would increase 600 percent?

The sweep of history may not have an inevitability, but there are discernible lessons. Flexibility and change are necessary for economic vitality. The capital market system is central to our country's ability to adapt, and it is fueled by the merger process. The net result is that America has prospered.

During our history, there has been a yin and yang, a balance of centrifugal forces, as to the role of mergers. Sometimes, the pace is too fast. Sometimes, the pain in adapting to industrial change is too much. Sometimes the process is subject to abuse. The government changes the antitrust laws, the states pass protective takeover statutes, the Delaware courts use their sense of smell and stop the greenmailers. But the discipline which the process creates for the whole economic system and the incentive for innovation are immeasurably valuable.

More narrowly, there are some clear lessons on doing deals:

Fundamentals   The difference in a deal is never the intricacy of a computer model but rather a fundamental understanding of the business and industry, and a strategy for coping with the inevitable changes.

Management   The impact of strong management is not apparent when things are going well, but when the rain comes, as it will, it makes the difference. Ted Forstmann's role at Gulfstream comes to mind. Through sheer tenacity and hands-on control, he turned a bad investment around. Success is never guaranteed, and businesses do suffer fatal wounds, but consistent effort and management insight significantly add to the final return.

Sensible Financing Looking at deals that did go wrong, many suffered a common problem—the mismatched book. In good times, it is possible to get away with financing long-term cash needs with short-term debt. Of course, one never knows when the good times will end, and the jolt can be sharp.

Even more difficult than analyzing the past is gazing into a Delphic crystal ball, prognosticating speculative profundities. Yet history is prologue and observations about the past do provide insight into the future course of events. Extrapolating, then, from the past, six trends in particular likely will continue to shape the future:

Cyclicality The deal business will continue to be cyclical with secular growth. We have experienced an unprecedented run of record-breaking years since the downturn of the early 1990s. However, the boom times will not last forever.

At the peak of the merger cycle, excesses will occur. There is a tendency to accept mediocrities into the ranks of takeover professionals, a dangerous indulgence. The nature of activity also varies with the financial circumstances and the mood of the times. Today there is a significant preponderance of stock deals. However, that will change again sometime in the next few years. Financial buyers alone have over $40 billion of committed capital to invest. The accounting gurus are revising the restrictive pooling rules which motivate strategic buyers in favor of stock deals. So the question is not whether there will be a resurgence of cash deals, but when.

The Danger of Belly Flops Of course, there is also a danger of belly flops. Poor strategic conception or tactical implementation can lead to problems with a merger or acquisition. The tribulations of AT&T in the computer sector, including the poorly executed NCR acquisition, Union Pacific's problems getting the freight trains to run on time after the Southern Pacific takeover, and alleged improprieties at Columbia/HCA all indicate the risks. As in all aspects of business, consistent follow-through, attention to details, quality leadership, and sometimes a bit of luck are necessary to a successful merger process.

Increasing Sophistication   The evolution of takeovers through the years has been a process of increasing sophistication. The cash deals of the 1980s represented an implicit repudiation of prevailing corporate valuation methods. Valuing companies based on book earnings understated a target's capacity to generate cash. Financial buyers saw the embedded opportunity and acted on it.

The greater role taken on by institutional investors has been another aspect of the increasing sophistication of the deal business. With their significant ownership percentages of most large corporations, institutional investors have been the vehicle for reuniting ownership and control. By acting in concert, they can bring considerable pressure on a board to accept an offer or take other value-maximizing actions. This process has only accelerated since the recent revision of the proxy rules made coordinated action less cumbersome, and will continue into the future.

The Delaware Pendulum Swings   In crafting the basic rules of takeover law, the Delaware courts have attempted to balance the interests of shareholders and other constituencies. The excesses of the 1980s hostile deals have been muted with the acceptance of the poison pill and the *Time* strategic merger ruling.

Delaware takeover law swings back and forth over a fairly narrow range of middle ground. The pill redemption issue surely will continue to come up until the Delaware Supreme Court clarifies the responsibilities of a board.

Securities Law Revisions   The creation of clear, fair securities laws has been critical to protecting the deal process over the long run. A system with integrity is crucial to the market trust behind mergers and acquisitions, and the standards still need to be elevated even after the Aircraft Carrier reforms.

Globalization   The global strategic imperative is a thread running throughout this book. No matter the industry, the impact is universal. We have barely begun global consolidation, and the pace will accelerate.

Layered on top of these trends, the Pistons also will continue to shape the deal flow. Regulations, technology, financial fluctuations, leadership, and the size-imperative will all drive change.

At this juncture, America is riding the crest of prosperity, and mergers are part of the story. It is largely an untold tale, a complex pattern missed because the focus is on individual transactions. Although conditions change, the time has come to take a realistic view of the merger process, not through rose-tinted lenses, but giving this important component of our economic development the recognition and sophisticated understanding it requires.

Bibliography

Much of the contemporary factual material in this book is drawn from memory, supplemented heavily by articles from leading business publications. Particularly important sources include *The Wall Street Journal, The New York Times, Business Week, Forbes,* and *Fortune.* My avocation is business history, and I have also drawn on many fine books that I have read over the years. A partial list follows:

Part One

Anders, George. *Merchants of Debt: KKR and the Mortgaging of American Business.* Basic Books, 1992.

Auletta, Ken. *Greed and Glory on Wall Street: The Fall of the House of Lehman.* Warner Books, 1987.

Baker, George P., and George David Smith. *The New Financial Capitalists: Kohlberg Kravis Roberts and the Creation of Corporate Value.* Cambridge University Press, 1998.

Brooks, John. *Once in Golconda: A True Drama of Wall Street.* Watson-Guptill Publications, 1969.

———. *The Takeover Game.* Truman Talley Books/Dutton, 1987.

Bruck, Connie. *The Predators' Ball: The Inside Story of Drexel Burnham and the Rise of the Junk Bond Raiders.* Penguin USA, 1989.

———. *Master of the Game: Steve Ross and the Creation of Time Warner.* Penguin USA, 1989.

Chernow, Ron. *House of Morgan.* Atlantic Monthly Press, 1990.

———. *Titan: The Life of John D. Rockefeller, Sr.* Random House, 1998.

Cray, Ed. *Chrome Colossus: General Motors and Its Times.* McGraw-Hill, 1980.

Fischel, Daniel. *Payback: The Conspiracy to Destroy Michael Milken and His Financial Revolution.* HarperBusiness, 1996.

Galbraith, John. *The Great Crash—1929.* Houghton Mifflin, 1988.

Groner, Alex. *The American Heritage History of American Business and Industry.* American Heritage, 1972.

Hearings Before the Subcommittee on Telecommunications, Consumer Protection, and Finance, of the Committee on Energy and Commerce, House of Representatives. U.S. Government Printing Office, 1984.

Hessen, Robert. *Steel Titan: The Life of Charles M. Schwab.* University of Pittsburgh Press, 1990.

Jacobs, Michael T. *Short-Term America: The Causes and Cures of Our Business Myopia.* Harvard Business School Press, 1991.

Johnston, Moira. *Takeover: The New Wall Street Warriors: The Men, the Money, the Impact.* Arbor House, 1986.

Josephson, Matthew. *The Robber Barons: The Great American Capitalists, 1861–1901.* Harcourt Brace, 1962.

Lacey, Robert. *Ford: The Men and the Machine.* Little, Brown, 1986.

Mair, George. *The Barry Diller Story: The Life and Times of America's Greatest Entertainment Mogul.* John Wiley & Sons, 1997.

McKee, Carl W. *Japanese Takeovers.* Harvard Business School Press, 1991.

Ravenscraft, David J. *Mergers, Sell-Offs and Economic Efficiency.* The Brookings Institution, 1987.

Salsbury, Stephen. *No Way to Run a Railroad: The Untold Story of the Penn Central Crisis.* McGraw-Hill, 1982.

Schoenberg, Robert J. *Geneen.* Norton, 1985.

Sloan, Alfred P. *My Years with General Motors.* Doubleday, 1996.

Smith, Roy C. *The Money Wars.* Truman Talley Books, 1990.

Sobel, Robert. *Dangerous Dreamers: The Financial Innovators from Charles Merrill to Michael Milken.* John Wiley & Sons, 1993.

———. *The Great Bull Market: Wall Street in the 1920's.* Norton, 1968.

———. *ITT: The Management of Opportunity.* HarperCollins, 1982.

———. *The Rise and Fall of the Conglomerate Kings.* Stein & Day, 1984.

Steiner, Peter O. *Mergers, Motives, Effects, Policies.* University of Michigan Press, 1975.

Stevens, Mark. *King Icahn: The Biography of a Renegade Capitalist.* Dutton, 1993.

Stewart, James B. *Den of Thieves.* Touchstone, 1992.

Stone, Dan G. *April Fools: An Insider's Account of the Rise and Collapse of Drexel Burnham.* Donald I. Fine, 1990.

Strouse, Jean. *Morgan: American Financier.* Random House, 1999.

Tarbell, Ida. *History of the Standard Oil Company.* Amereon Ltd., 1993.

Vanderbilt, Cornelius, Jr. *Farewell to Fifth Avenue.* Simon & Schuster, 1935.

Wall, Joseph Frazier. *Andrew Carnegie.* University of Pittsburgh Press, 1989.

Weidenbaum, Murray, and Kenneth Chilton. *Public Policy Toward Corporate Takeovers.* Transaction Books, 1988.

Part Two

Araskog, Rand V. *The ITT Wars.* Henry Holt, 1989.

Auletta, Ken. *The Highwaymen: Warriors of the Information Superhighway.* Random House, 1997.

Bollenbacher, George M. *The New Business of Banking: Transforming Challenges into Opportunities in Today's Financial Services Marketplace.* Irwin Professional Publications, 1995.

Brooks, John. *The Go-Go Years.* Dutton, 1984.

Brown, Stanley H. *Ling: The Rise, Fall, and Return of a Texas Titan.* Atheneum, 1972.

Chandler, Alfred D., and Herman Daems. *Managerial Hierarchies: Comparative Perspectives on the Rise of the Modern Industrial Enterprise.* Harvard University Press, 1980.

Clurman, Richard M. *To the End of Time: The Seduction and Conquest of a Media Empire.* Simon & Schuster, 1992.

Coll, Steve. *The Deal of the Century: The Breakup of AT&T.* Atheneum, 1986.

———. *The Taking of Getty Oil: The Full Story of the Most Spectacular and Catastrophic Takeover of All Time.* Atheneum, 1987.

Gart, Alan. *Regulation, Deregulation, Reregulation: The Future of the Banking, Insurance and Securities Industries.* John Wiley & Sons, 1993.

Grover, Ron. *The Disney Touch: How a Daring Management Team Revived an Entertainment Empire.* Irwin Professional Publications, 1991.

Harvey, Thomas W. *The Banking Revolution: Positioning Your Bank in the New Financial Services Marketplace.* Irwin Professional Publications, 1996.

Kadlec, Daniel J. *Masters of the Universe: Winning Strategies of America's Greatest Dealmakers.* HarperBusiness, 1999.

Mayer, Martin. *The Bankers: The Next Generation.* Dutton, 1997.

———. *The Money Bazaars: Understanding the Banking Revolution Around Us.* Dutton, 1984.

Mintzberg, Henry, Bruce Ahlstrand, and Joseph Lampel. *Strategy Safari: A Guided Tour Through the Wilds of Strategic Management.* The Free Press, 1998.

O'Connor, Richard. *The Oil Barons.* Little, Brown, 1971.

Pickens, T. Boone. *Boone.* Random House, 1988.

Porter, Michael E. *Competitive Strategy: Techniques for Analyzing Industries and Competitors.* The Free Press, 1984.

Rogers, David. *The Future of American Banking: Managing for Change.* McGraw-Hill, 1992.

Slater, Robert. *Jack Welch and the GE Way.* McGraw-Hill, 1999.

———. *The New GE: How Jack Welch Revived an American Institution.* Irwin Professional Publications, 1992.

———. *Ovitz: The Inside Story of Hollywood's Most Controversial Power Broker.* Mc-Graw-Hill, 1997.

Spiegal, John, Alan Gart, and Steven Gart. *Banking Redefined: How Superregional Powerhouses Are Reshaping Financial Services.* Irwin Professional Publications, 1996.

Wallace, James. *Overdrive: Bill Gates and the Race to Control Cyberspace.* John Wiley & Sons, 1997.

Wendel, Charles B. *The New Financiers: Profiles of the Leaders Who Are Reshaping the Financial Services Industry.* Irwin Professional Publications, 1996.

Yergin, Daniel. *The Prize: The Epic Quest for Oil, Money, and Power.* Simon & Schuster, 1991.

Part Three

Bernstein, Leopold. *Financial Statement Analysis: Theory, Application, and Interpretation.* Irwin Professional Publications, 1983.

Caplan, Lincoln. *Skadden: Power, Money, and the Rise of a Legal Empire.* Farrar, Straus & Giroux, 1994.

Cohen, Herb. *You Can Negotiate Anything.* Bantam, 1989.

Copeland, Tom, Tom Koller, and Jack Murrin. *Valuation: Measuring and Managing the Value of Companies.* John Wiley & Sons, 1995.

Cottle, Sidney, Roger F. Murray, and Frank E. Block. *Graham and Dodd's Security Analysis.* McGraw-Hill, 1988.

Dunlap, Albert J., and Bob Andelman. *Mean Business: How I Save Bad Companies and Make Good Companies Great.* Simon & Schuster, 1997.

Ehrbar, Al. *EVA: The Real Key to Creating Wealth.* John Wiley & Sons 1998.

Ferrera, Ralph C., Meredith M. Brown, and John H. Hall. *Takeovers: Attack and Survival, a Strategist's Manual.* Michie Dullerworth, 1987.

Fisher, Roger, and William Ury. *Getting to Yes: How to Negotiate Agreement Without Giving In.* Simon & Schuster, 1987.

Fleischer Jr., Arthur, and Alexander R. Sussman. *Takeover Defense.* Aspen Law & Business, 1995.

Freund, James C. *Anatomy of a Merger: Strategies and Techniques for Negotiating Corporate Acquisitions.* Law Journal Seminars Press, 1975.

Gaughan, Patrick A. *Mergers, Acquisitions, and Corporate Restructurings.* John Wiley & Sons, 1996.

Hamel, Gary, and C.K. Prahalad. *Competing for the Future.* Harvard Business School Press, 1994.

Hartz, Peter F. *Merger: The Exclusive Inside Story of the Bendix–Martin Marietta Takeover War.* William Morrow, 1985.

Hayes, Samuel L., and Philip M. Hubbard. *Investment Banking: A Tale of Three Cities.* Harvard Business School, 1990.

Hoffman, Paul. *Lions in the Street: The Inside Story of the Great Wall Street Law Firms.* Dutton, 1973.

Lowenstein, Roger. *Buffett: The Making of an American Capitalist.* Doubleday, 1996.

Mark, Howard. *Financial Shenanigans: How to Detect Accounting Gimmicks and Fraud in Financial Reports.* McGraw-Hill, 1993.

Mayer, Martin. *Lawyers.* Greenwood Publishing, 1980.

O'Glove, Thornton L., with Robert Sobel. *Quality of Earnings: The Investor's Guide to How Much Money a Company Is Really Making.* The Free Press, 1987.

Reich, Cary. *Financier, The Biography of André Meyer: A Story of Money, Power, and the Reshaping of American Business.* William Morrow, 1983.

Stewart III, G. Bennett. *The Quest for Value: The EVA™ Management Guide.* Harper-Business, 1991.

Thornhill, William T. *Forensic Accounting: How to Investigate Financial Fraud.* Irwin Professional Publications, 1994.

Tom, Willard K., and Abbott B. Lipsky Jr. *Antitrust Law Developments,* 3rd edition, Volume I. American Bar Association, 1992.

Wasserstein, Bruce. *Corporate Finance Law: A Guide for the Executive.* McGraw-Hill, 1978.

Key Takeover Cases

AMP Incorporated v. AlliedSignal Corporation, 168 F. 3d 649 (3rd Cir. 1999) ("control share acquisition" triggered upon acquisition of at least 20 percent of outstanding shares).

Basic, Inc. v. Levinson, 485 U.S. 224 (1988) (obligation to issue nonmisleading disclosure regarding merger negotiations).

Brown Shoe Co. v. United States, 370 U.S. 294 (1962) (antitrust).

Brunswick Corp. v. Pueblo-Bowl-O-Mat, Inc. 429 U.S. 477 (1977) (antitrust).

Carmody v. Toll Brothers, Inc., 723 A 2d 1180 (Del. 1998) (dead-hand poison pill impermissible).

Chiarella v. United States, 445 U.S. 222 (1980) (insider trading liability).

FTC v. Procter & Gamble Co. (Clorox), 386 U.S. 568 (1967) (antitrust).

Grand Metropolitan PLC v. The Pillsbury Company, 558 A.2d 1049 (Del. Ch. 1988) (court enjoins elements of defensive restructuring and orders pill redeemed).

Invacare Corporation v. Healthdyne Technologies, Inc., 968 F. Supp. 1578 (1997) (denying a bidder's motion to remove a dead-hand poison pill).

J.J. Case Co. v. Borak, 377 U.S. 426 (1964) (recognizing implied private right of action on behalf of shareholders for proxy violations).

Kennecott Copper Corp. v. FTC, 467 F.2d 67 (10th Cir. 1972) (antitrust).

Missouri Portland Cement v. H.K. Porter Co., CCH Securities Law Reporter, Para. 95,864 (S. Ct. 1977) (antitrust).

Moore Corporation v. Wallace Computer Services, Inc., 907 F. Supp 1545 (Del. 1995). ("just say no" defense approved).

Moran v. Household International Inc., 500 A.2d 1346 (Del. 1985) (poison pill is an acceptable preventive takeover defense).

Otis Elevator Co. v. United Technologies Corp., 405 F. Supp. 960 (S.D.N.Y. 1975) (antitrust).

Paramount Communications Inc. v. QVC Network Inc., 637 A.2d 34 (Del. 1994) (board may not unduly favor one party over another in a company sale).

Paramount Communications Inc. v. Time Incorporated, 571 A.2d 1140 (Del. 1990) (company need not forgo strategic merger in favor of a higher hostile bid).

Piper Aircraft Corp. v. Chris-Craft Industries, 430 U.S. 1 (1977) (bidder does not have standing to sue target for disclosure violations).

Quickturn Design Systems v. Shapiro, 721 A.2d 1281 (Del. 1998) (delayed-redemption poison pill invalidated on statutory grounds).

Revlon v. MacAndrews & Forbes, 506 A.2d 173 (Del. 1985) (board must maximize return to shareholders in a sale of company).

Smith v. Van Gorkom, 488 A.2d 858 (Del. 1985) (liability of directors for breaching duty of care).

Stanley Works v. FTC, 469 F.2d 498 (2d Cir. 1972) (antitrust).

TSC Industries, Inc. v. Northway, Inc., 426 U.S. 438 (1976) (defining materiality under securities laws).

United States v. Gillette Co., 828 F. Supp. 78 (D.D.C. 1993) (antitrust).

United States v. International Tel. & Tel. Corp. (Grinnell), 306 F. Supp. 766 (D. Conn. 1969) (antitrust).

United States v. Philadelphia National Bank, 374 U.S. 321 (1963) (antitrust).

United States v. Von's Grocery Co., 384 U.S. 270 (1966) (antitrust).

Unocal Corporation v. Mesa Petroleum Co., 493 A.2d 946 (Del. 1985) (discriminatory self-tender is a reasonable defensive response to a coercive hostile bid).

Index